MONEY IN POLITICS

FINANCING FEDERAL PARTIES AND CANDIDATES IN CANADA

W.T. Stanbury

Volume 1 of the Research Studies

ROYAL COMMISSION ON ELECTORAL REFORM
AND PARTY FINANCING
AND CANADA COMMUNICATION GROUP –
PUBLISHING, SUPPLY AND SERVICES CANADA

DUNDURN PRESS
TORONTO AND OXFORD

© Minister of Supply and Services Canada, 1991
Printed and bound in Canada
ISBN 1-55002-097-8
ISSN 1188-2743
Catalogue No. Z1-1989/2-41-1E

Published by Dundurn Press Limited in cooperation with the Royal
Commission on Electoral Reform and Party Financing and Canada
Communication Group – Publishing, Supply and Services Canada.

Note: Although copyright date states 1991, actual publication of this
material occurred in 1993.

Canadian Cataloguing in Publication Data

Stanbury, W. T., 1943–
Money in politics

(Research studies ; 1)
Issued also in French under title: L'argent et la politique fédérale
    canadienne.
ISBN 1-55002-097-8

1. Campaign funds – Canada. 2. Elections – Canada. 3. Political parties –
Canada. I. Canada. Royal Commission on Electoral Reform and Party
Financing. II. Title. III. Series: Research studies (Canada. Royal Commission
on Electoral Reform and Party Financing) ; 1.

JL196.S73 1991   324.271   C91-090513-4

Dundurn Press Limited
2181 Queen Street East
Suite 301
Toronto, Canada
M4E 1E5

Dundurn Distribution
73 Lime Walk
Headington
Oxford, England
OX3 7AD

CONTENTS

FIGURES

TABLES

8. CONTRIBUTIONS FROM INDIVIDUALS
AND THE IMPORTANCE OF THE TAX CREDIT

9. Direct-Mail Fund-Raising and Electioneering

10. Two Fund-Raising Techniques: Dinners and Major-Donor Programs

11. Contributions from Business and Commercial Organizations

12. CANDIDATE REVENUES AND EXPENDITURES, 1979–88

13. PROBLEMS WITH THE REGULATORY REGIME

FOREWORD

THE ROYAL COMMISSION on Electoral Reform and Party Financing was established in November 1989. Our mandate was to inquire into and report on the appropriate principles and process that should govern the election of members of the House of Commons and the financing of political parties and candidates' campaigns. To conduct such a comprehensive examination of Canada's electoral system, we held extensive public consultations and developed a research program designed to ensure that our recommendations would be guided by an independent foundation of empirical inquiry and analysis.

The Commission's in-depth review of the electoral system was the first of its kind in Canada's history of electoral democracy. It was dictated largely by the major constitutional, social and technological changes of the past several decades, which have transformed Canadian society, and their concomitant influence on Canadians' expectations of the political process itself. In particular, the adoption in 1982 of the *Canadian Charter of Rights and Freedoms* has heightened Canadians' awareness of their democratic and political rights and of the way they are served by the electoral system.

The importance of electoral reform cannot be overemphasized. As the Commission's work proceeded, Canadians became increasingly preoccupied with constitutional issues that have the potential to change the nature of Confederation. No matter what their beliefs or political allegiances in this continuing debate, Canadians agree that constitutional change must be achieved in the context of fair and democratic processes. We cannot complacently assume that our current electoral process will always meet this standard or that it leaves no room for improvement. Parliament and the national government must be seen as legitimate; electoral reform can both enhance the stature of national political institutions and reinforce their ability to define the future of our country in ways that command Canadians' respect and confidence and promote the national interest.

In carrying out our mandate, we remained mindful of the importance of protecting our democratic heritage, while at the same time balancing it against the emerging values that are injecting a new dynamic into the electoral system. If our system is to reflect the realities of Canadian political life, then reform requires more than mere tinkering with electoral laws and practices.

Our broad mandate challenged us to explore a full range of options. We commissioned more than 100 research studies, to be published in a 23-volume collection. In the belief that our electoral laws must measure up to the very best contemporary practice, we examined election-related laws and processes in all of our provinces and territories and studied comparable legislation and processes in established democracies around the world. This unprecedented array of empirical study and expert opinion made a vital contribution to our deliberations. We made every effort to ensure that the research was both intellectually rigorous and of practical value. All studies were subjected to peer review, and many of the authors discussed their preliminary findings with members of the political and academic communities at national symposiums on major aspects of the electoral system.

The Commission placed the research program under the able and inspired direction of Dr. Peter Aucoin, Professor of Political Science and Public Administration at Dalhousie University. We are confident that the efforts of Dr. Aucoin, together with those of the research coordinators and scholars whose work appears in this and other volumes, will continue to be of value to historians, political scientists, parliamentarians and policy makers, as well as to thoughtful Canadians and the international community.

Along with the other Commissioners, I extend my sincere gratitude to the entire Commission staff for their dedication and commitment. I also wish to thank the many people who participated in our symposiums for their valuable contributions, as well as the members of the research and practitioners' advisory groups whose counsel significantly aided our undertaking.

Pierre Lortie
Chairman

INTRODUCTION

THE ROYAL COMMISSION'S research program constituted a comprehensive and detailed examination of the Canadian electoral process. The scope of the research, undertaken to assist Commissioners in their deliberations, was dictated by the broad mandate given to the Commission.

The objective of the research program was to provide Commissioners with a full account of the factors that have shaped our electoral democracy. This dictated, first and foremost, a focus on federal electoral law, but our inquiries also extended to the Canadian constitution, including the institutions of parliamentary government, the practices of political parties, the mass media and nonpartisan political organizations, as well as the decision-making role of the courts with respect to the constitutional rights of citizens. Throughout, our research sought to introduce a historical perspective in order to place the contemporary experience within the Canadian political tradition.

We recognized that neither our consideration of the factors shaping Canadian electoral democracy nor our assessment of reform proposals would be as complete as necessary if we failed to examine the experiences of Canadian provinces and territories and of other democracies. Our research program thus emphasized comparative dimensions in relation to the major subjects of inquiry.

Our research program involved, in addition to the work of the Commission's research coordinators, analysts and support staff, over 200 specialists from 28 universities in Canada, from the private sector and, in a number of cases, from abroad. Specialists in political science constituted the majority of our researchers, but specialists in law, economics, management, computer sciences, ethics, sociology and communications, among other disciplines, were also involved.

In addition to the preparation of research studies for the Commission, our research program included a series of research seminars, symposiums and workshops. These meetings brought together the Commissioners, researchers, representatives from the political parties, media personnel and others with practical experience in political parties, electoral politics and public affairs. These meetings provided not only a forum for discussion of the various subjects of the Commission's mandate, but also an opportunity for our research to be assessed by those with an intimate knowledge of the world of political practice.

These public reviews of our research were complemented by internal and external assessments of each research report by persons qualified in the area; such assessments were completed prior to our decision to publish any study in the series of research volumes.

The Research Branch of the Commission was divided into several areas, with the individual research projects in each area assigned to the research coordinators as follows:

F. Leslie Seidle	Political Party and Election Finance
Herman Bakvis	Political Parties
Kathy Megyery	Women, Ethno-cultural Groups and Youth
David Small	Redistribution; Electoral Boundaries; Voter Registration
Janet Hiebert	Party Ethics
Michael Cassidy	Democratic Rights; Election Administration
Robert A. Milen	Aboriginal Electoral Participation and Representation
Frederick J. Fletcher	Mass Media and Broadcasting in Elections
David Mac Donald (Assistant Research Coordinator)	Direct Democracy

These coordinators identified appropriate specialists to undertake research, managed the projects and prepared them for publication. They also organized the seminars, symposiums and workshops in their research areas and were responsible for preparing presentations and briefings to help the Commission in its deliberations and decision making. Finally, they participated in drafting the Final Report of the Commission.

On behalf of the Commission, I welcome the opportunity to thank the following for their generous assistance in producing these research studies – a project that required the talents of many individuals.

In performing their duties, the research coordinators made a notable contribution to the work of the Commission. Despite the pressures of tight deadlines, they worked with unfailing good humour and the utmost congeniality. I thank all of them for their consistent support and cooperation.

In particular, I wish to express my gratitude to Leslie Seidle, senior research coordinator, who supervised our research analysts and support staff in Ottawa. His diligence, commitment and professionalism not only set high standards, but also proved contagious. I am grateful to Kathy Megyery, who performed a similar function in Montreal with equal aplomb and skill. Her enthusiasm and dedication inspired us all.

On behalf of the research coordinators and myself, I wish to thank our research analysts: Daniel Arsenault, Eric Bertram, Cécile Boucher, Peter Constantinou, Yves Denoncourt, David Docherty, Luc Dumont, Jane Dunlop, Scott Evans, Véronique Garneau, Keith Heintzman, Paul Holmes, Hugh Mellon, Cheryl D. Mitchell, Donald Padget, Alain Pelletier, Dominique Tremblay and Lisa Young. The Research Branch was strengthened by their ability to carry out research in a wide variety of areas, their intellectual curiosity and their team spirit.

The work of the research coordinators and analysts was greatly facilitated by the professional skills and invaluable cooperation of Research Branch staff members: Paulette LeBlanc, who, as administrative assistant, managed the flow of research projects; Hélène Leroux, secretary to the research coordinators, who produced briefing material for the Commissioners and who, with Lori Nazar, assumed responsibility for monitoring the progress of research projects in the latter stages of our work; Kathleen McBride and her assistant Natalie Brose, who created and maintained the database of briefs and hearings transcripts; and Richard Herold and his assistant Susan Dancause, who were responsible for our research library. Jacinthe Séguin and Cathy Tucker also deserve thanks – in addition to their duties as receptionists, they assisted in a variety of ways to help us meet deadlines.

We were extremely fortunate to obtain the research services of first-class specialists from the academic and private sectors. Their contributions are found in this and the other 22 published research volumes. We thank them for the quality of their work and for their willingness to contribute and to meet our tight deadlines.

Our research program also benefited from the counsel of Jean-Marc Hamel, Special Adviser to the Chairman of the Commission and former

Chief Electoral Officer of Canada, whose knowledge and experience proved invaluable.

In addition, numerous specialists assessed our research studies. Their assessments not only improved the quality of our published studies, but also provided us with much-needed advice on many issues. In particular, we wish to single out professors Donald Blake, Janine Brodie, Alan Cairns, Kenneth Carty, John Courtney, Peter Desbarats, Jane Jenson, Richard Johnston, Vincent Lemieux, Terry Morley and Joseph Wearing, as well as Ms. Beth Symes.

Producing such a large number of studies in less than a year requires a mastery of the skills and logistics of publishing. We were fortunate to be able to count on the Commission's Director of Communications, Richard Rochefort, and Assistant Director, Hélène Papineau. They were ably supported by the Communications staff: Patricia Burden, Louise Dagenais, Caroline Field, Claudine Labelle, France Langlois, Lorraine Maheux, Ruth McVeigh, Chantal Morissette, Sylvie Patry, Jacques Poitras and Claudette Rouleau-O'Toole.

To bring the project to fruition, the Commission also called on specialized contractors. We are deeply grateful for the services of Ann McCoomb (references and fact checking); Marthe Lemery, Pierre Chagnon and the staff of Communications Com'ça (French quality control); Norman Bloom, Pamela Riseborough and associates of B&B Editorial Consulting (English adaptation and quality control); and Mado Reid (French production). Al Albania and his staff at Acart Graphics designed the studies and produced some 2 400 tables and figures.

The Commission's research reports constitute Canada's largest publishing project of 1991. Successful completion of the project required close cooperation between the public and private sectors. In the public sector, we especially acknowledge the excellent service of the Privy Council unit of the Translation Bureau, Department of the Secretary of State of Canada, under the direction of Michel Parent, and our contacts Ruth Steele and Terry Denovan of the Canada Communication Group, Department of Supply and Services.

The Commission's co-publisher for the research studies was Dundurn Press of Toronto, whose exceptional service is gratefully acknowledged. Wilson & Lafleur of Montreal, working with the Centre de Documentation Juridique du Québec, did equally admirable work in preparing the French version of the studies.

Teams of editors, copy editors and proofreaders worked diligently under stringent deadlines with the Commission and the publishers to prepare some 20 000 pages of manuscript for design, typesetting and printing. The work of these individuals, whose names are listed elsewhere in this volume, was greatly appreciated.

Our acknowledgements extend to the contributions of the Commission's Executive Director, Guy Goulard, and the administration and executive support teams: Maurice Lacasse, Denis Lafrance and Steve Tremblay (finance); Thérèse Lacasse and Mary Guy-Shea (personnel); Cécile Desforges (assistant to the Executive Director); Marie Dionne (administration); Anna Bevilacqua (records); and support staff members Michelle Bélanger, Roch Langlois, Michel Lauzon, Jean Mathieu, David McKay and Pierrette McMurtie, as well as Denise Miquelon and Christiane Séguin of the Montreal office.

A special debt of gratitude is owed to Marlène Girard, assistant to the Chairman. Her ability to supervise the logistics of the Commission's work amid the tight schedules of the Chairman and Commissioners contributed greatly to the completion of our task.

I also wish to express my deep gratitude to my own secretary, Liette Simard. Her superb administrative skills and great patience brought much-appreciated order to my penchant for the chaotic workstyle of academe. She also assumed responsibility for the administrative coordination of revisions to the final drafts of volumes 1 and 2 of the Commission's Final Report. I owe much to her efforts and assistance.

Finally, on behalf of the research coordinators and myself, I wish to thank the Chairman, Pierre Lortie, the members of the Commission, Pierre Fortier, Robert Gabor, William Knight and Lucie Pépin, and former members Elwood Cowley and Senator Donald Oliver. We are honoured to have worked with such an eminent and thoughtful group of Canadians, and we have benefited immensely from their knowledge and experience. In particular, we wish to acknowledge the creativity, intellectual rigour and energy our Chairman brought to our task. His unparalleled capacity to challenge, to bring out the best in us, was indeed inspiring.

Peter Aucoin
Director of Research

ACKNOWLEDGEMENTS

I N THE COURSE OF THIS STUDY, I incurred a number of debts which, if they can't be requited, must be properly acknowledged. The largest debt is to the taxpayers of Canada, who provided money to finance the work. To the extent that the study helps to improve public policy in respect to party and candidate financing, taxpayers may realize a return on their expenditure.

I am deeply grateful to the three-score current and past senior officials of the Progressive Conservative, Liberal, New Democratic and Reform parties who were interviewed for the study. They provided answers to many questions, much data and the patience to explain arcane details to an outsider. I can only hope that I have both "got it right" and can provide them with information useful in their partisan endeavours.

I am indebted to Dr. Peter Aucoin, Director of Research of the Royal Commission on Electoral Reform and Party Financing, for selecting me to do this study. Dr. Leslie Seidle provided extensive and very helpful comments on matters of substance and style on several drafts.

The external referees provided hundreds of comments, corrections and suggestions for changes in the manuscript. Most of them were implemented. Some suggestions were not followed because they would have required work beyond the scope of the mandate for the study developed with the Royal Commission. Other proposed changes seemed to me to be matters of style about which reasonable persons can disagree.

For several months, Colleen A. Lee worked energetically as my research assistant. In particular, she was able to "recruit" virtually all the party officials who were selected for interviews – no mean feat given the heavy demands on their time. Gary Clark worked hard to create and manipulate various datasets on the computer. Some of the benefits of his labour will be seen in future papers.

I am indebted to the Dean of the Faculty of Commerce and Business Administration at the University of BC, and to my colleagues for letting me reduce and rearrange my teaching schedule in academic year 1990–91 so as to be able to work full time on this study in the fall of 1990.

Sandra Carter provided word processing services of exemplary quality and speed, despite the large number of tables and hundreds of pages of material not included in the study.

Finally, I am grateful for the comments and insights offered by the Chairman and members of the Royal Commission on Electoral Reform and Party Financing.

W.T. Stanbury
September 1992

ACRONYMS
AND CRYPTIC PHRASES

"Campaign expenses"	See "Other expenses."
CCF	Co-operative Commonwealth Federation, predecessor to the NDP
CEO	Chief Electoral Officer
CEO *Guidelines*	Documents issued periodically by the CEO which provide interpretations of the *Canada Elections Act* with respect to "election expenses" incurred by (a) parties and (b) candidates.
CLC	Canadian Labour Congress
Conservative party	Short form of Progressive Conservative Party of Canada (federal)
CPI	Consumer Price Index
"Election expenses"	Official election expenses of a party or candidate as defined in the *Canada Elections Act* and as interpreted by the CEO's *Guidelines* which have been issued from time to time.
Election period (or campaign period or writ period)	Period from the date the writs of election are issued to voting day. In 1988, the period was 1 October to 21 November.
Electoral cycle	This is the period between general elections. In measuring expenditures, revenues and government assistance to parties and candidates, this has been taken to be the period covering the year after the one in which an election is called to the year in which the next one occurs. Thus the last two complete cycles are 1981–84 and 1985–88.

ACRONYMS AND CRYPTIC PHRASES

F 155	List of the 155 largest financial enterprises in Canada compiled from the *Financial Post* annual listings (chap. 11).
FP 500	Financial Post 500; Canada's 500 largest non-financial enterprises as compiled by the *Financial Post* annually (chap. 11).
"Laurier Club"	Major-donor club operated by the Liberal Party of Canada for individuals contributing $1 000 or more annually.
LPC	Liberal Party of Canada
NCC	National Citizens' Coalition
NDP	New Democratic Party
Nominal dollars	Revenues or expenditures in the dollars of the year in which they are received/spent. Because of inflation it is useful to convert nominal dollar amounts to "constant dollars" of one year by using a price index such as the CPI. See "real terms."
Non-financial	These are business firms whose primary activity lies outside the financial sector (e.g., banking, insurance, securities) such as manufacturing, mining, retailing. See FP 500.
OCECE	Ontario Commission on Election Contributions and Expenses
OCEF	Ontario Commission on Election Finances (present name of OCECE)
"Other expenses"	These are outlays by candidates other than "election expenses" and "personal expenses" as reported by the CEO and are sometimes called "campaign expenses." They are financed out of tax-receipted contributions and are deducted by the CEO in the computation of a candidate's surplus (defined in chap. 12).
PAC	Political Action Committee, formed in the United States by firms, unions, trade associations and other interest groups to collect political contributions from individuals and organizations and to direct them to candidates and parties.
Participation rate	The percentage of firms or individuals, perhaps in a specific cohort, that contributed to a party (and/or candidate) in a year.
PC	Progressive Conservative Party of Canada (federal)

"Personal expenses"	Official personal expenses as defined in the *Canada Elections Act*, interpreted by the CEO in the *Guidelines*, the amounts of which are published by the CEO after each general election.
PMO	Prime Minister's Office
PQ	Parti québécois (operates at the provincial level in Quebec)
Pre-writ period	The period of time between a riding's nomination meeting and the day the election writ is issued (where the former precedes the latter).
PTA	Provincial or Territorial Association (Liberal Party terminology); often referred to as provincial association(s).
PTS	Provincial or Territorial Section (the NDP's terminology); often referred to as provincial section(s).
QLP	Quebec Liberal Party
Real terms	Revenues or expenditures deflated by the CPI (usually based on 1989 = 100.0) to produce revenues or expenditures in constant (1989) dollars.
Riding association (or political local association)	The organization of a party operating at the local or constituency level.
RPC	Reform Party of Canada
SME	Small and medium-sized enterprises
"Tax-receipted"	Contributions to a party or candidate for which a receipt for the tax credit is issued. Individuals or corporations may use the receipt to claim the federal income-tax credit for political contributions.
Tax receipting	The issue of receipts to individuals or corporations for contributions to a registered party or candidate. The maximum income-tax credit is $500 for a contribution or contributions totalling $1 150 in a year.
"The 500"	Major-donor club operated by the Progressive Conservative party for individuals contributing $1 000 or more annually.
Tory/Tories	Short, non-pejorative term referring to the Progressive Conservative Party of Canada.
Transfers	Amounts of money sent from one unit within a political party to another (e.g., from party headquarters to a candidate). The money becomes the revenue of the receiving unit.

Money in
Politics

PART I

INTRODUCTION
AND
OVERVIEW

1

INTRODUCTION

Money is essential to conduct election campaigns and to pay for the operation of political parties between elections. Joseph Israel Tarte, Laurier's chief organizer and fund-raiser in Quebec 1894–96, and who also organized election campaigns in Quebec and New Brunswick until 1902, wisely observed that "les élections ne se font pas avec des prières," or "prayers do not win elections." Jesse Unruh, who was speaker of the California legislature in the early 1960s, used a different metaphor when he observed that "money is the mother's milk of politics." More recently, Norman Atkins, who was chairman of the Progressive Conservative party's highly successful general election campaigns in 1984 and 1988, stated that "you can't run national campaigns on [the proceeds from] selling fudge" (quoted in the *Globe and Mail*, 14 March 1990, A9). Political parties need funds for at least three purposes: "first, to fight election campaigns; second, to maintain a viable inter-election organization; third, to provide research and advisory services for the party's leadership and elected representatives at various levels" (Paltiel 1977, 198).[1] In addition, parties need substantial sums to finance their periodic conventions and the candidates for leadership of a party have to pay for their campaigns.[2]

Money is the fuel of election campaigns and party activities between elections, but like gasoline, it is potentially dangerous. Money can corrupt the people and the political process, as well as providing the necessary means by which politicians compete for the voters' favour.

The focus of this study is on the financing of federal parties and candidates from 1 August 1974, when the *Election Expenses Act* came into effect, until 1990. It examines both the revenues and expenditures of parties and candidates, although there is more emphasis on the sources of revenues because more information is available on them. This study also tries to assess how well the 1974 legislation has worked and proposes some reforms.

While the primary statute, the *Canada Elections Act,* has been amended several times (see chap. 2), the key provisions of the 1974 legislation have not been fundamentally altered.[3] They provide for the registration of political parties and of candidates in each general election (or by-election).[4] Second, a substantial part of the cost of election campaigns incurred by parties and candidates is financed by taxpayers through income-tax credits for political contributions, and by the reimbursement of part of the "election expenses" of parties and candidates. Third, the 1974 legislation imposed controls on the "election expenses" that may be incurred by candidates and parties.[5] The fourth element of the regulatory regime is the requirement for parties to disclose their revenues and expenditures annually and for candidates to do the same for each election campaign. (Parties report only their "election expenses" after each election.) Further, both are required to file with the Chief Electoral Officer, who makes available to the public the names of all persons and organizations whose aggregate contributions during the year exceeded $100. Fifth, the election broadcasting activities of parties and candidates are regulated in several ways, including limits on the amount of time each may purchase for campaign commercials, the time period during which commercials may be broadcast and the allocation of free broadcast time during the campaign that must be supplied by broadcasters.

1. VALUES AND POLICY OBJECTIVES

Legislation embodies values and certain policy objectives. To begin to understand and assess a major policy initiative such as the *Election Expenses Act* of 1974, it is useful to understand the objectives that its sponsors sought to achieve. The principle of political equality is central to the concept of democratic government and has greatly influenced the legal constraints imposed on the financing of parties and candidates. Political equality is more than the right to vote; it necessarily includes the right of all adults to stand for election. It is almost immediately obvious that those with access to more economic resources will have an advantage over candidates not so well endowed, other things being equal.

It is often argued that the failure to regulate political financing violates the goal of political equality because it denies equality of opportunity for candidates competing for office, and because those with economic resources and who make large political contributions may be able to exercise disproportionate influence over politicians. The logic of controlling expenditures on election campaigns is that it obviates the need of candidates and parties to raise large or very large sums so as to compete on a roughly equal footing.[6] The need for large amounts of money for electoral contests opens up the possibility that the candidate will become obligated to those who make large contributions. This means that there may be inequality of influence among citizens – not based on the quality of their arguments or the number of people they may be said to represent.

Both at the time the reform legislation was enacted and since then there appears to have been quite widespread agreement about its objectives. It is commonly asserted that three principles are embodied in the *Election Expenses Act* of 1974. The first is to foster a measure of equality between candidates and registered parties. This principle was designed to ensure that every Canadian, irrespective of financial means, would have reasonable access to public office. The second is openness. The goal was to increase the public's confidence in the political process by ensuring that the sources of revenue and expenditures of parties and candidates are made public. The third principle relates to the participation of citizens and candidates. It was hoped that the general public would become more involved and participate fully in elections above and beyond just voting, by donating goods and services, by contributing money and by providing volunteer labour. Over the years these principles or policy objectives have become elaborated in terms of equity, participation and the prevention of corruption.

To achieve equity, government regulation of political money should seek to make more equitable the competition for political office by ensuring that the ability to raise money does not play too great a role in electoral outcomes, and by seeing that there is a substantial degree of equality among candidates and parties in respect to their ability to communicate with and persuade voters during election campaigns by limiting campaign expenditures. The participation objective implies that the regulation of political financing should seek to permit a wider range of Canadians to be candidates for office, to ensure that parties and candidates are able to present their positions fairly to the electorate so that voters may make an informed choice, and to encourage more Canadians to make political contributions. In order to prevent corruption, regulation should seek to increase the transparency concerning the sources of money to finance political activity and where it is spent and thereby to reduce its influence. Regulation should also ensure that candidates and parties are not improperly influenced by those able to provide large contributions (i.e., limit corruption), and it should ensure the public has confidence in the fairness of election campaigns.[7]

Paltiel (1977, 107–108) argued that "unequal and clandestine access to campaign funding" is a threat to the goals of promoting honesty in public life, reducing the costs of election campaigns and achieving the liberal principles of equity and equality of opportunity.

Corruption is viewed as a threat to the stability and integrity of the political and social order. High costs prevent the effective participation in the electoral process of those who do not have access to the means to conduct increasingly expensive and sophisticated campaigns. Liberal democracy is posited on the belief that in a fair fight untrammelled by the shackles of "unfair competition," the best man and the best policy will carry the day. (Ibid., 108)

Unfavourable perceptions about the financing of political parties and candidates may influence the public's perception of politicians. A national poll in March 1990 found that 57 percent of respondents said that politicians were "unprincipled"; 81 percent said they were more concerned with making money than helping people; and only 32 percent said they held generally favourable views about politicians (Gregg and Posner 1990, 54). A survey conducted for the Royal Commission on Electoral Reform and Party Financing in the fall of 1990 found that 39 percent of the adults surveyed believed politicians are "less honest" than the average person (Blais and Gidengil 1991, table 3.1). The same survey found that 30 percent believed there is more corruption in government than in business, and 64 percent "basically agreed" with the statement, "Most members of Parliament make a lot of money misusing public office" (ibid.). In response to the statement, "Anybody who gives money to a political party expects something in return, like a job or a contract," 43 percent "basically agreed," and 85 percent "basically agreed" with the statement, "People with money have a lot of influence over the government" (ibid., table 3.8).

Over 17 years have passed since the present regulatory regime was put in place in 1974. It is time to examine carefully its effects for there is some evidence that the regime is under some strain.[8] Consider the following:

- An increasing amount of money is being spent on election campaigns by parties and candidates over and above the "election expenses" that are subject to statutory limit (see chaps. 3, 4, 5 and 12).
- While the "election expenses" of parties and candidates are constrained by law, spending during elections by advocacy or interest groups is not. This raises serious questions about the equity and effectiveness of the constraints on "election expenses" (Hiebert 1991).
- Expenditures by all parties during interelection periods have grown far more rapidly than "election expenses," largely because there are no limits on expenditures other than "election expenses."

- In the last two general elections, there is some evidence to suggest that at least two parties have been able to reduce the effect of the limit on "election expenses" by increasing party expenditures prior to the election (see chaps. 4 and 5).
- There is considerable evidence that spending on areas of political activity *not* presently regulated, such as leadership campaigns, is substantial and is rising (see chap. 13).
- The fact that riding associations are essentially unregulated but are usually the beneficiaries of substantial surpluses from candidates' campaigns has resulted in a "black hole" in the current regulatory regime (see chap. 13). Much of the surplus enjoyed by many candidates is attributable to direct and indirect financial assistance provided by the federal government.
- Despite the fairly generous tax credit for political contributions, no more than 2 percent of adults and 9 percent of corporations made a political contribution in any year during the 1980s (see chaps. 8 and 11). However, about 40 percent of the 500 largest nonfinancial enterprises made a contribution to one or more of the three main parties during the years of the 1980s (see chap. 11).
- The amount, type, form and timing of the information required to be disclosed to and by the Chief Electoral Officer is inadequate to ensure that citizens, the media and policy analysts are able to understand how political parties and candidates raise and spend money. For example, considerable money raised by the NDP for which federal income-tax credits may be claimed is, in fact, spent on *provincial* political activities (see chaps. 3, 6 and 13). While "other expenses" now constitute some 15 percent of candidates' "election expenses," the amount is not disclosed in any of the CEO's published reports, nor is the surplus or deficit of each candidate; nor is the disposition of each candidate's surplus disclosed. Since disclosure is central to the effectiveness of the regulatory regime, these are serious omissions.

This study will examine these concerns and others in considerable detail. It concludes with a series of recommendations for improving the regulatory regime.

2. IMPORTANCE OF VOLUNTEERS

The resources of political parties and candidates are of two kinds: money (donated by individuals, corporations, unions and other organizations, or government subsidies), and volunteer labour. While this study focuses on the money revenues of parties, the importance of contributions in the form of labour donated by volunteers should not be understated.

Both the day-to-day operations of parties and their election campaigns depend greatly on volunteers. Wearing notes that "even in the days of sophisticated polling and advertising, a party's volunteer wing [is] of great value. A brilliantly conceived advertising campaign is no more than an artillery attack on the positions that have to be taken in hand-to-hand combat by an army of volunteers whose enthusiasm is built upon a self-reinforcing esprit de corps" (1981, 201)[9]. In the case of a priority seat, the NDP, for example, can sometimes deploy up to 500 volunteers. On election day, all 500 might be in action "pulling the vote" by foot canvassing and driving voters to the polls.

It is useful to think of a party as a club or an affinity group. Parties must focus on the needs of their members and on the ideas/ideals that attract them. At the national level, each party has a cadre of "expert" volunteers, individuals who have become skilled in the arts of organization and campaign techniques. There is often a big turnover in volunteers between election campaigns, and fewer volunteers are actively involved in party activities at the riding, provincial and national levels between elections. Each party faces the problem of recruitment to renew its crop of volunteers when the party is out of office. There is a trade-off between experience and enthusiasm, and between the comfort of old friends and allies and the need for new blood to carry on the line.

According to a former senior official in the federal Liberal party, with very few exceptions people work as volunteers for a political party only because they expect to get more out of it than they put in. The rewards received by the volunteer are both intangible and tangible. The intangible rewards include the following: the intrinsic satisfaction gained from the activity (participation in politics, camaraderie, competition); feelings of altruism – of helping others in a good cause, the practical workings of democracy; ideological satisfaction (seeing one's basic political values put into practice); and the psychological benefits of praise, expressions of esteem and recognition by others whose opinion is valued. According to one expert on Canadian parties, volunteers are vulnerable to "psychological patronage."

> Many of those leading figures in the volunteer wing, who are already
> established lawyers or businessmen, are often far more susceptible
> to the blandishments of what is called psychological patronage than
> the more traditional variety. These are the little courtesies, favours, an
> invitation to a prestigious government function, a flattering telephone
> call from Ottawa to ask for the local assessment of a current issue.
> (Just to indicate how little things count, one of the party's chief fund
> raisers recalls that he used to arrange to have his fund-raising team
> invited to lunch at the prime minister's residence once a year. His

special request to the staff of 24 Sussex was that lots of the residence's official match covers be put out because even a corporation executive liked to leave with a couple in his pocket!) (Wearing 1981, 192)

The tangible rewards of active participation in a party (current or potential) include the following: building a network that will advance one's economic or social status; earning promotion to a higher status position in the party – hence greater rewards; and building up IOUs that can be cashed in for benefits in the future (e.g., a position on a minister's staff, ability to get phone calls returned when representing clients dealing with government, ability to acquire "inside" information). The ultimate tangible reward is a seat in the Senate. This may require a few years to a decade or more of service to the party.

The volunteers' attachment to and participation in a party varies in intensity. It is likely influenced by the electoral cycle and by perceptions about the leader. It also competes with two other priorities: occupational and family responsibilities. A poor showing in public polls has an adverse effect on morale, recruitment, fund-raising and on the energy level of party employees and volunteers. A critical function for party regulars is to maintain contact with, and recruit new members for, the network of volunteers to be mobilized to help during election campaigns.

The requisites of an effective campaign operation are in serious conflict with party members' desire for participation and consultation. The former requires well-defined objectives, prompt, centralized decision making, tight discipline to implement decisions and expertise (not necessarily supplied by paid professionals). It also requires clear hierarchical relationships and division of labour, and close cooperation among the 10 to 20 core personnel who direct the campaign so as to be able to react quickly to changes in the environment, including the behaviour of other parties. At the same time, officials must find sufficient funds to be able to spend to the legal limit, but also control outlays so as to stay under the limit to avoid legal and political repercussions. Obviously, a campaign requires careful control over strategic information, such as polling data (Fraser 1989; Lee 1989; Frizzell et al. 1989). Participation, on the other hand, implies an effort to consult widely, an effort to involve many people in party activities, sharing information widely and devoting the time necessary to be able to work out differences.

The efforts of volunteers are not without cost to political parties. One of the "prices" volunteers extract from parties is the opportunity to make an input to the key decision makers in one or more areas of party activity. More experienced officials may not find this advice very useful, however. Another "price" such volunteers extract for their services is the right to exercise some power (autonomy) over a party activity – be it ever so humble. If they cannot be rewarded with money, they want a "piece of the action" where others defer to their judgement, preferences, instincts or clout. In a conventional hierarchy of paid employees, higher officials can rely more on pecuniary rewards (or the threat of their withdrawal) and their legitimate coercive authority to shape the behaviour of subordinates.

The value to campaigns of volunteers with specialized skills (e.g., computer skills, management of large-scale telephone operations) increases as campaigns become more sophisticated. The tighter the constraints on "election expenses," the more valuable are volunteers with these skills. At the same time, party officials suggest that it is difficult to recruit volunteers. People have less unscheduled time than they once had. Further, in recent years there has been considerable disillusionment with politics and parties. This is reflected in the willingness to work for a party or candidate as a volunteer (table 1.1).

3. COMPLEX FINANCIAL FLOWS

"The study of money in politics necessarily probes the organization of society in its relationship to the functions and actions of government" (Heard 1960, 4). The nature of power and influence is illuminated by studying the flow of funds from the rest of society to parties and candidates. Although the amounts of money moving through federal parties and their candidates are very modest by the standards of the United States or Japan,[10] the ways in which that money moves are almost Byzantine in their complexity and are not well known even within the parties themselves. Because of the complexity of the flows, the measurement of various aspects of party activities, particularly by *level*, is fraught with difficulty.

3.1 Financing Parties and Candidates

In order to try to "map" the various flows of funds associated with federal parties and candidates,[11] figure 1.1 has been prepared. It is useful to begin with the persons or organizations making contributions. They may make contributions to a candidate (flow 1), to a riding association (flow 2), to a provincial or territorial association of a party (flow 3) or to the national office of a party (flow 4). Several points should be noted here. Candidates (or more precisely their official agents) can provide tax receipts for contributions only during the official campaign period (from the day the writ is issued until voting day) *and* after they have filed their nomination papers. Second, some of the money that ends up in the hands of the federal or national office (party headquarters) is

Figure 1.1
Flows of funds associated with federal parties and candidates

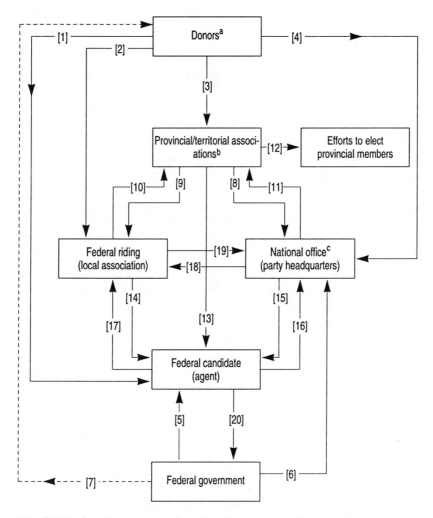

Note: Excludes financing of campaigns for party leadership or nomination campaigns.

aIncludes individuals, corporations, trade unions, interest groups and other organizations.

bThe NDP uses the term provincial or territorial "section."

cThe Liberal party uses this term; the NDP refers to the "federal office."

taken in by a PTA to which the official agent for the party has delegated tax-receipting authority (see chap. 3). Third, for the Progressive Conservative party – which has the clearest separation of the federal party from the various provincial PC parties – the PTA level does not exist. All donations for which tax receipts are issued must pass through the party agent (the PC Canada Fund) in Ottawa – except during election campaigns, when they can also be received and receipted by each candidate's agent.[12] Fourth, in 1987, the Liberal party rescinded the tax-receipting authority that had been delegated to the 12 PTAs that make up the federation that is the Liberal Party of Canada (see chap. 5).

The federal government plays a considerable role in financing parties and candidates. For example, in the last complete four-year electoral cycle ending in the 1988 election, the federal government provided, directly and indirectly (through tax credits), $66.7 million to parties and candidates (table 1.2). Flow 5 of figure 1.1 represents the government's reimbursement of half the "election expenses" of candidates who receive 15 percent of the votes cast. For the 1988 election, this amounted to $13.7 million (table 1.2). Flow 6 of figure 1.1 represents the government's reimbursement (sometimes called rebate) of 22.5 percent of each registered party's "election expenses," provided the party spends at least 10 percent of the limit based on running a full slate of candidates.[13] In 1988, the cost of this subsidy was $4.96 million (table 1.2).

Flow 7 of figure 1.1 represents the value of tax credits for political contributions claimed by individuals or corporations in filing their income tax return.[14] It is a dashed line because it is a "tax expenditure," that is, a reduction in the amount of revenue that would otherwise be collected.[15] This *indirect* subsidy amounted to $47.96 million in the period 1985–88, the last complete electoral cycle. In 1988 alone, the value of such income-tax credits was $18.85 million. Government funding for the previous electoral cycle, 1981–84, totalled $51.5 million. In constant 1989 dollars, the costs of the last two cycles were $63.6 million (1981–84) and $70.0 million (1985–88) respectively (see table 1.2). Michaud and Laferrière (1991) estimate the value of tax credits to have been equal to 30.7 percent of the income of federal parties in the electoral cycle 1981–84 ($118.9 million) and 29.0 percent for the cycle 1985–88 ($165.3 million). For the 1988 general election, they estimate that the federal government's contribution to the financing of federal parties and candidates amounted to 43.3 percent of parties' and candidates' expenditures ($63.5 million).

The level of government support for the 1984 general election amounted to $24.75 million out of total party and candidate expenditures of $57.1 million, or 43.3 percent. In terms of the expenditures of all parties and candidates over the last electoral *cycle* ending in 1988, the federal government's contribution in the form of reimbursements and tax credits was $66.7 million or 31.4 percent of the total (Michaud and Laferrière 1991).

Now consider the possible disposition of money given to a PTA (flow 3). The PTA might well transfer a substantial part of the contributions it receives to the party's national office (flow 8), perhaps because the PTA was merely acting with receipting authority delegated by the party's official agent. Even if the PTA raised the money by staging an event such as a dinner in the case of the Liberal party (1974–86) or the NDP, a specified fraction had to be sent to the national office. In the case of the NDP, during federal election campaigns, the PTSs transfer funds to the federal office ($2.2 million in 1988).[16] Through flow 9, money is transferred from the PTA to a riding association. This may occur as part of the riding's share of money raised by the PTA, or a donation made to a riding may be routed through a PTA in order to be eligible for the income-tax credit (receipting). Riding associations have no receipting power; they are not "registered entities" under the *Canada Elections Act,* unlike candidates during campaigns or parties (see chap. 13).

Money may move from the riding association to the PTA (flow 10), for example, where the riding holds a fund-raising event and a party's financing formula provides that the PTA receives part of the funds. From what can be ascertained, the amount of money moving through flow 9 is small (in the case of the Conservative party, it is zero, as the federal party has no PTAs). Flow 11 arises in several ways: first, the national office may simply be transferring to the PTAs its share of money raised at the national office. Second, in the case of the Liberal party, since 1987 all donations to the party are processed through the Federal Liberal Agency in Ottawa and the PTAs receive an annual budget to conduct their operations. In the case of the NDP, the 12 PTSs initially receive virtually all of the money raised by the party, other than that received by candidates during campaigns, and provide federal tax receipts under authority delegated by the party's federal agent. Only 15 percent of the money moves through flow 8. Since the amount of federally receipted funds (flow 3) greatly exceeds the federal office's receipts (flow 8), the individual PTS may spend the difference on its efforts to elect provincial members (flow 12). The annual amount in flow 12 for the NDP is usually several million dollars (see chaps. 3 and 6).

Turning now to the candidate's perspective, recall that a candidate's agent can provide tax receipts for contributions only during the official campaign period. The candidate through his/her agent can receive funds from several sources: from various donations (flow 1), from the riding association (flow 14), from the party's national office (flow 15) and from the federal government through the reimbursement of half the "election expenses," as discussed above (flow 5).

Within the party, a candidate can send funds to the riding association (flow 17), and/or to the national office (flow 16) and to the federal government (flow 20). These transfers typically occur in three situations. First, the candidate ends the election campaign with a surplus of funds. Under the *Canada Elections Act*, he/she must dispose of it by giving it to a local association or to the party (otherwise, it goes to the federal government). Second, the party, as a condition of having the leader sign the candidate's nomination papers may require him/her to assign some part of the reimbursement of "election expenses" to the party (should the candidate be eligible for reimbursement).[17] Technically, the amount assigned moves through flow 6, but it is really the candidate's money moving to the national office (flow 16). Third, each candidate must pay a deposit to the Chief Electoral Officer. It is returned if the candidate obtains 15 percent of the votes cast in the riding.

Flow 14 deserves comment. Flows from the riding association to the candidate may occur when a candidate has been nominated, but before the election has been called. Thus, the riding association may finance the pre-campaign activities of the candidate before the writ is issued. During this period, candidates may spend as much as they want, and the riding is not required to report the amounts given to the candidate (see chap. 13).

Finally, there are the flows between the national office (party headquarters) and the riding association. In the case of the Progressive Conservatives, contributions to any riding between elections for which the donor wants a tax receipt (flow 2) are routed through the PC Canada Fund in Ottawa (flow 19), which retains 25 percent and remits 75 percent to the riding association (flow 18).[18] Note that even though many riding associations have substantial funds, in part due to their receipt of the candidate's surplus (which in 1988 totalled $9.6 million according to the CEO (Canada, Elections Canada 1991, 10)), the national office usually knows little of their financial situation.[19] In contrast, in Ontario, where riding associations are a "registered entity" (like the party and each candidate), both their income statements and balance sheets must be reported to the Ontario Commission on Election Finances, and then made public.

Although figure 1.1 is complex, it does not show the flows from the various component entities (candidate, PTA, riding association and national office) to the persons and organizations who supply goods and services to the party or the flows associated with campaigns for the party's leadership.

3.2 Financing Leadership Campaigns

The *Canada Elections Act* does not regulate the financing of campaigns for the leadership of political parties. Given the amounts of money involved, the importance of the leader's role in political parties and the fact that public money helps to finance such campaigns, this omission is surprising.

Public money is used in leadership campaigns in two ways: where contributions benefit from a tax credit;[20] and where publicly paid staff of the candidate work on his/her campaign instead of their regular jobs. Further, when a cabinet minister is a candidate, part of his/her travel and related expenses (government phone lines, mailing privileges) might well benefit the campaign for the leadership.

Leadership candidates cannot *directly* provide official tax receipts, but contributions can be "routed through" the official agent of the party. There is no legal requirement covering how a leadership candidate must dispose of any surplus funds following a leadership convention, even if contributions benefited from the tax credit.

Recently, the Liberals and the NDP have imposed their own regulations on leadership campaigns (see appendix 13.1 to chap. 13). In the case of the 1990 Liberal leadership race, the provisions for disclosure – except for contributions routed through the Federal Liberal Agency – were less rigorous than now apply to contributions of $100 or more made to a registered party or candidate. Columnist Jeffrey Simpson pointed out the following:

> The Liberals have given themselves a system superficially transparent but fundamentally opaque. Anyone who earmarks a donation for a candidate, but sends it through the Liberal Party, becomes eligible for a tax deduction. Those donors' names, with the amounts they gave and the candidates they financed, will be made public.
>
> But anyone not wishing a tax receipt can give money to a candidate. The party will then publish only a list of those donors' names, identified as contributors to the party. There will no link to a candidate or report of the amount donated.
>
> The more you give, the less valuable the tax deduction, which is limited by law. Thus the largest donors, the very ones who might have a hook into a candidate, will not be known. The smallest donors, who will want the tax receipt, will be known. The system as designed stands the public interest on its head by publicizing those contributions of least importance and hiding those of potentially the greatest. (*Globe and Mail*, 19 January 1990, A6)

"Self-regulation" by political parties in the case of leadership campaigns can be difficult to enforce. Consider the case of the race for leader of the federal Progressive Conservative party in 1976:

> The biggest spender of all ... was apparently Montreal lawyer Brian
> Mulroney, who dazzled the media, if not the Conservatives, with a
> flashy, high-profile campaign. In defiance of party regulations,
> Mulroney – who has joined the Iron Ore Co. of Canada as executive
> vice-president and is apparently out of politics – refused to file a finan-
> cial statement showing what he spent and where he got the money.
> But knowledgeable sources estimate he spent $343 000, which works
> out to roughly $1 000 for each of the 357 first-ballot votes he received.
> (*Maclean's*, 28 June 1976, 17)

Figure 1.2 outlines the flows of funds associated with campaigns
for the leadership of a party. Donors (individuals, corporations, unions
and other organizations) are usually able to give money to a leadership
candidate in two ways. The traditional method of making contributions
directly to the candidate (i.e., to the chief fund-raiser) is illustrated by
flow 1 on figure 1.2. The second method is to donate the money to the
national party's official agent (flow 2), who, in turn, issues a receipt for
the income-tax credit to the donor, and passes the money along to the
leadership candidate (flow 3). Depending on the rules established by
the party, the party's agent may or may not retain a fraction of flow 2
funds before sending the money on to the candidate (flow 3). Note that
contributions directly to the candidate (flow 1) are subject only to the
disclosure rules established by the *party*, not the Chief Electoral Officer.
On the other hand, if the contribution is routed through the party's official agent (flow 2), all sums of more than $100 must be reported by the
party within six months after the end of the calendar year.[21]

The use of the federal tax credit for political contributions in leadership races is illustrated by the 1990 campaign for the leadership of the
Liberal party. Of the $6 million raised by the leadership candidates,
$1.95 million was routed through the national party agency (flow 2),
while about $4 million went directly to the candidates from the donor
(flow 1) (table 5.8).

Flow 4 in figure 1.2 indicates that a party may require all leadership
candidates to pay a fee to the party as a condition of their participation in the race. In the 1990 race for the leadership of the Liberal party,
each candidate had to pay a fee of 20 percent of their expenditures
above $250 000, but below the limit of $1.7 million. As a result, the
Liberal party received $608 151 from the candidates, who spent a total
of about $6 million (table 5.8).

The use of the party's tax-receipting authority to help finance leadership campaigns is discussed in more detail in chapter 13.

Figure 1.2
Flows of funds associated with campaigns for leadership of a party

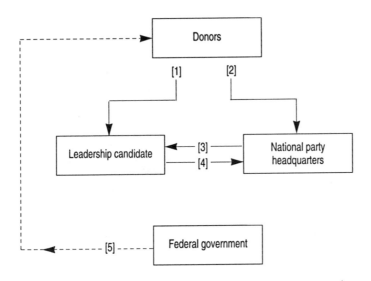

3.3 Financing Party Conventions

Figure 1.3 outlines the financial flows associated with party conventions, including leadership conventions. The delegate sends a cheque to the national party headquarters for his/her convention fees (flow 1 in figure 1.3). It is the practice of all the major parties to treat the payment of delegate fees for party conventions as *contributions;* hence, they issue a receipt for the income-tax credit for the amount received. The tax credit (flow 3) goes from the federal government to the delegate. Convention fees are designed to at least cover the costs of the convention and have become substantial. For example, each delegate paid a fee of $875 for the 1990 Liberal leadership convention. With the receipt for the political tax credit the *net* cost to each delegate was $467. The difference of $408, in effect, represents a subsidy to the delegates and party from other taxpayers. Party officials argue that policy and leadership conventions are central activities of the parties and it is entirely appropriate to issue tax receipts for delegate fees.[22]

The amounts of money involved in financing party conventions are large. For example, for the Liberal party leadership convention in June 1990 the amount of receipted revenue in the form of convention fees was $4.4 million. The party indicates that all of this was spent on the convention (flow 2 in figure 1.3). However, it appears the assistance from federal taxpayers may have been as much as $2 million.[23] This issue is discussed again in chapter 13.

Figure 1.3
Flows of funds associated with party conventions

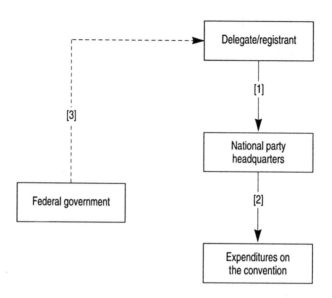

3.4   Financing Nomination and Pre-Writ Campaigns

While the amount of "election expenses" a candidate (or party) may incur during an election campaign is limited under a formula in the *Canada Elections Act*, expenditures to obtain a party's nomination as its candidate in a local riding are not regulated, nor are the candidate's expenditures after the nomination meeting but before the day the writ is issued (the pre-writ period). While Carty and Erickson (1991) indicate that 65 percent of candidates in 1988 won their nomination by acclamation and hence spent very little on their nomination "race," in a few cases large sums were spent on nomination races. Gray (1989, 18) states that in Metro Toronto some of the winners of Liberal party nominations spent from $50 000 to $100 000. Frank Stronach almost certainly spent much more to obtain the Liberal party nomination for York–Simcoe than he was allowed to spend on the election campaign itself (Lee 1989, chap. 6).

Figure 1.4 describes the flows of money associated with both the nomination races and the period between the nomination meeting and the day the writ is issued. (Note that in 20 percent of ridings in 1988, the nomination meeting occurred *after* the writ was issued (Carty and Erickson 1991).) Donors may make contributions to a candidate for the nomination to finance his/her nomination race (flow 1) or they may help to finance the nominee's pre-election campaigning in one or two ways. The donor can give the money to the local riding association (flow 2) which, in turn gives it to the candidate (flow 5); and/or the donor can give the money directly to the candidate (i.e., winner of the nomination race) (see flow 4). In either case, the donor cannot receive a receipt for the income-tax credit. Recall that a candidate cannot issue such receipts until the writ has been issued. In theory, the donor could route the contribution through the national party agent, but this is very seldom done because of the "tax" imposed (e.g., 25 percent in the case of the PC Canada Fund). According to a former president of the NDP, all three of the major parties are very reluctant to allow contributions in support of individuals seeking the nomination in a riding to be routed through the party so as to be eligible for a tax receipt.

In a few cases, substantial sums have been spent by candidates in the *pre-writ* period. For example, in the Toronto riding of Broadview–Greenwood, it is reported that Liberal challenger Dennis Mills had

Figure 1.4
Flows of funds associated with nomination races and pre-election campaigns

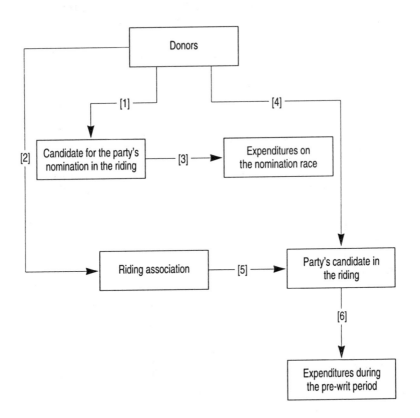

already spent $130 000 by the time the election writ was issued (*Globe and Mail*, 6 October 1988, A10). During his seven-month "pre-writ campaign," Mills worked almost full time in the riding. According to a newspaper report, Mills felt that pre-writ time and money are necessary for a challenger to build voter awareness (ibid.). Mr. Mills won the seat. To put his pre-writ expenses into perspective, note that Mr. Mills' official "election expenses" were $38 268 (89 percent of thelimit), his "personal expenses" were $1 161 and his "other expenses" were $7 422.

An example of flow 5 in figure 1.4 was noted in a newspaper article (*Vancouver Sun*, 16 August 1990, B6), which stated that the Trinity–Spadina association of the Liberal party told candidate Antonio Ianno that he could spend up to $2 000 to promote himself *after* he was nominated on 1 May 1988. The writ was not issued until 1 October. The author's own analysis of the 277 candidates with the largest total "other expenses" in 1988 indicates that they spent an average of $2 065 on pre-writ expenses, although 26 spent more than $7 000 (see chap. 12).

4. METHODOLOGY

The information contained in this study has been obtained from several different sources. First and foremost, the study draws upon information filed by the parties and candidates with the CEO. Unfortunately, very little of this information is available in electronic form (e.g., computer tape or disk).[24] Therefore, in order to determine the size distribution of contributions to parties in 1988, for example, it would have been necessary to scan 200 000 names and code the information for computer analysis. It is for this reason that contributions made by the 500 largest nonfinancial enterprises and the 155 largest financial enterprises could be tabulated only for the period 1983–90.[25]

Further, the review and analysis of the annual and post-election returns filed with and reported by the CEO found several problems. First, revenues and expenditures were reported inconsistently from year to year; for example, some parties report interest income as a negative expenditure in some years (see chap. 3). Second, some provincial revenues were reported by the NDP in some years and not in others (see chaps. 3 and 6). Third, there were occasionally large errors in the data reported by the parties (see chap. 5). Fourth, there were large inconsistencies in the data reported to and by the CEO with respect to intra-party transfers (see chaps. 3 to 6).[26] Fifth, it appears that some of the functional expenditure categories probably contain outlays on items that do not fall within the category, because the form provided by the CEO does not provide a sufficiently large number of categories (and the names of which have remained unchanged since 1974; see chap. 4). Sixth, the

CEO's principal publication on party and candidate revenues after each general election fails to report "other expenses" by candidates even though these amounted to about $4.7 million in 1988[27] (about 15 percent of "election expenses") and were financed out of contributions eligible for the income-tax credit (see chap. 12). Seventh, the CEO does not publish a report on each candidate's surplus or deficit.

In addition to the data that are filed with the CEO and made available to the public by him, the CEO kindly made available in printed and electronic form additional data collected in the course of the administration of the *Canada Elections Act*. Without such information it would not have been possible to describe and analyse candidates' surplus or deficit and "other expenses" for the 1988 election as outlined in chapter 12.

Some of the most original material in this study was provided by the Liberal, Progressive Conservative and New Democratic parties. While the data made available by each party were not the same,[28] they nevertheless provided new insights into the parties' methods of raising funds, and their costs.

To complement the figures provided by the parties, about 20 current and former officials in each of the three main parties were interviewed about their party's structure and financing. In addition, several officials of the Reform Party were interviewed by telephone. Some of the persons interviewed are, or have been, closely associated with the task of raising funds, others with running campaigns, while others have had extensive experience at the provincial and/or local level. All were extremely helpful, and in some cases spent several hours talking about their experiences. Any additional insights into the relationship between the structure of parties and their financing are largely due to the guidance provided by those interviewed.

A great deal of the published work on Canadian parties and their financing was also reviewed. The literature was particularly helpful in providing the details of the evolution of the regulatory regime and the characteristics of the parties and election campaigns.

5. STRUCTURE OF THE STUDY

This study is divided into five major parts. Part I provides an introduction to the study and an overview of the financing of the Progressive Conservative, Liberal and New Democratic parties. Chapter 2 examines the evolution of the present regulatory regime as it applies to the financing of federal political parties and candidates. It describes the decade-long process that resulted in the *Election Expenses Act* of 1974. It also reviews efforts made to modify the 1974 legislation through 1989, when the Royal Commission on Electoral Reform and Party Financing was appointed. Chapter 3 provides an overview of the revenues and expenditures of the parties, with the emphasis on the financial operations of the Progressive Conservative, Liberal and New Democratic parties in the period 1974–90.

Part II of this study analyses the organizational and behavioural aspects of the financing of the four leading parties in Canada. The Progressive Conservative party is the subject of chapter 4, while chapter 5 is devoted to the Liberal party. Chapter 6 focuses on the New Democratic Party, and chapter 7 examines the Reform Party. In each chapter, the focus is on the relationship between a party's organizational structure (and changes in its structure) and its financing. When the study was first undertaken, the importance of the basic design characteristics of a party's organization for its effectiveness in raising money was not appreciated. It appears that clear separation of its federal and provincial components has been an advantage to the Progressive Conservative party, while the Liberal party's structure as a federation has created difficulties for the party at the federal level.[29] The NDP has the most integrated structure in that all of its provincial or territorial sections (except Quebec) are dual-purpose, that is, the section operates at both the provincial and federal level. The Reform Party is the most recently established (1987), but it has grown enormously both in terms of members and revenues (more than the Liberal party in 1991). Its reliance on its members for funds is quite different from the other three parties.

Part III focuses on the methods by which *parties* raise money. Chapter 8 focuses on the role of individuals in supplying funds for the parties. An effort is made to ascertain the extent to which the federal government (really other taxpayers) subsidizes the contributions of individuals by means of the income-tax credit for political contributions. The importance of "large" contributions in terms of total party revenue is also assessed. Chapters 9 and 10 analyse in more detail some of the techniques used by the parties to raise money from individuals. Chapter 9 examines direct-mail fund-raising, which has been particularly successful for the Progressive Conservative party. Chapter 10 investigates fund-raising dinners and major-donor programs, notably the Conservative party's "The 500" and the Liberal party's "Laurier Club." Chapter 11 completes Part III of the study. It examines in detail contributions made to parties by corporations. Particular emphasis is given to contributions by Canada's 500 largest nonfinancial enterprises and by the 155 largest financial enterprises. Further, the importance of "large" contributions ($10 000+) to the Liberal and Progressive Conservative parties is assessed.

Part IV shifts the focus from parties to candidates. Chapter 12 describes the sources of revenues and categories of expenditures of candidates in the four general elections that have been subject to the 1974 legislation. Considerable detail is provided on candidates' "other expenses" in the 1988 election because they appear to be quite important in some cases, because such outlays are not controlled, and because the CEO provides no information to the public about them.

Part V of this study deals with the reform of the current regulatory regime. Reforms are likely to be most effective when informed by a thorough analysis of the limitations and failures of the present legislative and policy framework. Thus chapter 13 identifies and analyses the major problems with the regime. Chapter 14 summarizes the most important empirical findings, draws some conclusions and sets out some recommendations for improving the regulatory regime relating to the financing of federal political parties and candidates in Canada.

2

EVOLUTION OF THE REGULATORY REGIME

THE RAISING AND SPENDING of political money at the federal level in Canada since 1974 has been greatly influenced by the wide-ranging provisions of the *Election Expenses Act,* which came into effect on 1 August of that year. The Act established the framework within which parties and candidates have functioned through the four subsequent electoral cycles, which ended in the general elections of 1979, 1980, 1984 and 1988.

Because the regulatory regime[1] so greatly influences party and candidate financing, it is essential to understand its main elements and the forces and process that brought it about. Section 1 describes very briefly the limited number of legal provisions that governed the financing of federal parties and candidates prior to 1974. Section 2 outlines the process leading to the *Election Expenses Act* of 1974. The central elements of the 1974 reforms are also described in that section. Section 3 examines the efforts to change the 1974 regime, only some of which were successful.

1. SOME EARLY HISTORY, 1874–1974

The regulation of the financing of political parties and candidates in Canada can be traced to 1874, although some earlier provisions did exist.[2] At the time of Confederation, "only corrupt practices such as the giving and receiving of bribes, treating – notably with alcoholic beverages – and the conveyance of voters to the polls in questionable circumstances were considered to be illegal. The likelihood of corruption issuing from the moral and material indebtedness of candidates to those who had contributed to their campaigns was ignored" (Paltiel 1970b, 11).

In 1873, the Prime Minister, Sir John A. Macdonald, was found to be in receipt of large campaign contributions from the promoters of the Canadian Pacific Railway, who were vitally interested in a government contract and subsidy (Berton 1976). The resulting "Pacific Scandal" contributed to the defeat of the Conservatives in the election of 1874. Later, Macdonald observed that "the necessity for a party fund may be freely admitted, but the methods employed in its collection and distribution put a severe strain too often upon political morality" (quoted in Canada, Committee 1966, 14).

Reforms relating to election finance were made in the *Dominion Elections Act*, which was enacted in 1874 shortly after Alexander Mackenzie's Liberals came to power. The relevant provisions were "modelled fairly closely on the British Corrupt Practices Act of 1854" (Seidle 1980, 146), and relied on the basic premise that disclosure was sufficient to prevent corruption. The doctrine of agency was established. Both candidate and agent were required to produce a statement indicating how and where campaign funds were spent. Neither limits on election expenses nor disclosure of contributions was addressed. Nor was there mention of the matter of funds received by the candidate from the party, even though the parties were a main source of funds. No official was made responsible for administering or enforcing the law, which also was limited by its failure to define key terms (Canada, Committee 1966, 15–16).

According to the Committee on Election Expenses (the Barbeau Committee), "The law of 1874 ... failed on three basic counts: 1. it comprehended only the expenditure and not the income side of political finances; 2. it failed to recognize parties as collectors and spenders of money; 3. it failed to place the initiative for enforcement in any effective body or office. The result was legislation lacking in vision, ineffective in means, and impotent in action" (Canada, Committee 1966, 17).[3] The 1874 legislation did, however, set a pattern that has come to characterize subsequent efforts at reform prior to 1974: a public scandal arouses public opinion; the legislature responds with changes that are "high in moral content and low in enforceability" (ibid., 17).

A series of amendments was made to the *Dominion Elections Act* in 1908. The amendments specified that contributions from corporations were prohibited, if made directly to electoral candidates. However, since political parties remained undefined in law, the law was all but unenforceable.[4] The law of agency was strengthened by making it an indictable offence to contribute to a candidate other than through an official agent. Americans were prohibited from assisting in Canadian federal elections (Canada, Committee 1966, 18). The 1908 amendments "proved to be entirely ineffective in prohibiting big business from contributing to campaign funds ... There was no evidence that business contributions slackened after 1908; on the contrary, they may have increased" (ibid., 19).

In 1920, the ban on corporate donations of 1908 was widened to include all companies and associations, regardless of incorporation. Thus, trade unions were now included in the ban. Another amendment expanded the scope of disclosure by requiring that candidates reveal the names of contributors and the amounts they had contributed (Canada, Committee 1966, 21). Following the 1920 amendments to the *Dominion Elections Act*, no major law on the matter of political financing was enacted until 1974. However, efforts by J.S. Woodsworth and William Irvine of the CCF (predecessor of the NDP) led to the repeal in 1930 of the ban on contributions by corporations and labour unions.

The important elements of the *Canada Elections Act* with respect to the financing of parties and candidates prior to the enactment of the *Election Expenses Act* of 1974 can be summarized as follows:

- The Act provided for the registration of parties.[5]
- It required candidates to name an official agent to receive all contributions, and to pay all expenses (except the personal expenses of the candidate up to $2 000).
- It forbade private expenditures by the candidate's supporters, but the candidate or his/her agent could not be held responsible.
- It required that campaign expenses be presented for payment within one month of voting day and paid within 50 days; after 50 days, payment required the approval of a judge.
- It required that the agent present a detailed sworn statement of the candidate's finances to the constituency returning officer within two months of voting day. The returning officer was required to publish a summary of the report in a newspaper circulated in the constituency. The penalty for failure to submit a report was a fine of up to $500, or imprisonment for up to one year. Falsification of the report with an intent to mislead was also an offence: the offending MP could be barred from sitting in the House of Commons.
- The Act did not specifically assign responsibility for enforcement.

The effectiveness of these provisions is hard to determine without conducting a thorough search to find and review all the investigations and prosecutions made under the legislation. Such an activity was not within the scope of this study. However, the percentage of candidates failing to submit the required return (per section 63(3) of the *Canada Elections Act* before it was amended by the 1974 legislation) setting out their revenues and expenditures was as follows: 1962, 20 percent; 1963, 24 percent; 1965, 25 percent; 1968, 28 percent; 1972, 25 percent; and 1974, 24 percent (Seidle 1980, 149).

2. PROCESS LEADING TO THE *ELECTION EXPENSES ACT* OF 1974

2.1 Barbeau Committee

Dating the onset of a political process that results in a major piece of legislation is often arbitrary. In tracing the evolution of the *Election Expenses Act* of 1974, it seems appropriate to begin with 17 October 1964, the day that Maurice Lamontagne, Secretary of State in the Liberal government of Lester B. Pearson, established an "Advisory Committee to Study Curtailment of Election Expenses."[6] The Committee was to be chaired by François Norbert; however, he became ill and was replaced in January 1965 by Alphonse Barbeau, a Montreal lawyer.[7] The committee members were Gordon Dryden, secretary-treasurer of the Liberal Federation of Canada; A.R. Smith, a Conservative MP from 1957 to 1963; M.J. Coldwell, former national leader of the CCF; and Norman Ward, a prominent professor of political science from the University of Saskatchewan. The committee became known as the Barbeau Committee. Its report in 1966 formed the basis of the 1974 legislative reforms.

On 11 October 1966, the Barbeau Committee's final report was tabled in the House of Commons. According to Ward (1972, 340), the Committee "in essence ... accepted the Quebec plan [amendments of 1963].[8] The Barbeau Committee focused on changes that were likely to be "acceptable to the hard-headed MPS and party managers who would have to work with them" (ibid., 339). However, the changes it recommended were, by Canadian standards, "truly revolutionary" (Courtney 1978, 47).

In the view of Robin Sears, then federal secretary for the NDP,[9] three principles guided the Barbeau Report: equalization, access and participation.

> Those three principles – and the three tools the legislation used to implement them – are a kind of three-legged stool. If you don't have any one of the three, the whole operation tips over. *Equalization* in the money available to candidates to run their campaign and equalization in what they're permitted to spend to promote their

causes. *Access* of the electorate through the disclosure provisions and a more open administration of election finances – both contributions and expenditures. And *participation* through the tax credit system to encourage people to get involved in politics. The three tools were the limitations on expenditures, the disclosure provisions, and the public financing aspects of the Bill C-203. ("Round Table" 1981, 7–8)

The many recommendations of the Barbeau Committee (Canada, Committee 1966, chap. 4) can be grouped into six categories and summarized as follows:

1. Party registration and agency.
   - Each national party should be registered.
   - The party's official agent should be required to file the reports specified in the legislation.
   - The doctrine of agency between agent and candidate and between agent and party should be fully applied.

2. Subsidies to parties, candidates and donors.
   - Each candidate should be reimbursed for the cost of mailing one item of literature to every elector in his constituency.
   - Each candidate who receives 15 percent of the votes cast should be reimbursed with a sum equal to two cents for every elector toward his/her proven total expenses in purchasing space/time in any communications medium.
   - There should be an official "You vote at ..." card sent to every elector (to replace mailing of the preliminary list of electors to urban electors).
   - The Canadian Broadcasting Corporation (CBC) should negotiate the distribution of broadcast time among parties, subject to appeal to the Board of Broadcast Governors.
   - Broadcasters should be required to provide, free of charge, 50 percent of the broadcast time allocated to parties.
   - Broadcasters should be permitted to charge the Registrar of Election and Political Finance for the other 50 percent of the commercial value of the six-hour requirement at the published regular rate.
   - A limit of six hours of purchased broadcast time should be imposed on political parties.
   - If broadcasters offer free time, it should be divided equally among candidates.

- There should be a personal income-tax credit for individuals, consisting of 50 percent of donations of $1 to $20, 40 percent of those $21 to $100 and 30 percent of those $100 to $300. Receipts should be given only by official agents.
- Candidates' deposits of $200 should be returned if they receive one-eighth of the votes cast.

3. Limitations.
    - No restrictions should be placed on the size of contributions from individuals, unions, corporations or other entities.
    - Parties and candidates should be prohibited from campaigning on radio or television, or from using paid-print media, except during the last 28 days of the campaign.
    - Candidates' campaign expenditures on broadcast or print media (including billboards, posters and brochures) should be limited to $.10 per elector.
    - "Third parties," such as interest or advocacy groups, should be prohibited from purchasing broadcast or print media throughout the campaign period.
    - Payments to a scrutineer or agent at a poll or to anyone providing transportation of voters to the polls should be made an illegal practice.
    - The publication of polls during the entire campaign period should be prohibited.
    - Broadcasters, newspaper and periodical publishers should be prohibited from charging more than the usual local rates to candidates or the usual national rate to parties. Rates less than this must be made available to all parties.
    - All corrupt or illegal practices in related statutes should be retained "with a vastly increased emphasis placed on the enforcement of the law."

4. Disclosure and reporting.
    - The registered financial agent of each party should be required to provide the Registrar with a detailed statement of the party's income and expenditures within 60 days after an election, and with a similar statement annually. However, the names of donors should not be revealed.
    - The registered agent for each candidate should file with the Registrar within 30 days after an election a sworn statement reporting revenues and expenditures. The name and address of each donor and the amount donated should be provided.

- Persons soliciting funds on behalf of a national party should be registered.
- Broadcasters and publishers should report on the time/space sold or given free to parties/candidates.

5. Control and enforcement.
   - A Registry of Election and Political Finance, separate from the office of the Chief Electoral Officer, should be established under the direction of a Registrar, who would be responsible to the House of Commons for the enforcement of the legislation enacted pursuant to the Committee's report.
   - The Registrar would have the power to prescribe reporting forms, the audit of party and candidate records, the publication of annual reports and post-election reports and an annual report to Parliament. The Registrar would also pay the subsidies specified in legislation, pay broadcasters as specified in the legislation, prepare reports for the media and take legal action to enforce the new legislation.
   - The penalties upon conviction after prosecution should be greatly increased (e.g., conviction of a successful candidate and/or his/her agent would result in the unseating of the MP and disqualification from participating in a federal election for seven years). A party could be fined from $5 000 to $50 000, and the leader made subject to the same penalties as a candidate. The executive of a party would be liable for fines that the party could not pay.

6. Broadcasting.
   - The *Broadcasting Act* should be amended to ensure that no municipal or provincial election could affect the free use of the broadcasting media in a federal election campaign.
   - The *Broadcasting Act* should be amended to allow political parties to solicit funds in broadcasts.
   - The *Canada Elections Act* should be amended to ensure that political parties were prohibited from the use of foreign broadcasting media.

As a result of the Barbeau Committee's recommendations, the *Canada Elections Act* was amended in 1970 to institute the registration of political parties, the first step to their more extensive regulation. Another amendment permitted the candidate's party to be indicated on the ballot. In this regard, a further amendment to section 23(2)(*h*) of the Act was made in 1983, which specified that

> where the candidate has the endorsement of a registered party and
> wishes to have the name of the party shown in the election documents
> relating to him, an instrument in writing, signed by the leader of the
> party or by a representative designated by the leader ... stating that
> the candidate is *endorsed by the party*, shall be filed with the returning
> officer at the time the nomination paper is filed. (Canada, *An Act to
> amend the Canada Elections Act*, c. 164, s. 6(1) – emphasis added)

As Courtney (1978, 52) noted, this section "obviously enhances the
position of the leaders of recognized parties." The effect of this provision was to give the party leader veto power over the nomination
process at the riding level. The section was first invoked by Robert
Stanfield in 1974 in respect to Leonard Jones, the former mayor of
Moncton, whose views on bilingualism were at odds with the leader's.

2.2   Chappell Committee

In October 1970, the House of Commons Special Committee on Election
Expenses (Chappell Committee) was established. In its 1971 *Report*
(Canada, House of Commons 1971b), the Committee made 53 recommendations. The Committee proposed that there be a limit on candidate's election expenses as well as on party expenditures, that part of
each candidate's expenditures be reimbursed and that all donations
and expenditures for each candidate and party be disclosed after each
election. It also recommended that the CEO be solely responsible for the
administration of the new financing provisions, that the full doctrine
of agency be applied to candidates during elections and to parties during
and between elections and that the report of revenue and expenditures
by parties and candidates be audited. There was to be no limit on contributions (except a prohibition on nonresident individuals, corporations
and unions) and contributions were to be made a tax-deductible expense
up to the lesser of 2 percent of net income or $1 000 (ibid.).

2.3   Bill C-211

Bill C-211, which dealt with election expenses, was introduced on 16 May
1972. It was "seen as a pre-election sop designed to counter criticism of
the government's dilatory steps in this area with no possibility of enactment before dissolution ... [N]either the Progressive Conservatives,
who formed the Official Opposition, nor important elements of the
ruling Liberals were enthused [sic] by the project" (Paltiel 1977, 24). In
Bill C-211, the "election expenses" to be limited included only paid
broadcasting time, print advertisements in periodicals, and the cost of
printing, publishing and distributing any advertising material for the

purpose of promoting or opposing, directly or indirectly, a candidate or party. There was no overall spending limit on party expenditures, and the bill was strongly criticized by the NDP (Seidle 1980, 192).[10] The general election of 30 October 1972 produced a minority Liberal government with the NDP holding the balance of power. This fact was to influence the *Election Expenses Act* of 1974 in a number of ways, as will be described below.

2.4 *Election Expenses Act* of 1974

Bill C-203, the *Election Expenses Act*, was introduced on 22 June 1973. It received Second Reading on 12 July after three days' debate. Hearings by the Standing Committee on Privileges and Elections began on 18 October. The Committee proposed 169 amendments to the 38-page bill at the conclusion of its extensive hearings. The bill was returned to the House on 18 December; there followed four days of debate, ending on 3 January 1974 with its passage. Only one Social Credit and two NDP members[11] opposed it. The bill passed the Senate on 11 January and Royal Assent was given three days later. Rumours of scandals in Quebec and the Watergate Affair in the United States are said to have created an atmosphere conducive to reform in this period of Liberal minority government.[12] The final version of the bill was influenced by both Conservative party and particularly NDP amendments. According to David Lewis, then leader of the NDP, his party won three concessions: the criteria for reimbursement of expenditures on electronic media advertising by the parties; the scale of the tax credit; and the threshold for reimbursement of candidates' expenditures (Seidle 1985b, p. 131, n.19).[13] Privy Council president Allan MacEachen introduced 32 amendments of his own, many of which were in response to the Tories' questions (ibid., 117; Acker 1979, 79). Undoubtedly, Bill C-203 was, in the words of Mr. MacEachen, "probably the most comprehensive attempt at reform of electoral expenditures undertaken so far in Canada" (Seidle 1985b, 117).

The federal party and candidate financing reforms (Bill C-203) came into effect on 1 August 1974. As outlined below, the legislation contained many important provisions, most of which are still in force at the time of writing (1992).

2.5 Main Provisions of Act

Party Registration and Agency
The 1974 legislation required registered political parties to appoint a chief agent and an auditor responsible for filing information with the

Chief Electoral Officer. Only a person authorized by a party or candidate could incur "election expenses." The Act, however, specifically exempted interest groups or individuals who engaged in advertising during election campaigns, provided that they promoted discussion of public policy and did so in good faith.

All contributions to a candidate or a party in excess of $25 were required to be made to the chief agent of the candidate or the registered agent of the party. It was also made an offence to make a contribution of money that did not belong to the donor. All expenditures by registered parties or candidates of $25 or more were to be made through the registered agent and were to be vouched for by a bill stating the particulars and by a receipt.

Spending Limits

The 1974 legislation provided that each registered *party* could spend on election expenses no more than $.30 for each elector in each riding in which it had an official candidate during the period between the issue of the writs and election day.[14] The party campaign expenditure limit, however, excluded certain items, such as volunteer labour and grants by the parties to candidates.

Candidates were also subject to a spending ceiling. This was set at $1 per elector for the first 15 000, plus $0.50 for the next 10 000, plus $0.25 for each elector in excess of 25 000.[15]

"Election expenses" were defined in the Act as "amounts paid; liabilities incurred; the commercial value of goods and services donated or provided, other than volunteer labour; and amounts that represented the differences between amounts paid and liabilities incurred for goods and services, other than labour, and the commercial value of such goods and services where they were provided at less than their commercial value," where such amounts were paid, incurred or provided "for the purpose of promoting or opposing, directly and during an election, a particular registered party, or the election of a particular candidate." The Act gave some examples of what constitutes "election expenses": the cost of broadcasting and periodical advertising; the cost of acquiring the services of any person, including remuneration or out-of-pocket expenses; the cost of acquiring meeting space, providing light refreshment and promotional literature; and the cost of goods and services provided by any government or government agency.

Certain expenses were not "election expenses" for the purpose of determining whether or not a party or candidate had complied with the spending limitations in the Act. Specifically excluded by statute were (a) a candidate's travelling expenses; (b) the first $2 000 of a candidate's personal expenses; (c) the commercial value of certain free network broadcast time provided to registered parties; and (d) the outlays of a registered party to support a candidate's campaign expenses. (Such outlays were to be recorded by the candidate as campaign contributions and, if expended, were to be accounted for as part of his/her "election expenses.") By inference, certain other expenses were not "election expenses," such as, for example, the expenses of seeking a party nomination as a candidate, and the auditor's fee.

Reimbursement of Campaign Expenses

All candidates who received at least 15 percent of the votes cast and who complied with the requirements for submitting their report on election expenses were entitled to be reimbursed for a part of their election expenses by the federal government. The formula established in 1974 set the reimbursement as the sum of (1) the cost of a first-class letter to all electors; (2) $.08 for each of the first 25 000 electors, and (3) $.06 for every elector above 25 000.[16] For 21 very large/isolated constituencies, the candidate might be reimbursed for travelling expenses not exceeding $3 000.[17]

Advertising

Under the 1974 amendments to the *Broadcasting Act,* radio and television stations were required to make available up to 6.5 hours of prime time for paid advertising or political broadcasts by registered *parties* during the last four weeks of the election campaign. This time was allocated among the parties by the Broadcasting Arbitrator (since 1983) according to a formula based on the number of seats held and the party's popular vote in the previous election.[18] (The formula was modified in 1983 to include the number of candidates who had participated in the previous election.) The 1974 Act also set a maximum of 6.5 hours on advertising in the electronic media during the four weeks immediately preceding election day. No such limit applied to other media, such as print, although expenditures on other media (and electronic media) were to stay within the party's limit on "election expenses."

A broadcaster was not required to make time available to individual candidates. However, "once he does sell or contribute time to one candidate, he would be required by virtue of S.3 of the Broadcasting Act to make equitable time available to all other candidates in that riding, except ... where it is actually party time that is being turned over by a party to a particular candidate" (Boyer 1983, 456).

Network operators were required to make free-time programming periods available to registered parties during the period from 29 to

2 days before polling day. This time was to be in network reserved time periods, but did not have to be in prime time. The free time was allocated among the parties in the same proportion as the paid time, but the total amount was to be determined after consultation between the parties and the Canadian Radio-television and Telecommunications Commission (CRTC).[19]

Parties and candidates were not to advertise in a periodical publication or on television or radio prior to the 29th day before polling day. Advertisements giving notice of a meeting for nominating a candidate or meeting a party leader were not a breach of this rule if their cost did not exceed 1 percent of the candidate's limit in the previous election.

Section 99.3(*a*) of the *Canada Elections Act* required broadcasters to charge for political ads and programs the same rate that they would charge to any other person for an equivalent time on the facilities.

Disclosure

Under the 1974 legislation, every registered party was required to submit a detailed statement of revenues and expenditures annually. Candidates were to do the same after a by-election or a general election. The name of every person or organization who had donated more than $100 in cash or in kind to the party or to a candidate must be reported to the CEO.[20]

Each party's annual return was to be filed with the Chief Electoral Officer within six months after the end of its fiscal year. The return provided information in four categories: the identity of donors of $100 or more during the year; the amount of donations over $100; the operating expenditures of the party; and all other expenditures. A separate return was to be filed by each party[21] and each candidate within six and four months of an election respectively.

Where a candidate received a contribution of $100 or more from his/her local riding association, the sources of the association's funds were to be reported for each contributor giving $100 or more.

Tax Credits

In addition to reimbursing parties for electronic media advertising and reimbursing candidates for a substantial fraction of their campaign expenses, the federal government was to provide a tax credit for individuals and corporations, which was a deduction against taxes payable, not income. It was to be calculated as follows:

- 75 percent of amounts contributed up to $100, plus
- 50 percent of amounts contributed between $100 and $550, plus
- 33.3 percent of amounts contributed exceeding $550, up to a total tax credit of $500.

Therefore, the maximum tax credit ($500) was reached with a donation of $1 150. There was no statutory limit, however, on the total amount that a person, corporation, labour union or other organization might give to a party or candidate.

A candidate's agent could issue receipts for tax credits only *after* the individual had been nominated. Therefore, between elections, riding associations could receive funds, but could not themselves issue receipts for the tax credit. If the contribution to a riding association was made through the official agent of the national party, a tax receipt could be issued.[22]

It should be noted that some key recommendations of the Barbeau Committee (Canada, Committee 1966) were *not* incorporated into the *Election Expenses Act* of 1974:

- Broadcasters were not required to provide free of charge one-half of the allocation of broadcast time to the parties.
- The government was not required to pay the broadcasters for the other half of the parties' expenditures on election broadcasts. (The *parties* were given a 50 percent rebate on their expenditures for election media advertising.)
- The tax credit was increased from 50 percent of the first $20 to 75 percent of the first $100. The maximum total credit was raised to $500 for $1 150 versus $102 for $300. Both individuals and corporations were made eligible to receive the credit.
- The independent position of Registrar of Election and Political Finance was not created.
- Candidates' campaign expenditures on broadcast and print advertising were not limited to $.10 per elector, but total "election expenses" were capped.
- The publication of polls during the entire campaign period was not prohibited.
- The identity of contributors and the size of their donations to *parties* (as well as to candidates) were required to be made public.
- Registration of persons soliciting funds for a national party was *not* required.
- The tight deadlines for the filing of annual and post-election reports by the parties/candidates were lengthened considerably.

3. EFFORTS TO CHANGE THE 1974 REGULATORY REGIME, 1975–89

3.1 Bill C-5, 1977

The first amendments to the 1974 regulatory regime were enacted in 1977. Bill C-5 was introduced on 24 October and received Royal Assent on 20 December. It amended the *Canada Elections Act* in light of the recommendations of the Ad Hoc Committee comprised of MPs and representatives of the Liberal, Progressive Conservative and New Democratic parties. This committee was first convened in 1974 when the Chief Electoral Officer asked the leaders of all parties to discuss how the new legislation was to be implemented.[23] "The 'ad hoc committee' has always met in private and publishes no minutes" (Seidle 1985b, 124). By early 1976 it had prepared a package of about 40 amendments.

Bill C-5 has been described by Seidle as follows:

> Bill C-5 altered the rules for the registration of political parties. As the law stood after 1974, parties that had applied for registration would have become "registered parties" as soon as the writs were issued for the next general election. If the party did not nominate fifty candidates by nomination day, its registration would have been revoked. Nevertheless, for about a month any party that had filed an application for registration would have been a full-fledged party and, for example, could have taken advantage of the tax credit during that time. Several new parties had filed applications and a number of them did not appear to be very serious. Bill C-5 was aimed clearly at what the Chief Electoral Officer and a number of MPs saw as a weakness in the law. As a result, a "new" party's registration can now come into effect only when it has nominated fifty candidates during an election campaign.
>
> Bill C-5 also adjusted slightly upwards the candidates' spending limits in constituencies with fewer than the average number of electors. In addition, a number of definitions relevant to election spending were amended, but a section of the Bill that would have indexed the parties' and candidates' spending limits to inflation was defeated in committee. Bill C-5 received a fairly thorough examination by the Standing Committee on Privileges and Elections, which met nine times during a three-week period to discuss it. (1985b, 124)[24]

3.2 Development of Guidelines by CEO

It was out of the early work of the Ad Hoc Committee that the CEO prepared his first set of *Guidelines* for both candidates and parties in 1979. The official reporting forms for the candidate's official agent were developed and tested in by-elections in 1976, 1977 and 1978 (Seidle 1980, 221). A *Manual of Information* was published by the CEO in 1979 (Canada, Elections Canada 1979b). A more extensive one was published in 1980 (Canada, Elections Canada 1980a). For the 1979 election,

75 seminars were held in 46 locations, attended by about 2 500 officials, candidates, official agents and auditors (Canada, Elections Canada 1979c, 19).

3.3   Bill C-169, 1983

After the 1980 general election, the Ad Hoc Committee met again and by 1982 had formulated another set of amendments. These led to Bill C-169 in 1983. The next major amendments to the *Canada Elections Act*[25] were given First Reading on 17 October 1983, and Second Reading on 25 October after only one speaker for each of the three main parties spoke on the bill. Instead of referring the bill to the Standing Committee on Privileges and Elections, it was, by agreement, referred to the Committee of the Whole House. Then, after no further debate, it was given Third Reading and passed. Bill C-169 was given Royal Assent on 17 November 1983.

The amendments removed the "good faith" defence in section 70.1(4) for "third-party" (i.e., advocacy or interest group) activities during elections from the *Canada Elections Act*.[26] In addition, Parliament repealed and re-enacted section 72, which (i) required that all ads promoting or opposing the election of a registered party or candidate displayed during a campaign by a party or candidate or on their behalf be authorized by the party/candidate's agent and bear the latter's name; and (ii) made it an offence to print, publish or distribute ads that did not bear the name and authorization of the agent. The President of the Privy Council, who introduced Bill C-169, said the intent was "to equalize the chances of all candidates in all parties, by setting reasonable limits on election expenses and by guaranteeing reimbursement of a considerable part of those expenses. [However], this basic principle of equality is unfortunately ignored at times by groups or individuals, other than political parties and candidates, that make substantial election expenditures during an election campaign without going through a candidate or party. There is no record of these expenditures, which gives some candidates or parties an undue advantage" (Canada, H. of C., *Debates*, 25 Oct. 1983, 28295). Charles Cook (PC, North Vancouver–Burnaby) noted that the amendments had been discussed in all-party meetings "for at least a couple of years" (ibid., 28296). He was apparently referring to the Ad Hoc Committee, which provided advice to the Chief Electoral Officer. However, the amendments were not reviewed by the Commons Committee on Elections, Privileges and Procedure. Mr. Cook thought that the amendment regarding advertising by advocacy groups "will undoubtedly end up being tested in the courts" (ibid., 28297). He noted that it was more severe than that discussed by the Ad Hoc Committee, "but we agreed ... on the basis that it will be much easier to police" (ibid.).

Second, both candidate and party expenditure limits were indexed to the CPI, retroactive to 1980. Further, the limit on "election expenses" for candidates in ridings with fewer than 10 electors per square kilometre (i.e., large northern ridings) was increased substantially.

Third, the reimbursement provisions for parties were changed from one-half the cost of electronic media to 22.5 percent of total "election expenses." Note that in changing the reimbursement formula for party "election expenses," Parliament specified that a registered party would have to spend *at least* 10 percent of its permitted maximum to qualify. In 1984, this amounted to $630 000, if a party fielded a candidate in all ridings. In 1988, it amounted to $800 000.

Fourth, the requirement that the candidate's personal expenditures exceeding $2 000 be included in his/her "election expenses" was eliminated. According to Paltiel,

> a new loophole has been opened. There will no longer be a limit on the amount of "personal expenses" which a candidate may incur, nor will these be counted as "election expenses," they will only have to be "reasonable." However, no definition is provided for the latter term; all that will be required is a statement of such costs. (1985, 124)

Fifth, the reimbursement of a candidate's "election expenses" was changed from a formula based largely on postage costs of mailings to voters to 50 percent of the candidate's "election expenses." Between 1974 and 1983, the cost of a first-class stamp rose from $0.08 to $0.32. As a result:

> The relationship that existed at the time the Act was passed between reimbursements and spending limits has therefore been completely disrupted. The distortion is further aggravated by the size of the electoral district; the larger the electoral district, the more significant is the distortion. For example, in an electoral district with approximately 100,000 electors, the potential reimbursement at the present postal rates represents in excess of 99 per cent of the spending limits permitted, while in an electoral district with approximately 35,000 electors, that percentage is less than 65 per cent. (Canada, Elections Canada 1983, 30)

Sixth, significant amendments were made to section 99 of the *Canada Elections Act*, which concerned "political broadcasts." A Broadcasting

Arbitrator was appointed to carry out the provisions, including the allocation of free broadcast time.[27] The formula previously applied by the CRTC in allocating the 6.5 hours of paid prime-time broadcasting allocated to the parties was spelled out in legislation. It was retrospective, that is, based on the percentage of seats won in the past election, the percentage of votes received and the percentage of registered party candidates that ran in the past election. However, no party could receive more than one-half the total time.[28] Similar rules governed the allocation of *free* time.

Seventh, the 1983 amendments weakened the mechanism for verifying candidates' election expenditures. Under the 1974 Act, section 62.1(4) was enacted, which stated that the auditor "shall make a report ... on the return ... and shall make such examinations as will enable him to state in his report whether in his opinion the return presents fairly the information contained in the accounting records on which the ... return is based." This was amended in 1983 so as to require the auditor "to state in his report whether in his opinion the return presents fairly the financial transactions *contained in the books and records of the candidate*" (emphasis added). A similar disclaimer accompanies the auditor's report on the party's annual report to the CEO. This change, which limits the scope of the auditor's role, was the result of lobbying by the professional accounting bodies.

In summary, Paltiel states that the 1983 amendments

> were the product of the informal ad hoc committee of party officials with no standing in the law, accountable to no one, for whom the Chief Electoral Officer simply acted as a figurehead. The House of Commons simply adopted its recommendations, which were aimed principally at benefitting those already represented on Parliament Hill. (1985, 124; see also Canada, Elections Canada 1983, 67–78)

Paltiel, based on his review of the 1983 amendments (Bill C-169), argues that the role of the Ad Hoc Committee has resulted in the "colonization of the regulators by the regulated" (1987, 240). He notes that it

> is a common enough phenomenon and its consequences are known and predictable. While convenient to those charged with the administration of the act, its results may well frustrate the intentions of its originators, reinforcing the position of those represented to the detriment of outsiders and challengers (ibid.).

Activities of Advocacy Groups

The most controversial part of Bill C-169 consisted of the amendments designed to curb the activities of advocacy and other interest groups (so-called "third parties") during election campaigns. Rod Murphy (NDP, Churchill) stated that "all Members recognize that some of the most partisan, vicious and one-sided advertising takes place during election campaigns on behalf of so-called third parties" (Canada, H. of C., *Debates*, 25 Oct. 1983, 28299). In particular, Murphy was concerned about single-issue groups "pushing a very emotional issue to the extent that it clouds the real political issues of a campaign" (ibid.).

Prime Minister Trudeau said that Bill C-169 was "an amendment to ensure that the [National] Citizens' Coalition, or any other group with a lot of money, do not controvert the spirit of that law" (Canada, H. of C., *Debates*, 19 Jan. 1984, 556). Mr. Trudeau stated that the *Election Expenses Act* of 1974 was "written for a specific purpose, which was to destroy the inequality which arose from the power of money. We think it was a very progressive piece of legislation, putting every citizen and every candidate on an equal footing in so far as election expenses are concerned" (ibid.).

Paltiel referred to Bill C-169 as "a classic case of the rule-bound writing the rules to suit themselves" (1987, 234). Perhaps so, but the legislation did not go unnoticed.

> For a time, the pros and cons of the 1983 legislation and its quick parliamentary passage became the subject of editorials and articles on "op ed" pages. For the most part, editorial opinion strongly opposed the 1983 amendments. Among major newspapers, only the *Toronto Star* took the other side, arguing that the amendments "simply ensure that Canada's election spending limits won't be circumvented." As the campaign progressed, the NCC claimed the support of the Inter-American Press Association, the Canadian Daily Newspaper Publishers' Association, the Canadian Chamber of Commerce and the civil liberties section of the Canadian Bar Association. Never before had an amendment to the *Canada Elections Act* attracted so much attention. (Seidle 1985b, 126)

Paltiel called for an independent body, such as the Ontario Commission on Election Contributions and Expenses (now the Ontario Commission on Election Finances), to replace the Chief Electoral Officer.

In February 1984, Conservative MPs Vince Dantzer (Okanagan North) and Ron Huntington (Capilano–Howe Sound) apologized to their constituents in the House for supporting Bill C-169 (Canada, H. of C., *Debates*, 17 Feb. 1984, 1518). Hiebert suggests that

> The most damaging criticism of the regulations on interest-group spending, however, came from Opposition leader Brian Mulroney

who told the media that he regretted his party's complicity in supporting the amendments to the *Elections Act* and suggested that his caucus was "asleep at the switch" when it opted not to oppose the financial regulation of interest groups. (1989–90, 77)

A month earlier, the National Citizens' Coalition (NCC) had challenged the constitutional validity of sections 70.1(1) and 72 of the *Canada Elections Act*, as amended by Bill C-169. The NCC claimed that the amended sections prohibited the organization from using the print or electronic media to promote or oppose a candidate or registered political party during an election without their permission. The NCC argued that the amendments infringed or violated its rights to freedom of thought, belief, opinion and expression, as well as to freedom of the press as guaranteed under the *Canadian Charter of Rights and Freedoms*.

In his *Statutory Report*, quoted by Mr. Justice Medhurst of the Alberta Court of Queen's Bench, the Chief Electoral Officer conceded that the 1983 amendments had been enacted because the "good faith" defence had made it difficult to prosecute cases arising from the 1979 and 1980 elections. He also indicated that most of the suggestions for the amendments contained in Bill C-169 originated with the Ad Hoc Committee of paid party representatives dealing with election matters.

Mr. Justice Medhurst held that sections 70.1(1) and 72 of the *Canada Elections Act* were inconsistent with section 2(*b*) of the *Canadian Charter of Rights and Freedoms* and hence were of no force or effect on 25 June 1984 (*National Citizens' Coalition* 1985, 496).[29] Clearly, he said, a limit had been imposed on advocacy groups' freedom of expression. The judge found there was very little evidence to suggest that section 70.1 had been abused by advocacy groups in the 1979 and 1980 elections. Moreover, Parliament had not chosen the alternative of rewriting the "good faith" defence to make it more specific so that it preserved the right of freedom of expression while maintaining the intent of the 1974 legislation. Mr. Justice Medhurst held that "Fears or concerns of mischief that may occur are not adequate reasons for imposing a limitation. There should be actual demonstration of harm or a real likelihood of harm to a society before a limitation can be said to be justified" (ibid.). The Crown did *not* appeal. (The Minister of Justice was Donald Johnston.) Although the decision applied only to Alberta, the Commissioner of Canada Elections decided not to enforce these sections elsewhere in Canada.

The Chief Electoral Officer in his 1984 *Statutory Report* recommended, in light of the *National Citizens' Coalition* case:

that the question of third party advertising be looked at with a view
to striking a proper balance between the adequate control of election
expenses and the freedom of expression of Canadians. In my opinion,
the solution should probably lie in the imposition of certain restrictions
on third parties not amounting to a total prohibition. In this way, third
parties would be free to participate fully in the election campaign in
a manner that would strive to ensure fairness in the system. However,
news items and regular editorials should be specifically excluded
from the application of any new provision. (Canada, Elections Canada
1984d, 24)

He also recommended that "subsection 70.1(2) and section 13.7 be
amended to provide that a local association is guilty of an offence against
the Act if it incurs election expenses other than on behalf of a party or
candidate" (ibid.). The CEO commented on ways of dealing with the
problem of election expenses incurred by persons other than candidates and agents of registered parties.

It is proposed that persons who are not acting on behalf of candidates or political parties should be bound by the same rules during
an election as are the candidates and the political parties. This would
mean that:

- individuals and organizations, or associations of a non-political
  character, would be free to contribute funds or services to official candidates and parties of their choice;
- they could register as a party and nominate candidates dedicated to the aims of their organizations;
- individuals and organizations could obtain written authority
  from candidates or parties to incur election expenses on their
  behalf, the said expenses being chargeable against the expenditures of the candidate or the party. (Canada, Elections Canada
  1984, 73)

Seidle described the effect of the decision in the NCC case as follows:

The NCC judgement did not open the floodgates on a flurry of activity
by interest groups in the 1984 general election. Although it seems
some interest groups, particularly single-issue ones, were more active
than in the past, there is little evidence that they focussed their ener-
gies on campaigning for or against particular candidates or parties. A
notable exception was some anti-abortion groups which, as in past

elections, published "endorsements" of candidates whose views they found acceptable.

The National Citizens' Coalition, for its part, launched a series of newspaper advertisements [which] ... outlined the NCC's position on a number of national issues, suggested that readers ask their candidates about them, and printed the three parties' response to a questionnaire about the issues. The advertisements did not indicate specific approval for any party or candidates. The NCC apparently spent between $150,000 and $200,000 during the 1984 campaign. (1985b, 128)

3.4   White Paper on Election Law Reform, 1986

The Progressive Conservative government, elected in September 1984, tabled the *White Paper on Election Law Reform* in June 1986 (Canada, Privy Council Office 1986). It proposed that the *Canada Elections Act* "be completely redrafted" and enacted before the next general election. Most of the proposed changes dealt with issues other than financing. The financing-related issues included the following:

- application of the advertising "blackout period" to parties pending their registration;
- regulation concerning the publication of advertising by government departments or Crown corporations during the election period;
- prevention of the use of the Crown's printing facilities and the franking privilege (section 34 of the *Canada Post Corporation Act*) by incumbent MPs during the first 10 days of the election period;
- publication of the methodology of opinion polls published both between and during election campaigns;
- changes in the rules governing broadcasting by registered parties during elections;
- application of blackout periods to both candidates or persons acting on their behalf; and
- removal of the section forbidding nonresidents to canvass during an election.

Note that the White Paper did not address the problem of the definition of "election expenses." Yet, in his *Statutory Report*, the Chief Electoral Officer had stated that "the present definition of *election expenses* is so vague and imprecise that its application to various sections of the *Act* has become extremely difficult" (Canada, Elections Canada 1986, 10).

3.5   Bill C-79, 1987

Bill C-79, which consisted of many important amendments to the *Canada Elections Act*, was given First Reading on 30 June 1987. It was later given Second Reading, but did not go to committee. Hence it was not enacted before the November 1988 general election (which returned the Progressive Conservative party to power with a reduced majority).

Bill C-79 sought to implement many of the recommendations included in the 1986 *White Paper on Election Law Reform*,[30] which in turn had been based largely on recommendations made by the Chief Electoral Officer over the previous six or seven years. The bill dealt with a wide range of issues, ranging from extending the right to vote to federally appointed judges and the mentally disabled to requiring level access at polling places to altering procedures for enumerating and revising electoral lists and increasing the number of electors required for a person to be nominated as a candidate. It also included two general provisions relevant to campaigning and party finance and one relating to public opinion polls.

Elections Enforcement Commission

The bill proposed the establishment of a Canada Elections Enforcement Commission to enforce the *Canada Elections Act*. It would be composed of a chairman chosen by resolution of the House of Commons (seven-year term), and a representative of each party having 12 or more members in the House (three-year terms). One other commissioner representing the public (including other parties and independent members and candidates) would be appointed by order-in-council after consultation with the leaders of the parties with 12 or more members in the House (five-year term). The Commission would be able to appoint its own investigators or call on the Royal Canadian Mounted Police (RCMP). The Commission was intended to act as a replacement for the present Commissioner of Canada Elections, who is appointed by the Chief Electoral Officer.

Political Financing

The proposed changes affecting political financing included the following. The definition of "election expenses" was extended to include "the commercial value of printed material mailed pursuant to section 34 of the *Canada Post Corporation Act* and the postal costs of the mailing" (Canada, Bill C-79, s. 1(6)). Section 34 of that Act deals with the MPs' franking privilege (i.e., free mailings to constituents). Bill C-79 specified that where the value of donated goods or services exceeded $200, *and* were given by a person *not* in the business of providing such items, the value was to be based on the *lowest* amount charged for equivalent goods or services by a person supplying such goods/services on a commercial basis in the market area where they were donated. (If the value was less than $200, the donation was to be reported as zero.) The campaign expenditure limit for candidates was to be *increased* by $.15 per square kilometre of the electoral district up to a total of $10 000 (ibid., s. 55(2.1)(*d*)). The limitation on the *time period* in which the limit on campaign expenditures applied was extended to "every person who becomes a candidate and every person seeking the endorsement as a candidate, of a political party" (ibid., s. 56(1)). This would have begun to deal with the problem of campaign outlays before a candidate is nominated. Bill C-79 specified that all expenditures on election campaigns exceeding $50 (formerly $25) must be accompanied by a voucher specifying particulars and proof of payment (ibid., s. 57(2)). The right to spend up to 1 percent of the limit on "election expenses" at the previous election on advertising nomination meetings in the print and broadcast media during the blackout period was to be transferred from a potential candidate to the local association of a registered party or, where there was none, to the party sponsoring a candidate. Independent candidates who had to return to the Receiver General any surplus funds that remained after paying all their bills and receiving a reimbursement of their election expenses would have their money returned to them, with interest, if they decided to run in either of the next two general elections or in any by-elections during that period. The "broadcasting period" was to be defined to be the period between the 29th and 2nd days before polling day. Note that during this period parties and candidates could *not* advertise on radio or TV, publish ads in periodicals, or use a government publication for election advertising (ibid., s. 15). Local associations (ridings) could be made subject to essentially the same reporting rules as parties and candidates if they *agreed* to become registered. However, registration was to be voluntary and done through each party's chief agent.[31]

Public Opinion Polls
A new section (98.1) was proposed for the Act respecting commissioned polls on candidates and/or parties published in print or electronic media. The media were to be required to disclose the following in their reports: the identity of the polling organization; the identity of the person paying for the poll; the size of the sample, the dates of the first and last completed interviews; the margin of error if calculable; and the exact wording of each question the answers to which led to the reported results. The electronic media complained that the brevity of

their news items would not provide sufficient time to meet these requirements. The Progressive Conservatives agreed to drop the provision dealing with polls, because the electronic media could not comply in the context of their 30-second items.

Speakers for both the Liberal and New Democratic parties emphasized their frustration with the fact that Bill C-79 did not address the most important problem with campaign financing regulations, namely, the vague but vital distinction between "election expenses" (subject to limit) and "campaign expenses" (not limited by the *Canada Elections Act*) (Canada, H. of C., *Debates*, 16 March 1988, 13816–25). In short, one of the major problems identified in the 1985–86 affair of Marcel Masse (PC, Frontenac) was not addressed in Bill C-79.[32] Liberal and NDP MPs stated that the following expenditures by candidates were *excluded* from "election expenses," which were subject to statutory control:

- Payments to volunteers which are under the commercial value of their services or payments to cover the living and travel expenses of volunteers; section 2.1(*f*) of the *Canada Elections Act* specifies that "election expenses" include the cost of acquiring the services of any person, including remuneration and expenses paid to him, except where such services are donated or "provided at materially less than their commercial value."
- Auditors' fees, candidates' deposits and legal fees.
- Personal expenses of the candidate, including transportation expenses for their travel around the riding during the campaign (these can be huge in a geographically large riding).
- Costs of polling, which is described as research in the CEO's *Guidelines* and is deemed not to promote a party or candidate.
- Fund-raising expenses, such as letters to a "home list of preferred donors" seeking contributions are excluded, although they often advocate a party's position and attack rival parties – and then request a contribution.
- Donated services are excluded (Canada, H. of C., *Debates*, 16 March 1988; see also chap. 13).

3.6 "Campaign" or "Other Expenses" versus "Election Expenses"

According to opposition MPs, the Progressive Conservative party had the most to gain from not closing the "campaign expenses" loophole identified in the Marcel Masse affair (discussed in chap. 13). Their coffers were full, while the Liberal party was deeply in debt. Hence, the Tories had the $20 000 or so per riding to put into "campaign expenses" or "other expenses" such as reimbursement of volunteers' expenses while sticking to the $35 000 to $50 000 limit on official "election expenses" (Canada, H. of C., *Debates*, 16 March 1988, 13822).

Opposition MPs accused the Conservatives of delay, noting that the Ad Hoc Committee had been looking at "election expenses" since the summer of 1986 when the government had referred it to its *White Paper on Election Law Reform*. Further, Bill C-79 was discussed by the Committee after it was introduced. By starting debate on the Second Reading of Bill C-79 (on 16 March 1988) without any reference to the committee on "election expenses," the House Leader "precluded any possibility of the legislative committee making any legislative recommendations or amendments to Bill C-79 that deal with election expenses" according to NDP member Rod Murphy (Churchill) (Canada, H. of C., *Debates*, 16 March 1988, 13821–22). Patrick Boyer (PC, Etobicoke–Lakeshore) stated it was "unconscionable that it has taken so long to get this Bill [C-79] this far in Parliament" (ibid., 13829). Boyer said he had proposed nine months earlier that the noncontroversial parts of Bill C-79 be split off and enacted. The rest of the bill, including the sections relating to the "election expenses" issue, would wait until there was a consensus among all parties.

On 12 April 1988, the NDP forwarded to the government a letter setting out legal wording defining "election expenses." On 8 July the Honourable Doug Lewis (PC, Simcoe North), the government House Leader, said that negotiations were still going on with respect to Bill C-79. Murphy accused the Tories of delaying the definition issue until after the next election. In August, the House Leaders of all three parties discussed how to advance Bill C-79, which had still not gone to committee. Mr. Murphy pointed out that the government had not come forward with a new definition of "election expenses" as of 22 August. Donald Mazankowski (PC, Vegreville), the Deputy Prime Minister, said he had sent a letter to the House Leaders on 3 May 1988 informing them that a new definition would be included in the list of changes to be made in Bill C-79 (Canada, H. of C., *Debates*, 22 August 1988, 18623). On 15 September Mr. Lewis stated that the government was unable to proceed with Bill C-79 due to the "filibuster" by the NDP. Mr. Murphy again pleaded with the Conservatives to introduce legislation to redefine "election expenses" in light of the unanimous recommendation of the Commons Committee on Elections, Privileges and Procedure following its investigation of Mr. Masse's "election" and "campaign" expenses (ibid., 19294). Nothing was done, however. Bill C-79 was not enacted before the general election in November 1988, which returned the Progressive Conservative party to power.[33]

3.7 Royal Commission on Electoral Reform and Party Financing

On 15 November 1989, the federal government announced the creation of the Royal Commission on Electoral Reform and Party Financing with Pierre Lortie as chairman. Thus, further efforts to reform the regime regulating the financing of federal parties and candidates were put into abeyance until after the Commission issued its report.

4. CONCLUSIONS

Prior to the *Election Expenses Act* of 1974, there was little regulation of the financing of federal parties or candidates. What regulation there was stemmed from episodes of corruption, and most of the provisions proved to be ineffectual due to very limited enforcement.

The 1974 legislation began to take shape with the publication of the report of the Barbeau Committee in 1966. However, it was not until 1970 when the Chappell Committee was created that the issue of regulating party and candidate finances was again addressed by the House of Commons. Its second report in mid-1971 was followed by Bill C-211 in May 1972, but a general election in October intervened before the bill could be enacted. As a minority government dependent upon the support of the NDP, the Liberals introduced a bill that was substantially modified (Bill C-203) in June 1973. A significant number of amendments proposed by the opposition Progressive Conservative and New Democratic parties were accepted by the government of Pierre Trudeau.

While the new law was passed early in 1974, it did not apply to the 1974 general election. The *Election Expenses Act* embodied the following major elements: limits on the "election expenses" of both parties and candidates; extensive public disclosure; public subsidies in the form of income-tax credits, and reimbursement of part of candidates' and parties' "election expenses"; limits on broadcast advertising; and the provision of free broadcast time for parties during campaigns.

The work of interpreting the new regulatory regime was influenced by an informal Ad Hoc Committee of representatives from the major parties. They helped to persuade the Chief Electoral Officer to produce *Guidelines* specifying his interpretation of the *Canada Elections Act*. The various editions of the *Guidelines* have greatly influenced the interpretation of such key terms as "election expenses," which are defined in an ambiguous fashion in the *Canada Elections Act*. A series of fairly modest amendments was made in 1977 after the new regime had been in operation for only three years, but before the new legislation had been tested in a general election. In late 1983 Bill C-169 was enacted, amending a number of important provisions of the *Canada Elections Act*. One amendment was to have unforeseen consequences with respect to the ability of "advocacy groups" to participate in elections. In 1984, in the *National Citizens' Coalition* case, the Alberta Court of Queen's Bench held that the 1983 ban on "election expenses" by advocacy groups was unconstitutional, because it violated the freedom of expression as expressed in the *Canadian Charter of Rights and Freedoms.* Other changes indexed the spending limits, and altered the formulae for reimbursing parties and candidates.

Despite manifest problems with the financing regime and the urging of the Chief Electoral Officer, no new legislation has been enacted since 1983. There was a White Paper in 1986 and a major bill (C-79) in 1987, but the bill was not enacted before Parliament was dissolved prior to the November 1988 general election. The re-elected Progressive Conservative government launched the Royal Commission on Electoral Reform and Party Financing a year later.

3

PARTY REVENUES AND EXPENDITURES, 1974–90

An Overview

1. INTRODUCTION

THIS CHAPTER is the last of three that make up Part I of this study. It provides an overview of the revenue and expenditures of the three largest federal parties in the period 1974–90. In Part II, chapters 4 through 7 go into much more detail on the Progressive Conservative, Liberal, New Democratic and Reform parties respectively, relating their methods of financing to their organizational structure.

As will become clear, the *Election Expenses Act* of 1974 transformed the financing of federal political parties in Canada. Its most important consequence was to provide all the main parties with vastly larger sums to spend in the years *between* elections. At the same time, the "election expenses" of all parties increased in *real* terms between the 1979 and 1988 general elections, and – in 1988, for the first time – the New Democratic Party, like its two main rivals, spent close to the statutory limit. Hence, in the future, "election expenses" are unlikely to increase in real terms, because the limit is indexed to the Consumer Price Index. Note, however, that most party officials believe that the CPI understates the rate of inflation in the major items that go into election campaigns.[1]

The chapter is organized as follows. Section 2 provides a broad overview of the revenues and expenditures of the three largest parties between 1974 and 1990 in nominal dollars. Section 3 examines revenues and expenditures in constant 1989 dollars.[2] These two sections review the annual revenues and expenditures of the *federal office* of the NDP –

the first time this information has been published. The information filed with and published by the Chief Electoral Officer distinguishes between federally and provincially receipted revenue for the NDP, but does not provide any indication of the scale of the activities of the federal office of the NDP in the years between elections. This issue is addressed in more detail in chapter 6. Section 4 analyses the "election expenses" of federal parties for the four general elections (1979, 1980, 1984, 1988) since the *Election Expenses Act* came into effect. Section 5 examines the annual and cumulative surplus or deficit of each of the three main parties. Section 6 compares the overall ability of these parties to raise and spend money on federal politics. Section 7 sets out some major conclusions.

2. REVENUES AND EXPENDITURES IN NOMINAL DOLLARS

The growth of revenues and expenditures of the three main parties is documented in tables 3.1 to 3.3. In nominal dollars, the Liberal party's revenues and expenditures grew from about $2 million in 1974/75[3] to about $5 million in 1978. The Progressive Conservative party's revenues and expenditures grew even more rapidly during this period, from about $1.45 million in 1974/75 to about $5.5 million in 1978.[4] Comparisons with the NDP are very difficult because of several factors. First, the data reported by the NDP to the CEO include those for most of its provincial or territorial sections, while the data reported by the Liberals and Progressive Conservatives are for their federal activities only.[5] Second, while it is possible to identify "provincially receipted" revenues for the NDP and the rebates and subsidies paid to provincial sections by provincial governments (see table 3.1), it is not possible, using the data reported to the CEO, to separate federally and provincially related expenditures (except for federal "election expenses"). However, using data provided by party headquarters in Ottawa, a very good indication of the revenues and expenditures of the "federal wing" (in the form of the federal office) can be ascertained.

Third, as explained in detail in chapter 6, it appears that a substantial fraction of the NDP's federally receipted revenue in the interelection period is *not* spent on federal political activities. Therefore, the money is available for efforts to elect *provincial* members. The NDP's *total* revenue rose from $2.6 million in 1975 (the first full year under the legislative reforms of 1974) to approximately $4.2 million in 1978. However, about $784 000 of the 1978 revenue was provincially receipted revenue.[6]

Omitting election years for a moment, in 1981 Liberal party revenues ($5.6 million) and expenditures ($5.1 million) were about the same as they were in 1978. Because the CPI increased by 35 percent over the period, they fell in real terms. By 1983, Liberal party revenues had increased to $7.7 million, while expenditures were $6.3 million, so that the party had a substantial surplus. It was to be the last for some time. In 1985, the Liberals' fiscal fortunes hit a low: revenues amounted to only $6.2 million (below those for 1982 even in nominal dollars), and expenditures were $8.1 million. Hence, a deficit of $1.9 million followed the huge deficit in election year 1984 of $5.2 million.

While Liberal party revenues jumped sharply to $10.7 million in 1986, expenditures were $11.2 million, so another substantial deficit was recorded. Then revenues slumped in 1987 and another deficit was reported. Liberal party revenues rose dramatically to almost $18 million in election year 1988 and the party even generated a surplus of almost $900 000.[7] However, in 1989, the party raised only $6.4 million and spent $7.1 million. The important point is not the deficit, but rather the fact that, in *nominal* dollars, the Liberal party revenues were below those of 1982. The sharp increase in Liberal revenues and expenditures in 1990 is an anomaly reflecting the leadership race (won by Jean Chrétien) and convention in Calgary in June 1990. These events generated the following amounts of revenue: $4.4 million in delegate fees for the convention, which were treated as contributions to the party; $1.95 million in contributions to leadership candidates routed through the Federal Liberal Agency; and $608 000 in fees paid by leadership candidates to the party (table 5.8). When these items are deducted, Liberal party revenue in 1990 totalled $6.8 million, while expenditures totalled $7 million, amounts very close to the 1989 level.

The Progressive Conservative party has been the money-raising and spending champion among federal parties since 1978. Although the progress was uneven, excluding election years, annual revenues and expenditures rose from $5.5 million in 1978 to $8.5 million in 1982. Then they jumped to $14.8 million in revenues and $13.2 million in expenditures in 1983. This was, as table 3.1 reveals, more than double the level of the Liberal party and almost triple the NDP's federally receipted revenues. The PCs' expenditures in election year 1984 – even excluding $6.4 million in official "election expenses" – were $20.8 million. By comparison, the Liberal party spent $12 million over and above its "election expenses" of $6.3 million.[8]

The Progressive Conservatives' expenditures fell somewhat in the years before the 1988 election (e.g., $11.7 million in 1985 to $14.1 million in 1986), and in two of the three years, the party generated substantial surpluses (e.g., $3.4 million in 1985). In any event, the PCs were able to outspend their rivals during the period 1985–87 by a large margin.

In election year 1988, the Progressive Conservative party spent $21.1 million in addition to $7.9 million in official "election expenses." The comparable figures for the Liberal party were $10.2 million and $6.8 million, respectively. In 1989, while PC revenues and expenditures fell to $14.5 million and $12.8 million, both figures were double that of the Liberal party, and double the federally receipted revenues of the NDP. Note that the PCs' revenues in 1990 ($11.3 million) were $3.2 million below the 1989 level and were also below the level of the Liberal party ($13.8 million), although, as has been explained, the Liberals' revenues were increased by almost $7 million due to the 1990 leadership race and convention. The NDP's total revenues in 1990 were up by almost 11 percent over 1989 to $15.4 million, but this figure includes $6.4 million in sectionally receipted revenue, so that federal revenues were $9.04 million in 1990 (see table 3.2).

As noted above, it is difficult to compare the revenues and expend-itures of the NDP to the figures provided for the Liberal and Progressive Conservative parties. The central problem stems from the organiza-tional structure of the NDP and the fact that the Chief Electoral Officer has not required the party to segregate, on the expenditure side, its federal from its extensive provincial activities.[9] Further, the CEO has not reported the data filed with him on a consistent basis.[10]

Two measures of the revenues and one of expenditures of the federal level of the NDP are given in table 3.2. Column 1 provides an estimate of "federal revenues," which consist of federally receipted contributions plus other income, and the reimbursement of "election expenses" for federal general elections. As noted above, a good part of this revenue was not expended on federally related political activity. A second measure of the NDP's federal revenues (column 2) consists of the revenues of the party's federal office plus revenues collected by the federal office to fight federal elections. As shall be explained in chapter 6, part of these election revenues comes from levies on the party's provincial sections. Note that the first measure of NDP federal revenues (column 1) is much larger than the second (column 2). The difference is largely attributable to the fact that a major part of the money raised by the NDP using the federal income-tax credit for con-tributions is spent on provincial political activities. This point is care-fully documented in chapters 6 and 13.

With respect to expenditures, NDP officials interviewed for this study stated that the *federal office's* outlays are a good measure of the activities of the "federal wing" of the party. Further, each federal elec-tion is treated as an activity for which revenues and expenses are sepa-rately identified (see chap. 6). Transfers to riding associations have not been included in the estimates of the NDP federal wing's expenditure because they reflect outlays from federally receipted revenues and because almost all of the amount goes to the provincial sections for provincial activities according to the federal office's accountant. Hence column 3 in table 3.2 slightly underestimates the NDP's expenditures on federal political activity. Three things should be immediately apparent about the data in table 3.2. First, the NDP's "federal revenue" has substantially exceeded the expenditures of the federal office in every year between 1974/75 and 1990, even in the election years (1979, 1980, 1984, 1988). Second, the NDP's federal revenue is far below the party's total revenue as reported in table 3.1. The difference is attributable to provincially receipted (or sectional) revenues. Third, with the exception of election years, the federal office's revenues were typically less than one-third of total federal revenues. Virtually all of the difference went to support the provincial activities of the NDP (see chaps. 6, 13).

New Democratic Party officials emphasize that the NDP is a single, highly integrated party that operates at the federal and provincial levels and in some cases participates in municipal politics. The federal and provincial "wings" of the NDP are interwoven in financial and operational terms. However, there are different views concerning whether the difference between the federal office's revenues and its expenditures is used almost entirely on activities aimed at electing provincial governments or whether it also supports considerable activity within provincial sections whose objective is to elect federal MPs.[11] Party officials interviewed by the author indicate that the expenditures of the NDP's *federal office* quite accurately reflect the amounts spent on activities designed to elect federal MPs (outside of general elections). It has been suggested that the transfer of federal revenues to provincial sections is used to finance federally oriented work in provincial offices under the direction of provincial sections. However, a former party president who has also been a federal candidate indicates that, outside of the period of federal elections, the provincial sections devote little effort to federal politics. Moreover, the history of the party indicates that the federal "wing" was grafted on to a party that grew out of provincial politics. Only in recent years has there been an effort to increase the representation in the highest councils of the NDP of party members whose primary focus is on federal politics (see chap. 6). Even if only a quarter of the federally receipted revenue transferred to the NDP's provincial sections was used for federal politics, the central policy issue is whether federal taxpayers should subsidize the activities of any party at the provincial level.

The NDP's *federal* revenue, reported in table 3.2, grew from

$2.3 million in 1976 to $5.6 million in 1980, an election year. By comparison, the Liberal and Conservative parties each raised $7.5 million in 1980. NDP federal revenue fell off to only $3.9 million in 1981, but grew to almost $6 million in 1983. This figure was below that of the Liberals, $7.7 million, and less than one-half of that of the Conservatives' revenue in 1983, $14.8 million. NDP federal revenues rose to $9 million in 1984, only three-quarters of the Liberals' level and 40 percent of the Tories' revenue in this election year (table 3.2). NDP federal revenues were almost one-third lower in the next three interelection years (in the range of $6.3 million to $6.985 million), but rose to $13.8 million in election year 1988. Despite the increase, the NDP *federal* revenues amounted to 77 percent of the Liberal revenues and 51 percent of the Progressive Conservative revenues (as reported in table 3.1). The revenues of the federal wing of the NDP in 1989 were only 56 percent of the 1988 level, but increased substantially in 1990 to just over $9 million (table 3.2).

On the expenditure side, with the exception of 1988, the NDP's outlays at the federal level (i.e., by the federal office) have been far below those of its two main rivals. In nominal terms, NDP federal expenditures increased from only $476 000 in 1976 to $714 000 in 1978. Because of the general elections, they rose to $3.3 million in 1979 and $4.2 million in 1980. They fell to less than one-third the 1980 level for the next three years before rising to $6.7 million in election year 1984. Again, in the next three interelection years, the NDP's federal expenditures fell to one-third of what they had been in 1984. However, in election year 1988 they rose very sharply to $11.5 million, an amount that was within shooting distance of that of the Liberal party ($16.9 million), but still far below that of the Progressive Conservative party ($29.0 million).

An update to 1991 on the figures in table 3.1 is given in table 3.1a. It indicates that, while the Progressive Conservative party's revenues in 1991 ($12.3 million) were up almost $1 million over 1990, they were still well below those of 1989 ($14.5 million). The Liberal party's revenues fell from $13.8 million in 1990 to $7.2 million in 1991. The difference is very largely attributable to the leadership campaign and convention in 1990. The NDP's revenues rose sharply in 1991 to $19.9 million, up from $15.4 million in 1990. Most of the difference was attributable to an almost $3 million increase in the revenues of the party's *provincial* sections. The Reform Party had revenues of $6.6 million in 1991, a large increase from $2.7 million in 1990. The figures for 1991 indicate that all four parties had a surplus. The NDP's was the largest, $1.16 million.

3. REVENUES AND EXPENDITURES IN CONSTANT 1989 DOLLARS

Between 1974 and 1990, the CPI rose from 34.9 to 104.8, an increase of 300 percent (see table 3.3). Therefore, to make more useful comparisons of the three main parties' revenues and expenditures over time, it is useful to recast the nominal dollar amounts into constant dollars, 1989 dollars in this case.[12] While the CPI may not be the best possible deflator, there is no better one available that reflects the changing prices of those goods and services purchased by political parties.[13]

Table 3.3 provides party revenues and expenditures in 1989 dollars. The financial strength of the Progressive Conservative party can easily be seen by looking at its average revenue in the three interelection periods. From 1976 to 1978, the party averaged $9.8 million in revenue (in 1989 dollars). This amount increased by 40 percent to $13.7 million a year during the period 1981–83. It then increased again to $16.7 million a year in the period 1985–87. Moreover, as shall be made clear, in election years, the Tories were able to increase their revenues by far more than the amount needed to pay for official "election expenses" (see figure 3.1).

While the Liberal party raised more money than the Conservative party in the period 1976–78 ($11.5 million in 1989 dollars), its average revenue (in 1989 dollars) in the next two interelection periods was substantially below that for the 1976–78 period: an average of $9.20 million per year in the period 1981–83 and only slightly better in 1985–87, $9.75 million annually in 1989 dollars. The point is that the Progressive Conservative party, in real terms, was able to raise $4.5 million per year more than the Liberal party in the period 1981–83, and $6.9 million per year more in the period 1985–87. The gap was even larger in 1989 (see table 3.3). If the effects of the Liberals' 1990 leadership race and convention are removed, the Conservative party generated about $4.5 million more revenue in 1990 than did the Liberal party.

A very useful indicator of the financial strength of the Progressive Conservative party, relative to its rivals, can be seen in its ability to outspend them in election years on activities *not* included in official "election expenses" (table 3.1). The figures can be summarized as follows:

Party expenditures other than "election expenses" in election years in 1989 dollars
(thousands of dollars)

	1979	1980	1984	1988
PC	9 690	8 372	25 649	22 190
Lib.	5 180	6 296	14 814	10 689
PC – Lib.	4 510	2 076	10 835	11 501

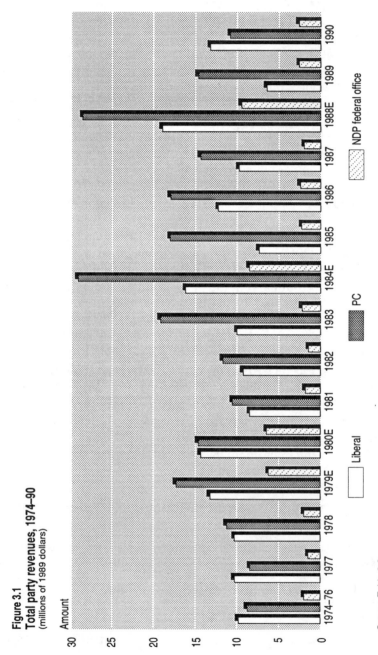

Figure 3.1
Total party revenues, 1974–90
(millions of 1989 dollars)

Source: Table 3.3.

These figures indicate that the Conservative party was able to outspend the Liberal party in terms of outlays other than "election expenses" in election years by $4.5 million in 1979 and $2.1 million in 1980.[14] However, in 1984, the "gap" was $10.8 million and in 1988 it was $11.5 million. To put these two figures into perspective, note that the "election expenses" of both parties were about $7.9 million in 1984, and $8.3 million for the Conservative party and $7.2 million for the Liberal party in 1988 (as measured in 1989 dollars). It appears also that the NDP's federal office increased its nonelection expenditures in 1988, but it did so on a tiny scale compared to the Conservative party.

Again the NDP presents a serious problem if its federal activities are to be compared to those of the other main parties. The "NDP I" figures given in table 3.3 are for the party as a whole, including most of its provincial sections. Like the federal Progressive Conservative party, the NDP has been able to increase its revenues and expenses in real terms. For example, expenditures averaged $6.6 million per year in the period 1976–78, while in the last interelection period, 1985–87, they averaged $15.26 million per year. In 1989 and 1990, total NDP expenditures (in 1989 dollars) averaged $13 million, somewhat below the 1985–87 period. These figures, however, include a large component of provincial activity.

The "NDP II" figures include only the revenues and expenditures of the *federal office*, including the revenues associated with elections and the federal office's figures for "election expenses" (which are slightly larger than those reported to the CEO).[15] While the federal office's revenues and expenditures have grown substantially in real terms, they were always far below the levels of the other two main parties. For example, the NDP federal office average annual expenditures in inter-election years grew from $1.38 million in the period 1976–78 to $1.46 million in the 1985–87 period. Recall that the comparable figure for the Liberal party in the last period was $9.75 million, while that for the Conservative party was $16.7 million. While the NDP's federally receipted revenues (*not* the revenues of the federal office) exceed the expenses of the federal office, typically by several million dollars, the difference is used to finance the activities of the NDP's provincial sections, whose focus is largely on provincial rather than on federal politics.

Figure 3.2 illustrates the ability of the Progressive Conservative party since 1981 to spend much more than its two main rivals outside of "election expenses." As we shall see in section 4, the difference in "election expenses" between the PCs and Liberals on the one hand and the NDP on the other has been closing over the past four elections. What is difficult to determine is to what extent the demonstrated ability of the Conservative party to greatly outspend its two main rivals *outside* of the 50 to 60 days of the official campaign period contributed to its ability to win on election day in 1979, 1984 and 1988. This matter is addressed in chapter 4.

Figure 3.2
Party expenditures excluding "election expenses," 1974–90
(millions of 1989 dollars)

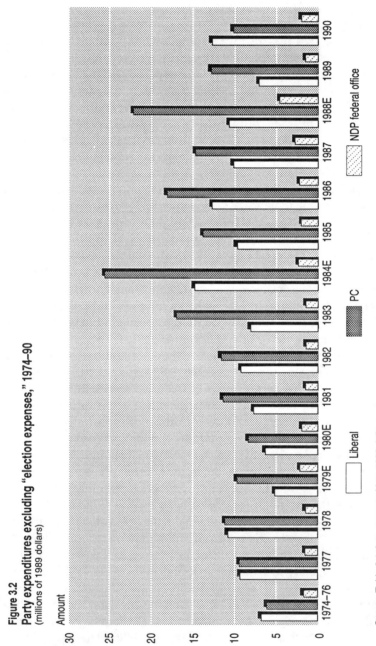

Source: Table 3.1 data converted into 1989 dollars.

4. PARTY ELECTION EXPENSES

There have been four general elections since the *Election Expenses Act* of 1974 came into effect: 1979, 1980, 1984 and 1988. The "election expenses" of all registered parties increased from $10.1 million in 1979 to $17.6 million in 1984 and to $22.4 million in 1988 (table 3.4; figure 3.3). In real terms (1989 dollars), the increase was much smaller – from $18.9 million in 1979 to $21.75 million in 1984, to $23.56 million in 1988. Parties other than the Progressive Conservatives, Liberals and NDP have never accounted for more than 2.6 percent of the "election expenses" of all parties combined.

In nominal and real terms, the NDP has had the greatest increase in the level of "election expenses"; it has also spent a higher fraction of the statutory limit on "election expenses": from 49.1 percent in 1979 to 74.0 percent in 1984, to 88.2 percent in 1988 (see figure 3.4). Indeed, in 1988 it went closer to the limit than did the Liberal party (85.7 percent) because of the Liberals' financial straits (see chap. 5). Even in 1979, the Conservative party (87.7 percent) was closer to the limit than the Liberal party (86.2 percent), and the Conservative party went even closer in

Figure 3.3
"Election expenses" by party, 1979, 1980, 1984, 1988 general elections
(millions of dollars)

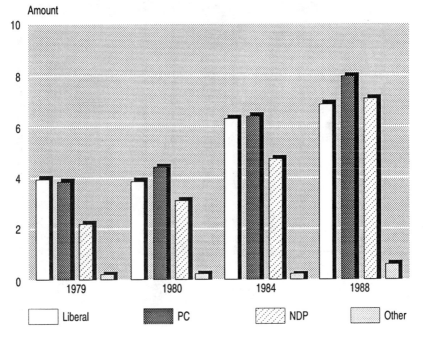

Source: Table 3.4.

1984 (99.96 percent) and 1988 (98.95 percent). Given the practical problems with controlling and coordinating party spending in a general election, it is a remarkable achievement to be able to get so close to the limit and not exceed it. Officials of all three main parties told the author that budgeting for anything over 95 percent of the limit is very risky because of the complexities of a national election campaign. Therefore, the ability of the PCs to spend 99.96 percent of the limit in 1984 and 98.95 percent in 1988 is remarkable, to say the least.

Table 3.4 also provides the data on the federal government's reimbursement of the parties' "election expenses." In 1979 and 1980, the *Canada Elections Act* provided that parties would be reimbursed for 50 percent of the media costs of broadcast (radio and television) advertising. Then, as now, the total amount of such advertising by *all* parties was limited to 6.5 hours and could only be broadcast between the 29th and 2nd days before voting day. In 1983, the Act was amended to change the reimbursement formula to 22.5 percent of a party's "election expenses" (up to the limit), provided the party spent at least 10 percent

Figure 3.4
Party "election expenses" as percentage of statutory limit,
1979, 1980, 1984, 1988 general elections

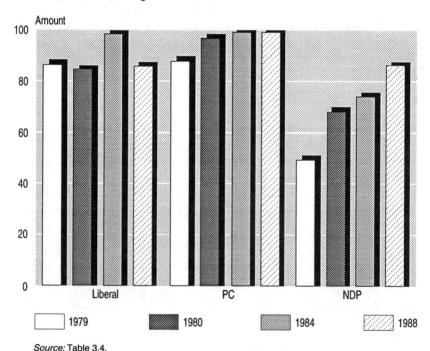

Source: Table 3.4.

of its spending limit ($800 000 in 1988). Overall, the reimbursement amounted to 19.9 percent of the total "election expenses" of all parties in 1979, and 22.2 percent thereafter. As indicated in table 3.4, the amount of reimbursement received by parties other than the three main parties has been minuscule. Even in 1988, the reimbursement to these other parties was $49 000, while they spent $604 000.

Michaud and Laferrière (1991) estimate that over the electoral cycle 1981–84, the federal government's contribution to federal parties in the form of tax credits to donors amounted to 30.7 percent of party revenues. For the last electoral cycle (1985–88), the tax credits amounted to 29.0 percent of all parties' revenues (table 3.4).

The composition of the three main parties' "election expenses" is described in table 3.5. Advertising costs (print, radio and TV) have consumed more than half of each party's total outlay, except the NDP in 1984 and 1988. For the Progressive Conservative party, advertising absorbed 71 percent and 70 percent in 1979 and 1980 respectively, but this category fell to 50 percent in 1984 and rose to 60 percent in 1988. For the Liberal party, advertising accounted for 62 percent of total "election expenses" in 1979, 68 percent in 1980, but only 56 percent in 1984 and 1988. For the NDP, advertising accounted for 60 percent of "election expenses" in 1979 and 1980, but only 38 percent in 1984 and 44 percent in 1988.

It is clear from table 3.5 that broadcast or "electronic" advertising accounts for the bulk of each party's expenditures on advertising.[16] Print advertising for the Progressive Conservatives accounted for from only 3.2 percent of total "election expenses" in 1984 to 13.1 percent in 1980. The comparable figures for the Liberals were 10.4 percent (1980) and 14.7 percent (1979), while those for the NDP were 3.3 percent (1984) and 14.4 percent (1979). Within the electronic advertising category, television is far more important (in terms of expenditures) than radio. In 1988, for example, the Conservative party spent $2.4 million on television as compared to $1.56 million on radio. However, the NDP spent slightly *more* than the Tories on television ($2.5 million), but only $477 000 on radio.

For the Progressive Conservative and Liberal parties, travel expenses typically absorbed one-sixth to one-seventh of total "election expenses." For the NDP, the percentage was somewhat lower. The NDP's figure for 1984 ($146 000) is suspect, for internal party records indicate the cost of the leader's tour at $531 000 (see chap. 6). In 1988 the NDP leader's tour cost $1 258 000, and the "travelling" expenses reported to the CEO were $1 037 000. On a proportionate basis, therefore, it appears that the figure for "travelling" in 1984 should be over $430 000, or about 9 percent of total "election expenses," not the reported 3.1 percent.

The "other expenses" category includes "hire of premises," "salaries and wages," "administrative expenses," "national office expenses," but the CEO does not report these items separately. It should be noted that in all four general elections, the NDP spent a much higher fraction of its total "election expenses" on the "other" category, and that this category has consumed a larger proportion of the NDP's "election expenses" over time. For example, in 1979, "other" expenses accounted for 28.4 percent of the NDP's total "election expenses," versus 20.1 percent for the Liberal party and only 12.2 percent for the Conservative party. In 1988, the NDP's fraction had increased to 41.0 percent, while the Liberals' had increased to 25.8 percent and the PCs' had increased to 20.8 percent. If such "other" expenses are largely overhead costs, one would expect them to *fall* as a percentage of the total as the NDP was able to get closer to the legal limit on total "election expenses." The reason for the NDP's higher percentage may lie in the trade unions' supply of volunteers to NDP campaigns and the fact that the party pays a larger fraction of its organizers than do other parties. Where volunteers are on leave from their regular jobs, the party has to record their pay as an "election expense," even though the union is paying the person on leave for the campaign.

Some historical perspective on the importance of broadcast advertising can be gained from the figures in table 3.6. In real terms (1989 dollars), party outlays on radio and television advertising grew from $5.4 million in the 1965 election to $9.2 million in the 1972 election, and then fell to $7.8 million in the 1974 election – the last one in which election expenses were not subject to a limit. In the last four elections, expenditures on radio and television ads were between $9.1 million (1984) and $10.5 million (1980 and 1988). In other words, it appears that party outlays on electronic advertising have doubled between the 1965 and 1988 general elections. In the elections of 1979 through 1988, expenditures on broadcast advertising (see table 3.6) were increased as a fraction of the total "election expenses" of the parties.

The data indicate that electronic advertising absorbed a much larger percentage of total party "election expenses" in the 1979–88 period than in the 1965–74 period. However, in the earlier period, a much larger fraction of party (or national campaign) expenditures consisted of transfers from headquarters to individual candidates. For example, in 1974, the Liberal party spent $5.5 million on the election, of which $2.6 million consisted of transfers to candidates. In 1979, the party spent $3.9 million, but transfers to candidates amounted to about $300 000 (Paltiel 1975, 190, 192; Seidle and Paltiel 1981, 238). In the past two elections, Conservative party headquarters transferred much less to candidates (see chap. 4). The reasons why the national campaigns transfer much less money to candidates appear to be that candidates have found it much easier to raise money with the aid of the income-tax credit, and because most are eligible to have half their "election expenses" reimbursed by the federal government.

Under the CEO's 1988 *Guidelines*, a number of potentially important election-related outlays are *excluded* from a party's "election expenses." These include:

- polling and research expenses (which could easily amount to from $400 000 to $800 000 during the campaign);
- fund-raising costs (these could amount to one-third of the gross revenue from direct mail, which could amount to from $1 million to $2 million);
- costs of developing party policies or election strategy;
- costs of training candidates or election organizers; and
- all the party's internal costs "not incurred as an integral part of endeavours furthering the external exposure of the party" (Canada, Elections Canada 1988a, 4).

These exclusions might easily have totalled $4 million to $5 million in the case of the Progressive Conservative party in 1988. The issue is discussed in more detail in chapter 13.

5. "BOTTOM LINE"

While the financial difficulties of the Liberal party in the period 1985–89 have been the subject of numerous newspaper articles (see chap. 5), the amounts of annual surplus or deficit of the other parties are less well known. Table 3.3 indicates that over the 16-year period 1974/75 through 1990, the Progressive Conservative party and the Liberal party ran a deficit in 7 years. For the NDP as a whole (i.e., including its provincial sections), there were deficits in 8 of the 16 years. The NDP's federal office had deficits in 6 of the 16 years for which we have data (see NDP II in table 3.3).

The surplus or deficit of each of the three main parties in each of four periods since the new regulatory regime was in effect, determined by which party was in power, has been examined in table 3.7. While the Clark government was in power from the spring of 1979 to early 1980, the data are only available by calendar year, so 1979 was chosen. The data indicate that in *nominal* dollars, all three parties ran a cumulative surplus during the period 1 August 1974 to 31 December 1978, when the Liberal party held power in Ottawa under Pierre Trudeau.

As might be expected, the surplus of the party in power was larger (by almost $1 million) than that of the Conservative party. However, the NDP's surplus (for the party as a whole) was even larger ($1.8 million). The federal office's surplus was tiny, suggesting it just broke even over the initial 53 months under the 1974 legislation (NDP II in table 3.7). Despite the fact that 1979 was an election year, the Progressive Conservative and Liberal parties were able to generate a slight surplus, while the NDP as a whole had a comparable deficit.

Table 3.7 indicates that in the period 1980–84 when the Liberal party held power under Mr. Trudeau, both the Liberal and the Conservative parties had large cumulative *deficits:* $3.56 million in nominal dollars for the PCs, and $2.56 million for the Liberals. In both cases, most of the cumulative deficit occurred in 1984 when the Conservatives had a deficit of $3.75 million and the Liberals' deficit was $5.28 million (see table 3.3). The reasons for the Liberals' very large deficit in 1984 are discussed in chapter 6. During the last Liberal regime, the NDP as a whole had a modest cumulative deficit in nominal dollars ($453 000), while the NDP federal office had a comparable surplus ($563 000).

Table 3.7 makes it clear that the Progressive Conservative party was apparently able to capitalize on its electoral victories in 1984 and 1988 to achieve a cumulative *surplus* of $4.8 million in nominal dollars in the period 1985–90, while the Liberal party had a cumulative *deficit* of $2.2 million during the same period. Note, however, that although the Progressive Conservative party ran a $2.03 million deficit in election year 1988, the Liberal party ran a decent *surplus* ($881 000). The Liberals' problems stemmed from a large deficit in 1985 ($1.97 million) and smaller deficits in 1986, 1987 and 1989 (table 3.3). In the period 1985–90, with the Progressive Conservative party in power in Ottawa, the NDP as a whole had a cumulative deficit of just under $2 million in nominal dollars, while the federal office's deficit was almost as large ($1.84 million).

When the surplus or deficit figures are recast in terms of *constant* 1989 dollars, the large size of the cumulative surpluses in the 1974–78 period can be seen. For example, in 1989 dollars, the Liberal party had a cumulative surplus of $3.7 million during the period 1974–78, versus over $4 million for the NDP as a whole and $1.5 million for the Conservative party. By comparison, the Liberals' cumulative deficit in the 1980–84 period was $2.57 million, and in the 1985–90 period it was $2.66 million. For the Conservatives, the surplus of $1.5 million during the period 1974–78 was followed by deficits totalling $4.84 million during the last Trudeau government (1980–84). These deficits, however, were offset by a cumulative surplus of $5.5 million (all in 1989 dollars) in the period 1985–90 when the Conservative party held power in Ottawa (table 3.7).

The NDP as a whole had a cumulative surplus of $4.1 million (in 1989 dollars) in the period 1974–78, but since that time had cumulative *deficits* of $655 000, $1.44 million and $2.5 million in the three successive periods. While the NDP's *federal office* had a cumulative deficit of $2 million in the period 1985–89, this is largely attributable to the fact that less than one-half of the federally receipted revenues generated by the NDP are given to the federal office, which is also responsible for financing the federal general elections. The cumulative deficit between 1985 and 1990 was almost entirely due to the federal office's deficit of $2.6 million (1989 dollars) in 1988, an election year.

In general terms, table 3.7 indicates that, since 1979, the Liberal party and the NDP (as a whole) have run large, cumulative deficits, while the Progressive Conservative party has been able to run a slight cumulative surplus. The record indicates that the Conservative party has been able to benefit from holding office (1985–90), while the Liberals failed to do so during their last term in power (1980–84). In particular, the Liberal party had a deficit of $5.3 million in 1984, the year in which the Conservatives came to power.

6. COMPARING THE THREE MAIN PARTIES: AN OVERALL VIEW

The Liberal party held power for two-thirds of the 17-year period for which we have data on the financing of parties (and candidates) under the legislation instituted effective 1 August 1974. Yet, while it was in power, the Liberal party did *not* dominate the Conservative party in terms of the ability to raise and spend money on nonelection activities. As indicated earlier in table 3.4, the three main parties were fairly evenly matched on official "election expenses" by 1988. In terms of *total* party revenues in 1989 dollars, the Liberal party raised only 9 percent more than the Conservative party in the almost five-year period after the *Election Expenses Act* came into effect and before the short-lived Clark government came to power (table 3.8). However, during the last Trudeau government (1980–84), the Liberal party raised only 68.4 percent of the amount raised by the opposition Conservative party. Moreover, in absolute terms, the difference was almost $27 million in 1989 dollars, or over $5 million annually. The gap between the Liberal and Conservative parties on the expenditure side was not so great. Table 3.8 indicates that during the first four years and five months under the 1974 legislation, the Liberal party spent only $1 million more than the Conservative party, again in 1989 dollars. In the period 1980–84, the Conservatives spent $29 million more than the

Liberals – almost all of the difference was outside official "election expenses."

Then, when the Liberal party under John Turner's leadership fell from electoral grace in September 1984, matters got worse in terms of the party's ability to raise and spend money aside from "election expenses." Between 1985 and 1990, the Progressive Conservative party raised almost $104 million, versus $68 million for the Liberal party. Indeed, the Liberals' fiscal problems were such that, in 1988, its "election expenses" were only 85 percent of the statutory limit, and in absolute terms were below those of the NDP. The Liberal party's expenditures, excluding "election expenses" over the same period, were $63.1 million in 1989 dollars, versus $89.9 million for the Conservative party.

The Liberal party's failure to dominate the Conservative party in terms of party financing, even while in power, reflects a number of structural features of the party, and its implicit assumption that, as the "natural governing party," it had little need to change its methods of raising money. Party officials have suggested that the weaknesses of the old methods of raising money (which relied heavily on donations from large corporations) were real but simply not apparent when the party was in power (chap. 5).[17] Moreover, the party failed to appreciate the implications of the new technologies and of how much it was relying on being in power to facilitate fund-raising. Specifically, the party failed to expand its funding base, most notably by failing to create a major direct-mail effort before 1986. While there are clear signs of renewal in terms of new policies instituted in 1987–89,[18] it is not obvious that the party has the capability of raising money between election years on a scale that is comparable to the Progressive Conservative party. In mid-1991, the Reform Commission of the Liberal party summarized the party's financial problems very succinctly: "We don't raise enough money by our current methods to fight national elections, staff our Party, and pay off our debt" (1991, 4). In fact, in 1991, the Reform Party, which was founded in 1987, raised almost as much money as the Liberal party (table 3.1a).

Comparisons of the revenues and expenditures of the Liberal and Conservative parties with those of the NDP are complicated by two factors: first, the NDP reports its revenues and expenditures to the CEO on an integrated basis that combines federal and provincial activities; second, between general elections, the federal activities of the NDP most comparable to its major rivals are those of its federal office, but its expenditures are not reported to the CEO (however, the NDP kindly provided them to the author). On the revenue side, the data for the NDP in table 3.8 are for all federally receipted contributions and other federal revenues. Between 1 August 1974 and 1978, the NDP raised almost $30 million (in 1989 dollars), but this was only 39 percent of the amount raised by its two main rivals. While NDP revenues rose to $40.8 million in the period 1980–84 (the last Trudeau government), its two rivals raised $142.5 million, so the NDP's revenues as a percentage of its major rivals declined to 28.6 percent. Like the other two major parties, the NDP's total revenues fell slightly in the first five years of the Mulroney government relative to the previous five years when the Liberal party was in power. The crucial point, however, is that the NDP's revenues fell to 25.3 percent of those of its two major rivals combined.

At the *federal* level, NDP expenditures were far below the party's revenues raised using the federal tax credit. More importantly, expenditures at the federal level by the NDP (the federal office) were far below those of its two main rivals (except during the 1988 election). For example, from 1974 to 1978, revenues were over four times expenditures. The difference – recorded as a surplus in table 3.8 – was in fact transferred to the NDP's provincial sections, which used it largely for provincial activities. In the period 1980–84, the NDP's federal revenues were double its federal expenditures, but its expenditures were only 13.2 percent of those of the Liberal and Conservative parties combined (up from 10.2 percent in 1974–78). Over the period 1985–89, federal expenditures of the NDP were only 55.2 percent of revenues. However, the NDP's federal office outlays (including those for the 1988 general election) amounted to only 14.2 percent of its two main rivals combined. Compared to its single best-financed rival (the PCs), the NDP was outspent by over four to one during the first five years of the Mulroney government (excluding "election expenses" in 1988).

The provisions of the *Election Expenses Act* of 1974 have benefited the New Democratic Party a great deal. However, much of the benefit – for example in the form of higher revenues – has *not* gone into the federal office, except during elections. The federal tax credit for political contributions has been used to raise far more money for the NDP as a whole than is spent by the federal office outside of "election expenses." The NDP, as an integrated party, has chosen to use the federal tax credit as a vehicle to help finance its provincial ambitions.[19] In most years between 1974 and 1990 the federal office's budget (all sources of revenue) to promote the election of federal MPs was less than the amount of money flowing to provincial or territorial sections for the purpose of electing *provincial* governments from money raised using the *federal* tax credit (chap. 6).

While the federal office of the NDP receives 15 percent of revenues generated by the party's provincial sections using the federal income-tax credit for political contributions to registered parties, the federal office's other sources of revenues generate only modest amounts of money, and some of these sources depend upon the generosity of the provincial sections. In contrast, in the Progressive Conservative party there is a clear separation between federal and provincial politics. When the federal Conservative party (PC Canada Fund) retains 25 percent of the money raised by riding associations between elections in "exchange" for the use of its (federal) tax-receipting authority, it is dealing with a local organization *solely* devoted to electing a *federal* government. Moreover, the Ottawa headquarters of the federal Conservative party has complete autonomy from provincial Conservative parties. Further, federal headquarters has not agreed to accept any constraints on the sources of funds it can tap in order to accommodate riding associations.

Trade unions continue to be an important source of revenue for the NDP, through affiliation dues, cash contributions and contributions of goods and services. However, their importance in financing federal elections declined from 43 to 44 percent of the total election-related revenue in 1979 and 1980 to 34 percent in 1984 to 25 percent in 1988 (chap. 6). In large part, this decline is a result of the increase in party spending on "election expenses" – from 49 percent of the statutory limit in 1979 to 88 percent in 1988 – and the fact that union contributions have not been raised accordingly.

Officials in the three main parties and many citizens see the role of trade unions in financing the NDP as closely analogous to that of corporations in financing the Progressive Conservative and Liberal parties. The analogy, in fact, is not a close one for several reasons. First, trade union locals that are affiliated with the NDP pay annual affiliation dues that provide a regular source of income for the NDP; there is no corresponding relationship between corporations and the Progressive Conservative or Liberal parties. Second, it appears that a higher fraction of trade union locals give money or services to the NDP than do corporations (although 40 percent of the 500 largest nonfinancial corporations contribute to one or both parties).[20] Third, except in the 1979 and 1980 elections, the resources provided by unions have been a smaller fraction of the NDP's revenues than have been corporate contributions of the Liberal or Conservative parties' revenues. However, union contributions that are centralized through the Canadian Labour Congress might give that body more influence. Fourth, a much greater fraction of the unions' contributions to the NDP's federal election campaigns consists of goods and services than is the case for corporate contributions to the Liberal or Progressive Conservative parties. Indeed, in 1979, 1980 and 1984, the value of unions' contributions in the form of goods and services greatly exceeded their cash contributions; in 1988, union cash contributions were double their contributions in kind.

Although the "federal wing" (federal office) of the NDP does not spend nearly as much as its main rivals between elections, in 1988 it closed the gap with respect to "election expenses" (see figure 3.3).[21] In 1988, for the first time, the NDP ran a truly national federal election campaign. The party spent over $2 million in Quebec, compared to only about $50 000 in the previous election. It also spent more on "election expenses" in 1988 than did the Liberal party. For the first time, the NDP had to worry about "hitting the limit," rather than trying to shift outlays into the "election expenses" column so as to benefit from the 22.5 percent reimbursement. One effect of making such a major effort in Quebec was that "election expenses" in other provinces fell below the 1984 level in real terms.

7. CONCLUSIONS

While the revenues and expenditures of the three main parties and the Reform Party are explored in much more detail in Part II of this study (chaps. 4–7), it is possible to draw certain conclusions at this point. First, the *Election Expenses Act* of 1974 has enabled the three main parties to raise and spend money on activities other than official "election expenses" on a scale far beyond the levels of the 1950s, 1960s or early 1970s. Further, in constant dollars, these expenditures grew quite rapidly from 1974 to 1984, then fell off, but rose sharply again in 1988, only to fall to a level in 1989 and 1990 roughly equivalent to 1978 and 1979 (figure 3.2).

Second, the "election expenses" of both the Conservative and Liberal parties rose at about the rate of inflation between 1979 and 1988. They rose more rapidly for the NDP because it was able to increase its expenditures from 49 percent to 88 percent of the statutory limit.

Third, while the three main parties are annually raising and spending large sums by historical standards, they have not been able to accumulate surpluses. Indeed, the record reveals that only the Progressive Conservative party has been able to generate a (modest) cumulative surplus since 1974, while the Liberal party has had a substantial accumulated deficit, although it has been able to reduce its debt in the period 1989–91. Comparisons with the figures for the NDP are very difficult because of the integrated nature of the party and the complexity of its intraparty financial flows. For the NDP as a whole, the cumulative surplus of the 1974–78 period has been more than offset by subsequent deficits; this is also true of the NDP's federal office. However, when the NDP's federally receipted revenue is compared to the expenditures of its federal office, it is clear that very substantial surpluses were generated (over $44 million in the period 1980–90; see table 3.8). These were transferred to the party's provincial sections, which used the money largely on provincial rather than federal political activity.

In contrast to the parties, as will be documented in detail in chapter 12, *candidates* as a group have generated surpluses totalling $8 million in 1984 and $9.6 million in 1988. These, however, have gone largely to riding associations, although the Liberal party and, to a lesser degree, the NDP have sought to "capture" part of the surplus by requiring that part of the candidates' reimbursement be paid to the party (see chaps. 5, 6).

Fourth, the problem for the Liberal and Progressive Conservative parties has not been to raise the money to pay the official "election expenses" for the last four general elections – in large part because such outlays are limited by law. Rather, it has been to pay for the large rise in "operating expenses" in election years 1984 and 1988 in the case of the Conservative party and 1984 in the case of the Liberal party. This issue is addressed in more detail in chapters 4 and 5 below.

PART II

PARTY FINANCING

4

PROGRESSIVE CONSERVATIVE PARTY

1. INTRODUCTION

IN TERMS OF ITS CAPACITY to raise and spend money, the Progressive Conservative party has been by far the most successful in Canada of the major parties in the period 1981–90.[1] Even during the last Liberal government under Pierre Trudeau (1980–84), the Conservative party raised $84.6 million, as compared to $57.9 million by the Liberal party (both in 1989 dollars) (table 3.8). Once it gained power, the party was able to widen this gap. Between 1985 and 1990, it raised $103.7 million, while the Liberal party raised only $67.6 million (table 3.8).

The seeds of the Conservatives' ability to raise money were planted very shortly after the *Election Expenses Act* of 1974 came into force. Because it spent so many years in the political wilderness, the Conservative party could not rely on the people or other resources associated with being the government-of-the-day. Being in opposition appears to have made the party more open to new fund-raising techniques and more "business-like" methods of organization. The Conservative party sought the help of consultants to the U.S. Republican party in establishing its fund-raising strategy, particularly direct mail, corporate contributions and major-donor programs (see chaps. 9–11). By the late 1970s, the party's direct-mail operation was in high gear – party officials had been willing to invest in the building of a large list of individuals who were willing to donate money to the party.

The Conservative party centralized all authority for the issuing of receipts for the income-tax credit for political contributions in the PC Canada Fund.[2] Further, headquarters retained 25 percent of all revenues raised by riding associations that were funnelled through the Fund. Conflicts over fund-raising and spending have been reduced by the fact that the Conservative party is not a federation like the Liberal party, or a single, integrated party like the NDP. The Conservative party has not been burdened by conflicts over access to membership lists, as were its two main rivals. The clear separation of federal and provincial Progressive Conservative parties[3] has clarified and simplified the role of both, although one level has been able to draw upon the resources of the other at election times.

The federal Progressive Conservative party has strongly encouraged its candidates to become less dependent on money from party headquarters than its rivals.[4] As importantly, the Conservative party has also successfully encouraged its candidates to raise more money so that more of them can spend close to their legal limit on "election expenses."

This chapter is organized as follows. Section 2 examines the organizational structure of the federal Progressive Conservative party and relates it to fund-raising techniques and the sharing of revenues. Section 3 examines party revenues and expenditures, including financial transactions between headquarters and riding associations and candidates. This discussion reviews the activities of the party between elections, including its capacity to greatly increase operating expenditures during election years. Section 4 examines the organization of the party's election campaigns between 1979 and 1988. In section 5, the activities and financing of riding associations are discussed. Finally, the conclusions are set out in section 6.

2. ORGANIZATIONAL STRUCTURE

Officially, the national Progressive Conservative party is the Progressive Conservative Association of Canada. The PC Canada Fund is the official agent of the party. Unlike the NDP and the Liberal Party of Canada, the Progressive Conservative party does not have any provincial/territorial associations or sections that have a *dual* role of electing federal MPs and electing members to a provincial legislature. Therefore, its key entities are the 295 riding associations and the national headquarters in Ottawa. Dyck describes the structure of the Progressive Conservative party as follows:

> The national Progressive Conservative Party is less a federation of provincial units than the Liberals, and the two wings of the party are generally quite independent ... The federal-provincial relationship varies from one part of the country to another, being closest and somewhat integrated in the four Atlantic provinces, variable in Ontario, and more confederal in the Prairies. The federal party was particularly dependent on the Ontario organization in the Stanfield era and under Mulroney, when the Big Blue Machine moved on to Ottawa,

whereas, under Clark, relations were more distant. There is virtually no provincial wing in British Columbia, and the total truncation occurs in Quebec, where, since 1935–36, there has been no provincial Conservative Party at all ... In every province there is a complete set of federal riding associations and executives alongside existing provincial organizations. (1989, 198–99)

Provincial organizations elect a certain number of members of the National Executive of the Progressive Conservative party and a number of delegates to the biannual General Meeting. National headquarters is under the authority of the National Executive and is run on a day-to-day basis by the party's National Director.

In terms of financing, the federal party has only two levels: the local (riding) associations, and the national level represented by the PC Canada Fund, the party's official agent. The simpler organization of the party units and associated flows of funds can be seen by comparing figure 4.1 to figure 5.1 (chap. 5) for the Liberal party and figure 6.1 (chap. 6) for the NDP. Dyck describes the financing of the Conservative party as follows:

[T]he two wings of the party rely basically on their own fund-raising efforts. That is not to say that requests for funds are not frequently submitted to Ottawa, especially from the Atlantic region. The federal party does usually help provincial parties at election time, primarily through the provision of personnel, expertise and services ... Provincial parties are not obliged to contribute to the federal party's budget, and there are virtually no joint fund-raising events in any province. Ontario officials say, for example, that it is too complicated to agree on the split of the take, as well as to receipt the proceeds properly under different federal and provincial legislation. Instead, federal and provincial fund-raising dinners in the province alternate. (1989, 200)[5]

In light of the new regulatory regime that came into effect 1 August 1974, the federal Progressive Conservative party carried out a complete assessment of its fund-raising operations in 1974 (Seidle 1980, 240). The changes included setting up the PC Canada Fund (a non-share capital corporation) as official agent and starting a direct-mail operation. For about two years, the Tories had a Treasury Committee to solicit funds from large corporations and wealthy individuals. It was disbanded in late 1976 (ibid., 241).

The PC Canada Fund coordinates all fund-raising activity and also oversees the preparation and control of the federal party's expenditure budget. Since it was established, the Fund has received 25 percent of

Figure 4.1
Flows of funds relating to Progressive Conservative party and its candidates

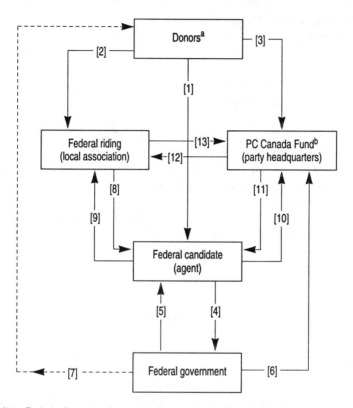

Note: Excludes financing of campaigns for party leadership or nomination campaigns.
aIncludes individuals, corporations, trade unions, interest groups and other organizations.
bOfficial agent for federal Progressive Conservative party.

tax-receipted funds raised by local associations (ridings) between election campaigns. The "tax" is not applied during campaign periods, when each candidate's agent can issue receipts for the income-tax credit. If ridings want to provide donors with a tax receipt between elections, the contribution must pass through the PC Canada Fund, which retains 25 percent. Local associations that object to the 25 percent "tax" have to recognize that, for most individual donors and small firms making contributions, the tax credit is probably an important part of their decision to make a donation to riding associations (see chap. 8). Therefore, the ability to provide donors with a tax receipt probably offsets the effect of the 25 percent "tax" and, on a net basis, the riding would appear to be better off under this arrangement.

Although the Progressive Conservative party headquarters began some major intitiatives in 1981 and 1982,[6] the period between the elections of 1984 and 1988 was the first time that the party made a sustained effort to engage in political organization between elections. There was a concerted effort to make the operation of the Conservative party more "professional" after Mr. Mulroney became leader in 1983. The activities involved more polling, tours by ministers and the leader, the development of the party organization at headquarters and at the riding level, and the appointment of full-time field organizers based in each region. In general terms, the party sought to create a "permanent election machine." However, efforts to make the party more effective by means of "professionalization" have not been without cost. The increase in the number and responsibilities of paid staff is likely to reduce the perceived importance of volunteers, who are regarded as amateurs (recall chap. 1).

3. PARTY REVENUES AND EXPENDITURES

3.1 Overview

The Progressive Conservative party's revenues and expenditures in nominal dollars for the period 1974–90 are given in table 4.1. In nominal dollars, party expenditures rose from $3.5 million in 1976 to $7.5 million in 1981 to $12.8 million in 1989, but dropped to $10.6 million in 1990 (all nonelection years).[7] In 9 of the 16 years, the amounts of contributions by individuals and from business or commercial organizations were very close (figure 4.2). In 1979, 1980 and 1988, all election years, the amounts of corporate contributions were substantially larger than those by individuals.[8] For example, in 1979 the amounts were $5.0 million from corporations versus $3.2 million from individuals; in 1988, the comparable figures were $14.4 million and $10.2 million respectively. In 1981, 1982 and 1983, however, individuals gave substantially more than corporations. Over that period, individuals gave $18.6 million, while corporations gave only $10.3 million.

Except in election years when the reimbursement of part of the party's "election expenses" was received, other sources accounted for only a modest percentage of the Conservative party's revenues – never more than 10 percent, and usually only 3 percent to 4 percent. Although the federal reimbursement amounted to 22.5 percent of party "election expenses" in 1984 and 1988,[9] the growth in the total revenues of the Conservative party in these election years was so great as to reduce the importance of the reimbursement to only 6.6 percent of total revenue in 1988 and 6.1 percent in 1984 (see table 4.1).

Election years aside, two categories of expenditures, "operating expenses" and "transfers to party associations," account for virtually all of the party's total expenditures. Most of the latter category consists of returning to ridings their share of the revenues they have raised but have had receipted through the party's agent, the PC Canada Fund – see section 3.4 below.

Because each federal party's "election expenses" are constrained by law, the greatest expansion of party activities has occurred in the periods between election campaigns. Such activities have included making greater efforts to communicate with the membership, holding national policy conferences every two years and giving party support for the political component of ministers' activities. The Progressive Conservative party began in the late 1970s to engage in regular polling and other forms of research that may cost as much as $1 million annually[10] in order to monitor shifts in public opinion and, more importantly, to identify issues that could be the focus of the party's efforts in Parliament and/or in the next general election. Between elections, it is necessary for the party's executive apparatus to maintain the network among party officials. Given Canada's geography, enlarging the base of skilled volunteers participating in the party's governance and administration requires considerable sums. Building the party also requires putting party organizers in the field. In 1990, the Tories had 19 field organizers working to strengthen riding associations and increase the likelihood of electing new MPs and re-electing the incumbents.[11] The distribution was as follows: BC, 2; Ontario/Quebec, 5 each; and other provinces, 1 each. (By comparison, in the late 1970s, the party had only 4 or 5 field organizers.) Organizers help to increase riding (and party) membership. They help to raise funds so that local associations are financially independent ("Ottawa is not a money tree"), and help associations to remain active between elections. A year before an election is expected, the field organizers help to train association executives and volunteers for specific tasks, such as acting as the official agent or as campaign or communications manager. National headquarters produces detailed training manuals for such tasks.

Three categories account for the bulk of the Progressive Conservative party's operating expenses (table 4.2). In most years over the period 1974/75–1990, wages, salaries and employee benefits absorbed about 27 percent to 40 percent of operating expenses. Since 1979, the "printing and stationery" category has accounted for 23 percent to 37 percent of operating expenses. Party officials indicate that for 1987 to 1990 this category included, among other items, the printing and mailing expenses associated with direct-mail fund-raising; postage; professional, polling and other outside services; computer services; outside translation services and outside photography services (table 4.3). These items were included in "printing and stationery" because the form on which the

Figure 4.2
Progressive Conservative party sources of revenues, 1974–90
(millions of dollars)

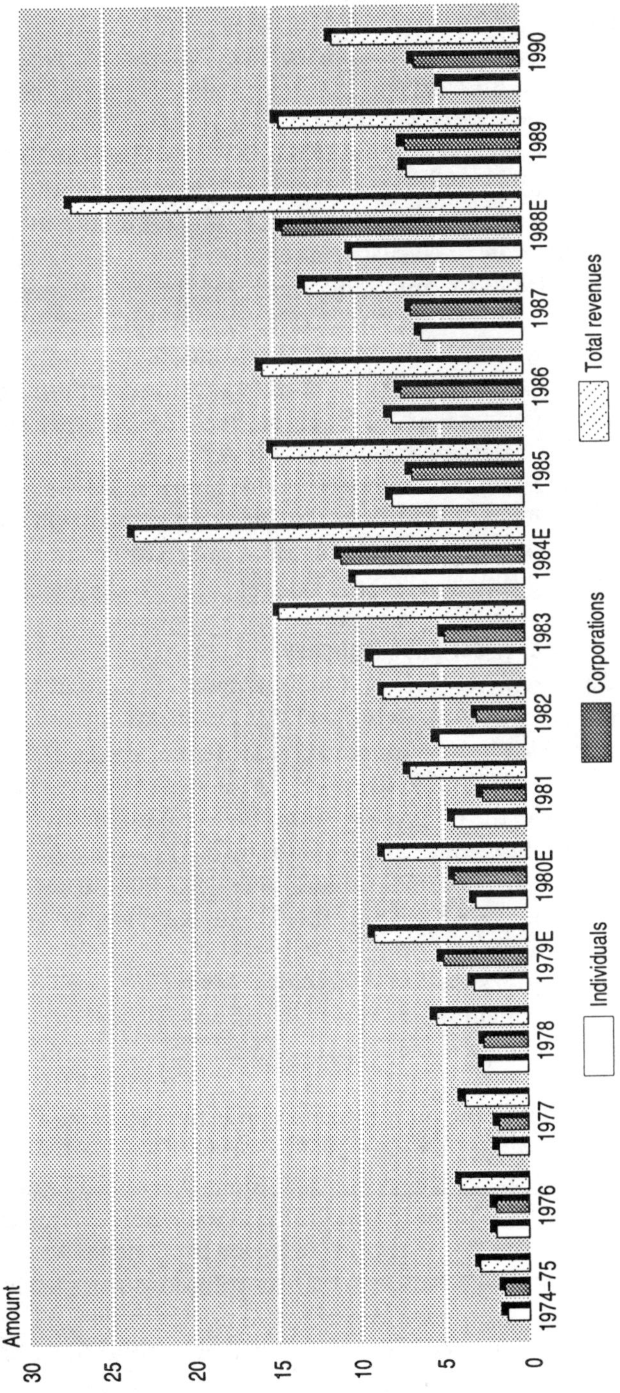

Source: Table 4.1.

party must report its operating expenses annually to the CEO does not contain separate categories for these outlays. The "printing and stationery" category grew from less than 7 percent of operating revenues in 1974/75 and 1975/76 to 13.8 percent in 1977, to 18.3 percent in 1978, and then to 26.7 percent in 1990. This increase is largely attributable to the Conservatives' growing emphasis on direct-mail fund-raising (see chap. 9) and to their expenditure on polling and other forms of research, particularly during election campaigns and in the year or so prior to the date the writs are issued.

The third most important category is "travelling expenses," which typically accounted for about 15 percent of total operating expenses (table 4.2). Expenditures on party conventions and meetings appear to have declined in importance. They were at a high of 33.8 percent in 1975/76, reflecting the convention at which Joe Clark was elected leader. In 1983, this category accounted for 23.9 percent of operating expenses, despite the fact that the party held a national general meeting in Winnipeg in January and a leadership convention in Ottawa.[12] In 1986 and 1989, party conventions absorbed only 8.3 percent and 8.7 percent of operating expenses.[13]

3.2 Changes under Brian Mulroney

The Conservative party had a large debt when Brian Mulroney was elected leader in 1983, according to W. David Angus, a Montreal lawyer whom Mr. Mulroney appointed chairman of the PC Canada Fund in 1983.[14] The data in table 4.1 reveal that, in five of the years from 1974/75 through 1982, the Progressive Conservative party had a deficit in terms of its annual revenues and expenditures. The *cumulative* deficit at the end of 1982 (in nominal dollars) was $577 600. In 1983, total party revenue rose to $14.8 million from $8.5 million the year before and there was a surplus of $1.57 million (table 4.1).

Mr. Angus stated that, between September and December 1983, the PC Canada Fund organized major fund-raising dinners in 13 cities, at which the new leader spoke. Further, Angus said he built up and galvanized teams of fund-raisers across the country. The party was able to capitalize on the widespread disaffection with the Liberals under Pierre Trudeau (leader since 1968). During this period, Angus said, the Conservative party raised sufficient funds that by the beginning of 1984 it was debt-free. Table 10.1 indicates that the net revenue in 1983 from national fund-raising events featuring the party leader was $1.55 million. However, table 4.1 indicates that contributions from individuals rose sharply from $5.2 million in 1982 to $9.1 million in 1983, while those from corporations rose less: from $2.92 million in 1982 to $4.82 million in 1983. Hence, the total increase in corporate and individual contributions could have eliminated the debt, if total expenditures had not increased. However, the Progressive Conservatives' operating expenditures rose from $7.3 million in 1982 to $10.98 million in 1983 (table 4.1).

Mr. Angus indicated that he quickly recognized that not only was there a large debt, but that the administration of party finances left much to be desired. For example, the party deposited its revenues in one bank and paid its bills out of another, thus paying interest at the latter while it had substantial deposits at the former. Angus said that he soon began to rely on Nick Locke, who had been appointed director of administration at party headquarters in Ottawa early in 1982. After the 1984 election, Locke was made Executive Director of the PC Canada Fund and soon greatly improved its operation, according to Angus.

Angus also indicated that the party's fund-raising is divided into several major directorships, including direct mail, "The 500" and corporations.[15] Angus indicated that he receives reports on revenues weekly, and statements for each of 10 cost centres monthly.[16] The Fund is responsible for all fund-raising activities and administers the party's expenditure budget process and controls spending. The budget has to be approved by the National Executive. However, Angus emphasized that the allocation of funds within the budget is controlled by political decision makers rather than financial decision makers. The level of expenditures between elections is driven by the amount of revenue that can be raised and by the need to build up reserves for the next election. It is clear that revenues between election years are influenced by the party's and the leader's standing in the polls, amongst other factors.

Angus stated that a corporate approach was applied to the operation of the PC Canada Fund. All 25 Board members of the Fund are encouraged to belong to "The 500," which requires a personal annual contribution of at least $1 000. They are also encouraged to pay all their own expenses (including travel to the monthly meetings) and each fund-raiser is given a specific revenue target. All PC Canada Fund directors, as well as David Angus, are volunteers. The value of the free services they provide to the party is substantial.

3.3   Fund-Raising Techniques

Senior party officials stated that the set of fund-raising techniques used by the Progressive Conservative party has changed relatively little since the late 1970s, although there have been numerous refinements. The party has learned to target its appeals for funds more directly. This can be seen in its use both of direct mail and of "The 500" to raise larger amounts from individuals (see table 4.4). While some techniques are more efficient than others (i.e., less costly per dollar of revenue), the party relies on a portfolio of revenue sources. There is no doubt that the base of financial support has been broadened. The importance of big business as a source of funds has declined, particularly from the period prior to the 1974 legislation. The Conservatives have learned a great deal about providing individuals or corporate executives with a good reason to give to the party. Fund-raising has become more of a team effort, according to David Angus.

Conservative party fund-raising techniques include the following:

1. Sustaining memberships: the mail is used to solicit renewal annually, then individuals receive eight to ten direct-mail appeals asking for $10 to $1 000. The average contribution is between $90 and $100 (see chap. 9).
2. "The 500": this appeal is aimed at individuals willing to contribute at least $1 000 each year (see chap. 10).
3. Fund-raising events (e.g., dinners): these events are sold via mail (50–60 percent), especially if they are an annual function; and the rest are sold by telephone and personal solicitation (see chap. 10).[17]
4. Corporate canvass: this solicitation is made by telephone, mail and/or in person. The best prospects are those firms that gave in previous years. In election years, the party asks for double the regular donation. Corporations are divided up among PC Canada Fund directors by the province in which their head office is located; special teams solicit contributions from lawyers, engineers, accountants and small and medium-sized enterprises (see chap. 11).
5. The 25 percent "tax": the PC Canada Fund receives 25 percent of contributions made to riding associations between campaign periods.

A principal role of the party leader in fund-raising is to sign direct-mail appeals (the signatory is an important part of the package), deliver speeches and/or mingle with people at fund-raising events and to motivate the volunteers who solicit contributions and manage the fund-raising process.

During election campaigns, the Conservative party makes only a few changes in its fund-raising activities except for the following: requesting that corporations double their regular contributions; increasing the frequency of direct-mail appeals by asking for extra funds to pay for "election expenses"; and eliminating special events, such as dinners, during the campaign.

Contributions from individuals accounted for between 37.7 percent and 61.7 percent of the Progressive Conservative party's total revenue between 1983 and 1990 (table 4.4). The importance of this source dropped in election years to 43.3 percent in 1984, and 37.7 percent in 1988. In those years, contributions from corporations rose, for example, from 32.6 percent in 1983 to 47.0 percent in 1984, and to 53.2 percent in 1988. Further, in election years, the party obtained the 22.5 percent reimbursement on its "election expenses," but as noted in table 4.1, this source provided only a tiny fraction of its total revenue (e.g., 6.6 percent in 1988). In 1990, individuals contributed $4.7 million to the Progressive Conservative party (as compared to $6.35 million from corporations). Only 84 individuals gave the Tories $2 000 or more in 1990 (a total of $259 443). By comparison, 101 individuals gave the Liberal party $289 922 in 1990 (chap. 8).

The Conservative party has been by far the most successful of the national parties in using direct-mail fund-raising. Gross revenues from this technique accounted for between 52 percent and 75 percent of the total amount of contributions from individuals (table 4.4). The "major-donor" program, aimed at obtaining larger contributions from individuals, raised $1.94 million in 1985 and $2.48 million in 1988 or 12.8 percent and 9.2 percent of total revenue in those years.

Contributions from corporations accounted for between 44 percent and 56 percent of total party revenue between 1984 and 1990.[18] The 500 largest nonfinancial enterprises in Canada (FP 500) and 155 largest financial enterprises (F 155) jointly accounted for from 7.6 percent to 16.0 percent of total party revenue (table 4.5). The Conservative party has been more successful in raising money from many more corporations than the Liberal party. This may be due to the Conservatives' direct-mail solicitation of small and medium-sized firms (see chap. 11). A large number of small businesses are sustaining donors who respond to an annual appeal. A senior party official stated that about one-third of the members of "The 500" are the owners of small private corporations (chap. 10).

Large contributions ($10 000 or more) from corporations accounted for from 5.3 percent to 25.4 percent of total party revenues between 1983 and 1990 (table 4.5). In 1990, 107 corporations made contributions of $10 000 or more to the Conservative party (versus 86 to the Liberal party) for a total of $2.46 million or 38.8 percent of all corporate contributions and 21.8 percent of total party revenue. There appears to be an upward trend in the importance of these large corporate contributions, but this measure ignores inflation. Adjusting for the increase in the CPI, a contribution of $7 760 in 1983 or $8 770 in 1986 was equivalent to $10 000 in 1989.

The Conservative party (like the Liberal party) has not raised much money from interest groups (other than corporations) (for more detail, see Stanbury 1986a, 459–60). A former senior PC staff member said that some interest groups have what amounts to their own political action committee. For example, the Pharmaceutical Manufacturers' Association (PMAC) gives on behalf of its members.[19] David Angus points out that such groups have not been the focus of Conservative party fund-raising efforts. Second, many interest groups are nonprofit organizations and must limit their spending on political activity (trying to influence public policy) in order to ensure that contributions to them are tax-deductible to the donor.[20]

3.4   Financial Transactions with Riding Associations and Candidates

Some party officials who were interviewed by the author stated that few riding associations do much fund-raising between elections, arguing that the 25 percent "tax" imposed by the PC Canada Fund is a disincentive to fund-raising, even though the riding gains the benefit of the use of the tax credit. Some ridings simply live off any surplus from the previous election that the candidate transferred to the riding association. This can be considerable (see chap. 12). Between elections, riding associations range from moribund, with very little money, to highly active, with well-financed organizations. The category into which a particular association falls may well vary over time.

As noted in figure 4.1, donors' contributions to the Progressive Conservative party or its candidates may be made to three entities: to a federal candidate during an election campaign (flow 1), to a federal riding association (flow 2) and/or to the PC Canada Fund at party headquarters (flow 3). Riding associations can make transfers to their candidate (flow 8) and the candidate's agent can transfer funds to the riding association (flow 9), usually in the form of surplus left after the end of an election campaign. Flow 12 in figure 4.1 includes 75 percent of the amount of contributions intended for a riding association between election campaigns that were routed through the PC Canada fund in order to obtain the tax receipt. It also may include transfers from party headquarters to assist ridings that find it difficult to raise sufficient funds to finance their operations, including supporting the local Tory candidate. The PC Canada Fund also makes transfers to some candidates directly (flow 11), and it may receive money from candidates, although it has never "taxed" a portion of candidates' surpluses as have the Liberal and New Democratic parties.

The federal government provides receipts to donors to claim the income-tax credit on political contributions (flow 7). It reimburses the PC Canada Fund for 22.5 percent of the party's "election expenses" (flow 6), and it reimburses candidates for 50 percent of their "election expenses," if they receive 15 percent of the votes cast (flow 5). The government keeps the $200 deposit of any candidate who fails to obtain 15 percent of the votes cast (flow 4).

Despite the views of party officials about the lack of effort of local associations to raise funds during the periods between election campaigns, between 1983 and 1990 riding associations raised an average of $2 million annually from contributions and from the revenue from dinners and other events for which the PC Canada Fund issued tax receipts.[21] The Fund's 25 percent share amounted to an average of $601 000 annually (table 4.6). Party officials stated that the amount retained by headquarters is far less than the cost to headquarters of the organizers in the field who are financed by headquarters. While the centralization of tax receipting helps party headquarters to monitor the fund-raising activities of the ridings, some money raised at the local level does not go through the PC Canada Fund. If a donor does not request a tax receipt, he/she can give money to the local association between elections and the latter is not required to report it to the CEO, as it is not a "registered entity." Thus, there is no public disclosure of these contributions.

Table 4.6 describes the amounts raised by ridings that flowed through the PC Canada Fund between 1985 and 1990. The gross revenue is recorded as contribution revenue in table 4.6,[22] and the "net revenue to ridings" in table 4.6 is part of the "transfer to party associations" in table 4.7. In 1989, for example, ridings raised (after expenses) $937 000 from fund-raising events for which tax receipts were issued, and had 74.9 percent of this amount returned to them by the PC Canada Fund. Ridings also raised $1 231 000 in contributions for which tax receipts were issued, and received 77.4 percent of this from the Fund.[23] In 1988, the ridings' share of contributions routed through the PC Canada Fund was very slightly under $3 million (table 4.6).

The share of the revenue transferred by headquarters to the ridings (local associations) that passed through the PC Canada Fund ranged from 77.5 percent to 96.0 percent between 1985 and 1990 (table 4.7). Note how small is the amount transferred by headquarters for "riding or candidate support." Even in election year 1988 it amounted to only $232 000, yet the party's total expenditures exceeded $29 million (see table 4.1). However, the CEO (Canada, Elections Canada 1988c, 3–339) reports that PC candidates stated that they received $1.04 million from party headquarters. One party official suggested that the difference probably consists of advances rather than unrequited transfers and that the two have not been properly distinguished. Also, party officials stated that if a donor makes a cheque payable to the PC Canada Fund, but asks that part or all of the money go to one or more candidates, the Fund issues a receipt, discloses the donation and transfers the money as requested to the official agent of the candidate(s).

After the 1974 legislation came into effect, the Conservative party established a policy of encouraging its candidates to become less dependent upon money from headquarters. For example, in 1979 only 12.8 percent ($776 000) of the total revenues of PC candidates came from headquarters (table 12.3). By 1988, this was reduced to 7.8 percent ($1.04 million). In contrast, 41.2 percent ($2.7 million) of Liberal party candidates' revenues in 1979 came from headquarters. The ratio for the Liberal party dropped to 17.5 percent in 1988. The comparable figures for the NDP over the last four elections were 23.9 percent, 24.5 percent, 24.6 percent and 23.2 percent respectively.

More importantly, the Progressive Conservative party encouraged its candidates to raise more money to ensure that they could spend to the limit on "election expenses." As a group, PC candidates in the 1984 and 1988 elections raised much more money than their Liberal rivals: $11.3 million compared to $8.4 million in 1984; $13.4 million compared to $9.6 million in 1988. In the 1979 and 1980 elections, Liberal candidates had raised about 7 percent more than PC candidates. As more Tory candidates raised more than they were permitted to spend on "election expenses," their surplus increased and, in almost every case, the surplus was transferred to the riding association. Therefore, riding associations had more money to finance local activities between elections and to attract strong candidates for the next election.

After recent election campaigns, the PC Canada Fund sought a contribution from every riding association in which the candidate had a surplus, with a view to obtaining part of that surplus. Some associations contributed; most did not, however. Some 78 percent of Conservative party candidates in 1988 had a surplus and the average amount of the surplus was about $20 000 (see chap. 12). This means that Tory candidates had a total surplus of $4.6 million after the 1988 election to divide between their riding association and the national party. The figures on party revenues in table 4.1 do not indicate how much of the surpluses went to the party, but officials say that very little was transferred to the PC Canada Fund. Some officials at Conservative party headquarters believe strongly that some riding associations have substantial liquid assets, although the riding associations disclose very little information about their finances, particularly to party officials in Ottawa.

3.5   Rise in Operating Expenses in Election Years
In 1984 and 1988, there appears to be an interesting pattern with respect to the Conservative party's operating expenditures (those excluding transfers to ridings or candidates). In 1983, a nonelection year, they totalled $10.98 million. Then, in 1984, an election year, they rose sharply to $18.16 million. The year following, however, they fell to $9.91 million – lower than the pre-election year. A similar pattern recurred with respect to the next general election. In 1987, operating expenses were

$11.49 million. They rose to $17.77 million in election year 1988. Then they fell to $10.68 million in 1989. No similar pattern occurred in election years 1979 and 1980, as can be seen from table 4.1. Indeed, operating expenses in 1981 were far *above* those in 1980 or 1979.

A considerable amount of money can be spent with good effect in the year or so prior to the issue of the election writs. Yet virtually all of these outlays will *not* be included in the party's legally limited "election expenses," because they do not fall within the statutory definition (as interpreted by the CEO), even if they are incurred during the campaign period. The activities that will not be included in the definition "election expenses" include the following: outlays for policy/issue development, focus groups and polling; collection/preparation of materials for commercials that are not aired; preparation of "speech modules"; training of organizers; establishment of a communications network (e.g., prior to the 1984 election the Tories distributed fax machines to some ridings to permit rapid communications with party headquarters); and selection of the campaign team and meetings with them to discuss strategy tactics and lines of communication (see chap. 13). Party officials indicated that, in 1984 and 1988, all expenditures that were "election expenses" as defined in the *Canada Elections Act* were included as part of their spending limit, even if they were incurred outside the campaign period. The problem lies, in part, with the specific *exclusions* from the definition (based upon the wording of the legislation and the CEO's *Guidelines*), the definition of "normal administrative costs of maintaining the party as an ongoing entity" (Canada, Elections Canada 1988a, 4) and the allocation of the costs of the party's national office. Two of the most important exclusions are polling and other research expenses, and the production costs of commercials not used in the campaign. For the 1988 campaign, the Conservative party was said to have employed cameramen for many months before the election was called to photograph the Prime Minister in action, with a view to creating material for campaign advertisements. These expenses were included as "election expenses" to the extent that footage was included in advertising materials used during the writ. The significance of these expenses and those for polling can be seen in what the Conservative party spent on "professional, polling and other outside services." In 1987, the party spent $1.08 million. In 1988, this category increased to $3.05 million, and in 1989 it fell to $1.14 million.

3.6 Net Revenues Available to Headquarters

It costs money to raise money for a political party (or candidate). Some indication of the costs can be found in table 4.8, but the author has been able to obtain information on the *direct* costs of only two of the methods of fund-raising used by the Conservative party.[24] For example, the costs of operating the PC Canada Fund are not available from the party. Nor did the party make available any estimate of the *indirect* costs of raising money. A more detailed analysis of the costs of raising money by means of direct mail can be found in chapter 9, while the costs of national fund-raising events are discussed in chapter 10. It is entirely possible that at least one-third of the party's gross revenue is absorbed by the costs of generating the contributions from individuals, corporations and other organizations. Moreover, this figure makes no provision for the value of the time of volunteers who help to solicit contributions.

By deducting even some of the costs and the constituencies' share of gross revenues, it becomes clearer that the Conservative party has had somewhat less money to spend on party activities at the national level than is implied by the figures in table 4.1. In 1988, for example, gross revenues totalled $27.0 million, but net revenues were $22.4 million. Yet a substantial part of this amount is not available to do the party's work because it includes other costs of raising the $22.4 million. These might well have amounted to another several million dollars in 1988. Note that the "net revenue available to headquarters" is substantially overstated in 1983, 1986 and 1989, when party conventions absorbed $2.62 million, $955 000 and $929 000 respectively. While the Conservative party tries to ensure that delegates' fees cover convention expenses, the convention expenses must be deducted from operating expenses to ascertain the amount of money available to finance the ongoing work of party headquarters between election campaigns.

4. ELECTION CAMPAIGNS

For party activists, success in election campaigns is by far the most important objective of their efforts. The conditions for success were altered somewhat by the *Election Expenses Act* of 1974. In particular, beginning with the 1979 general election, the problem for the Progressive Conservative and Liberal parties was far less how to raise money for the campaign than how to spend it for the best effect. The legal limit on "election expenses" (which rose from $4.38 million in 1979 to $8 million in 1988, if a party ran a full slate of candidates) placed a premium on getting the "biggest bang for the buck," *and* on not violating the legal limit. The latter is a difficult management task because of the short duration of the campaign period (as little as 50 days), the geographic scope and the dynamics of election campaigns, and the number of persons involved in the campaign. Moreover, all parties had to contend with the even greater importance of the leader's tour and of television advertising, where the price of such advertising rose more rapidly than the limit on "election expenses," which for the 1984 and 1988 elections was indexed to the increase in the Consumer Price Index.

Paltiel has described contemporary election campaigns as follows:

> Contemporary campaign technologies and strategies, guided by professional consultants using highly sophisticated sample surveys and polling techniques, are inextricably linked to the exploitation of the advantages and avoidance of the limitations of the electronic media. The election battle is reduced to a joust between knights of each faction with the mass media serving as the lists for the contenders, whose every thrust is guided by their professional handlers. Success and the fate of their parties are credited to the avoidance of gaffes, charisma, skilled performance and presentation, and the manipulation of the media by the consultants and advertisers in their service. The homogeneity of election campaign coverage encouraged by concentrated cross-media ownership, pack journalism, and campaign strategists, together with the emphasis on personality, reinforce the drift towards an undifferentiated and politically less meaningful party system. (1989a, 335)

4.1 Centralization and Professionalization of Election Campaigns

Under John Diefenbaker, the Progressive Conservative party held power from 1957 to 1963. The Tories did not regain power until 1979, when Joe Clark formed a minority government for 259 days. The 1979 general election was the first under the regulatory regime enacted in 1974. That regime and the party's new leader altered the way the Progressive Conservative party conducted the 1979 and 1980 campaigns.

> The improved state of Progressive Conservative finances went hand in hand with a systematic approach to campaign planning. The somewhat fragmented nature of past campaigns, with a good deal of expertise being provided by activists in Toronto in addition to the campaign organizers at the national level, was not repeated. Joe Clark appointed Lowell Murray as campaign chairman in 1977, and it was clear from then on that the next campaign would be run from Ottawa, though with a decentralized structure based on campaign committees in the provinces ...
>
> The national and provincial organizers agreed on financial activities to cover election costs ... The board of directors of the PC Canada Fund was required to approve each plan, and it was consulted on the anticipated fund-raising activities. The board did not, however, say yes or no to particular programs or items of expenditure. (Seidle and Paltiel 1981, 256)

Senior party officials stated that, since the 1979 general election, the organization of Conservative party campaigns has changed little, and that individuals have a large impact on the way they carry out their assigned responsibilities. The major components of the campaigns are polling, policy/strategy development, advertising and communications, the leader's tour and campaigning at the riding level. According to Harry Near, director of the Conservative party's 1988 campaign, between 1979 and 1988 election campaigns became more decentralized, that is, regional considerations became more important in the leader's tour as well as in advertising and ministerial tours.[25] Voters were targeted more narrowly. The 1988 Tory campaign was more decentralized or "cellular" than previous ones. Not only was there the traditional separate campaign in Quebec, but the campaign in English Canada was "regionalized." Moreover, there was a finer division of labour in the performance of campaign tasks relating to advertising, the leader's tour, polling, the media, policy development and legal and financial matters. Campaigns also became an exercise in capital rationing in light of the statutory limits on "election expenses." According to a senior Tory advisor and strategist, the focus of election campaigns during the 1980s was on three things: (1) the leader's tour, which is the means to get the party's message to the voters through the news media;[26] (2) paid media, notably television ads, which are expensive; and (3) direct marketing, which is the targeting of specific groups of voters using direct mail and telephone calls.[27]

The importance of polling and other forms of voter research (e.g., focus groups) is likely to increase in light of the evidence that a large fraction (more than the majority) of the electorate has no long-term attachment to any party. Volatility is the norm, according to the pollsters for both the Liberal and the Conservative parties. More voters are making and/or changing their voting decisions during the campaign. Why has this occurred? A senior Tory strategist referred to four factors. First, elections have become driven by television in terms of the party's effort to shape the nightly news via the leader's tour[28] and the growing percentage of the total campaign budget that is spent on television ads. Second, fewer people have a strong allegiance to any one group or institution. Third, parties, politics and politicians are held in low esteem (Gregg and Posner 1990, 54; Blais and Gidengil 1991). Fourth, interest groups are playing a greater role in politics; in 1988, this fact was evident in the general election (Hiebert 1991).

Because the focus of the leader's campaign efforts is to get his/her message on the nightly national television news (as well as on the local television news), the settings and formats of the leader's appearances have to be chosen with that central fact uppermost in mind (Fraser 1989; Lee 1989). Large crowds of enthusiastic supporters often make a good backdrop for "visuals," on which television coverage tends to focus. The leader's tour has changed somewhat in the most recent campaigns, according to party officials. First, greater care is now exercised in the choice of stops and "events." Second, the detail involved in the advance work has greatly increased. Third, the linkage of the tour to polling in terms of themes, language and locations is closer. Fourth, much more effort goes into the production of sound bites and good visuals for the national news, which has a huge audience. Fifth, scheduling has become more complicated: in 1988 Mr. Mulroney crossed the country almost three times in 50-odd days, with one day a week off to attend to business in Ottawa.

When a party is in power, the leader's tour is a more complicated and expensive operation than when the party is in opposition. A greater number of persons has to be moved about for at least two reasons: there are more reporters and cameramen on the Prime Minister's plane, and more security personnel are required. Moreover, it is difficult to determine how the costs of the leader's tour should be allocated: for example, which costs should be charged to the party's "election expenses," and which ones should be paid for by the federal government because the leader is also the Prime Minister? The danger of the tour, according to campaign officials, is that it isolates the leader and senior advisors from reality. The tour makes it impossible for the leader and his/her "handlers" to get a feel for local/regional issues and to be able to listen to the constituents.

Advertising, particularly on television, is the most effective and efficient way of getting a party's message across. Recall from chapter 3 that the Progressive Conservative party spent over 40 percent of its total "election expenses" in 1979 and 1980 on television advertising. However, in 1984 and 1988, the percentage was only 27.5 percent and 30.8 percent respectively. The use of television advertising by political parties has become more sophisticated in terms of the nature of the appeals (aided by polling) and the targeting of particular groups of voters.[29] Further, parties are better able to measure the results of advertising, and they have been able to reduce the production time for television ads to about 48 hours, if necessary. While television ads have more "reach" (depending upon the choice of programs into which they are inserted), radio and print can be more narrowly targeted, and these media can be linked to local candidates.

The use of technological wizardry in future Canadian general elections is likely to be constrained only by the legal limit on a party's "election expenses" (Axworthy 1991).

5. RIDING ASSOCIATIONS

Successful political parties in Canada require the combination of a skilful leader, effective organization at party headquarters and a large number of local riding associations that nominate and support attractive candidates. As noted previously, since the 1974 party/candidate financial legislation came into effect, the policy of the federal Progressive Conservative party has been to encourage both riding associations and candidates to become financially independent of party headquarters. While we have some evidence on the financial flows among various units within the party, the author could not obtain information about the state of finances of riding associations. Party officials in Ottawa stated that they too have little information on this subject.

5.1 Strength of Riding Associations

The organizational and financial "health" of riding associations depends on a number of factors, but the key is the willingness of a small group of individuals with some political/organizational skills to devote time and energy to the affairs of the association. Crucial to these efforts is finding an attractive candidate – preferably one with many friends willing to work on his/her behalf. Thus, the strength of local associations is often fairly closely tied to the ambitions and energy of a few people. The ambitions may be those of a would-be candidate who, with a few friends, breathes new life into a local association so it can be a vehicle for his/her desire to become an MP (and preferably a cabinet minister in short order). The group of friends who makes this possible – often greatly helped by the broader tide of public support for the leader/party – may cease to be active in the riding association if their MP/friend is defeated at the next election. Even if he/she is re-elected, the rising demands of other responsibilities (family, profession/ business) may reduce the involvement of members of the core group. As a result, the riding association may become less active and even atrophy.

What is the significance of a party's membership base? It provides a modest revenue base. A growing base provides a sense of momentum, which, in turn, attracts more members; most people want to identify with a winner. A growing membership helps to create a bandwagon effect. As importantly, a large membership provides a base for the recruitment of volunteer election workers. It is critical for the party executive to provide training for volunteers during the pre-campaign period, and to develop plans as to how best to use the energy, enthusiasm and skills of the volunteers. However, an incumbent MP may prefer a riding association that has only a few members,[30] an executive that is beholden to him/her, and a set of association nomination rules that are to his/her advantage. The disadvantage is that he/she may end up with a political base that is too small to win the seat in the next election.

Progressive Conservative party officials state that their party – unlike the NDP – does not pay for any expenses of its candidates' campaign organizers (except perhaps for their child-care expenses). Campaigns, however, have become somewhat more sophisticated. Because there are 10 to 12 key positions, it is virtually impossible for a handful of the candidate's friends to run his/her campaign.[31] As the rules and guidelines proliferate, the skill required to be an official agent has grown. More candidates are spending a higher fraction of the statutory limit on election expenses (see chap. 12). This requires more careful budgeting and control over expenditures. More "high-tech" hardware is being used, such as fax machines and microcomputers. Telephone banks have largely replaced the foot canvass.[32] Where the limit on "election expenses" binds, candidates make a greater effort to spend money on "other expenses" that help the cause, but are not "election expenses" that are subject to limit (see chap. 12). Campaign costs are rising faster than the CPI to which the limit on "election expenses" is indexed. Local campaign-related expenditures whose prices have increased faster than the CPI include the following: travel, media advertising, brochures and rental space (in most major cities).

Party officials indicated that most party members, even those at the executive level, have a local/regional rather than *national* orientation for several reasons. First, individuals join the party through a riding association. Second, the riding is the electoral unit; federal governments are formed only when a party elects a member in a plurality of the seats in the House of Commons. Third, most of the individual's contacts with other members and officials occur at the local/regional level; for example, while there is a *national* convention every two years, an active local association may meet for business or pleasure several times a year. Fourth, parties tend not to have a periodical national internal newsletter linking all members to the national office: in 1990, for example, the Tories ceased publishing their newsletter (because Liberal party national headquarters does not have a list of its members, it could not send out a national newsletter). Fifth, the individual MP (or candidate) is seen by association members as the personification of the party (although in elections, the role of the leader is of great importance). Sixth, most members fail to understand that voting decisions are influenced far more by the electorate's perceptions of a party's leader and of the party as a whole, and rather less by the virtues of the individual candidate (Heintzman 1991).

The perception of at least some party notables who reflect a local/regional orientation is that the requirement to pay the PC Canada

Fund 25 percent of contributions to local associations between election campaigns is an unfair "tax" levied by an insensitive and distant headquarters. Further, they argue that the Fund should permit fund-raisers for candidates and riding associations to approach companies that have their headquarters or major plants in the area.[33] Finally, it is argued that the use of party membership lists in direct-mail appeals sent from headquarters reduces the amount of money a riding can raise from its own members ("our own people"). However, officials at PC headquarters stated that they have evidence contrary to this claim.

5.2 Campaigning at the Riding Level: A Case Study

Prior to 1978, Vancouver Centre had been an almost moribund federal riding for the Conservative party because the riding was held by Ron Basford, a Liberal MP and cabinet minister. Then a group of younger party activists led by Lyall Knott decided to "take over" the PC riding association in order to get the nomination for Pat Carney, whom they enthusiastically supported. These energetic and skilled amateurs raised money, generated publicity and, of course, benefited from the disaffection with the Liberal party in the West. Carney was almost elected in 1979 and then beat the odds by being elected in 1980 against the tide back to the Liberals. She became the shadow Minister of Energy and, in 1984, she became the Minister of Energy in the first Mulroney government.

Over the past decade, the Vancouver Centre PC riding association has been able to raise $50 000 to $100 000 "in a good year."[34] More than 90 percent of this amount is tax-receipted. The association has used a number of techniques to raise money. First, it tries to hold two events per year for which admission is charged or the hat is passed. For example, one social event featured John Crosbie as the guest speaker. Some 350 members of the riding association (and friends) each paid $75 and the event netted about $20 000. Second, the riding association's mailing list has several thousand names. In 1989, 1 000 targeted letters were sent out signed by the president or a member of the fund-raising committee. The typical donation was $100, but the odd cheque for $1 000 was received. Third, local corporations were solicited on an individual basis by association members, the appeal being that the money was to support a popular MP and cabinet minister (Kim Campbell), not party headquarters. According to the president of the riding association, there is a clear understanding in the Conservative party that "every source is fair game for every level of the party." The riding association developed a list of Vancouver businesses which were contacted by mail and then by telephone by a volunteer fund-raiser. Toward the end of the year, an extra push was made emphasizing the benefits of the income-tax credit, which could be recouped by the donor within the next few months.

One of the problems of financing campaigns at the riding level is the need for substantial sums (e.g., $10 000) even before the election writ has been issued. The sophisticated candidate will rent space for campaign headquarters, install up to 12 telephone lines, purchase supplies and even print 40 000–50 000 brochures. Suppliers almost always demand immediate payment or a substantial deposit.

The Vancouver Centre riding association has focused its pre-election activities in the 90–120 days prior to the issue of the writ. It has opened a campaign office, spent freely on advertising in local community papers, set up the campaign team and raised more money. In 1984, the riding began spending the money on Ms. Carney's behalf well before she was re-nominated and in the period after she was nominated but before the writ was issued. In 1988, substantial pre-election expenditures on publicity and on the campaign infrastructure had been made when Pat Carney decided to retire late in the game for reasons of poor health. For example, in the summer of 1988, the riding had placed a four-page special section in the community newspapers, which, according to party officials, looked more like the editorial pages of the newspapers than like an advertisement. The riding association had already run a campaign school and trained about 75 people before the writ was issued. The campaign committee had been selected (individuals had to agree to be ready to keep their commitment for a six-month period).[35] It was the strength of the riding association that made it possible to recruit Kim Campbell, then a Social Credit MLA. She could be assured that considerable money was in the bank and more than enough money would be raised. Moreover, Vancouver Centre had a large and active membership from which to recruit campaign volunteers. Ms. Campbell won in a close race over two strong rivals, including the president of the national NDP. In doing so, she spent more on "other expenses" than she did on official "election expenses." In total, she spent $40 000 more than did the second-placed candidate.

5.3   Regional Fund-Raising by Ridings

In figure 5.1 and in the text, the point was made that there are only two types of organizational units in the federal Progressive Conservative party: the riding associations and the national party headquarters. In terms of fund-raising, this picture is slightly misleading, because party officials indicate that, in several provinces, clusters of riding associations have banded together to facilitate their efforts to raise money between general elections. One of the earliest and best known of such efforts is "PC Metro," which consists of Conservative party supporters within the Metro Toronto business community.[36] In Quebec, in recent years, there have been clusters of ridings that have cooperated with each other informally by co-hosting fund-raising events such as barbeques, golf tournaments and dinners. Not only do such events help to raise money for the ridings involved, but they also provide an opportunity for party officials, volunteers and supporters to get together to "schmooze" about party business. Party officials emphasized the importance of these events in sustaining enthusiasm and participation in the party at the local level. They noted that ridings in Quebec tend to be more "proactive" in organizing events between election campaigns. It is common for cabinet ministers to attend these events, or even be part of the "draw" to increase attendance. Such events facilitate communications between the party élite and some of the important volunteers at the riding level.

While the ticket price for events organized by a group of ridings is seldom over $50, the net amount of money raised for each of the ridings can be substantial in terms of the riding's annual revenues and expenditures. The PC Canada Fund will issue tax receipts for the net amount that is eligible as a contribution (retaining 25 percent), but finds that the administrative costs of the receipting and handling process fail to justify the issuing of receipts for contributions under $10. PC Canada Fund officials indicated that the availability of receipts for such amounts is unlikely to be important in attracting participants to events organized by a riding or group of ridings.

A rather more formal regional fund-raising effort for ridings on Vancouver Island existed for a short period in the mid-1980s.[37] In early 1984, a small group of Vancouver Island professional and business people created the PC Island Group (PCIG) to raise money primarily for the five federal ridings on Vancouver Island, only two of which were then held by Tories. The founders of the PCIG believed that in both the 1979 and 1980 elections, PC candidates across Vancouver Island had, on average, raised only a fraction of the amount that they had spent, and that their "election expenses" had run well below the statutory limit.[38] Moreover, the data on contributions filed with the Chief Electoral Officer revealed that the Conservative party had not raised very much money from individuals or corporations on Vancouver Island prior to 1984.

A handful of well-connected Island residents was recruited to act as fund-raisers, largely by means of their personal contacts. Taking a page from Brian Gallery's efforts on behalf of "The 500" (see chap. 10), the PCIG sought to raise individual contributions of at least $1 150 – the amount that exhausts the federal personal income-tax credit for political contributions ($500). Some donors made their contribution through a small business that they owned. Donors received receipts for the tax credit from the PC Canada Fund. By the end of the 1984 election campaign, over 120 individuals had contributed $1 150 (or more). One fund-raiser obtained over 20 such donations from in and around the small town of Campbell River located in the middle of a riding that had been represented for some time by an able NDP member! He found, as did the other PCIG fund-raisers, that many of the people and firms that contributed a total of $428 000 in 1984 had never before been asked to make a contribution to the party.[39] What were these contributors to get in return for their support? They were to receive invitations to lunch or breakfast meetings with a series of three or four cabinet ministers each year; access to a 1-800 telephone number and to a coordinator of the PCIG who would provide information in response to queries about dealings with the federal government, including advice concerning how to relate effectively with a minister's office; and a periodic newsletter.

For the 1984 election, the Progressive Conservative candidates in all five Island ridings raised far more than they could spend on "election expenses" – from $56 524 to $90 973, with an average amount of $68 394. Second, the PC candidates' "election expenses" increased to between 87.6 percent and 97.4 percent of the statutory limit (Canada, Elections Canada 1985). The Conservative party candidates won three of the Vancouver Island seats (an increase of one), while the NDP won two (a loss of one seat). Despite such success, PCIG ceased to exist less than two years after it had begun, largely because certain of the riding associations and MPs did not want to compete with other sources of access to Ottawa and to ministers in particular, according to a former party official familiar with the events. They apparently resented the fact that, even though they had benefited from increased revenues to their election campaign, the PCIG seemed to be more successful in getting cabinet ministers to attend party functions on Vancouver Island. PCIG had some "clout" in Ottawa precisely because it could raise substantial money for the party (even though most of the funds stayed at the local level). Some of the Vancouver Island PC riding associations and MPs apparently viewed PCIG's activities as a zero-sum game that diminished their modest amount of power.[40]

In 1988, NDP candidates won all six Vancouver Island ridings (one more seat had been added since 1984). Contributions to the six PC candidates averaged $50 396 in 1988, down from an average of $68 394 in the five Vancouver Island ridings in 1984.[41]

6. CONCLUSIONS

In electoral terms, the Progressive Conservative party was long dominated by the Liberal party prior to 1984. In financial terms, the foundation of the Conservative party's electoral victories in 1984 and 1988 was built in the first few years after the *Election Expenses Act* came into force on 1 August 1974 and in the revamping of the party organization in the early 1980s, which provided it with the ability to generate much more revenue than its rivals.

The Progressive Conservative party has been able to raise more money for several reasons. First, it has adopted methods that were proven to be effective in the United States, such as direct-mail and major-donor programs, and it has skilfully modified such programs to reflect Canadian conditions. (These are discussed in more detail in chapters 8 to 11.) Second, the PCs have broadened both their corporate and individual contributor bases. For example, in 1976 the party obtained 23 400 contributions from individuals, slightly less than the Liberal party (see table 8.2). However, the Conservative party increased the number of contributions to 99 300 in 1983, as compared to 66 700 for the NDP and 33 600 for the Liberal party. While the numbers have fallen substantially since then, they remain far above those of the Liberal party (but far below those of the NDP): for example, in 1989 the Conservative party received contributions from 40 200 individuals versus 20 000 for the Liberal party and 89 300 for the NDP.[42] On the corporate front, the number of firms making a contribution to the Conservatives increased from only 2 000 in 1974/75 to a peak of 21 300 in 1984 (see table 11.2). Between 1974 and 1990, the Liberal party never received more than 7 500 contributions from corporations. In the period 1987–90, the Conservative party obtained 39 900 contributions from corporations, as compared with 22 800 for the Liberal party. These numbers make up for the fact that the *average* size of contributions to the Liberal party is slightly larger than is that to the Conservative party. Third, the Conservatives have the most diversified "portfolio" of fund-raising techniques and sources. They have assiduously and successfully cultivated a variety of flowers in their fund-raising garden, such as direct mail, telephone solicitation, dinners, major-donor programs and the traditional direct solicitation of corporations. The Conservative party has been much more effective than the Liberal party in differentiating its appeals for funds among potential donors in terms of socio-economic status. The most obvious example is "The 500," the fund for individuals who give more than $1 000 annually (see chap. 10).

The Progressive Conservative party expanded its "operating expenditures" in election years 1984 and 1988. The apparent purpose of such increases is to pay for campaign-related activities that are not classified as official "election expenses." For example, in 1984 such expenditures were almost double what they were in 1983 or 1985.[43] More important, the increase in 1984 (and in 1988) over the previous year far *exceeded* the amount the party was allowed to spend on official "election expenses."

The Progressive Conservative party has been largely successful in its efforts to establish a clear division between the financing of riding associations and the financing of candidates. Only modest sums are transferred from headquarters to ridings or candidates, aside from contributions routed through the PC Canada Fund and for which the Fund retains 25 percent. Indeed, in 1984 and 1988, a majority of Conservative candidates had a surplus (the total was about $4.3 million in 1988) and the surplus was transferred to their riding association. In the future, there is likely to be increased tension about the "fiscal balance" within the party.

Even so, the federal Progressive Conservative party appears to face a number of challenges to its fiscal dominance. Some members of the Quebec caucus support the adoption of "financement populaire," as exists in the province of Quebec (see chap. 8). The key provisions are that only electors may make contributions and that contributions to each party (including its candidates) are limited to $3 000 per year. If such a change were adopted, and even if the limit was set at $5 000 as proposed by some Progressive Conservative MPs, the Conservatives would face difficulties in funding their activities, as would the other major parties. The second challenge stems from the rise of the Reform Party, which may be obtaining contributions that formerly went to the Progressive Conservative party. (In 1990, the Reform Party received donations from 23 462 individuals averaging $88 each, while the Conservative party received donations from 27 702 individuals averaging $169 each (see chap. 8).)

Even though its fund-raising base is both diversified and broad, the Conservative party has to cope with declining revenues in periods of political unpopularity. This means that party activities have to be scaled down, or substantial deficits could be incurred, such as those that plagued the Liberal party under John Turner (see chap. 5). Note that in 1989 dollars, the Progressive Conservative party raised an average of $16.7 million per year in the period 1985–87. In 1989, it raised $14.5 million, but in 1990 its revenues fell to $10.8 million (in 1989 dollars). Thus about two years before the next federal election, the Conservative party has been able to raise far less than it raised in 1983 ($19.0 million in 1989 dollars). If this trend is ominous, it is less depressing when compared to the position of the Liberal party. If the effects of the 1990 leadership race and convention are removed, the Liberal party was able to raise only about $6.5 million in each of 1989 and 1990 – less than half the amounts raised by the Progressive Conservative party. By comparison, the NDP's *federally receipted* revenue in 1989 was $7.7 million and it was $8.6 million in 1990 (both in 1989 dollars). Therefore, while the Conservative party's revenues have been sliding, they remain ahead of their two main rivals. At the same time, the Reform Party raised $6.6 million in 1991 (as compared to $12.3 million for the Tories, and $7.2 million for the Liberal party), and may already have more money set aside for the next election than the Progressive Conservative party.

5

THE
LIBERAL PARTY
OF CANADA

Probably no area of the [Liberal] party's activities matches the
complexity of its financial operations.

(Banister and Gibson 1984, 16)

Many Liberals are astonished that they cannot join the LPC at the
national level where Party policy and financing are developed.

(Liberal Party of Canada, Reform Commission 1991, 25)

1. INTRODUCTION

T HE APHORISM that "the child is father of the man" applies to the
financing of the Liberal Party of Canada in the sense that the party's
history has strongly shaped how the party responded to the far-reaching
1974 legislation. Indeed, in some ways (e.g., its federated structure),
the financial operations of the Liberal Party of Canada continue to reflect
basic choices made more than half a century ago. While some of the
earlier milestones in the evolution of the party are described below, it
is useful to set out briefly the "inheritance" of the party in 1974 in the
sense of the factors that were to influence how its financing later evolved.
The Liberal party had been in power in Ottawa since 1963 and for some
two decades before 1957. Moreover, it formed a majority government
after the election of July 1974 under Pierre Trudeau. The Liberal party
was reluctant to change a winning financing formula under which virtually all revenues came from a few hundred large corporations. The operations of the national office were modestly funded between elections
prior to 1974,[1] and it was dependent upon money saved from contributions to election campaigns and from transfers from provincial associations, which had a considerable degree of autonomy. The Quebec
wing of the party was operated between and during elections entirely

separately from the rest of the Liberal party (Davey 1986). The Liberal Party of Canada was (and is) a federated structure whose "members" consist of 12 provincial or territorial associations. Individuals join a riding association and/or a PTA, not the party at the national level. The national office did not (and does not) have a list of the members of the LPC.[2] Eight of the 12 provincial/territorial associations were (and are) "dual purpose" organizations, that is, they seek to elect both provincial members and federal MPs. The weight given to the two objectives varied across PTAs and varied over time.

Of greatest significance was the fact that the Liberal Party of Canada held power in Ottawa for such a long period. It is often said that the nonparliamentary side of a party atrophies when it is long in power.[3] When the Liberal party formed the government, it received certain benefits useful in its electoral efforts (e.g., the analytical and planning resources of the PMO, the government's vast publicity machine, natural visibility and the capacity to direct expenditures for best political effect). It also faced certain dangers. Over time, the Cabinet tended to focus more on the bureaucratic requirements of governing and less on political matters. The party, with its obvious focus on politics and electioneering, tended to be neglected until a few months before the next election. Yet good planning requires about two years of systematic preparation before a general election. An obvious problem arose when it was necessary for the Cabinet to accept direction from the key campaign strategists, whose job it was to ensure victory at the polls. The experience of the Liberal party since the Conservative party came to power in 1984 has been that it takes a long time to throw off the weaknesses in a party bred by many years in power.

This chapter is organized as follows. Section 2 briefly outlines the evolution of the Liberal party and its methods of financing prior to the *Election Expenses Act* of 1974. Section 3 addresses the party's initial responses to the new legislation, and some of the implications of its federated structure. Section 4, the core of the chapter, analyses party revenues and expenditures over the period 1974 to 1990. Section 5 offers a more detailed examination of the Liberal party's finances from the early 1980s, under John Turner's leadership from mid-1984 to mid-1990, and then under Jean Chrétien's leadership. Finally, section 6 draws some conclusions.

2. EVOLUTION PRIOR TO 1974

2.1 Creating the Federation
Wearing indicates that "the organizational beginnings of the Liberal party go back well into the nineteenth century, when riding associations

were created to elect Reformers to the pre-Confederation legislatures" (1981, 6). He explains how provincial offices and conventions were well established before any national office existed.[4] "Before 1932, sporadic attempts were made to amalgamate these provincial associations into some kind of national organization." While the National Liberal Organization Committee (NLOC) was created in 1919 with a head office in Ottawa, "as soon as the party regained power in 1921, everyone lost interest in the new organization" (ibid., 7).

In 1931, stung by the Beauharnois scandal (Donovan and Winmill 1976) and wanting to distance himself from the party's fund-raisers, Mackenzie King revived the NLOC, and in 1932 the National Liberal Federation[5] was established. "It was to be a true federation in which federal and provincial interests would have an equal voice" (Wearing 1981, 8). The Federation soon began to exhibit the inherent strains that continue to plague it to this day. There were conflicts over money – who should be responsible for raising it and how it should be spent.[6] The party had to contend with its dual provincial and federal orientation, that is, the relative efforts to be spent on provincial versus federal politics. Further, there were differences over the parliamentary versus nonparliamentary influence within the party. Then when the party was in power, there were the conflicts between running the government versus paying attention to *party* matters.

Wearing notes that "a federated structure ... conflicted with the mobilization model of a participatory party, because the intermediate bodies [PTAs], in a sense, broke the direct link between the individual Liberals and their charismatic leader" (1981, 157). While waves of reform or attempted reform have washed over the LPC since the late 1950s, the party remains a federation of 12 PTAs, and the advocates of bottom-up policy making remain frustrated by the fact that the policy is most often made by the leader and his close advisors (Wearing 1989).

2.2 Federal-Provincial Linkages

Wearing notes that, at least prior to the 1960s, "part of the accepted political wisdom in Canada [was] that federal success was dependent on having a strong provincial base, not least because of the value of provincial patronage" (1981, 13).[7] It was the Tories, however, who in the late 1940s and 1950s "pioneered the establishment of an effective national office which operated between elections and which adopted the strategy of building up provincial Conservative parties" (ibid., 14). The strategy paid off with John Diefenbaker's victory in 1957.

A major step toward centralization in the LPC was taken in 1962 when (now Senator) Keith Davey set up a federal election campaign committee in each province (Davey 1986). The chairman was appointed by the leader (Lester B. Pearson). Part of the committee's responsibility was to recruit attractive candidates. This naturally led to conflict with the executives of some riding associations (Wearing 1981, 30). The 1962 campaign was also the first in which the Liberals used polling (supervised by U.S. pollster Lou Harris) to help devise campaign strategy and shape party advertising. Wearing (ibid., 35) credits Keith Davey with three main organizational innovations in the 1962 election campaign: polling and statistical analyses of ridings to allocate resources strategically; standardized nationwide advertising; and workshops to train campaign managers.

2.3 Raising Money

The Liberal party's Treasury Committee (responsible for raising money from corporations) recommended in 1964 that the PTAs assume responsibility for funding 20 percent of the Federation (i.e., the national office), but "the idea was abandoned as being unrealistic" (Wearing 1981, 61). The national office of the LPC, according to Wearing "has always had to overcome a kind of Cinderella problem within the party" (ibid., 14). He continues,

> its duties, chiefly those of keeping the party alive between elections, are mundane; the leader tends to see it as being less responsive to his own needs than his personal staff on Parliament Hill; the fund raisers see it as a drain on election funds; the parliamentary caucus want to use it as an MP's re-election office; and the provincial organizations see it as yet another manifestation of distant, insensitive Ottawa. (Ibid.)

Wearing (1981, 148) states that the Liberal party's Ottawa office had a staff of 26 to 28 in 1968. The cost of operations in 1969 was $377 000, up from $146 000 in 1963. By 1979, the national office had a budget of $600 000. While the PMO's staff went from 44 to over 90 in the same period, the LPC national office shrank by about half to 18 (ibid., 214).

Prior to the *Election Expenses Act* of 1974, the Liberal party was financed very largely by donations from a few hundred medium- to large-sized corporations (Paltiel 1970b; see also chap. 11). It was (and still is) the task of the Revenue Committee (formerly the Treasury Committee) to solicit funds from these firms. The party's Finance Committee is responsible for raising money from members and supporters and for generally ensuring a broad base of financial support.

Under John Aird, John Godfrey and their fellow Liberal fund-raisers in the 1960s and 1970s, corporations were asked for substantial contributions in the name of "supporting the democratic process" and "supporting free enterprise" in very general terms. The appeal was generally quite successful, but a few donors wanted some advantage from government.[8]

> In time, the federal Treasury Committee got such a reputation for scrupulosity that some companies began donating directly to candidates. One fund raiser complained, "the smart cookies ... think they get more value for their money if they donate to candidates rather than to the Party, and of course they are right." In one instance, a large company was chastised for making donations exclusively to individual candidates and told that companies who give to political parties know that they get no benefit, other than the "satisfaction of knowing that they are good corporate citizens." (Wearing 1981, 182)

2.4 Election Spending prior to 1979

The "election expenses" of both parties and candidates have been limited by law since 1 August 1974. To put into perspective expenditures during the last four general elections (1979, 1980, 1984 and 1988), it is useful to compare them to party and candidate outlays for election campaigns before the 1974 legislation was in effect. Such comparisons are difficult, however, for several reasons. First, for elections prior to 1979, parties did not have to disclose their election revenues or expenditures. While candidates were required to disclose their "election expenses," about one-quarter failed to do so (Seidle 1980, 149). Second, for the Liberal party, no estimates of party or candidate election outlays for the 1958, 1962 and 1963 general elections have been published. Further, the candidates' returns were not audited. Third, the campaign expenditures of the Liberal (and Conservative) party prior to 1979 appear to have included substantial transfers to candidates, but it is difficult to be sure that the figures do *not* include double counting (i.e., transfers from the party that are still included as part of its expenditures rather than being included only in the candidates' expenditures).

For the 1945 election, after 22 years in power, the Liberal party had amassed one of the largest war chests in its history, almost $5 million (Paltiel 1970b, 37). Funds for the general elections raised by the Liberal party came largely from 300 to 400 donors, in amounts ranging up to $75 000. Substantial gifts in kind (e.g., broadcasting time, advertising space) were also received. While comparisons across more than four decades are hazardous, the Liberal party's 1945 election fund amounted to some $32.5 million in 1989 dollars. By comparison, in 1988, the party spent $6.8 million on "election expenses" and all Liberal candidates spent $9.7 million on "election expenses" (Canada, Elections Canada 1988c, 3–339).

The Liberals' incomplete estimate of their election spending in 1965 by national and provincial campaign committees was $3.5 million (or $15.8 million in 1989 dollars).[9] Candidates reportedly spent $2.6 million, or $11.7 million in 1989 dollars. By comparison, in the 1979 election (the first under the 1974 legislation), the Liberal party spent $3.9 million ($7.3 million in 1989 dollars), while Liberal candidates spent $6.2 million ($11.6 million in 1989 dollars).

The Committee on Election Expenses (Barbeau Committee) estimated that the national parties together spent in excess of $8 million on the 1965 election campaign, and that all candidates spent a similar amount for a total of about $16 million (Canada, Committee 1966). To put these figures in context, it should be noted that all parties spent $22.04 million in 1988, which was just below the maximum permitted. If the increase in the CPI is applied to the 1965 figure of $8 million it amounts to $33.9 million in 1988 dollars. The candidates of all parties spent a total of $31.34 million in 1988.[10] Therefore, if the 1965 expenditures are translated into 1988 dollars, it is possible to conclude that candidate outlays in 1965 were slightly greater than those in 1988.

The Liberal party's incomplete estimate of its election spending in the 1968 election by national and provincial campaign committees was $4 million (or almost $16 million in 1989 dollars). Candidates were estimated to have spent $3.5 million (almost $14 million in 1989 dollars). Thus the 1979 "election expenses" ($18.9 million) were well above those in 1968.

In the 1972 general election, the national campaign spending by the Liberal party was $6.5 million[11] ($22.2 million in 1989 dollars). This figure should be compared to the Liberal party's "election expenses" of $7.3 million in 1979, $7.8 million in 1984 and $7.2 million in 1988, also in 1989 dollars. Again, the evidence indicates that party election expenditures after the 1974 legislation came into effect were substantially *lower* than they were in the 1945, 1965 and 1972 general elections (in real terms).

The Liberal party raised $6.2 million for the 1974 election and spent $5.5 million ($15.8 million in 1989 dollars). Expenditures by headquarters totalled $1 493 000 (Paltiel 1975, 190, 192), while some $2.6 million was distributed to candidates. Expenditures by the Liberal candidates who filed a return with the House of Commons were $4 961 127. This was the last election prior to the coming into effect of the *Election Expenses Act* of 1974. Party expenditures plus candidates' expenditures (net of transfers from headquarters to candidates) converted into 1989 dollars indicate that the Liberals' campaign expenditures in 1974 totalled $22.6 million. In 1979, under the new rules, party plus candidate "election expenses" totalled $18.9 million in 1989 dollars. The apparent effect of the new legislation was to reduce election outlays by the Liberal party and its candidates.

3. RESPONSES TO THE *ELECTION EXPENSES ACT* OF 1974

3.1 Financing the Party

Shortly after the *Election Expenses Act* came into effect on 1 August 1974, the Liberal party named registered agents for each PTA. At the beginning of 1976, the final responsibility for reporting donations was transferred from the chief agent to a corporate body, the Federal Liberal Agency.[12] However, unlike the PC Canada Fund, the Agency "assumed no responsibility for fund-raising or for promoting donations to the party" (Seidle 1980, 226).

The formula for apportioning money raised at the riding or constituency level of the Liberal party established in 1974 was as follows: 25 percent to the PTA, 25 percent to the riding for operating expenses and 50 percent to a trust fund to be used by the riding in the next election. This remarkable arrangement, which gave no share of the revenue to the federal office, was still in operation in 1979 (Seidle 1980, 226). The national office was dependent on an assessment on each PTA negotiated with the chairman of the Treasury Committee of each PTA. However, the national office retained authority to obtain contributions from corporations solicited by the Treasury Committee (later the Revenue Committee).

In the mid-1970s, the Liberal party's Finance Committee sought to develop "sectoral fund-raising," or efforts "directed at the segment that falls between major corporations (the preserve of the Treasury Committee) and individuals and organizations that might contribute to constituency associations" (Torrance Wylie, senior Liberal party official, quoted in Seidle 1980, 227). The Liberal party's ability to raise funds was hampered by the limit of $25 000 ($50 000 at election time) imposed on contributions from a single source by Pierre Trudeau (Urquhart 1978). (An informal limit of $100 000 had previously been in effect.) The move, said to be instigated or at least supported by Senator Keith Davey, was strongly opposed by the party's fund-raisers (e.g., Senator John Godfrey).

Seidle states: "In the opinion of leading Liberals, the reliance on the constituency as the major basis of fund-raising was far from successful during the 1974–1979 period. One problem was that constituency associations have no real incentive to raise significant amounts of money" (1980, 230). Why? Because "election expenses" are constrained, and most ridings need little money between elections. Moreover, if the candidate gets 15 percent of the vote, one-half of his/her "election expenses" are reimbursed by the federal government.

Despite the party's structural problems, its total income rose from $2.2 million in 1974/75 to $5.0 million in 1978 (table 5.1). During the same period, operating expenses, which exclude transfers to ridings or PTAs, rose from $1.0 million to $3.4 million.[13] Yet Seidle states that "it was plain that the Liberal Party was in financial difficulty" in the summer of 1979 (1980, 231).

Seidle reports that "both in 1972 and soon after the passage of the Election Expenses Act, leading Liberals had pressed for the introduction of direct mail ... This was opposed by several people at the top level of the party, some of whom felt it would not work because they felt it would not accord well with the party's structure" (1980, 226). Others argued that nothing could replace personal contacts in raising money at the riding level. Hence, nothing was done. Then, after the 1979 election, a special committee under treasurer Gordon Dryden recommended that the Liberals introduce direct mail (ibid., 231, no. 1). However, direct-mail solicitations enjoyed only a modest success from 1979 and 1982 (see chap. 9).

In retrospect, it is clear that the Liberal party made a strategic error when, shortly after the 1974 legislation came into effect, it failed to ensure that the national office would get a fraction of all moneys raised by riding associations or by PTAs using the federal party's tax-receipting authority. However, in 1979 and 1980, the national office moved to capture a fraction of the federal government's reimbursement of one-half of each candidate's "election expenses" (see flow 16 in figure 5.1).

In the months before the 1979 election, the national campaign committee devised a plan by which candidates would channel part of their reimbursements back to the national campaign committee. Candidates were subsequently asked to sign a pledge form that was sent to the chief electoral officer. After the election, when each candidate's return had been submitted and verified in the office of the chief electoral officer, part of the reimbursement was sent to the candidate and part to the Liberal party national office. Nearly all candidates in Ontario and Quebec signed the necessary "pledge forms"; in Quebec candidates handed over half their reimbursements, and in Ontario the usual amount was one-third. In other provinces a small number

Figure 5.1
Flows of funds relating to Liberal party and its candidates

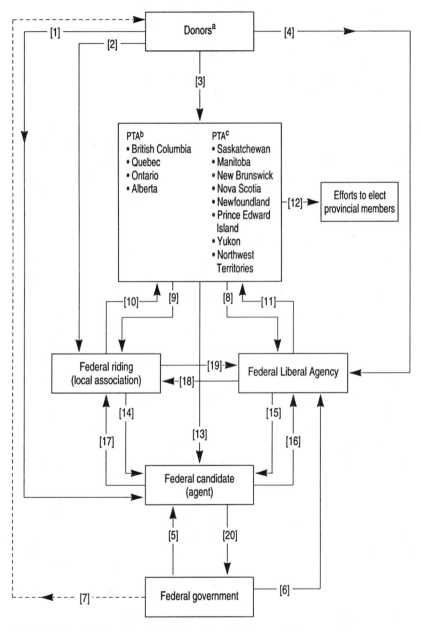

Notes: Excludes financing of campaigns for party leadership or nomination campaigns.

[a]Includes individuals, corporations, trade unions, interest groups and other organizations.

[b]Federal part of LPC in four provinces.

[c]In eight provincial/territorial associations, both federal and provincial wings are in same organization. These "dual" associations *also* engage in provincial politics. See flow 12.

PTA = Provincial/territorial association.

of candidates were asked to return some money to the provincial committee, although the pattern varied widely. The amount gained at the national level from candidates in Ontario and Quebec was $830 000, over one-fifth of the Liberal party's reported expenses ... [In the 1980 election] candidates were asked to return part of their reimbursement to the national party, and the amount returned accounted for about $1 million of the funds required for the 1980 election. (Seidle and Paltiel 1981, 253–54, 255).[14]

The shift in the composition of the national office's election expenditures was dramatic. In 1974, the Liberal party spent $5.5 million on the election, of which $2.6 million consisted of transfers to candidates (Paltiel 1975). In 1979, the party spent $3.9 million, but only about $300 000 was transferred to candidates. However, this did not solve the fiscal imbalance within the party.

3.2 Provincial/Local Orientation

Senior officials at the national level of all three major parties emphasize the local/provincial orientation of the so-called national or federal parties. The problem is most acute for the Liberal and New Democratic parties. There are several reasons for this. First, individuals join a party at the constituency or riding level, and in this way become members of their provincial/territorial association (section), which maintains "party" membership lists.[15] The Liberal Party of Canada (1986a, 3) points out that "individual members of the Liberal Party cannot belong directly to the Liberal Party of Canada. Rather, each Liberal joins a provincial or territorial association, either directly or by joining one of the riding associations [federal or provincial] which make up the provincial or territorial association. In turn, the provincial or territorial association belongs to the LPC. Therefore, the only 'members' of the LPC are provincial and territorial Liberal associations."[16] This explanation does not make clear that 8 of the 12 member organizations of the LPC are those that *combine* federal and provincial parties.[17] Article 2 of the 1990 LPC Constitution specifies several criteria for membership: being age 14 and over, ordinarily resident in Canada, and not a member of any other federal political party within Canada. Individuals may not hold membership in more than one federal constituency (riding) association. There are, however, no standard criteria for membership in a constituency association (Liberal Party of Canada, Reform Commission 1991, 6).

Second, for many individuals, the national party and its headquarters in Ottawa are remote and of questionable relevance. The national centre–periphery conflict is reflected in each federal party.[18]

National officials (many of whom do not work in Ottawa) emphasize that many party members identify more strongly with either their federal riding association or with their provincial riding and/or PTA than with the national party and its headquarters. Third, eight of the PTAs that make up the LPC are "dual purpose" entities in the sense that they have two electoral targets. They seek to win sufficient seats in the provincial or territorial legislature to be able to form a government, *and* they seek to elect MPs to represent federal ridings in their province/territory. The "dual purpose" PTAs have certain advantages as seen from their own perspective: the national level can be treated as a "milch cow" to support either provincial or federal activity at the riding level; and they are eligible to use both the federal and provincial income-tax credit system (8 of 10 provinces have such a credit). On the other hand, money raised by the Ontario, Quebec, BC and Alberta "federal-only" associations from their members (and riding associations) can only be used for *federal* activities (see figure 5.1).

All of these factors make it difficult for Liberal party headquarters to obtain the resources and organizational support for those activities that are designed to advance the interests of the party at the *national* level. The problems have been reflected in repeated efforts to alter the division of responsibilities and flows of money within the party,[19] the latest being the Interim Report of the Reform Commission of the Liberal Party of Canada (1991) published in July 1991.

4. PARTY REVENUES AND EXPENDITURES, 1974–90

4.1 Revenues

The Liberal party's annual revenues and expenditures over the period 1974 to 1990 are set out in table 5.1. Contributions from individuals and corporations accounted for the bulk of revenues, except in election years where "other income" (which includes transfers from candidates to the party) and the reimbursement of part of the party's "election expenses" were of some importance.[20] The complex web of financial flows associated with the party is mapped in figure 5.1.[21]

The relationship between the total value of contributions from individuals and those from business and commercial organizations (corporations) has been far less regular for the Liberal party than for the Progressive Conservative party. In only half the years between 1974 and 1990 were the amounts reasonably comparable. In 1979, 1980, 1987, 1988 and 1989 (three being election years) the amounts contributed by corporations substantially exceeded total contributions from individuals. For example, in 1988 corporations donated $8.45 million as compared to $4.75 million from individuals. In 1979 corporations donated $3.88 million, while individuals gave only $1.18 million. There appear to be two reasons why, in both relative and absolute terms, the Liberal party has been less successful than the Conservative party in raising money from individuals. First, the party was much slower than the Conservative party in making a serious effort to use direct-mail fund-raising (see chap. 9). Second, in its many years in power prior to the 1974 legislation, the Liberal party came to rely on no more than 500 firms to supply over 90 percent of its funds in election years, and on less than 200 firms to provide much smaller amounts in interelection years. Subsequently, the Liberals made far less effort than the Tories or the NDP to reduce their dependency on corporate donations by trying to obtain more money from individuals. By the late 1970s, the Conservative party was receiving donations from more individuals than the Liberal party, while the average size of contributions from individuals favoured the Liberal party (see chap. 11). In 1982, 1985, 1986 and 1990, however, the Liberal party raised more money from individuals than from corporations. The increase in contributions from individuals in 1986 is largely attributable to the well-attended policy convention in Ottawa. The delegates' fees were treated as contributions so that party members could obtain the tax credit on fees of over $400.

The effect of a leadership convention on the composition of Liberal party revenues can be seen when figures for 1989 are compared to those for 1990, when Jean Chrétien won the leadership race to replace John Turner. In 1989 individuals accounted for 37.6 percent of the Liberal party's *receipted* revenues (table 5.2a). In 1990, they accounted for 61.8 percent of such revenues, which included $4.4 million in convention fees and $1.95 million in contributions to leadership candidates routed through the Federal Liberal Agency in order to obtain tax receipts. In both cases, most of the money came from individuals. In *absolute* terms, contributions from individuals increased from $2.4 million in 1989 to $7.4 million in 1990 (table 5.1).

The relative weakness of the Liberal Party of Canada in raising money from individuals in most years is illustrated by the data in table 5.2. In each of the years between 1985 and 1989, the Quebec Liberal Party (led by Robert Bourassa) was able to raise more money from individuals than the LPC despite the fact that the Quebec Liberal Party had a population base only 26 percent as large as the LPC and the Quebec income-tax credit for political contributions was less generous than the federal tax credit.[22] Moreover, the Quebec Liberal Party persuaded more persons to contribute in every year between 1983 and 1988 than did the federal Liberal party. Finally, in 1988 and 1989, the average contribution by individuals to the Quebec Liberal Party was greater than that to the federal Liberal party.

The financial flows within the Liberal Party of Canada between party headquarters and the PTAs and ridings have been, and continue to be, more complicated than they are in the Conservative party (chap. 4). Dyck states that they "have always been a nightmare":

> Since the new federal election-finance legislation of 1974, there has been a trend toward greater individual contributions, with less reliance on corporate donations. One result was a heightened competition for funds among federal, provincial, and constituency levels of the party. Another effect was an even closer cross-level link in those places where no equivalent provincial legislation was available and where the federal tax credit was used for provincial party contributions. A third change occurred after the debacle of 1984 when the federal party simply had no money to spare and hoped that its provincial branches would help it reduce its own deficit ... many provinces now also provide tax credits and/or public subsidy of election expenses, so in these cases there is less need to depend on the national party. In Ontario, in particular, the law virtually prohibits federal-provincial transfers of party funds, and the federal and provincial parties usually alternate fund-raising events, federal one year and provincial the next. Except for Quebec and Ontario, there continue to be some joint fund-raising efforts, and the proceeds from a dinner featuring either the federal or provincial leader will usually be shared. Even in Alberta, federal mps (from other provinces) may do fund-raising events, the proceeds of which are divided between the two organizations.
>
> [In November 1986] the federal party established a new Financial Management Committee which included five provincial party representatives and adopted a new financial plan. This involved retrenchment at both federal and provincial levels and, at least until the federal party's debt was eliminated, a closer federal-provincial financial relationship. (Dyck 1989, 190–91)[23]

Beginning in 1987 and continuing through early 1989, the Liberal party made a series of changes in its financial arrangements (described in more detail in sections 5.5 and 5.7) that assigned to party headquarters the following revenue sources:

- 100 percent of donations from firms on the Revenue Committee's (previously the Treasury Committee) list;
- 100 percent of the revenue from the Laurier Club;[24]

- 100 percent of the net revenue from the federal leader's dinners;
- All of the federally receipted revenue raised by PTAs,[25] less transfers to the PTAs for their operating costs;
- 100 percent of direct-mail revenues from lists created by headquarters prior to 1990; and
- 50 percent of the net revenue raised from membership lists provided by a PTA for that purpose (as of 1990).[26]

The Revenue Committee, which consists of fund-raisers from each PTA, divides up the list of target corporations by province/territory. The focus is on the top 500 nonfinancial and 200 financial enterprises, most of which have their headquarters in Ontario and Quebec. Former party president Michel Robert acknowledged that the party has been less successful with small and medium-sized enterprises than with large corporations, except in BC. He noted that, in Quebec, the provincial Liberals under Robert Bourassa have been quite successful in tapping the owners or executives of these small to medium-sized firms.

Since the beginning of 1989,[27] the Liberal party's PTAs and constituency associations have had the following sources of revenue:

- membership dues;[28]
- revenues from local events (dinners, social events, sale of party paraphernalia);
- "popular fund-raising," that is, contributions solicited from individuals and small and medium-sized firms (within the PTA or riding); and
- 50 percent of the net revenues from direct mail to a PTA's membership list used by Ottawa in 1990 (all PTAs but Quebec and New Brunswick were involved).[29]

Article 3(2)(i) of the LPC Constitution states that the PTAs, "in their respective constitutions provide for a procedure for determining the allocation of revenues between federal constituency associations and the provincial and territorial associations, as agreed from time to time."

Quebec is not a province like the others within the Liberal Party of Canada. No centralized direct-mail effort has been established in Quebec, but ridings and candidates may use this technique. The Quebec PTA has made a greater effort to raise funds by "sectoral collection." A finance committee often targeted small and medium-sized enterprises by selling tables of eight (at $125 each) at an annual banquet and through personal contacts with professional bodies and ethno-cultural communities, letters and phone calls. Money raised by the federal wing of the party in Quebec has stayed in Quebec in the past. Since the series of changes in party finances were made in 1987 and 1988, national head-quarters receives a fraction of it, although the amount has varied over time. Between elections, revenues raised locally are distributed 25 percent to the riding, 25 percent to a riding trust fund for the next election and 50 percent to the LPC (Quebec). Michel Robert told the author that about 10 percent of Quebec Liberal candidates had created trust funds that they effectively controlled. (These are *not* the riding association trust funds that hold money until the next election.)[30] These trust funds have been financed in part from the candidate's surplus, which is given to the riding association after the election campaign and is then moved into the trust fund. However, in the last four elections, LPC head-quarters has obtained part of each candidate's reimbursement of their "election expenses," and thus the surplus available to be transferred to the riding association is reduced.

Table 5.2a examines the Liberal party's revenues in 1989 and 1990 by source in a way that distinguishes the revenues associated with the leadership race and convention in 1990. Corporate donations (excluding those in the form of purchase of tickets to the leader's dinners) fell from $2.34 million in 1989 to $1.82 million in 1990. Popular fund-raising and special events are the sources of revenues used by the ridings and PTAs. Combined, they raised $1.71 million in 1989 but only $1.27 million in 1990. Direct-mail gross revenues, however, rose sharply, from $1.04 million in 1989 to $1.73 million in 1990.

4.2 Expenditures

Most of the Liberal party's expenditures fall into three broad categories: operating expenses, transfers to party associations (notably PTAs, riding associations and, in election years, candidates) and "election expenses" (see table 5.1 and figure 5.2). The pattern of "election expenses" has been discussed in chapter 3. One point should be emphasized, however. Because of its financial problems, the Liberal party was able to spend only $6.84 million in the 1988 election – far below its legal limit of $7.98 million. Moreover, the party was *not* able to increase operating expenditures sharply in 1988 over the previous year as it had been able to do in the previous election year, 1984. In 1983, the Liberals' operating expenses were $4.6 million. They rose to $11.2 million in 1984 and then fell to $7.25 million in 1985. However, a substantial part of the increase was attributable to expenditures on the leadership convention in 1984.[31]

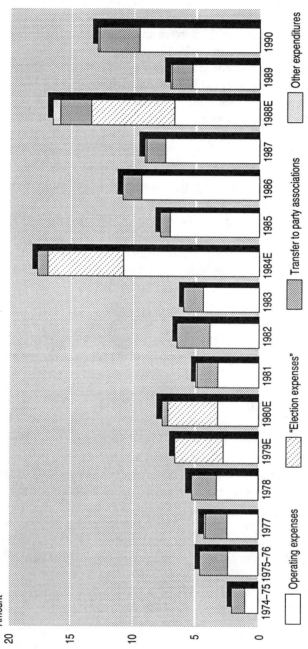

Figure 5.2
Analysis of Liberal Party of Canada expenditures, 1974–90
(millions of dollars)

Source: Table 5.1.

Transfers to PTAs, Ridings, Candidates

It is clear from table 5.1 that "transfers to party associations"[32] fluctuate much more than the Liberal party's operating expenses (which are analysed in detail in table 5.3). For example, transfers rose from less than $1 million in 1974/75 to $2.3 million in 1975/76. From $1.74 million and $1.86 million in 1977 and 1978, they fell to only $7 134 in 1979 and $388 572 in 1980, both election years, because of the nature of the intraparty financial flows. Recall that from 1974 to 1980 at least, ridings were allowed to keep *all* of the money they raised using the federal tax credit, the right to issue receipts for which was delegated by the Liberal party's official agent to the PTA/ridings. During the period of the election campaign, the agents for each candidate may issue tax receipts; there is no need to route the money through the party's agent.

Although figure 5.1 maps in a general way the flows of funds into and within the Liberal party, measuring the *size* of the flows is difficult because the figures provided by the party to the Chief Electoral Officer and by candidates to the CEO and other figures from the party do not agree. This can be seen by examining the figures in table 5.2b. In 1979, Liberal party *candidates* reported receiving $2.7 million from party headquarters. However, party headquarters reported to the CEO that its transfers to candidates in 1979 were *minus* $810 386. In other words, transfers from candidates to headquarters *exceeded* those from headquarters to candidates by $810 386. A similarly huge discrepancy in the figures occurred in 1980: candidates reported receiving $1.546 million from headquarters, while headquarters stated it received a *net* $1.098 million *from* candidates. Recall that in 1979 and 1980, Liberal party headquarters sought to recover one-half the amount that candidates received in reimbursement from the federal government ($3.59 million in 1979 and $3.66 million in 1980; see table 1.1). Even if the party had succeeded, the amount could not explain the discrepancy in 1979 and 1980 reported in table 5.2b.

In 1984, Liberal candidates reported receiving $2.77 million from party headquarters, while headquarters reported a transfer of $474 212 to candidates. The difference *cannot* be explained by headquarters' "tax" on the federal government's reimbursement of candidates' "election expenses" because the party imposed it only in Quebec in 1984. In 1988, the discrepancy reported in table 5.2b was about $1.2 million, but the figure reported by headquarters *excluded* the $2.274 million headquarters collected from candidates' reimbursement (which totalled $4.656 million).

The complexity of the intraparty financial flows is further illustrated by table 5.2b. The party reported substantial transfers to ridings (column 4) and PTAs (column 5) in election years. These correspond to flows 18 and 11 in figure 5.1. At the same time, *candidates* reported receiving substantial sums from their PTA and/or riding association (column 2, table 5.2b). The transfers to PTAs from headquarters can include several things: the PTA's share of contributions routed through the Federal Liberal Agency; "grants" from headquarters to PTAs reflecting the PTAs' operating costs; and transfers to pay for regional "election expenses." Moreover, transfers to a PTA may, in turn, be transferred to a riding association or a candidate. Table 5.2b indicates that, in election years 1979 and 1984, Liberal party headquarters transferred fairly modest sums to PTAs. However, in 1980 and 1988, the amounts were much larger ($612 000 in 1980 and $931 000 in 1988).

Transfers from Liberal party headquarters to ridings in election years were substantial in 1979, 1980 and 1988, but much smaller in 1984 (column 4 in table 5.2b). The figure of $1.16 million in 1988 should be compared to that of $1.625 million raised by ridings (table 5.6). The difference suggests that headquarters was retaining some fraction of revenues raised at the local level but routed through the Federal Liberal Agency in order to be eligible for the receipt for the tax credit for political contributions.

If election years are ignored, transfers to "party associations" (which includes PTAs and ridings) as reported in table 5.1 appear to account for a declining fraction of the Liberal party's total expenditures. Between 1974/75 and 1977 they accounted for from 42 percent to 49 percent of total expenditures. In the period 1981–83, such transfers accounted for from 26 percent to 39 percent of total expenditures. In the period 1985–87, the range was only 11 percent to 16 percent. Then, in 1989, transfers amounted to 22 percent of total Liberal party expenditures. In 1990, $578 000 was transferred to riding associations and $788 000 to PTAs.[33] The former amount reflects contributions to riding associations that were routed through the Federal Liberal Agency in Ottawa and then returned to the riding via the PTA (see flows 2, 19, 11 and 9 in figure 5.1). The transfer to PTAs reflects the new arrangements (beginning in 1989) in which all their revenues go to the Federal Liberal Agency, while the PTAs receive a grant to cover their operating costs (see section 5.7 below for more detail).

Composition of Operating Expenses

The composition of the Liberal party's operating expenses is examined in table 5.3. These operating expenses exclude "election expenses" in 1979, 1980, 1984 and 1988 and transfers to PTAs and ridings in all years. The salaries, wages and benefits of employees have consistently been the largest category, typically accounting for 30 percent to 40 percent of total operating expenses. The two exceptions were 1984 and 1990 when leadership conventions occurred and salaries and wages dropped to 11.3 percent and 19.1 percent respectively.

Not surprisingly, expenditures by the Liberal party on "party conventions and meetings" varied greatly between 1974 and 1990: from less than 3 percent (1974/75, 1987–89) to over 25 percent (1980, 1984, 1990). In 1986, when John Turner's leadership was in doubt, the party's convention in Ottawa absorbed 18.4 percent of its total operating expenses. Note, however, that the party has tried to ensure that convention revenues more than offset costs. The details for the 1990 leadership convention (which cost $4.4 million) are provided in table 5.8.

Advertising and broadcasting expenses declined as a percentage of operating expenses from 6.3 percent to 7.9 percent in the period 1977–79 to less than 1 percent in 1982 and 1983. Then they increased to 11.1 percent to 12.3 percent from 1985 to 1989 (table 5.3). The importance of the "printing, stationery and postage" category has tended to decline: in 1974/75 and 1975/76, it was 10 percent of operating expenses; between 1984 and 1990, this category ranged from 1.0 percent to 5.1 percent.

Bank charges and interest only became an issue in 1980 (3.9 percent) and they remained at about that level to 1985, when they rose to 6.6 percent, reflecting the huge deficit incurred in 1984 (some $5.4 million). In 1989, bank charges absorbed 11.8 percent of the Liberal party's operating expenses. Given the fact that the party had almost $7 million in total liabilities – largely bank debt (see table 5.7) – the interest on these debts ($648 528) implies an interest rate of under 10 percent in 1989.

Details of Expenditures, 1983–90

Additional details of the Liberal party's expenditures in the period 1983–90 are set out in table 5.4. These data come from party records and there are a few slight differences from the totals reported in table 5.1. The data in table 5.4 reveal several interesting insights into Liberal party expenditures during the years in which the party experienced severe fiscal stress. First, despite the cutbacks in 1987 and 1988 (see below), party administration continued to be the largest single component of total expenditures (excluding "election expenses" in 1984 and 1988). For example, in 1983, it accounted for 49.3 percent of total expenses. In 1989, after considerable cost cutting, party administration accounted for 37.6 percent of total expenditures.

Second, after John Turner became leader (June 1984), the party's expenditures to support his office swelled greatly. In 1984, they were only $138 174 (Turner became Opposition Leader in September), but in 1985 this category of expenditures rose to $1.14 million and remained at that level in 1986 when the party's total operating expenses were $9.6 million. While some cuts were made, the Leader's Office received almost $1 million from the party in 1987 and 1988 (when total operating expenses were about $7 million), before being reduced to $478 617 in 1989 and $512 733 in 1990.

Third, table 5.4 indicates that the Liberals spent substantial sums in generating revenues from direct mail. For example, the party spent just over $1 million annually in 1983 and 1985, and hit a peak of $1.37 million in 1986. These efforts bore fruit, but the net revenue was far below that of the Progressive Conservative party. Moreover, the Liberal party's costs of generating contributions from direct mail were a much higher percentage of gross revenues than were those of the Conservative party (see chap. 9).

Money Available to Headquarters

One of the most interesting aspects of party financing is to determine how much of a party's gross revenue is spent to generate the revenue and how much is left to spend on political activities. Further, it is useful to determine how much of the net revenue is retained by party headquarters rather than transferred to provincial associations or to ridings. For the Liberal party, it has been possible to provide a reasonable estimate of the difference between gross revenue, net revenue and the amount available to party headquarters to spend on political activities (table 5.5).

Three types of outlays have been deducted to determine the *net* revenue available to headquarters. The first is the cost of raising funds. This category includes the costs (for one year) of direct-mail campaigns, the official agent's operations, fund-raising at the PTA level and the Revenue Committee. During the period 1983–86, the Federal Liberal Agency (the party's official agent) delegated its tax-receipting function to official agents in each of the 12 provinces/territories. The second category of deduction from the party's gross revenue consists of transfers of funds to other units in the party: PTAs, riding associations and candidates in election years. The other units are the ones that subsequently incur the expenditures for goods and services. These intraparty transfers are deducted from the party's gross revenue because these funds are then *not* available to headquarters for running the party at the national level. The third deduction is expenditures on party conventions and conferences. While these are important activities, they are episodic and are designed to be self-financing, that is, the delegates' fees (which are included in the total party revenue) are designed to cover the total costs. Thus, in order to determine the amount available for the ongoing activities of party headquarters, it is useful to deduct them.

Election years aside, table 5.5 reveals that the net revenue available for Liberal party headquarters amounted to from 44 percent to 60 percent of gross revenue between 1983 and 1989. In 1990, party headquarters had available only one-third of the gross revenue of $13.78 million, largely because of the cost of the leadership convention ($4.4 million) and the "pass through" of $1.95 million in contributions to leadership candidates. Even so, on a net basis, headquarters had more money for its ongoing activities in 1990 ($4.58 million) than it did in 1989 ($3.38 million). These data alone are indicative of the fiscal stress experienced by the federal Liberal party.

The net revenue available to pay for the ongoing operating costs of party headquarters in election year 1984 was only $53 000 (table 5.5). One of the reasons why the figure was so low is because the costs of administering the Federal Liberal Agency seemed to be very high ($2.3 million), far above the level in other years.[34] Recall that in 1984 the Liberal party ran a deficit of $5.3 million (table 5.1). The improvement in the party's finances by election year 1988 is reflected in the net revenue available to headquarters, $6.7 million (table 5.5). In 1988, the party had a surplus of $882 000 (table 5.1), in part because its "election expenses" were over $1 million below the statutory limit.

Intraparty Finances

Within political parties, money is fugacious. It moves in many directions and sometimes in opposite directions between the same two entities within the party. It is extremely difficult to identify and measure all the flows of money, not only because of the limitations of party accounting systems but also because the "sharing" arrangements change over time.

Table 5.6 is the result of a special effort by Liberal party officials to link types of revenues to the *level* within the party at which they were raised (see figure 5.1). In 1988, 88 percent of Liberal party revenues were raised at the national level, although 73 percent of this amount was actually collected by the PTAs. This paradox results from two facts. First, as noted above, the Liberal Party of Canada is a federation of 12 PTAs. Second, early in 1987, party headquarters ended the national Federal Liberal Agency's delegation of tax-receipting authority to each of the PTAs. Therefore, as of 1987, a dollar collected, for example, by the Saskatchewan Liberal Association,[35] was deemed to be raised at the national level because it had to be receipted in Ottawa. As a result, in 1988 and 1989 – unlike the practice in many years prior to 1987 –

the federal side of the PTAs did not raise any money "on their own." The costs of their federal operations were met by a transfer from Ottawa. One of the effects of the change in arrangements made in 1987 was to greatly reduce the financial autonomy of the federal side of the 12 PTAs.

Table 5.6 indicates that ridings raised only 12 percent of total revenue in 1988, but this figure hardly tells the full story. In 1988, according to table 5.4, ridings received $1.16 million from party headquarters.[36] It appears that PTAs ("other party organizations") received $931 451, while candidates received $485 146. On the other hand, Liberal candidates were required to transfer some $2.27 million to headquarters to help pay for the national election campaign ("election expenses" totalled $6.84 million). This money came from half of the federal government's reimbursement of candidates' "election expenses." The connection back to the riding associations is this: as a group, Liberal candidates normally have a substantial surplus after paying all the campaign-related costs and receiving the reimbursement (see chap. 12). The surplus is usually given to the candidate's riding association. And so the money goes round and round. (As shall be seen in chapter 6, the movement of money within the NDP is even more complex.)

4.3   Bottom Line and Balance Sheet

The surplus/deficit line in table 5.1 summarizes in stark terms the financial problems of the Liberal party, beginning in 1984. In seven of the nine years between 1974/75 and 1983, the Liberal party had a surplus. The cumulative surplus in nominal dollars was $4.56 million. As table 5.1 indicates, the party ran a deficit of $5.3 million in 1984, which more than offset the previous cumulative surplus. From 1984 to 1990 the Liberal party ran a deficit in five of the seven years. The cumulative *deficit* in nominal dollars over this period was almost $7.5 million. In contrast, during the period 1984 to 1990, the Progressive Conservative party had a cumulative *surplus* of just over $1 million in nominal dollars (table 4.1).

The balance sheet of the Liberal party over the period 1983–90 (table 5.7) reflects the party's financial plight during the period that John Turner was leader. The members' equity (i.e., assets minus liabilities) stood at $3.38 million at the end of 1983. Within 12 months, after running the 1984 election largely on borrowed money, the members' equity was *minus* $1.9 million. The problem worsened as annual deficit followed annual deficit. By the end of 1987, the members' equity was *minus* $4.8 million. The Liberal party's figures for 1988 contain a large error, namely, that the amount of assets in the form of election rebates receivable was overstated by $2.27 million. Hence, the members' equity was minus

$6.2 million, not minus $3.93 million, as indicated in table 5.7. More recently, the party has been making some progress in reducing its debt, which amounted to $3.8 million at the end of 1990 according to a party official. The equity had been reduced to minus $4.16 million.

5. EVOLUTION OF THE MANAGEMENT OF PARTY FINANCES IN THE 1980s
While the previous section documented the pattern of revenues and expenditures for the Liberal party over the period 1974–90, the purpose of this section is to describe and analyse in some detail the problems that have beset the party beginning in 1984. The large deficits generated in 1984, 1985 and 1989 (table 5.1) reflected a number of factors, notably the organizational design of the party itself.

5.1   The Seeds of the Problem
Long an observer of the Liberal party, Joseph Wearing indicated that the party's "internal financial management was a mess" in the early 1980s:

> A special financial review committee revealed an appalling fragmentation in the raising and spending of funds both at the national level and between the national, provincial, and constituency levels. For example, three bodies raised money at the national level: the Liberal Agency that issued receipts and reports to the Chief Electoral Officer and also had responsibility for the direct mail campaign; the Treasury Committee, a shadowy group of well-connected businessmen who went after large donations from the major corporations; and, finally, "senior political figures" (often cabinet ministers when the party was in power) who had good financial connections in their home province and a major role in the allocation of those funds. Funds were disbursed by the party's national office, the leader's office, the Liberal Agency, and, during elections, by another ad hoc committee. (1989, 278–79)

Banister and Gibson pointed to other problems as well:

> There are basically two ills which plague the health of the party's finances. The first is that the $6 million pie is not big enough. The party has no consistent method of raising money from its members or other potential donors. The second inadequacy which contributes to a less than effective party, is division of the money raised among the different levels ... The ridings, aside from making this contribution if any, maintain riding trust funds (held by the official agent of the province/territory) for election purposes, and the balance goes to pay for riding maintenance costs. As an example, the formula could be

40 percent-riding maintenance, 35 percent-riding trust account, and 25 percent-provincial/territorial member organization. There is no set amount earmarked for the national party, and generally nothing is assigned. (1984, 18)[37]

The weakness of the "centre" relative to the PTAs and the ridings in the early 1980s was indicated as follows:

> The national executive has never been able to, perhaps not felt it necessary to, negotiate revenue-sharing arrangements directly with the provinces/territories and/or ridings ... [N]o national fundraising campaign has never been mounted by the national executive, nor has the executive been able to ensure that door-to-door fundraising campaigns are undertaken by each member organization. The national office continues to rely on the treasury committee for its funding – a source over which the national executive has no control. (Banister and Gibson 1984, 17)

No wonder Banister and Gibson noted that "the bulk of the money in the Liberal party is collected at the local level and remains there" (1984, 29). (This had changed by 1988, as table 5.6 makes clear.)

According to senior Liberal party officials, Pierre Trudeau left the party in 1984 without any debt, but also without a surplus.[38] Most argued that there should have been a large war chest, given the fact the Liberal party had held power since 1963 (except for the Clark government's 259 days in 1979–80), and had formed a *majority* government from 1968 to 1972, 1974 to 1979 and 1980 to 1984. One former senior party official contended that no party in power should generate a *surplus*, while others have suggested there should have been a $20 million surplus when Trudeau resigned. It would have been "immoral and dangerous" for the party, according to Torrance Wylie, a former senior party official, to use the fact of being in government to generate a large surplus. In any event, the Liberal party's financial management left much to be desired in the early and mid-1980s. For example, Wearing (1989, 278) states that "party finances were in such confusion that when Iona Campagnolo became president in 1982, she could not get a financial statement on the total operations of the party – other than the information that the party had a $2.6 million debt (later $4.6 million) and that she should get rid of it!"

5.2 Huge Deficit in 1984/Leader's Office
The Liberal party's financial problems, which reached crisis proportions in 1988 and continued to dog the party in 1991 under its new leader

Jean Chrétien, began in 1984. In 1984, a year in which the party had a leadership race and convention and had to fight a general election, the Liberal party took in $13.0 million (including reimbursement of its "election expenses"), and spent $18.3 million (including $6.3 million on "election expenses" and $2.85 million on the leadership convention). The result was a deficit of $5.3 million (table 5.1). The party's problems were exacerbated when it lost power, electing only 40 MPs to the Tories' 211. During the campaign, according to Weston (1988, 114), John Turner's election tour overspent its budget by $1 million and fund-raising fell $2 million short of its target.[39] Not only was the party heavily in debt, "worse, the party lacked most of the modern fundraising technology needed to mop up that much red ink" (ibid.).

In an interview following the defeat of his party in the 1984 general election, Liberal leader John Turner commented on the party's lack of preparation for the summer campaign:

> I inherited a party without policy, without preparation, without money and without recruitment. I do not blame [party president] Iona Campagnolo for that. The party was really run out of the Prime Minister's Office for the past number of years, and she was not given the scope to do anything. During 1983, the Tories raised $14 million, the NDP raised $8 million and the Liberals only $6 million. We would not have been better prepared in October or November. Everybody would have taken the summer off. The Liberal party was only held together by a loyalty to Trudeau. (*Maclean's*, 19 November 1984, 10i)

Senator Keith Davey strongly disputes the contention that the Liberal party was not ready for the 1984 election:

> Soon after John Turner won the leadership [in June 1984], one damnable piece of political mythology almost became part of Liberal folklore. This was the notion that the party he inherited was simply not ready for an election. Marc Lalonde and I had structured a campaign team as well as a campaign committee, complete with chairmen in every province. A candidate search was well under way. (1986, 328).

One of the most important and controversial categories of expenditures made by the Liberal party over the next five years was that on the Leader's Office. Party outlays to support the Leader's Office rose from $138 174 in 1984 to $1.14 million in 1985 and $1.12 million in 1986. They fell slightly to $955 000 in 1987 and $994 000 in 1988.

Headquarters' support for the Leader's Office dropped to $479 000 in 1989 and $513 000 in 1990.[40]

5.3 Initial Efforts at Reform

A new financing agreement, worked out by the party's Financial Management Committee and designed to help the party eliminate its reported $3 million debt, was announced in June 1985.[41] The new arrangements meant that "25 percent of all money raised at the constituency and provincial level would be turned over to the national office" (*Globe and Mail*, 13 June 1985, 9). In addition to this, funds generated by the central office's direct-mail program would be split 50–50 with provincial/territorial associations.

In addition to the revenue-sharing programs, Liberal party president Iona Campagnolo also announced that the party would, for the first time, release a consolidated financial report that would "bring all three levels of financing together" (*Globe and Mail*, 13 June 1985, 9). Further, the party also agreed to reveal the activities of the Treasury Committee, a group described in a newspaper report as one "that has pursued donations from the corporate sector, the previously secret 'bagmen' who, before the advent of election-spending rebates ... and income-tax credits ... used to provide a much larger share of total party financing" (ibid.).

In the spring of 1985 when the Liberal party was in dire straits financially,[42] John Turner asked Senator Leo Kolber to become its chief fund-raiser. Previously, Kolber had headed the party's Quebec Treasury Committee, which solicits contributions from larger corporations.[43] Senator Kolber understood that he was also to take charge of party spending. According to Kolber, Turner "reneged" on this commitment to him because of the view of other party officials (notably president Iona Campagnolo) that this would give too much power to one person. Kolber believed that unless spending could be controlled and made more effective, raising more money would be far less likely to reduce the huge deficit incurred in 1984. Kolber wanted to completely overhaul what he called the party's "archaic" methods of financing and budgeting. While the Progressive Conservative party had placed fund-raising on a "very business-like basis" and had centralized the receipting process through the PC Canada Fund, the Liberal party organization was – in Kolber's view – a collection of provincial "fiefdoms." According to Kolber, Ontario "collects zilch" and "only looks after its own offices," that is, it contributed little to the operation of the national party. Senator Kolber sought to obtain money from various (provincial) trust funds and those riding associations with substantial bank accounts. He was unable to get any money from these sources, however.[44]

In 1986, the Liberals began "Project 200," a "discreet special project to raise $5 million and wipe out the party's huge debt" (*Globe and Mail*, 13 September 1986, A5). The plan, headed by Senator Kolber, involved soliciting donations of $25 000 each from 200 companies and individuals. Kolber and one aide were to meet the prospective donors personally. Senator Kolber stressed, at the time the party's plans became public, that the appeal was "to foster a two-party system – no more, no less" (ibid.) and would target individuals such as "the Thomsons [and] the Eatons" (ibid.). With party official Herb Metcalfe as his executive assistant,[45] Kolber spent nine months travelling across Canada to meet some 235 chief executives or wealthy individuals, seeking one-time contributions of $25 000. He stated that he raised $2.5 million, including his own cheque for $25 000.[46] In 1985, the Liberal party received 102 contributions of $10,000 or more from corporations, up from 54 in 1985. In 1987, the party received 104 of these large contributions. However, the *average* size of these contributions increased only by about 10 percent (see table 11.6).[47] According to Kolber, the persons he met were, for the most part, sympathetic to the Liberal party's financial plight, and many who had never given to the party before made contributions. The effort foundered, however, when one or more of the people Kolber contacted told him about the efforts of John Addison, a Toronto car dealer, to raise money to create a trust fund for the education of John Turner's children (see chap. 13). Kolber was furious that he had not been told of Addison's activities.

In 1985, the Liberals, at the behest of Senator Kolber, announced that they would be forming a new leader's club (the Laurier Club; see chap. 10) for donors of larger amounts, which would be modelled after the highly successful Progressive Conservative club, "The 500" (*Vancouver Sun*, 3 May 1985, A12). It would target "business and professional people, key supporters across the country, who are willing to come on and get involved at a certain level" (ibid.). John Swift, John Turner's chief of staff, also explained that, as part of the incentive to participate, members would get such benefits as newsletters, and there would be meetings of 100 to 200 members with Turner, where their views would be solicited. At the time that the Liberal party announced its plans, "The 500," according to PC Canada Fund chairman David Angus, was generating "over two million bucks a year" (ibid.).

In early 1986, Senator Kolber sought to emulate the Conservative party by having all tax-receiptable contributions to the Liberal party processed centrally, with the national executive deciding the amount to be returned to the ridings and PTAs. "Understandably, the independent fiefdoms throughout [the Liberal party] threatened revolt at the mere mention of such a scheme, in part because a lot of Liberals saw a lot of money being frittered away" (Weston 1988, 179). A year later, however, this change was made.

Just before the November 1986 convention, Senator Kolber "presented a seven-point plan to put all fundraising under one roof in Ottawa." The plan was said to have been met with "shrugs," and "Kolber's frustration hit the boiling point" (Weston 1988, 179, 180), largely because by 1986 the party's post-1984 election debt of $3.2 million had increased to almost $6 million (ibid., 172).[48] One insider had estimated late in 1986 that the party needed to raise $22 million in two years to cover the debt, run the party and break even after paying for the 1988 election expenses. The Liberal party raised $8.9 million in 1987 and $17.9 million in 1988 (including reimbursement and transfers from candidates), but it spent $9.3 million and $17.0 million respectively. Therefore, the members' equity, which stood at *minus* $4.3 million at the end of 1986, was reduced only slightly to minus $3.9 million two years later (see table 5.7).

5.4 November 1986 Convention

The November 1986 party convention in Ottawa turned into a battle over Turner's leadership in which he was supported by the well-funded efforts of an ad hoc group known as "The Friends of John Turner." As a result, there was much less interest in the series of potentially important changes to the party constitution. Banister and Gibson (1985, 5–7) indicated that the "fundamental themes" in their proposal for reforming the Liberal party[49] were the following:

- the need to enhance the links between the parliamentary and nonparliamentary wings and to ensure "meaningful policy input by the ordinary Party member";
- the need to establish clear lines of accountability for all elected and nonelected party officials;
- the need to enhance the national presence of the party, while respecting the federal structure and maintaining the optimal degree of decentralization;
- the need to inject a degree of professional expertise into party operations and streamline party structures, without affecting the party's basic voluntary character;
- the need to broaden the base of the party.

One of the potentially useful changes that was made in the party's constitution (new financial reporting requirements) was not adhered to, so the national office was no better informed about the resources of the ridings. Other changes gave the appearance of "democratizing" the party. More committees were formed. There was more communication between committees. More groups were recognized (e.g., Aboriginal peoples). The new, more participatory approach had important consequences for party expenditures: it increased the party's overhead costs in the form of higher secretarial, travel, accommodation and transportation costs associated with committee meetings.

The November 1986 convention brought in some new party officers, including Michel Robert as president. Turner made Robert the party's chief financial officer in December 1986 while Senator Kolber remained as chairman of the Revenue Committee. Gino Francolini, who had been chairman of the Financial Management Committee, resigned in December 1986.

5.5   Financial Restructuring and New Fund-Raisers in 1987

In January 1987, the national executive of the Liberal party decided that all money would be funnelled through the Ottawa headquarters and that the money would be shared with the PTAs and the riding associations according to centrally determined budgets. This move led to a series of conflicts between the provincial organizations and head office. On 19 January, the national executive announced that it would be imposing new and tougher measures for the party that would override the revenue-sharing deal that had been worked out by the national finance committee and the PTAs in 1985. The deal was reportedly the result of tough lobbying by Michel Robert, the new party president, and Douglas Richardson, the leader's principal secretary (*Globe and Mail*, 23 January 1987, A10). Under the new arrangements, all funds coming into the Liberal party would be receipted centrally by the Federal Liberal Agency (*Globe and Mail*, 19 January 1987, A5). This would allow the Ottawa office to see how much money was being raised, as well as allow it to generate a single computerized list of members and donors. Fifty percent of all money raised at the riding level using the federal tax credit for donations was to be automatically returned to the riding. The other 50 percent was to be divided between national and provincial offices (PTAs). In addition, all fund-raising for the party, with the exception of fund-raising using direct mail, was to be decentralized (ibid.).

Apparently the Financial Management Committee, which had strong representation from the PTAs, had determined that the PTAs could retain 50 percent of all the money they raised up to the point that the amount retained by the PTA equalled the PTA's expenditure budget for that year. After that point, party headquarters in Ottawa would get all of the additional revenue raised by the PTA. However, the plan approved by the national executive would have party headquarters set each PTA's budget; all revenues raised by each PTA would then be sent to Ottawa, which would return to each PTA sufficient funds to meet its budgeted expenditures (*Globe and Mail*, 23 January 1987, A10). Moreover, as part of the financial restructuring, the budget at national headquarters was cut drastically. The assistance to the Leader's Office was to be cut by one-third and the combined expenses of the national headquarters, the Federal Liberal Agency and the fund-raising section were to be cut by $650 000. The total reduction in spending was over $1 million and 25 people were fired. In addition to the cuts in the headquarters' budget, the executive committee announced that the budgets of the PTAs would also be cut by 25 percent.

The effect of the restructuring in 1987 compelled the previously autonomous PTAs to yield all fund-raising, except purely local riding events, to Ottawa. Moreover, the PTAs' budgets were actually cut by 30 percent. Marie-André Bastien, the party's secretary-general, stated:

> "De facto, we are not the same federated party ... They are not the same autonomous groups." After four years of pressure, the Quebec wing also yielded its master mailing list to Ottawa, and Ontario is transcribing its records for Ottawa now. (*Globe and Mail*, 2 January 1988, A5)[50]

Liberal leader John Turner had to move very quickly to quell a revolt by the PTAs against the new financing plan. The Ontario, Quebec, Manitoba and Alberta associations strongly resisted what they reportedly saw as an attempt at a "power-grab" by the central party organization (*Globe and Mail*, 23 January 1987, A10). Although the changes were endorsed by the national executive, they had to be ratified by the various PTAs that made up the Liberal party federation.

As part of the efforts to deal with the party's fiscal crisis, the executive decided to require all candidates in the next election to sign over to the party 50 percent of the amount of reimbursement of their "election expenses" by the federal government (*Globe and Mail*, 4 February 1987, A5). The means of enforcement was the fact that the party leader must sign every candidate's nomination papers. The scheme was expected to raise more than $2 million.[51] The initiative was opposed by the presidents of several PTAs. The president of the Alberta PTA said the move amounted "to taxpayers directly subsidizing the central federal party operation instead of the local candidate." The president of the Manitoba PTA said that candidates would have to raise more money.

Recall that party headquarters "taxed" candidates' reimbursement in 1979 and 1980, but in 1984 only the Quebec association did so.

The Liberal party announced in May 1987 an ambitious plan to raise $23 million in revenue over the next two years. In announcing the plan to the Ontario wing of the party, Michel Robert said that such a large amount was necessary in order to "rid the party of its existing $5 million debt; cover normal operations in the meantime; (and) build up a $10 million war chest for the next election" (*Toronto Star*, 9 March 1987, A1). At the same meeting, delegates were reported to have overwhelmingly approved changes to the way in which Ontario riding associations dealt with their membership lists. Responsibility for the lists was to be handed over to the provincial office in Toronto, which would also keep $2.50 of each membership fee to cover its administrative costs. In addition, the provincial office was given the authority to set uniform membership fees for all of the ridings. Previously ridings had individually established the fee, with a ceiling of $15 (ibid.).

As described in table 5.1, Liberal party revenues fell from $10.7 million in 1986 to $8.9 million in 1987 and then doubled to $17.9 million in 1988. The annual deficit fell from $447 527 in 1986 to $392 609 in 1987. However, in 1988 there was a surplus of $881 537, which was quite remarkable considering 1988 was an election year. On the other hand, it can be argued that it is easier to raise money during an election campaign.

Senator Leo Kolber resigned as the Liberal party's chief fund-raiser in February 1987. He was the third senior financial officer to quit in three months. However, newspaper reports stated that Kolber was known to be on the list of party officials Turner wanted removed from their posts.[52] Kolber had also been in conflict with other party officials over his demand to gain more control over the party's fund-raising system (*Vancouver Sun*, 18 December 1986, A12). In March, the party announced that Gerald Schwartz, president of Onex Capital Corporation, would replace Senator Kolber as chief fund-raiser (*Toronto Star*, 9 March 1987, A1).

5.6 Crises in 1988

In February 1988, it was reported that the Liberal party's financial situation was so desperate that it was having problems meeting the monthly payroll (*Globe and Mail*, 20 February 1988, A10). Newspaper accounts said that the payroll was covered after a "scramble around town" by one of the party's most senior staff members. Also in February 1988, a newspaper article predicted that the Liberal party would be called on to implement more austerity measures at a meeting of financial managers that was to be held in March. The paramount concern for the party, according to the article, was not the continuing debt or the cash-flow problem, but rather the "fact that the party (was) still not setting aside sufficient money to meet campaign start-up costs such as chartering planes, producing reams of materials and hiring campaign workers" (*Globe and Mail*, 22 February 1988, A5).

The Liberals' Financial Management Committee responded by creating a special "election-readiness fund" at its March meeting.[53] The Committee decided that one dollar of every five raised in 1988 would be put into the special fund. Money allotted to the fund was to come from all revenue sources, including direct-mail campaigns, riding activities, corporate fund-raising and special events. In addition to creating the special fund, the Committee also decided to make further cuts in the money given to the Leader's Office. The decision meant that the party at both the national and provincial levels would lose 20 percent of the money already allocated for their budgets that year. This cut came in addition to earlier substantial cuts to PTAs' budgets.

In March 1988, party officials confirmed that not only did the Liberal party owe $4.7 million to the Royal Bank of Canada, but it also had several other large outstanding debts (see table 5.7) (MacKenzie et al. 1988, 15). These debts included $600 000 in unpaid bills and outstanding accounts, as well as $395 000 owed in overdue remittances to riding associations. Further, "the size of the Liberals' debt [appeared] to be discouraging the very donations that could reduce it" (ibid.). Corporate donations to the party were also said to have been hampered both by John Turner's performance and by the party's opposition to free trade, which did not please most of the business community. The shortage of money prompted one Liberal to ask, "What are we going to offer Air Canada on deposit to charter a plane. How are we going to set up a computer network, a communications system, a facsimile system?" (ibid.).

Columnist Jeffrey Simpson argued that the Liberals' financial problems "cannot be placed on the fundraisers themselves, since the Liberals have tried several of the best in the country" (*Globe and Mail*, 8 March 1988, A6). Moreover, "they have also geared up to tap the direct mail market" (ibid.). Rather, despite a strong showing in the polls, the problem was that "neither the party nor its leader John Turner can evoke much enthusiasm for the political battle, even from within the Liberal ranks" (ibid.). Simpson noted that the party had not been able to get money from the various trust funds "scattered across the country" – at least two in Nova Scotia, three in Ontario and one each in New Brunswick and Manitoba (*Globe and Mail*, 24 March 1988, A6).

In April 1988, the Liberal party officials announced that, in order to ease the party's financial situation, lay-offs and further budget cuts were necessary. One-quarter of the national office staff was laid off and a further $350 000 was cut from the budget for the Leader's Office.[54] Most of the cuts were made as a result of the shifting of 20 percent of the party's resources to the special election fund (*Vancouver Sun*, 23 April 1988, A7). Another report described the moves as a "victory for Mr. [Michel] Robert, who [had] been campaigning for a cut of up to 50 percent in spending to ensure the party has money set aside for an election before the vote is called" (*Globe and Mail*, 23 April 1988, A1).[55]

In June 1988, the Liberal party decided to postpone its national convention scheduled for later that year in order to help put the party onto solid financial ground before the next election. Michel Robert denied that the move was designed to mask intraparty controversy or prevent an evaluation of the party's leadership.[56] In addition to the postponement, the national executive also decided to give up one floor of the party's Ottawa headquarters. The Liberals also outlined a new "two-point" fund-raising plan (*Globe and Mail*, 20 June 1988, A3). The first element of the plan consisted of an appeal to all members of the party, asking them for a donation of $100. The second element was the selling of $500 "Victory Bonds" (*Vancouver Sun*, 9 September 1988, A1). The bonds would have a duration of five years, during which time the party would keep the interest received. After five years, the principal would be returned to the investor. Because of the complications associated with the tax treatment of the interest, no "Victory Bonds" were ever issued. According to Liberal party financial statements, the party raised only $28 900 and netted a mere $5 596 from the appeal to members.

In an effort to generate funds for the upcoming 1988 general election, the Liberal party designed a scheme to obtain financial support from its own national executive, elected and appointed party officials (*Globe and Mail*, 20 June 1988, A3). Alfred Apps, the Toronto lawyer heading the fund drive, secured a commitment of $600 from each of the 40 members of the national executive and, according to a newspaper article, intended to ask the same of the "more than 1 000 elected and appointed officials in the party" (ibid.). In addition, members of the party at all levels were asked to contribute $100 each to the party's election readiness fund. This "Popular Campaign" generated a net revenue of $116 843 according to party records (see table 5.6).

Corporate donations were especially difficult to raise prior to the 1988 general election because of the party's stance on free trade. Frank Stronach, organizer of the 1988 Confederation Dinner, admitted that "it's a little more cumbersome than it would have been in other years," and Elvio DelZotto, president of the Ontario association, confirmed this, stating "I'm not going to say it doesn't have an impact"

(*Globe and Mail*, 27 June 1988, A1). Some business executives who had been long-time Liberal supporters were angered by Turner's impassioned attacks on the Free Trade Agreement and made it clear that they were supporting the Progressive Conservative party (*Financial Times*, 26 September 1988, 9). The problems in fund-raising were magnified in part because the Liberal party has been generally more dependent on corporate funds than the Progressive Conservative party (see chap. 11).

5.7 New Chief Financial Officer/New Policies in 1988

The Liberal party announced in August 1988 that party president Michel Robert was being replaced by Michael Robinson as chief financial officer of the party. Mr. Robinson, president of the Public Affairs Resource Group and a long-time party worker, was also appointed as head of the Financial Management Committee. Mr. Robinson immediately began to take a series of steps to improve the Liberal party's finances. He negotiated with the bank holding the party's major debt an agreement under which the 1988 general election campaign would be financed. Expenditure limits were established and the bank was given first claim on both the federal reimbursement of 22.5 percent of the party's "election expenses" and the 50 percent "tax" to be imposed by headquarters on the candidates' reimbursement of their "election expenses." Second, Mr. Robinson began enunciating a new philosophy under which LPC headquarters and the party's PTAs and riding associations would each have certain exclusive revenue sources with which to finance their expenditures. In other words, Robinson wanted to disentangle much of the intraparty financial flows so that headquarters would begin to have revenue sources commensurate with its responsibilities. The third element of Robinson's new strategy was to significantly reduce the LPC's debt by raising revenues and reducing expenditures. Robinson was to institute further changes in 1989.

For the November 1988 general election, the Liberal party spent $6.84 million on "election expenses," well below its statutory limit of $7.98 million. The NDP spent more on "election expenses" ($7.06 million) than the Liberal party. In 1988, the Liberal party had total revenues of $17.9 million, including $1.54 million in rebates on its party election expenses from the federal government, and $2.27 million as its 50 percent share of the reimbursement of *candidates'* election expenses. Total expenditures in 1988, including transfers of $2.57 million to PTAs and local riding associations, were $17.0 million. As a result, the Liberal party had a surplus of $882 000 in 1988 (see table 5.1).

The scale of the Liberal party's financial operations in 1988 was dwarfed by the Progressive Conservative party's gross revenues of

$27.0 million and total expenditures of $29.0 million. The greatest differential between the Liberals and the Tories in 1988 was in their regular operating expenses (i.e., excluding "election expenses"). The Liberal party's outlays fell from $7.64 million in 1987 to $6.95 million in 1988 and $5.5 million in 1989. In comparison, the Conservative party's operating expenses rose from $11.5 million in 1987 to $17.8 million in 1988, and fell to $10.7 million in 1989.

Effective 1 January 1989, the headquarters of the Liberal party gained *exclusive* use of the following sources of revenues: donations from the Revenue Committee's list of large firms; the Laurier Club; nationwide direct mail; and leader's dinners. PTAs and riding associations were given exclusive use of the following revenue sources: door-to-door canvassing; solicitation of individuals, and small- and medium-sized businesses; membership dues; local dinners and social events; and direct mail within their own area.

Early in 1989 the party's financial situation looked a little brighter. The election campaign cost several hundred thousand dollars *less* than anticipated (*Globe and Mail*, 9 January 1989, A11). Riding associations were given more incentive to raise more money, particularly from individuals. In fact, from their own sources the PTAs and riding associations were allowed to keep 100 percent of the money raised – even if they used the federal tax credit. Party officials indicated that more effort would be put into direct mail in an effort to catch up with other parties, particularly the Conservatives (see chap. 9).

5.8   Chrétien Becomes Leader

The national convention scheduled for October 1989 in Calgary at which there was to be a vote for or against a leadership review had to be rescheduled in light of John Turner's announcement on 3 May 1989 that he was resigning as leader. The Liberal party's 1989 policy convention thus became a leadership convention on 20–23 June 1990. Jean Chrétien, who had been runner-up to John Turner in 1984, won the leadership on the first ballot with 2 652 votes versus 1 176 for Paul Martin, MP and son of a former cabinet minister, 499 for MP Sheila Copps, 267 for Tom Wappel, an anti-abortion activist and Toronto MP, and 64 for MP John Nunziata.

With the aid of additional data provided by the Liberal party, it is possible to examine the financing of the 1990 leadership race and convention. The candidates together reportedly spent $6 million, of which the winner spent $2.45 million (table 5.8).[57] (While the party had put a limit of $1.7 million on candidates' expenditures, the limit excluded certain expenditures, including the "tax" on candidates' revenues imposed by the party itself (see appendix 13.1 in chapter 13).) In addition, the Liberal party spent $4.586 million on the convention (as reported to the CEO; $4.4 million per table 5.8). However, the convention broke even (table 5.8), in part because the delegates' fees were treated as contributions for which a tax receipt was issued. Therefore, the cost of the leadership race and convention was about $10.5 million. To put this in perspective, note that the Liberal party's non-convention-related revenues in 1990 totalled $5.7 million (table 5.2a). This figure does not include the $608 151 generated by the tax on part of the leadership candidates' expenditures, the convention fees, or the $1.95 million in contributions to candidates routed through the Federal Liberal Agency. Tax receipts were issued for such contributions, so federal taxpayers subsidized both the delegates to the leadership convention and some contributions to the candidates.

The financial pressures on the Liberal party continued in 1990. A newspaper report in November 1990 indicated that the new leader had ordered each of the 80 MPs to raise $10 000 for the party (*Globe and Mail*, 17 November 1990, A1–2). The party was said to have a debt of $3.7 million, and fund-raising was proving to be difficult in the face of a recession after an extraordinarily expensive leadership campaign. Noncorporate contributions were said to be especially low. Mr. Chrétien's fund-raising brunch in Montreal in October "was not a sell out and he [was] not likely to reach the goal of 1 500 tickets at $500 each, at the [Confederation] dinner in Toronto" later in November. Regardless of the problems, the brunch generated $65 000 in net revenue, while the Confederation Dinner netted $320 000 (see chap. 10).

In 1990, the Liberal party grossed $1.7 million from its direct-mail appeals, including a year-end campaign that generated $175 000. Donations from Quebec – where Jean Chrétien had been subject to strong political and editorial criticism – were said to be comparable to other regions. The party was able to reduce its debt by about $1 million to $3.8 million at the end of 1990. There was grumbling about the new leader's edict that all Liberal MPs or their riding associations were to give $12 000 to party headquarters before the summer of 1991, while other ridings were to give $4 000. This scheme was intended to generate $1.85 million for headquarters. Corporate donations were down in 1990, "probably because of aggressive corporate fundraising among the three leading contenders in [the 1990] Liberal leadership race," according to Sheila Gervais, secretary-general of the party (*Globe and Mail*, 26 February 1991, A6).

In January 1991, the LPC's national executive made some changes designed to better coordinate the revenue-raising and expenditure activities in the party. The Revenue Committee (which consists of the chief national fund-raisers in the 12 PTAs) is now required to establish a fund-raising plan and targets. The anticipated level of revenue establishes the limit for total expenditures. The Management Committee sets the priorities for the party for the same fiscal period. The rest of the process is outlined as follows:

> The revenue projections and overall priorities are then turned over to the [Financial Management Committee of 17 persons] which, led by the Chief Financial Officer, negotiates the level of funding available to each sector of the Party. The Management Committee then reviews the work of the FMC and recommends final budgetary numbers to the National Executive ...
>
> The budgets of the PTAs are based on various factors related to the needs and financial status of the Party in each province or territory. In most cases, the amount of the LPC transfer [which totalled $630 000 in 1991] is tied to a Revenue Committee Fundraising target in that PTA ... Once disbursed, the allocation of these funds within the province or territory is the responsibility of the PTA. Except in Alberta, Ontario, Quebec and British Columbia, there is no way of knowing whether the funds are being used for national or provincial purposes. (Liberal Party of Canada, Reform Commission 1991, 12–13)

In January 1991, Donald Johnston, president of the LPC, announced plans to cut in half the $3.7 million debt[58] of the Liberal Party of Canada (*Globe and Mail,* 21 January 1991, A4). He said that the annual cost of servicing the debt was about $500 000 (see table 5.9). To reduce the debt, the party planned to raise more money (about $6 million to $7 million) rather than to cut expenditures by going after its traditional sources "in a very systematic way," said Mr. Johnston. In February 1991, Senator Leo Kolber was appointed as chair of the Revenue Committee. It had been restructured by Johnston to establish national committees for each of the main headquarters' revenue sources (Treasury Committee list, Laurier Club, direct mail and leader's dinners). Each committee was to have a mirror committee in each of the 12 PTAs. Further, the Laurier Club was being revitalized (see chap. 10).

The Reform Commission of the LPC (1991, 15), whose Interim Report was published in July 1991, identified two major concerns with party fund-raising: "the decreasing level of funds which are being raised and the dependence of the Party on corporations for a large proportion of its financing." The commission noted that the Conservative party had generated several times as much net revenue from direct mail as had the Liberal party (see chap. 9). The Reform Commission stated that the changes made in recent years in fund-raising responsibilities and intra-party financial arrangements remained the focus of some criticisms. For example, it was suggested to the Commission that

> the current split of funds raised at the riding level creates a disincentive in constituency associations to raise more money between general elections. It is argued that many constituency associations are not inclined to raise funds in non-election years when any funds raised are subject to a sharing formula with the provincial associations, preferring instead to concentrate their fundraising during the election writ period when they are entitled to keep 100 percent of the funds they raise. (Liberal Party of Canada, Reform Commission 1991, 17)

Thus, some of the major problems that had afflicted the Liberal party in the late 1970s remained in 1991, albeit to a lesser degree. The party's federated structure continued to shape its financing.

In 1991, the Liberal party raised $7.2 million and spent virtually the same amount so that it had a surplus of only $7 000. It collected $3.35 million from 26 396 individuals and $3.41 million from 3 799 business organizations (table 3.1A). Operating expenditures totalled $14.8 million in 1991, including $553 000 in interest on its debts. In addition, the party transferred $1.23 million to its constituencies and $1.17 million to provincial and other party organizations (annual return filed with the CEO). While total revenues were up over 1990 (when the 1990 figures are adjusted for the leadership race and convention), the party was not able to generate a sizeable surplus to be used to pay down its debt.

A newspaper report indicated that the Liberal party's budget for 1992 was about $2.9 million, of which $500 000 was earmarked to reduce the party's substantial debt (*Vancouver Sun*, 2 January 1992, A3). Thus, it is very likely that the Liberal party will spend substantively less in 1992 than will the Reform Party, which raised $6.6 million in 1991 and spent $6.3 million (see chap. 7).

6. CONCLUSIONS

The Liberal party held power for two-thirds of the 17-year period for which we have data on the financing of parties (and candidates) under the reforms instituted effective 1 August 1974. Yet while it was in power, the Liberal party did not dominate the Conservative party in terms of its ability to raise and spend money on nonelection activities (the parties have been fairly evenly matched on official "election expenses"). In terms of *total* party revenues in 1989 dollars, the two parties raised the following amounts while the Liberals were in power and then while the Conservatives were in power (computed from table 3.8):

Period	Liberal	Progressive Conservative
1974–78 (Lib.)	$40.2 million	$36.9 million
1980–84 (Lib.)	$57.9 million	$84.6 million
1985–90 (PC)	$70.3 million	$98.2 million

These figures indicate that in the period after the *Election Expenses Act* came into effect and before the Clark government came to power, the Liberal party raised some 9 percent more than the Progressive Conservative party. However, during the last Trudeau government (1980–84) the Liberal party raised 31.6 percent *less* than the amount raised by the opposition Progressive Conservative party. Moreover, in absolute terms, the difference was almost $27 million in 1989 dollars. The Conservative party raised $28 million more than the Liberal party during the period 1985–90.

Then, when the Liberals under John Turner's leadership fell from electoral grace in September 1984, matters got worse in terms of raising and spending money between election years, and on operating expenses other than official "election expenses" in election years. Indeed, the Liberal party's fiscal problems were such that, in 1988, its "election expenses" were only 85 percent of the statutory limit and in absolute terms were below those of the NDP. Between 1985 and 1989, the Liberal party's total revenues in 1989 dollars were $54.5 million, versus $92.9 million for the Tories (computed from table 3.8).[59] The Liberals' expenditures, excluding "election expenses" over the same period, were $50.4 million in 1989 dollars, as compared to $79.7 million for the Conservative party.[60]

The Liberal party's failure to dominate the Conservatives in terms of party financing even while in power reflects a number of structural features of the party and its assumption that, as the "natural governing party," it had little need to change its methods of raising money. Further, while the Treasury (now Revenue) Committee had a list of major firms to be contacted for donations, not all the firms on it were approached for funds on a regular basis. The party failed to expand its funding base, most notably by failing to create a major direct-mail effort before 1986.

The critical structural problem for the Liberal party appears to lie in its organizational design: it is a federation of 12 PTAs, 8 of which have "divided loyalties," i.e., they seek to elect both federal MPs and provincial members. In effect, the Liberals have failed to build a distinct federal party beyond its provincial and territorial associations, particularly the "dual purpose" ones. It has been suggested that the party was very successful in gaining and retaining office for many years at the federal level because voters were able to identify with particular leaders (e.g., St-Laurent and Trudeau), rather than because of the effectiveness and support of its component PTAs. In terms of building a national, centrally controlled party, the Liberals were hampered greatly because the Ottawa office did not (and still does not) have a national membership list or even have access to those of the PTAs because of the party's federal structure.[61] Although Raymond Garneau persuaded the LPC (Quebec) in 1988 to vote 72 to 3 in favour of giving its membership list to national headquarters, this was not, in fact, done. Moreover, there has been a lack of clarity in the roles and responsibilities of the organizational units in the party: national headquarters, PTAs and riding associations. This is compounded by a failure to match fund-raising abilities and spending responsibilities for each unit, or to work out stable arrangements for the movement of funds among the component parts of the organization. The arrangements have sometimes been vague and they have been subject to change in order to reduce conflict. (In this sense, they mirror the nature of federal-provincial fiscal arrangements.)

The Liberal party's financial woes from 1984 through 1988, which stemmed in large part from the large deficit in 1984 ($5.3 million), were exacerbated by a number of factors. First, the almost regular threats to John Turner's leadership reduced the public's confidence in the party and hence their willingness to contribute to a party that was in disarray. The party's low standing in the polls (this was partly a reflection of the well-publicized threats to Turner's leadership) made it much more difficult to raise funds. Second, a large amount of party money was devoted to supporting the Leader's Office – at a time when the party was raising less money than it spent. Third, there were numerous changes in senior party personnel during the Turner years. This is both cause and effect of the party's problems. Confusion and conflict at the top levels of the party were exacerbated, in turn, by the huge debt, poor revenues and the need to make cuts in expenditures. Conflict delayed the cuts until 1987 and 1988. Fourth, the Liberal party's direct-mail solicitations, which began in earnest only in 1986, generated only one-fifth to one-tenth of the net revenue that the same technique generated for the Conservative party (see chap. 9). Fifth, in the wake of the 1984 debacle, there were strong grass-roots pressures to increase participation and consultation, although the reform process had begun earlier. The democratization and reform of the Liberal party resulted in the establishment in 1988 of some 19 committees, each with an average membership of 15. A substantial amount of money went to support the committees and new groups within the party.[62] Sixth, the Liberal party had almost no experience in Opposition prior to 1984. Because of the many years in government, the party's financing and organizational machinery had atrophied, as many of its functions as an "election machine" had been taken over by the PMO. By not being "in the wilderness," the party did not go through a process of organizational renewal that included the adoption of new techniques to raise money. "The [Liberal] party suffers from years in government when popular fundraising was not necessary. We never learned how to do it," according to Donald Johnston, who became president of the LPC in 1990 (*Maclean's*, 10 December 1990, 20). Seventh, the fact that the Liberal party had two leadership races (1984, 1990) while the Conservative party had only one (1983) during the same period absorbed about $10 million which might well have been used to finance the party. Eighth, the Liberals adopted a number of policy positions that probably adversely affected the party's ability to raise money. The most obvious was (and is) its opposition to the Canada–U.S. Free Trade Agreement. While John Turner's impassioned criticism of the FTA during the leaders' television debates in the 1988 election campaign increased support for the Liberals, the party's position announced in 1987 (including the use of its majority in the Senate to push the Conservative party into an election before it was enacted) no doubt alienated business firms. Yet the Liberal party was (and is) more dependent upon donations from business than is the Conservative party, which through direct mail receives more money from individuals. Also, the Liberals' internal conflict over their position on the Meech Lake Accord not only demoralized traditional supporters who believed in a strong central government and no "special treatment" for Quebec, but also probably hindered fund-raising because of doubts about the party's ability to "manage itself" and to form an effective government.

Can the Liberal party restore its electoral and fiscal fortunes? Joseph Wearing has examined the history of the Liberal party over several decades prior to 1980. He offered the following observation on its cycles of decline and renewal:

> Looking at the history of the Liberal party in perspective, one can clearly see a cyclical pattern of decay and renewal; the decay coming after a number of years in power and the renewal prompted by electoral defeat, either threatened or actual. During the periods of decline, the parliamentary party and the leader have become progressively more isolated from opinion in the party and in the country at large, while the volunteer or extra-parliamentary wings have grown disillusioned and uninterested. The sobering reality of electoral losses has then prompted the parliamentary leadership to take the volunteer wing more seriously. (Wearing 1981, 235)

There are clear signs that the renewal phase was well under way with a series of changes made in the period 1987–90:

- In 1987, the tax-receipting process was centralized (when it was taken away from the agents in the 12 provinces/territories).
- Each organizational sub-unit was required to present a proposed budget for review by a committee at party headquarters.
- Beginning in 1989, closer links were forged between efforts to raise money and control party expenditures through the party's chief financial officer.
- After 1988, the amount of money transferred from the party to the Leader's Office was greatly reduced (table 5.4).
- In 1988, "election expenses" were held down to the amount of revenue that could be raised (in fact, there was a respectable surplus in that year).
- In 1988, all candidates were required to turn over 50 percent of the reimbursement of their "election expenses" to party headquarters.
- Effective 1 January 1989, the headquarters of the Liberal party gained *exclusive* use of the following sources of revenues: the Revenue Committee's list of large firms, the Laurier Club, nationwide direct mail and leader's dinners. PTAs and riding associations were given exclusive use of the following revenue sources: door-to-door canvassing, solicitation of individuals and small- and medium-sized businesses, membership dues, local dinners, social events and direct mail within their own area.
- In 1990, the new leader strongly encouraged MPs and other ridings to transfer funds to headquarters.
- In July 1990, the Reform Commission published its Interim Report.
- In 1989 and 1990, the Liberal party's debt was reduced substantially.

However, it is not clear that the Liberal Party of Canada has the capability of raising money between election years on a scale that is closely comparable to the Progressive Conservative party. Moreover, both parties face more competition, notably from the Reform Party, which has been rapidly growing in terms of both membership and financing (see chap. 7).

6

NEW
DEMOCRATIC
PARTY

1. INTRODUCTION

Because the *Election Expenses Act* of 1974 was enacted by a minority Liberal government dependent upon the support of the New Democratic Party, the latter's MPs were able to influence the legislation in ways that particularly helped their party: the criteria for reimbursement of part of each party's "election expenses"; the size of the tax credits for contributions; and the lowering of the threshold for reimbursement of candidates' "election expenses" to 15 percent of the votes (recall chap. 2). Because a very high proportion of contributions to the NDP are less than $100, the party and its candidates benefit from the highest rate of subsidization (75 percent) by federal taxpayers in terms of the tax credit. On the other hand, the trade unions and other labour organizations that provide substantial funds for the NDP (particularly in election years) cannot claim the tax credit. At the same time, the *dues* paid by members to their unions are tax-deductible expenses.

As we shall see, of all of the major parties the NDP has the most complex (and dynamic) set of intraparty flows of financial resources, and of human resources in the form of election organizers. This is a reflection of the integrated nature of the party, its philosophy of redistribution from units with more resources to those with less, and a desire to maximize the political effectiveness of the party's traditionally scarce resources.

This chapter is organized as follows. Section 2 provides a very brief review of the history and expenditures of the CCF/NDP prior to 1974. Section 3 examines the organizational structure of the party and how it influences the way the NDP is financed. Section 4 describes the important ways in which the NDP responded to the *Election Expenses Act* of 1974.

Section 5 describes and tries to sort out the complex flows of funds within the party. Revenues and expenditures are analysed in section 6, including the ways in which the federal office is financed. Section 7 examines the role of trade unions in financing the NDP, while section 8 reviews the very modest role of corporate contributions. Section 9 is devoted to elections, and describes changes in the party's campaign practices and how federal elections are financed by the NDP. Finally, the conclusions are set out in section 10.

2. THE EARLY PERIOD

The Cooperative Commonwealth Federation, predecessor to the NDP, was established in 1932 when western agrarian parties combined forces with several labour groups and other political organizations from eastern Canada. Soon the intellectuals of the League for Social Reconstruction took an active role in the new party (Young 1969). The CCF's political strength lay at the provincial level in Saskatchewan, BC and Ontario. The structure was decentralized, and fund-raising was centred on the constituency – very largely provincial rather than federal constituencies (Seidle 1980, 165–66).[1]

The NDP, which replaced the CCF, was formed in 1961 (Young 1969). Its structure provided for union locals to affiliate with the party and to provide ongoing financial support for it. In addition, an accord with the provincial parties gave the federal office sole access to the national offices of the party's trade union affiliates to collect funds for federal election campaigns (Seidle 1980, 166). Moreover, the unions' affiliation dues were an important source of funds for the federal office between elections. Seidle suggests that the NDP and the CCF "existed in a sense as the 'creature' of the provincial parties. The NDP's success in federal elections has been closely related to the strength of the various provincial parties" (ibid., 249), notably those in Saskatchewan, Manitoba, BC and Ontario. It was not until 1974 that the NDP elected an MP in Nova Scotia, and it elected its first MP in Newfoundland in 1979. It did not elect its first MP from Quebec until it was successful in a 1990 by-election, despite a major effort in the 1988 general election.

The total expenditures of the NDP's federal office grew from $164 122 in 1965 to $207 251 in 1968, but fell back to $165 300 in 1970 (all in nominal dollars), although it should be noted that 1965 and 1968 were election years. Expenditures grew unevenly to $279 700 in 1974 (Paltiel 1974, 1975). The NDP's expenditures on federal election campaigns between 1962 and 1968 ranged from $162 000 (1963) to $569 000 (1968) (Paltiel 1970b, 1975). The party's election expenditures in 1974, the last year prior to the reforms embodied in the *Election Expenses Act*, were only \$354 000,[2] or about \$1 million in 1989 dollars. In the 1988 election, as we shall describe in detail below, the NDP spent just over \$7 million on "election expenses" – more than the Liberal party.

3. STRUCTURE OF THE PARTY

In seeking to understand the financial operations of the NDP, it is useful to begin with a brief discussion of its unique organizational structure. In the NDP, financial flows (mapped in figure 6.1) reflect the party's organization, and the organization strongly reflects the party's origins and the success of particular provincial sections. Dyck states:

> The NDP is by far the most integrated of the three main Canadian political parties. Its national predecessor, the CCF, was literally a federation of provincial parties after 1938 (Young 1969), and the NDP maintains this structure in many ways. Its constitution does not use the term "federation," but it does provide for a fully autonomous provincial party in each province. While there [may be] no provincial party representation on the federal executive, the leader, president, secretary, and treasurer of each provincial [or territorial] section sit on the federal council. (1989, 207)[3]

> One joins the NDP in one's province of residence, and this entails an automatic membership in the national party as well. The relative vitality of federal and provincial constituency associations varies across the country, and, at least in the western half, the provincial ridings have traditionally been the party's centres of gravity. However, even in the three provinces where it has held power – Manitoba, Saskatchewan and British Columbia – there are now separate federal and provincial riding associations of about equal strength and activity. (1989, 208)

The NDP is the most "integrated" party in the sense of combining the twin foci of electing provincial members and electing federal MPs.[4] Terry Morley's description of the situation in BC is appropriate for the rest of the nation – except Quebec:

> There is but one New Democratic Party in British Columbia, and the modes of provincial and federal activity are never permitted to diverge. Any person joining the British Columbia New Democrats is also considered to be a member of the New Democratic Party of Canada. Those who toil in the service of the party must work in the interests of candidates both for the legislature and for Parliament. It is seen as right and proper so to do. The idea is one social democracy under two leaders. (1991, 100)

Figure 6.1
Flows of funds relating to New Democratic Party and its candidates

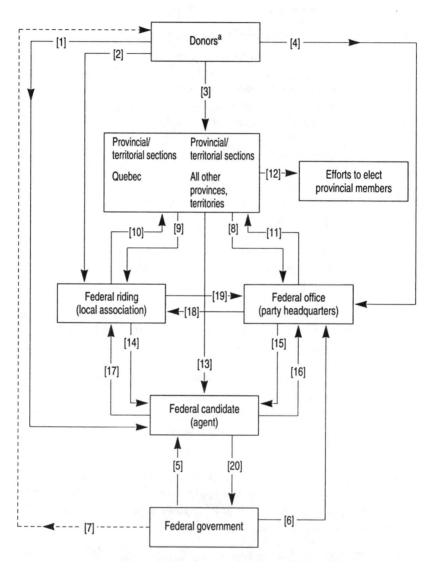

Notes: Excludes financing of campaigns for party leadership or nomination campaigns.

[a]Includes individuals, corporations, trade unions, interest groups and other organizations.

Prior to the constitutional changes made in December 1989, two-thirds of the 150 members of the NDP's chief governing body, the Federal Council, were individuals wearing a "provincial hat." The membership of the Federal Council was as follows:

- 50 members from among party officers, nationally elected, and from affiliates;
- 48 members from 12 PTSs, all ex-officio; and
- 48 members elected at PTS conventions, including youth and women delegates.

The composition of the Federal Council was changed in December 1989 to include the following:

- 36 members, 3 from each PTS;
- 12 women delegates, 1 from each of the 12 PTSs;
- 12 youth delegates, 1 from each of the PTSs;
- 24 members, 2 from each PTS convention;
- 60 members from the 12 Councils of Federal Riding Associations; and
- 6 representatives of the parliamentary caucus.

In other words, prior to 1990 neither the parliamentary caucus nor federal ridings were directly represented on the NDP's highest governing body. The previous composition of the national Council reflected the origins and provincial focus of the party, as did its financing.

At the 1989 Convention of the NDP, article XII was added to the party's constitution. Clause c of article XII states that "[f]or the purposes of federal individual membership in the province of Quebec, membership shall be open to every resident of Quebec, regardless of race, colour, religion, sex or national origin, who undertakes to accept and abide by the constitution and principles of the Federal Party and who is not a member or supporter of any other federal political party." In March 1991, the general council of the federal NDP severed the "fraternal ties between it and the NDP of Quebec." In July 1990, the latter had endorsed the sovereigntist Bloc québécois in a by-election. The federal NDP has about 1 500 members and the provincial party has about 550 in Quebec (*Globe and Mail*, 12 March 1991, A4).

It is hard to escape the conclusion that the federal wing of the party is still largely controlled by the party's provincial and territorial sections which created it. This is because of the strength of the NDP in BC (the party formed the government in 1972 and 1991), in Ontario (where it first formed a government in 1990), in Saskatchewan (where it has elected a number of provincial governments since 1944, including one in 1991) and in Manitoba (where the party has been a force since it first formed a government in 1969). At the federal level, the NDP's ability to elect MPs has been concentrated in less than 100 key ridings in the same provinces.

Between elections, the federal office in Ottawa delegates to the PTSs its tax-receipting authority, and receives 15 percent of the money raised by them. The PTSs use this power to raise money, most of which stays at the PTS level, and only a fraction of which finds its way through the labyrinthine set of intraparty transfers to either federal ridings or to the national office.[5] Although there is now a Council of Federal Riding Associations in each province and territory, it has no authority to issue federal tax receipts and hence no ability to raise money strictly for the federal wing, whether at the riding level or for the federal office. The result is that the federal office, directly or indirectly, receives only a fraction of the revenues generated through the use of the federal tax credit for political contributions. (For example, in 1990, total federal revenues were $8.6 million, of which $7.4 million came from federally receipted contributions, but of this the federal office received only $2.7 million.) Very few of the senior officials in the Ottawa office know how much money for which federal tax credit receipts have been issued ends up being used to try to elect provincial MLAs. They were surprised by the data set out in table 6.4. On the basis of the score of interviews conducted with party officials for this study, it appears that few officials are concerned about the use of the federal receipting power to solicit contributions that are subsequently used to finance the party's activities at the provincial, or even at the *local*, level.

4. RESPONSE TO THE 1974 LEGISLATION

Virtually all senior officials in the three major parties agree that the NDP has benefited the most from the *Election Expenses Act* of 1974. When the legislation was enacted, the NDP saw immediately the potential of the tax credit as a way to raise much more money from individuals. According to Robin Sears, then a senior party official, the NDP was better able to adapt to the new provisions for the following reasons:

> There is the unitary structure of our party – we do not have independent provincial and federal organizations anywhere. We convened a meeting in Halifax in the fall of [1974] to say, OK, is everyone going to play by these rules? Yes. Then every dollar raised by the party for any purpose is going to come under the purview of this legislation? Yes. Every dollar therefore will be taxed. So that where we have a powerful provincial organization but are weaker federally, we benefit.

> Conversely, where we have a strong incumbent federal MP, as was
> the case in Newfoundland, his association with the provincial party
> benefitted them provincially. ("Round Table" 1981, 11)

The tax credit for political contributions created "instant affluence" for
the NDP. Sears said in 1981 that "we're among the biggest beneficiaries
… we went from average expenditures on local campaigns of $2 to
3 thousand to $12 to 15 thousand currently, our national budget multi-
plied five times, the staff in my office multiplied four times" ("Round
Table" 1981, 9, 11).

However, the prospect of interprovincial and federal-provincial
transfers of funds within the party prompted a legislative response in
Ontario. "It is widely felt that the NDP's decision to use the federal tax
credit for provincial purposes helped bring about the passage of the
Election Finances Reform Act in Ontario in 1975" (Seidle 1980, 253).
This legislation prohibited transfers (except for small amounts during
elections) from a federal registered party to any registered entity in
Ontario: candidate, party or local (riding) association. Seidle and Paltiel
explain how the NDP adapted to the 1974 legislation:

> The NDP was able to fit the financial provisions of the 1974 changes
> into its party structure by deciding to use the tax credit for both federal
> and provincial purposes. In this way, party members whose primary
> loyalty was to the provincial organization could raise funds, with the
> tax credit's incentive, and help both the provincial and the federal levels
> of the party. A decision made when the legislation came into effect
> was that 15 percent of all money raised, anywhere in the party, would
> go to the federal office. The remaining 85 percent is returned to the
> appropriate province and divided among the provincial office and the
> federal and provincial ridings from which it originated. The formulas
> vary from province to province, but it is fair to say that over half of
> what is returned to the province goes, at least initially, to the provin-
> cial party office or the appropriate provincial riding. (1981, 246–47)

The extensive use of the tax credit had some effects that some senior
party officials have found disturbing. It increased the role of paid professionals versus volunteers between elections. Indeed, it made it possible
to expand greatly the scope and scale of party activities between elections, although the NDP has not been able to match the level of expenditures of the Liberal party and particularly of the Progressive
Conservative party. However, in the 1988 general election, the NDP
spent *more* than the Liberals and moved within a few percentage points

of the statutory limit. As the party is perceived to be more affluent, some officials indicate that it has become harder to recruit volunteers at the riding level, where they play the largest role. As more union and party staffers have come from the "outside" to take the key positions in local campaigns, there is a tendency for local volunteers to withdraw. Further, it has been suggested that people are less inclined to donate if all the party wants is their money – and not their help as a volunteer. A somewhat different view is expressed by other experienced party organizers. They argue that with the growth in the number of two-income households, it is harder to recruit volunteers, but people are quite willing to donate as a way of supporting their party (aided by the tax credit of $75 on the first $100). Further, there is a danger that, as more money is available to finance paid campaign workers, volunteers will become less involved. Given the tight constraints on "election expenses" at the candidate level, this seems unlikely, however.

5. INTRAPARTY FINANCIAL FLOWS

The relationship between the financing of federal and provincial parties/candidates in Canada is complicated by two factors: first, whether or not a province has its own income-tax credit for political contributions; and, second, whether rules exist that govern the flow of funds into or out of a province raised using the provincial or federal tax credit. In 1991, the situation was as follows:

- Only Saskatchewan and Newfoundland do *not* have provincial tax credits (i.e., in those provinces the party cannot issue receipts for tax credits or deductions for political contributions to provincial parties/candidates).
- Ontario, New Brunswick and Alberta have legislation prohibiting the transfer of money raised provincially (using provincial receipts) to be used federally, and vice versa.
- Manitoba, Nova Scotia and BC are more permissive about flows between the provincial and federal levels.

In general, the NDP's stated approach to financing the party is that money should flow from the riding or constituency level up to the provincial section, and then up to the federal level. Therefore, it is only necessary to send money from the federal office down to a PTS where the party is weak in that province. Historically, the party's capacity to raise money for elections has been greatest at the riding level, although the party has made extensive use of direct mail between elections. In Manitoba, Nova Scotia and BC, for example, contributions to the NDP, which must be made through a PTS, are divided, and a federal receipt is issued for one part of the contribution and a provincial receipt for the other part. This is done so as to maximize the total value of tax credits available to the individual, and hence to encourage larger contributions to the party. For example, Roger Howard, the treasurer for the BC section, has used a computer algorithm to divide each individual's contributions to the party so as to maximize the value of the total federal plus provincial tax credits to the person. For example, if a person has contributed $200 to the party, he/she would receive a provincial income-tax credit of $75 and a federal income-tax credit of $75. If the person received only a single receipt from either government, the total value of the credit would be $125 rather than $150 (Morley 1991).

In 1988, the BC section of the NDP raised $4 million. Of this amount, 43.7 percent was federally receipted and 55.5 percent was provincially receipted (see table 6.1). In 1989 and 1990, the fraction of BC sectional revenue that was federally receipted dropped to 27.1 percent and 29.6 percent respectively. The reason that the percentage was higher in 1988 is that, during the federal election, a considerable part of the revenue consisted of donations specifically earmarked for federal candidates.

For the NDP as a whole, it is very difficult to separate the various levels of the party in accounting terms, because ridings have quotas of funds to be raised, which are then transferred to both the provincial and the federal level, and because each PTS outside Quebec has dual responsibilities (figure 6.1). Moreover, there is a rough form of "equalization" across provinces to reflect the differential strength of the party and hence the ability to raise money. In general, Ontario, Manitoba, Saskatchewan, Alberta and BC subsidize the operations of the NDP both federally and provincially in the rest of the country. While described by party officials themselves as "byzantine," the system "works," according to one senior official, because it is flexible (there are many *different* agreements between the federal office and PTSs), and because it allows individuals and organizational units to participate at more than one level. Redistribution within the NDP is made more difficult, but is not stopped, by the fact that in Ontario, New Brunswick and Alberta legislation prevents federal-provincial financial flows in both directions. Ways are found to achieve the party's objectives by other means.[6]

The integration of the NDP in terms of financial flows between the federal office and the provincial sections has been described as follows:

> The NDP is also uniquely integrated in its finances. To a large extent, the federal party is financed by its provincial wings, and the latter are obliged to send the former 15 percent of all provincial monies received,

plus 60 percent of [union] affiliation fees. How the 15 percent is raised varies from one provincial party to another. In some cases, the membership fee is split among federal, provincial and/or constituency parties, but in such provinces as Ontario, New Brunswick, and Alberta, legislation now prohibits the direct cross-level flow of funds. The Ontario party manages to fulfil its federal commitment by sending all affiliation fees to the federal party (not just 60 percent) and sets up a federal account in its guise as a branch of the federal party, raising money in other ways to make up the difference. From time to time, a provincial wing falls into arrears with the federal party, especially in the wake of a provincial election, but no branch has been chronically delinquent. Although it draws from its provincial wings, the national NDP in turn assists provincial parties, especially in Atlantic Canada and more recently in Quebec. (Dyck 1989, 209)[7]

This account fails to emphasize the use of the federal tax credit by PTS and riding associations who, in effect, pay the federal office only 15 percent of what they raise.[8] It also ignores the fact that part of the money raised using the federal tax credit ends up being utilized for provincial, or even municipal (not federal), politics. Further, because financial arrangements within the NDP are dynamic, this account does not recognize the fact that there are "windows" or short periods of time when a riding or PTS can keep more of the money it raises. Morley (1991, 108) notes that when pre-election windows are in effect, revenue received by an NDP riding in BC is shared as follows: 15 percent to the federal office, 25 percent to the provincial section, 30 percent to pay down the riding's election quota and 30 percent to the riding. During an election window, 40 percent goes to the PTS, while 60 percent goes to the riding, but the riding gets some cash only after its election quota has been paid. In BC, there are even election windows for municipal NDP organizations, during which they can retain 60 percent of the funds they collect instead of the normal 15 percent (ibid., 109).

The NDP's official agent in the federal office appoints an official agent in each of the provincial sections. Each agent has the authority to issue receipts that can be used to claim the federal tax credit for political contributions. Within each PTS, all "receiptable" fund-raising passes through the PTS's agent (including that at the riding level) between elections. In general, the candidate's agent collects money for the campaign in the riding, although in 1988 in BC all candidates' revenues had to flow through the PTS. In general, 15 percent of funds raised through the PTS (both provincially and federally receipted revenues) is supposed to go to the federal office, while the balance is divided between the PTS and the riding in different ways.[9] There have been some exceptions to this general rule[10] – and these have been a source of persistent conflict within the party. For example, some provincial sections have been very slow to remit the 15 percent to the federal office. In BC, Saskatchewan and Manitoba the PTS ran a lottery whose expenses are not revenue-shared, and some PTSs were unable to cover their own operating and electoral expenses,[11] so they did not pay the 15 percent. In the late 1980s, the party's financial strength lay in BC, Saskatchewan, Manitoba and Ontario.

The sources of funds for the NDP's federal office in the 1980s (excluding general elections) were as follows: 60 percent of the affiliation dues from those unions affiliated with the party; 15 percent of every dollar raised at the local or PTS level, whether federally or provincially receipted; 100 percent of direct-mail solicitations (but some PTSs were also active in such appeals); and 100 percent of fund-raising events (e.g., dinners at which the leader spoke – a very modest source of funds). It is clear that the federal office of the NDP has been – to a surprising degree – dependent upon transfers from PTSs. It could control expenditures, but it had far less control over its sources of revenues. The federal office's 15 percent share has not been paid during provincial election campaigns, even if federal tax receipts were issued for donations. To finance federal election campaigns, the federal office received transfers from the PTSs, each of which negotiated a "quota" (or agreed payment) with Ottawa.[12] As explained in more detail below, the PTSs have in some cases collected part of their federal quota by "taxing" a portion of the federal government's reimbursement of half of candidates' "election expenses" – see section 9 below. In general, it can fairly be said that the financing of the NDP has been vastly more complex and dynamic than that of other parties since the *Election Expenses Act* of 1974 was enacted.[13]

6. PARTY REVENUES AND EXPENDITURES

This section begins by examining the finances of the NDP largely as they are reported to and by the Chief Electoral Officer. Since the late 1970s, virtually all of the revenues and expenditures of the party's PTSs have been included in the returns filed with and published by the CEO.[14] However, the CEO has not been consistent in the way he has reported several items. Provincially receipted revenues were not included in the NDP's total revenues as reported by the CEO prior to 1980, although the party provided this information to the CEO. Second, even after 1980, the CEO excluded rebates or subsidies paid to PTSs by provincial governments. However, these amounts have been included in tables 6.2 and 6.3.

6.1 The NDP as a Whole

The information on NDP finances published by the CEO that is given in tables 6.2 and 6.3 is correct, but is *not* comparable to the data published for the Liberal, Reform and Progressive Conservative parties, except for "election expenses." While the data for the Liberal, Reform and Progressive Conservative parties do fairly accurately represent the funds raised and spent for the purposes of advancing the cause of the party at the *federal* level between elections,[15] the figures for the NDP are an amalgam of revenues and expenditures raised for and spent on activities at *both* the federal and provincial level.[16] For example, while in 1989 the NDP reported to the CEO that the party had total revenues of $13.86 million and operating expenditures of $8.87 million, the *federal office* raised $2.57 million and spent $1.53 million (table 6.5). The difference is hardly trivial. While it is true that the NDP's annual filings with the CEO indicate that the return incorporates data from its provincial sections except Ontario, the information return provides only the following clues that it represents greater activity at the provincial than at the federal level:[17] $6.03 million is described as provincially receipted revenue, $3.61 million as transfers to PTSs and ridings, and $92 182 as revenue from provincial rebates and subsidies. An effort is made to distinguish the federal and provincial operations of the NDP in section 6.3.

The revenue side of the NDP as a whole greatly exaggerates the size of the party's "federal operations." For example, in 1986 and 1987, provincially receipted revenues were comparable to federally receipted revenues but, in 1990, federal revenues were substantially larger (table 6.2). As importantly, provincially receipted revenue is growing quite rapidly. For example, in 1979 it was $1.3 million, in 1984, $3.2 million and in 1990, $6.4 million (table 6.2). In 1991, provincial sections raised $9.3 million of the NDP's total revenues of $19.9 million (table 3.1a).

The composition of the NDP's revenue sources is quite different from that of its major rivals, as indicated in table 6.3. The major sources of NDP revenues are contributions from individuals and trade unions. In 1989, for example, 83.1 percent of federally receipted contributions came from individuals, and 14 percent came from trade unions. The rest came from sources for which no receipts could be issued.[18] In 1986, the comparable figures were 77.9 percent and 18.1 percent respectively, and in 1976, they were 80.4 percent from individuals and 15.3 percent from trade unions. Unfortunately, the NDP does not provide a comparable breakdown of provincially receipted revenues, but it is likely to be similar to that for federally receipted revenues. However, some provincial sections (e.g., Saskatchewan) are more willing than others to accept corporate contributions, so that source may be somewhat more important.

For the party as a whole, the NDP had a cumulative surplus of $4.1 million in the period 1974–78 (in 1989 dollars). Subsequently, the NDP as a whole ran cumulative deficits (in 1989 dollars) of $655 000 in 1979, $1.44 million in 1980–84 and $2.51 million between 1985 and 1990 (table 3.7). Table 6.2 indicates that over the past decade (1981–90), the party has had a deficit in six years, although it had a surplus of $1.36 million in 1989 and one of $1.18 million in 1990. In 1991, the party had a surplus of $1.16 million (table 3.1a).

6.2   Disaggregating the Party Data

It is critical to appreciate that, within the NDP, many key individuals wear several hats, which they switch depending upon the demands of the moment. If a provincial election is looming, they don their provincial hats and seek resources (money and skilled organizers) from other units within the party in order to achieve electoral success. When a federal election is called, they put on their federal hats and shift their focus of attention to that election.[19] Many senior officials in the NDP appear to view the party as essentially a common pool for which resources are collected at whatever level in whatever geographic area they may most easily be found. These resources are viewed by many party officials as quasi-collective bounties that may be used to best effect regardless of their origins or even of the purpose the donor intended for them. Within the party there is much argument over which organizational units should provide how much money to others needing it to achieve the party's objectives. There are strong disagreements too over which targets of expenditures are of truly strategic significance for the party – ones worthy of the expenditure of much energy and money from the limited stock of resources (organizational expertise and dollars) available.

A variety of financing issues have created controversy within the NDP. There has been conflict over the requirement that the federal office receive 15 percent of provincially receipted revenues (except during provincial elections). At the same time, federally oriented officials believe that the federal office should get more than 15 percent of federally receipted revenues. Direct-mail solicitations made by the federal office shortly before or during a provincial election campaign have been another source of conflict. There have been disputes over whether the party should accept contributions from corporations; each province has its own policy. As in the Liberal party, there has been conflict over the sharing of membership lists with the federal office. Conflict has resulted from the desire of the provincial sections for a fraction of the revenue generated by "prospect" mailings by the federal office.[20] Conflicts over the flow of money within the NDP are probably exacerbated by the fact that officials at the national and PTS levels are largely ignorant of the income statements, balance sheets and trust accounts of the riding associations, except in the case of provincial ridings in Ontario where the information must be publicly disclosed.

6.3   Federally Receipted Revenues Used to Finance Provincial Activity

To identify how much federally receipted revenue is, in fact, used to advance the party's goals at the provincial level, table 6.4 has been prepared. It identifies all federally receipted revenues[21] and other revenue received by the federal level of the NDP from 1974 to 1990, including reimbursement of party "election expenses" incurred in federal general elections. Outlays by the NDP on federal politics include the operating expenses of the party's *federal office* and the party's outlays for federal general elections. It should be noted, however, that most of the party's field organizers are on the payroll of the PTSs.[22] The organizers work on both federal and provincial ridings, as directed. Hence, the federal office's expenditures may be *understated* to the extent that these organizers work on federal ridings between or during elections.[23] Correspondingly, on the revenue side, it could be argued that the PTSs should keep a larger share of federally receipted revenues to reflect the fact that they pay for most of these organizers.

Table 6.4 reveals that the NDP's federal revenues have substantially exceeded federal expenditures (i.e., those for the purpose of electing MPs and of running the federal office) in every year since the 1974 legislation came into effect. Between 1974/75 and 1980, the difference ranged from $1.4 to $2.9 million annually. From 1981 to 1984, the difference ranged from $2.4 million to $4.8 million annually. From 1985 to 1990, the difference ranged from $2.3 million to $6.5 million annually. From 1974/75 to 1984, the excess of federal revenues over federal expenditures, that is, funds available for provincial use out of money raised using the federal income-tax credit, *exceeded* provincially receipted revenues of the NDP. In other words, the provincial sections of the NDP have been handsomely financed by federally receipted revenues. Even party officials do not know to what extent federally receipted money is used for provincial activities. When asked whether the "difference" figure in table 6.4 (except during election campaigns) went very largely to support provincial political activities, federal party officials said that it did so.

In election years, particularly in 1980, the difference between federal revenues and federal expenditures has been much lower. In election years, the NDP PTSs have been required to transfer funds to the federal level to pay for the campaign. These transfers became significant in 1984 and 1988, $1.6 million and $2.2 million respectively (see table 6.4). However, it could be argued that these sums were simply a small part of the federally receipted revenues recycled back to the federal level. But this is not the case because, in at least one province (BC), where all candidates were required to sign over *all* of the reimbursement of their "election expenses" to the PTS, the reimbursement was almost enough to pay for its share of the federal campaign in 1988. In other words, in the case of BC at least, no provincial money which the donors had reason to believe would be used for electing provincial MLAs was used to pay for federal election expenses.[24] Note that in the case of Saskatchewan, which does not have a tax credit for political contributions, the NDP issues receipts for individuals to claim the *federal* tax credit for their contributions. The federal office, however, sends 85 percent of the money to the provincial section, which is then devoted to electing both members of the Saskatchewan legislature and federal MPs.

It appears that the NDP's rationale for the use of the federal tax credit can be summarized as follows. First, the NDP is a properly registered party at the federal level and, as such, it (and its federal candidates) is entitled to issue receipts for political contributions, which individual and corporate donors may use to claim the tax credit. Second, the NDP is a single, integrated party that attempts to elect representatives at both levels of government. It deploys money raised by the party in whatever ways it can best achieve its objectives. Third, it may well be that federally receipted funds are used to elect provincial MLAs, but that is not prohibited by federal law, and the party files with the CEO details of the party's revenues and expenditures as a single entity.[25]

6.4 Financing the Federal Office

The revenues and expenditures of the "federal wing" (federal office) of the NDP are described in table 6.5. These data are the most comparable to the data provided by the other two parties, particularly on the expenditure side (except for "election expenses"). The federal office of the NDP is, in financial terms, a much smaller operation than that of its two main rivals in the years *between* elections. To illustrate this point, consider the expenditures (in nominal terms) of the three major parties in just three years:

Total Expenditures
(thousands of dollars)

Party	1977	1983	1989
PC	4 233	13 199	12 824
Liberal	4 187	6 277	7 115
NDP (federal office)	688	1 130	1 530

In 1977, the NDP's federal office spent less than one-sixth of what the Conservative or Liberal parties spent. In 1983, despite almost doubling its expenditures (in nominal dollars), the NDP spent only 18 percent of what the Liberal party did and only 8.6 percent of what the Conservative party spent. In 1989, the comparable figures were 21.5 percent and 12 percent respectively. Note, however, that the NDP federal office ran a large surplus in 1989 ($1.04 million).

In real terms, the NDP federal office's outlays (in 1989 dollars) averaged $1.29 million annually during the period 1975–78. In the next interelection period, the amount increased slightly to $1.46 million annually. There was, however, a major increase in the period 1985–87, to $2.36 million per year. Then there was a large drop to $1.53 million in 1989 and $1.49 million in 1990 (see table 3.3).

The dependency of the federal office on the financial goodwill of the provincial sections can be seen in the composition of its revenues (table 6.5). The bulk of the NDP federal office's revenue comes from its 15 percent share of all federally receipted revenues and 15 percent of (some) provincially receipted revenues. Note that, in 1989, if the federal office had received 15 percent of all federally or provincially receipted revenues, it would have received $1.98 million rather than the $1.41 million reported in table 6.5. The second major source of revenue for the federal office is "affiliated members' dues." These dues come from unions affiliated with the NDP and are designed to provide the federal office with funds on an ongoing basis. In general, 60 percent of the dues go to the federal office and 40 percent to provincial sections. The critical point is that, despite the growing amounts of federally receipted contributions (table 6.3), the federal office's share of these revenues ranged from 22 percent to 33 percent in the period 1981–90, excluding election years.

Table 6.6 indicates that the total members' equity grew in an irregular fashion from $131 254 in 1974 to $393 655 in 1981. By the end of 1983, the members' equity in the NDP rose to $908 601 and thereafter gradually increased to $1.52 million at the end of 1986. Table 6.6 indicates that the members' equity fell to minus $949 887 at the end of 1988. This was due largely to deficits of $719 000 in 1987 and $1.93 million in 1988. However, the party ran a surplus of $1.36 million in 1989. Hence, by the end of 1989, the members' equity recovered to $85 357.

The composition of the federal office's assets illustrates the financial integration of the party. From 1980 to 1987, the largest single asset, reported in table 6.6, consisted of amounts due from provincial sections. This is money raised at the PTS level using the federal or provincial tax-receipting authority. The federal office is dependent upon the goodwill of the provincial sections to forward even the 15 percent of such revenues it is supposed to receive. Officials of strong provincial sections are able to "hold the federal party up for ransom on policy issues" because they can threaten to stop the flow of funds to the federal office. Of particular importance is the fact that the federal office had few "independent" sources of revenue in comparison with the Progressive Conservative and Liberal parties' headquarters.

Former NDP leader Ed Broadbent has said that party MPs are deeply split over equity (in the form of redistribution within the party) versus local autonomy.[26] He was particularly frustrated by the failure of riding associations and PTSs to provide basic information on members to the federal office (e.g., name, address, telephone number). He believes that most party members would be shocked if they realized that the federal office (national headquarters) has no list of party members. In Broadbent's view, arguments couched in terms of the "principle of local autonomy" are really about money. Control over money provides power within the party, so those who control money are unwilling to give it up – or they demand something in return for transferring funds to others. According to Broadbent, it is not simply the inertia of history that explains why the NDP is still dominated by its provincial sections. As described in section 2 above, a potentially important change was made in the composition of the NDP's key governing body which might increase the influence of the federal wing of the party.

7. TRADE UNION SUPPORT

7.1 The Significance of Affiliation

The NDP, unlike the Liberal or Progressive Conservative parties, permits trade unions and farm organizations to be affiliated to the party.[27] The formation of the NDP in 1961 "combined organized labour and individual members represented through constituency associations with the balance of power held by the latter" (Archer 1990, 24). Archer states that "in theory, the NDP welcomes affiliation of national, regional or local labour organizations, but in practice only the affiliation of local ones is encouraged. Only local organizations ever have affiliated with the party, a legacy of the relationship between organized labour and the CCF" (ibid.).

The number of union members affiliated with the NDP rose from 5.0 percent of total union membership in 1961 to 14.6 percent in 1963,[28] then fell gradually to 10.4 percent in 1974, to 8.7 percent in 1979 and to 7.3 percent in 1984 (Archer 1990, 37).[29] In April 1985, some 730 union locals were affiliated with the NDP, representing 267 350 members.[30]

Of these, 202 300 were in Ontario, 30 500 in BC, 10 500 in Saskatchewan and 12 000 in Manitoba (ibid., 38). The decline in the percentage of union members affiliated with the NDP between 1963 and 1984 is largely attributable to the fact that national organizations, very largely public service unions, accounted for the bulk of the growth in union membership in Canada over this period, and the fact that most did not affiliate with the party.[31] Between 1966 and 1984, the percentage of the paid nonagricultural work force that was unionized rose from 30.7 percent to 39.2 percent, and membership in national unions rose from 445 000 to 2.05 million, or from 25.6 percent to 56.1 percent of total union membership (ibid., 42, 43).[32] Archer concluded that "if public sector unionists are excluded ... affiliation has remained stable, and is static at rates below those expected in 1961 when the NDP was formed" (ibid., 44).

While affiliation fees "contribute a very modest proportion of the NDP's revenues" (table 6.8), the main purpose of affiliation "is to provide a 'cue' to union members that there is an important link between the party and organized labour" (Archer 1990, 25). Archer's analysis of the 1979 election found that "members of affiliated locals are three to four times more likely to vote NDP than are non-unionists and also significantly more likely to do so than members of non-affiliated unions. Nonetheless only a minority of NDP-affiliated unionists voted for the party" (ibid., 77). While union affiliation is valuable to the NDP, it opens up the party to the charge that it is dominated by labour.[33] Archer emphasizes that the NDP "is not a labour party or a party controlled by organized labour. Rather, it is a social democratic party with links of varying strength to the union movement, some of which are purposefully weak" (ibid., 39).

Even though BC is Canada's most heavily unionized province, few of its unions are affiliated with the NDP. The BC-based unions believe that a formal separation of the two entities is healthier. It also means that the unions retain greater discretion in making contributions to the NDP. Ontario has the greatest number of affiliated union locals. One prominent NDP official said that, in general, the BC-based unions make less effort to influence the party than do the Ontario-based unions that are affiliated. According to party officials, some union leaders have more difficulty in balancing their different hats – hence they are inclined to try to influence party matters, perhaps because they see themselves as major stakeholders. Some union leaders feel the party should be more accountable to the unions.[34]

7.2 Financial Assistance

Trade unions and related labour organizations provide a number of types of financial assistance to the NDP: annual affiliation dues,[35] which are important for the ongoing operations of the federal office between general elections; contributions in cash during general elections; and contributions of goods or services, primarily in the form of the time of officials and members who take a leave of absence to work as campaign organizers at the national or riding level. Very few people in the NDP worry about the party's reliance on unions for contributions; many feel the unions should give more.

Affiliation dues are split 60 percent to the federal office and 40 percent to the PTS in which the union operates. Affiliation dues in 1990 were $0.20 per union member per month (as compared to $0.05 in 1961). Any amount provided by a union above the amount of affiliation dues, whether in cash or in kind (e.g., volunteer labour paid by a union), is considered to be a "contribution" to the party. The annual affiliation dues paid by those union locals affiliated with the NDP are funnelled through PTSs. They are subtracted from the PTS's contribution to the federal office. Since many of the affiliated unions have their headquarters in Ontario, their dues effectively reduce the amount that the Ontario PTS must raise to meet its "quota" for the federal office.

Between elections, with very few exceptions,[36] unions make some contributions, but total affiliation dues are usually greater than such contributions (table 6.8). The CLC's commitments to the party for an election are based on its canvass of unions'/locals' willingness to contribute. A rough version of the election campaign budget is set about two years in advance, based on the expected level of contributions from the unions and the quotas (transfers) expected from each PTS.

Financial support from labour organizations (unions, provincial federations of labour and district labour councils) to the NDP in nonelection years has typically been in the range of 13 percent to 20 percent of total federal revenue over the period 1974–90 (table 6.8). In election years, the fraction was higher, but it has declined over the past four elections: from 32.5 percent in 1979 to 25.6 percent in 1984 to 19.8 percent in 1988. The decline between 1984 and 1988 was largely due to the large increase in total federal revenue: from $9.0 million in 1984 to $13.75 million in 1988. Even in election years, therefore, labour organizations have not provided as high a fraction of the NDP's federal revenues as corporations do for the Liberal and Progressive Conservative parties (chap. 11).

Table 6.8 indicates that union affiliation dues doubled (in nominal dollars) between the late 1970s and the late 1980s, from just over $300 000 to over $600 000 annually. In real terms, however, the affiliation dues did not increase (the CPI increased from 49.0 in 1978 to 104.8 in 1990). Contributions from labour organizations outside election years increased from under $100 000 annually prior to 1977 to over $500 000 in each of 1986, 1987 and 1990.

Table 6.9 indicates the sources of all contributions of $1 000 or more to the federal NDP from labour organizations in 1988. While *contributions* over $100 (in cash or in kind) are identified by source in the annual return filed by the NDP, affiliation dues are not so identified. In 1988, the sum of the two totalled $2 718 000 (Canada, Elections Canada 1988c, 1–11). Contributions over $1 000 totalled $1.49 million, of which the lion's share came from the Canadian Labour Congress ($1 014 192).[37] There were 43 contributions of $1 000 or more and 15 of $10 000 or more.[38] By comparison, in 1988, the Progressive Conservative party received 299 contributions of $10 000 or more from corporations, and the Liberal party received 171 such contributions (table 11.6). The key point is that a minority of Canada's largest unions supported the NDP to the extent of at least $10 000 in the last general election.

In 1989, the federal NDP received $672 577 in affiliation dues and $334 112 in contributions. As table 6.10 indicates, there were 19 contributions of $1 000 or more and 9 of $10 000 or more, including a total of $58 800 from the Canadian Steelworkers' Union. By way of comparison, the Conservative party received 118 contributions of $10 000 or more from corporations, while the Liberal party received 83 such contributions. The average in both cases was about $22 000 (see table 11.6). In 1990, the NDP received $535 765 in contributions of $1 000 or more from labour organizations (table 6.10a).

It is important to understand that, in election years, much of the union support is in kind and so is counted as contributions (which are not limited) and as "election expenses" at either the party level or candidate level. As union members and staff become more highly paid and the rate of increase in their incomes exceeds the CPI, the "value" of their services on the expenditures side may become a decidedly mixed blessing for the party, because many candidates are running up against statutory limits on expenditures (see chap. 12). The crucial point is that contributions in kind are not fungible – they cannot be converted into other valuable forms of campaign activity. So it is ironic that, as the unions pay more of their members to work on NDP election campaigns, a smaller fraction of "election expenses" is available for advertising and for other cash outlays. No wonder NDP officials have complained loudly that the rules regarding volunteers are biased against them (see chap. 13). NDP volunteers, who have developed considerable campaign skills, are employees who have to remain on salary during campaigns. Their rivals, however, the NDP contends, attract many more self-employed professionals or others able to forego one or two months' income during a campaign. Hence, the only amounts chalked up against official "election expenses" in regard to such volunteers are their expenses for travelling, accommodation and meals.

8. CORPORATE CONTRIBUTIONS

The NDP has a welter of different policies toward contributions from corporations (other than those from the small businesses owned by supporters). In some provinces (e.g., Nova Scotia), the party refuses to accept corporate donations. Others, such as Manitoba and Saskatchewan, solicit them, but put a limit ($5 000 or $10 000) on individual corporate contributions. Still others engage in what some party officials have called hypocrisy: for example, the BC section sends corporate contributions through the federal office and then belabours the federal officials for taking money from big business while benefiting from a large part of such contributions. Under a 1981 policy, provincial sections that do accept such contributions must ensure that the donations are from Canadian firms with good labour practices who agree with the party's policies. In 1984, one firm's cheque for $5 000 was returned, according to a senior official, because it did not meet such criteria.

A newspaper story that appeared in 1988 illustrates the differences within the NDP regarding contributions from corporations:

> The present system also lets the provinces operate independently from the Ottawa office. But such independence does yield inconsistencies. While some sections only accept money from "mom and pop" businesses, others, such as Manitoba, are less selective. The Manitoba NDP accepts corporate money, limiting each donation to 0.5 percent of the party's total revenues ...
>
> In contrast, the federal party does not accept money from publicly traded companies or ones with what it regards as particularly objectionable traits. Still, such corporate heavyweights as John Labatt Ltd. and Northern Telecom Ltd. show up on government records as federal NDP contributors. Although other provinces point to Manitoba as the culprit, the prairie NDPers deny that they are responsible. Even some corporations appear confused about how their money ended up on federal lists: "Where the contribution originated is not clear," says a spokeswoman for the accounting firm of Coopers & Lybrand, which gave $1 000 to the NDP in 1986. Other companies have no doubt about why they gave. "That was the first time they asked us," says Arthur Price, president of Husky Oil Ltd. Husky gave $7 000 to the NDP during the 1986 Saskatchewan election, a chunk of which ended up going to the federal New Democrats.

Some NDP executives see nothing wrong with the trend to more business donations. Says Ron Johnson, federal coordinator of the British Columbia NDP, "There's no reason why there can't be NDP bankers. Besides, I don't think we make claims to be purer than the driven snow." For the rank and file, however, corporate donations may yet prove too rich for socialist blood. (*Financial Times*, 6 June 1988, 11)

Between 1974 and 1990, corporate contributions to the NDP ranged from $14 000 to $263 000 annually in nominal dollars (table 6.3). As a percentage of federally receipted revenues, corporate contributions ranged from 0.6 percent (1984) to 6.3 percent (1977). In absolute terms, contributions from corporations were greatest in 1988. The party reported 25 contributions of $2 000 or more from corporations, a total of $148 000 (table 6.11). Some of the large contributions were $25 000 from John Labatt Ltd., $17 500 from Nova Corp of Alberta and $10 000 from McDonald's Restaurants of Canada. Credit for the much larger amounts in 1988 was claimed by then senior party official Bill Knight. When corporations called and said they wanted to donate, he said that he gladly accepted their money and fought off the objection of some of the "purists" in the party. Knight noted that two Ontario insurance companies had employees vote on which party should receive a cheque from the company. In both cases, they voted for the NDP and the insurers sent in their cheque. In 1989, total contributions from corporations dropped to $54 323 from $262 524 in 1988. In 1990, the NDP collected $141 509 from corporations. The largest contribution was $4 000.

The rationale for corporations to make contributions to the NDP is hard to fathom. The party has generally favoured extensive government intervention of all types and higher corporate income taxes. Perhaps the rationale is based on the idea that such contributions support competition among parties, which is necessary if democracy is to function well. In any event, it is clear that corporations have not been an important source of revenue for the NDP.

9. ELECTIONS: FINANCES AND CAMPAIGNING

9.1 Election Revenues and Expenses

The 1974 *Election Expenses Act* has contributed greatly to the NDP's ability to fight federal elections. In 1974, the last campaign under the "old rules," the party (aside from candidates) was able to spend $380 436. In 1979, its "election expenses" as reported to the CEO grew to $2.19 million (table 6.12). In real terms, the increase was *four*fold. In each succeeding election, the NDP's outlays increased in real terms:

from \$4.09 million in 1979 to \$5.25 million in 1980, to \$5.84 million in 1984 and \$7.42 million in 1988 (all in 1989 dollars). In summary, in real terms the NDP's "election expenses" in 1988 were seven times greater than in 1974.[39]

A major shift in the organization and control of the NDP's general election campaigns occurred in the 1970s. They became far more centralized and this trend was evident in 1979.

> Ed Broadbent had argued strongly for a party with "muscle and resources" at the federal level; even during his bid for the NDP leadership, he had advocated a new approach to election organization. After the 1975 convention, he kept his promise, and a federal Election Planning Committee began its work early in 1976. It was composed of about twenty people representing various branches and functions of the party: the leader's office, fund-raising, research, party organization. The Election Planning Committee was responsible for drawing up an election budget, which was approved by the finance committee of the party's national executive. The Election Planning Committee had to justify the expenditure, but responsibility for obtaining the necessary funds remained with the finance committee. (Seidle and Paltiel 1981, 259)

Party officials emphasize that the 1988 campaign was the most centralized of all previous NDP campaigns, with the exception of the specialized campaign conducted in Quebec (Fraser 1989; Caplan et al. 1989; Lee 1989).

Note that the figures for "election expenses" provided by the federal office, reported in table 6.12, are somewhat greater than those reported to the CEO. For example, in 1988, the party's figure was \$7.74 million, versus \$7.06 reported by the CEO. For the purpose of the 22.5 percent reimbursement of "election expenses," outlays on goods and services, which are also recorded as contributions on the revenue side (e.g., payment of the wages of a volunteer campaign worker), were excluded from the amounts of "election expenses" eligible for reimbursement. Also, the CEO's practice is to deduct any revenue received from media personnel from the cost of the leader's tour. Therefore, the CEO (Canada, Elections Canada 1988c, 2–1) reports the *net* cost of the leader's tour as \$766 789 while the NDP (in table 6.12) records the gross cost as being \$1 258 490 and also records \$540 717 on the revenue side.

Evidence of the greater importance of the leader's tour, as measured by gross expenditure, is seen in the fact that it cost \$343 000 in 1980, \$531 000 in 1984 and \$1.26 million in 1988. As a percentage of total party expenditures on the election, tour costs rose from 10.9 percent in 1980 to 16.2 percent in 1988. Expenditures on media (principally television) advertising rose from 33.2 percent of campaign expenses in 1974 to 48.6 percent in 1980; they then fell to 41.0 percent in 1988.

If the slightly more than $2 million expenditure in Quebec is removed from the NDP's "election expenses," the party's outlays in 1988 were about 10 percent *below* those in 1984 in real terms.[40] In other words, expenditures were reduced in provinces where the party had a much greater chance of winning more seats in order to provide more money for the Quebec campaign. In the 1984 election, the party spent only about $50 000 in Quebec, according to its officials. The NDP did not win one of Quebec's 75 seats in 1988, although some senior officials claim that the party's first "truly national campaign" won votes for NDP candidates outside Quebec.[41]

For no other party has it been possible to ascertain election-related revenues. It appears that only the NDP segregates each general election so carefully on the revenues side. This is probably due to two factors. First, as we shall see, the NDP finances federal elections in a way quite different from that of the Liberal and Progressive Conservative parties. Second, for the NDP, the amounts of nonelection spending in election years are much smaller than its "election expenses." As noted above, they are also much smaller than those of the other two major parties. Third, the NDP believes that information on how election campaigns are financed should be in the public domain.

While the Liberal and Conservative parties appear to finance general elections by soliciting larger contributions from individuals and corporations as well as by urging more of them to make a contribution, the NDP's method of financing elections relies heavily on its PTSs and on trade unions. Contributions from individuals made directly to the federal office – despite the more extensive use of direct mail in 1984 and 1988 – are of modest importance in financing the NDP's federal election campaigns. Their importance was greatest in 1988, but even then such contributions accounted for only 10.3 percent of total election revenue (table 6.12). Second, levies or quotas imposed on the PTSs have grown in importance from 17 percent in 1979 and 12.3 percent in 1984 to over 30 percent in 1984 and 1988.[42] These quotas are the subject of vigorous negotiations. It must not be assumed, however, that all PTSs participate. For the 1988 election, over 90 percent of the amount raised through quotas came from BC, Saskatchewan, Manitoba and Ontario – where the party is politically and financially stronger. Further, one should not assume that the "provincial quotas" at election time represent a reversal of the large annual flow of federally receipted revenues to the PTSs. In some provinces (e.g., BC, but not Saskatchewan) individual candidates have been required to assign part or all of the 50 percent reimbursement of their election expenses to the provincial association in order to help it meet the amount ("quota") it has agreed to transfer to the federal office.

To finance the 1988 federal election, the federal office negotiated a quota for each PTS.[43] BC's approach to meeting its obligation of $585 000 was probably unique.[44] The BC provincial council decided to require the candidates in all federal ridings to transfer to the party all reimbursements of "election expenses."[45] (This amounted to $558 127 (Canada, Elections Canada 1988c, 3–259).) Further, the official agents of candidates in federal ridings in BC were not allowed to issue tax receipts for contributions. Rather, the BC PTS issued the receipts for the federal income-tax credit (under authority delegated from the NDP national office). The BC PTS then kept 35 percent of the contribution up to a certain level, then 25 percent beyond it. The balance (65 percent to 75 percent) flowed back to the federal candidate's official agent. In other words, the BC PTS was able to exercise virtually complete control over the benefits intended to go to candidates in federal ridings through reimbursement and use of the income-tax credit. No wonder, as an NDP official pointed out, the candidates in the federal ridings were very angry about this arrangement.

In every election since the *Election Expenses Act* has come into effect, the federal reimbursement of party "election expenses" has been the second most important source of funds to the NDP in fighting federal elections. In 1979, it amounted to 19 percent of total revenues and in 1980 it was 22.8 percent. In 1984 and 1988, the rebate was 22.5 percent of official "election expenses," although as a percentage of revenue, reported in table 6.12, the figures are slightly different.

As noted earlier, trade unions and labour organizations are a major source of revenues for the NDP's federal campaigns. They provide cash ("contributions") and "goods and services." For the 1980 election, unions' cash contributions accounted for 12 percent of NDP revenues, and their contributions in kind amounted to over 31 percent. In the 1979, 1980 and 1984 elections, the unions' contributions in kind substantially outweighed their cash contributions. In 1988, the unions' cash contributions amounted to 17 percent of total revenue (the bulk of this came from the CLC, which raised the money from its affiliates).[46] In addition, unions gave "goods and services" amounting to 8 percent of the revenues to finance the 1988 election. These contributions in kind occur when union members (or officials) take leave from their regular job and act as volunteer campaign organizers. Where the union pays individuals their wages while they act as organizers, the amount must be reported as a contribution by the union (or another organization that pays the volunteer's wages) *and* as an "election expense." In 1984, cash contributions from unions amounted to 12 percent of total NDP election revenues, but contributions in kind ("goods and services" in table 6.12) amounted to 22 percent. From the perspective of national campaign officials, cash contributions are much more useful, because cash is entirely fungible, while the payment of volunteers' wages is a contribution whose use is highly restricted and which must be spent in the sense of being reported as an "election expense," even if the volunteer does little for the national campaign or for a candidate.

Contributions in kind from unions include the time of campaign organizers, office space and supplies. The release of organizers from their regular employment is coordinated centrally,[47] but some are the result of arrangements with union locals. During each federal election, the CLC and some individual unions run a "strictly internal campaign" to reach union members through union papers, telephone canvasses and even direct mail. These efforts, because they directly advocate support of the NDP, must be included in the party's official "election expenses."[48]

Prior to 1986, donations from unions (as opposed to annual affiliation dues) were raised on a case-by-case basis, typically only for general elections. In 1986, the "nickel fund" was established by the CLC to generate money to fund political activities by the CLC.[49] A percentage is set aside for federal election and pre-election expenses. The fund also provides money for provincial elections (see table 6.7). In addition, union locals receive requests for funds for federal and provincial elections and by-elections. As a result of the efforts to combine the contributions of various unions, the CLC was able to provide the federal office with a cheque for $1.04 million for the 1988 election campaign.

9.2 The 1988 Election Campaign: From a Federal to a National Party

Party officials stated that, after the 1984 election, the NDP was able to increase the percentage of electors who identified themselves as NDP supporters from 5 percent to 6 percent in 1984 to a peak of 20 percent to 23 percent in the 1988 campaign. However, a party must also be able to engage its "identifiers," that is, it must get them to vote for its candidates. The polls in 1988 showed that Ed Broadbent had a truly national following. Party officials felt that the NDP had an obligation to respond by making acceptable the notion of three national parties, not two major parties and one minor party. This meant that the NDP had to campaign much more vigorously in Quebec and the Maritimes. (In 1984, the leader's tour made only brief stops in Montreal and Quebec City. It did not get to Newfoundland and made only downtown appearances in Moncton, Halifax and Charlottetown. Moreover, in 1984 the leader visited only two cities in Alberta.)

In 1988, the NDP went from the regional/targeted campaign of 1984 and earlier to a truly national campaign in which the party made a huge effort in Quebec. Party officials stated that there is a world of difference between the two types of campaigns. The strategy was not simply to increase the number of targeted ridings from 60 in 1984 to about 125 ridings in 1988.[50] Rather, a campaign infrastructure had to be created in Quebec almost from scratch (a point not appreciated by NDP leaders in western Canada). The full-scale campaign in Quebec required a separate francophone advertising agency. This resulted in numerous coordination meetings. The campaign required assistance in "team building" from a psychologist. The Quebec campaign cost $2.0 million to $2.2 million, according to party officials.

The 1988 campaign was different from previous ones in several ways: the leader's tour was more diverse (weeks one to seven were national in focus, while the remaining weeks were more regional); media buys concentrated much more on television commercials and very little on print commercials; the structure of campaign management was more centralized; and the amount of money raised was much greater as a result of reliance on direct-mail appeals. In general, the new campaign techniques have been beneficial to the NDP, but some party officials indicated that they were worried by the greater centralization of election campaigns. Evidence of centralization can be seen in the party's increased expenditures on national television ads and its emphasis on the leader's tour in order to generate nightly television coverage. Nightly polling was also conducted during the campaign. At the same time, party officials said that the biggest change in the NDP's organization for the past two general elections has been the creation of a formal and broadly based organization committee. Control by a few "notables" (particularly by the federal secretary) and by a small number of staff members was said to have been reduced. This organizational change is said to reflect the greater democratization of politics within the NDP.

Party officials stressed that in 1988, the NDP's commercials were much more professional than in previous campaigns and cost as much as $200 000. (In one advertisement, $650 was paid to a food designer for a macaroni and cheese casserole that was part of a family scene.) The party went from simple "talking heads" commercials to the visually oriented "On Golden Pond" commercial. As one senior official put it, some of these more abstract and artistic efforts made some supporters uncomfortable because they were not sufficiently different from the Liberals' and Tories' commercials.

For the 1988 election, the NDP's official "election expenses" totalled $7.06 million, so the party outspent the Liberal party ($6.84 million) but not the Progressive Conservative party ($7.92 million).[51] NDP *cash* outlays in 1988 were almost double those of 1984, and the party spent a higher fraction of its statutory limit. However, in real terms, the amount of money spent by the NDP outside Quebec in 1988 was 10 percent below that spent in 1984. In any event, the NDP "broke even" on the 1988 campaign when the party rebate of 22.5 percent of election expenses was taken into account.

Of the $2 million that the NDP spent in Quebec,[52] party officials stated that some $1.8 million went for radio and TV advertising and other forms of publicity, using the party's own temporary ad agency that had been created by drawing upon the services of individuals in the private sector. The balance was spent on staff, including teams of organizers to run local campaigns. The party did not transfer funds directly to candidates. Indeed, candidates were required to agree to turn over to the party 50 percent of the reimbursement of election expenses from the federal government. This agreement was struck when the NDP's support was in the 30 percent to 40 percent range. However, many NDP candidates in Quebec did not receive 15 percent of the votes cast[53] and ended up with debts of $8 000 to $10 000, according to party officials.

The characteristics of local campaigns in Quebec in the 1988 election were as follows. There was a core campaign staff of up to five persons. Typically these were union or party employees whose salary and expenses (about $18 000 to $20 000) had to be reported as contributions and election expenses. About 20 ridings had the benefit of experienced teams of up to five campaign organizers in 1988. Leaflets for distribution to each household in up to three "waves" were used in many ridings (at a cost of about $6 000 per "wave").

The high cost and lack of success of the Quebec campaign in 1988 created further vigorous debate within NDP ranks. A split appears to have emerged between the members of the party's leadership cadre (staff, caucus and the federal council) who supported the scale of the party's efforts in Quebec, and grass-roots supporters who were less enthusiastic about the campaign and wanted more money spent outside Quebec. In the latter's view, increased spending on carefully selected ridings outside the province would have yielded a greater number of seats for the party.

9.3 Local Campaigning

NDP organizers state that the basic task at the riding level during general elections has not changed; it is still a matter of identifying the party's voters and getting them to the polls. The means, however, have changed and have become less visible. For example, the foot canvass has more or less been replaced by telephone banks using volunteers who are given less than an hour's training, and are given a script. Party officials state that the use of volunteers at the local level must be more sophisticated. At least some volunteers need to be able to manage a telephone bank and use microcomputers. As importantly, paid organizers need to better learn how to motivate them and utilize their skills. An experienced NDP organizer stated that an MP's staff is very important to his/her re-election campaign. In some cases, three or four people work full-time on the campaign once the writ has been issued. The financial arrangements for such workers vary: some staff members take their vacation time during the campaign; some go on leave of absence and the riding association pays their salary; some go on leave without pay and their expenses become "election expenses" for the candidate.

Officials stated that, prior to the 1988 election, the NDP set up 48 weekend workshops to train some 2 000 volunteers as campaign organizers at the riding level.[54] Training was done in two rounds. The first focused on how to organize prior to the election call; the second was devoted to how to run a campaign. In this way, with some experience, volunteers could become skilled operatives, and energetic and willing amateurs could become capable organizers. Moreover, in some cases the newest volunteers had skills (such as running microcomputers) that old hands lacked. In general, they were more open to applying the new technologies to politics. The NDP campaign training focused on the skills needed by the key persons in the NDP's approach to local campaigns: campaign manager; telephone-bank coordinator; foot-canvass coordinator; sign coordinator (optional, depending on local custom); candidate's coordinator (optional, depending on the candidate's need for assistance with the media); and election day coordinator (getting party supporters to the polls). Such individuals were often recruited from the staff of trade unions, and much less frequently from the central staff of the party or party adherents with other jobs who had developed expertise in running some aspect of a local campaign. Some individuals, often working as teams, moved across the country and worked on both federal and provincial elections.

10. CONCLUSIONS

The provisions of the *Election Expenses Act* of 1974 have benefited the New Democratic Party a great deal. However, much of the benefit – for example in the form of higher revenues – has *not* gone to the *federal* wing of the party, except during federal elections. Data reported in this chapter reveal that the federal tax credit has been used to raise far more money for the NDP as a whole than is spent by the federal office, except for "election expenses." The NDP, as an integrated party, has chosen to use the federal tax credit as a vehicle to help to finance its provincial ambitions. In most years between 1974 and 1990, the federal office's budget (all sources of revenue) to promote the election of a federal government was less than the amount of money flowing to provincial sections for the purpose of electing *provincial* governments from money raised using the *federal* tax credit.

While the federal office of the NDP receives 15 percent of revenues generated by its provincial sections using the federal income-tax credit for political contributions to registered parties, the federal office's other sources of revenues generate only modest amounts of money and some of these sources depend upon the generosity of the provincial sections. In contrast, in the Progressive Conservative party, there is a clear separation between federal and provincial politics. When the PC Canada Fund retains 25 percent of the money raised by riding associations between elections in "exchange" for the use of its (federal) tax-receipting authority, it is dealing with a local organization *solely* devoted to electing a *federal* government. Moreover, the Ottawa headquarters of the federal Conservative party has complete autonomy from provincial parties and has exclusive control over all of the various methods of raising funds.

The commonly made comparisons concerning the revenues and expenditures of the NDP, Progressive Conservative and Liberal parties based on data published by the CEO fail to recognize that the NDP's revenue figures included provincially receipted revenues (i.e., those used to finance the party at the provincial level) and the expenditures include the federal office and the party's *provincial* sections. Except in election years, the comparisons can be misleading, because the NDP's outlays on *federal* activities are seldom one-third of its federally receipted revenues and the latter was only slightly larger than provincially receipted revenues.

Trade unions, through affiliation dues, cash contributions and contributions of goods and services, continue to be an important source of revenue for the NDP. However, their importance in financing federal elections has declined from 43 percent to 44 percent of the total revenue in 1979 and 1980 to 34 percent in 1984, to 25 percent in 1988. In large part, this decline is due to the increase in party spending on election expenses (from 49 percent of the statutory limit in 1979 to 88 percent in 1988) and the fact that union contributions have not been raised accordingly.

While the federal office of the NDP is now spending as much as its main rivals on "election expenses," it remains far behind in expenditures between elections. The NDP's federal office's expenditures in 1977 were less than one-sixth of those of the Liberal and Progressive Conservative parties. In 1989, the federal office's expenditures had fallen to 12 percent of the Conservatives' expenditures, but had increased to 21.5 percent of the Liberals' expenditures.

Officials in the three main parties and many citizens see the roles of trade unions in financing the NDP as closely analogous to that of corporations in financing the Progressive Conservative and Liberal parties. The analogy is, in fact, not a close one, for several reasons. First, trade union locals that are affiliated with the party pay annual affiliation dues that provide a regular source of income for the NDP; there is no corresponding relationship between corporations and the Conservative or Liberal parties. Second, it appears that a higher fraction of trade union locals give money or services to the NDP than do corporations (although each year about 40 percent of the 500 largest nonfinancial corporations contribute to one or both parties). Third, except in the 1979 and 1980 elections, the resources provided by unions have been a smaller fraction of the NDP's revenues than corporate contributions are of the Liberal or Conservative parties' revenues. Fourth, a much greater fraction of the unions' contributions to the NDP's federal election campaigns consists of the services of organizers than is the case for corporate contributions to the Liberal or Progressive Conservative parties. Indeed, in 1979, 1980 and 1984, the value of unions' contributions in the form of goods and services greatly exceeded their cash contributions. (In 1988, union cash contributions were double their contributions in kind.)

In 1988, for the first time, the NDP ran a truly national federal election campaign. The party spent over $2 million in Quebec, as compared to only about $50 000 in the previous election in 1984. For the first time, the party had to worry about "hitting the limit," rather than trying to shift outlays into the "election expenses" column so as to benefit from the 22.5 percent reimbursement. One effect of making such a major effort in Quebec was that "election expenses" in other provinces fell 10 percent below the 1984 level in real terms.

In 1988, the BC section may have set an example of how the financially stronger provincial sections west of the Ottawa River will pay for their quotas levied to help finance federal elections. BC imposed a 100 percent "tax" on the reimbursement paid to candidates, which almost covered its quota obligations for the election campaign.

Changes made in the composition of the NDP's national governing body in December 1989 may increase the power of federally oriented officials and precipitate increases in the funding of the federal office. On the other hand, the election of NDP governments in Ontario in September 1990 and in BC and Saskatchewan in the fall of 1991 may prevent any shift of power and money within the New Democratic Party. It is not clear which development will prevail.

7

THE
REFORM PARTY
OF CANADA

The Reform movement has started a fire of resentment and anger among English Canadians that rages beyond mere political issues and smoulders at the very heart of Canada. In releasing this populist fury, the party challenges the foundation of our social contract, our parliamentary traditions, and the political compromises that have preserved the union.

(Sharpe and Braid 1992, 189)

People who have been led to believe that the Reform Party is a one-man band with the organizational sophistication of a pink lemonade stand are mistaken.

(Manning 1992, 332)

1. INTRODUCTION

THE PURPOSE OF THIS CHAPTER is to examine the financing of one of the newest and most rapidly growing parties in Canada. The Reform Party of Canada was formed in 1987 and became registered as a federal party on 21 October 1988, only one month before voting day in the last general election.[1] This chapter describes the origins, development and financing of the Reform Party, and examines its candidates' revenues and expenditures in the 1988 election. Writing about the financing of the Reform Party is a challenge because of the very fluid political environment in Canada in 1991 and because the revenues of the party have been growing so rapidly. In 1988, its first full year of operation, the party raised $799 000; in 1991 it raised $6.6 million, almost as much as the Liberal party.

In the 1988 general election, 12 registered parties presented candidates. While each of the three main parties (Progressive Conservative, Liberal and NDP) had a candidate in all of the 295 ridings, the other nine parties presented a total of 539 candidates ranging from nine for the

Social Credit party to 88 for the Libertarian party.[2] The Reform Party of Canada ran 72 candidates, all in the four western provinces.

The origins of the Reform Party are sketched in section 2. The party's activities in 1988, including the general election, are the subject of section 3. Sections 4 and 5 review developments concerning the RPC in 1989 and 1990 respectively. Section 6 examines the party's methods of fund-raising. Section 7 describes developments related to the Reform Party in 1991 and 1992. The conclusions are set out in section 8.

2. ORIGINS

2.1 The Western Assembly

According to Dobbin (1991, 76), Preston Manning[3] and Stan Roberts, former head of the Canada West Foundation, formed the Reform Association of Canada in 1986.[4] It established core groups in Edmonton, Calgary and Vancouver.[5] Manning had been following closely political developments in western Canada for years. By 1986, "there were signs that another populist movement was in the making in western Canada" (Manning 1992, 7). A new party could be the vehicle "through which that movement could express itself in the federal arena" (ibid.).

A series of events in 1986 led to the decision to hold the "Western Assembly on Canada's Economic and Political Future" in Vancouver on 29–31 May 1987 and to seriously explore the possibility of establishing a new political party. First, in August 1986, Ted Byfield wrote a column in *Alberta Report* arguing strongly that "the West needs its own party." Second, only two years after coming to power in Ottawa, it was becoming clear to westerners that the Progressive Conservative party, after decades of strong support in the West, was unresponsive to their concerns.[6] Third, in September 1986, "a small group of oilpatch lawyers and executives" began regular meetings "to discuss ways and means, including political action, to secure greater constitutional equality for the resource producing regions through Senate reform and political action" (Manning 1992, 129). Fourth, in the same month, Manning wrote a memorandum "A Western Reform Movement: The Responsible Alternative to Western Separatism" and circulated it to Ted Byfield, Jim Gray (a prominent petroleum executive) and David Elton. This led to a meeting on 17 October to discuss if the time was ripe – as Manning thought – to "create a new federal political movement" (ibid., 132). Fifth, the federal Cabinet's decision in October to award the CF-18 contract to Canadair in Montreal rather than to Bristol Aerospace, which had submitted a lower bid and outranked Canadair in technical competence, "showed westerners exactly how much influence their

PC members and cabinet ministers had in the new government when push came to shove" (ibid., 127). Sixth, for another meeting of those inclined to take action, in November Manning prepared a presentation entitled "Proposal for the Creation of a Western-Based Political Party to Run Candidates in the 1988 Federal Election" (ibid., 133). Thus, the decision was taken to organize the Western Assembly on Canada's Economic and Political Future in Vancouver on 29–31 May 1987.

Francis Winspear, an 84-year-old Victoria accountant (formerly from Edmonton), is said to have approached Stan Roberts and said: "If you feel as I do and want to change the political system, I'll give you the money to form a party." With a cheque for $100 000,[7] Roberts and Manning planned the "assembly of the Reform Association for Vancouver in May 1987" (Dobbin 1991, 76). According to Manning (1992, 136), the Vancouver assembly had two goals. The first was to develop a "Western Agenda for Change" that a majority of westerners could support. The second was to determine the best political vehicle to advance this agenda over the next few years, including the next federal election.

The organizers decided in advance to limit attendance at the Vancouver meeting to 300 persons. Delegate Selection Committees for each of the four western provinces were to select 60 delegates and the Conference Steering Committee would choose another 60 delegates at large. Delegates were to be "sane and responsible citizens, capable of mature and balanced judgments on important issues and capable of accurately representing the concerns and aspirations of fellow citizens," according to a pre-conference document produced in January 1987 (Dobbin 1991, 77). The response in Alberta was strong; over 2 600 Albertans applied for delegate status (despite the fee of $200). Applicants were refused on several bases: their radical beliefs, their failure to be Canadian citizens or over 18 years of age, or simply because too many had applied. The final count of voting delegates was as follows: Alberta, 100; BC, 58; and Saskatchewan and Manitoba, 38. In addition there were 350 non-voting delegates at large, about 100 visitors and 23 observers and resource people (Manning 1992, 135). According to Manning (ibid., 135), most of the delegates had been connected in some way with one of the three traditional parties: the majority were ex-Liberals and ex-Tories. Moreover, there was more than a hint of Social Credit present, probably reflecting the large contingent from British Columbia and Alberta. At the end of the meeting, delegates voted on the following set of alternatives for "advancing the West's Agenda for Change":

• Working within an existing federal party.
• Creating/supporting a new, broadly based pressure group.

- Creating/supporting a new, broadly based federal political party.
- Other (ibid., 142).

Seventy-seven percent voted for the third option. Delegates approved a resolution to form a steering committee to plan a founding assembly for the new party in Winnipeg by the end of November.

Prime Minister Mulroney sent a letter to the Assembly that described his apprehension that the meeting might result in the formation of a new party with interests that would be detrimental to the country as a whole and to the West as a region. Certainly the new party was to adversely affect support for the Progressive Conservative party in the West.

2.2 Founding Convention

The founding convention (assembly) of the Reform Party of Canada was held in Winnipeg on 31 October to 2 November 1987. At that time, the party had 2 500 members[8] (Dobbin 1991, 79). Some 262 delegates (who each paid a fee of $200 and their own travel and hotel expenses) attended the meeting: 129 from Alberta, 76 from BC, 51 from Manitoba and 6 from Saskatchewan (Manning 1992, 145). The delegates had to address a wide range of matters in establishing the new party. They had to debate and approve its constitution, choose a name (30 were reviewed), select the party's colours and symbols, elect members to the party's governing body (executive council), debate and adopt a statement of principles and choose a leader (ibid., chap. 8). Two candidates, Preston Manning and Stan Roberts,[9] ran for the leadership. However, Roberts quit the race the night before the vote,[10] citing improprieties in the registration of his delegates and the failure of the party to fully account for all of its financial activities (*Winnipeg Free Press*, 2 November 1987, 1, 4). Thus Preston Manning became leader of the party.[11] According to Sharpe and Braid (1992, 5), Manning's timing in launching the Reform Party was "excellent." He "moved ... just before English Canada's discontent began to explode into a true fury over Meech Lake, the national debt, the Goods and Services Tax, Quebec's law against English signs, the rise of the Bloc Québécois, and criminal charges against Tory politicians" (ibid.).

Organizers stated that the purpose of the Reform Party was to respond to western concerns and to reform government. The new party would avoid entering into provincial politics, however, and concentrate its efforts on the national stage. While Manning said that "the core of this party's mission is achieving economic justice for the West," he suggested that the Reform Party would try to replace the Progressive

Conservative party (Dobbin 1991, 80). Manning said it had "a congenital inability to govern" and that it could not be considered "an appropriate vehicle for the implementation of a reform program" (ibid.). He announced that the party planned to field at least 50 candidates in the next federal election. The delegates voted on what they considered to be the most important priorities/policies for the party: a "Triple E" (elected, equal, effective) Senate; no special status for Quebec unless Atlantic Canada, the West and the North were given similar treatment; the use of national referendums on key issues; and reducing government subsidies to farmers by eliminating tariffs and taxes on inputs used by farmers (*Winnipeg Free Press*, 3 November 1987, 5). At the close of the convention, Manning estimated that the party needed $1.2 million in order to establish constituency organizations in every province in western Canada. He also stated that the party would require $3 million for the next election.

Many federal politicians dismissed the formation of the party and its members. Progressive Conservative party MPs described the new party's adherents as "disgruntled fringe members whose only rallying point is their disaffection with Eastern Canada" (*Winnipeg Free Press*, 3 November 1987, 1, 4). Some, however, were worried that the new party might split the vote in some ridings, to the detriment of Tory candidates (ibid.). After the founding convention, the *Globe and Mail* devoted a lengthy editorial to the new party. It said that some of the party's positions "are conventional, but the flavour is reactionary and parochial" (4 November 1987, A6). As a regionally focused party, "the Reform Party demonstrates the virtue of national parties that reconcile local perceptions to a greater and healthier whole" (ibid.). At the same time, the *Globe and Mail* said that the party's support in Alberta and BC "reflects honest emotions and convictions ... [and] expresses the powerlessness many Westerners feel within our federal system" (ibid.). It concluded that the Reform Party did not appear to be a "logical invention."

2.3 Initial Financial Support

At the Winnipeg assembly and the founding meetings, the party collected over $250 000, mainly from farmers and small businessmen (*Financial Post*, 27 April 1988, 17). The assembly, however, left the Reform Party with a debt of $89 000. (The party received all of the assets of the Reform Association.)

In December 1987, Francis G. Winspear is said to have donated $100 000 to the party.[12] This contribution represented almost one-third of the party's total revenue for the year. Winspear also suggested that other wealthy Edmontonians had supported the party "very generously"

(*Globe and Mail*, 1 December 1987, A10). Manning accepted the large donation, but stated that the party had to seek a broad base of financial support. At the end of 1987, the Reform Party had a deficit of $30 700, according to financial statements it filed with the Chief Electoral Officer. Three years later, at the end of 1990, the party reported a surplus of $646 000.[13]

3. PARTY ACTIVITIES IN 1988

3.1 Development of the Organization

In January 1988, the Reform Party of Canada secured preliminary registration as a federal party. To complete its registration (and be eligible to issue tax receipts), the party would have to nominate 50 candidates in the next federal election. A nonprofit corporation, Reform Fund Canada, was incorporated to act as the party's official agent and to be responsible for the collection and disbursement of funds.

Manning (1992, 157) identified three main tasks necessary to build the new party in 1988: developing constituency (riding) organizations, raising money (without the benefit of the tax credit) and creating an administrative structure at party headquarters (then in Edmonton). These he delegated to others so he could concentrate on two matters: explaining the aims and positions of the Reform Party to people in western Canada through speeches and media coverage; and further developing the party's policy platform "to rebut the charge that we were offering simplistic solutions to complex problems" (ibid.).

In April 1988, Manning approved the creation of "The Reformer," a party news tabloid, first edited by a 19-year-old university student. It was soon to become "our most effective communications tool" (Manning 1992, 156). The paper was used to diffuse the party's ideas to members and nonmembers. It became a vehicle for encouraging participation at the grass-roots level. For example, "any technique to raise membership, money, and support that worked was written up in *The Reformer* or disseminated via the constituency development workshops or the party grapevine" (ibid., 230).

In an interview in the spring of 1988, leader Preston Manning stated that he looked beyond the West, and hoped to make the Reform Party one that would represent all areas in Canada with resource-based regional economies (*Financial Post*, 27 April 1988, 17). He mentioned possible future areas of support in Northern Ontario, rural Quebec and Atlantic Canada. The profile of the party was raised nationally when five directors from Joe Clark's Progressive Conservative party Yellowhead Riding Association "defected" to the Reform Party. The stated reason for their switch was dissatisfaction with the treatment of western Canada by the federal government (*Globe and Mail*, 29 March 1988, A5). In August 1988, the party held a policy assembly in Calgary and produced a set of proposals that became part of its policy "blue book" and that were highly critical of the Mulroney government (Dobbin 1991, 81–82).

Financially, the Reform Party was described in the spring of 1988 as living "hand to mouth," dependent upon volunteers and well-wishers to provide "anything from computers to tables and chairs" (*Financial Post*, 27 April 1988, 17). However, its fund-raising efforts bore fruit. In 1988, the Reform Canada Fund had total revenues of $799 134 and a net operating surplus of $86 542 (table 7.1). Manning (1992, 183) states that almost all of the party's revenue came from the sale of memberships (at $10 per year) and contributions from *members* ($688 400). The number of party members had increased from 2 500 to 3 000 in October 1987 to about 23 000 a year later when the federal election was called.

3.2 Federal Election

The Reform Party ran candidates[14] in 72 of the 86 seats in the four western provinces in the 1988 federal general election (see table 7.3). Its election strategy reflected the maxim "Never attempt to execute complex strategies with raw troops" (Manning 1992, 161). Every riding was on its own and had to do the best it could. Financially, individual candidates were better off than the party, which could not issue receipts for the tax credit until 21 October when the registration requirements were met.

In Alberta, nine Reform Party candidates finished in second place, including leader Preston Manning who lost to former Progressive Conservative party leader Joe Clark by 6 700 votes in Yellowhead.[15] As table 7.4 indicates, two-thirds of all Reform Party candidates in 1988 finished in fourth place, while 11 percent finished in third place (mostly in Alberta). Overall, the Reform Party received 7.3 percent of the votes cast in the West (Dobbin 1991, 81). Manning (1992, 181) notes that the party's candidates obtained 275 000 votes (178 000 in Alberta or 15.4 percent of the popular vote – ahead of the Liberal party at 13.7 percent). According to Manning (ibid., 183), in the six weeks after the federal election, the Reform Party obtained 3 000 new members.

Reform Party candidates raised $1 001 600 for the 1988 election. They spent $995 695 on "election expenses" and $57 696 on personal expenses (Canada, Elections Canada, 1988c, 3–339).[16] However, the *party* itself spent only $112 400 (ibid., 2–1) – perhaps because it was registered so close to election day. The tax credit for political contributions was not available to the party prior to 21 October 1988, when it became a registered federal party, although each candidate's agent could issue tax receipts once the candidate filed his/her nomination papers.

During the period 21 October (when it became a registered party) to 31 December 1988, the Reform Party received $129 570 in the form of contributions from 384 individuals. Twenty-five people gave $1 000 or more. The two largest contributions were $6 100 and $15 000 (from Mr. F.G. Winspear). In addition, the party received $42 000 from corporations, including $10 000 from Canadian Occidental Petroleum (1988 annual return filed with CEO).

In Alberta, Reform Party candidates raised an average of $19 900 each, and spent an average of $19 400 on "election expenses." As table 7.3 indicates, this was more than rival Liberal party candidates and only slightly below that of NDP candidates. The only Reform candidates who received 15 percent of the votes cast, and hence were eligible for reimbursement, were in Alberta. The average amount received by the 11 who obtained reimbursement was $6 200, well above that for Liberal candidates, but only one-third that of Progressive Conservative candidates.

In BC the Reform Party had a candidate in 30 of the 32 ridings. On average, they raised $12 300 and spent $12 200 on "election expenses." Their "election expenses" averaged only one-half those of Liberal candidates and less than one-third those of PC and NDP candidates (see table 7.3). The 12 Reform candidates in the 14 federal ridings in Manitoba spent an average of $8 800 on "election expenses," only one-third that of their nearest rival, NDP candidates, and less than one-quarter the amount spent by PC candidates. As table 7.3 indicates, the Reform Party ran only four candidates in the 14 Saskatchewan ridings. All finished in fourth place. They were able to spend an average of only $5 400 – only one-eighth the average of Conservative and NDP candidates.

Of the 72 Reform candidates in 1988, 10 were able to raise $28 900 or more, with the top fund-raiser collecting $53 443. Leader Preston Manning raised $50 000 for his battle with Joe Clark (see table 7.5). Twenty-one Reform candidates in 1988 recorded a surplus, even though 10 of them did not obtain reimbursement.[17]

At the end of 1988, the Reform Party had assets of $181 600, liabilities of $125 800 and a surplus of $55 800 (as compared to a deficit of $30 700 a year earlier).

4. ACTIVITIES IN 1989

The Reform Party recorded two notable victories in the federal political arena in 1989. It elected its first MP: Deborah Grey was elected in Beaver River (Alberta) in a by-election in March 1989.[18] She received 11 154 votes, more than her three other opponents combined. Grey campaigned on a platform that opposed deficit spending, enforced bilingualism and the Goods and Services Tax. The party provided $13 520 to assist Ms. Grey (table 7.1).

On 16 October 1989, Albertans elected Stan Waters, the candidate of the Reform Party,[19] as their choice for a vacant seat in the Senate.[20] Waters collected 259 293 votes (41.7 percent of the total),[21] almost twice that of his nearest rival (Dobbin 1991). Manning (1992, 206) states that Waters' campaign cost $250 000, including $90 000 for television advertising. Dobbin (1991, 92) states that Mr. Waters raised $173 000 for the race (almost four times the amount raised by the Liberal party runner-up). Less than 5 percent came from individuals contributing $40 or less. Most of the money is said to have come from corporations or corporate executives – including $10 000 from Mr. F.G. Winspear and $10 000 from a company of which Mr. Waters was a director (ibid.). Waters actively promoted the idea of a "Triple E" Senate during his campaign. Prime Minister Mulroney, however, waited until June 1990 before appointing him to the Senate. In effect, Waters became the first elected Senator in Canada's history.

Preston Manning continued to be the most visible and most effective representative of the Reform Party, promoting his views on governmental reform and fiscal responsibility. In 1989, the Reform Party distributed over 80 000 copies of the Meech Lake Accord, mainly to party members (Manning 1992, 238).[22] Manning frequently spoke on the issue of constitutional reform. In 1989 Manning is said to have made over 250 speeches, mainly in western Canada (Dobbin 1991, 81). Party membership reached 26 000 in October 1989 (Manning 1992, 215).

The 1989 assembly on 27–29 October in Edmonton attracted over 1 000 voting delegates when registration had to be cut off due to lack of space. Much of the time was devoted to the internal organization of the party: the relationship of the members to the executive council; clarification of the roles of the leader, the executive council and the riding associations; the election of a new executive council; and the affirmation of Manning as leader. A task force was set up to consider the issue of expanding the party outside the West; it was to report by May 1990. The delegates voted down a resolution to have the party enter provincial politics (Manning 1992, chap. 12).

In 1989, the Reform Party raised a total of $1.41 million, of which $1.21 million consisted of contributions from individuals. The Reform Party reported 7 360 donations from individuals, with an average of $154 each (table 7.2). (Note that the revenues in 1989 reported by the Reform Canada Fund in table 7.1 do not agree with the figures reported to the CEO in table 7.2. Party officials could not explain the differences.) Virtually all contributors were party members according to party officials.

It is important to draw attention to this fact because, throughout its short history, the Reform Party has relied far more than the Liberal, Progressive Conservative and New Democratic parties on contributions from members, obtained very largely by direct-mail solicitation. The key to the Reform Party's ability to raise so much money from its members lies in the fact that the membership list of the party is maintained by headquarters rather than by the riding associations or provincial sections/associations, as in the case of the Liberal, Conservative and New Democratic parties. Further, like the Progressive Conservative party, the Reform Party does not have provincial/territorial sections situated between riding associations and its national headquarters (figure 7.1).

Figure 7.1
Flows of funds relating to Reform Party and its candidates

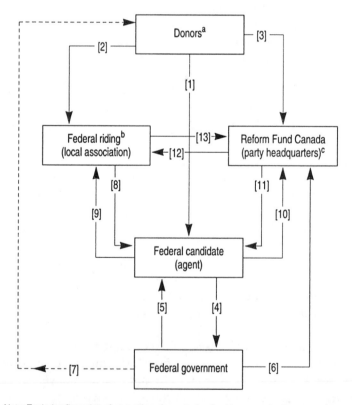

Note: Excludes financing of campaigns for party leadership or nomination campaigns.
[a]Includes individuals, corporations, trade unions, interest groups and other organizations.
[b]A total of 225 federal ridings outside Quebec.
[c]Official agent for Reform Party of Canada.

In 1989, the Reform Party received from individuals some 3 806 donations of *at least* $100 (an average of $202).[23] The average was above that for the Progressive Conservative party ($170), the Liberal party ($119) and the NDP ($67). In 1989, some 69 individuals donated $1 000 or more (the average was $1 757), while 11 individuals gave the Reform Party $2 000 or more (the largest amount being $16 000).

Some 245 businesses contributed a total of $141 200 to the Reform Party in 1989. The party received only two corporate contributions of $5 000 or more ($9 000 and $15 000 respectively, the latter from a numbered company). Expenses did not, however, increase as dramatically, and the Reform Canada Fund had an operating surplus of $219 000 for the year (see table 7.1).

For 1989, the Reform Party reported $952 268 in operating expenses, including $318 964 for wages and salaries, $104 029 for advertising and $277 572 for printing and stationery (table 7.1a). Total Reform Party spending in 1989 as reported to the CEO was $965 788. The party reported that the Reform Canada Fund had expenditures of $897 300 in 1989. While the Fund reported a surplus for the year of $219 300, the party reported a surplus of $385 130 based on total revenues and expenses reported to the Chief Electoral Officer. It is not clear why this difference exists.[24] At the end of 1989, the Reform Party had $410 400 in assets and liabilities of $135 200. Thus the party's surplus had increased to $275 100 from $55 800 a year earlier.

5. ACTIVITIES IN 1990

Between October 1989 and the summer of 1990, the Reform Party's membership grew from 26 000 to 44 000, including 24 000 members in Alberta, 14 000 in BC and 5 000 in Manitoba/Saskatchewan (Manning 1992, 215, 245). According to Sharpe and Braid (1992, 8), the Reform Party began 1990 with 27 000 members and ended the year with 54 000. "Canada has not seen a new federal party grow so explosively since the Progressives burst out of the West and Ontario to finish second to Mackenzie King's Liberals in the 1921 election" with 65 seats. Manning (1992, 226) credited Prime Minister Mulroney as the individual who did the most to increase membership[25] and contributions to the Reform Party in 1990.

In January and February 1990, Manning and "senator-in-waiting" Stan Waters toured Alberta and spoke to 7 000 people in 30 communities (Manning 1992, 227). The party distributed 60 000 "Notice of Termination of Employment For Cause" pink slips that could be sent to MPs (ibid., 227–28). The party moved its headquarters to Calgary from Edmonton and built up its paid staff. Members of the executive council focused on building the party at the constituency level. "This included writing a constituency development manual and organizing a workshop program, and with the help of local coordinators, putting on constituency development seminars across the west" (ibid., 228). In addition, the party organized "lunches for the curious" in Calgary, and the Vancouver Quadra riding association raised $30 000 at a fundraising dinner at which Manning, Waters and Deborah Grey spoke (ibid., 229). The leader made his first exploratory tour of Ontario and the Atlantic region in March 1990, often speaking at meetings of service clubs.

The growing strength of the Reform Party in Alberta could be seen in an Angus Reid poll in September 1990. Decided voters would, according to the poll, cast their votes as follows (*Vancouver Sun*, 19 October 1990, A14): Reform Party of Canada, 36 percent; Liberal party, 31 percent; Progressive Conservative party, 18 percent; and New Democratic Party, 17 percent. Private polling by the Conservatives showed that, were an election held in the fall of 1990, the Reform Party could have won as many as 40 of the 86 western Canadian seats, including 20 of Alberta's 26 federal ridings.

The Reform Party's support was not limited to Alberta. A Gallup poll conducted in 1990 across the Prairies showed that decided voters would cast ballots in a federal election in the following way:[26] New Democratic Party, 37 percent; Liberal Party, 23 percent; Reform Party of Canada, 23 percent; and Progressive Conservative party, 16 percent. In the summer of 1990, Manning visited 30 of BC's 32 federal ridings and spoke at 45 public events to more than 8 000 people and did over 100 interviews with reporters (Manning 1992, 246). Manning even made a short trip to Quebec in the fall of 1990 to speak and to participate in a television program.

The Reform Party attracted a great deal of interest in Ontario in 1990. Over 1 600 persons joined the party and 24 informal riding associations were organized in 1990. The party also established its first Reform Clubs on college campuses and universities. In the fall of 1990, 700 people turned out in Orillia to hear Preston Manning speak, and many cited his "credibility" as the reason they found the party appealing (*Maclean's*, 29 October 1990; *Financial Times*, 22 October 1990, 6). Manning also met with over 50 "blue-chip" Ontario guests at a dinner arranged by prominent industrialist Conrad Black and Hal Jackman, long publicly identified with the Progressive Conservative party,[27] on 5 September. Manning (1992, 252) has noted that "senior business executives, with a few rare exceptions, are not in a position to identify openly at the outset with a populist, bottom-up political movement dedicated to 'changing the system.' " Yet the dinner did result in a few contributions from the guests, according to Manning.[28] Expansion into Ontario would require a change in the party's constitution, which then did not allow it to expand outside the West. However, Ontario members formed an ad hoc committee for expansion into Ontario in July 1990 (ibid., 265). This issue was addressed at the next party convention in April 1991.

In 1990, the Reform Party generated $2.21 million in *contributions*, an increase of 64 percent over the 1989 level (table 7.2). Almost 94 percent of this amount consisted of donations from individuals. In addition, the party raised $479 860 in membership dues of $10 per year and $51 526 in other revenue. Thus total revenue in 1990 was $2.75 million.[29] Because the party has not filed a comparably amended return for 1989, only the amount of contributions can be compared (table 7.2). The number of contributions from individuals rose by 319 percent to 23 462 in 1990 (versus 27 702 for the Progressive Conservative party, 36 361 for the Liberal party and 116 448 for the NDP). However, the *average* contribution by individuals to the Reform Party dropped from $154 in 1989 to $88 in 1990 (versus $169 for the Conservative party, $205 for the Liberal party and $52 for the NDP).

The Reform Party raised very little money from corporations in 1989 ($141 000) and in 1990 ($138 000). (The NDP raised $141 509 from corporations in 1990 and $54 323 in 1989 (table 6.3).) In 1990, the Reform Party received only one corporate contribution of $10 000 or more (as compared to 86 for the Liberal party and 107 for the Progressive Coservative party). Given the Reform Party's strong support for competitive markets and private enterprise (Dobbin 1991; Manning 1992), its modest support from the business community seems surprising. On the other hand, in 1989 and 1990 the Reform Party was seen largely as a western protest/populist party well out of the mainstream of Canadian politics. As the party continued to grow, gain ever more coverage in the media and rise in the polls, perceptions of it began to change. As noted below, in the fall of 1991 the party launched a major effort to obtain contributions from corporations.

The Reform Party's operating expenditures in 1990 ($1.72 million) were far below those of the Progressive Conservative and Liberal parties, but they were fairly close to the expenditures of the NDP's federal office ($2.1 million). The growth of the party is reflected in several expenditure categories in table 7.1a: equipment purchases, special projects, salaries and "postage and mailhouse."[30] The last category absorbed $220 042 in 1990, suggesting greater expenditures on fund-raising, notably by direct-mail solicitation. At the end of 1990, the Reform Party had a surplus of $646 000.

6. METHODS OF FUND-RAISING

The Reform Party has relied very heavily upon contributions from individuals to finance the party (which accounted for approximately 90 percent of total revenue during the period 1988–90). However, the party is unique in the specific source of those contributions: it has relied very largely upon its *members* to finance the party.[31] (The second major source of revenues has been the $10 annual membership fee.) Beginning in 1988, the party launched its "sustainer" program, which consists of direct-mail appeals to members. From the beginning, the Reform Party has maintained a centralized list of party members. Party officials were astonished to learn that none of the three main parties have such a list at their headquarters, for the reasons discussed in chapters 4, 5 and 6. The object of the Reform Party's appeals is to get members to renew their membership annually (and pay the annual dues of $10) and to get them to make further contributions to the party. Officials state that the number of mailings has increased steadily from two in 1988 to six in 1991. Seven or eight mailings were planned for 1992. Manning (1992, 228) notes that every eight weeks he and the chief fund-raiser Donna Larson (responsible for the "sustainer" program) and two other members of the party's executive council "produced a long, newsy fundraising letter for distribution to our entire membership. These letters were vitally important to keep our members informed as the party expanded, and as a means of soliciting feedback. Almost 80 percent of our revenue was also generated by these letters" (ibid.).

While the Reform Party has rented lists from other organizations for direct-mail solicitations, officials indicate that little money was raised this way and not much effort was made to go through the expensive and time-consuming process of "prospecting" so as to build up a productive "house" list of potential donors other than current members. (Direct-mail techniques are discussed in more detail in chapter 9.) The main reason that this approach has not been adopted is that party membership was growing rapidly (from 2 500 in November 1987 to 110 000 in February 1992) and because the "sustainer program" was bringing in so much money from members. The number of contributions from individuals rose from 7 360 in 1989 to 23 462 in 1990 to 43 176 in 1991 (table 7.2). The figure for 1990 suggests that about half the members of the Reform Party made contributions because the party states that 47 986 persons paid annual dues of $10 in 1990.[32] Party headquarters and constituencies share the annual membership dues on a 50:50 basis. Party officials state that between 1987 and the end of 1991, some 132 000 persons joined the party. With a membership of about 95 000 at the end of 1991, the figures suggest the party has been quite successful in getting individuals to renew their membership (although almost one-half of the members in December 1991 had joined the party during the previous 12 months and so have not yet been solicited to renew their membership for the first time).

Party officials state that, in 1990, some $1 112 300 was raised by direct-mail solicitation at a cost of $259 000 or 23.3 percent of gross revenue. Thus, direct-mail revenues amounted to 40.5 percent of total party revenues of $2.75 million in 1990. In 1989, the Reform Party raised $1 898 000 by means of direct mail at a cost of $274 000 or 14.4 percent of gross revenue. Thus direct-mail contributions amounted to 33.9 percent of total party revenues of $5.6 million.[33] In 1988, the party spent $110 000 to raise an estimated $600 000 by means of direct mail (the party could not provide the exact figure). The figures for 1988–90 suggest that the Reform Party's costs of raising money through direct-mail solicitation was far less than that for the Liberal party or the NDP and somewhat less than that for the Progressive Conservative party (see chap. 9).

Reform Party officials state that, in 1991, the average donation generated by direct mail was between $90 and $100. (Table 7.2 indicates that the average size of donations from individuals in 1991 was $110.) They indicate that the response rate was about 30 percent. As the data in chapter 9 indicate, this is a very high response rate. The party has found that the response rate is higher when the direct-mail solicitation is accompanied by a questionnaire. For example, in the fall of 1990, the questionnaire had two parts: the first sought demographic information on members, while the second contained questions designed to elicit members' views about policy issues.

Figure 7.1 describes the flows of funds associated with the Reform Party. The party has a simple two-level structure: party headquarters (in Calgary), and some 220 local riding associations (all outside Quebec). Party officials state that the Reform Canada Fund, the party's official agent, takes 5 percent of contributions to riding associations outside the official campaign period that are routed through the Fund so that the donor can obtain a receipt for the tax credit. They stressed that the 5 percent figure is based on an analysis of funds, costs of handling the funds and issuing the receipt. The officials were surprised that the PC Canada Fund retains 25 percent for the same service. Donations made directly to party headquarters are retained entirely by headquarters, "notwithstanding that the contribution was received by the Constituency to be forwarded to Head Office" (Reform Party of Canada 1991, 33). Cash donations such as "passing the hat" and anonymous donations are kept by the entity that organizes the event and no receipts for the tax credit are issued. Party policy "is to allocate a portion of a donation to issuance or renewal of a membership unless the donor specifically indicates otherwise" (ibid., 34).

The revenue figures reported to the CEO (table 7.2) include contributions to riding associations that pass through the Reform Canada Fund (for the purpose of issuing a receipt for the tax credit) and are sent back to ridings. Thus, the Reform Party did not report any "transfers to riding associations" on the *original* table filed with CEO.[34] On the amended filing, the party states that $653 145 was transferred to constituency associations. However, party officials stated that, in 1990, some $512 600 was raised by ridings but routed through the Reform Canada Fund so that donors could receive a receipt for the tax credit.[35] The ridings' 95 percent share totalled $486 970 in 1990 (table 7.1a). The difference between the total amount transferred to ridings in 1990 ($653 145) and their 95 percent share of contributions to ridings ($486 970) consisted of the ridings' 50 percent share of the annual membership dues collected by party headquarters. Party officials emphasize that riding associations are financially independent of party headquarters. Only very small amounts of money were provided to a few associations in 1988 and 1989.

Rallies have been a substantial source of income for some riding associations. They retain all of the net revenue, which can be considerable if over 1 000 people pay $10 each to attend.[36] The associations organizing the rally need only pay party headquarters for Mr. Manning's travel and hotel expenses. For example, on 30 November 1991, Manning attracted 4 300 to a rally in Edmonton (*Maclean's*, 16 December 1991, 14). Allowing for the rental of the hall, the event probably netted at least $38 000.[37] Manning was able to attract crowds of over 3 000 about a score of times in 1990 and 1991.

7. DEVELOPMENTS IN 1991 AND 1992

7.1 Growth in Membership and Public Opinion Polls

In January 1991, Preston Manning stated that the Reform Party had 55 000 members (*Globe and Mail*, 16 January 1991, A5). Some 26 000 were in Alberta, 19 000 in BC, 7 000 in Saskatchewan and Manitoba and 3 000 in Ontario (*Vancouver Sun*, 26 January 1991, B5). In February 1991, a poll taken by the NDP's pollster, David Gotthilf, indicated that, of committed voters, 30 percent in the Prairies and 23 percent in BC supported the Reform Party. Yet Gotthilf said the members of the Reform Party were not representative of western Canada, i.e., they were mostly elderly and non-urban (*Vancouver Sun*, 15 February 1991, A12). Manning asked, "Why is it when our members had memberships in those other parties they were outstanding citizens contributing to the political process and their eccentricities were dismissed?" (ibid.).

An Angus Reid poll taken on 23 March 1991 showed the Reform Party was in first place in Alberta with 33 percent of decided voters, ahead of the Progressive Conservative party in British Columbia with 16 percent of decided voters and last in Manitoba/Saskatchewan with 11 percent (*Globe and Mail*, 31 March 1991, D4). Another Angus Reid poll conducted in late April and early May found that the Reform Party's support had risen to 17 percent nationally,[38] versus 30 percent for the Liberal party, 26 percent for the NDP and 16 percent for the Conservative party.

A poll of 1 500 adults outside Quebec in November 1991 found that 46 percent of those interviewed are "very likely" or "somewhat likely" to vote for the Reform Party. The figure was 44 percent for persons in Ontario and the Atlantic provinces (*Maclean's*, 6 January 1992).

On 4–6 April 1991, the Reform Party – now with 62 000 members (Manning 1992, 270) – held a convention (assembly) in Saskatoon that attracted some 1 400 registrants, observers from the Liberal, Progressive Conservative and New Democratic parties and from the governments of the United States and the United Kingdom. It received extensive coverage in the media.[39] There were 823 voting delegates and 450 non-voting delegates at large.[40] Delegates spent more than six hours debating policy issues. The assembly's decisions became part of the party's "blue book" of principles and policies. According to Manning, "the most significant thing about the April assembly's policy decisions was that they strengthened or added important elements to the Reform Party's concept of New Canada and reflected a conscious attempt to move away from positions that could be interpreted as extreme or parochial" (1992, 272). However, agricultural policy proved to be the most conflict-ridden topic and Manning obtained agreement to schedule an extra session at 5:30 AM on Sunday to hammer out a draft policy statement. More than 150 delegates met for two hours and approved a policy that would gradually move Canadian agriculture from extensive reliance on government subsidies toward the competitive market (ibid., 363).

Gordon Shaw, vice-president of the Reform Party, told the assembly that "the country is begging for leadership. The issues are the same in the West as in Ontario and the Atlantic provinces" (*Maclean's*, 15 April 1991, 18). However, Manning stated that the party would not run candidates in Quebec in the next election. He argued that other federal parties cannot represent Quebec and the rest of Canada at the same time.[41] Delegates voted down a motion that the Reform Party enter provincial politics (more generally, see Dobbin 1991, 136–38). Manning opposed the motion because it would impose a drain on the party's resources and distract it from its efforts at the federal level.

Almost 97 percent of the delegates voted to expand the party to the rest of Canada in a "straw vote" (Manning 1992, 281). However, the delegates approved four "safeguard resolutions" before the vote: entrenching the commitment to "Triple E" Senate reform in the party constitution; providing for representation by population in the composition of party assemblies and representation by equal number of members of the executive council; requiring a "double majority" vote at assemblies to carry resolutions designed to change party policy; and providing for a special party referendum on eastward expansion by party members in western Canada (ibid., 227). Within eight days, the Reform Party sent ballots to 56 649 members eligible to vote (those living in the four western provinces) and, of 24 042 that were returned, 92 percent favoured having the party expand into Ontario and the Atlantic provinces (but not Quebec) (*Financial Post*, 6 June 1991, 3).

In early April the Reform Party said it had some 6 000 members in Ontario and membership was growing at the rate of 20 percent per month (*Globe and Mail*, 8 April 1991, A1). On 22 April 1991, the Prime Minister compared the Reform Party to Quebec separatists, saying "both are preparing for a breakup ... the road to their success runs straight through the failure of Canada" (*Globe and Mail*, 23 April 1991, A1). A Conservative party organizer noted that at least 15 of the 32 seats in Metro Toronto were won by margins of less than 3 000 votes in 1988. "You don't think I could find 3 000 voters angry enough to go Reform now in every single riding in Metro? They (Reform) are potent" (*Globe and Mail*, 26 April 1991, A6).

By June 1991, the Reform Party had over 70 000 members, including 30 000 in Alberta, 21 000 in BC, 10 000 in Manitoba/Saskatchewan and 10 000 in Ontario (Manning 1992, 293). Manning began a tour of Ontario cities in June designed to raise the Reform Party's visibility and membership base in that province. By that time, the party had established a riding association in 85 of Ontario's 99 federal ridings.[42] Party headquarters in Calgary could not keep up with the 200 to 300 membership applications arriving daily from Ontario (Sharpe and Braid 1992, 29). In his tour from Thunder Bay to Ottawa to Toronto, Manning stated that "the heart of our platform, and our reason for being resides in those reforms designed to get Canada's constitutional, economic and parliamentary houses in order during the 1990s" (*Financial Post*, 10 June 1991, 1). Manning emphasized that, to be more than a protest vehicle, the Reform Party must offer constructive alternatives to the current political realities. As for not running candidates in Quebec in the next federal election, Manning asked, "Would you trust a leader of a federal party who comes from Quebec, dependent upon Quebec seats, to represent Ontario's constitutional interests at negotiations?" (ibid., 4).

Manning's speeches generated substantial revenue at $10 per person. In June, more than 8 000 tickets were sold in Toronto; in Ottawa, 2 500 persons turned out to hear Manning (*Vancouver Sun*, 6 June 1991, A1). During the summer of 1991, Manning spoke to approximately 12 000 people at five meetings and two luncheons in Ontario. Some 1 100 new members were enrolled at these events (Manning 1992, 295). By the end of 1991, the party had 30 000 members in Ontario, according to party officials.

In September 1991, the Reform Party released its proposals for changing the constitution, "Shaping Canada's Future." Newspaper reports indicated that in 1991 the party hired a pollster and campaign strategist (Frank Luntz) who had worked for the Republican Party in the United States. It also commissioned a national poll from a Canadian firm, and hired a major advertising firm (Hayhurst Communications) – said to be a "veteran of political image-making" (*Globe and Mail*, 9 September 1991, A1, A2).

Newspaper reports indicated that the Reform Party expected to have $20 million[43] at its disposal to fight the next federal election, which it expected in 1993 (*Globe and Mail*, 9 September 1991, A1, A2). It appears that this amount is for both the party and its candidates. If the limit on party "election expenses" increases by 30 percent to reflect the increase in the CPI over five years, the 1988 limit of $8 million for a full slate of 295 candidates becomes $10.4 million. If the party runs candidates in all ridings outside Quebec, its limit on "election expenses" would be about $7.8 million in 1993. If the party ran 220 candidates and each spent the estimated average limit on candidates' "election expenses" in 1990 of $61 000, candidates would need $13.40 million. This amount is before the 50 percent reimbursement for those candidates who receive at least 15 percent of the vote in their riding. Therefore, the total expenditure of $7.8 million for party "election expenses" and $13.4 million for candidates would amount to $21.2 million.

7.2 Court Challenge in Respect to Advertising Time

On 12 August 1991, the Reform Party filed an action in the Alberta Court of Queen's Bench claiming that the limits on paid advertising during election campaigns violate section 2(*b*) of the *Canadian Charter of Rights and Freedoms* (*Globe and Mail*, 16 August 1991, A5). Section 2(*b*) specifies that everyone has the right to "freedom of thought, belief, opinion and expression, including freedom of the press and other media of communication." Party officials had been engaged in discussions with the Broadcasting Arbitrator and other federal parties seeking to increase its allotment of 10 minutes of advertising time in the next federal election. By comparison, the Progressive Conservative party will get 173 minutes, the Liberal party, 110, and the NDP, 71 minutes. Four other parties, including Reform, will share 26 minutes for a total of 6.5 hours, as provided under the *Canada Elections Act*. The party had argued that the Broadcasting Arbitrator has the power to change the ratio of allotted time when the formula is "unfair to any of the registered parties or contrary to the public interest." Party official Diane Ablonczy (who was also named as a plaintiff) argued that "it really looks like the legislation was meant to prevent new parties from breaking into the political process" (*Globe and Mail*, 16 August 1991, A1).

The suit asks the court to strike down sections 307, 309(3) and 310 of the *Canada Elections Act* or to declare them to be ultra vires of Parliament (*Financial Post*, 16 August 1991, 4). It is argued that the constraint on the party's right to advertise "infringes upon and impacts adversely on the right to a free and fully informed vote." If the suit fails, the Reform Party could have plenty of money to spend on television and radio advertising, but be unable to spend it. In the 1988 federal election, radio and television advertising absorbed 50.4 percent of the Progressive Conservative party's "election expenses." The comparable figures for the Liberal and New Democratic parties were 44.6 percent and 42.1 percent respectively (table 3.5).

In its brief to the Royal Commission on Electoral Reform and Party Financing, the Reform Party (1990b) argued that the method of allocating paid broadcast advertising time "is unfair and favours established parties ... In a democratic country, it is inconsistent that the voices of established parties are so favoured ... and the voices of small or new parties are effectively stifled." The party proposed that each registered party be allowed to buy an equal portion of the 6.5 hours available on every station. If a party did not buy its full share, that time would be split equally among the other parties. Moreover, the Reform Party does not want any restrictions on activities of advocacy groups during election campaigns. This issue is addressed in chapters 13 and 14. The party won its case at the level of the trial court.

7.3   Seeking Contributions from Corporations

In September 1991 the Reform Party launched a major campaign to raise much more money from corporations as part of an effort to broaden its sources of funds. The party had previously not devoted much effort to obtaining money from corporations, largely because it had grown so rapidly and because its members had supplied sufficient funds to meet its expenditures and leave it with a surplus each year ($86 500 in 1988, $219 300 in 1989 and $493 000 in 1990). Total party revenue rose from $799 000 in 1988, to about $6.6 million in 1991.[44] In 1991, the Reform Party obtained $490 743 from 2 286 corporations (table 7.2).

In September 1991 the Reform Party's chief fund-raiser, Cliff Fryers,[45] said he expected to obtain from $2 million to $3 million from corporations in 1992. The campaign involved 3 000 letters to business leaders and 1 000 personal visits to companies:

> Mr. Fryers said that corporate Canada will donate to the party because of the tradition of supporting all major federal parties, a method of bolstering the democratic process. But he added that captains of industry also want to ensure they have access and influence into Reform circles. (*Globe and Mail*, 9 September 1991, A2)

Fryers said that Canadian Pacific Ltd., one of Canada's largest firms, had given the Reform Party $25 000 so far in 1991. Donations had also been received from Pan Canadian Petroleum and Canadian Occidental Petroleum. The focus of the party's efforts is on companies in the *Financial Post 500*. In Fryers' view, corporations should contribute to the Reform Party so that they can "cover all their bases," because the party is expected to hold a major bloc of seats in the next Parliament (Hutchinson 1991, 19). Fryers indicated that corporations are a natural part of the Reform Party's constituency given its support for free enterprise and competitive markets with less government intervention (ibid., 27). Further, substantial contributions from corporations give the Reform Party respectability, according to Fryers. They indicate that the party is taken seriously by an important set of interests. Sharpe and Braid (1992, 107) argue that the challenge facing the Reform Party is "to get the serious money flowing from Toronto, since the other major source of federal political money in Canada, Montreal, will be virtually impossible to tap. Well-heeled anglophone federalists will not see much point in giving money to a party which invites Quebec to leave Canada and does not plan to run candidates in the provinces."

Leader Preston Manning has observed that, because large companies have "an increasingly intimate relationship with government" as tax collector, regulator and giver of grants, "senior executives simply cannot afford, regardless of their personal political inclinations, to 'get on the wrong side of the governing party' for long, nor can they risk identification with political innovations that may turn out badly" (1992, 253).

7.4   The "Save Canada Campaign"

At the end of October 1991, the Reform Party launched its "Save Canada Campaign" to raise $12 million from individuals with which to fight the next general election. Some 3 000 volunteers were to canvass the party's more than 90 000 members during the campaign period 6 November 1991 to 6 February 1992 (*Vancouver Sun*, 30 October 1991, A5). Although the party is opposed to government subsidization of political parties,[46] it said that receipts would be issued for the federal tax credit (*Globe and Mail*, 29 October 1991, A6). Cliff Fryers stated:

> We do not believe in running a government or an election on borrowed money ... We have identified $12 million as the minimum amount required to operate an effective election campaign and we want that funding securely in place well before the next election is called. (*Vancouver Sun*, 30 October 1991, A5)

Fryers said that the Reform Party was hoping to benefit from the dissatisfaction Canadians have with existing parties and so generate contributions from persons other than the party's members. Fryers said,

> We cannot fight a campaign on dribs and drabs from our various members ... We need concerted public money to do that. We will get that. The fact of the matter is, there are so many disaffected Canadians who will register their disaffection by giving us funds. (Ibid.)

In its first week, the "Save Canada Campaign" raised $700 000, according to Mr. Fryers (*Vancouver Sun*, 2 December 1991, A4).

In the "Save Canada Campaign," the Reform Party used a pyramid-type organizational structure based on having thousands of party members each personally solicit contributions from people they know in the party and, to a lesser extent, persons outside it. This approach has two benefits, according to party officials. First, people are likely to contribute larger sums when asked to do so by a friend or acquaintance on a face-to-face basis. (This strategy is based on the experience of charities.) Second, in asking for money, potential donors are asked about their opinions and ideas. Reform Party officials suggest that polling data make it clear that people are alienated from politics in Canada and believe that no party cares about their ideas and concerns. The Reform Party is trying to signal to its members and potential supporters that it does listen to them. Party officials emphasize that such an approach requires plenty of time and effort to organize and manage because so many people are involved working on a voluntary basis. The contrast to a massive direct-mail effort could not be greater.[47]

Central to the strategy of the "Save Canada Campaign"[48] was to use individuals who had made their own commitment to the party with a contribution of $1 000 to $5 000 as canvassers to approach people in similar social and economic circumstances and ask them to do the same. Party officials emphasized the importance of the canvasser disclosing to the persons being solicited the extent of the canvasser's financial commitment to the party. By launching the campaign near the end of the year, individuals were encouraged to give more by issuing a cheque, eligible for the tax credit on their 1991 tax return, and one or more post-dated ones eligible for a tax credit in 1992. Moreover, by splitting any donation over $1 150 over two years, the individual reduced his/her net after-tax cost of the total amount of the contribution to the "Save Canada Campaign."

Pratkanis and Aronson (1991, 123–27) explain that research on persuasion indicates that one of the most effective techniques is participatory self-persuasion. It can be induced by group discussion, by getting someone to role-play an opponent's position or by asking a person to imagine adopting a course of action. The technique is consistent with the values of participation, self-reliance and deciding for one's self. They point out that politicians are using the technique when they "send out questionnaires and surveys asking for our opinions in 'helping to plan the next election campaign' " (ibid., 127). Face-to-face solicitation of funds where the potential donors are also asked for their opinions also benefits from another powerful technique of persuasion, namely, reciprocity. Research has shown that where potential donors receive something from the person contacting them *prior* to a request for funds, they are more likely to contribute and contribute larger amounts (ibid., 178–83). By asking for people's opinions, the solicitor creates a sense of obligation that the "target" can requite by making a donation. Where people are frustrated by what they feel is the unwillingness of politicians to listen to their views, concerns and complaints, a sympathetic representative of a party provides not only an audience, but also an apparent channel of communication to the party leadership. It does not seem unreasonable to believe that people would, indirectly, be willing to pay for this opportunity to express their opinions. Besides, writing a cheque to a party that is overtly challenging the orthodoxy of the party in power and the official Opposition is a way of giving "voice" to one's frustration.

Party officials blamed bad weather and the worsening recession for their decision to end the first phase of the "Save Canada Campaign" at the end of 1991 (*Vancouver Sun*, 3 January 1992, A4). Only $2 million had been raised, far short of the $12 million target. However, the machinery was still in place and would be revived later in 1992. Party officials told the author that the vigour of the campaign was less than expected because the revenues were being split with riding associations on a 50:50 basis and the executives of many riding associations believed that they already had enough money to meet their needs. In any event, Reform Party officials said they were confident that, when the campaign was reinstituted, it would generate the planned $12 million before the next federal election. A newspaper report in April 1992 indicated that only $3.5 million had been raised by the "Save Canada Campaign," but party officials expected to raise $6 million by the fall of 1992 (*Vancouver Sun*, 3 April 1992, A5).

In 1991, the Reform Party raised a total of $6.6 million from donations from the sale of memberships and other sources (table 7.2). It transferred $2.1 million to its constituency associations (table 7.1a). Therefore, the Reform Party raised almost as much revenue as the Liberal Party of Canada ($7.2 million). Between 1990 and 1991 the Reform Party increased its total revenues by 140 percent. The increase between 1989 and 1990 was 94 percent (table 7.2). The number of contributions from individuals rose from 7 360 in 1989 to 23 462 in 1990 to 43 176 in 1991 (20 477 of which were over $100). By comparison, the Liberal party received 26 396 contributions from individuals in 1991, while the Tories received 27 391 and the NDP received 94 080 (table 3.1a). In terms of the average size of contributions from individuals, the Reform Party in 1991 ($110) trailed the Liberals ($127) and the Tories ($196), but exceeded the NDP ($78).

The Reform Party's efforts to obtain more money from business organizations began to pay off in 1991. The number of contributions from corporations increased to 2 286 from 274 in 1990. However, the average business contribution in 1991 ($215) was far below that of the Liberal party ($898) and the Progressive Conservative party ($900). In 1991 the Reform Party received 26 contributions from corporations in the range of $2 000 to $4 999 and it received five in the range $5 000 to $9 999 (in fact, all were for $5 000 exactly). It received four contributions of $10 000 or more. The largest corporate contributions were from Canadian Pacific Ltd. ($25 000) and Prowest Professional Partition People ($25 000), while the Bank of Nova Scotia gave $20 000 and Canadian Occidental Petroleum gave $10 000.

In May 1992 the Reform Party announced that it hoped to collect between $5 million and $10 million from corporations now that it was firmly established as a national force. A party spokesman said that corporations will give it money because of the party's pledge to make it easier for business to operate (*Calgary Herald*, 31 May 1992, A8).

Table 7.1a indicates that one-third of the party's total expenditures in 1991 consisted of transfers to constituency associations. As noted above, the amount of these transfers reflects the revenue-sharing arrangements within the party. Party headquarters retains only 5 percent of contributions raised at the constituency level and 50 percent of membership fees (currently $10 per year). The expenditure data for 1990 and 1991 provided by the Reform Party in table 7.1a indicate the limited value of the categories provided by the CEO, the first 10 listed in the table. In 1990, one-half of the Reform Party's operating expenditures was reported in seven categories established by the party. Obviously, this makes comparisons over time extremely difficult, as the figures in table 7.1a make clear.

7.5   Developments in 1992

Early in January 1992, Ray Speaker resigned from the Cabinet of the Alberta Progressive Conservative party to run for the Reform Party nomination in Lethbridge. He was first elected to the provincial legislature in 1963 as a Social Credit member. He was a founding member of the Reform Party (*Globe and Mail*, 4 January 1992, A1–A2).

In January, Preston Manning's book *The New Canada* was published and parts of it were excerpted in the *Financial Post*. It was closely followed by another book on the Reform Party by journalists Sydney Sharpe and Don Braid (1992). With Dobbin's book in 1991, the Reform Party and its leader had become the subject of three books published in a six-month period.

Reform Party members were invited to purchase "New Canada Signature Design Collection of wearables, playables and just plain usables" designed by Alfred Sung. A limited-edition framed print of the party logo numbered and signed by Preston Manning cost $150 (*Financial Post Magazine*, January 1992, 10).

Rallies in Ontario featuring a speech by Manning in January drew large crowds. A breakfast at 7:30 AM drew 600; a rally in Pickering attracted 4 000; one in Hamilton (a Liberal party stronghold) was attended by 2 200.[49] In January, the party welcomed its 100 000th member, a 16-year-old Ontario girl.[50] Within two months, the party had 110 000 members (*Vancouver Sun*, 13 March 1992, A19).

On 28 February, "The Journal," the news/public affairs program with the largest television audience in Canada, devoted an entire program to the Reform Party.

In a newsletter circulated in early March 1992, party officials described a new method by which individuals can donate fairly large sums to the party. A Calgary member called "Anne" arranged to purchase a life insurance policy with the Reform Party named as the beneficiary. The ownership of the policy was then transferred to the party. "Anne" then made a donation to the Reform Canada Fund to cover the annual premium for which she received a receipt for the tax credit for political contributions. In subsequent years, "Anne's" donations to cover the annual premium will be eligible for the tax credit. The party is able to borrow against the cash value of the policy.

The transaction resulted in considerable controversy and publicity in the newspapers, including a cartoon in the *Globe and Mail* on 13 March (A16). A party fund-raiser in Winnipeg resigned in protest. The party's spokesperson denied that the story in the newsletter constituted a sales pitch to get other members to do the same thing. The NDP's spokesman on electoral reform "criticized the scheme as a 'disgraceful' way of having taxpayers subsidize life insurance policies" (*Globe and Mail*, 11 March 1992, A4). The Minister of State for Finance said the arrangement was "highly unethical and, on the first blush of investigation, we find it totally illegal" (*Globe and Mail*, 12 March 1992, A4). The Minister of National Revenue stated that "you cannot transfer life insurance policies to political parties for political tax credits" (*Vancouver Sun*, 12 March 1992, A4). Two weeks later, the minister said, "Strictly speaking from a legal standpoint, that is allowed [tax credits for contributions to pay the premiums on a policy owned by a party] but that's like circumventing the law and I find that just as unethical and wrong as actually breaking the law but it's not breaking the law" (*Globe and Mail*, 28 March 1992, A5). Only one member of the Reform Party had made use of this method of contributing to the party.

In 1992, party headquarters and some riding associations began what are expected to be a series of 10 leader's dinners. The first one in Winnipeg charged only $50 per plate, so it is not surprising that very little net revenue was produced. The dinners planned for Vancouver and Toronto were expected to charge $175 per plate. Net revenues are to be shared equally between the riding(s) helping to organize the dinner and party headquarters.

An Angus Reid–Southam News poll of 1 502 Canadians conducted between 21 February and 4 March 1992 found that 13 percent of decided voters support the Reform Party, while 41 percent support the Liberal party, 22 percent support the NDP and 15 percent support the Conservative party. Outside Quebec, Reform's support was slightly higher than that of the Tories (*Vancouver Sun*, 11 March 1992, A4).

Another national poll of 1 501 adults by the same firms conducted 18–25 March put the Reform Party's support outside Quebec at 20 percent, versus 15 percent for the Conservatives, 24 percent for the NDP and 40 percent for the Liberals (*Vancouver Sun*, 28 March 1992, A20).

The strength of the Reform Party's support in Alberta resulted in intense competition for the party's nomination in some ridings. In Medicine Hat, for example, the winner by two votes is said to have spent $8 000 on the campaign. This was far above the party's guideline spending cap of $3 000. In Edmonton–Strathcona, the runner-up's campaign was estimated to cost $5 000 to $7 000. A party official said that, in other ridings, nomination contestants spent up to $10 000 – but did not win (*Vancouver Sun*, 2 July 1992, A5).

Leader Preston Manning will be running in Calgary–Southwest, which is held by Bobbie Sparrow for the Progressive Conservative party. In 1988, she received 32 000 more votes than the Reform candidate. The Reform Party states that it has 3 000 members in the riding (*Vancouver Sun*, 7 July 1992, A5).

8. CONCLUSIONS

The Reform Party is widely perceived by those outside western Canada as the latest in the series of western Canada-based "protest" parties doomed to a short political life. Even the party's leader Preston Manning argues that populist movements – of which the Reform Party is one – "are more 'human' than traditional parties. They do not go on forever ... They fulfil a purpose ... They beget offspring ... and then they die, sometimes with the satisfaction of seeing their progeny carry on" (1992, 50).[51] From his study of five previous populist movements in the West, Manning has concluded that they go through four distinct phases in relation to traditional parties. "First, the new group is ignored, dismissed as irrelevant ... Second, it is ridiculed and disparaged ... Third, as the new movement continues to gain support, its basic positions, ideology, and leadership are subjected to systematic attacks, substantive criticism and deliberate misrepresentation" (ibid.). The Reform Party reached this stage in the fall of 1990. Fourth, "if the new party survives and continues to grow by increasing its 'market share' at the expense of others, the traditional parties begin to steal significant portions of the new group's ideas, platform and language" (ibid., 259). According to its leader, the Reform Party had reached the fourth stage by the fall of 1991. One of the reasons it did so is that the Reform Party had moved to broaden its base by establishing riding associations in Ontario and in Atlantic Canada and by seeking to attract the core supporters of the Progressive Conservative and Liberal parties (*Vancouver Sun*, 25 January

1992, A8). Political scientist Roger Gibbins states that the Reform Party is not a regional movement for two reasons: "the western Canadian electorate has been nationalized in the sense that their concerns are not parochial any more. And second, the primary issues the Reform Party is addressing are not really regional. It's a much more broadly based movement" (quoted in Sharpe and Braid 1992, 6).

The Reform Party has been able to raise and spend money in the 1988 election on a scale that previous protest/populist parties could not.[52] The Reform Party had its founding convention in November 1987. In 1988, it raised $799 000 and in 1989 it raised $1.35 million (in contributions). Then in 1990, it raised $2.21 million ($2.75 million, including other sources of revenue). In all three years, it had a surplus – in 1990, the surplus was almost half a million dollars. In 1991, the Reform Party raised a total of $6.6 million, including $5.2 million in contributions from individuals and corporations. Late in 1991 it launched a major campaign to raise $12 million in contributions from individuals to fight the next election. The Reform Party also launched another campaign in the fall of 1991 to raise $2 million to $3 million in 1992 from corporations. Between 1989 and 1991, the party had obtained some 75 percent of its total revenues from contributions from individuals.

If Reform candidates obtain the level of support in the next federal election that the party enjoyed in public opinion polls in 1991 and early 1992, many of its candidates will cross the 15 percent threshold and hence be reimbursed for one-half their "election expenses." The amount of revenue that could flow through to riding associations or party head-quarters in the form of candidate surpluses could be considerable. Perhaps because it was able to become registered as a federal party only one month prior to the 1988 election, the Reform Party spent only $112 400 on "election expenses." Because it did not spend 10 percent of its limit, the party was not eligible for the 22.5 percent reimbursement. In the next federal election, there is little doubt that the Reform Party will be able to spend enough in "election expenses" to be eligible for reimbursement.

The rapid growth in financial support for the Reform Party would appear to call into question the arguments that certain provisions of the *Canada Elections Act* and other legislation that relate to the financing of political parties act as a "barrier to entry" to new parties. Critics point to four main barriers:

- To become registered, a party must nominate 50 candidates for the forthcoming election.[53]
- Only those candidates who receive 15 percent of the votes cast are

eligible to have one-half of their "election expenses" reimbursed by the federal government.

- A registered party must incur "election expenses" of at least 10 percent of the maximum permitted to receive reimbursement for 22.5 percent of its "election expenses" from the federal government.
- The rules under which the allocation of paid broadcast advertising time is determined do not favour newer, smaller parties.

Looking at the fourth barrier first, it should be noted that a party's allotment of broadcast time is based on its popular vote in the previous general election and the number of seats it obtains. While the Reform Party obtained 7.3 percent of the popular vote in western Canada, it did not elect an MP until a subsequent by-election in March 1989. Therefore, while it has been able to raise substantial sums – indeed it may be able to spend close to the limit on the party's "election expenses" in the next general election – the Reform Party may not be able to purchase more than 10 minutes of time for television and radio commercials. (In 1988, the Conservative, Liberal and New Democratic parties spent from 42 percent to 50 percent of their "election expenses" on broadcast advertising.) While the Reform Party will be free to use other media (notably print and direct mail), it is widely believed that television advertising is a very important tool of political campaigning. While it is expensive, it appears to be more efficient in reaching large audiences, particularly marginal voters. More importantly, television ads are believed to have a greater impact on voters (Lee 1989; Fraser 1989). According to Karl Strubel of Strubel and Totten, an experienced American campaign strategist-for-hire,

> Television is the most dominant force in our society ... we're going into ... a post-literate period. Most people can read, they just *don't*. It's easier to get the information given to you in a passive medium like television. It is only natural that as the most dominant instrument in society, campaigns employ it more. (Quoted in Mulgrew 1991, 40)

The effect of the 50-candidate rule for registration as a party had the effect of *delaying* the registration of the Reform Party until 21 October 1988, only one month before voting day, although the writs had been issued on 1 October. While this rule prevents *parties* from issuing receipts for the tax credit for political contributions, it does not prevent candidates' agents from doing so once the candidate has been nominated (and the writs have been issued).

The requirement that candidates must receive at least 15 percent of the votes cast before they are eligible for the 50 percent reimbursement of their "election expenses" certainly limited the number of Reform Party candidates who were able to obtain reimbursement. In 1988, 11 Reform Party candidates received a reimbursement (totalling $162 122). Bertram (1991) shows the effect on Reform Party candidates if the threshold for reimbursement had been reduced below the required 15 percent in 1988: 12.5 percent, 18 candidates; 10 percent, 25; 5 percent, 39; and 0 percent, 72. He shows that, if the reimbursement of candidates was based on the *party* gaining 2 percent or more of the national popular vote, all 72 RPC candidates would be eligible. However, if the party had to obtain 5 percent of the popular vote, none of its candidates would have been reimbursed.

The rule for the reimbursement of 22.5 percent of a party's "election expenses" requires the party to incur expenses of at least 10 percent of the maximum permitted. However, the maximum depends on the number of candidates a party nominates. As noted above, in the next federal election, if the Reform Party runs a candidate in every riding outside Quebec, its "election expenses" would be limited to an estimated $7.8 million (in 1993) as compared with $10.4 million for a party running a candidate in every riding. From the Reform Party's record in raising money between 1988 and 1991, the 10 percent minimum will not be an issue. However, the upper boundary may well inhibit the Reform Party's campaign efforts because the limit on broadcast time will require higher expenditures on other campaign techniques to compensate for the lack of television and radio advertising.

In summary, while there are legal "barriers to entry" for new parties, they appear to have had little effect on the growth of the Reform Party in federal politics between 1987 and early 1992. The party's growth (from 2 500 members in November 1987 to 110 000 in February 1992) appears to have been fuelled by increasing cynicism about incumbent politicians of all stripes and by the hostility toward the Progressive Conservative party and its leader. Joining and/or giving money to the Reform Party is a way of signalling displeasure with the status quo. In this context, the Reform Party has been little troubled by legal "barriers to entry." However, critical issues remain to be determined, notably the party's legal challenge to the allocation of time for broadcast advertising in the next general election, when it seems likely that the Reform Party will be a serious contender for seats in the West and Ontario.

PART III

ANALYSIS
OF SOURCES
OF PARTY REVENUE

8

CONTRIBUTIONS FROM INDIVIDUALS AND THE IMPORTANCE OF THE TAX CREDIT

~

1. INTRODUCTION

IT IS GENERALLY AGREED that one of the most important changes fostered by the *Election Expenses Act* of 1974 is that it greatly broadened the financial base of the Liberal and Progressive Conservative parties. Previously, both had relied on a few hundred corporations to finance their election campaigns (Canada, Committee 1966a; Paltiel 1970b, 1974). These parties have been able to increase greatly the number of donations from individuals. The NDP, which had very little money at all prior to 1974, has also been able to raise much larger sums from individuals. This may have been due to the advent of the then generous income-tax credit for political contributions. The growth in the number and importance of contributions from individuals was probably also stimulated by the use of the direct-mail method of solicitation. The Tories were the first to use this technique and have been the most successful by far. However, the NDP and Liberal party soon followed, although they did not make extensive use of the technique until the mid-1980s. Because of the importance of this technique, it is addressed in a separate chapter (chap. 9).

This chapter is organized as follows. Section 2 describes the number and importance of individual contributors to parties and candidates.

Section 3 examines the importance of "large" contributions by individuals, defined as contributions of $2 000 or more to a party in one year. Section 4 assesses the importance of the personal income-tax credit for political contributions in relation to the amount of such contributions to parties and candidates. Tax credits are analysed by province and by income level. Section 5 examines the proposal that the federal government adopt the *financement populaire* approach to financing parties and candidates adopted in Quebec in 1977. Finally, section 6 offers some conclusions.

2. NUMBER AND IMPORTANCE OF INDIVIDUAL CONTRIBUTORS

2.1 Number of Contributions from Individuals

Within three years after the *Election Expenses Act* of 1974 had come into effect, all parties in Canada combined were receiving 109 000 contributions from individuals[1] (table 8.1). In fits and starts the number of contributions from individuals rose to almost 149 000 in 1982. Then it jumped sharply to 205 000 in 1983. The total rose to 211 000 in 1984, an election year, and stayed almost at that level in 1985 (203 000). Then the total number of contributions by individuals to all parties fell to 159 000 in 1987 but, as expected, it rose sharply in 1988, an election year, to over 208 000. However, the number of contributions from individuals dropped sharply to 166 700 in 1989, then rose to 218 423 in 1990, but dropped to 194 793 in 1991.

Much of the increase in the number of contributions from individuals in 1990 is attributable to the increase in the number of contributions received by the Reform Party: 7 360 in 1989 versus 23 462 in 1990. In addition, the number of contributions to the Liberal party increased from 19 970 in 1989 to 36 361 in 1990. Much of this increase is attributable in large part to the 1990 Liberal leadership race and convention. Almost $2 million in individual and corporate contributions to leadership candidates was routed through the Federal Liberal Agency and hence reported to the CEO. Note that contributions from individuals fell to 26 396 in 1991.

The total number of contributions by individuals to *candidates* in the four elections since the new legislation came into effect rose from 67 323 in 1979 to 104 807 in 1988 (table 8.1a). The data in table 8.1a reveal some interesting differences by party. First, in all four election years, when contributions to party and candidates are combined, the Progressive Conservative party was able to generate many more contributions from individuals than the Liberal party, but fewer than the NDP (except in 1984). From 1979 and 1980 to 1984, contributions by individuals to the

Conservative *party* almost tripled, but then they fell dramatically (38 percent) between the 1984 and 1988 elections. However, the number of contributions by individuals to Conservative *candidates* fell only slightly between 1984 and 1988. In election year 1988, the number of contributions from individuals to the New Democratic Party was almost double the level in 1979 and 1980. However, the number of contributions by individuals to NDP *candidates* increased more slowly, from 13 800 in 1979 to 22 500 in 1988 (table 8.1a). On a combined basis (party plus candidates), the number of contributions from individuals to the Liberal party has shown the slowest rate of increase of the three main parties: from 31 600 in 1979 to 57 700 in 1988. Contributions to the *party* showed a bigger increase than those to *candidates*. The Liberal party's problem is that its two main rivals have been able to attract contributions from many more individuals than it has been able to do.

The pattern of the total number of contributions from individuals to the Progressive Conservative, Liberal and New Democratic parties over the period 1974–90 is somewhat surprising, given the growing intensity of direct-mail fund-raising by all of them. For the three-year period straddling the 1984 election, the average total number of contributions from individuals was 200 600. However, the average for the three years straddling the 1988 election was only 177 900. (The number was 180 500 in 1990.) This pattern should be disturbing to the parties, because the drop in the real value of the tax credit (described below) should affect the average size of contributions in real terms, but not the number of contributions. Indeed, in light of the strenuous efforts by all three major parties to use the direct-mail technique, it would seem reasonable to expect more, rather than fewer, contributions from individuals in recent years. Perhaps the decline is attributable to the growth in the use of direct-mail solicitations by interest groups and charities. Perhaps the drop is attributable to the rising disaffection for the political system generally. (The latest survey data on political disaffection are discussed in Blais and Gidengil 1991; see also Gregg and Posner 1990.)

The pattern of the number of contributions from individuals varied widely across parties and across time. Perhaps the most extraordinary development was the ability of the Progressive Conservative party to increase the number of contributions it received from individuals. In the first decade after the *Election Expenses Act* came into force, the number of such contributions increased from under 7 000 annually to 99 300 in 1983 and 93 200 in 1984 (table 8.2). Indeed, in the early 1980s, the Conservative party, on average, received more contributions from individuals than did the NDP, which is proud of its ability to get individuals to support the party financially. However, the Tories were far less successful in the latter part of the 1980s (the peak was in 1983). The average number of contributions from individuals in the period 1986–90 was 42 800 per year, versus 80 100 per year in the previous four-year period. As noted in chapter 3, the total revenues of the Conservative party greatly outpaced those of the Liberal and New Democratic parties between 1985 and 1990 (table 3.8). Further, as will be discussed in chapter 9, the Conservative party's gross revenues from direct mail were far larger than those of the Liberal or New Democratic parties, although direct mail accounted for a varying fraction of the value of contributions from individuals. The Conservatives' problem can be seen by noting that, in 1990, the total value of contributions from individuals ($4.7 million) was only slightly more than the amount raised from this source in 1981, $4.3 million. (Both amounts are in *nominal* dollars and over the period of CPI rose by 58 percent.) The fall in the average number of contributions from individuals in the period 1985–90 versus 1982–85 may reflect the drop in the Conservatives' popularity, as measured by the Gallup or Decima polls, *between* the 1984 and 1988 elections and after the 1988 election. In 1990, for example, the Conservatives' popularity hit a record low for any previous federal government.

The differences among the Conservative, NDP and Liberal patterns in the number of individuals making a contribution to the party can easily been seen in the following data (computed from table 8.2) on the *average* annual number of contributors in four-year intervals.

Period	PC	Liberal	NDP[a]	Total
1974–77	14 191	14 204	50 778	79 173
1978–81	37 853	19 445	62 440	119 738
1982–85	80 069	29 805	77 420	187 294
1986–90 (5 yrs.)	42 779	30 263	100 523	173 565

[a]These figures are for federally receipted contributions only.

The NDP's pattern was like the slow and steady tortoise. The average number of individual contributions doubled between 1974–77 (50 800) and 1986–90 (100 500). Note that the NDP's average number of individual contributions exceeded that of the other two parties in three of the four periods. Indeed, in the first period (1974–77), the NDP had an average of 3.6 times as many contributions from individuals as the

Liberals or the Tories. However, in the 1982–85 period, the Tories slightly outperformed the NDP although the NDP's average number of contributions (77 400) was 2.6 times the Liberals' (29 800) (table 8.2).

The Liberal party has been the least effective of the three main parties in increasing the number of contributions from individuals. The average number per year doubled between 1974–77 (14 200) and 1982–85 (29 800); however, it barely increased in the period 1986–90. In the period 1986–90, the Liberals averaged 30 300 contributions from individuals annually, but this was only 71 percent of the number enjoyed by the Conservative party (42 800) and 30 percent of the NDP's number of contributions (100 500).

Voting and making a political contribution are both forms of participation in the political process. However, only a small fraction of voters makes a contribution. The three years in which the total number of contributions from individuals to federal parties was highest were 1984 and 1988 (election years), and 1990. The percentage of *electors* contributing to a federal party was 1.26 percent in 1984 and 1.18 percent in 1988.[2] The comparable figure for 1990 was 1.21 percent. If we add the number of contributions by individuals to *candidates*, the percentage rises to 1.78 percent in 1984 and 1.77 percent in 1988.

The number of individuals contributing to a party and/or candidate in relation to the party's popular vote in the last two general elections is as follows:[3]

Party	1984 (%)	1988 (%)
PC	1.5	1.0
Liberal	0.8	0.7
NDP	3.4	4.4
All three	1.7	1.6

Source: Michaud and Laferrière (1991).

By comparison, Michaud and Laferrière (1991) estimate that 2.4 percent of the persons voting in the Quebec provincial election in 1989 made a political contribution to a party and/or candidate. For Parti québécois supporters, the figure was 4.9 percent, while for the Quebec Liberal party, it was only 0.7 percent. In 1988, the comparable figures were 2.5 percent for the Parti québécois, 3.1 percent for the Liberal party and 2.6 percent for all parties combined.[4] Therefore, with the exception of NDP supporters, a substantially smaller fraction of voters at the federal level makes a political contribution during the election year than is the case in provincial politics in Quebec. In any event, despite the inducement of a tax credit of 75 percent of the first $100 in contributions and 50 percent of the next $340, only a tiny percentage of electors also made a contribution to a party and/or candidate. Yet, this tiny percentage has provided more than one-half of the total revenue of the four main parties combined. In particular, the Progressive Conservative and Liberal parties have been able to eliminate their almost total dependency on a few hundred large corporations, as was the case prior to the reforms of 1974. Over three-quarters of the NDP's revenues has come (outside of elections) from individuals; over 90 percent of the Reform Party's revenues between 1988 and 1991 have also come from individuals.

2.2 Average Size of Contributions

To some degree, the Liberal party's weakness in getting money from a larger number of individuals has been made up by the larger size of the contributions the party has received. In 11 of the 18 years between 1974 and 1991, the average contribution by individuals to the Liberal party exceeded that to the Progressive Conservative party and, in all 18 years, the Liberals' average exceeded that of the NDP (table 8.2). Yet in the period 1987 through 1989 and in 1991, the Liberals fell behind the Tories, a fact that does not bode well for the Liberals. The increase in the average contribution to the Liberal party from $119 in 1989 to $205 in 1990 is almost certainly attributable to the leadership race and convention because the average fell to $127 in 1991. In 1990, the party took in $4.4 million in delegates' fees at $875 each (table 5.8), which were treated as contributions. In addition, $1.95 million in contributions (from individuals and corporations) to candidates was routed through the Federal Liberal Agency, and those by individuals are included in the figures used to compute the average contribution from individuals.

The average annual contribution by individuals to the Liberal party, in nominal terms, ranged from $85 in 1981 to $205 in 1990. The comparable figures for the Conservatives were $75 (1978) and $196 (1991), while those for the NDP were $32 (1976) and $78 (1991). Even though the average contribution to the Conservative party and the NDP increased substantially (table 8.2), it did not keep up with the rate of inflation, as the data in table 8.3 indicate. While the average contribution in terms of 1989 dollars (using the CPI as the deflator) varies substantially in the period 1974–90, the trend for all parties is clear: in real terms, the size of the average contribution by individuals has fallen. For example, in the period 1974–76, the average for the Liberals was about $300, while during the years 1987–89, the averages were $131, $163 and $119 respectively. For the Conservative party, the average contribution from individuals was $284 in 1974 and $253 in 1975. It fell to $119 in 1983, rose again to $199 in 1988, but fell to $161 in 1990. While the long-term trend as measured from 1974–75 to 1989–90 has been downward, the data in table 8.3 indicate that between 1974 and 1975 and 1983, the average contribution fell from over $250 to $119. Thereafter, however, it *increased* to $199 in 1988, and then it fell somewhat to $161 in 1990. The higher average contributions in 1974 and 1975 (in 1989 dollars) were associated with small numbers of contributors (e.g., 10 300 in 1975). However, the lowest average size of contribution in 1983 was associated with the highest number of contributors (99 300) to the Progressive Conservative party. As the average contribution rose in the late 1980s, the number of contributions from individuals fell; for example, in 1988, when the average had risen to $199, the number of contributions was 53 900. Note that this is more than double the number of contributions in 1976 and 1977, when the average contribution (in 1989 dollars) was virtually the same as it was in 1988 (tables 8.2, 8.3).

In real terms, the long-term trend for the average amount contributed by individuals to the NDP, the party most dependent upon contributions from individuals, has been downward. In the last five months of 1974, the NDP's average contribution was $132. Thereafter, the average fell to $90 in 1975 and then to $80 in 1979. After rising to $88 in 1980, the average contribution from individuals to the NDP in 1989 dollars fell to $58 in 1982. The figure moved up and down again as table 8.3 indicates but, in 1988 and 1989, the average ($69, $67) was well below the average for the 1970s. In 1990 the average fell to $50, but it rose to $72 in 1991 (although the number of donors fell from 116 448 in 1990 to 94 080 in 1991).

The average of the 17 232 contributions by individuals to the other nine registered parties in 1989 was $154. This exceeded the average for two of the three main parties: Liberals ($119), Conservatives ($170) and NDP ($67). The range for the nine smaller parties was from $103 for the Green Party to $427 for the Party for the Commonwealth of Canada (232 individuals gave $99 036). The Communist party received $328 286 from 986 individuals, for an average of $333. In 1990, 37 837 donations were made by individuals to the nine other parties. The average contribution was $85. For the party with the largest number of contributions from individuals in 1990, the Reform Party (23 462), the average was $88. The party with the second largest number of contributions was the Christian Heritage party (9 226) and its average was $52 – the same as for the Confederation of Regions Western party (2 956). While the

Communist party received only 710 donations from individuals, the average contribution in 1990 was $465. In 1991, the Reform Party received 43 176 contributions from individuals, an increase of 84 percent.

2.3   Importance of Contributions by Individuals

Table 8.5 provides the data on political contributions by individuals to the three largest parties. In nominal dollars, the Progressive Conservative party collected only $1.3 million from individuals in the first 17 months after the tax credit was available (1 August 1974 to 31 December 1975). By 1979 and 1980, contributions had increased to over $3 million. Then, in the next two election years (1984 and 1988), individuals donated over $10 million. After the 1984 and 1988 elections, however, contributions dropped sharply. For example, in 1988, the Progressive Conservatives collected $10.2 million from individuals, but in 1989 the amount fell to $6.85 million, and in 1990 the amount was only $4.7 million.

While the NDP's *federally receipted* contributions from individuals reported in table 8.5 were generally above those of both the Liberals and Tories in the 1970s (as discussed in chap. 6), they grew slowly. For example, between 1977 and 1981, this form of revenue for the NDP ranged from $2.2 to $2.9 million annually. Over the next two years, contributions from individuals rose sharply to $5.0 million in 1983, a level not reached again until 1986, despite the fact that 1984 was an election year. In the next election year, 1988, the NDP was able to raise $7.8 million from individuals. While this was $3 million more than the Liberals, it was $2.4 million less than the Tories collected from individuals. In 1989, they collected $6.85 million; in 1990, the amount was down to $4.7 million.

Except for 1984, 1986 and 1990, the Liberal party raised less money from individuals than the NDP in the period 1977–90 (table 8.5). Between 1976 and 1981, the Liberals were able to raise an average of only about $2 million annually from individuals. This increased substantially in 1982 and 1983 (about $3.2 million). While the Liberals raised $5.2 million in 1984, this was only half as much as the Tories received from individuals. Then revenues from individuals dropped sharply in 1985, but rose to a high of $5.75 million in 1986, only to fall to $3.5 million in 1987. In 1988, contributions revived to $4.7 million, but this was less than half the amount raised by the Tories. In 1989, the Liberal party raised only $2.4 million from individuals.[5] Even in nominal terms, this was less than the party raised in any year between 1982 and 1988. The sharp rise to $7.44 million in 1990 is largely attributable to $4.4 million in convention fees, and $1.95 million in contributions (from individuals and corporations) to leadership candidates passed through the Federal Liberal Agency so that the donors were eligible for a receipt for the tax credit. In 1991, the Liberals received $3.35 million from individuals, less than the amount received by the Reform Party, $4.74 million.

When the total contributions by individuals to the three main parties are converted to constant 1989 dollars, in 1975, the first full year when the tax credit was available, the total value of contributions by individuals was $11.9 million. This rose to $13.9 million in 1976, but did not rise appreciably above this level until 1982, when individual contributions amounted to $16.6 million. In real terms, they rose to a peak of $24.0 million in 1984 or double the level of 1975. However, the level of such contributions dropped to $15.6 million in 1987, was even lower in 1989 ($15.2 million) and yet lower in 1991 ($14.7 million). The level of contributions in 1988 was only slightly below that of 1984.

As noted above, the *average* level of contributions by individuals for all three parties *fell* in real terms between 1974 and 1991 (table 8.3). However, the pattern for total annual contributions in *real* terms is different. During the period 1974–77, contributions to the three main parties averaged $13.2 million annually.[6] In the period 1978–81, the comparable figure was $13.9 million. However, in the next four-year period (1982–85), the annual average rose to $20.4 million. However, it fell slightly to $18.7 million during the succeeding five-year period, 1986–90. The drop is largely attributable to the decline in contributions by individuals to the Conservative party (table 8.5).

Contributions from individuals vary in their importance to each of the three main parties, as measured by the percentage of total party revenue that they represent.[7] In nonelection years, individuals typically have accounted for 75 percent of the NDP's federal revenues (figure 8.1). In 1979, 1980 and 1984, the percentage dropped to about 50 percent. (It was 57 percent in 1988.) The percentage has dropped in election years for several reasons. First, the party receives the reimbursement of its "election expenses." Second, trade unions make substantial cash contributions and contributions in kind in election years. Third, the NDP raises money from its provincial sections to fight elections. If this money comes from contributions for which federal receipts have been issued, the money is treated as an intraparty transfer, not as a contribution to the party (see chap. 6).

In most years over the period 1974–90, the Progressive Conservative party received more money in the form of contributions from individuals than did the Liberal party. Further, contributions from individuals were a more important source of revenue to the Conservative party than to the Liberal party. Prior to the 1979 election, from 44 percent to

Figure 8.1
Percentage of total party revenues contributed by individuals, 1974–90
(percentages)

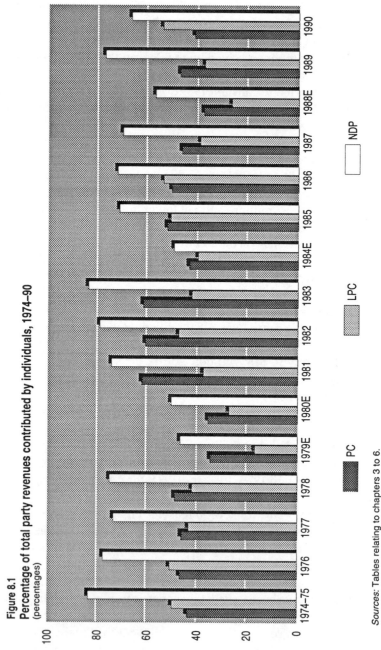

Sources: Tables relating to chapters 3 to 6.

49 percent of Conservative party revenues came from individuals. This dropped to about 35 percent for the election years of 1979 and 1980, then it rose to 61 percent–62 percent during the early 1980s. The ratio dropped to 43 percent in election year 1984, rose to 52 percent in 1985, then declined gradually to only 38 percent in 1988, an election year; it rose to 47 percent in 1989, but dropped to 41.5 percent in 1990. Almost all of the decline in the relative importance of individual contributions in the case of the Conservative party in election years is due to the rise in corporate contributions.[8]

The Liberal party obtained one-half of its total revenues from contributions from individuals in the mid-1970s. Then the percentage began to fall, reaching a low of only 17 percent in 1979, an election year. The percentage rose to 27 percent in 1980, another election year, and then increased sharply to 38 percent in 1981 and 47 percent in 1982. While it fell slightly thereafter, it was still 40 percent in the election year of 1984. It then rose to a peak of 54 percent in 1986, only to decline sharply to 26.5 percent in 1988, another election year. In 1989, the Liberals obtained 37 percent of their total revenue from individuals. The sharp increase to 54.1 percent reflects the special circumstances of the leadership race and convention described above. What happened to the Liberals in 1979, 1980 and 1988 when contributions from individuals were only 17 percent, 27 percent and 27 percent respectively? In 1979, contributions from individuals fell by $917 000 over 1978, while corporate contributions rose by $1 388 000 between 1978 and 1979.[9] Moreover, the reimbursement amounted to 10.2 percent of party revenues in 1979, and "other income" rose by $844 000 in 1979 (most of the latter increase was due to the assignment by candidates of part of the reimbursement of their "election expenses").[10] In 1980, individuals contributed $2.3 million to the Liberal party, up from $1.2 million in 1979, but only slightly higher than the amount in 1978 ($2.1 million). Corporate contributions in 1980 totalled $3.7 million, up from $2.5 million in 1978. "Other income" was almost $1.1 million in 1980 (again reflecting assignment of part of their reimbursement by candidates). The reimbursement accounted for 10.9 percent of total Liberal party revenues in 1980. In 1988, contributions from individuals to the Liberal party totalled $4.7 million, up from $3.5 million in 1987. However, corporate contributions rose from $5.3 million in 1987 to $8.5 million in 1988. "Other income" was $3.1 million, including about $2.27 million in assignment of candidate reimbursement. This category amounted to 17.6 percent of party income. In the previous two years, "other income" was less than $141 000. The 22.5 percent rebate amounted to 8.5 percent of total revenue in 1988.

In summary, the drop in the relative importance of individual contributions to the Liberal party in election years 1979, 1980 and 1988 reflects
the rise in other sources of revenues in those years, notably the reimbursement of part of the party's "election expenses" by the federal
government, and the "tax" imposed by party headquarters on the candidates' reimbursement of their "election expenses." In addition, in each
of these years, contributions from corporations rose in absolute terms
over the previous year. These years provide some insight into the way
the Liberal party has financed its activities in election years. The party
has relied on more corporations giving higher average contributions
(chap. 11), the 22.5 percent federal reimbursement of "election expenses"
and compulsory transfers from the party's candidates (except in 1984,
as noted in chap. 5).

3. LARGE CONTRIBUTIONS BY INDIVIDUALS

While large contributions (defined as those of $2 000 or more in a single
year)[11] by individuals may result in the odd newspaper story, they are
not an important source of revenue for Canada's three largest political
parties. Between 1983 and 1990, the largest single contribution to the
Liberal party ranged from $3 000 in 1985 (from each of three persons)
to $40 000 in 1988. For the Conservative party, the comparable figures
were $15 000 in 1983 and 1987 to $54 919 in 1989.[12] In 1988, the former
chairman of BCE Inc. (which owns Bell Canada) gave $40 000 to the
Tories *and* $25 000 to the Liberal party. Interestingly, all of these contri-
butions pale beside the contributions to the NDP by Mrs. Irene Dyck, a
Calgary widow. She has been the party's top individual contributor for
the entire period 1983–90. Her largest donation occurred in 1983, when
she gave $453 365 to the NDP. Thereafter the amounts ranged from
$23 165 (1985) to $215 767 (1984). Her contribution in 1983 is equivalent
to a contribution of $638 000 in 1991.[13]

The number of contributions of $2 000 or more in the period 1983–90
to the Conservative party ranged from 45 in 1983 to 295 in 1988 (table
8.13).[14] The Liberal party obtained few large contributions: their range
was from 15 in 1985 to 101 in 1990. In 1990, $1.95 million in contribu-
tions from individuals and corporations was routed through the Federal
Liberal Agency. This amount included 33 contributions of $2 000 or
more from individuals (totalling $103 050).[15] The NDP usually received
10 or 11 large contributions in each year. However, the party did better
in 1983 ($N = 21$), 1988 ($N = 39$), 1989 ($N = 26$) and 1990 ($N = 19$). In every
case, virtually all of the NDP's contributions were in the $2 000 to $4 000
range (table 8.13).

While the Tories received 963 contributions of $2 000 or more between 1983 and 1990, the Liberal party received 396 and the NDP received only 146. For the Conservatives, 61 percent of the "large" contributions from individuals were made in the election years of 1984 and 1988. The comparable figures for the Liberals and NDP are 31 percent and 34 percent respectively. In 1984, individuals who made large donations ($\geq$ \$2 000) seemed intent on "sending the Liberals a message," since the number of such contributions to the Tories outnumbered those to the Liberals by ten to one. In 1988, the ratio was only three to one (table 8.13). The average size of these contributions of \$2 000 or more ranged from a low of \$2 978 (for the Liberals in 1983) to a high of \$5 233 (for the Liberals in 1986).

Of the 1 525 contributions of \$2 000 or more between 1983 and 1990 reported in table 8.13, only 73 were over \$10 000, and 32 of them were made in the two election years, 1984 and 1988. The vast majority (79 percent) of contributions of \$2 000 or more between 1983 and 1990 were in the range of \$2 000 to \$4 000.

Between 1983 and 1990, "large" contributions (i.e., $\geq$ \$2 000) from individuals accounted for between 1.1 percent and 7.9 percent of the total value of contributions by individuals to the Liberal party (table 8.14). For the Progressive Conservative party, such contributions accounted for from 1.5 percent to 11.3 percent of the value of all contributions from individuals. These data strongly suggest that neither of these parties is heavily dependent upon a fairly small number of individuals who make large contributions to finance the party. Even in 1984 and 1988, when 278 and 295 individuals contributed an average of \$3 900 each, they accounted for only about 11 percent of the Progressive Conservative party's revenues from individuals. But individuals accounted for only 43.3 percent and 37.7 percent of total revenue of the Conservative party in 1984 and 1988 respectively (figure 8.1).

4. IMPORTANCE OF THE TAX CREDIT

One of the major innovations in the *Election Expenses Act* of 1974 was the provision for two types of government assistance in the financing of political parties and candidates: reimbursement of part of candidates' and parties' "election expenses," and the income-tax credit for contributions by individuals or corporations to parties and/or candidates. In general, party officials and academics have suggested that the effect of the tax credit has been to stimulate contributions by individuals by lowering the net after-tax cost of such contributions. Heretofore, it has not been possible to test this proposition, but with the aid of data provided to the Royal Commission on Electoral Reform and Party Financing by the Department of National Revenue on the *use* of the tax credit, more insights into the importance of the tax credit in stimulating contributions by individuals can be gained.

The structure and level of the tax credit for political contributions has not changed since 1974. It provides for a tax credit of the following:

- 75 percent on the first $100 of political contributions;
- $75 plus 50 percent of contributions between $100 and $550; and
- $300 plus 33.3 percent of contributions between $550 and $1 150.

The maximum tax credit is $500. At the outset, it must be appreciated that the *value* of the tax credit in real terms has declined since 1974, because the provision has been unchanged. Between 1974 and 1990, the Consumer Price Index trebled. As a result, a contribution of $100 in 1974 is the same in real terms (1989 dollars) as a contribution of just over $300 in 1990. The net after-tax cost of a contribution of $100 in 1974 would be $25, while the net, after-tax cost of the same contribution in real terms in 1990 ($300) would be $125, because the larger contribution in nominal terms is subject to the lower rate of credit on the amount over $100.

The tax credit for political contributions should be compared to that for contributions to charity. The tax credit for charitable contributions varies slightly depending upon the provincial income tax the individual pays, but in the case of a BC resident in 1991, the tax credit for charitable contributions was 26.6 percent on the first $250 and 45.4 percent on amounts above $250. Individuals may save their receipts for up to five years and thereby get a larger portion subject to the higher rate (*Financial Post*, 16 December 1991, 17). The tax credit for political contributions is more generous on contributions up to $1 150 in a year. At that level, the political tax credit is $500, while the tax credit for charitable contributions is $430. However, the maximum tax credit for political contributions is $500, while that for charitable contributions is 20 percent of the individual's taxable income, i.e., on a taxable income of $40 000, the maximum tax credit for charitable contributions is $8 000. This would require contributions of over $17 475. According to the Canadian Centre for Philanthropy, in 1990 Canadians gave $4.7 billion to charities, or about 0.8 percent of their pre-tax income.[16] A Decima poll conducted in September 1991 found that 77 percent of individuals claimed they had made contributions to non-religious groups in 1990. The median contribution was $62, up from $50 in 1989 and $42 in 1987 (ibid.).

The motives for making a political contribution are many and probably interrelated. Individuals give for ideological reasons, because they are asked to do so, to support a friend or associate, because they admire certain attributes of the candidate or party, to signal their displeasure with *other* parties or candidates, or because as party members they are solicited and are expected to make a contribution. Where the tax credit fits in is difficult to determine, although parties and candidates emphasize in their solicitations of all kinds that the tax credit reduces the *net* cost of making a contribution. The growth in the number of individuals making political contributions has already been described (tables 8.1, 8.1a, 8.2). For whatever reason, all three main parties have been able to attract many more contributors than they were able to do prior to 1974. In terms of the total number of dollars contributed by individuals to the three main parties, table 8.5 suggests that peaks may have been reached in 1984 and 1988 when individuals gave $24 million (in 1989 dollars) to the Progressive Conservative, Liberal and New Democratic parties.

A substantial fraction of individuals did *not* claim the tax credit for their political contributions, but the fraction that did so appears to be rising. For example, while only 45 percent of individuals making a contribution between 1974 and 1977 claimed the tax credit, just over half did so in 1979 and 1988, when a much larger number made a contribution to a party and/or candidate (table 8.4). In 1981 and 1982, the percentage claiming the tax credit rose about 58 percent, after which it fell to the 51 percent to 54 percent range until 1986. In 1986 and 1987, almost two-thirds of individual donors claimed the credit. The rate dropped to 59 percent in 1988, an election year in which over 313 000 people made a political contribution.

Massicotte (1991) indicates that the percentage of individual contributors who claimed the Quebec income-tax credit[17] for political contributions ranged from 31 percent to 52 percent between 1978 and 1988. In six of the years, the claim rate was under 40 percent. The value of contributions reported to the Quebec Department of Revenue as a percentage of contributions to the parties between 1983 and 1988 was typically over 15 percentage points higher than that for the federal tax credit, except in 1986 and 1987. Massicotte (ibid.) offers several reasons why a substantial fraction of individual contributors, particularly small contributors, does not claim the Quebec tax credit. First, people lose their tax receipts. Second, some contributors do not pay income tax and hence cannot claim the credit. Third, some people do not claim the credit to which they are entitled on their income tax return for "fear of political reprisals." Moreover, such behaviour is most common among those giving less than $100 and for whom the legislation guarantees anonymity. The last reason seems surprising, but Massicotte insists that such a fear exists, even if some consider it somewhat far-fetched. To this list, another reason could be added: the value of the credit for a contribution of, say, $50 in Quebec is only $25.

The data in table 8.2 indicate that, in nominal terms, the average contribution by individuals to the NDP never exceeded $70 in the period 1974–90. Thus, it is reasonable to infer that probably more than half the contributions were less than $100. Hence, they were eligible for the maximum rate of tax credit, 75 percent. On the other hand, the absolute size of the credit for a $80 contribution is only $60, whereas the tax credit on a $500 contribution is $275. However, relative to the gross income and taxes payable of the donor of $500, the tax credit may be less significant than the $60 tax credit is to the donor of an $80 contribution. Table 8.2 indicates that it was not until 1984 that the average contribution by individuals to the Conservative party exceeded $100 in nominal terms. For the Liberal party, the average was under $100 in 5 of the 17 years between 1974 and 1990. In summary, it appears that many individuals making political contributions are eligible for the maximum *rate* of tax credit (i.e., 75 percent on the first $100). However, in real terms, a contribution of $100 in 1989 is equivalent to a contribution of $36 in 1974, $59 in 1980, $81 in 1984 and $92 in 1987.[18]

Table 8.4 indicates that the average value of the tax credit[19] for political contributions by individuals was in the range of $58 to $67 (in nominal dollars) between 1974 and 1981. Then the average increased in an irregular trend to $95 in 1988. In constant 1989 dollars, the average value of the tax credit fell from about $180 in 1974 and 1975 to $100 in 1988.

The total value of the federal tax credit for political contributions increased from under $3 million annually prior to 1977 to over $8 million in 1983 in nominal dollars (table 8.6). In election year 1984, the value of the credit for political contributions jumped to $13.6 million. The subsidy averaged $8.7 million over the period 1985–87. Then, the amount surged to $17.5 million in 1988, an election year. In constant 1989 dollars, the value of tax credits for political contributions totalled $145.1 million between 1974 and 1988 (table 8.6). The amount exceeded $10 million in all four election years, and in 1983 and 1986. The value of the tax credits rose from $3.6 million in 1974 (when they were only available effective 1 August) to between $6 million and $8 million annually between 1975 and 1978. Between the 1980 and 1984 elections, the value of tax credits was in the range of $7.4 million to $10.7 million per year. During the next three interelection years, 1985–87, tax credits amounted to between $8.4 million and $11.3 million (table 8.6).

The data in table 8.6 indicate that the taxpayers, through the tax credit, paid for about 50 percent of the value of political contributions made by individuals to parties and candidates. In election years, perhaps because a larger number of people made a contribution, the percentage was lower, typically 46 percent versus 52 percent in the period 1985–87. Note that between 1980 and 1988, no more than 1.4 percent of all individuals filing a taxable[20] tax return ("tax filers") claimed the tax credit for political contributions (table 8.7).

The Department of National Revenue indicates that only a tiny fraction of tax filers claimed the tax credit for political contributions. Table 8.7 indicates that no more than 1.8 percent of male tax filers claimed the tax credit in the period 1980–88. Male tax filers were, on average, twice as likely to claim the tax credit for political contributions as female tax filers (and they were also twice as likely to make a contribution in the first place). However, if a high proportion of the men were married and had a higher income than their spouse, this difference is not surprising.

The data in tables 8.1 and 8.7 indicate that, despite the existence of a rather generous tax credit for political contributions (particularly those below $100) and the parties' expanded use of direct-mail appeals, not more than 2 percent of electors made a political contribution even in an election year.[21] Is the problem that the parties (and candidates) have failed to ask for contributions from a sufficiently large fraction of the population? What is known about the direct-mail "prospecting" efforts of all three parties (which obtain a contribution from 1 percent to 2 percent of those receiving the appeal) and the use of the parties' much smaller "house" list (where the response rate is usually about 15 percent to 20 percent) suggests that, in fact, Canadians' willingness to *make* political contributions is far less than they *say* it is.

Ken Carty has raised a number of thoughtful questions about the interpretation of the data on the percentage of individuals claiming the tax credit for political contributions. First, if the credit is as important to party fund-raising as has been suggested, why did it take seven years before at least one-half of the donors claimed it? Second, why is the percentage of individuals claiming the credit in election years 1984 and 1988 *less* than in adjacent years? Further, he noted that the absolute number of persons claiming the tax credit and the average contribution rose in 1984 and 1988 (table 8.2). Thus, it seems plausible to believe that more of these election-year-only donors would claim the tax credit to reduce their net cost of making a political contribution to a candidate and/or party. Finally, he asked if there were differences in the "claim rate" by party. Unfortunately, the data provided by the Department of National Revenue and reported in the tables were not disaggregated by party.

The general thrust of these points is that the availability of the tax credit (which was quite generous in 1974) may be of modest significance to parties and candidates in their efforts to obtain contributions from individuals. Perhaps there are two groups of individuals who make donations: one that is "price sensitive" and hence claims the tax credit, and the other that is not influenced by the availability of the tax credit and does *not* claim it. Certainly the *parties* believe that the existence of the tax credit is helpful in soliciting contributions, since they all feature the details of the credit in their direct-mail appeals.[22] All parties treat convention fees as contributions for which they can issue a receipt for the individual to claim the tax credit. On a fee/donation of $875, such as that for the 1990 Liberal leadership convention, the value of the tax credit is substantial ($408).

Perhaps many people are induced to make a contribution because of the tax credit or to make a larger contribution because of it – because they like the idea of having "the government" (actually other taxpayers) subsidize part of their contribution. However, a substantial fraction of donors does not bother to *claim* the credit because (i) in their mind, they have already "received" the benefit when they make the contribution and think of its *net* cost when they write their cheque; (ii) they lose their receipt for the tax credit; (iii) the amount of the tax credit is quite small relative to the total tax bill of most middle- to upper-income persons; and (iv) donors not only require a receipt, but must also make the effort to find where to claim the credit on the tax return and fill out the appropriate part of the form. Thus, the fact that no more than 65 percent of individuals *claim* the tax credit is not proof that it is not much of an incentive to make a political contribution. There is, as the poet said, "many a slip between cup and lip."

4.1 Tax Credits by Income Level

The distribution of the federal tax credit for individuals making a political contribution by level of income between 1980 and 1988 is given in tables 8.8 to 8.10. In terms of the *number* of tax filers claiming the tax credit for political contributions, between 1980 and 1988 between 57 percent and 63 percent were in the range of $15 000 to $50 000 in taxable income. Another 15 percent to 23 percent of filers were in the income range of $50 000 to $100 000 (table 8.9). As expected, the average size of the tax credit claimed rose as the donor's level of income increased. For example, in 1988, the average credit for those with an income under $30 000 was about $70. For those with an income of $100 000 to $250 000, it was $173, while for those over $250 000 it was $233 (table 8.8). A tax credit of $70 implies a contribution of $93, while a tax credit of $233 implies a contribution of $416. It should be noted that of the 184 410 tax filers claiming the tax credit for political contributions in 1988 (compared to 313 142 contributions from individuals), only 19 450 (or 10.5 percent) had an income over $100 000.

In terms of the dollar value of tax credits for political contributions, an increasing fraction is claimed by persons with a taxable income over $30 000: from 56 percent in 1980 to 72 percent in 1985; this was followed by a slight decrease to 68 percent in 1986 and 1987, and then an increase to 72 percent in 1988 (table 8.9). Obviously, comparisons of income levels and amounts of tax credits over the period 1980–88 are made difficult by the fact that all the figures in tables 8.8 to 8.10 are in nominal dollars. However, between 1980 and 1988, the CPI increased by 62 percent. Unfortunately, it is not possible to adjust the income classes for inflation, although it is possible to convert the amount of the tax credit into constant 1989 dollars. This was not done for tables 8.8 to 8.10 because the income classes could not also be corrected.

The concentration of the value of tax credits is easily seen in table 8.8. In 1987, for example, 32.2 percent of tax filers had taxable income of under $15 000, but they accounted for only 7.7 percent of the value of tax credits. On the other hand, 42.9 percent of political tax credits were claimed by individuals with a taxable income of $50 000 or more. These individuals accounted for only 7.3 percent of taxable returns. In 1985, 6.1 percent of taxable returns over $50 000 accounted for 46 percent of all political tax credits. The only income group for which the proportion of political tax credits was about equal to the proportion of taxable returns was the group in the $30 000 to $50 000 range (table 8.10).

4.2 Tax Credits by Province

The distribution of political tax credits by province/region can be found in tables 8.11 and 8.12. Between 1980 and 1988, the average tax credit claimed by individual tax filers in the Atlantic region, Quebec, Ontario and Alberta was almost always *above* the national average. However, the average credit for BC and Manitoba/Saskatchewan tax filers was *below* the average in most years. This *may* be attributable to the strength of the NDP in BC, Manitoba and Saskatchewan[23] and the fact that the NDP has been able to obtain contributions from more individuals than the other parties, although the average size of contributions to the NDP has been well below that for the Tories or Liberals (table 8.2).

When the total value of tax credits obtained by individuals is examined in comparison to the number of tax filers by province/region, a rather different picture emerges. While Manitoba and Saskatchewan accounted for 8.0 percent of taxable returns in 1987, they accounted for 21.9 percent of the value of tax credits claimed and for 26.2 percent of the number of tax filers claiming a tax credit for political contributions.

In 1987, tax filers in BC accounted for 16.5 percent of the value of tax credits, but only 11.3 percent of the number of taxable returns. In contrast, Quebec accounted for 13.8 percent of the value of political tax credits, 11.2 percent of all returns claiming a tax credit, but 25.3 percent of the total number of taxable returns. In other words, tax filers in Quebec were *far* less likely to make a political contribution to a federal party than were residents of Manitoba/Saskatchewan or BC. However, when they did contribute, their average contribution was substantially larger. Table 8.11 indicates that, in 1987, the average tax credit for Quebeckers was $92, while that for Manitoba/Saskatchewan residents was $62 and that for BC residents was $55. These tax credits translate into average contributions of $109, $83 and $73 respectively. However, the higher average value of Quebeckers' contributions did not make up for the much lower fraction of Quebeckers who made a political contribution for which they claimed the tax credit. In 1987, 0.35 percent of Quebeckers with a taxable income made a political contribution for which they claimed a tax credit.[24] The comparable figures for Manitoba/Saskatchewan and BC were 2.57 percent and 1.57 percent respectively. In other words, Manitoba/Saskatchewan taxpayers were over seven times as likely to make a political contribution as were taxpayers from Quebec. BC residents were 4.5 times as likely to make a contribution to a federal party as Quebec residents.

Table 8.12 indicates that Ontario residents, who accounted for 37.5 percent of taxable income-tax returns filed by individuals in 1987, accounted for 32.3 percent of the value of tax credits and 28.6 percent of the number of individuals claiming a tax credit. In other words, Ontario residents were somewhat less likely than the average Canadian to claim a political tax credit, but their average contribution ($118) was above the national average ($100).[25] Given the lower average income of persons living in Atlantic Canada, it is not surprising to find them "underrepresented" in terms of the value of tax credits for political contributions (6.2 percent) relative to the percentage of taxable returns (8.5 percent) in 1987. The figures for Alberta were 8.9 percent and 8.9 percent respectively. Note that, while we have focused on 1987, there would be very little difference in the pattern if we had examined 1980 or 1985 (table 8.12).

The interprovincial differences in the use of the tax credit for political contributions can be seen when one examines the number of tax filers claiming the credit in 1984 and 1988 (peak years) as a percentage of the number of electors in those two federal general elections. Table 8.12a indicates that electors in Manitoba/Saskatchewan had the highest rate of use of the tax credit (over twice the national average), while Quebec had the lowest – less than half the national average. BC was also well above the national average, while the Atlantic provinces and Alberta were below it. Ontario was very close to the national average. Note that Manitoba/Saskatchewan electors' use of the tax credit for political contributions was 5.7 times that of Quebec in 1984 and 4.4 times it in 1988. Recall, however, that the average contribution (and tax credit) of Quebeckers was 41 percent higher than Manitoba/Saskatchewan electors in 1984 and 53 percent higher in 1988 (table 8.11).

5. *FINANCEMENT POPULAIRE*

The purpose of this section is to discuss a proposal for reforming the law concerning political contributions that would have particular significance for contributions from individuals. In the past few years, some federal Conservative MPs from Quebec have argued that *only* registered voters should be permitted to make contributions to candidates and parties, and that the size of such contributions be limited to perhaps $5 000 annually.[26] These two changes are described as *financement populaire* (or "popular fund-raising"). The MPs proposed that the federal government adopt legislation like that enacted in Quebec in 1977.

Under the Quebec legislation, the *Act to govern the financing of political parties*, enacted by the Parti québécois, only registered voters can contribute to a political party and/or to a candidate. Their total donations to each party (including its candidates) are limited to $3 000 per year. Further, the name of each person contributing $100 or more must be made public. It should be emphasized that this innovation by the Parti québécois was seen as having two rather different types of virtues. First, it would make political financing more democratic and lessen the possibility of corruption. Second, it would provide the PQ with a tactical advantage over the provincial Liberal party, which was then heavily dependent upon corporate contributions. The tactical advantage did not last long (Massicotte 1991; Angell 1990a, 1990b).

5.1 Gérin's Proposal

In March 1986, the federal Progressive Conservative party announced that it was forming a committee to examine the possibility of limiting individual contributions to the party to $5 000 and eliminating corporate donations entirely (*Globe and Mail*, 17 March 1986, A4). However, the party would retain its traditional financing structure for the next two years, even if the proposal was adopted. The most outspoken proponent of the proposal was Quebec MP François Gérin (Megantic–Compton–Stanstead), who pointed to the success of the Quebec Liberal party in raising $8 million annually in Quebec.[27] The proposal had the strongest support from Quebec MPs, who stated that this would help the party to counter its image as the party of "large corporations, rich people and white male Canadians" (ibid.). The debate on the issue was halted when Michel Côté, then Minister of Consumer and Corporate Affairs, introduced a motion to refer the plan to a committee. However, Gérin raised the matter at a meeting of the Quebec caucus of the Conservative party in early February 1987. The caucus unanimously recommended that corporate and union contributions to all federal political parties be prohibited. The Quebec caucus also proposed an unspecified limit on contributions from individuals (*Toronto Star,* 9 February 1987, A1–A2). The caucus proposed four reforms to deal with what the Prime Minister called a "serious problem of perception about morality": *financement populaire,* registration of lobbyists, tougher conflict of interest rules and more controls on patronage.

At a weekend convention of the Progressive Conservative party's Quebec wing in March 1987, following the André Bissonnette and Roch LaSalle scandals (see Harrison 1988, chap. 16; Hoy 1987, chap. 16), the issue of *financement populaire* was again raised. The Quebec wing of the federal Conservative party voted unanimously for a law to ban corporate donations to political parties and to limit contributions, but the amount was not specified (*Financial Times,* 28 August 1988, 34).

In an interview in October 1987 on the merits of his plan, Gérin pointed to his own riding. He said that, by knocking on doors in August, he and party members had raised $58 300 in contributions from 2 800 individuals[28] (*Financial Post,* 5 October 1987, 4). The move to *financement populaire* would, he argued, also clean up the current image of the party and help to raise its standing in the polls. Businesses should also support the reform, Gérin insisted, because many of them donate "only because it is expected of them" (ibid.).

In November, what the newspapers called the "fund-raising feud" reached a new intensity. Gérin and other supporters threatened to boycott a party fund-raising dinner in Montreal featuring the Prime Minister, stating that they did not believe in that type of fund-raising (*Globe and Mail,* 13 November 1987, A1). They also complained that average people were being discriminated against because they could not afford the ticket price of $250. At a seminar held in his Eastern Townships riding, Gérin told 50 Tory supporters and businessmen that donations by large corporations – to any political party – give the appearance of buying the party and "embarrasses" him. He added that he had no time for those who take the role of party bagmen, and stated that they were "a public danger."[29]

In August 1988, Lucien Bouchard, the federal Secretary of State, produced a paper on ethics that proposed to limit political contributions to $5 000 per year and to permit only individuals to make such contributions (Bouchard 1988). The Prime Minister said he was willing to legislate this proposal, if other parties would agree to it (*Globe and Mail*, 23 August 1988, A6). Columnist William Johnson argued against the proposal, although he agreed with Mr. Bouchard that it "would limit, both in fact and in the minds of the electorate, the risks of patronage and of conflicts of interest" (*Vancouver Sun*, 23 August 1988, B3). Johnson argued that "there has been no evidence of scandals or chronic and serious abuse of trust that would justify such a drastic restriction of freedoms." It would exclude unions, associations and corporations from political life. In Johnson's view, most people take part in public life as members of associations. Hence, to deprive them of this right – except as members of political parties – "is to strike a terrible blow against freedom of speech and freedom of association."[30]

In a newspaper interview a few days before the 1988 general election, Prime Minister Mulroney stated that *financement populaire* "fits with a logical and fundamental approach to attack the root of many potential conflicts of interest" (*La Presse*, 16 November 1988, quoted in Gérin 1990, 15). The Prime Minister said that he was determined to bring in legislation to forbid contributions from corporations and trade unions and to limit the size of contributions from individuals. "The adoption of such a law on citizen-based financing is part of this concern for transparency."

According to an official of the Quebec wing of the Progressive Conservative party, for the 1988 general election, 71 of 75 ridings in Quebec raised funds for their campaigns solely through donations from electors that were limited to $5 000 per year (Falardeau 1990).[31] Companies, corporations, trade unions and syndicates were prohibited from contributing to the campaign. Each riding association raised about $30 000 this way. Data reported by the CEO indicate that the Conservatives raised an average of $43 820 in the 75 Quebec ridings.[32]

In April 1989, the Quebec wing of the Conservative party sent a questionnaire to each of its 75 constituency associations in Quebec. Some 49 constituencies (representing 78 percent of Quebec Conservative MPs) replied. The answers from volunteers and riding officials to several specific questions are worth noting. Although the majority of the ridings in Quebec financed the 1988 campaigns using *financement populaire*, 71 percent of the ridings said that they considered the financing campaign "not very successful" or "a failure." However, almost all ridings (86 percent) favoured the use of *financement populaire* to finance the riding between elections. Finally, when asked if they would press for the adoption of *financement populaire* at the next national convention and push for all parties to raise funds this way, 81 percent of respondents replied that they "did not believe in this concept of fundraising" (Falardeau 1990).

Four years to the day after he had proposed a resolution calling for *financement populaire* at a Progressive Conservative party convention, François Gérin testified before the Royal Commission on Electoral Reform and Party Financing. According to Gérin (1990, 3), *financement populaire* would "limit the clout in party circles of the professional fundraisers who are real political parasites with disproportionate influence on parties." Further, *financement populaire* "will give political parties back to those who are their ultimate source of power, their members and those who vote for them." Gérin (ibid., 16) suggested that political parties are hesitant to endorse *financement populaire* because they fear its decentralizing effects that would reduce the power of the present "establishment figures." In Gérin's view (ibid., 5–6), political contributions by corporations are "not disinterested acts." He noted that about half the donations of $5 000 or more are given exclusively to the party in power. When one of the members of the Royal Commission asked "whether corporations might not contribute to political parties as part of their civic responsibilities, Mr. Gérin replied they can contribute by paying more income tax. He also said their individual shareholders are free to contribute and there was no evidence individual shareholders endorsed the donation policies of the corporate managers" (*Globe and Mail*, 13 March 1990, A8).

Financement populaire "requires true citizen participation, but it also requires true decentralization of party organizations and decision making" (Gérin 1990, 8). Moreover, Gérin (ibid., 9) argued that *financement populaire* will require the party to "get closer" to voters and "regularly seek their views on its main policy directions." This has certainly not occurred in Quebec where the Quebec Liberal party under Robert Bourassa has been able to raise the bulk of its considerable funds from "social activities" that amount to paid access opportunities.[33] Gérin (ibid., 10) advocated that public funding take the form of $1 per vote in general elections transferred to each party. He stated that, if this had been applied in the elections from 1974 to 1988, the Liberals and Conservatives "would have got about as much as they received from corporations and unions."

Gérin (1990, 13) indicated that his August 1987 fund-raising efforts in his own riding generated $62 710 from 3 162 individuals. A limit of $1 000 was placed on contributions. According to Gérin, in mid-1988 Lucien Bouchard was able to raise $85 000 from 1 600 individuals using the *financement populaire* approach to his by-election race. Gérin (ibid., 14) claimed that the Progressive Conservative party's candidates in Quebec raised $2.5 million for the 1988 general election.[34] For the 1988 election, Mr. Gérin reported that he raised $8 922 from 95 individuals and received $27 104 from the Conservative party, for a total of $36 026. His "election expenses" were $38 815 and his "personal expenses" were $3 680. He received $21 137 in reimbursement (Canada, Elections Canada 1988c, 3–136). In light of what he said about his fundraising in 1987, it is hard to understand why Mr. Gérin received $27 104 from the Conservative party, although it is possible that this amount consisted of money raised by Mr. Gérin before the writ was issued and routed through the PC Canada Fund so that donors could receive a receipt for the tax credit. While the Conservative party made only modest transfers to candidates in 1988, Quebec candidates received over half the total amount.

The case for *financement populaire* was taken up by Allan R. Taylor, chairman and chief executive officer of the Royal Bank of Canada, in a speech in February 1991.[35] Taylor (1991, 10) argued that limiting contributions to electors would increase public participation in political parties: "to remain healthy [the] system needs constructive ideas and dedicated people." In his view, "the current system of corporate fundraising doesn't help with that broader purpose – the continuing democratization of our politics." Taylor (ibid., 12) stated that the purpose of looking closely at the Quebec model "is to strip away any possible suggestion of unfairness or impropriety, or undue influence." It is not clear, however, that *financement populaire* in Quebec has eliminated all of these concerns (Massicotte 1991; Angell 1990a, 1990b).

In light of the fact that two of the most vocal supporters of *financement populaire* inside the Progressive Conservative party caucus, François Gérin and Lucien Bouchard, left the party to join the separatist Bloc québécois in May 1990, it is unlikely that the Conservative party will push this "reform." Moreover, the idea attracted little support from the persons and organizations presenting briefs to the Royal Commission on Electoral Reform and Party Financing. The author's interviews with over 60 officials/advisors of the three main parties found virtually no support for the idea. As one senior NDP official put it, "the Tories and the Liberals have the corporations as a major constituency and we have the trade unions. All of us try to raise money from individuals. We see no reason to prevent people from making donations through organizations such as trade unions rather than as individuals." Almost without exception, the interviewees stressed the importance of full disclosure of the source and amount of political contributions as the best protection against the possibility of contributions influencing a party or a candidate. Further, those familiar with the situation in Quebec argued that limiting donors to electors leads to subterfuges to "get around" the law. In their view, it is very hard to enforce this element of *financement populaire*. In Quebec, the Liberal party has made extensive use of "access opportunity" events to raise money from corporate executives and professionals, rather than relying on many donors each making a modest contribution. Finally, some interviewees emphasized that, if it becomes more difficult (and costly) for parties and candidates to raise money to carry out their important tasks, there will be pressure on government to increase the financial assistance it provides. As noted in chapter 1, over the last electoral cycle (1985–88), the federal government's tax expenditures and cash subsidies (reimbursements) amounted to 31.4 percent of the expenditures of all parties and candidates (some $66.7 million in nominal dollars).

6. CONCLUSIONS

One of the major transformations wrought by the *Election Expenses Act* of 1974 has been a great reduction in the dependence of the Progressive Conservative and Liberal parties on a few hundred large corporations for almost all of their funds. While no more than 1.8 percent of federal electors ever made a contribution to a party and/or a candidate in any year in the period 1974–90, the number of contributions by individuals to a party rose from 85 000 in 1975 to 205 000 in 1983 and to 218 000 in 1990. In election years 1984 and 1988, the number was 298 000 and 313 000 respectively (1.8 percent of electors), reflecting the number of contributions to candidates as well. For the three larger parties combined (PC, Liberal, NDP), the average number of donations from individuals rose from 79 000 annually in the period 1974–77 to 120 000 in the period 1978–81, and then to 187 000 in the period 1982–85. However, the annual average dropped to 174 000 annually over the last five years, 1986–90. This drop is largely attributable to the reduced number of individual donations to the Progressive Conservative party. Between 1982 and 1985, the number of contributions averaged 80 000 per year, but dropped to 43 000 per year in the period 1986–90. On the other hand, the Liberal party's average rose very slightly, while the NDP's rose from 77 000 per year in the period 1982–85 to 101 000 between 1986 and 1990. Because federal politics in Canada has become so dynamic, it is not clear whether the setbacks experienced by the Tories and the success of the NDP in the period 1986–90 will continue.

In terms of contributions from individuals as a percentage of total party revenue, it is clear that the NDP relies most on this source (over 75 percent in half the years between 1974 and 1990)[36] and the Liberal party relies on it the least, particularly in election years (figure 8.1). In 12 of the years between 1974/75 and 1990, the Conservative party obtained a larger share of its total revenues from contributions from individuals than did the Liberal party. However, except for election years, both the Liberal and Progressive Conservative parties now obtain about half of their revenues from individuals. Moreover, both are raising and spending far, far more between elections than was the case prior to the *Election Expenses Act* of 1974.

Large contributions from individuals, defined as those of $2 000 or more, have not been an important source of revenues for any party. Between 1983 and 1990, they accounted for from 1.5 percent to 11.3 percent of the total value of all contributions from individuals to the Progressive Conservative party. For the Liberal party, the comparable figures were 1.1 percent to 7.9 percent.

There appears to be something of an "election year effect" in terms of the *number* of contributions to the three main parties from individuals. For example, in 1988 the Tories had 54 000 contributions versus 39 000 in 1987 and 40 000 in 1989. The NDP received 118 000 contributions from individuals in 1988 versus 88 000 in 1987 and 89 000 in 1989 (table 8.2). The effect was not present, however, for the Liberals and Tories in the 1979 and 1980 elections or for the NDP in 1984.

All of the three main parties face a challenge in terms of the shrinking size of the *average* contribution from individuals in *real* terms. For example, in 1974 and 1975, the average contribution to the Progressive Conservative party was $284 and $253 in 1989 dollars. In 1990 and 1991, it was $161 and $180 respectively. (It fell to a low of $119 in 1983, the year in which the Tories had a record number of donors, 99 300.) For the Liberal party, the average contribution from individuals in 1974–76 averaged almost $300. In 1989, it was $119, and in 1991, it was $117. For the NDP, the average contribution in 1974 was $132 and it was $90 in 1975. It fell to $67 in 1989 and $50 in 1990 but recovered somewhat to $72 in 1991. Perhaps this decline in the average contribution from individuals in real terms is simply the result of the greater *number* of contributions from individuals. But the donor base is still a tiny percentage of the population; for example, only 1.8 percent of electors in 1988 made a contribution to a party and/or candidate. A better explanation may lie in the fact that the formula for the income-tax credit for political contributions has not changed since 1974. Contributions up to $100 (in nominal terms) are eligible for a tax credit of 75 percent. However, a contribution of $100 in 1974 was, in terms of constant 1989 dollars, equal to a contribution of $300 in 1990. The *net* after-tax cost of a contribution of $100 in 1974 was $25. The net cost of a $300 contribution in 1990 (equivalent in 1989 dollars to $100 in 1974) was $125. If donors wanted to make the same contribution in real terms, their net cost rose greatly after 1974. Thus, it seems reasonable to infer that average contributions have not kept pace because their real net after-tax cost to the individual has increased substantially since 1974. It has done so because the tax credit formula has not been changed since it was enacted.

The net cost of political contributions to individuals is higher than the application of the formula suggests because, prior to 1980, less than 50 percent of the individuals making a contribution claimed the tax credit (table 8.5). Since that time, the fraction has increased somewhat, although the peak (for the period 1974–88) was 64.9 percent in 1986. The (unweighted) average for the period 1974–79 was 46.4 percent. It rose to 53.9 percent in the period 1980–84 and to 60.6 percent in the period 1985–88. In light of these figures, it is important to reconsider the importance of the tax credit in assisting parties and candidates in raising money from individuals.

Although the average tax credit did not exceed $100 (in nominal terms) between 1974 and 1988, and was less than $70 in most years, the median tax credit[37] was probably somewhat smaller. Smaller amounts are easier to overlook in computing one's income taxes, particularly if a receipt must be filed with the return. However, in *real* terms, the average value of the tax credit *fell* from $186 in 1974 to $100 in 1988. Yet, despite the decline of the average value of the tax credit, the percentage of persons claiming it rose – from 46.1 percent in 1974 to 58.9 percent in 1988. The real value of the credit in 1986 and 1987 was even lower ($97–$82 in 1989 dollars), but almost 65 percent of individual donors claimed it. The rising long-term trend in the fraction claiming the tax credit suggests there may be a social learning process at work, that is, it takes a long time for people to learn to use the tax credit in the sense of following through on the paperwork *after* they have made the political contribution. Parties can help. For example, in BC the NDP issues the receipt for the tax credit between January and February of the year following the year in which the contribution(s) has (have) been made. Thus it arrives in the mail close to the time when most people file their income tax return, i.e., in April.

One of the most interesting findings was the large interprovincial differences in the propensity of individuals to make political contributions. In 1984 and 1988, for example, taxpayers in Manitoba/Saskatchewan were 5.7 and 4.5 times as likely to make a contribution to a federal party as were Quebec residents. However, the average *contribution* of Quebeckers was 41 percent and 53 percent higher than that of Manitoba/Saskatchewan residents claiming the tax credit. The difference may be due to the strength of the NDP in Manitoba/ Saskatchewan relative to Quebec. Overall, a higher percentage of NDP voters made a political contribution than supporters of other federal parties.

At the insistence of a few Quebec MPs, the Progressive Conservative party has discussed the possibility of adopting the *financement populaire* approach to the regulation of party and candidate fund-raising. The two key elements of this approach are: permitting only electors to make contributions and putting a limit on the amount any individual can contribute to a party/candidates in any year, say, $5 000. Party officials responsible for its financing were not enthusiastic. Two of its most important advocates have left the Conservative party for the Bloc québécois, so the proposal is unlikely to gain much visibility or support. None of the five dozen current or former officials in the Progressive Conservative, Liberal or New Democratic parties interviewed by the author in 1990 supported the idea of legislating *financement populaire*.

APPENDIX 8.1
FINANCEMENT POPULAIRE IN QUEBEC

Since 1 April 1978, only electors have been entitled to make contributions to political parties in Quebec. Moreover, electors may give no more than $3 000 in a single year to any party. While the subject of *financement populaire* in Quebec is addressed in much more detail elsewhere (Massicotte 1990; Angell 1990a, 1990b), it is useful to review some of its salient characteristics, particularly the Liberal party's use of social events (including "access opportunities") to finance its activities.

Between 1978 and 1988, the annual total revenues of the Quebec Liberal party ranged from a low of $1.1 million in 1981 to a high of $10.1 million in 1985 (in nominal dollars). The range for the Parti québécois was $1.8 million (1987) to $6.9 million (1985)[38] (table A8.1; note that between 1978 and 1988, the CPI rose by 94.3 percent).

Contributions (all from electors) accounted for 66.3 percent of total Liberal party revenues between 1978 and 1988. For the PQ, the comparable figure was 62.8 percent. As noted in table A8.2, the PQ relied more heavily on membership dues (15.8 percent of total revenues versus 10.3 percent for the Liberals). The importance of contributions varied considerably from year to year. For the Liberal party, contributions accounted for 80 percent or more of total revenues in two years (1978, 1979) but for as little as 38 percent in 1982. The range was almost as great for the PQ (table A8.1).

Both parties experienced extraordinary variation in the number of receipts issued for contributions. The number issued by the Liberals rose from 64 500 in 1978 to 124 400 in 1979, only to fall to 11 000 in 1981. Then the number recovered to 50 000 in 1983. While the number of receipts rose to 61 800 in 1985 and 66 500 in 1987, Massicotte (1991, tables 1.A1 and 1.A2) explains that the number of contributors to the Quebec Liberal party was about 70 percent of the number of receipts in the period 1985–88. (For the PQ, the difference was much smaller, typically less than 2 percent.) The number of receipts for contributions reported by the PQ rose from 93 900 in 1978 to a peak of 168 900 in 1981 (when Liberal fortunes were at their lowest). Then the number of receipts issued by the PQ fell to 23 600 in 1986 and 22 100 in 1987 (table A8.1).

Not only has the number of contributors to the PQ fallen greatly from the late 1970s, but the average level of contributions has been modest and well below those to the Liberals from 1986 to 1988. In nominal terms, average contributions to the PQ were in the range of $20–25 in the period 1978–82. Since that time, they have been in the range of $33 to $38,[39] except for 1985, an election year, when the average was $64. Recall from table 8.2 that these amounts were below even the average contribution to the NDP (which was far below the average for the PCs and Liberals).

While the average contribution to the Quebec Liberal party was below that for the PQ in 1979 and 1980, it was substantially above the PQ's average in most other years; for example, in 1981, the Liberals' average contribution was $65 versus $20 for the PQ; in 1984, the comparable figures were $64 and $38 respectively. While the average contribution to the Liberals between 1985 and 1988 (reported in table A8.1) should be reduced somewhat to reflect the difference between receipts and contributors, the gap between the two parties in the late 1980s was large indeed (Massicotte 1990). The gap widened in 1989: $253 for the Liberal party versus $49 for the PQ.

In December 1985, the Quebec Liberal party returned to power under Robert Bourassa. The party's method of raising money moved toward increasing use of social functions (ranging from cocktail parties to golf tournaments) at which the attendance of one or more cabinet ministers is advertised and for which tickets are sold for up to $1 000 per person. The growth in the use of social activities as a method of fund-raising can be noted from the fact that, in 1984 when it was not in power, the QLP raised only $222 570, or 6 percent of its total contributions from this source, according to Angell (1990a, 21). In 1985 (the general election was in December), the Liberal party raised 30 percent of all contributions from social activities (table A8.1). In 1986, the amount from this source was up to 66.7 percent of contributions and in 1987[40] it rose to 73.5 percent of contributions (ibid., 21).[41] In 1988, social activities accounted for over 80 percent of money raised by QLP (a total of $9.75 million). However, in 1989, there was a huge drop to just 6 percent, a change that merits further research (table A8.1).

Massicotte (1990, 15) states that 50 of the 264 events in 1988 required a contribution of $1 000 or more and accounted for about 35 percent of the revenues from such social events. Because these events typically involved about 30 contributors, they amounted to an "access opportunity" where individuals were able to press their concerns on the minister or ministers present on a face-to-face basis. For example, Premier Bourassa had a $1 000 per person cocktail party in his riding of St. Laurent in August 1987. It raised $101 850 for the QLP (Angell 1990a, 11). According to one newspaper account in 1987, businessmen attending a dinner at $125 a plate were promised a meeting with the president of the Treasury Board – if they paid an extra $375 (*Globe and Mail*, 25 November 1987, A8). According to this account:

> St. Hyacinthe Liberal MNA Charles Messier got into hot water recently when the PQ released a copy of a letter he sent out to local businessmen, inviting them to attend a benefit dinner. Referring to Mr. Gobeil [Paul] as "a man with great influence within the present Government," the letter held out the promise of a personal meeting with him, "in consideration of a supplement" of $375 over the "regular" dinner price of $125, for a total of $500. "Esteemed for his enterprising spirit, he [Mr. Gobeil] will no doubt understand and listen to the desires and needs of the business people of the region," the letter said. Embarrassed Liberal organizers quickly cancelled the meeting with Mr. Gobeil, a former executive with the Provigo food conglomerate. (Ibid.)

Sometimes the access events are organized by businessmen. For example, in May 1987, some paving and construction firms invited their confreres to participate in a QLP fund-raising golf tournament, which had an entry fee of $1 000. The ministers of tourism, agriculture and transport attended. The PQ member bringing this event to the attention of the legislature stated that the firms receiving an invitation had received contracts from the Liberal government worth more than $26 million since the party returned to power in December 1985 (Angell 1990a, 22).

In the Liberal party, fund-raising is apparently based on quotas for each riding, which averaged about $30 000 in 1987. The quota or target "is determined with a precise formula that takes into account the 'socio-economic level and wealth index' as well as the number of Liberal voters in the last election" (Angell 1990a, 22). According to the party's director general, John Parisella, "each riding fund raiser who is planning a dinner sends his choice of 'star' and two substitute choices to party headquarters." Because they are the focus of the access events, cabinet ministers bear a heavy load. The "stars" among them "make at least 25 appearances."

> The big gun, Mr. Bourassa himself, is brought out only for special occasions. During the three-month campaign, he will have attended four dinners – one in his Montreal-area riding of St.-Laurent, one for party caucus president Michel Bissonnet, one for Speaker of the House Pierre Lorrain, and one for the ethnic wing of the Liberal Party. Mr. Parisella would not put an estimate on Mr. Bourassa's worth as the best drawing card. (*Globe and Mail*, 25 November 1987, A8)

Angell (1990b, 19) describes the access events in the form of social activities as "a businessman renting a cabinet minister and donating the price of the rental to the minister's party fund." There is nothing wrong with the idea of the businessman telling his troubles to the minister and indicating what he wants the government to do about them. However, if "the minister promises to do anything for the businessman, or if he promises him a government contract, that is an offence called 'influence peddling' " (Angell, 1990a, 20).

As Angell (1990a, 4) emphasizes, the creation of paid access opportunities[42] is an effective technique only for the party in power. Moreover, it cannot be used by some parties when they are in power because their supporters would resent the idea of ministers "cozying up" to businessmen, "whom they regard as their natural enemies." Angell makes the strong claim that this method of fund-raising – raised to a high art by the Liberal party in Quebec – "is more like the traditional types of government-party financing: toll gating, or even the traditional Quebec system of 'kickbacks', or, in French, 'ristournes' " (ibid.).

Alfonso Gagliano, chairman of the federal Quebec Liberal caucus, explained in a newspaper interview in early 1989 how companies fund the Quebec Liberal party, despite the fact the law prohibits donations from corporations, trade unions or any other organization (Montreal *Gazette*, 30 January 1989, A8). The company pays a bonus to the executive on the understanding that the individual will make a corresponding donation to the party (up to $3 000 per annum). The individual has to pay income taxes on the bonus, but receives the receipt under which he/she can receive a tax credit for the contribution. According to Gagliano, both major parties[43] are aware of the practice, as are many donors: "All you have to do is ask any businessman," he said (ibid.). The circumvention of the law "isn't something new, this is a reality. Everybody does it." Gagliano argued that the Quebec Tories who advocated *financement populaire* at the federal level were just creating a smokescreen to cover up the scandals of the Mulroney government. In Gagliano's view, "It's useless to change a law that won't settle anything" (ibid.).

Bernard Roy, former principal secretary to the Prime Minister, has been impressed by Quebec's legislation and noted that other provinces have followed suit to some extent (New Brunswick, Ontario). However, the prohibition on corporate (or union) contributions is "a bit of a sham." Not only do corporations indirectly contribute through their executives, but the law is also circumvented by large anonymous cash contributions at party functions (rallies, speeches, etc.) and by paid access opportunities at $1 000 per head. Roy emphasizes that, in designing the regulation of political finance, much of politics is a matter of perception, that is, *limits* on contributions would reassure the public that candidates and parties are not beholden to contributors.

9

DIRECT-MAIL FUND-RAISING AND ELECTIONEERING

If there's any key to success in direct mail fund raising, it's this: you have to mail, and mail, and mail some more.

(Warwick 1990, 67)

1. INTRODUCTION

DIRECT-MAIL FUND-RAISING by political parties or candidates consists of letters to individuals (or organizations) that solicit a contribution for a party and/or candidate. The donor sends a cheque to the party/candidate by mail. While direct-mail solicitations may be of the "Dear householder/occupant" variety, most are addressed to specific individuals. Indeed, the "personalization" of direct mail is one of the ways in which parties/candidates have sought to improve the effectiveness of their appeals.

In general, there are two types of direct-mail solicitations: those designed to solicit donations and those whose purpose is to sell merchandise.[1] At least four types of organizations are involved in fund-raising by direct mail: political parties/candidates; interest groups (e.g., various environmental groups, civil-liberties groups); charities (e.g., Oxfam, Easter Seals); and religious organizations. Since the 1970s, there has been a vast growth in direct-mail fund-raising by all four types of organizations. Canadians receive about 300 pieces of direct mail each year (Mitchell 1990, 65). The emerging technology of database marketing seems to point the way toward more personalized and differentiated direct-mail appeals by political parties and candidates in Canada.[2] Canadians who dislike direct-mail solicitations can take solace from the fact that the volume of direct mail in the United States is much larger in proportionate terms.[3]

While the use of direct mail as a way of raising funds for political parties can be traced back at least to World War I,[4] the technique first began to be used in Canada on a systematic basis shortly after the *Election Expenses Act* was passed in 1974.[5] It was the opposition parties (notably the Progressive Conservatives and NDP) that led the way rather than the Liberal party, which was then long used to being in power. By the late 1980s, political parties/candidates had to compete in an increasingly crowded "market." In some cases, it has been suggested that the growing number of solicitations by a single party (perhaps a dozen annually) has resulted in "donor fatigue" and in lower returns relative to the rising costs of direct-mail campaigns.

Section 2 of this chapter describes some of the technical aspects of direct-mail fund-raising by political parties. Section 3 provides an overview of the use of direct mail as a fund-raising technique by the Progressive Conservative, Liberal and New Democratic parties. Section 4 examines the Progressive Conservative party's very successful direct-mail program. Section 5 reviews the Liberal party's efforts to use this method of fund-raising. Not only was the Liberal party slow to use and develop the technique, but the latter generates much smaller amounts of net revenue than it has for the Progressive Conservative party, although the Liberals take in more than the NDP. Section 6 examines the New Democratic Party's use of direct mail. Section 7 describes the Progressive Conservative party's use of direct mail as an electioneering vehicle. The conclusions are set out in section 8.

2. TECHNICAL ASPECTS

The components of a direct-mail "package" or "piece" include the outer envelope,[6] the postage, the letter, the reply device, the reply envelope and possibly other enclosures such as a brochure or a "front end premium" (Warwick 1990, chap. 3).[7] Direct-mail expert Mal Warwick suggests that the controllable factors that influence the success or failure of a direct-mail appeal are the following: the list selection; the "offer"; the copywriting; the format (i.e., size, shape, colours of the envelope and its inserts); and the design of the "piece" (ibid., 46–48). He emphasizes that "successful direct mail fund-raising has little to do with statistics or with letter-writing. It's a long-term process that requires intelligent planning and careful, consistent management" (ibid., 3).

Parties and other organizations send their direct-mail appeals quite frequently – often monthly – because most people make their contributions from current discretionary income (Warwick 1990, 17). Such appeals attempt to tap several types of giving: annual contributions for ongoing activities; capital contributions based on special appeals related to evident needs; and deferred contributions, i.e., from wills and bequests. Users of direct mail think of donors as having a four-stage cycle: interest (willingness to open the envelope, read the letter and send a first-time contribution); support (a second, more generous gift); commitment (larger donations, possibly in response to a greater effort by the recipient organization); and legacy (gifts, plus other forms of active involvement such as time volunteered, and ultimately a bequest in their will) (ibid., 112).

The cost of a direct-mail solicitation in 1900 ranged from $0.40 to $0.50 per "piece" for a "prospect" or "donor acquisition" mailing to about $1.00 for a "house list" mailing using a personalized salutation (interview with Stephen Thomas, September 1990).[8] Personalized letters, which in the case of political contributions might contain a reference to each individual's MP, thank the recipients for previous donations and refer to a specific future electoral race. This technique requires an elaborate computer program and the highest quality laser printer.

Economies of scale are quite substantial: for example, a mailing of 100 000 pieces that costs $0.50 each would cost $0.40 if 700 000 pieces were mailed. The most extreme case of economies of scale is the Easter Seals campaign, which consists of a bulk delivery to every household in Ontario. In 1990, this campaign cost 16.5 cents per piece, including the postage of $0.07. The balance covered the letter, the outgoing envelope and the reply envelope (Thomas interview, 1990). The least individuated version of direct mail is the "householder" solicitation that is delivered by Canada Post to every household in a defined area (grouped by "postal walks"). Such items cost $0.08 or $0.09 per household in 1990.

Large direct-mail operations, such as those run by the political parties, regularly test different versions of their packages. For example, a mailing of 300 000 pieces might consist of 200 000 items that use a standard or "control" package and two other batches of 50 000 each with a new or test package. The three versions are randomized within the mailing. The messages in direct-mail efforts may first be tested on focus groups to identify both "good issues" and the language used by voters to describe these issues. However, skilled practitioners often can create successful appeals solely on the basis of their own experience and intuition.

Political direct-mail efforts compile mailing lists from several sources: previous donors (this year and last year);[9] "lapsed donors" (those who gave more than two years ago); contacts lists (e.g., those who bought tickets to leaders' dinners); marked lists (those whose names are generated by door-to-door canvasses during election campaigns) (such lists belong to the riding associations); and rented lists (those whose names appeared on lists of groups such as Oxfam, Save the Children or Amnesty International) (these lists are often exchanged rather than rented). The criteria for selecting lists for a prospect mailing include: donor history (have they given before?); "mail responsiveness" (how frequently have they made donations to other organizations?); recency (how up to date are the addresses?); and accuracy and affinity (how "close" are the persons on the list to the profile of those likely to send money to the party/candidate?) (Warwick 1990, 56).

Rented lists can be found through list brokers.[10] In 1990, there were 900 direct-marketing lists available for rent or exchange. They ranged from lists of 405 000 senior citizens, 52 900 business leaders in small towns, 30 000 subscribers to *Playboy* and 420 psychologists (Mitchell 1990, 71). Info Direct (an affiliate of Bell Canada) rents out lists of names, addresses and postal codes of 6.5 million telephone subscribers in Quebec, Ontario, Manitoba and BC. The renter is permitted to keep only the names of persons who make a donation and use them in their "house list."

A prospect mailing might well combine lists from several sources and involve 300 000 to 400 000 names. The purpose of "prospecting" is to create a house list of persons with a higher probability of giving – namely those who have previously donated in response to a prospect mailing. Warwick (1990, 15) explains that direct-mail fund-raising is based on getting a response of approximately 1 percent from prospects but a response of 10 percent or more from the few individuals who previously gave as prospects.[11] "The only reason direct mail fund-raising works is that someone who does send you a first gift is very likely to send another when asked."[12] Prospect or donor acquisition mailings seldom break even. Indeed, most public-interest organizations expect to *lose* 15 percent to 30 percent of their investment in such mailings (ibid., 16). Warwick (ibid., 18) suggests that donor acquisition mailings typically have a response rate in the range of 0.5 percent to 2.5 percent, while "resolicitation," "donor renewal" or "house list" mailings typically have a response rate of 6 percent to 12 percent.

3. OVERVIEW OF PARTIES' DIRECT-MAIL REVENUES AND COSTS
Before examining in sections 4 through 6 the experience of each of the three main parties in using direct mail as a fund-raising technique, they are compared on a number of dimensions.

3.1 Importance of Direct-Mail Revenues
For the Progressive Conservative party, direct-mail gross revenues accounted for from 51.5 percent to 74.6 percent of total contributions to

the party from individuals in the period 1983–90 (see table 9.1). Direct-mail gross revenues as a percentage of *total* party revenues fell from 38.8 percent in 1983 and 37.2 percent in 1985 to 24.1 percent in 1988 and 21.5 percent in 1990. Note that in election year 1988, direct mail generated $1 million *less* gross revenue than it did in 1984 (table 9.1).

For the Liberal party, direct-mail gross revenues accounted for from 23.4 percent to 47.9 percent of total contributions from individuals between 1985 and 1990. Direct-mail gross revenues accounted for from 9.6 percent to 18.7 percent of total Liberal party revenues over the same period (table 9.1). The weakness of the Liberals' direct-mail efforts compared to those of the Tories can be seen in these figures.

For the federal office of the NDP, direct-mail gross revenues accounted for 24.4 percent to 31.3 percent of federally receipted contributions from individuals between 1987 and 1990 (table 9.1). As a fraction of all the revenues raised at the federal level of the NDP,[13] the gross revenues from direct mail accounted for from 15.4 percent to 21.9 percent over the period 1987–90 (table 9.1).

The Progressive Conservative party's advantage in direct-mail fund-raising is illustrated by the figures for the *net* revenue each party received from direct mail (table 9.2). The net revenue is calculated by deducting the direct costs of direct-mail efforts from the gross revenue they generate. Between 1985 and 1990, the Tories' annual *net* revenue from direct mail exceeded that of the Liberals by from $1.03 million to $3.87 million (in nominal dollars). Over the period, the Conservatives generated some $15.7 million (in nominal dollars) *more* net revenue from direct mail than did the Liberal party. This amounted to an average of about $2.6 million each year. Between 1987 and 1990, the Conservative party generated $9.3 million *more* in net revenue (an average of $2.32 million annually) from direct mail than did the federal office of the NDP (table 9.2).[14]

3.2   Costs of Direct-Mail Fund-Raising

It costs money to raise money, but some parties are more efficient in the use of direct mail, that is, their direct-mail expenses constitute a lower percentage of their gross revenues. One of the reasons why the Conservative party's net revenues from direct mail have outpaced that of their rivals is that the party has been much more efficient (as well as more effective) than either the Liberal party or the NDP in using the direct-mail fund-raising technique. Between 1983 and 1990, expenses accounted for from 17.7 percent to 28.1 percent of the Conservative party's annual gross revenues from direct mail (table 9.3).[15] In contrast, expenses absorbed 60 percent or more of the Liberal party's direct-mail revenues from 1985 to 1990, except in 1988 when the ratio was 34.2 percent and in 1990 when it was 43.9 percent (table 9.3). For the NDP, expenses absorbed from 39.9 percent to 64.9 percent of direct-mail gross revenues between 1987 and 1990.[16]

Why is the Progressive Conservative party's expense ratio for direct mail so much lower than that of the Liberal party and of the NDP's federal office? There are probably two reasons. The first is that the Tories started their direct-mail program much earlier and made more extensive use of this technique than did the other parties. Therefore they have more experience with this technique. The second is that, because they have more experience, by 1983 the Conservatives had already incurred the high "front end" costs of developing a large (and productive) house list. As noted above, a list is built from prospecting, using purchased lists, and such activity seldom makes money. This can be observed in tables 9.3 and 9.4. The former indicates that the Conservative party's promotional or prospect mailing between 1985 and 1990 generated a total of $2.48 million in gross revenue, but cost $2.40 million. (By comparison, the Conservative party collected $23.7 million from its house list between 1985 and 1990 at a cost of $4.0 million.) Table 9.4 indicates that, between 1986 and 31 August 1990, the Liberal party's 15 prospect mailings generated $1.91 million in revenue, but cost the party $2.22 million. But note that these expenditures do not include *indirect* expenses associated with the Liberals' direct-mail program. As table 9.5 indicates, these were quite high in 1985 and 1986 when the party was making a major effort to expand its direct-mail program.

Third, by greatly varying over time the effort they put into their direct-mail efforts, the Liberals failed to get into the range of higher net returns. For example, the Liberal party sent out 12 direct-mail appeals in 1986 and 1987 (table 9.4). In 1986, five of these were prospect mailings; in 1987 there were four prospect mailings (table 9.5). Then the number of prospect mailings dropped to two in 1988, 1989 and 1990. This fact bodes ill for the Liberal party over the next few years: without continual prospecting, the much more productive in-house mailings quickly "depreciate" in their ability to generate revenues (at about 20 percent per year due to people moving). Warwick (1990, 106) emphasizes that "direct mail is a *process*, not a passing event." It requires continuous prospecting because of "attrition": "people die or move without leaving forwarding addresses, their financial circumstances change, and so do their interests and loyalties" (ibid.).

Fourth, because the Liberal party made a sustained effort to use direct mail only nearly a decade after the Progressive Conservative party, it entered an increasingly crowded market. Not only were other parties sending out up to a dozen appeals each year, but hundreds of charities and interest groups were also employing this technique to raise funds. As a result, it was probably harder for the Liberal party to generate substantial sums from direct mail, and the costs of doing so were higher.

4. PROGRESSIVE CONSERVATIVE PARTY

4.1 The First to Use the Technique

The Progressive Conservative party responded more quickly to the opportunities presented by the new technology of very large computerized direct-mailing lists and the generous tax credit in the 1974 *Election Expenses Act* to raise money from individuals. The Conservatives were also driven by "a deficit of nearly $1 million [remaining] from the 1972 and 1974 elections, in addition to a long-term debt" (Seidle and Paltiel 1981, 239). The PC Canada Fund was put in place effective 1 August 1974, the date the new legislation came into effect. Not only was the Fund to be the party's official agent, but it was intended to be a vehicle for raising money and managing it better (recall chap. 4).

Seidle and Paltiel describe the genesis of the Conservative party's very successful direct-mail efforts as follows:

> Not long after the establishment of the PC Canada Fund, David McMillan, the fund's national coordinator until mid-1979, visited Republican party offices in the United States. He was subsequently responsible for adapting the American direct-mail efforts to the needs of the Progressive Conservative party. Lists of potential contributors were purchased from newspaper and magazine publishers. Tens of thousands of letters are dispatched at a time, and those who reply with a contribution can be approached over and over again. The initial costs of direct mail were high, but after extensive "prospecting" the Progressive Conservatives began to get a return on their outlay. Extensive research allowed the party to determine which sorts of lists would provide the most prospective donors. The tax credit provides a direct incentive for political contributions, and this is emphasized in the letters sent out. An additional advantage of direct mail is that many people who might not normally give to political parties or who might not normally be approached by local canvassers can be asked for a donation. (1981, 242)

After the Tories were defeated in the 1980 election, contributions slumped. This prompted the use of a new technique, a telephone canvass:

"Fifteen students were hired to ask for contributions from those who had given to the Progressive Conservatives in the 1976–1979 period, and in two weeks some $450 000 was raised" (Seidle and Paltiel 1981, 258, n.33).

Even prior to 1983 when Brian Mulroney became leader, the Progressive Conservative party had the U.S. consulting firm of Odell & Roper on retainer. In fact, Robert Odell had been hired to help the party implement changes in its financing in light of the 1974 *Election Expenses Act*. The consultants helped to design and improve the party's direct-mail efforts. They even drafted the copy for direct-mail appeals and, during the late 1980s, Odell continued to attend some meetings of the 25-person Board of Directors of the PC Canada Fund to provide advice.

The Conservative party's direct-mail effort includes at least 12 mailings annually, including "prospecting" efforts. W. David Angus, head of the PC Canada Fund, stated that during the 1984 election campaign, an additional seven mailings were made in a 30-day period. A Conservative party official stated:

> Our "in-house" direct mail programme is targeted at prior donors to our Party. The "promotional" programme, on the other hand, aims to attract new donors to PC Canada Fund and thereby incurs substantially higher costs by mailing to large numbers of prospective donors, generally from purchased lists.
>
> Direct mail costs are included as part of the "printing and stationery" expense on our Statement of Receipts and Expenditure. Such costs include both the production expenses, i.e., paper, letter-shop and handling, as well as mailing costs.[17]

Part of the direct-mail effort is a "sustaining membership program" that provides the donor with membership in the PC Canada Fund in return for a tax-receiptable contribution. Angus indicated in 1990 that those responding to the Conservatives' direct-mail appeals contribute an average of $90 to $100.

Progressive Conservative party fund-raising is based on a multilayer approach designed to tap all "markets" by using the most appropriate method, ranging from direct mail, telephone solicitation, personal contacts, opportunities to meet with senior members of the party and special events such as dinners featuring the leader. It is based on the idea that there are many people willing to give who have never been asked to donate. For example, in the mid-1970s, the party received a cheque for $5 000 – an unheard-of amount from a direct-mail appeal. When the donor was contacted by telephone, she said she had simply never before been asked for a contribution.

Party officials state that the cost of raising money by direct mail is about 100 percent of the revenue from prospecting lists, but only 15 percent to 20 percent of that from the party's house list. In any event, overall between 1983 and 1990, only about one-quarter of direct-mail gross revenues were absorbed by expenses (table 9.3).

4.2 Criticisms of Progressive Conservative Party Direct Mail

Direct-mail solicitations of political contributions are usually viewed as a private matter between the "asker" (the party or candidate) and the "giver." However, at certain times, the content of the mail is brought to light in the press. For example, popular columnist Allan Fotheringham, after receiving a personal, plastic, sustaining membership card from the Conservative party and a "Dear Friend" letter from PC Canada Fund Chairman David Angus, devoted an entire column to criticizing the appeal. He said, in part:

> The card is engraved with my name – "Fotheringam"... my first name and initial are mixed up ... it is addressed to a city where I no longer live and to an employer where Fotheringam hasn't worked for years ...
> The plastic card isn't quite as thick as an Amex or a Visa card, but a lot of people might like to have it in their wallets, in case it impresses a cop the next time they are picked up for impaired walking. The fact that you are a personal friend of David Angus might impress them.
> Close friend Angus, appealing to high principle, points out that up to 75 percent of my donation can be written off my income tax. If Fotheringam will contribute $100, it will cost Fotheringam only $25. Who pays the rest? Well, the ordinary taxpayer of course. It's called democracy. (Fotheringham 1986, 64)

In April 1986, the Public Service Alliance of Canada accused the Progressive Conservative party of soliciting "federal public servants at work, urging them to join the party and contribute $25, $50, $100 or more" (*Vancouver Sun*, 5 April 1986). Alliance president Daryl Bean stated that he was "amazed" that several people had reported receiving the letters at work. "It's one thing to get a letter of this sort at home. It's another to have them mailed to the office. Even if it was inadvertent, that's no excuse. They should be better organized than that," he said (ibid.). Nick Locke, executive director of the PC Canada Fund, said that the letters were not specifically mailed to public servants. He added that, because the mailing lists are based mostly on magazine subscription lists, letters might have gone to those who subscribe to magazines through work.

In a mailing by the PC Canada Fund in May 1987, the party asked
for contributions to a $560 000 fund to save Canada from a "Soviet-
style government" under the "radical left agenda" of the NDP. The letter
was four pages long, and was signed by Conservative party President
Bill Jarvis. NDP leader Ed Broadbent said that the letter would be
"supremely funny" if it did not "question the loyalty and motives of
thousands of NDP supporters" (*Vancouver Sun*, 5 June 1987). While some
Tory MPs applauded the letter, officials at party headquarters, including
Mr. Jarvis, refused to comment. Columnist Jeffrey Simpson, in calling
for an apology from the Conservative party, wondered if the party had
been spooked by the NDP. "How else to explain the piece of garbage
masquerading as a fund-raising letter recently published by
Conservative party headquarters?" (*Globe and Mail*, 20 June 1987, A6).

At the opposite end of the scale from mass mailings is the small
targeted direct-mail effort. This type of mailing is sent to specifically
selected individuals, chosen because they meet a particular criterion. In
January 1990, the Conservative party sent out such a mailing, designed
to elicit support for the government's GST bill (*Globe and Mail*, 12 March
1990, A4). The letter was sent to "fewer than 5 000 businessmen who are
not regular party supporters," according to Nick Locke. The mailing,
signed by John Craig Eaton (chairman of Eaton's of Canada Limited),
called upon the recipient to support the "courage" of the Mulroney
government in introducing the GST and addressing the issue of the national
debt. The letter, written on Eaton's corporate letterhead, also asked for a
donation of "$250, $500 or more" to provide the Prime Minister with a
vote of confidence. Although some western Canadians were reported to
have returned their membership cards to protest the mailing and to be
considering cancelling their Eaton's accounts, Locke described the response
to the letter as "good." A spokesman for the T. Eaton Co. distanced the
retail operation from Mr. Eaton's actions, stating that the letter was a
"personal thing" that had nothing to do with the retail operation.

It is impossible to use direct-mail fund-raising without offending
someone. This does not mean that the game is not worth the candle.
Indeed, for the Conservatives, direct mail has been one of the party's
most important vehicles for raising large amounts of money, as the data
in table 9.1 indicate.

5. LIBERAL PARTY

5.1 Slow Start

The Liberal party was much slower than the Progressive Conservative
party to use the direct-mail technique to raise money to pay for its
activities. Seidle and Paltiel explain:

> Shortly after the passage of the Election Expenses Act [in 1974], the
> Liberals made a couple of important decisions that affected fund
> raising in subsequent years. The first was that the constituency would
> be used as the major organizational basis of fund raising. Although
> some party activists, both in 1972 and after the passage of the act, had
> pressed for the introduction of direct-mail solicitation of donations,
> this was strongly opposed because of uncertain returns and because
> it was thought it would not accord with the party's structure. More
> important, leading Liberals argued that nothing could surpass the
> face-to-face approach in seeking donations at the local level. (1981,
> 237)

To add to the difficulties of financing the national office, party officials
proposed a formula under which *none* of the money collected was to go
to party headquarters in Ottawa (recall the discussion in chap. 5).[18]
This "system" of financing the national office lasted only five years.
Fiscal necessity became the mother of changes in the party's methods
of fund-raising.

> In mid-1979 Liberal party finances were in very bad shape, and a party
> committee under Gordon Dryden, the national treasurer, was set up
> to investigate the possible introduction of direct-mail fund-raising.
> The Liberals improved over 1979 in their solicitation from individ-
> uals: in 1980, 17,670 people contributed nearly $2.3 million, or
> 37 percent of total Liberal party contributions. Nevertheless, the
> Liberals could not deny the clear success of the Conservatives' venture
> in this area, and despite some opposition from within the party, direct
> mail began to be used at the national level in early 1981. (Seidle and
> Paltiel 1981, 239)

Within the Liberal party, the Ontario provincial association was
the pioneer in using direct mail. The direct-mail effort got to a break-
even point in about 1975–76. Then its efforts were taken over by headquarters. But the technique was not pursued effectively until some
years later.

The Liberal party was slow to use direct mail, according to former
party director Torrance Wylie, for several reasons. First, the party structure meant that headquarters had no central membership lists and little
or no access to provincial membership lists. Second, the method
conflicted with existing fund-raising methods; most provincial associations and MPs balked, even though they were not using direct mail
themselves. Third, the party did not see the benefits of a well-funded

national headquarters. Finally, Wylie said that party officials did not appreciate the potential amount of revenue that could be obtained by using the direct-mail technique. Opposition to it, however, was not based on any philosophical objections to the technique.

While the Liberal party began its national direct-mail efforts in 1981, little money was raised. Officials failed to appreciate that it was necessary to spend money prospecting in order to build up a house list of persons who were more receptive to direct-mail appeals. Further, the absence of a central list of party members and the unwillingness of provincial/territorial sections to share their lists made the job of creating a large house list very difficult. The Liberal party hired U.S. consultants and obtained advice from Democratic Party officials. However, the poor initial results from direct mail discouraged the Liberals from restructuring and staying the course over the several years necessary to build up a rewarding direct-mail operation.

5.2 A Serious Effort

Howard Stevenson, a direct-mail specialist, was hired as a consultant in 1981 and joined the Liberal party's staff in April 1982 to develop its limited direct-mail activities. "Three years later, he walked away shaking his head ... describing his efforts as an exercise in utter frustration" (Weston 1988, 177). When Stevenson arrived, direct-mail letters were being written by an American company that was selling most of its services to the Democratic Party. Leader John Turner seldom agreed to sign the appeals. A party official said Turner thought such appeals were "tacky." Most direct-mail solicitations were then signed by party president Iona Campagnolo or treasurer Gordon Dryden.

The absence of any effective direct-mail effort by the Liberal party showed up in the total revenues of each of the three main parties between 1980 and 1984. The Progressive Conservative party raised $32 million, while the NDP raised $18 million and the Liberal party raised only $16 million (table 3.1). According to Gordon Dryden, "Essentially, we were a decade behind in the [direct mail] game. It was the worst mistake the party ever made on the financial side" (quoted in Weston 1988, 177). Banister and Gibson noted:

> As a very important additional duty, the Federal Liberal Agency has been charged with the development of direct mail solicitation for funds, which is an undertaking in which we seriously lag the Conservatives. Given the lead time for the development of efficient lists, this can be expected to become a major source of revenue within three to five years. (1984, 15)

Stevenson faced problems in "trying to sort out all the conflicting demands from within the party as to what should be said in the letters" (Weston 1988, 178). MPs' views were solicited, as were those of Turner's staff, but "the only people who knew what they were doing were in the United States writing the stuff" (ibid.). The party was also slow to capitalize on potential opportunities to use a direct-mail solicitation. For example, when a refinery was to be closed in the east end of Montreal in 1985, Senator Leo Kolber, then the chief fund-raiser, wanted the Liberal party to send a direct-mail appeal to people in the area. However, the complex web of approvals necessary to get the letter out would have taken three months, so the idea was scrapped. The party's biggest problem, however, lay in its organizational structure, which made it difficult to build up a mailing list with the names of people likely to respond.

When Stevenson quit in 1986, the direct-mail program was breaking even, according to Weston (1988). The data in table 9.5 indicate that in 1985 the Liberal party generated $404 000 in net revenue from direct mail. In 1986, the net revenue was even smaller, only $378 000.

When Marie-Andrée Bastien was appointed as secretary general of the party in early 1987, she was concerned about its deteriorating financial situation and decided to champion direct mail as a way of increasing revenue. Bastien's efforts were built around a Canadian consultant (Coburn Direct Marketing) and in-house staff, notably Linda McGreevy. The party's chief fund-raiser (Gerry Schwartz) did not support Bastien's initiative because of the risk, that is, the chance that the front-end costs would not be recouped through contributions. However, party president Michel Robert authorized the new, larger-scale direct-mail effort.

According to Bastien, the Financial Management Committee set an objective of $1 million *net* revenue during the first year (1987), in the expectation that she would fail. Bastien was able to revive and expand direct mail, despite the opposition of Schwartz, who wanted the party to focus on soliciting larger contributions from individuals and corporations. The number of mailings was seven to ten per year for a total of 25 while Bastien was in Ottawa (table 9.5). Some of the early mailings were to "householders" (i.e., they were not personally addressed) and were not pre-tested. Later letters were tested, personally addressed and mailed to individuals with particular attributes thought to predispose them to respond to the party's appeal. The direct-mail letters were signed by various party officials, such as Senator Michael Kirby, John Turner (only once), House Leader Herb Gray, chief financial officer Michael Robinson and Marie-Andrée Bastien (several times).

Occasionally, party officials disagreed about who should sign a particular letter.

In 1987, net revenue from direct mail rose to $666 000, even though gross revenue fell slightly. However, in 1988, Bastien's efforts began to pay off. Net revenue was $1.43 million (table 9.5). Bastien indicated that a mailing of some 10 000 letters signed by Senator Michael Kirby asking for $500 was a major factor in this success. She said that this particular approach of asking a much smaller number of people for a larger contribution had never been tried before in Canada. Also in 1988, the Liberals did a mailing of an audio cassette on free trade to 10 000 to 13 000 "upscale" potential donors. It was said to have been very successful. Sometimes direct mail hits the jackpot. A Liberal direct-mail piece sent to a vice-president of Union Gas resulted in a $20 000 cheque from the company. Apparently the company had not been approached by a member of the Treasury Committee.[19]

But the battle over access to membership lists continued. As noted in chapter 5, the membership lists in the Liberal party are administered by the federal riding associations and the provincial/territorial associations. They "own the names." The lack of a national list in Ottawa is attributed to a lack of trust in national headquarters. The constituency associations and PTAs fear that Ottawa will use the names to solicit direct-mail contributions at their expense.[20] Yet the ridings and the PTAs often do not use the names for their own direct-mail campaigns.[21] Direct-mail experts argue that, even if they did so, it is unlikely that fund-raising by party headquarters in Ottawa would diminish the amount given to ridings (candidates) or PTAs. It was not until 1990 that Liberal party headquarters and several PTAs were able to negotiate an agreement under which the headquarters could use the PTAs' lists in its direct-mail efforts, with each PTA receiving one-half of the revenues. Ottawa was allowed to keep the names of those who made a donation for its house list.

As of June 1990, the Liberal party's national headquarters still did not possess a complete list of party members. Despite previous agreements to do so, only six of the PTAs had provided the central party with their membership lists. This continues to reflect what the party's chief financial officer, Michael Robinson, has called "distrust" between the grass roots and the national party. Robinson said that this lack of confidence stems, in part, from a time in the mid-1980s when constituencies would "raise funds, send them to Ottawa expecting to get their share of the funds returned, and it didn't happen. There was a great deal of resentment built up and we're still trying to overcome that" (quoted in *Financial Post*, 11 June 1990, 5). Robinson adds that the establishment of a central membership list is essential and that the lack of this has left the Liberals "far too dependent on corporate contributions." With a central list, the Liberal party could greatly reduce its dependence on corporate funds. Even if a list could be generated, chief BC fund-raiser Bob Annable has said that the party is so far behind the Conservative party that it could not catch up by the next federal election in 1993. Annable, who has been one of the party's most successful fund-raisers, has called for the party to become more "professional" in its approach to generating funds. He stresses that the Liberals must learn to tailor their product to the "market" in recognizing why individuals donate. Annable has made use of dinners, meetings with politicians and automatic pay deductions as tools in his fund-raising efforts.

In 1990, the Liberal party started a development council under its direct-mail program. Those who become members (not just party members) are asked for a donation of $50 or more. The objective is to create a dialogue: donors receive a newsletter, and periodic questionnaires whose results are shared with the caucus. The first mailing generated 1 800 donors (the target was 1 200), with an average contribution of about $85. The party plans four to six mailings each year to create a type of affinity group that could become the basis of a direct national membership for the federal party.

Secretary General Sheila Gervais has said that the Liberal party is gradually improving its position and that it has raised more money in the past few years than it has spent. Still, she admits to scepticism about the central office at the local level. In 1990, party headquarters established a target net revenue for the direct-mail program. Any amount over the target was to be put into prospect mailings. With the decline in prospect mailings in 1988 and 1989, both gross and net revenues were lower in 1989 than they were in 1987. Net revenues in 1989 were only $378 000, back to the level of 1986 (table 9.5). In 1990, the Liberals' direct-mail gross revenues were $1.74 million and the net revenue was $976 500 (table 9.5). The greater revenue and lower cost of raising it in 1990 appears to be reflective of the greater consistency in the direct-mail program following the hiring of the firm of Bruce, Moore, Russell of Ottawa in 1989 to manage the direct-mail program.

To address the national party's organizational and financial problems, various reforms have been proposed. As noted in chapter 5, in its "Interim Report" in July 1991 the Reform Commission of the Liberal party proposed that the party create a national membership list. The Commission was well aware of its potential value in direct-mail fund-raising.

5.3   Criticisms of Liberal Party Direct Mail

Like the Conservative party, some Liberal party direct-mail efforts have met with criticism. One columnist (Jamie Lamb) was critical of a direct-mail piece in which the "pitch" took the form of a letter, signed by MP Donald Johnston, which included a questionnaire, a "Confidential Budget Survey," for the reader to fill out. It also included a "Response Form" that allowed for a special contribution that would allow Johnston to "get the real story on the Tories' budget out to millions of concerned Canadians." The columnist was outraged that the questions were "so slanted as to receive only one possible answer from a true Liberal party follower" (*Vancouver Sun,* 10 July 1985, A4). He concluded that the only purpose of the mailing must be to "raise money from Liberals so that the party can conduct more sweeping polls."

Even an effort by the Liberals to be innovative in direct-mail appeals resulted in criticism by another columnist. Judd Buchanan, then president of the party, announced in September 1986 that the Liberal party would be offering a "money-back" guarantee to its donors. They were supposed to "get back every penny by December 31 if they (didn't) agree that the Liberals (were) an effective opposition alert to the concerns of Canadians and ready in terms of policy and personnel to form the next government of Canada" (*Financial Post,* 6 September 1986, 7). Columnist Don McGillivray argued that

> instead of keeping the spotlight on the Mulroney government's mistakes, Buchanan's gimmick invites people to look for flaws in the Liberal party, of which there are plenty. What's more, it suggests that nobody in his right mind would donate to the Liberals without the right to reclaim the cash. (Ibid.)

Despite these and other criticisms, the test for the party is whether direct-mail appeals are successful in financial terms. This requires more information than is usually available to newspaper columnists.

6. NEW DEMOCRATIC PARTY

The use of direct mail by the NDP began with the Ontario provincial party in 1975. The federal office began using the technique in 1978. It is an important source of funds for the federal office, although the latter does not keep all of the revenues direct mail generates. They are shared according to a formula negotiated with the provincial sections.[22] (Direct-mail campaigns at the provincial level must send 15 percent to the federal office, except during provincial elections.[23]) Senior federal officials have argued that, since the federal office was bearing the risk of financing the heavy "front end" expenses of prospect mailings, it should keep 100 percent of the revenues raised. The additional net revenue would be used to finance the next general election. Thus, it is argued, each provincial/territorial section would benefit by having its quota for that election reduced because the federal office would have more money in the bank to pay for "election expenses." Officials at the PTS level seldom find this argument convincing. Officials in the provincial sections see the national office's direct-mail effort as "poaching by the feds." They see the "pot" of money that can be tapped as fixed in size – hence there is less money left for them to collect. At the federal level, from 15 percent to 22 percent of total party revenue came from direct mail in the period 1987–90 (table 9.1).

6.1 The Party's Approach to Direct Mail

NDP members and supporters show their support and commitment by responding well to direct-mail appeals.[24] At the federal level and in several provinces, the party uses a direct-mail consultant, Stephen Thomas & Associates.[25] Senior NDP officials consider that the party's direct-mail effort has been a success on several levels. It has provided a steady cash flow – the banks are prepared to lend money on it. The house list, which took some time to build up and costs money to maintain, has been "very lucrative," particularly in 1988 when the level of expenditure on the general election was the highest in the party's history. According to one NDP official, direct-mail appeals during the election "brought in millions of dollars."[26] Direct mail increases the party's contact with individuals (members and thousands of others through the prospect lists). It is also a vehicle to get out the party's message, as the letters are typically three to four pages (single-spaced), much of which is devoted to describing the "good work" the party is doing.[27] "Direct mail fund raising is a form of advertising, which is based on repetition" (Warwick 1990, 118).

The NDP divides its direct-mail efforts into three categories: annual appeals, predetermined "specials" chosen three months ahead of time[28] and "wild card" specials that are instant mailings following exogenous events likely to stimulate responses (e.g., the BC NDP always keeps two sets of envelopes and paper on hand for such opportunities). NDP guidelines specify that 50 percent of the costs of direct-mail campaigns are classified as "election expenses" but the fraction may be more or less; for example, 90 percent of prospect mailings but only 50 percent of the costs of mailings using the house list may be counted as "election expenses." Within the NDP, direct-mail efforts are kept separate from efforts to obtain contributions by means of pre-authorized cheques.

This service is offered to supporters as a convenient form of sustained giving and is often part of the effort to recruit new members or to encourage existing members to indicate their support.

The NDP direct-mail effort – like that of the Liberal party – has been inhibited by the fact that membership lists are controlled by the 12 PTSs. Therefore, the national "house list"[29] was not built from party membership lists but by "prospecting" from lists rented from Amnesty International or Oxfam. The objective was to create a list of "direct-mail responsive people." One of the best rented lists turned out to be composed of senior citizens in BC. These people may or may not vote for the NDP, but it is clear that some do give it money – sometimes several times a year. The party has found that people in BC, Ontario and the Prairies are more responsive to direct-mail appeals than are those in Newfoundland. In some cases, direct-mail appeals are linked to membership drives and telephone solicitation.

The NDP, like other parties, has tried to modify its direct-mail efforts to differentiate and sharpen its appeals to groups of voters likely to be more responsive to such messages.[30] Voters with a similar socio-economic/demographic profile (even in geographically disparate locations) have been sent messages that are carefully crafted to appeal to themes of particular concern to them. Perhaps the ultimate limit of this approach would be millions of letters, each uniquely designed to appeal to the political sentiments of individuals based on their ascriptive characteristics, gleaned from careful research. The object is to obtain money or individuals' votes by making them believe that the party supports/opposes what they support/oppose. The individuals may even be used to identify the issues they find most salient. The first step is a broadly targeted letter from the party – perhaps from the leader – that solicits the views of the recipient. A brief closed-end questionnaire may be used or responses may be more open-ended so that the recipient identifies the salient issues ("top of the mind" response) in his/her own words. Second, the party can use these replies to develop differentiated messages that are targeted to what it believes are like-minded individuals. Third, the replies at stage one can be organized and used for a telephone call in which the caller provides information on the party's position on the matters of concern to the voter, and solicits his/her vote and/or asks for a contribution.[31]

One of the challenges parties face in direct-mail fund-raising is that most are active at two levels of government. Each level wants to use direct mail to raise money. However, if direct-mail solicitations are not coordinated, particularly when the list of "targets" contains many of the same people, there is a danger of "donor fatigue" and wasted resources. The problem is compounded when riding associations or provincial organizations wish to solicit people *outside* their geographic area. Direct-mail consultant Stephen Thomas suggests that Canadians understand federalism and recognize the logic of party appeals that are differentiated by as many as four levels: federal, provincial, riding (federal and provincial) and even municipal. He believes that the NDP is able to raise more money by adopting a form of limited "competitive" approach to fund-raising.[32] Thomas handles direct mail for the NDP's national office, as well as for its provincial sections in Ontario,[33] BC and Manitoba, so it is in his interest to advocate more mailings. In only two other provinces is the party active in direct mail: Saskatchewan and, to a lesser extent, Alberta.

Morley (1991, 112) states that, in 1989, the BC provincial section mailed 18 direct-mail pieces, eight to targeted groups and ten to party members. (Gross revenues totalled $1.3 million in 1989.) In the same year, the NDP's federal office mailed eight house and four prospect pieces. According to Morley, party members became angry about what they saw as an excessive number of direct-mail solicitations. They believed that the federal direct-mail efforts inevitably siphon off funds that might otherwise be raised by a provincial section for the next provincial election. In 1988, a federal mailing went out at the start of a provincial election campaign in Saskatchewan, which raised the ire of officials in that provincial section.[34]

A review of 23 direct-mail packages sent by the NDP between 1988 and 1990 indicates that all envelopes contained a window for the recipient's name and address. However, the return address did not always identify the party as the sender, especially in a prospect mailing, where the ability to get the letter opened is key. Prospect mailings that have been very successful are those that have resembled an "official government mailing," as pieces that focused on taxes have shown. The content of the letter varied according to the topic of the particular package. The date was not specified on a prospect mailing, but was more likely to be used on an annual mail-out or house mailing. The salutation also varied. Past donors were usually addressed as "Dear Friend." Almost all letters were sent on some sort of "letterhead." The length of the letter varied, typically from two to four pages, with prospect letters being the longest. Only recycled paper was used and this fact was noted on the letter. The signatory was typically the leader or the federal secretary.[35] With the change from long-time leader Ed Broadbent to the new leader, Audrey McLaughlin, more pieces were signed by prominent MPs. The leader was always referred to on a first-name basis. Funds were requested in all but one mailing, the election thank-you. Almost all mailings also explained the advantage of the federal income-tax credit, using a specified amount ($50–$100) of contribution.[36]

The reply package was quite standard. The donation card was typically headed by a "Yes [name of person who signed the letter], I agree with you!" message. The amount of the donation requested was specified, with the smallest amount being between $20 (most prospects) and $50 (election and annual appeals). Donations could be payable by cheque or by Visa or Mastercard. Space was also given to correct any errors in the name or address. For prospect mailings, the recipient could also request future mailings in French. Tax credit information was included in all mailings, with the prospect and special pieces being the most specific on how the credit works. Return envelopes were always postage-paid.[37] However, some prospect mailings mentioned that, when the sender affixed a stamp to the envelope, the party saved money.

The NDP has found that lists of magazine subscribers tend to be the most productive: they are "clean," that is, up to date, and the people tend to be more direct-mail responsive. The rental fee is usually $90 per 1 000 names, with a minimum of 5 000 names (interview with Stephen Thomas, September 1990). It is also possible to rent the telephone book in electronic form from Info Direct for selected geographic areas where the individuals are thought to be responsive to a party's direct-mail solicitation. In BC it is possible to link the voters' list to BC Tel's directory in electronic form.

Response rates (the percentage of recipients who mail back a cheque) have varied widely, depending on the type of list employed and the particular appeal. As noted above, 1 percent is a bench-mark for a prospect list. For the NDP house list, the return has usually been 15 percent to 20 percent. However, for some mailings, the response rate was over 30 percent. For the NDP annual membership drives, renewal rates have typically been 60 percent to 70 percent. Telephone follow-up can increase the response rate, but it also increases the cost. The average donation generated by *renewal* mailings was over $60 (interview with Stephen Thomas, September 1990). The response rate from the NDP's prospect mailings has been high by the usual direct-mail standards: the average contribution to the NDP has been about $50. This is about double the level obtained by charities using the same technique, according to Stephen Thomas. Thomas said that he could detect no increase in contributions to the Ontario NDP after 1986, when the highest rate (75 percent) of tax credit was increased from $100 to $200 and the maximum was increased from $500 to $750.

Despite its systematic and sustained approach to direct mail, the federal office of the NDP never raised as much as $1 million annually in *net* revenue between 1987 and 1990 (table 9.6). During that period, the NDP's federal office generated a total of $3.1 million in net revenue from direct mail, as compared to $3.24 million by the Liberal party and $12.4 million by the Conservative party. Moreover, the NDP's expense ratio has been much higher than that of the Conservative party: 65 percent, 57 percent, 40 percent and 51 percent as compared to 22 percent, 25 percent, 22 percent and 20 percent for the Conservative party during the period 1987–90 (table 9.6). Even on its house list, the NDP spent $702 000 to raise $3.4 million between 1988 and 1990 and these costs *exclude* printing and postage, professional fees and processing (see table 9.6). In contrast, the Conservative party spent $1.79 million to raise $11.19 million from its house list between 1988 and 1990 (table 9.3).

Another measure of the NDP's costs of using direct mail can be gained from the experience of the BC section. The treasurer of the BC section of the NDP stated that its gross revenue in 1990 was $3 937 000 (interview with Dr. Roger Howard, March 1991). Of this, $1 502 741 was raised via direct mail. The costs of the direct-mail appeals amounted to $537 564 or 35.8 percent of the gross revenue from direct mail. In 1989, the BC section raised $1 306 042 from direct mail at a cost of $367 076, or 28.1 percent of gross revenue. The treasurer indicated that the BC section estimates that the cost of prospect mailings is 70 percent of the gross revenues, while the costs of mailings to persons on the house list usually amount to 35 percent of gross revenues. These data suggest that the NDP's federal office has been less efficient in using direct mail than has the BC section.

6.2 "Sweepstakes," an NDP Innovation

New Democratic Party officials have said that the use of "sweepstakes" offers in their direct-mail appeals has been particularly successful. The sweepstakes offered persons receiving the direct-mail "piece" the chance to win a trip for two to a specified location or with a specific airline. An analysis of three sweepstakes packages (one for the federal NDP and two for provincial wings, BC and Ontario) found that, in all three cases, the outer envelope offered the opportunity for the recipient to win a possible vacation for two. It featured photos or graphics promoting the destination of the prize package. The party's name was used on the envelope in two of the three cases, as indicated below:

Federal: "The New Democrats want you to win a Dream Vacation for two in France"

Ontario: "You could win a trip anywhere in Canada Air Canada flies"

British   "BC New Democrats, Here Comes The Sun. Summer 1990
Columbia: Draw – Win! A Free Sun-Filled Vacation for 2 in either: Hawaii or Mexico"[38]

Depending on whether or not the sweepstakes package was being sent to a prospect or house list, the salutation varied. In the letters analysed, the salutation was "Dear Friend" (Ontario and federal) or "Dear Supporter" (BC).

With respect to the contents of the letter, two of the three began with a description of the vacation package being offered by the party. The letter then shifted to a statement about the current state of government in Canada and asked for the recipient's support for the NDP. One letter began with a statement and then offered a description of the prize. Note that in only one case (BC mailing) did the statement that the person did *not* have to make a donation to enter the contest appear on a sheet separate from the letter. In all three cases, the letter was signed by the "Secretary" of the particular party involved.

The entry form for all of the sweepstakes mailings was on the same page as a form that stated something to the effect of "Here/Enclosed is my tax-deductible donation," and contained suggested amounts to give (from $35 to $250, or own amount). The appropriate tax credit was outlined and the "real cost" of the donation after the credit was indicated.[39] All of the sweepstakes packages contained a "reply" envelope that did not require postage. Each listed the particular draw on the front of the envelope, and was addressed to the relevant party headquarters. There were no messages on the back of the envelopes. Each package contained other enclosures, e.g., the federal one included a glossy, legal-sized "poster" of the trip itinerary.

Party officials were not prepared to provide revenue and expense data for specific sweepstakes mailings. They did say that the most successful mailing by the federal office was a sweepstakes package in 1988 that generated $325 000 in gross revenue.[40]

6.3   Criticisms of NDP Direct-Mail Efforts

Like its rivals, the NDP has attracted criticism for its direct-mail efforts. A December 1985 newspaper story offered a strong attack against a direct-mail prospect mailing sent out by the NDP (*Globe and Mail*, 20 December 1985, A4). The letter itself involved a fund-raising pitch from NDP leader Ed Broadbent that focused on the theme that the current Canadian tax system is unfair. However, the controversy over this mailing was in the packaging of the piece:

> The campaign [was] based on an unsolicited mailing to tens of thousands of Canadians in an official-looking envelope that had the words Taxation Notice in both languages in red letters on the front. In size and colour, the envelope [resembled] those used by the federal Department of Revenue. (Ibid.)

The campaign reportedly "delighted" party officials with its unusually high response and donation rate. The first test-mailing resulted in a large 17 percent response rate that, according to spokesperson Julie Mason, convinced the party to use it nationally. However, the mailing polarized the caucus and caused some public complaint.[41] NDP MP Lynn McDonald (Broadview–Greenwood) reported that she found the mailing "shocking." She added that she, and other MPs, had received complaints from the public that described the campaign as "disturbing, unfair camouflage of junk mail and a blot on the NDP's integrity." Ms. McDonald concluded that, while the message was worthwhile, the "gimmick" upset people (*Globe and Mail*, 20 December 1985, A4).

Despite the controversy raised by the "Tax Notice" campaign, the NDP used a similar type of direct-mail appeal in 1989. The August 1989 "prospect" mailing was packaged in a brown envelope (one very similar to those used by the federal government) and carried the label "Goods & Services Tax Notice" on the front.[42] Inside was a request for support, and money, to fight the proposed GST.

Business columnist Terence Corcoran was highly critical of a direct-mail piece from the NDP, signed by Ed Broadbent, that purported to deal with tax reform:

> Careful readers who plow through the remaining three pages of the letter might realize that what Broadbent is actually talking about is something other than tax cuts.
>
> [Tax reform] is a godsend for the NDP ... [and] in the hands of a skilled propagandist it is even more of a godsend. Broadbent, in his *Dear friend* letter, manages to completely divorce government spending from rising taxes and convey the impression that the only reason that taxes are rising is because corporations and wealthy Canadians are not paying enough.
>
> But what makes Broadbent's letter stand out as a masterpiece of direct-mail propaganda is its request that readers join him in "citizens campaign for basic tax reform based on fairness"... Broadbent is using a tax loophole [the tax deductible credit] to raise money from people who want to close tax loopholes ... The final effrontery is in a postscript, in which Broadbent says the letter was "Neither printed or mailed at public expense" ... That's an outright lie. Where does he think the 75 percent deducted cost comes from? (*Financial Times*, 14 July 1986, 1)

It is obvious that the NDP and other parties in their direct-mail solicitations are caught between the demands of what is likely to be effective (the world of advertising) and the demands of accuracy and public rectitude as political parties.

7. DIRECT-MAIL ELECTIONEERING

As a fund-raising technique, direct mail has certain attractive characteristics – other than the fact that it can generate substantial sums for parties. First, it can be an important source of information about issues for voters.[43] The letters often contain two or three pages of information about a party's or candidate's policies and positions. It is a good vehicle to convey political ideas in a more substantive form than the "sound bites" on television news or on political commercials. Second, direct mail is "involving." It asks for action and thus is a method of countering political alienation. Sending a cheque is a way of giving "voice" to one's political views. Third, it may be an efficient method not only to raise funds but also to get a party's message across, because it appeals directly for support (Warwick 1990, 266–67).

Dennis Young, a senior NDP official, argues that only about one-half of a direct-mail effort is directed toward raising funds. The other half consists of getting the party's message out to hundreds of thousands of supporters and potential supporters. This can be vital when the party is sliding in the polls, as was the NDP in 1983-84. In some cases, the NDP uses direct mail *not* to raise funds, but to "move" voters to become NDP voters or to build support for the party. For example, to help build a base in Quebec, in 1987 and 1988 the NDP sent a letter via bulk mail to every household in some 15 to 20 "priority" ridings. The letter included a return coupon indicating that the recipient wanted more information about the party. Individuals who returned the coupon were then contacted by telephone. Subsequently, they were contacted in person in an effort to sign them up as members. The response was good enough to suggest that the program should be extended. However, according to party officials, the members recruited in this fashion tend to be in the lower income levels – hence less able to respond to direct-mail appeals for contributions to the party.

The Progressive Conservative party draws a clear distinction between fund-raising direct mail and "political" direct mail. In the case of fund-raising direct mail, the objective is to raise money from large numbers of people, and it is expected that only 1 percent to 15 percent of recipients will respond with a cheque. The letter is usually long and involves an emotional appeal. Political direct mail is usually focused on marginal voters and it is designed to persuade the individual, often at an emotional level, to vote for the party. The letter is usually signed by a political actor, such as the leader, a minister or a candidate. In 1984 and 1988, the Conservatives' fund-raising direct-mail consultants were kept away from the political direct-mail efforts. The party's political direct-mail efforts culminated in the "Target '88" program.

Target '88 was the name of a Progressive Conservative party program that integrated the most modern techniques of individuated direct mail, telephone banks and computers. It was another campaign technique imported from the United States; in this case, the consultant was Mary Ellen Miller, an Oklahoma-based Republican Party organizer. The technique was first tried out in 1984, but its significance was not appreciated by senior party officials – even though in ridings in which it was used the Conservatives' vote was said to be above the national average, and the party obtained a larger share of the undecided vote (Lee 1989, 261).

Target '88 was launched in mid-summer 1988 under Pierre Fortier's direction, using four ridings, one of which was a blind control. It was so successful – resulting in a 65 percent response rate – that it was extended to 40 ridings during the campaign. In summary terms, the program worked as follows:

1. In each of about 40 ridings, a list of about 5 000 electors was prepared containing what officials believed was a high fraction of undecided voters. (The lists were prepared on the basis of Decima's polling.)
2. A customized letter was prepared for each voter signed by the Prime Minister. It contained a "magic paragraph" near the end asking for the person's "help in shaping and implementing a bold new plan for Canada's future."[44] A reply envelope was enclosed. From the 40 ridings (200 000 voters) in which Target '88 was used, an astounding 130 000 recipients replied – in long hand on their own paper (Lee 1989, 262).
3. A few days later all the recipients received a telephone call asking if they had received the PM's letter, thanking them for writing back, and asking them what they believed was the most serious issue facing the country today.
4. Later, the targeted voters received *another* letter from the Prime Minister, which relied on information previously supplied by the recipient. In particular, it responded – from a bank of 33 standard responses kept in a computer file – to the concerns voiced in the voter's previous letter. The real objective "was to persuade him that what he thought actually mattered" (Lee 1989, 262).
5. Later, the voter received from a party worker "calling for the Prime Minister" another call, reinforcing the second letter from him.

6. Finally, on voting day, there was another call on behalf of the Prime Minister offering help to get to the polls.

The reported response rate of 65 percent was 30 times higher than projected from expectations based on experience with direct-mail programs. Lee offers two reasons for the very high response rate: "Target 88 invited involvement from an electorate that had previously felt disengaged, voiceless and powerless" (1989, 261). Second, their involvement was solicited by "none other than the prime minister himself" (ibid.).

The direct, personal solicitation of electoral support is not resented; rather, it is generally welcomed. More important for the party, it is likely to convert undecided voters into supporters. The technique is based on the simple psychological fact that people like to be asked. In a sense, what Target '88 did was to employ the same principles used by Jimmy Carter in his run for the presidency before the 1976 election. "Carter ... turned a new key: getting thousands and thousands of voters to feel they had a stake in his victory" (Matthews 1988, 60–62). He had solicited their views and their support on an individual basis (ibid.). Carter applied, and Prime Minister Mulroney copied, the most effective way to gain a person's loyalty – let that person do you a favour. Those who give you a helping hand are also likely to look out for you further down the road. As a result of being asked for their views and being given some indication that they were being taken seriously, uncommitted voters found it easier to offer their political support when asked for it by the Prime Minister. Matthews puts it this way:

> The little secret shared by smart politicians ... is that people get a kick out of being propositioned. The smart politician knows that in soliciting someone [for their opinion, for money, for volunteer labour, for their vote] he is not so much demanding a gift or service, he is offering [the person an opportunity] to get involved. [The candidate] is simply offering a chance to join in the political action, to be part of his success. He is selling stock in himself, and in the process he is creating a network of stockholders. (Ibid., 63)

While expensive, Target '88 generated much useful data for those forming campaign strategy in Ottawa and for candidates. In fact, the telephone calls were made locally using the candidate's phone bank, but using a script provided by headquarters. The local candidate could use the information to solicit both votes and volunteers. Some targeted voters who were deemed influential might be asked to write notes to their neighbours saying why they intended to vote for the Conservative party (Lee 1989, 263). At headquarters, the voters' replies provided material for references to individuals for the Prime Minister's next speech in their community. More important, the program created an enormous "focus group" in each of the ridings in which it was used. The information they provided supplemented the nightly national and riding-specific tracking polls (ibid.).

Each riding's share of the cost was said to be $5 000 and the services of 10 volunteers (Lee 1989, 264). However, the value of Target '88 "is a matter of some dispute" in a campaign such as that of 1988, which saw such large and non-uniform swings in political support.[45] It seems most useful in close races in ridings that have tended to shift back and forth between two parties. Progressive Conservative party strategists estimate they won 35 ridings in 1988 by less than 2 percent of the vote (ibid., 264).

Several points should be noted about this program, which senior Conservative party strategists call "the way of the future" or "new dawn."[46] First, it is expensive (the party refused to provide details), but demographic analysis is a significant expense that can be incurred outside the official campaign period and be deemed – under the CEO's 1988 *Guidelines* for parties – *not* to be an "election expense" because it is part of the ongoing polling program.[47] These expenses include the identification of undecided voters in each of the ridings in the program. Second, in order to be efficient, the program requires a large and continuous polling database. As Lee (1989, 261) noted, "to reach undecided voters, Fortier consulted Decima's riding-profile polls and national tracking." Such a database is expensive, but no party – even the far wealthier Conservative party – has avoided the temptation to cut the polling budget when times are tough financially or where current information seems less relevant. Yet it is continuity in at least some of the key series of a database that makes it most valuable. Between election years, a national party could run (at the 1990 level of costs) a "gold plate" polling program for $750 000 or $1 million annually, according to Allan Gregg and Martin Goldfarb respectively. The third point about a program such as Target '88 is that it requires close cooperation between national headquarters and participating ridings. Even at the fairly modest cost to the ridings in 1988 (about 10 percent of their election expenses limit), some notable candidates turned down Target '88, for example, Maureen McTeer, who lost by 9 000 votes in Carleton–Gloucester, an Ottawa suburb (ibid., 264–66). Money was clearly not the problem in her case. She raised $50 862 and reported spending $49 447 on "election expenses," $222 in "personal expenses" (Canada, Elections Canada 1988c, 3–8) and another $25 652 on "other expenses."[48]

8. CONCLUSIONS

The tax credit provisions in the *Election Expenses Act* of 1974 probably stimulated efforts by all three main *parties* to use the direct-mail technique to solicit contributions from individuals. However, the data in chapter 8 on the rate at which individuals claim the tax credit (about 61 percent in the period 1985–88) suggest that the importance of the credit as a determinant in the individual's decision to make a contribution may have been overestimated.

The Progressive Conservative party started its direct-mail operation in 1975. It was closely followed by the federal office of the NDP in 1978. The Liberal party, because of its organizational structure and perhaps because it had been so long in power, failed to see the potential of direct mail and made its first effort only in 1981, when it had little success. This was followed by another, stronger, effort in 1983. Between 1985 and 1990, the Progressive Conservative party's *net* revenue from direct mail exceeded that of the Liberal party by between $1.03 million and $3.87 million annually. Part of this difference is due to the Tories' much lower costs of using this technique, which ranged from 18 percent to 28 percent of annual gross revenues between 1983 and 1990. Between 1987 and 1990, the Conservative party's net revenue from direct mail exceeded that of the federal office of the NDP by from $1.09 million to $4.0 million annually.

For the Conservative party, direct mail accounted for between 52 percent and 75 percent of the value of contributions from individuals over the period 1983–90. For the Liberal party, the comparable figures were 23 percent to 48 percent between 1985 and 1990. Data for the NDP indicate that direct mail is a less important source of revenue for the federal wing, accounting for 24 percent to 31 percent of total federally receipted contributions from individuals in the period 1987–90.

All three parties have met with criticism in the media for some of their direct-mail pieces. All three have relied at one time or another on the proposition that

> the key to direct mail is to make the reader angry or scared. To do so, says liberal direct mail consultant Roger Craver, "You've got to have a devil. If you don't have a devil, you're in trouble!" The devil in these letters is some person or group that is visibly and actively working against the soliciting group's interests. (Berry 1989, 59)

The NDP has been an innovator in direct mail by using "sweepstakes" offers that often give those who return a reply card (even if they do not make a donation) a chance to win a free holiday.

The future of direct mail as a fund-raising technique for parties appears to be limited only by the saturation effect of previously "responsive" donors receiving more than a dozen such appeals annually. It appears that the increasing number of appeals by all parties and the growth of indirect mail fund-raising by charities and interest groups have resulted in diminishing returns for all.

The Progressive Conservative party undertook a major innovation in using direct mail as a *campaign* technique in a limited number of ridings in 1988 (Target '88). It appears that the "experiment" was successful (Lee 1989). However, wider use of the technique will probably be constrained only by the limit on official "election expenses" in what Thomas Axworthy (1991) calls "the age of capital-intensive politics."

10

Two Fund-Raising Techniques
Dinners and Major-Donor Programs

1. INTRODUCTION

THIS CHAPTER EXAMINES two fund-raising techniques that produce a moderate amount of net revenue for both the Progressive Conservative and Liberal parties.[1] The first is fund-raising dinners, which have had a long history and today are one of the activities where a party leader can make an important personal contribution to his/her party's fund-raising activities. The second technique, major-donor clubs, is of much more recent vintage, although such clubs existed in a slightly different form in the early 1970s. Major-donor clubs are designed to raise larger donations from individuals (at least $1 000 per person annually in the case of both the Liberal and Progressive Conservative parties). The specific methods employed – largely imported from the United States – are based on the idea of market segmentation in which the party appears to provide a set of services or opportunities for individuals not available to those unable to make a sufficiently large donation.[2]

The chapter is organized as follows. Section 2 deals with the revenues and costs of fund-raising dinners. The focus is on the Liberal and Progressive Conservative parties. The NDP makes little use of this form of fund-raising because the ticket prices it is able to charge for such activities are so low that it gains little revenue from this source. Section 3 examines the Liberal and Conservative parties' major-donor programs. Emphasis is placed on "The 500" program, which is one of the Progressive Conservative party's fund-raising innovations, although the concept originated in the United States. The conclusions are briefly set out in section 4.

2. FUND-RAISING DINNERS

The fund-raising dinner is one of the oldest forms of raising money for political purposes. It combines food and wine with a chance for the party faithful and others to meet in a social situation. For the organizers, the primary objective is to raise money, but the event may also provide the leader with a large and receptive audience.

The existence of the tax credit for political contributions has probably helped the parties to raise the price of tickets to fund-raising dinners. However, the credit is allowed only on the part of the ticket price that is left *after* expenses. Under the tax credit system, for example, this means that a $500 dinner ticket that has a profit of $400 provides a $225 tax credit. The net after-tax cost of the dinner to the person attending is $275.

Party officials stress that such dinners require weeks of planning, and a large number of volunteers to arrange the venue, the head table guests, the tickets and the mailing list. The majority of tickets, according to a Liberal party official, have tended to be purchased by corporations, law firms and accounting firms in the larger centres and by individuals in the smaller centres. Larger firms tend to buy tickets for both major parties' dinners.

2.1 Progressive Conservative Party

The PC Canada Fund annually organizes major fund-raising dinners featuring a speech by the leader in Vancouver, Calgary or Edmonton, Toronto and Montreal. From time to time, similar dinners are organized in Ottawa, Winnipeg, Halifax, London and Quebec City. The ticket prices have been between $150 and $500 a person since 1986. Corporations and professional firms (lawyers, accountants, engineers) are approached to buy tables of eight or ten. For example, at the 1986 event in Toronto, 2 100 guests, many from major corporations, paid $400 each to hear the Prime Minister's message (*Globe and Mail*, 25 November 1986, A3).

In December 1986, the Tories put a new twist on the traditional fund-raising dinner. Instead of the usual "dinner and speeches," the main focus of the evening was the Montreal Symphony Orchestra, with a program of Verdi and Strauss. As a newspaper reporter stated,

> There was no rubber chicken ... and little political rhetoric ... (the) Quebec Conservative caucus was introduced. The prime minister

spoke for five minutes, then the politicians took their places with everyone else. (*Vancouver Sun*, 8 December 1986, A6)

The report went on to state that the Conservative party had "blazed the trail in political fund-raising in Canada for years, and Sunday's event was their latest innovation" (ibid.). The event brought out 2 300 people, who donated a total of almost $500 000.

On 6 November 1990, the Progressive Conservative party held a $500-per-person fund-raising dinner in Toronto. The speaker was the Prime Minister, who drew 1 700 paying guests (*Vancouver Sun*, 7 November 1990, A10). The PC Canada Fund probably netted about $625 000 from the event, based on the typical relationship between gross and net revenue that existed in 1990 (table 10.1). On 2 December 1990, the PC Canada Fund changed the dinner idea into a Sunday brunch in Montreal at $500 per person. Eleven teams of party officials and volunteers were each responsible for selling tickets for 20 tables of eight. Their target donors were run through a computer to ensure that no duplication occurred in the personal solicitation efforts.

Since he became leader of the Progressive Conservative party in mid-1983, Brian Mulroney has been personally active in fund-raising for the party by occasionally signing direct-mail appeals, and by speaking at an annual dinner for members of "The 500" and at national fund-raising dinners sponsored by the party. For example, in December 1991, Prime Minister Mulroney gave speeches at a series of major fund-raising dinners. "In a week, the Prime Minister had attracted several thousand people, and raised $2 million," according to a report in the *Globe and Mail* (9 December 1991, A5).[3] The dinner in Calgary is said to have attracted 850 people at $350 each (*Maclean's*, 16 December 1991, 13). In his speeches, Mulroney "aimed at Tories leaning to the Reform Party" and offered them "a carefully crafted blend of economics and patriotism, mockery and appeals to regional self-interest, heart and wallet" (*Globe and Mail*, 9 December 1991, A5). Raising $2 million through a series of dinners would appear to be a considerable achievement at a time when 77 percent of the population said they disapproved of the performance of the Conservative government.[4] The revenues and expenses associated with these dinners (which the party calls "national fund-raising events") are set out in table 10.1. Between 1983 and 1990, such dinners *netted* between $927 000 and $1.70 million annually. Expenses ranged from 25.5 percent to 41.5 percent of gross revenue.

Net revenue from national dinners as a percentage of *total* Conservative party revenues ranged from 3.4 percent in 1988 (when total party revenue was a record $27.0 million) to about 7 percent in the period 1985–87, 11.1 percent in 1989 and 15.1 percent in 1990. In 1990, dinners generated a record net revenue of $1.70 million, the largest amount in nominal terms since 1983. On the other hand, total party revenues were $11.3 million – less than they were in 1983 in nominal dollars (table 10.1).

2.2 Liberal Party

On 18 December 1978, the Ontario wing of the Liberal party erased its debt when it held a highly successful fund-raising dinner. Almost 2 000 people gathered to hear Prime Minister Trudeau speak, and the event provided the party with a net profit of $225 000 (*Ottawa Citizen*, 10 January 1979, 17). In 1979, Liberal organizers reported that they cleared about $120 from each $150 dinner ticket, whereas the Conservative party was said to net only $75 from a $150 dinner ticket (ibid.). However, the data in table 10.1 indicate that, by the mid-1980s, the Conservative party was netting a higher fraction of the ticket price, perhaps because the price had been raised more quickly than the costs of the events had increased.

Senator Keith Davey takes credit for being the first party official to raise over $1 million from a fund-raising dinner. He states:

> One of my greatest challenges ever as an organizer was to attract four thousand people, at $250 each, to hear Pierre Trudeau speak on December 13, 1983, at the CNE Coliseum. The press cynically dubbed it "The Last Supper"... I wanted to achieve this important goal by means of one stylish event and was convinced it would attract the party faithful ... Equally important, I wanted to provide Pierre Trudeau with a speaking opportunity before a blue-ribbon audience of area Grits and community leaders, not to mention the media and the Toronto business Establishment ... What a wonderful evening it was – complete with a head table of sixty-eight outstanding Canadians. Everyone from Cardinal Carter to Willie Upshaw, from Betty Kennedy to John Candy was there. (1986, 299)

In general terms, fund-raising dinners featuring the leader as speaker have been a more important source of revenue to the Liberal party than they have been to the Conservative party. Between 1987 and 1989, the net revenues from such dinners accounted for between 12.3 percent and 20.2 percent of the Liberal party's total revenues (table 10.2). The comparable figures for the Conservative party between 1983 and 1989 were 3.4 percent to 11.1 percent. In absolute terms, between 1987 and 1989, the Liberal party generated $5.3 million in net revenues from dinners, while the Conservative party generated only $3.5 million (table 10.1). In 1990, the Conservatives obtained $1.70 million from dinners, while the Liberals generated only $664 000 from this source (only half the amount raised in 1989). The reasons why the net revenue from dinners as a percentage of total Liberal party revenues fell from 20.2 percent in 1989 to 4.8 percent in 1990 lie in the doubling of party revenues attributable to the leadership race and convention and the halving of net revenues from dinners (table 10.2).

The Liberal party's expenses for fund-raising dinners between 1987 and 1990 ranged between 31.7 percent and 36.3 percent of gross revenues, while those of the Conservative party ranged between 25.5 percent and 41.5 percent (table 10.2). Comparisons are difficult to make between parties and even over time for a party, for several reasons. First, the expense ratio depends in large part on the strategy adopted by the party, which may change over time. For example, the party could decide to set a fairly modest ticket price, serve a less expensive meal and hope to increase its total net revenue by attracting a larger number of supporters. Alternatively, the party could set a high ticket price, offer high-quality food, wine and service, and hope that there would be sufficient attendance to generate a large amount of net revenue for the event. Second, a substantial component of the cost of organizing a fund-raising dinner is fixed, that is, the cost is independent of the ticket price, the quality of food or wine or the number of persons attending. Thus a dinner that fails to sell the expected number of tickets will have a high expense ratio. Third, the assignment of certain costs to the dinner is arbitrary. One approach is to record as expenses only those items that the Department of National Revenue requires to be deducted from the ticket price in computing the portion of the ticket price that will be eligible for the tax credit for political contributions. Another approach is to assign to a dinner a substantial part of the indirect costs associated with a fund-raising dinner. Such costs would include the time of the paid employees who helped organize the dinner.[5] As will be discussed in more detail in chapter 13, there is an asymmetry in the way that the Department of National Revenue treats revenues raised from direct mail or personal solicitation and those generated by fund-raising dinners. While it may cost $0.25 to $0.60 to generate $1 in contributions from direct mail, these costs are *not* deducted from the $1 for which the party (or candidate) issues a tax receipt. The expenses of a dinner, however, are deducted from the ticket price to compute the amount eligible for the tax credit.

The Liberal party's biggest annual fund-raising dinner is the Confederation Dinner in Toronto. Table 10.2 provides details of the revenues and expenses from this event for the years 1987–90. During this period, the dinner accounted for almost 30 percent of the net revenues generated by the leader's fund-raising dinners, even though its expense ratio was higher than that of other dinners.

The task of recruiting the party faithful and others willing to pay up to $500 for a ticket (but receive a tax receipt for a contribution of only $325) requires the mobilization of party officials and experienced volunteers. This is no easy task. Frank Stronach, chairman of Magna International Inc., the organizer of the 1988 Confederation Dinner, generated some negative publicity because of the tactics he used to sell tickets for the event (*Globe and Mail*, 6 October 1988, A2). Admittedly the Liberals, with their anti–free trade stance, were not a popular choice for corporate ticket buyers, and Mr. Stronach and his team of Magna executives organized all levels of the firm in an effort to counter this. However, the Liberal party received many complaints about the number of letters that people received from different Magna companies. One Magna supplier was reportedly angry that one of the letters he received "explicitly (tied) his contract with a Magna company to his support for the Liberal dinner" (ibid.). Commenting on the letter, Mr. Stronach admitted that "Some of my managers might not be diplomatic, and I wouldn't have written a letter quite like that." He added that his managers were "non-political, but this worry about free trade is the reason they are so supportive of the Confederation Dinner" (ibid.).

Data provided by the Liberal party show that, in 1987, leader's dinners held in Quebec accounted for 42 percent of the total *gross* revenues that the party received from dinners. This fell to 21 percent in 1988 and 9.5 percent in 1989. In absolute terms, gross revenues from dinners in Quebec fell from $1.1 million in 1987 to only $192 000 in 1989. However, the expense ratio for the dinners in Quebec was much lower than for those in other provinces: 18.1 percent in 1987, 19.6 percent in 1988 and 22.9 percent in 1989.

2.3 New Democratic Party

In the NDP, the leader's role in fund-raising has been fairly limited. Both Ed Broadbent and Audrey McLaughlin have signed direct-mail appeals. According to party officials, Broadbent did not spend much time on internal financial matters. He did, however, favour major banquets that might provide an audience of up to 1 000 people. While described as fund-raisers, these events netted only modest amounts and absorbed the time of the limited number of staff officials. Moreover, the NDP could charge only $100 or less for tickets in contrast to $250, or more commonly $500, charged by the Conservative or Liberal parties for similar events.

Since the organizational costs and costs of food and wine are virtually independent of the ticket price, a high ticket price is needed to bring in much net revenue. The banquets, however, helped to reinforce the support of the faithful and they were said to be "media hits." More were held in 1986 and 1987 when the party and the leader were rising strongly in the polls.

3. MAJOR-DONOR PROGRAMS

Only the Tories and the Liberals have major-donor programs that seek donations of at least $1 000 a year from individuals. On the other hand, the NDP has had the good fortune to obtain the generous support of Mrs. Irene Dyck[6] who between 1983 and 1990 contributed an average of $153 593 each year to the NDP, including $453, 365 in 1983!

3.1 "The 500"

The origins of the Progressive Conservative party's major-donor program, "The 500," lie in the "The Early Bird Club" started by Joe Clark and Senator Finlay Macdonald in 1980, when Mr. Clark was leader. The idea was to create a vehicle to raise annual contributions of at least $1 000 each from individuals. The present name of the program reflects the idea of raising at least $1 000 from 500 individuals. Some 49 individuals have been members of "The 500" for the decade since it was founded.

Shortly after Brian Mulroney was elected leader in June 1983, Brian Gallery[7] was appointed to develop the nascent major-donor program. Gallery and his team took the idea, applied his knowledge of marketing and developed "The 500" into a major Conservative party fund-raising vehicle. The growth[8] of "The 500" from 800 to 900 members in 1984 (only one year after Gallery took charge) to a peak of 2 400 in 1988 and then to 1 300 in 1989 stemmed from the ability to identify and target a previously untapped market for political contributions. This market consists of business executives, professionals (lawyers, accountants, engineers) and owners of small businesses who, according to Gallery, "believe in good government" and are willing to contribute as individuals[9] to a party they believe can make a difference. This point is reinforced in "The 500" 's communications. A pamphlet announcing the program's tenth anniversary put it this way:

> People often ask: "Can I really make a difference?"
> The answer for members of The 500 is YES! Since 1980, the members of The 500 have proven that by joining together and supporting the P.C. Party and its candidates they can make an impact on the future of Canada.

Other parties have tried to emulate The 500, but neither Opposition party has succeeded. No other group has been as successful in recruiting members, raising funds and supporting winning campaigns.

The 500 is a national leader ... a political force ... that has helped to bring positive change to the P.C. Party and to Canada.

Conservative party officials claim that they were the first to introduce the major-donor concept to Canadian politics[10] and based "The 500" on a similar program used by the Republican Party in the United States. For an annual donation of $1 000 (with a $450 tax credit) and a "commitment to the Prime Minister and the Progressive Conservative Party of Canada," an individual can become a member of this group (*Globe and Mail*, 10 January 1987, A4). "The 500" does not advertise itself as an exclusive club per se, but, as a newspaper article reported, "the notion is salted into every line" (ibid.). Those who receive an appeal to join "The 500" have been chosen from a list of persons selected on the basis of income level/occupation. The literature sent to members or potential members stresses the unique benefits open to this special group of donors. The members may have an opportunity to meet the Prime Minister, participate in forums that provide an opportunity to learn about recent government policies and to talk to those in charge, and can ask an official of "The 500" should they need any special information or assistance.

A newspaper report of an annual conference of "The 500" in Toronto described the gathering as one in which the

drinks are free ... The hors d'oeuvre are fresh. The stripes on the suits are very wide and very blue. Displayed discreetly in the corner of each lapel is a small pin which says simply "500". Nibbling and sipping, the group sorts out into small clusters around each minister, and hangs on every word. And the PM is coming for lunch. (*Globe and Mail*, 10 January 1987, A4)

Party officials point out that members pay a cost-recovery registration fee to attend such events.

It appears that the club characteristics of "The 500" are appealing to individuals who are able to give $1 000 annually to a political party. Their donations are not anonymous; they are reported by the Chief Electoral Officer each year and made public by him. The individual receives recognition (e.g., lapel pin, tie, newsletter, invitations), an opportunity to "network" among what party officials describe as a "fascinating group of individual Canadians" and each receives individuated benefits[11] from joining the club (in particular, local opportunities to meet party notables and to attend the national conference).

The costs of the operation are modest: a full-time executive secretary in Ottawa; the cost of mailings to solicit renewals and new members; and the costs of the dinner with members of the Honour Roll, which may be attended by the Prime Minister.[12] Members receive the "Info 500" newsletter quarterly. It contains pictures of club activities, news of members' activities and information about party activities. Members who phone the secretary to request them are sent copies of ministerial speeches and policy documents in the public domain. However, this service is little used. Brian Gallery suggests that something like "The 500" cannot be run by paid staff. It has to be run by a fairly high-profile, gregarious person with a very large circle of friends and acquaintances. The job requires plenty of time to manage the marketing efforts, travel to reinforce the efforts of the local presidents and hundreds of phone calls to ensure that the "access events" go off without a hitch (despite the uncertainties of ministers' schedules).[13]

"The 500" is seen as a burden on the time of the Prime Minister and his ministers, according to Gallery, because they have very heavy schedules and are reluctant to take on more. So Gallery tries to schedule meetings with "500" members in conjunction with a public event in the same city. The Prime Minister is requested to attend only two events: dinner with the members of the Honour Roll and a speech at the national convention of "The 500" (after which he and his wife Mila "work the crowd"). The 1990 national conference of "The 500" had to be cancelled because of a conflict in the Prime Minister's schedule. Some ministers make as many as three appearances each year on behalf of "The 500." Some, such as Michael Wilson, John Crosbie and Don Mazankowski, are in greater demand than others. In mid-1990, only about 50 of 150 members of "The 500" in the Montreal area turned out to meet Benoît Bouchard, then Minister of Transport. He gave a short speech, followed by a question-and-answer session. Even when they are unable to come to such events, members "like to be asked," according to Gallery.

Part of the strategy of "The 500" is getting members involved in running the organization itself. As chairman of "The 500," Gallery seeks out members to serve as presidents in each of a score of major urban centres. Their job is to use personal contacts, telephone calls and the mail to enrol additional members. Titles are assigned that reflect the various responsibilities assumed by these volunteers. Therefore, in each of 22 urban areas there is a president, vice-president and board of directors. To recruit members, "The 500" has sent out some 10 000 letters, sometimes several times each year. The letters have been signed by various individuals, including the Prime Minister.

As already mentioned, a strong incentive is offered to those who recruit three new members. Such persons are put on the Honour Roll and are personally thanked for their efforts at a dinner following the completion of the program. The Prime Minister attempts to attend this special event and offer his thanks for the significant contribution these individuals have made to funding the party. Although attendees pay their own travel and accommodation costs to this event, the dinner itself is funded out of revenues generated by the program. The Honour Roll recorded 240 names in 1988 and 80 in 1989, according to Gallery.

"The 500" also holds an annual national conference in Ottawa for members and their spouses. (Members must pay their own travel and accommodation, in addition to a cost-recovery registration fee.) The conference begins with cocktails and is often attended by several members of the Cabinet. The next morning there is a question-and-answer session with a handful of ministers, followed by lunch with the Prime Minister. The conference ends with a dinner dance.

> 500 members are joined by Members of Parliament and other Party leaders to review the accomplishments of the past year, to exchange ideas and make recommendations, and to enjoy the camaraderie of a team that will have an impact on the direction the Party will take in the years ahead.
>
> The 1990 National Conference will be different because it is an important opportunity for all 500 members to be recognized for their special contribution to the success of the P.C. Party of Canada since 1980. (500 *Tenth Anniversary*, pamphlet)

Members of "The 500" are eligible for tax receipts. A contribution of $1 000 has a net after-tax cost of $550.[14] In return, the individual gains some measure of exclusivity – much more than would be gained by spending the same amount to purchase two $500-a-plate tickets for a dinner with the Prime Minister and his wife. Then there is the matter of social differentiation. "The 500" would appear to offer an opportunity to (hopefully) impress friends and acquaintances with casual comments about having had a drink with such well-known ministers as Michael Wilson or John Crosbie, or having met the Prime Minister.

What motivates people to join "The 500"? Party officials suggest that there are a variety of motives: responding to the invitation of a friend or respected acquaintance or being given an opportunity to participate in politics and being flattered for having been asked to join what most perceive as a group of action-oriented Canadians. A small percentage, Gallery notes, think that membership provides access –

beyond the local informal meetings with cabinet ministers and the national conference. Some are doubtless disappointed by Gallery's response to requests from members for help in dealing with the federal government. Gallery indicated that he emphasizes to all that he is not a middleman, lawyer or lobbyist. He avoids making any effort to assist individuals seeking contracts, beyond referring them to the relevant minister using a one-line letter.[15] However, he will make a greater effort to have a case re-examined by the minister in the few cases where he concludes that the individual has been unfairly "caught in the toils of the system." Gallery believes that a very few members "try him out" to see how far he will go to provide help in light of their contribution to the party. Directors of "The 500" are quick to point out that membership does not result in any special access to inside information and that their membership appeal does not imply that failure to join will leave the individual, somehow, on the "outside." Gallery has said that "Anybody who can write a cheque for $1 000 is smart enough to know that, of all ways, this is the least [effective] way they are going to lobby or do anything. These are supporters of the party and there is a little bit of togetherness" (*Vancouver Sun*, 3 May 1985, A12).

In August 1986, opposition members criticized the government for an activity of "The 500" (*Globe and Mail*, 16 August 1986, A11). Their anger erupted after it was learned that Mr. Mulroney, who had missed two major meetings of his full Cabinet, and a one-day special session of the House, and had assigned increasing responsibility to Deputy Prime Minister Don Mazankowski, was to be the major speaker at a "500" fund-raiser in October. Opposition members charged that the Prime Minister "after playing hide-and-seek with his Cabinet all this summer and removing himself from day-to-day chores, is taking part in a high-priced scheme that gives the wealthy access to the Prime Minister in exchange for cash for Tory coffers" (ibid.).[16]

Table 10.3 indicates that the gross revenues[17] of "The 500" ranged from 7.2 percent to 12.8 percent of the total Conservative party revenues between 1984 and 1990. With the exception of 1985 and 1986, direct costs were a very small percentage of gross revenues. The net revenue from "The 500" has ranged from $1.13 million in 1990 to $2.44 million in 1988, an election year. As we shall now describe, the Conservative party's club for individuals who make large contributions has far outpaced the Liberal party's comparable effort.

3.2 The "Laurier Club"
While the Liberal party's counterpart to the Conservatives' "The 500" was not established until 1985, the Liberals were innovators in Canada

in the concept of raising larger sums from individual donors. Wearing (1981, 185) states that the Red Carnation Fund was established by the Liberal party in 1970. It was to coordinate already established provincial organizations and initiate new ones in provinces where they did not already exist. The Fund would seek donations of between $100 and $500 from individuals, with two-thirds of this amount going to the provincial association and one-third to the federal party for interelection maintenance. The Fund was astutely conceived of as appealing to relatively apolitical professional and business people. The general approach was based on the theme – "Support the democratic two-party system in this country." In contrast to the personal solicitation used in later major-donor programs, the Red Carnation Fund was based on direct mail. A prospective donor would receive from a cabinet minister or senator an "individualized" letter (produced by an automatic typing machine) that was intended to soften him up for the visit by "My friend, Sam Jones, [who] will be around to see you in the next few weeks." All contributors would receive a letter of thanks from the Prime Minister (signed by an ingenious automatic signature machine that uses a pen to recreate a signature exactly) and donors of $500 or more would get an annual Christmas card. When the Prime Minister was in town, donors would have precedence in meeting him and would be given a red carnation to wear at prime ministerial functions (ibid.). The Fund "was slow in getting off the ground," but, in 1972, in the face of an impending election, the Ontario association raised $30 000. It was not part of the Liberal party's fund-raising strategy after the 1974 reforms became law.

In May 1985, the Liberal party announced that it was establishing its own major-donor program. In doing so, John Swift, chief of staff for leader John Turner, stated that "similar efforts have been used very successfully by the Democrats in the States, by the Republicans, [and] by [British Prime Minister] Margaret Thatcher" (*Vancouver Sun*, 3 May 1985, A12). The target group for the new "Laurier Club" was to be "business and professional people, key supporters across the country, who are willing to come on and get involved at a certain level" (ibid.). Following the pattern of "The 500," members of the Liberal club would also receive a "newsletter," and there would be meetings of 100 to 200 people with the leader where their views would be solicited (ibid.). Ironically, only one month before this announcement, a Liberal MP had criticized the Tories for this style of fund-raising.

The "Laurier Club" has, on average, generated from one-eighth to one-quarter the net revenues of "The 500" (tables 10.3 and 10.4). Between 1986 and 1989, the "Laurier Club" 's net revenues were in the range of

$154 000 to $416 000. The "Laurier Club" 's contribution (as measured by gross revenues) to the Liberal party's total revenues ranged from 2.5 percent to 4.7 percent between 1986 and 1989. Note also that gross revenues in 1989 were less than half those of 1986, 1987 or 1988. They fell to only $94 000 in 1990 (table 10.4).

The Liberal party's weakness relative to the Conservative party in appealing to individuals willing to donate $1 000 or more annually could be the result of a number of factors. First, the party has been out of power since September 1984. Therefore, it cannot offer dinners or cocktails with a cabinet minister. In other words, the Liberal party has not been in a position to supply "access opportunities" that businessmen would perceive as valuable. Second, as leader, Mr. Turner was not popular with business executives in light of his stand on free trade and his apparent support for more government intervention on a number of fronts, yet business executives are the primary constituency for the "Laurier Club." Third, the success of the Conservative party's major-donor club may have reflected the high level of energy and special skills of the individual (Brian Gallery) who heads it. As described in chapter 5, between 1986 and 1988 Senator Leo Kolber, the Liberals' chief fund-raiser, was preoccupied with a variety of other initiatives to raise money and control party expenditures. Under less stressful circumstances, he might have been able to make the "Laurier Club" a stronger vehicle for raising money for the Liberal party. Senator Kolber was reappointed chairman of the Revenue Committee in February 1991 and, according to party officials, the "Laurier Club" is being reinvigorated.

3.3   New Democratic Party

The NDP does not have a major-donor program like its two main rivals. Data for the period 1987–90 reveal, however, that the party has had some success in attracting contributions of $1 000 or more from individuals. Table 10.5 indicates that the NDP received an average of 290 contributions of $1 000 or more and 23 of $2 000 or more each year between 1987 and 1990.[18] The peak year was 1988 when the NDP received 380 contributions from individuals in the range of $1 000 to $1 999, and 39 of $2 000 or more.[19] In 1989, the NDP received more contributions of $2 000 or more from individuals (22) than did the Liberal party (17), although the Conservative party received almost four times as many (82). The average size of "large" contributions ($2 000 or more) to the NDP was larger than those made to the Liberal or Conservative party, but this was attributable to the very large donations of Mrs. Irene Dyck. Between 1983 and 1990, she gave the NDP a total of $1.23 million in nominal dollars.

3.4 Understanding Access Opportunities

Officials of all parties deny that political contributions "buy anything" in terms of influence with the party and particularly with the government in the case of the party in power. Rather, potential donors – particularly those responsible for what might be a large contribution from a corporation – are told that money should be given to "support the democratic political system." Political contributions, fund-raisers argue, are simply part of being a "good corporate citizen." However, as shall be seen in chapter 11, except for the largest firms, only a tiny fraction of corporations make a political contribution. For executives of large corporations or owners of a small business or professional practice, it may be hard to justify political contributions if they cannot expect to receive any benefit thereby. It is common, however, for party officials to argue that, while contributions, notably large ones, do not "buy influence," they do facilitate "access."[20] They see no harm in taking contributions to facilitate access. But is it really harmless?

Normally, gaining access is a precondition to influencing the behaviour of government. (Indirect access may be obtained through the media, that is, a prominent report of certain statements or actions by an interest group may have the effect of "opening the doors" of a minister. Indeed, one of his/her aides may contact the group to discuss their concerns or to set up a meeting.) In parliamentary systems, it is much more important to have easy access to cabinet ministers, parliamentary secretaries and chairs of committees than it is to have such access to ordinary backbenchers. Access can mean a variety of things. For example, it can ensure that a person's telephone calls are returned promptly; it may increase the odds of receiving sympathetic consideration of the person's subsequent requests. In addition, access usually involves the ability to gain a face-to-face meeting, which others may fail to gain, or to gain as promptly. The value of access may lie largely in its *timing*, that is, in being able to make representations before the relevant issue is cast in stone, or just before the crucial points have been decided.

There is always excess demand for a minister's time. How can he/she decide to allocate it? One way is to answer first those calls from people known to the minister. The identity of large contributors is no secret, not only because such names must be reported to the CEO for annual publication, but also because those who make large donations seldom hide their light under a bushel. Political contributions may buy access to key individuals rather than to their executive assistants or aides. Such contributions may make a group's representations more effective because the group will be *known* to the member/minister. There is already the basis of a *personal* relationship as well as a business one.

If one takes at face value the strong denials of senior party officials that large political contributions "buy nothing" in terms of benefits for donors, then one is left with the possibility that the extra attention paid to members of the Conservative party's major-donor program ("The 500") is really designed to create an illusion. By providing members with "access opportunities" in the form of cocktail parties with one or more ministers where the number of attendees is small, and with an opportunity to attend the annual national meeting at which the Prime Minister speaks and "works the crowd," the party gives the impression that access opportunities are valuable, while knowing that they produce no tangible benefit for the donors. The donors may believe there is a benefit – perhaps long delayed, and only indirectly related to the donation. Party officials would likely reject this explanation. Rather, they might say that what they are providing is an opportunity for wealthy and powerful people to signal to each other (and to those of lower status) just how important/influential/wealthy/well connected they are. In the logic of advertising, the various rewards and forms of recognition are themselves essentially neutral. It is the donor (buyer) who imbues the opportunities with importance because of his/her psychological needs, and who projects these needs onto the "items" made available by the party. For the party and the cabinet ministers, the intimate dinners and other "access opportunities" may be seen as just another form of ritual behaviour in which they participate in order to help the party. They have no intention of allowing those gaining access to influence the substantive performance of their role as important public officials.

But what about the vast majority of citizens who cannot afford to participate in a major-donor club? How can the party explain to them that the "recognition and rewards" it provides, largely in the form of access opportunities,[21] signify *nothing* in terms of influencing government decision making, without also providing the large donors with evidence of cynicism or even duplicity? It may well be that such major-donor programs can succeed largely because of their calculated ambiguity. In any event, it seems wrong to treat the matter of access lightly, if major-donor programs or other forms of party fund-raising do, in fact, result in more/better access for donors. It may be useful to think of access as providing a slight "edge" to those who have it, relative to other persons also seeking to influence public policy.

In summary, to the extent that they provide even a small edge, political contributions may be useful to the contributor who seeks to influence public policy. That edge may be access or more rapid access to a minister when normally the person would have to make his/her case to a ministerial aide or parliamentary secretary. The edge may simply be a slightly more sympathetic eye when the minister reviews a file. It may consist of having another look at a firm's case before the final decision is rendered. The point is that, as long as political contributions are used to distinguish one person's (or firm's) representations from another in the slightest way, then such contributions can be said to produce a benefit. Whether that benefit is worth the cost to the donor is quite another matter.

4. CONCLUSIONS

Fund-raising dinners are one of the oldest forms of raising money for parties and candidates. While the Liberal and Progressive Conservative parties make considerable use of this technique, the New Democratic and Reform parties do not do so. The net revenues from dinners featuring the party leader amounted to between 3.4 percent and 15.1 percent of total Conservative party revenues during the period 1983–90. For the Liberal party, dinners featuring the leader generated from 12.3 percent to 20.2 percent of total party revenues in the period 1987–89. Even in absolute terms, the Liberal party generated more net revenues from dinners than did the Conservative party during the period 1987–89. In 1990, however, the Conservative party's net revenue from dinners ($1.70 million) was almost three times that of the Liberal party ($664 000).

While the idea of major-donor programs can be traced back to efforts by the Liberal party to raise larger sums from individuals through the Red Carnation Fund in the early 1970s, it was not until 1983 that the Progressive Conservative party launched the modern form of the major-donor program, "The 500." Under the energetic leadership of Brian Gallery, "The 500" solicits annual contributions of at least $1 000 from individuals. This program generated from 7.2 percent to 12.8 percent of the total revenues of the Conservative party between 1984 and 1990. The Liberal party launched its counterpart, the "Laurier Club," in 1985. Between 1986 and 1990, this program raised from 0.7 percent to 4.7 percent of total Liberal party revenues. In 1986 and 1987, the ratio was 4.3 percent and 4.7 percent respectively. In 1988 and 1989, the ratio dropped to 2.5 percent and 2.9 percent respectively.

While the NDP does not have a major-donor program, each year between 1987 and 1990 the party generated from 209 to 419 contributions of at least $1 000. However, the NDP was far less successful than its rivals in raising contributions of $2 000 or more. From 1987 to 1990, it received an average of 23.5 such contributions annually, versus 133 for the Conservative party and 62.8 for the Liberal party.

11

CONTRIBUTIONS FROM BUSINESS AND COMMERCIAL ORGANIZATIONS

1. INTRODUCTION

W HEN MEMBERS OF PARLIAMENT legislated the *Election Expenses Act* in 1974, they were well aware of the fact that, for decades, less than 500 donors, mainly medium-sized to very large corporations, had been supplying the Liberal and Progressive Conservative parties with almost all of their funds. Although there was no talk of *financement populaire* (in the sense of allowing only electors to make political contributions) in the Barbeau Commission (Canada, Committee 1966), the Chappell Committee (Canada, House of Commons 1971b) or the debates surrounding the *Election Expenses Act*, it was clear that the intent of the reforms was to diversify the revenue base of the two oldest and largest parties. The reforms were also to ensure that, if corporations continued to make large donations, annual public disclosure would all but eliminate the possibility of some form of quid pro quo for such donations. As described below, the fear expressed by some, including prominent Liberal fund-raiser Senator John Godfrey (Canada, Senate 1974), that disclosure would lead to reduced willingness to donate appears to have had very little effect on donations from corporations.[1] While the Liberal and Progressive Conservative parties continued to raise substantial sums from corporations, they began to raise roughly comparable amounts from individuals (described in chap. 3).

At the same time, there has been a dramatic change in the Liberal and Progressive Conservative parties' perception of the role of contributions from corporations.[2] Leading fund-raisers within both parties contend that corporations are failing to meet their social obligations to support the democratic system by making contributions that reflect the scale of their operations. Only a tiny fraction of business enterprises make political contributions (typically less than 3 percent, except in election years when the percentage doubles). Even among the 500 largest nonfinancial enterprises in Canada, only 40 percent made an annual contribution to any political party in the period 1983–90. Moreover, fund-raisers have suggested that the contributions from major corporations have not kept pace with inflation. That perception will be examined in this chapter.

The chapter is organized as follows. Section 2 provides an overview of the size and significance of contributions from corporations to the Progressive Conservative, Liberal and New Democratic parties. Section 3 reviews the use of the tax credit for political contributions by corporations. Section 4 analyses political contributions of the 500 largest *nonfinancial* corporations in Canada (the *Financial Post 500*) over the period 1983–90. These contributions generally account for a rather modest fraction of all contributions from corporations and for an even smaller fraction of total party revenue. Section 5 analyses the contributions of the 155 largest *financial* enterprises in Canada over the period 1983–90. Section 6 offers some conclusions.

2. CORPORATE CONTRIBUTIONS: OVERVIEW

2.1 Their Importance as a Source of Revenue

During the period 1974–90, contributions from corporations accounted for about half of the Progressive Conservative and Liberal parties' total revenues (table 11.1).[3] However, in both cases, the importance of corporate contributions has varied considerably. For the Conservatives, the fraction ranged from 33 percent to 37 percent between 1981 and 1983 to 51 percent to 56 percent in 1974/75, 1979, 1980, 1987 and 1988. In general, corporate contributions have been a larger fraction of the Conservatives' total revenues in election years than in interelection years – even though election year revenues include the partial reimbursement of "election expenses" from the federal government. For the Liberal party, corporate contributions as a percentage of total revenues ranged from 37.4 percent in 1982 and 39.5 percent in 1985 to 60.2 percent in 1987 and 61.5 percent in 1989 (table 11.1). The drop to 33.2 percent in 1990 is attributable to the leadership race and convention in June won by Jean Chrétien.[4]

Partly because of its philosophy and the opposition of most

provincial sections to corporate contributions, the NDP receives little money from business organizations.[5] At the *federal* level, the NDP received from 4.0 percent to 6.3 percent of its federal revenues from businesses between 1975 and 1978. However, from 1982 to 1990, corporate contributions were typically less than 1 percent, the exceptions being 2.5 percent in 1986 and 1.9 percent in 1988 (table 11.1).

2.2 Contributions in Dollars

Contributions from corporations to the Progressive Conservative party, in nominal dollars, rose from $975 000 in 1974/75 to $5.0 million in 1979, an election year, then dropped to $2.57 million in 1981. They increased sharply in 1983 and again in 1984, another election year, to $11.0 million. Then they dropped to an average of about $7 million in the interelection years of 1985–87. The peak was reached in 1988 ($14.4 million); then corporate contributions to the Conservative party dropped by over one-half to $6.9 million in 1989, $6.35 million in 1990 and $6.66 million in 1991 (table 11.1).

In *real* terms (1989 dollars), corporate contributions to the Conservative party have increased dramatically in election years: from $9.4 million in 1979 ($7.4 million in 1980) to $13.6 million in 1984 to $15.1 million in 1988. However, the change in corporate contributions to the Conservative party between elections has been far less consistent. For example, in 1974/75, the total was $2.6 million, and in 1981 and 1982 the level was only about $3.9 million (table 11.1). However, between the 1984 and 1988 general elections, corporate contributions in real terms averaged $7.9 million annually, well above the average of $4.7 million between the 1980 and 1984 elections. Since the 1988 election, contributions from corporations to the Conservative party averaged $6.37 million (from 1989 to 1991), well below the average between the 1984 and 1988 election years ($7.9 million annually).

After 1977, with the exception of 1981, the Progressive Conservative party was able to raise more money – in some years much more – from corporations than was the Liberal party (table 11.1). In nominal dollars, the Liberal party raised $2.3 million from corporations in 1977. This increased to $3.9 million in 1979 (an election year), fell to $2.5 million in 1982 and then increased to $5.3 million in election year 1984. Then corporate contributions to the Liberals dropped by more than half in 1985, only to recover sharply in 1986 and 1987. Corporate contributions peaked in the election year of 1988 at $8.4 million, only to drop sharply in 1989. The 1990 figure for the Liberal party ($4.56 million) was inflated by contributions to leadership candidates routed through the Federal Liberal Agency. The figure for 1991 was $3.4 million, below the level in 1989 ($3.93 million).

In *real* terms (1989 dollars), the Liberal party raised more from corporations in the 1979 election year ($7.25 million) than it did in 1984 ($6.6 million), but was able to increase the amount in the next election year ($8.9 million in 1988). It seems clear that, in real terms, the Liberal party has not been able to increase total contributions from business organizations between elections. In 1977 and 1978, the average was $5.1 million. This fell to an average of $4.0 million in the period 1981–83 and then, in the period 1985–87, returned almost to the level of 1977–78 of $4.8 million (table 11.1). This amount fell to $3.9 million in 1989. The increase to $4.36 million in 1990 is very likely attributable to the contributions to leadership candidates routed through the Federal Liberal Agency since it was $3.13 million in 1991, well below the amount for 1989.

The Liberal party, therefore, faces a major challenge in raising contributions from corporations, which at one time were relied upon to support the party more generously. The gap between it and the Progressive Conservative party is documented in table 11.1. In the first 41 months under the 1974 *Election Expenses Act,* the Liberals raised some $724 000 (in nominal terms) more from corporations than did the Tories. Since that time, however, the situation has been reversed (except for 1981), and the gap has widened. For example, in the 1979 and 1980 election years, the Conservative party raised $1.8 million more from corporations than did the Liberals. In the next two election years, 1984 and 1988, the Tories' advantage was a huge $5.7 million and $4.9 million respectively (in nominal dollars). The Conservatives' advantage *between* election years increased as well. This is most easily seen by looking at the corporate contributions in real terms (1989 dollars). During the period 1981–83, the Conservative party received an average of $4.7 million annually from corporations, versus $4.0 million for the Liberal party. In the next interelection period, 1986–87, the Tories averaged $7.9 million, while the Liberals generated only $4.8 million.[6] From 1989 to 1991, the Conservative party collected $8.0 million (in 1989 dollars) *more* than did the Liberal party, despite the fact that the Liberals' 1990 figure was inflated by corporate contributions to leadership candidates.

Another useful way to compare the Liberal and Conservative parties' capacity to raise money from corporations is to group the years between 1974 and 1991 into the periods when each party was in power and to put the amounts into constant 1989 dollars (table 11.2a). Between 1974 and 1978 when the Liberals were in power, they raised a total of $19.1 million (1989 dollars), or $1.36 million more from corporations than did the Tories. In 1979, when the Progressive Conservatives formed a minority government under Joe Clark, the party raised $9.4 million from corporations or $2.14 million *more* than did the Liberal party. Since that time, the Tories have been able to maintain or increase the gap. In the period 1980–84, the Progressive Conservative party raised $35.1 million, compared with $25.0 million for the Liberal party, or an average of $2 million a year more. After they came to power in October 1984, the Tories did even better relative to the Liberals. The Conservatives under Brian Mulroney raised $57.8 million from corporations between 1985 and 1991 compared to $34.5 million for the Liberal party – an average difference of $3.33 million per year (1989 dollars).

2.3 Number of Contributions from Corporations

The strength of the Conservative party in raising money from corporations has been in persuading a much larger number of firms to make a donation rather than in the average size of those donations, which have consistently trailed those to the Liberal party (table 11.2). The advantage of the Conservatives over the Liberals was evident in the period 1974–78, when Liberals obtained 18 314 contributions from corporations versus 21 697 for the Conservatives (table 11.2a). In election year 1979, the Conservative party generated twice the number of corporate contributions (7 752) than did the Liberal party (3 737). However, even under the last Liberal government of Pierre Trudeau, the Tories obtained 31 000 *more* contributions from corporations than did the Liberals. After the Mulroney government came to office, the Conservatives' lead in corporate contributions continued. In the period 1985–91, the Tories generated 39 157 more contributions from corporations than did the Liberals. However, on an *annual* basis, the Conservatives' advantage over the Liberals fell from 6 200 in 1980–84 to 5 594 in 1985–91. This is attributable largely to the decline in the average annual number of contributions to both parties between 1980–84 and 1985–91. For the Tories, the drop was from 12 222 to 10 817, while for the Liberals it was from 6 028 to 5 223 (table 11.2a).

The growing difference in the ability of the Conservative and Liberal parties to obtain contributions can be seen in another way. In the period 1974–78, the number of contributions from corporations to the Liberal party was 84.4 percent of the number for the Conservative party. By the period 1980–84, this figure had dropped to 49.3 percent, and in the period 1985–91, it dropped even further to 48.3 percent.

2.4 Overall "Participation Rate"

The term "participation rate" is used to refer to the fraction of corporations that make a contribution to one or more parties and/or candidates in a year. Combining the number of corporations giving to parties with those giving to candidates in election years, we find that the total number of corporations making a political contribution amounted to from 2.4 percent to 9.1 percent of the total number of corporations between 1980 and 1988 (table 11.7). In election years 1980, 1984 and 1988, the percentage was at the high end of the range: 5.7 percent, 9.1 percent and 6.7 percent. In nonelection years, only 2.4 percent to 3.3 percent of corporations made a political contribution to a party during the 1980s.

2.5 Average Size of Contributions

In 13 of the 17 years between 1974/75 and 1991, the average contribution by corporations to the Liberal party exceeded that to the Conservative party. In some years (e.g., 1979, 1984, 1986) the Liberals' average was more than $200 above the Tories' average. In the period 1985–90, the average contribution to the Conservative party was 78.8 percent of that to the Liberal party, up from 69.2 percent in the period 1980–84. However, with the exception of the period 1974–78, the Liberal party was *not* able to use its higher average contribution to offset the Conservative party's larger number of contributions from corporations.

In nominal dollars, it appears that the average contribution from corporations has increased. In *constant* 1989 dollars, the average appears to have decreased for the Tories, but not for the Liberals (table 11.2). In 1974/75 and 1975/76, the average corporate contribution to the Liberals was $1 111 and $1 253 respectively (1989 dollars). While the average was higher in the election years of 1979 and 1980, the average fell to $608 in 1982 and $454 in 1983. Between 1985 and 1987, the average was $765 to $962. In 1990 and 1991, the Liberals averaged $779 and $824 respectively, somewhat *below* the average of the mid-1970s. Another way to describe the pattern of average contributions is to say that, after 1975, the average size dropped in 1981–83 (a recession), then more or less returned to pre-recession levels, if the two election years are excluded.

Contributions by corporations seem to have been subject to an "election year effect" in that the average size of corporate contributions increased noticeably in election years. For example, in 1979, the average contribution from corporations to the Liberals (in 1989 dollars) was $1 938, almost double that for 1978, $1 010. For the Conservative party, the figures were $1 181 and $663 respectively. In 1984, the average contribution by corporations to the Liberals was $1 015, versus $454 in 1983. The figures for the Tories were $638 and $299 respectively. However, the effect was not so great in 1988. The average contribution in 1987 for both parties was well above that of 1983 but below that of

1978. In terms of the *number* of corporate donors, the "election year effect" benefited the Tories, but not the Liberals in 1984 and 1988.

When the average contribution from corporations in 1989 dollars is computed by the period during which different parties were in power, it is observed that the average contribution to the Liberals fell from $1 043 in 1974–78 to $830 in the period 1980–84. However, it increased to $945 in the period 1985–91 when the Conservatives under Mulroney were in power. For the Conservatives, the average contribution by corporations in the period 1974–78 was $818, but it fell to $574 in the period 1980–84, when the Liberals were in power. (However, the Tories enjoyed a great increase – 149 percent – in the annual average *number* of contributions.) In the next period, 1985–91, the average contribution to the Conservative party increased to $763. However, this was *lower* than the average in the period 1974–78 (table 11.2a).

2.6 Contributions to Candidates

In election years, corporations give to candidates as well as to parties. The number of contributions from business or commercial organizations to candidates of each of the Progressive Conservative, Liberal and New Democratic parties is given in table 11.3. The total number to Conservative party candidates increased from 9 515 in 1979 (which represents an average of 34 contributions per candidate) to 17 639 in 1984; it then declined to 13 849 in 1988. For Liberal candidates, the number of contributions increased from 7 028 in 1979 to 8 867 in 1980, and then declined slightly to just over 8 000 in each of the next two general elections. These figures indicate, for example, that Liberal candidates received twice the number of contributions from corporations for the 1988 election than did the Liberal party. For Conservative party candidates, the figures were 13 849 and 9 435 respectively. The average contribution, however, to Conservative candidates was $451 versus $736 to the Conservative party (derived from table 12.4). The average contribution by a corporation to Liberal candidates in 1988 was $330 versus $1 167 to the Liberal party.

The average contribution (in 1989 dollars) to Conservative party candidates fell between the 1979 ($407) and 1984 ($314) elections, and then increased in 1988 ($353). However, the average in 1988 was well below the 1979 level. For Liberal party candidates, much the same pattern occurred. The average (in 1989 dollars) dropped from $387 in 1979 to $342 in 1980; it rose slightly in 1980 ($355), but then fell to $339 in 1988.

The average contribution to the Conservative and Liberal parties in election years has typically been about three times that to candidates (table 11.3a). The pattern of the number of corporate contributors to parties and candidates in election years has been quite different for the Liberal and Conservative parties (table 11.3a). For the Conservatives, the number of corporations giving to the *party* rose dramatically from 7 752 in 1979 to 21 286 in 1984, then dropped to 14 032 in 1988. A similar pattern occurred in the number of contributions to Conservative *candidates:* from 9 515 in 1979 to 17 639 in 1984 and then to 13 849 in 1988. In contrast, the number of corporate contributions to the Liberal *party* increased steadily over the four elections between 1979 (3 737) and 1988 (7 238). The number of contributions to Liberal party *candidates* grew between 1979 (7 028) and 1980 (8 867), but then the number declined to 8 052 in 1984 and 8 209 in 1988.

2.7 Largest Contributions

Despite the sometimes heated rhetoric about large contributions from corporations, the largest contribution to either of the Progressive Conservative or Liberal parties between 1983 and 1991 was $150 000 (table 11.4). Typically, the largest contribution was in the range of $50 000 to $80 000.[7] To put these sums in context, it is useful to consider corporate contributions in 1968 and 1972 (table 11.5). While we have data only for contributions to the Liberal party from corporations head-quartered in Ontario, it is reasonable to believe that such contributions are indicative of those to the Conservative party as well. To gain a more accurate picture, we would also need the comparable list for Quebec-based firms.[8]

The highest contribution in 1968 was $90 000 from Imperial Oil Ltd. In 1989 dollars, this is equivalent to $357 143. In 1990, Imperial Oil was the largest single contributor to both parties, $75 000. This was one-fifth the contribution to the Liberals in 1968, when both amounts are converted into constant 1989 dollars. The highest contribution in 1972 was $125 000 from the Canadian Imperial Bank of Commerce. This is equivalent to a contribution of $426 621 in 1989. It appears, therefore, on the basis of Liberal party data, that the largest contributions have declined very greatly in real terms between 1968 and 1972 and the mid- to late-1980s.

2.8 Contributions of $10 000 or More

How important are "large" contributions from corporations to the Liberal and Conservative parties? A large contribution is arbitrarily defined as one of $10 000 or more in nominal terms. (Between 1983 and 1990, the CPI increased by 35 percent, which means that a contribution of $13 500 in 1990 was equivalent in real terms to a contribution of $10 000 in 1983.)

The number of "large" contributions from corporations to the Conservative party increased markedly, from 43 in 1983 to 198 in 1984, an election year, falling to an average of 106 per year in the interelection years, and then rising to 302 in election year 1988 and falling again to 107 in 1990 (table 11.6). Overall, from 1983 to 1990, the Conservative party received 1 086 large contributions from corporations versus 761 for the Liberal party. The greatest differences occurred in election years, i.e., 198 to the Tories in 1984 versus 113 to the Liberals and 302 versus 174 in 1988. The average size of these corporate contributions of $10 000 or more changed very little between 1984 and 1990 for either party: about $22 000 for both (table 11.6).

Large contributions from corporations have accounted for a substantial fraction of the value of all contributions from corporations for both parties. Between 1984 and 1990, large contributions from corporations accounted for from 40.5 percent to 47.1 percent of total corporate contributions to the Liberal party. The comparable figure for the Conservative party was more variable, ranging from 29.6 percent to 48.3 percent (table 11.6). These large contributions were generally more important as a percentage of Liberal party than Conservative party total revenues. For six of the past eight years, the figure for the Liberals was in the range of 18 percent to 28 percent, usually over one-fifth of total revenues. Table 11.6 indicates that large corporate contributions to the Conservative party accounted for as little as 5.3 percent of total revenue (1983) to as much as 25.7 percent (1988).

The difference between the Conservatives and Liberals in terms of dollars of revenue from corporate contributions of $10 000 or more was almost $2 million in 1984 and almost $3 million in 1988. These amounts represent 35 percent and 51 percent of the *difference* in total corporate contributions received by the two parties in these election years. (To put the figures in perspective, recall that each party had a limit of $8 million on its "election expenses" in 1988 and a limit of $6.4 million in 1984.) Between 1983 and 1990, the Conservative party was able to raise $8.4 million (in 1989 dollars) more than was the Liberal party in the form of corporate contributions of $10 000 or more. This difference in large contributions accounted for 29 percent of the lead in total corporate contributions enjoyed by the Conservatives over the Liberals between 1983 and 1990 ($28.9 million in 1989 dollars).

Table 11.6a provides the distribution of corporate contributions of $10 000 or more in 1988. It indicates that 38.1 percent of these large contributions to the Tories were in the range of $10 000 to $14 999, versus 39.7 percent for the Liberals. On the other hand, 8.9 percent of large contributions to the Tories were $50 000 or more, versus 8.6 percent to the Liberals. In absolute terms, in a year in which a record for large contributions was established, only 27 corporate contributions to the Conservative party and 15 to the Liberal party exceeded $50 000.

3. USE OF THE TAX CREDIT BY CORPORATIONS

Only about one-fifth of the business or commercial organizations that make political contributions claimed the federal tax credit during the period 1982–88. According to the Department of National Revenue (DNR), between 1982 and 1988 some 3 500 to 6 000 corporations claimed the tax credit for political contributions (table 11.7). This number amounted to from 11.9 percent (1988) to 30.6 percent (1985) of the number of business organizations reported to the Chief Electoral Officer by the parties as having made a contribution to a party and/or a candidate. The number of corporate contributors calculated in this fashion is somewhat overstated for two reasons. First, the same firm may give to both the Liberal and Conservative parties. (This is quite common among Canada's largest 500 nonfinancial and 155 largest financial firms, as will be seen.) Second, the figure for candidates consists of the number of contributions to candidates by a business or commercial organization. Therefore, if the same firm made more than one donation to the same candidate or made one or more contributions to several candidates, the figure in column 2 of table 11.7 will be overstated.

All things considered, however, the possible "double counting" in columns 1 and 2 of table 11.7 is unlikely to inflate the totals by more than 10 percent. Hence, we can safely conclude that at least two-thirds of all firms contributing to parties and/or candidates do not claim the tax credit. For those that do, the benefit ranged from $162 in 1982 to $244 in 1988 in nominal dollars (table 11.7). The maximum federal tax credit for corporations (and individuals) in any year is $500, which is reached on a contribution of $1 150. Table 11.2 indicates that the average corporate contribution to the Liberal party in 1988 was $1 167, and in 1989 it was $1 019. The comparable figures for the Conservatives were $1 023 and $736 respectively. In other words, the average contribution in 1988 was close to the amount at which the tax credit ends ($1 150). The fact that the average contribution by corporations has not increased in real terms over the period 1974–78 to 1985–91 (table 11.2a) may be attributable to the fact that the tax credit provisions have been unchanged since they came into effect in 1974 and therefore have declined in value in real terms.

It should be noted that the percentage of firms claiming the tax credit for political contributions between 1982 and 1988 (20.1 percent) was less than half the fraction of individuals who did so (57.4 percent) (table 8.5). Further, while the percentage of individual donors claiming the tax credit over the period 1980–88 increased, there has been no upward trend in the percentage of corporations claiming the tax credit for such contributions.

Why have so few corporate contributors claimed the tax credit? There are several possible reasons. First, relative to the taxes payable of most corporations, the amount of the tax credit is probably rather small – the average credit in the period 1982–88 was about $200 in nominal terms. The maximum tax credit is $500. Second, the tax credit is not much of an incentive for firms making a *large* contribution, but it may have an effect on contributions as large as $2 000 or $3 000 because the credit would amount to 25 percent of the former and 17 percent of the latter amount. Donors may think of the tax savings in terms of the *average* benefit rather than of the fact that, at the margin, there is no tax credit for any amount above $1 150. If the tax credit is not much of an incentive to make a contribution, then even if a substantial contribution is made, the corporation may not "bother" to claim the credit, particularly when the date of the contribution and the date of filing the tax return are separated by as much as 16 months. Third, there is likely to be a slip between the cup and the lip with respect to the receipt for the tax credit, that is, like individuals, corporations can lose their receipts and therefore cannot claim the tax credit.

Because such a modest fraction of corporations claims the tax credit, the subsidy by taxpayers with respect to corporate contributions is far less than it is with respect to political contributions by individuals. For example, in 1988, some 184 410 individuals claimed tax credits worth $17.5 million, as compared to only $1.33 million going to 5 471 corporate donors (table 8.4). In 1984, 151 308 individuals claimed tax credits worth $13.6 million, versus 7 561 corporations claiming $1.6 million in tax credits.

In 1988, the value of the tax credit was equal to only 4.3 percent of the total value of corporate contributions to parties and to candidates combined.[9] The figure for 1984 was 6.8 percent.[10] In other words, even in election years when corporate contributions and the amount of the tax credit claimed increase, the amount of the subsidy to parties and candidates by means of tax credits for corporate contributions is modest: it never exceeded $1.6 million (in nominal dollars) from 1977 to 1988.

The DNR has provided data on political contributions by "small" corporations (those eligible for the Small Business Deduction) and all others (table 11.8). As was noted in table 11.7, the number of corporations reporting a contribution to DNR was *far lower* than the number reported by the parties and candidates (in election years). By comparing columns 3 and 4 in table 11.7 it seems clear that the number of corporations making a political contribution, shown in table 11.8, is essentially the same as the number that also claimed the tax credit, although the number claiming the credit in 1988 exceeded the number reporting a donation in 1988. Since credits can be shifted from one year to the next, it is likely that this occurred in 1988. In any event, the average contributions by "small" corporations in the 1980s ranged from $179 (1983) to $723 (1985). For all other corporations, the average political contribution ranged from $1 231 (1982) to $3 734 (1988). Note, however, that the total amount of contributions reported by DNR typically amounted to one-quarter of the amount reported by the parties and candidates (table 11.8).

A higher percentage of "small" corporations than all other corporations made a political contribution. Using the DNR data, the figures were 1.2 percent versus 0.3 percent in 1988, for example. In 1980, the comparable figures were 2.6 percent and 0.7 percent. It is impossible to know if the difference is attributable to a higher reporting rate by "small" corporations for which the income-tax credit is likely to be more important. Alternatively, individuals who own or control a "small" corporation may make their political contributions through their business rather than through their personal chequing account.

The distribution of political contributions by size for both "small" and other corporations in the 1980s is found in table 11.9. It must be interpreted with caution because the distribution is based on firms that *also* claim the tax credit and, on average, only 20 percent of firms making a contribution did so.

4. CONTRIBUTIONS BY FIRMS IN THE FINANCIAL POST 500
This section describes the frequency and size of contributions to the Liberal and Progressive Conservative parties by firms in the *Financial Post 500* (FP 500), the 500 largest nonfinancial enterprises in Canada.

4.1 Size/Importance of the FP 500
Some idea of the size of the firms in the FP 500 can be determined from their sales revenues as reported in table 11.10. In 1989, for example, the average sales revenues of the 50 largest nonfinancial enterprises were $5.4 billion. The size dropped quickly as one goes down the ranks of the FP 500. For example, the sales of firms ranked 151 to 200 averaged $574 million, while those at the bottom, 451 to 500, averaged only $127 million. Between 1983 and 1989, the sales revenues of firms in the FP 500 typically grew by 40 percent, which was above the increase in the CPI (28.9 percent) during the same period.

Marfels (1988, 65) reports that, in 1983, the 100 largest nonfinancial enterprises in Canada accounted for 52.2 percent of all corporate assets. The largest 500 nonfinancial firms' share of all corporate assets was 68.2 percent. Marfels (ibid., 66) also indicates that in 1982 the 100 largest manufacturing firms in Canada accounted for 47.1 percent of total manufacturing value added. In light of the merger boom in the period 1986–89, and the historically high number of large mergers, it is quite likely that the concentration of corporate assets (and revenues) has increased somewhat since 1983.

4.2 "Participation Rates"

The participation rate is defined here to be the percentage of corporations in some category that made a contribution to either the Progressive Conservative or the Liberal party, or both, in a given year (or period). To put the rates cited below in context, recall that only 2.4 percent to 9.1 percent of *all* corporations made a contribution to a party (or to a candidate) in the years 1980 to 1988.

First, the big picture: between 1983 and 1990, the average participation rate for firms in the FP 500 was 40.3 percent (table 11.11a). The percentage of firms making a contribution to either or both the Conservative and Liberal parties ranged from a high of 50.4 percent in 1984, an election year, to a low of 34.2 percent in 1988, also an election year. Between 1983 and 1990, there was a noticeable decline in the overall participation rate among the firms in the FP 500.

The fraction of the FP 500 firms making a donation to either the Conservative or the Liberal party, or to both, fell from 47 percent in 1983 and a high of 50 percent in 1984 to about 35 percent in each of the years 1986–90. This trend of declining participation in the political system was present in each of the five cohorts (i.e., 1 to 100, 101 to 200, etc.). The greatest decline occurred in the bottom cohort (401 to 500). The fraction of firms making a political contribution fell from 40 percent in 1983 and 43 percent in 1984 to 16 percent in 1988 and 23 percent in 1989. What must be particularly troubling to party officials is the fact that, while 251 firms in the FP 500 made a contribution to one or both parties in election year 1984, in election year 1988 the number was down to 171. As table 11.11 indicates, the biggest drop in this form of participation occurred among the firms ranked 301 to 400, from 36.5 percent to 22.5 percent.

The participation rate of firms in the FP 500 was lower among smaller (lower-ranked) firms within the FP 500 than it was among larger firms during the 1980s. This can be seen clearly in table 11.11b. For the period 1983–85, the fraction of firms making a contribution to one or both parties fell from 59.6 percent for firms in the top 100 to 37.7 percent for firms ranked 301 to 400 and 401 to 500. The decline in the participation rate was even greater in the period 1986–90: from 53.4 percent of firms in the top 100 to 37.8 percent for firms ranked 201 to 300 and to 21.6 percent for those ranked 401 to 500.

4.3   Frequency/Amount of Giving to Both Parties

Both the Liberal and the Progressive Conservative party fund-raisers urge large corporations to make substantial donations to *both* parties. Between 1983 and 1990, firms in the FP 500 made 1 611 contributions to the Liberal and/or Conservative parties (table 11.11a). Of the firms that made contributions, 58 percent gave to both parties, while 30 percent gave only to the Conservative party and 13 percent gave only to the Liberal party. The fraction giving only to the Liberal party fell from 31 percent in 1983 and 1984 to 14 percent in 1985 and 1986 and then to a low of only 8.8 percent in 1988 (table 11.11a). The fraction of firms making a contribution *only* to the Conservative party ranged from 20.9 percent to 36.7 percent over the period 1983–90. The fraction giving *only* to the Liberal party ranged from 8.8 percent to 17.4 percent (table 11.11a).

These figures provide some insight into the conventional wisdom that larger firms tend to give to both "free enterprise" parties because they do not wish to be seen as partisan and they want to be able to deal effectively with whichever party forms the government. The data clearly indicate that, among firms in the FP 500 that made a political contribution in any year between 1983 and 1990, the highest percentage of firms giving to both parties was 68.0 percent in 1987. However, table 11.11b indicates that a higher fraction of firms in the top 200 gave to both parties than was the case for those ranked from 201 to 500. Perhaps smaller firms among the FP 500 believed that, by supporting only the Conservatives when they looked like the successors to the Liberals in 1983 and 1984, and then when they became the government, they increased the odds that they would gain more favourable treatment when dealing with the federal government. Perhaps firms in the top 200 that make political contributions believe that any attempt to make contributions in a strategic fashion is likely to be counterproductive or subject to misinterpretation by the media, the public and others.

The strongest evidence of giving only to one party is found among firms ranked 201 to 500 in 1983 and 1984. In 1983, 42.5 percent of their contributions went only to the Liberals; in 1984, the fraction was 44.9 percent. Then the firms ranked 201 to 500 shifted to the Tories: in 1985, 55.1 percent of their contributions went only to the Conservative party, and in 1986 the fraction was 39.4 percent. In contrast, a large percentage of the larger firms, that is, those ranked in the top 200, gave to *both* parties. For example, in 1984, 84.5 percent of the top 200 firms making a contribution made one to both parties. In 1988, the comparable figure was 77.2 percent. In the off-election year of 1989, the figure was the same as 1988 (table 11.11). Overall, the propensity of firms in the FP 500 to give to *both* the Liberal and Conservative parties is much lower in firms ranked 201 to 500 than in those ranked in the top 100. For the period 1983–85, on average, 45.7 percent of firms in the top 100 gave to both parties, while only 14 percent to 15.7 percent of firms ranked lower than 201 did so. In the period 1986–89, on average, 40 percent of firms in the top 100 gave to both parties. This dropped to 18.5 percent for firms ranked 201 to 300 and then to only 7.3 percent for those firms ranked 401 to 500.

If firms are grouped into those that gave to *both* parties and those that gave only to one party, we find that, in the period 1983–85, a major difference exists between firms in the top 200 versus those that were ranked from 201 to 500: 40.9 percent of the firms ranked 1 to 200 gave to both parties, while 15.2 percent gave only to one party; in contrast, 14.6 percent of firms ranked 1 to 200 gave to both parties while 23.7 percent gave to only one party. As table 11.11b makes clear, among the firms that gave only to one party in the period 1983–85, 14.7 percent gave only to the Conservative party, while 5.7 percent gave only to the Liberal party. The pattern was somewhat different in the period 1986–90: among the top 200 firms, 33.3 percent gave to both parties while 14.8 percent gave to only one. Among the firms ranked 201 to 500, 13.7 percent gave to both, while 15.2 percent gave only to one party. As in the previous period, among those firms supporting only one party, the Conservative party was favoured over the Liberal party (11.7 percent versus 4.5 percent) (table 11.11b).

Using the data for 1990, the proposition that larger firms tend to give equal or almost equal amounts to both the Conservatives and the Liberals was examined in more detail. Among firms in the FP 500, which range in size in terms of sales from $126 million to $18.5 billion, of the 179 firms that made a contribution to the Conservative party, 39.1 percent gave *only* to that party, while 18.4 percent gave "about equally" (the contribution to one party was within 10 percent of that to the other). The comparable figures for the 140 firms that gave to the Liberal party were 22.1 percent (to the Liberals *only*) and 23.5 percent ("about equally"), respectively.

A majority of firms in the FP 500 making a contribution in 1990 gave to *both* parties: 61 percent in the case of those giving to the Conservatives as compared with 78 percent of firms giving to the Liberals. However, of those making an unequal contribution to both parties, three times as many favoured the Tories as the Liberals (table 11.11c). The pattern of average contributions in 1990 is highly distinctive. The contributions of the firms making "about equal" contributions were the largest, about $13 500 to each party, or 73 percent above the average for all firms (which was remarkably similar for the two parties). The lowest average contribution was among the firms giving only to *one* party: $3 191 in the case of the Conservatives and $2 554 in that of the Liberals. What is startling is the similarity of the average contribution by firms making unequal (by more than 10 percent) contributions to both parties. In 1990, those favouring the Conservatives gave them an average of $11 615, as compared with $5 204 to the Liberals. Firms favouring the Liberals gave them an average of $11 695, as compared with $5 256 to the Tories (table 11.11c).

In an effort to understand the characteristics of those firms making "about equal" contributions and those giving to only one party, their average size in relation to their *rank* on the FP 500 was computed. It is clear that the firms making "about equal" contributions are, on average, substantially larger (have a lower rank number) than those that give only to one party. The average rank of the former was 134 (sales revenues of $806 million), while that of firms giving *only* to the Tories was 263 ($360 million in sales) and those giving *only* to the Liberals was 230 ($414 million).[11] This suggests that more large firms tend to give "about equal" amounts to both parties than do small firms, which are more likely to give only to one party or to give the two parties substantially unequal amounts.

While definitive conclusions await a comparable analysis of the contributions by firms in the FP 500 in other years, the data for 1990 suggest that only limited empirical support exists for the idea that large firms in Canada making political contributions give "about equally" (within 10 percent) to both the Liberal and Progressive Conservative parties. Those making the largest total contributions do so, but those making smaller contributions tend to give only to one party.

4.4 Importance of Contributions by FP 500 Firms to the Parties

The total value of contributions from firms in the FP 500 to the Liberal and Conservative parties is now examined (table 11.12). Despite their enormous importance to the corporate sector and to the economy as a whole, the 500 largest nonfinancial enterprises in Canada typically accounted for only about one-fifth of the value of all contributions by corporations to the Liberal and Conservative parties between 1983 and 1990. For example, in 1989, the FP 500 accounted for 18.9 percent of all corporate contributions to the Tories and 23.1 percent to the Liberals. These percentages were somewhat *lower* in election year 1988, although that for the Liberals was higher in election year 1984 (26.0 percent). It is somewhat surprising to find that the FP 500 firms, which account for 68 percent of all corporate assets in Canada, provide only one-fifth of the value of contributions by corporations to the Liberal and Conservative parties.

It is perhaps understandable that senior officials in both parties are frustrated with the top management of the FP 500 firms. First, in their view, too few firms make *any* contribution to either party (as we have seen, typically only 40 percent of the FP 500 firms made an annual donation in the period 1983–90). Second, the contributions of the largest firms are seldom commensurate with the firms' size (as we shall see, the largest among the FP 500 give less relative to their size than lower ranked firms). Third, many large firms do not support *both* the Liberal and Conservative parties with contributions of the same amount. Fourth, in the perception of the senior officials, contributions from the FP 500 have failed to keep up with the rate of inflation.

These are strong criticisms and most have empirical support. However, corporate executives could argue with considerable force that political contributions are, on balance, likely to have *negative* consequences for their firm. To begin with, the public may well assume that a contribution is being made to ensure access or to achieve certain beneficial actions by government or by a party when it does become the government. Yet, the members of the board of directors asked to approve political contributions could argue that the shareholders' money is being spent on something for which nothing can be expected in return (all parties emphasize that contributors should expect nothing in return), and that if the contribution were made in exchange for the promise of a benefit, it would be illegal. Further, the maximum tax credit is small ($500), and contributions are not tax-deductible expenses under the federal *Income Tax Act*.[12] The problem of negative perceptions is so great that even where a corporation simply sends in its cheque to a party and asks that no party representative telephone or call in person, adverse inferences may be drawn merely because the firm has made a donation. Hence, contributors "stand out" and may well be subject to question.

Corporations that decide to give to one or more political parties are faced with several subsidiary questions: How much to give? Should the amount increase in an election year? Should candidates as well as parties receive a donation? Should the amount be the same for both the Conservative and the Liberal parties? What about the NDP?[13] It is no easy task to develop a defensible contributions policy for corporations (Stanbury 1986a, chap. 10).

In every year but 1986, the Conservative party received more from the FP 500 firms than did the Liberal party (table 11.12). In some years, the difference was significant: for example, $1.9 million to the Tories versus $1.4 million to the Liberals in 1984, and $2.0 million to the Tories versus $1.6 million to the Liberals in 1988, both being election years.

The election year effect is quite apparent in most cohorts of the FP 500. It can be seen very clearly in the average contribution for all firms in the FP 500 making a contribution (table 11.12a). In 1989 dollars, the average contribution in 1984, an election year, was double that in 1983. The average contribution in 1985 to the Conservatives was 61 percent of that in 1984. For the Liberals it was 72 percent. In 1988, the average contribution (in 1989 dollars) to the Tories by FP 500 firms was $16 200 – up from $8 100 in 1987. The effect was not so great in the case of contributions to the Liberal party: from $8 100 in 1987 to $13 400 in 1988.

As indicated by table 11.12a, the size of the average contribution by firms in the FP 500, in real terms, has varied considerably over the period. However, it appears that it has increased over time. For example, the average contribution to the Conservative party in 1983 and 1985 combined (omitting the election year) was $5 794. The average for 1989–90 was $8 202. The comparable figures for contributions to the Liberal party were $6 415 and $7 518 – indicating some growth in the average contribution in real terms. However, in real terms, total contributions from firms in the FP 500 to the Liberal party were lower in 1988 than they were in 1984; the Conservatives, however, enjoyed a slight increase. Overall, the party fund-raisers' argument that contributions from the FP 500 firms have not kept up with inflation is not true when these firms are considered as a group. It may be, however, that the fund-raisers' perceptions are based on the pattern of contributions of a small number of firms that have traditionally made large contributions.

4.5   Contributions by Size Cohorts

The average size of contributions by cohort among the FP 500 firms is given in table 11.13. Figures are provided for all firms in the cohort, as well as for those that actually made a donation. The average contribution of the 50 largest nonfinancial enterprises in Canada in 1989 was $10 625 to the Conservative party as compared to $8 804 for the Liberal party. In both 1984 and 1988, the "election year effect" can be seen in almost every cohort of 50 firms. For example, in 1987, the top 50 donated an average of $8 343 to the Conservatives and $7 895 to the Liberals. In 1988, the comparable figures were $13 341 and $11 897. The largest election year effect occurred in 1984 for firms ranked 301 to 350. Their average contribution to the Liberal party rose from $271 in 1983 to $2 296 in 1984 and then fell to $1 356 in 1985. The comparable figures for the Conservative party were $697, $3 054 and $1 248, respectively.

In general, average contributions fell as the rank of firms within the FP 500 declined. There were, however, some notable exceptions. For example, after 1983, firms ranked 301 to 350 gave more to both parties than those ranked 251 to 300. For example, in 1988, the former gave an average of $4 315 to the Conservatives and $3 188 to the Liberals, while the latter gave $2 495 and $2 618, respectively.

In relation to their sales revenues, Canada's 100 largest nonfinancial firms gave *less* to political parties than did those ranked lower among the FP 500 (table 11.14). In 1988, for example, total contributions to either party per million dollars of sales for the 50 largest nonfinancial firms were $4.69. Firms ranked 51 to 100 gave an average of $7.50 per million dollars of sales and those ranked 100 to 150 gave $11.58. Contributions relative to sales in 1988 were the highest among those firms ranked 301 to 350, $29.80 per million dollars of sales. Then the level dropped sharply, but was higher in the 351 to 400 and 451 to 500 cohorts than it was among the top 50. While the levels vary across the years, the same general pattern can be found in other years in the 1980s (table 11.14).

Table 11.14 also measures the proportionate size of contributions to each party separately, but does so *only* for those firms making a contribution, not for all firms in the cohort. With some exceptions, larger firms within the FP 500 gave *less* per million dollars of sales than did smaller firms. For example, in 1988, firms ranked 151 to 200 gave $21.29 to the Conservatives and $16.78 to the Liberals. In contrast, among the top 50, the contribution rate was $5.15 to the Conservatives and $4.05 to the Liberals. Note that one of the reasons *why* the contribution rate ($ per million dollars of sales) increased among smaller firms is that a declining fraction of those firms in cohorts made a contribution (recall table 11.10).

4.6 Contributions and Ownership

Wearing and Wearing (1990) examined the relationship between political contributions and foreign ownership among the 250 largest nonfinancial enterprises in Canada in 1984 to 1986. Some of their results are summarized in table 11.15. The biggest difference between those firms that are domestically owned and those that are foreign-owned can be seen in the percentage of firms making large contributions. Over the three years, twice as many Canadian-owned firms made contributions of $10 000 or more as did foreign-owned firms. The Pearson correlation coefficients for the propensity to make a contribution and the percentage of Canadian ownership ranged from .17 to .21, and were all statistically significant at the .01 level (ibid., 119). Further, the authors found support for their hypothesis that the "degree of removal from the British political tradition is inversely related to both propensity to make contributions and size of contributions" – even when the size of the firm is taken into account (ibid., table 4).

5. CONTRIBUTIONS BY THE LARGEST 155 FINANCIAL ENTERPRISES

Using four categories of large financial enterprises (financial institutions, life insurers, property and casualty insurers, and investment dealers) a list of the 155 largest financial enterprises was compiled by the author from the *Financial Post*'s annual rankings (F 155).[14]

5.1   Size/Importance of the F 155

Some idea of the size of the firms in the F 155 can be seen in table 11.16. In 1990, for example, the 25 largest financial institutions (which include the banks and trust companies) had average assets of $32.2 billion. It is the five largest chartered banks that greatly increase the average size of the 25 largest financial institutions reported in table 11.16. On the other hand, those institutions ranked 76 to 100 averaged assets of $541 million. The average size of the top 25 life insurance companies measured in terms of their assets was $8.36 billion in 1990. (Note that the 15 largest property and casualty insurers in the F 155 were measured in terms of their revenues, not their assets.)

In terms of annual *revenues*, the size of the top 25 financial firms ranged from $423 million to $14.6 billion in 1990. By comparison, the range of revenues for firms in the largest 25 nonfinancial firms was $4.3 billion to $18.5 billion. The size, in revenues, for those nonfinancial firms ranked 76 to 100 was $1.18 billion to $1.58 billion – much larger than the firms ranked 76 to 100 on the FP's list of financial institutions: $33.0 million to $127.1 million (*Financial Post 500*, Summer 1991).

5.2   "Participation Rates"

In the years between 1983 and 1990, an average of 35.5 percent of firms in the F 155 made a contribution to either or both of the Progressive Conservative and Liberal parties (table 11.18a). The comparable figure for the firms in the FP 500 (i.e., nonfinancial firms) was 40.3 percent (table 11.11b). The variation in the "participation rate" among the four categories of firms in the F 155 was substantial. While 87 percent of the largest 15 investment dealers made a contribution, only 23 percent of the 15 largest property and casualty insurers did so. Forty-seven percent of the top 25 life insurers made a contribution to one or both of the Liberal and Conservative parties, but only 27 percent of the 100 largest financial institutions did so (table 11.18).

Between 1983 and 1990, the overall participation rate of firms in the F 155 declined. For example, in 1983 and 1984, about 40 percent of the firms made a political contribution to the Liberals or the Conservatives or to both parties. In 1989 and 1990, only 31 percent did so (table 11.18a). The overall participation rate among firms in the FP 500 also declined, from 47.0 percent in 1983 and 50.4 percent in 1984 to 35.6 percent in 1989 and 42.0 percent in 1990 (table 11.11b). The "participation rate" among the financial institutions ranked 51 to 100 declined between the early and late 1980s (table 11.18). The rate was 26 percent in 1983 and 1984. However, between 1985 and 1989, it fell to 11.2 percent. In 1989, it was only 4 percent. In no other category within the F 155 did the annual "participation rate" vary much between the early and late 1980s.[15]

It is not clear why the participation rate for property and casualty insurers is so much lower than that for investment dealers. Is it because so many of the former are foreign-owned (recall the discussion in section 4.6 above)? Is it because the investment dealers have been interested in handling the privatizations of the Mulroney government (Stanbury 1988b) and handle other financial transactions for the government? In any event, for all the firms in the category, the average political contribution by the top 15 property and casualty insurers never exceeded $907 in the period 1983–90, while average contributions by the top 15 investment dealers were typically several times this amount and in 1988 amounted to $24 759 to the Conservative party and $16 301 to the Liberal party (although this was an election year).

5.3   Importance of Contributions by the F 155

The total value and importance of the political contributions by the 155 largest financial enterprises to the parties over the period 1983–90 is described in table 11.17. In six of the eight years, firms in the F 155 provided more than 10 percent of the Liberal party's revenue from all corporations, but in no year was this true for the Conservative party. For example, in election year 1984, the Liberal party received 11.6 percent of total contributions from corporations from F 155 firms versus 6.3 percent for the Conservative party. In the next election year, 1988, the comparable figures were 10.9 percent and 8.0 percent respectively. Note, however, that in each year between 1983 and 1990, the Conservative party received more money than the Liberal party from the F 155 and in 1988 the difference was quite substantial, $224 000. In general, it appears that in most years the difference between Liberal and Conservative revenues from the F 155 firms was less than it was from firms in the FP 500 (table 11.12).

Revenues from the F 155 never accounted for more than 8.6 percent of either party's *total* revenue in the period 1983–90. In most years, the figure was 4 percent to 5 percent. Contributions from the F 155 to both parties increased in real terms (1989 dollars) between the early 1980s and the late 1980s: for the Conservative party they averaged $575 000 per year in the period 1983–85; in the period 1986–90, such contributions averaged $585 200 annually; the comparable figures for the Liberal party were $484 000 and $519 000 respectively.

5.4 Average Contribution

The average contribution per firm in 1989 dollars by firms in the F 155 to the Progressive Conservative party varied greatly over the period 1983–90. In 1983 it was $4 607; then it rose to $14 862 in 1984, an election year, only to fall to $9 333 in 1985 (table 11.17a). However, by 1987 the average contribution to the Tories had risen to the 1984 level. Then in 1988 the "election year effect" was evident, for the average rose to $23 549, only to fall to $13 778 in 1989 and to $9 244 in 1990. In six of the eight years, the average contribution to the Liberal party exceeded that to the Progressive Conservative party, although in all years the number of firms among the F 155 giving to the Conservatives was greater than that to the Liberals (table 11.17a).

As table 11.19 indicates, average contributions by firms within the F 155 varied greatly by category. For example, by far the largest average contributions came from the 25 largest financial institutions, where the big contributions of the five largest chartered banks dominated the category. For example, in 1984 the top 25 gave an average of about $18 000 to each party, and in 1988 they gave an average of $23 234 to the Conservatives and $22 219 to the Liberals. In contrast, the top 25 life insurers gave an average of $3 322 to the Conservatives and $3 482 to the Liberals in 1984, and $5 338 to the Tories and $3 449 to the Liberals in 1988. These huge differences existed despite the fact that the *participation* rate of the two categories was very similar.

Another unusual characteristic of the political contributions by the 15 largest investment dealers in the 1980s is their rapid increase in total amount. For example, in 1983 the dealers gave an average of $3 127 to the Conservative party and an average of $1 403 to the Liberal party. By 1986, the contributions averaged just over $9 000 to each party. Then in 1989, the average almost doubled again, to $18 791 to the PCs and $15 869 to the Liberals.

5.5 Frequency/Amount of Contributions to Both Parties

Over the period 1983–90, two-thirds of firms in the F 155 that made a contribution made it to *both* parties (versus 58.3 percent for the FP 500).

One-quarter of the contributions went only to the Conservative party and 8.3 percent went only to the Liberal party (table 11.18a). The comparable figures for the FP 500 were 30.2 percent and 13.0 percent respectively (table 11.11b).

A more detailed analysis of the propensity of firms in the F 155 to make similar contributions to both parties was done for 1990 (based on only 140 firms; see table 11.11c). Of the 41 firms making a contribution to the Conservative party and the 28 firms making a contribution to the Liberal party, 37 percent gave *only* to the Tories compared with 7 percent giving only to the Liberals. Forty-two percent giving to the Tories made an "about equal" contribution to the Liberals, while 61 percent giving to the Liberals made an "about equal" contribution (within 10 percent) to the Conservatives. Finally, 22 percent of the large financial firms giving to the Liberals gave to both parties, but unequally, that is, they gave at least 10 percent more to one party than to the other. The comparable figure for those giving to the Tories was 32 percent. In both cases, however, more firms favoured the Tories over the Liberals.

The average contribution for firms making about an equal contribution to *both* parties (over $17 000) was much higher than that of firms that gave only to the Conservative party ($2 547) or only to the Liberal party ($1 500) (table 11.11c). However, among the firms that gave to *both* parties but gave more than 10 percent more to one than to the other, those that favoured the Liberals gave an average of $20 400 to them as compared to $11 000 to the Tories. The average for those firms favouring the Conservative party was much lower: $6 100 to the Tories as compared to $3 500 to the Liberals (table 11.11c). The high average contribution of those firms that gave "about equally" to both parties is dominated by five of the six largest banks.[16] Their average contribution to the Conservative party in 1990 was $49 316 as compared to $40 850 to the Liberal party.

5.6 Contributions Relative to Size

Are political contributions by firms in the 155 largest financial enterprises in Canada proportionate to the size of the firms? This question is answered in table 11.20, which measures average contributions to *both* parties in terms relative to the firm's assets. For example, in 1988 contributions by the 25 largest financial institutions amounted to $1.66 per million dollars of their assets.[17] For firms ranked 26 to 50, the comparable figure was $1.23, while that for the top 25 life insurers was $1.37. Note that for the top 15 property insurers the figure relates to revenues, that is, it is $1.90 per million dollars of *revenue*. The key point to be seen in table 11.20 is the typical *decline* in the dollars of contributions per million dollars of assets as the size of financial institutions decreases. For example, in 1989, the top 25 firms gave 72 cents per million dollars of sales, the next 25 gave 76 cents and those ranked 51 to 75 gave only 25 cents. The bottom quartile gave only 3 cents per million dollars of sales. While the relationship is *not* perfectly consistent (e.g., see 1983 or 1987), it stands in sharp contrast to what was observed with respect to firms within the FP 500 (nonfinancial firms), where smaller firms generally made larger contributions than did the largest firms.

The major reason for this relationship is that (despite big contributions by the five largest banks) the average size of the top 25 financial institutions is vastly greater than that of the next 25 financial institutions, so that smaller contributions are a larger percentage of the assets of smaller financial institutions. Table 11.16 indicates that in 1989, for example, the average assets of the top 25 were $32.8 billion, while the average for the next 25 were only $3.0 billion. (The average size of the top 25 life insurers was $7.34 billion in assets.) In 1985, for example, each of the top five banks gave the Liberal and Conservative parties $35 000 each and their average size was $73.1 billion in assets. Hence their contributions to both parties amounted to an average of approximately .0001 *cents* per *million* dollars of assets. However, the banks did double their contributions in election years 1984 and 1988. To put the five banks' contributions in further perspective, recall that in 1988 investment dealer Merrill Lynch gave $106 047 to the Conservative party and $43 782 to the Liberal party; the five biggest banks gave an average of $81 954 to the PC party and $80 613 to the Liberal party. In terms of assets, however, Merrill Lynch is tiny relative to the banks – less than 1 percent of their size.

5.7 How Much Should Corporations Contribute?

None of this, however, answers the enormously difficult question of how much a financial (or nonfinancial) firm *should* give to political parties. As we have seen, on average 59.7 percent of the FP 500 and 64.5 percent of the F 155 did *not* make any contribution to the Liberal or Conservative party between 1983 and 1990. Among those that contributed, the amounts ranged from a few hundred dollars to somewhat over $100 000. But note that the largest-ever contribution by a corporation, $150 000 in 1984 by Candor Investments, was *not* made by a firm among the 500 largest nonfinancial or 155 largest financial enterprises in the country. Indeed, one of the insights obtained in the course of the analysis for this chapter is that political contributions are not even roughly proportionate to the size of the firms making them – even if the nongivers are ignored entirely. For 1983, 23 of 88 contributions of $10 000 or more to the Liberals or Conservatives were not made by firms in the FP 500 or in other groups of large firms compiled by the *Financial Post*. In 1984, the comparable figures were 112 of 311 (Stanbury 1986a, 449).

The problem for boards of directors is that they are called upon by both the Liberal and the Progressive Conservative parties to give generously, roughly in relation to their size,[18] in equal amounts to both parties each year and to double their contributions in election years. Yet they are told they can expect *nothing* in return (no favours, no advantages), except the knowledge that they are supporting "the democratic political system" in which parties compete for the voter's favour. For example, in raising funds for the Liberal party, Senator Kolber said he "did not promise a bloody thing" (interview, 1990). At the same time, the board members have a fiduciary responsibility to the firm's shareholders. Most business executives interpret this to mean maximizing profits subject to obeying the laws of the land. Since there can be no economic advantage to the corporation from making political contributions – indeed, there may even be disadvantages, as noted above – it does not seem rational for directors to make such contributions. Perhaps the directors take the view that giving to political parties is much the same as making a contribution to various charities that importune the firm. They give in order to be seen as "good corporate citizens." However, the vast majority – about 95 percent in most years – do not make a political contribution, and most that do give very modest amounts relative to their economic resources.

On the matter of what may be "exchanged" for political contributions, Senator Kolber made a number of interesting statements. He said that, when a party forms the government, it is logical for that party to solicit contributions from those firms that have government contracts. When the Liberal party was in power, Kolber could help major corporate contributors to gain access to ministers (except on tax matters), so that they could have another look at the firms' problems. According to Senator Kolber, ministers were not swayed by political contributions.

Senator Kolber believes that corporate contributions should be limited to $10 000,[19] because with larger amounts there is the danger of abuse due to the expectation that such contributions entitle the donor at least to gain access to decision makers. Kolber argued that, from the perspective of a corporation, political contributions have only negative implications. The public believes they are made in order to gain advantage; if nothing is expected, others ask why the shareholders' money is being used for such donations. Still others argue that with the federal tax credit all taxpayers are subsidizing the corporation's political preferences (although the limit on the credit is $500).

6. CONCLUSIONS

The *Election Expenses Act* of 1974 transformed the ways in which the Liberal and Progressive Conservative parties financed their operations. The work of Paltiel and others indicates that, prior to the 1974 legislation, these two parties obtained over 90 percent of their funds from the several hundred largest enterprises in Canada. However, between 1974 and 1990, only about one-half of the total revenues of the Conservative and Liberal parties came from business organizations of all sizes. The growth in the *number* of contributions to these parties by corporations was remarkable. In the case of the Conservative party, the number rose from an annual average of 4 900 in the period 1974–78 to 12 200 in the period 1980–84 to 10 800 (a drop) in the period 1985–91. The comparable figures for the Liberal party were 4 100, 6 000 and 5 200 respectively. While the *average* contribution to the Liberal party was consistently higher than that to the Conservative party, the Tories more than made up for it in the number of contributions. The Progressive Conservative party generated $10 million (1989 dollars) more from corporations than did the Liberal party in the period 1980–84. Then in the period 1985-91, the Conservative party generated $23.3 million (1989 dollars) more than the Liberal party.

In contrast to the Liberal and Progressive Conservative parties, the NDP, no doubt reflecting its different political philosophy, has obtained very little money from corporations. While the Reform Party, launched in 1987, has obtained some money from corporations, it did not begin to make a major effort to solicit contributions from corporations until the fall of 1991.

Data for the period 1982–88 indicate that only from 11.9 percent to 30.5 percent of firms making a political contribution *claimed* the tax credit. (The range for *individuals* over the same period was 50.7 percent to 64.9 percent.) For those claiming the tax credit, its average value ranged from $162 to $244 (versus $73 to $90 for individuals over the same period, 1982–88). It appears that the tax credit (which has a maximum value of $500) has not been very important in stimulating the increase in the number of corporations that give to the Liberal and/or Conservative parties. While the maximum tax credit has little effect on the net after-tax cost of a contribution of several thousand dollars or more, most contributions are $2 000 or less. For a contribution of $2 000, the tax credit reduces the net cost by 25 percent to $1 500. Perhaps the low rate of claiming the tax credit is attributable to three factors: first, a tax credit of $200 to $400 may be only a tiny fraction of the total taxes payable by the corporation; second, the firms may lose their tax receipts and hence be unable to claim the tax credit on their income-tax return; third, the tax credit is not much of an incentive for making large contributions because it has a maximum value of $500 and this amount has been unchanged since 1974.

While the Liberal and Conservative parties have increased the number of contributions from corporations, they have been less successful in increasing the average level of contributions in real terms. For the Conservative party, the average (in 1989 dollars) in the period 1974–78 was $818 ($1 043 for the Liberal party). During the period 1980–84, the average dropped to $574 ($830 for the Liberals). However, in the period 1985–91, the average contribution to the Conservative party was $763 (1989 dollars) as compared to $945 for the Liberal party.

While both parties greatly broadened their "corporate base" after 1974, only a tiny fraction of all corporations made political contributions to a party and/or candidate between 1980 and 1988. In election years 1980, 1984 and 1988, the percentage was 5.7 percent, 9.1 percent (the record) and 6.7 percent respectively. (Recall that, in 1984 and 1988, some 1.8 percent of *electors* made a contribution to a party and/or candidate.) In interelection years, the participation rate was only 2.4 percent to 3.3 percent. The participation rate (computed annually) for larger firms, the 500 largest nonfinancial enterprises (FP 500) and 155 largest financial enterprises (F 155) was much higher. The average for the FP 500 between 1983 and 1990 was 40.3 percent, while for the F 155 it was 35.5 percent. In both cases, however, the rate declined noticeably over the period. It also declined within each grouping as the average size of firm declined. For example, on average, over the period 1986–90, the participation rate of firms in the top 100 of the FP 500 was 53.4 percent, while for the firms ranked 401 to 500 it was 21.6 percent.

Neither large contributions (those of $10 000 or more) nor contributions from large corporations (FP 500 or F 155) dominated the Liberal or Conservative parties' sources of revenue in the period 1983–90. The amount collected in the form of large contributions accounted for from 18 percent to 28 percent of the Liberal party's total revenues in the years between 1983 and 1990. For the Conservative party, the percentage was 5.3 percent to 25.5 percent (in election year 1988). The average number of large contributions was 136 per year for the Tories (peak of 302 in 1988) and 95 for the Liberals (peak of 174 in 1988).

Contributions by firms in the FP 500 (which jointly accounted for 68.2 percent of all corporate assets in Canada in 1983) accounted for from 5.6 percent to 11.4 percent of the Conservative party's total revenues between 1983 and 1990. For the Liberal party, the comparable range was 7.9 percent to 14.2 percent. As a percentage of contributions from all corporations, the FP 500 could be said to be "underrepresented" in the sense of their share of all corporate assets. Contributions from the FP 500 accounted for from 13.3 percent to 22.2 percent of contributions from all corporations to the Conservatives between 1983 and 1990. The figures for the Liberal party were somewhat higher: 18.9 percent to 30.3 percent. As for the F 155 (largest financial enterprises), they accounted for 2.9 percent to 8.6 percent of the Liberal party's annual revenues over the period 1983–90. The range for the Conservative party was 2.0 percent to 5.1 percent.

There is considerable evidence of an "election year effect" in political contributions from corporations. This refers to the sharp increase in the average *contribution* in election years and, in most cases, an increase in the *number* of firms making a contribution. The jump in the average contribution to the Conservatives was apparent in all four general elections, while a significant increase in the total number of corporate contributions was apparent only in 1984 and 1988. Consider the last election: in 1988 the Tories received contributions averaging $1 075 (1989 dollars) from 14 032 firms. In 1987, the Tories received 9 188 corporate contributions averaging $797. For the Liberals, the election year effect was clearly evident only with respect to the average size of donations. For example, in 1984 the average was $1 015 (1989 dollars) as compared with $454 in 1983 and $765 in 1986.

Among the FP 500 and F 155 enterprises, the election year effect was confined to a sharp rise in the average level of contributions – largely because both parties' fund-raisers ask firms to double their usual contribution in election years. For example, among the FP 500 firms, the average contribution to the Conservative party in 1988 was $16 169 (1989 dollars), while that to the Liberal party was $13 424. By comparison, the average in 1987 was $8 137 and $8 132 respectively, while that in 1989 was $8 905 and $7 622 respectively (all in 1989 dollars).

This chapter has provided some evidence to suggest that only a *minority* of larger firms (e.g., those in the FP 500 or F 155) make "about equal" contributions to both the Liberal and Conservative parties. For example, in 1990, only 18.4 percent of FP 500 firms giving to the Tories ($N = 179$) also gave about an equal amount (within 10 percent) to the Liberal party. For firms giving to the Liberal party ($N = 140$) the fraction was 23.5 percent. By comparison, 39.1 percent of firms giving to the Conservatives gave *only* to the Tories; 22.1 percent of firms giving to the Liberals gave only to the Liberals. However, in the case of the F 155 (actually 140 in 1990), 41.5 percent of firms giving to the Tories ($N = 41$) gave about an equal contribution to the Liberals. For firms contributing to the Liberal party ($N = 28$) 60.7 percent gave about an equal amount to the Conservative party (i.e., within 10 percent). It should be noted that in both the FP 500 and F 155, the firms making "about equal" contributions also made the largest average contribution on a combined basis.

PART IV

FINANCING
CANDIDATES

12

CANDIDATE
REVENUES
AND EXPENDITURES,
1979–88

1. INTRODUCTION

T HIS CHAPTER FOCUSES on the financing of general elections since the
adoption of the *Election Expenses Act* of 1974 from the perspective of
candidates rather than parties. While a brief account of all four elections conducted under the 1974 legislation (and its amendments) is
provided, much more emphasis is placed on the revenues, "election
expenses," "personal expenses," reimbursement, "other expenses" and
surpluses of candidates in the 1988 general election. This was done not
only because it was the most recent election, but also because it was
the one for which data could be obtained in an electronic form, thus
permitting a much more detailed analysis.

Section 2 begins with an overview of the revenues and expenditures of candidates in the general elections of 1979, 1980, 1984 and 1988.
Section 3 focuses closely on the sources of candidates' revenues and the
number of contributions to their campaigns made by individuals and
corporations. Section 4 examines candidates' expenditures over the past
four elections and describes how close candidates came to the statutory
limit on "election expenses." Section 5 describes candidates' "other
expenses" in the 1988 election. These are campaign-related expenditures
other than "election expenses" and "personal expenses" which are
financed out of contributions for which tax credits are issued. Unlike
"election expenses," "other expenses" are not subject to a statutory
limit. Section 6 reviews the reimbursement of candidates' "election
expenses," while section 7 examines candidates' surplus after reimbursement. The surplus is an important source of revenue for riding

associations, although the Liberal party and, to a lesser extent, the New Democratic Party headquarters effectively reduced the amount available for riding associations in 1988 by requiring virtually all of their candidates to sign over part of their reimbursement. The conclusions are set out in section 8.

2. OVERVIEW

Between the general elections of 1979 and 1988 the total number of candidates increased from 1 427 to 1 578; however, much of the increase was accounted for by the increase in the number of ridings from 282 in 1979, 1980 and 1984 to 295 in 1988. As noted in table 12.1, the three main parties (Progressive Conservative, Liberal and NDP) ran a full slate of candidates in all four elections, with the exception of the NDP in 1980, which fielded candidates in all but two ridings.[1]

2.1   Revenues

Total revenues[2] of all candidates rose from about $15.6 million in 1979 and $15.4 million in 1980 to $24.3 million in 1984 and $32.5 million in 1988. However, in constant 1989 dollars (using the Consumer Price Index as the deflator)[3] candidates' total revenues were as follows: 1979, $30.8 million; 1980, $26.2 million; 1984, $30.0 million; and 1988, $34.1 million. In real terms, therefore, the total revenues of candidates *fell* by 8.5 percent between 1979 and 1980 (probably due to the short period between these general elections), returned to the 1979 level in 1984 and then rose by 13.7 percent between 1984 and 1988.

While the lion's share of revenues went to candidates of the three main parties, the average revenues of candidates of other parties rose from $1 155 in 1979 to $1 438 in 1984 to $3 899 in 1988. NDP candidates have had the highest rate of increase in total revenues: from $2.3 million in 1979 to $6.8 million in 1988, an increase of 195 percent, well above the rate of inflation of 78 percent. Progressive Conservative party candidates' revenues increased from $6.1 million in 1979 to $13.4 million in 1988, an increase of 120 percent, also well above the increase in the CPI. Contributions to Liberal party candidates grew more slowly: from $6.56 million in 1979 to $9.63 million in 1988, an increase of only 47 percent. Hence, in constant 1989 dollars, Liberal party candidates raised $12.26 million in 1979, but only $10.12 million in 1988. However, in 1988, Liberal party candidates raised, on average, 41 percent more than their NDP rivals, but only 72 percent of the average of their Conservative party rivals.

2.2   "Election Expenses"

In nominal dollars, total "election expenses" for all candidates rose from $15.9 million in the 1979 election to $31.34 million in the 1988 election. In 1989 dollars, the increase was much smaller, from $29.76 million in 1979 to $32.96 million in 1988 (recall that, in 1983, the limits on candidates' "election expenses" were indexed to the Consumer Price Index retroactive to 1980). Therefore, as more candidates spent closer to the limit, total "election expenses" rose in terms of nominal dollars, but did not increase in real terms.

By party, candidates' "election expenses" in nominal dollars rose most rapidly for the NDP – by 174 percent between 1979 and 1988 (table 12.1). This is far ahead of the CPI, which rose by 78 percent during the same period. The "election expenses" of Progressive Conservative party candidates rose by 97 percent to $11.9 million in 1988, also outpacing inflation. In absolute terms, in 1988, Conservative candidates spent, on average, 62 percent more than their NDP rivals and almost 23 percent more than Liberal candidates.

The decline in financial strength of the Liberal party can be seen in its candidates' "election expenses" over the past four general elections, which mirror the decline in revenues. In 1979 the 282 Liberal candidates spent slightly more than their Conservative party rivals. However, the growth in Liberal spending between 1979 and 1988 (56 percent) was less than the rate of inflation (78 percent). The result is that Liberal candidates, on average, have fallen well behind the Tories, and their lead over the NDP has been reduced from 132 percent in 1979 to 32 percent in 1988.

For at least two reasons, the interparty differences in "election expenses" are less than the differences in revenues. First, while contributions are not limited, "election expenses" are constrained, and a larger fraction of candidates of all parties have been spending a higher fraction of the limit. NDP candidates as a group spent only 34.4 percent of their total limit on "election expenses" in the 1979 election, but in 1988 this had increased to 52.8 percent (table 12.19). For Conservative party candidates, the fraction increased from 77.6 percent in 1979 to 89.0 percent in 1984, but dropped slightly in 1988 to 85.8 percent. The recent financial problems of the Liberal party can be seen in the fact that its candidates (as a group) spent only 70 percent of the limit on "election expenses" in 1988, a drop of eight to nine percentage points from the previous three elections (table 12.19). Second, NDP candidates, who are less able to raise contributions, can rely on the reimbursement of about half of their "election expenses" (provided that they receive at least 15 percent of the popular vote). While they end up with lower surpluses or larger deficits than Conservative and Liberal candidates, NDP candidates have been able to reduce the inequality in average "election expenses" over time, but they have not closed the gap.

2.3 "Personal Expenses"

The *Canada Elections Act* distinguishes "personal expenses" from "election expenses" and does not impose limits on the former, although only certain types of expenditures properly fall into the category of "personal expenses." These consist largely of the candidate's travel and accommodation expenses to, from and within the riding during the campaign (see chap. 13). As table 12.1 indicates, such expenses have never exceeded 9 percent of "election expenses" over the past four elections, and have grown less than the rate of inflation over these elections.[4]

2.4 Reimbursement and Surplus/Deficit

How important is the federal government's reimbursement of 50 percent of a candidate's "election expenses" in terms of the financing of campaigns at the riding level? To answer this question, the author sought to determine if contributions (including transfers from party headquarters or from the riding association) covered "election expenses" and "personal expenses." Hence we defined the term "campaign surplus"[5] (or deficit) as total revenues minus election expenses and personal expenses. The data in table 12.1 yield several important conclusions. First, for all the candidates combined in each of the past four general elections, revenues just about covered both "election" and "personal" expenses. The "campaign *deficit*" fell from $1.7 million in 1979 to $1.3 million in 1980 and 1984 to $542 000 in 1988. In other words, even *before* reimbursement, in the *aggregate*, candidates took in almost enough money to cover their "election expenses" and "personal expenses." Note, however, that by combining the experience of some 1 500 candidates, the large amount of variation in their individual circumstances is ignored. As will be documented for the 1988 election, some candidates took in far more than they needed to cover their "election" and "personal" expenses, while others raised very little money and thus were unable to spend as much as their rivals.

Second, the data in table 12.1 indicate that the 500 to 700 candidates not running under the banner of one of the three main parties turned their "campaign deficit" of $569 000 in 1979 into a slight *surplus* in 1988 ($47 000). No doubt, they were driven to raise more money in contributions to cover their expenses because very few such candidates get 15 percent of the popular vote and therefore are not eligible for the reimbursement. Indeed, table 12.1 indicates that the total amount of reimbursement going to these candidates fell between 1979 and 1988, even in nominal terms.

Third, in 1979 and 1980, the candidates of all of the three main parties had a "campaign deficit." However, in 1984 and 1988, Conservative party candidates as a group had a surplus, while the NDP and Liberal candidates continued to have a slight deficit. (In 1988, the average deficit for Liberal party candidates was $1 834, while that for NDP candidates was $2 939.) The key point is that, in 1988, taking all 1 578 candidates as a group, contributions covered all but 1.7 percent of their "election expenses" and "personal expenses." Hence, it could be claimed that virtually all of the federal reimbursement of $13.74 million was "unnecessary" in the sense of ensuring that all candidates *as a group* had sufficient funds to cover the two categories of expenses specifically recognized in the *Canada Elections Act.*

The "post-reimbursement surplus" for all candidates rose from $6.8 million in 1979 to $9.9 million in 1984 and then to $13.2 million in 1988 (table 12.1). However, the Chief Electoral Officer puts the surplus for candidates at over $8.0 million in 1984 (Canada, Elections Canada 1989a, 47) and $9.6 million in 1988 (Canada, Elections Canada 1991, 10).[6] The difference arises because the CEO takes into account the candidates' "other expenses" not recorded in his report published after each general election.[7]

Even these figures strongly suggest that, in the aggregate at least, the 1974 reforms that established the reimbursement and the tax credit for contributions have proved to be something of a cornucopia for many candidates. However, in order to help recover part of the cost of the national campaign that supports candidates, the Liberal party[8] has forced virtually all of its candidates to sign over part of the reimbursement to the *party.* The NDP applied a similar policy, but less widely (chap. 6). Their "stick" is the fact that the party leader must sign each candidate's nomination papers. Much of the reimbursement flows through to the candidate's surplus (or reduces his/her deficit). The effect of this is to reduce the net amount of a candidate's surplus that finds its way into the coffers of the riding association.

As will be documented in section 7 below, even on an *individual* basis, a high fraction of Liberal and Progressive Conservative candidates and a smaller fraction of NDP candidates ended up with a surplus in 1988, even taking into account "other expenses." However, the reimbursement formula has not been of much assistance to candidates of parties other than the Conservative, Liberal and New Democratic parties. Table 12.1 indicates that the ratio of reimbursement to "election expenses" for these candidates fell from 36.5 percent in 1979 to only 7.4 percent in 1988. In contrast, the ratio for all candidates of the three main parties as a group was 54.7 percent in 1979 and 47.0 percent in 1988. Even allowing for changes in the formula in 1979 and 1980 (which was based on 50 percent of expenditures on electronic media) as compared to 1984 and 1988 (22.5 percent of total election expenses), the difference reflects the fact that few candidates of minor parties are able to win 15 percent of the vote and hence become eligible for reimbursement. For example, in 1988 the Reform Party fielded 72 candidates, but only 11 were eligible for reimbursement (chap. 7). The figures for 1979 reflect the fact that 103 Social Credit candidates had $599 000 in election expenses and received $359 000 in reimbursement (Canada, Elections Canada 1980b, 5).

3. CANDIDATE REVENUES

3.1 Sources of Revenues

It may be useful to examine more generally the flows of funds within parties, and to and from candidates and the federal government. These are outlined in figure 12.1. Candidates can receive money from national party headquarters (flow 1), from a PTA (flow 10), from their local riding association (flow 8) or from the federal government in the form of the 50 percent reimbursement of their "election expenses" if they obtain 15 percent of the votes cast (flow 13). (In order to focus on intraparty flows, contributions from donors such as individuals, corporations or unions have been omitted from figure 12.1.) Flow 15 illustrates the situation when parties "tax" away part of a candidate's reimbursement from the federal government. Flow 9 illustrates candidates' disposition of their surplus by giving it to their local riding association. Flow 4 shows funds passing from a riding association to party headquarters, which most often occurs between campaign periods when donations to the riding association are routed through the party's official agent (e.g., PC Canada Fund or the Federal Liberal Agency) in order to obtain a receipt for the tax credit. The net amount is returned to the riding association in flow 2. Parallel arrangements occur with respect to the provincial associations of the Liberal party and provincial sections of the NDP.

Tables 12.2 and 12.3 provide an analysis of the candidates' sources of revenues by party for the four general elections under the 1974 legislation.[9] There are some important differences in the way each of the three main parties finances its candidates' campaigns. Note that trade unions accounted for from 14 percent to 18 percent of NDP candidates' revenues in the past four elections as compared to less than 1 percent for Conservative and Liberal candidates. Second, with the exception of 1988, Liberal party candidates relied more heavily on transfers from party headquarters ("registered parties") than did their rivals. For example, in 1979 some 41 percent of Liberal candidates' revenues came from this source as compared to only 13 percent for Conservatives and

Figure 12.1
Flows of funds within federal parties and to and from candidates and federal government

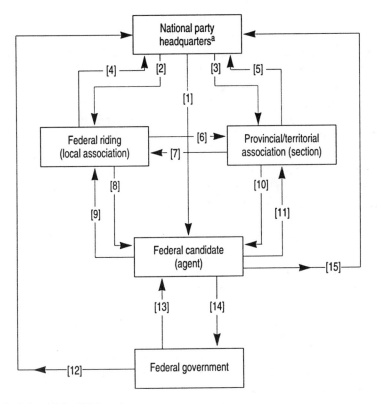

aIncludes party's official agent.

24 percent for NDP candidates. While the Liberal candidates' dependence on transfers from headquarters dropped to 25 percent in 1980 (the same level as for the NDP but above the Conservatives' 17 percent), it rose to 33 percent in 1984 (versus 25 percent for the NDP and 11 percent for the Conservatives). In 1988, largely due to the central office's fiscal problems, Liberal candidates, on average, received only 18 percent of their total revenues from headquarters.[10] This, however, was double the Conservative candidates' level of support (8 percent), but below the NDP's level (23 percent). In general, the Progressive Conservative party has sought to reduce its candidates' dependence on party headquarters to finance their campaigns. At the same time, Conservative party headquarters has never required that candidates sign over a

portion of their reimbursement to headquarters as the Liberals did most extensively in 1979 and 1980, when many candidates had to give the central office one-half of their reimbursement, and in 1988, when all candidates had to do so. Great care must be exercised using the data on intraparty transfers. For example, the CEO indicates that in 1988, Conservative party candidates received $1.04 million from party headquarters. Party officials at headquarters indicate that "riding and candidate support" amounted to $232 000 in 1988 (table 4.7). The difference is very likely attributable to the following factors. First, contributions earmarked for specific candidates are routed through the PC Canada Fund. The Fund retains 25 percent of such contributions if they are made before the writ is issued, but nothing afterward. Second, contributions generated by the direct-mail efforts of a candidate or a group of candidates are paid into the PC Canada Fund and then transferred to the candidate(s). In both these cases, the transfers to candidates do not represent help from headquarters but the receipt of money raised by the candidates themselves. Third, in a few cases, Conservative party headquarters makes loans or advances to candidates. It is possible that these are treated as transfers by the candidate's agent and the error is not caught by the CEO's auditor. The author found several of these in the sample of 277 candidates' returns that were examined to ascertain their "other expenses."

The data in tables 12.2 and 12.3 suggest that there was a slight trend for a larger fraction of candidates' revenues to come from what the CEO calls "political organizations." This term refers to local associations or riding associations and provincial and territorial associations (PTAs).[11] While NDP candidates obtained from 14 percent to 21 percent of their revenues from riding associations and PTAs over the past four elections, Conservative party candidates obtained 8 percent, 13 percent, 6 percent and 10 percent in 1979, 1980, 1984 and 1988 respectively. The comparable figures for Liberal party candidates were 7 percent, 11 percent, 9 percent and 15 percent. If we combine revenues from party headquarters and those from riding associations and PTAs, a clearer picture of the greater dependency of NDP and Liberal candidates on "party sources" emerges. For example, in 1979 Conservative party candidates received 21 percent of their funds from "party sources" as compared to 48 percent for Liberal party candidates and 42 percent for NDP candidates. In 1988, the comparable figures were 18 percent for the Conservatives, 33 percent for the Liberals and 44 percent for NDP candidates. Table 12.4 provides more detail on the amounts transferred from parties and riding associations to candidates over the past four elections. These figures are difficult to interpret, however. Officials from all parties state that, during election periods, contributions from individuals (and, to a lesser extent, from corporations) are sent to party headquarters but are earmarked for a particular candidate or riding association. When these are passed on to the candidate or riding association, the money shows up as a transfer from the party. Therefore, where transfers from the party to a candidate form a substantial part of a candidate's revenues, it would be incorrect to conclude that the candidate is "dependent" upon help from headquarters to finance his/her campaign. It is simply not possible to separate contributions "routed through" party headquarters from money paid out of headquarters' own resources to the candidate. Further, it should be noted that the majority of candidates of the three main parties in 1984 had a surplus, and in most cases this money was assigned by the candidate's agent to the riding association. According to the CEO, the total of candidates' surpluses in 1984 was $8 million, while in 1988 it was $9.6 million. It may be that part of the surplus of 1984 was "recycled" in 1988 as transfers from riding associations to candidates. Note that, for the three main parties, the amount of transfers from riding associations (and PTAs/PTSs) to candidates in 1988 was $4.25 million, or just over half the amount of surplus generated by all candidates in 1984.

The problems of accounting for intraparty financial flows, particularly in election years, can be seen in the data in table 12.4a. This table looks at these intraparty flows from two different perspectives, that of the recipients and that of the entity making the transfer. For example, in 1979 all Liberal candidates combined reported that they received $2.7 million from party headquarters. However, the party reported that it transferred *minus* $810 000 to its candidates; in other words, headquarters received more from candidates than it transferred to them. In 1979, the Liberal party sought to obtain about half the amount of reimbursement received by each candidate and it obtained about $1 million.[12] Even taking this amount into account, it is not possible to reconcile the two sets of figures reported in table 12.4a. The same is true of the Conservative party. For example, in 1988 party headquarters reported transferring $3.34 million to candidates. Candidates, on the other hand, reported receiving $1.04 million. Is the difference attributable to the party counting contributions to candidates routed through the PC Canada Fund, which it reports as a transfer to candidates, while the candidate reports only those amounts over and above such contributions? Party officials could not account for the differences. Interestingly, the Chief Electoral Officer has never publicly commented upon the disparities reported in table 12.4a, even though he receives and publishes the information presented in the table.

In each of the past four general elections, the single most important source of revenue for candidates consisted of donations from individuals. There is, however, some variation in the relative importance of this source across parties. Tables 12.2 and 12.3 indicate that Conservative party candidates, on average, raised from 38 percent to 45 percent of total revenues from individuals over the past four elections, as compared to 27 percent to 39 percent for Liberal party candidates and 34 percent to 44 percent for NDP candidates.

Business organizations contributed from 31 percent to 40 percent of the total revenues of Conservative party candidates over the last four general elections. The range for Liberal candidates was 22 percent to 28 percent. Given the policy of some of the NDP's provincial sections not to accept contributions from business organizations, it is not surprising that the party's candidates received only 2 percent to 3 percent of their revenues from this source over the past four general elections.

It is important to appreciate that the major recipient of candidates' surplus is the riding associations.[13] Since headquarters has not "taxed" the reimbursement going to Conservative party candidates, virtually all of their surpluses end up in the coffers of the riding associations. This was true of the Liberals in 1984, when only the Quebec PTA imposed a 50 percent tax on reimbursements to help finance the central campaign effort. In 1979 and 1980, many Liberal candidates were required to give half their reimbursement to party headquarters to finance the national campaign. In 1988, all Liberal candidates were required to do so and the party collected $2.27 million from its candidates.

Less is known about the NDP, but it appears that, prior to 1988, a candidate's reimbursement was not "taxed" by either a PTS or the Ottawa office. In 1988, however, the BC provincial section met its quota of funds to be sent to Ottawa to help pay for the national campaign by requiring all candidates in the province to transfer all of their reimbursement to the provincial section, which used the funds to meet its quota.[14] The total amount of the reimbursement of candidates' "election expenses" (over $500 000) almost covered the BC section's share of the NDP's national campaign budget (chap. 6).

3.2 Number of Contributions

The number of contributions from individuals and the total of all contributions to candidates by party for the past four general elections is reported in table 12.5. It indicates that the number of contributions from individuals grew from 67 300 in 1979 to 104 800 in 1988. While this is substantially greater than the increase in population, it indicates a low level of participation in the political process in the form of making a contribution. The data suggest that, even in 1988, only one-half of one percent of individuals[15] of voting age made a contribution to a candidate's campaign. In 1984, all the parties reported that they received 211 000 contributions from individuals; the figure for 1988 was 208 000 (chap. 8). Since some contributions going to candidates are routed through the party (or riding association or PTA) rather than being sent directly to the candidate's agent, the total number of individuals making a contribution in the past two general elections was less than 298 400 in 1984 and 313 100 in 1988. Therefore, only 1.8 percent of electors in Canada made a contribution to a party or candidate in the years in which the last two general elections occurred.[16]

Table 12.5 indicates that, for both the Liberal and Conservative party candidates as a group, individuals have accounted for 70 percent to 75 percent of the total number of contributions in the past four elections. However, Conservative party candidates have been able, with the exception of 1980, to obtain a substantially larger number of donations from individuals than have Liberal party candidates (and, as can be seen in tables 12.2 and 12.3, to raise more money). For example, in 1984 Conservative candidates received 42 247 contributions from individuals versus 21 185 for Liberal candidates. The difference in 1988 was not so great: 40 329 versus 27 106.

The data in table 12.5 indicate that, in the past four elections, 90 percent of the donations to NDP candidates as a group have come from individuals. However, the number of such contributions has been far below the Tories' level and somewhat below the Liberals' level. For example, in 1979 the figure for the Tories was 27 597, versus 13 765 for the NDP and 18 525 for the Liberals. Although the gap was reduced in 1980, it increased again in 1984 and 1988, so that, in 1988, the number of contributions to Conservative party candidates was 79.3 percent above that for NDP candidates (and 48.8 percent above that for Liberal party candidates).[17] In terms of average revenue per candidate, table 12.3a reveals that individuals provided $7 850 to NDP candidates in 1988 as compared to $12 597 to Liberal party candidates and $20 758 to Conservative party candidates. In terms of the average size of contributions from individuals, the Conservatives led in 1988 with $152, followed by the Liberals with $137 and the New Democrats with $103. In other words, not only did the Tory candidates receive more contributions from individuals in 1988, but the average size of such contributions was 11 percent larger than those to Liberal party candidates and 48 percent larger than those to NDP candidates. The disparity in average size of contributions from individuals was less in 1984: $111 for Conservative candidates, $112 for Liberal candidates and $86 for NDP candidates.

The disparity in the average amount of revenue from individuals was mirrored in the total revenues for candidates in 1984 and 1988 (table 12.3a). In 1988, on average, Conservative party candidates obtained $45 395 compared to $32 647 for Liberal party candidates and only $23 074 for NDP candidates. In other words, on average, Tory candidates raised 39 percent and 97 percent more than their Liberal and NDP rivals. Note that the average amount raised by Tory candidates was still slightly *below* the average limit on candidates' "election expenses" of $46 900 in 1988.[18]

Table 12.3a indicates that NDP candidates were able to increase their average revenue proportionately much more than either of their rivals between 1984 and 1988 (from $13 047 to $23 074). In 1984, Tory candidates had 37 percent more revenue than Liberal candidates and 206 percent more than NDP candidates.

3.3   Revenues of Candidates in 1988

Total Revenues
Obviously, averages based on 295 candidates can conceal as much as they reveal. Table 12.6 provides the distribution of candidates' total revenues by party for the 1988 federal election. It indicates that 18.4 percent of Conservative party candidates raised over $60 000 (recall that the average limit on "election expenses" was $46 900), while only 6.2 percent of Liberal party and 1.3 percent of NDP candidates were able to raise this amount. At the other end of the distribution, some 47.6 percent of NDP candidates raised less than $20 000, compared to 23.5 percent of Liberal party candidates and only 7.5 percent of Conservative party candidates. Candidates of all other parties raised the least amount of money in 1988: 80.3 percent raised less than $10 000.[19]

Categories of Revenues
Total revenues of candidates in 1988 could be "broken down" into four categories: contributions of $100 or less from all sources, contributions of over $100, donations of goods and services, and revenues generated by fund-raising functions. This was done for each of the total revenue cohorts for each party (table 12.7). The importance of small cash contributions – those of $100 or less – from individuals or businesses declined as candidates' total revenues rose, although the rate of decline was quite different by party. For example, such cash contributions accounted for 44 percent, 27 percent, 23 percent and 28 percent of Conservative, Liberal, NDP and Other candidates' revenues where their total revenue was under $10 000. However, contributions of $100 or less accounted

for 20 percent, 15 percent and 1 percent for Conservative, Liberal and NDP candidates raising $60 001 to $70 000 in 1988. In general, fundraising functions generated only a tiny fraction of candidates' total revenues, regardless of party or the amount of total revenue raised; in most cases, the amount was 3 percent or less of candidates' total revenues.

Contributions of goods and services declined as a percentage of the total revenues of candidates of all parties. However, goods and services were generally much more important to NDP candidates than to other candidates. For example, in the $30 001 to $40 000 cohort, they accounted for 20.4 percent of the NDP candidates' revenues as compared to 5.1 percent for Conservative candidates and 7.8 percent for Liberal candidates. A similar pattern can be seen in the next three revenue cohorts (table 12.7).

Cash contributions of over $100 accounted for at least half of the total revenues of candidates in 1988 in all revenue cohorts and for candidates of all parties. For the three main parties, contributions of over $100 accounted for at least 65 percent of candidates' revenues for virtually all revenue cohorts above $10 000 (table 12.7).

Revenues by Province

Table 12.8 provides data on average revenues per candidate by party and by province for the 1988 federal election. The data reveal the regional strengths and weaknesses of each party in terms of its candidates' ability to generate revenues. In general terms, the data indicate that Conservative candidates led in total revenues and "election expenses" in every province, while the NDP and Liberal candidates jockeyed for second and third position. NDP candidates outperformed Liberal candidates in the three western provinces, while the Liberals were number two and the New Democrats number three in the other provinces. The story in more detail now follows. While the average revenue for all Conservative party candidates was $45 400 in 1988, substantially larger sums were raised in Newfoundland ($55 600), New Brunswick ($55 300), Saskatchewan ($51 300) and BC ($53 200). The weakest provinces were Manitoba ($31 973), PEI ($35 809) and the Yukon/NWT ($35 391). The average revenue of Conservative party candidates in Quebec ($43 820) was slightly below the average. In Ontario the average revenue was very slightly below the national average.

By far the biggest variation in average revenues by province occurred within the NDP, which for the first time sought to run a truly national campaign in the 1988 election by spending some $2 million of its $7.1 million party "election expenses" budget in Quebec. While the 295 NDP candidates raised an average of $23 075, those in BC ($44 782) and Saskatchewan ($40 495) raised far more, while candidates in Ontario ($25 382) and the Yukon/NWT ($27 773) had revenues slightly above the average. In BC, NDP candidates raised (and spent) far more than Liberal candidates ($24 600). While they raised, on average, $8 370 less than their Conservative rivals, NDP candidates in BC spent only $1 175 less than them on "election expenses" (table 12.8).

In Alberta and Saskatchewan, NDP candidates, on average, raised more than their Liberal rivals. In Saskatchewan, NDP candidates raised, on average, $10 790 *less* than Conservative party candidates (but spent only $1 730 less). In Quebec, however, the NDP candidates trailed badly, raising an average of $14 071 and spending $17 053 on "election expenses." In contrast, the Progressive Conservative candidates raised $43 820 and spent $42 474, while the Liberal candidates raised $35 735 and spent $37 486 (table 12.8).

Liberal candidates in Ontario, Quebec and the Maritimes raised more than the average for all 295 candidates ($32 647). Nova Scotia had the highest average ($40 428). The Liberals were weakest in Alberta, where candidates raised an average of only $16 273, less than Reform Party candidates ($19 922).

Top Fund-Raisers

In 1988, some candidates were able to raise sums far in excess of the average limit on "election expenses" ($46 900). The money-raising champion was Barbara McDougall (PC – St. Paul's, Toronto), who collected $130 626; but as table 12.9 indicates, 200 candidates raised as much as the average limit on "election expenses." Five hundred candidates raised $31 272 or more – which, if the candidate spent the limit on "election expenses" and received 15 percent of the vote, would leave him/her with a balance of $7 850 before "personal expenses" and "other expenses" that are not subject to statutory limit. These are discussed below.

As might be expected from the averages for all candidates, Conservative party candidates dominated the top 100, 200 and 300 fund-raisers in the 1988 election. They accounted for 68 percent of the top 100 (those who raised at least $55 648) and 56.3 percent of the top 300 (those who raised at least $39 899) (see table 12.10). The comparable figures for Liberal candidates were 24 percent and 24.3 percent respectively. Six NDP candidates placed in the top 100, while 17 percent of the top 300 fund-raisers in 1988 were NDP candidates. While candidates of the three main parties dominated the money-raising sweepstakes, 5 Christian Heritage and 2 Reform Party candidates (out of 693 candidates of "other" parties) were also among the top 300 fund-raisers in 1988.

A more detailed examination of the characteristics of the top

100 fund-raisers reveals that 67 percent were incumbents (see table 12.11). Moreover, 78 percent of these incumbents had been government MPs or cabinet ministers. About 70 percent of the Mulroney cabinet members between 1984 and 1988 who ran again in 1988 ranked in the top 100 fund-raisers among some 1 578 candidates.[20]

Of the 28 cabinet ministers who were among the top 100 fund-raisers, 25 (or 89 percent) won their seat. The electoral success rate for incumbent government MPs (58 percent) was very close to that for challengers (55 percent) in this group of the top 100 fund-raisers (table 12.11).[21] Overall, 71 percent of those who were among the top 100 fund-raisers were elected. Great care, however, needs to be taken in interpreting any causal relation between being a top fund-raiser and achieving electoral success. Since expenditures are limited for all candidates, the ability to raise money may simply be a reflection of the candidate's popularity and the widely held prior belief that he/she will win and subsequently hold a cabinet post, or perhaps become an opposition party critic. A high percentage of incumbent opposition party MPs and even challengers who placed in the top 100 fund-raisers could be classified as "notables," that is, they had been cabinet ministers when the Liberal party was in power or were highly visible and well-known individuals in their own right.

The distribution of the top 200 fund-raisers by province and by party in 1988 is given in table 12.12. It indicates that only seven candidates of parties other than the PC, Liberal or New Democratic parties were among the top 200 fund-raisers. Three provinces (BC, Ontario and Quebec) accounted for 74 percent of the top 200 fund-raisers. In BC, for example, 39 percent of the candidates of the three main parties were among the top 200. In Ontario, the comparable percentage was 23.6 percent, while in Quebec it was 18.7 percent. On the other hand, none of the candidates of the three main parties in PEI or the Yukon/NWT was among the top 200 fund-raisers.

Table 12.13 indicates that 62 percent of all winning candidates in 1988 and 66 percent in 1984 also raised the most revenue. The data indicate that the odds against a candidate winning in 1988 if he/she ranked third in the riding in terms of revenue were 16 to 1. In 1984, the odds were 25 to 1. These results, however, should be treated with caution. What is needed is a multivariate model of electoral success that also recognizes that there is a statutory limit on "election expenses" but no limit on "other expenses."

Sources of Revenues

There are some interesting differences by party and province in the way candidates financed their 1988 election campaigns. In Ontario, for example, Conservative party candidates obtained 47 percent of their revenues from individuals, while in Quebec this source provided 61 percent, but in BC it provided only 38.0 percent of candidates' revenues (table 12.14). On the other hand, corporations provided only 6 percent of the reported revenues of PC candidates in Quebec as compared to 36 percent in Ontario and 53 percent in BC. Recall from chapter 8 that, in 1988, a majority of Conservative party candidates in Quebec used *financement populaire* to obtain the money for their campaign, although 71 percent described the technique as "not very successful" or "a failure." However, table 12.8 indicates that, on average, PC candidates in Quebec raised $43 820, far more than Liberal candidates ($35 735) or NDP candidates ($14 071).[22] Table 12.14 indicates that PC candidates in Quebec were much more dependent on party headquarters (18 percent) than their counterparts in Ontario (3 percent) and BC (4 percent). Further, a larger fraction of Quebec Conservative party candidates' revenue (13 percent) came from riding associations than was the case for Conservative candidates in Ontario (2 percent) or BC (4 percent). Again, as noted in section 3.1, great care must be used in interpreting the transfers from headquarters to candidates. For the Conservative party at least, most of the money consisted of contributions earmarked for candidates that were sent to headquarters in order to qualify for a tax credit receipt.

In Ontario and BC, Liberal party candidates in 1988 obtained about 44 percent of their campaign funds from individuals. In Quebec, the figure was only 29 percent. Quebec Liberal candidates were even more dependent on riding associations or PTAs (12 percent) and national party headquarters (31 percent) than were Conservative or NDP candidates (5 percent and 13 percent respectively). Business organizations accounted for 27.3 percent of Ontario Liberal candidates' revenues as compared to 27 percent in Quebec and 29 percent in BC. Even in Ontario, party-related sources accounted for 26 percent of Liberal candidates' revenues. In BC, the comparable figure was 24 percent.

Cross-province comparisons are most difficult for the NDP because of the way the BC provincial section handled contributions in the 1988 election. NDP candidates (more precisely, their agents) were required to have the BC provincial section receive and provide receipts for the tax credit for all contributions from individuals. Then the provincial section kept a fraction of the revenues to pay for its share of the national campaign effort and returned the rest to the candidates.[23] As a result, the federal party, provincial sections and riding associations accounted for 73 percent of BC NDP candidates' revenues in 1988. Trade unions accounted for another 18 percent. In Quebec, the picture was rather different because contributions went directly to the candidate's agent rather than to the provincial section, as was done in other provinces. Individuals accounted for 60 percent of total revenues (which were on average one-third of those in BC), while national headquarters accounted for 13 percent and the Quebec PTS or riding associations supplied 5 percent. In Ontario, NDP candidates received 53 percent of their funds from individuals, 23 percent from trade unions (versus 12 percent in Quebec) and 14 percent from the Ontario PTS or riding associations (table 12.14).

This analysis reveals that the data reported by candidates to the CEO and published by him may be misleading. Because the NDP chose to route all contributions in BC in 1988 through the provincial section, the public is presented with an incomplete picture of NDP candidates' sources of revenues. Moreover, the total *number* of contributions to candidates reported by the CEO becomes meaningless. In the extreme case where the PTS was able to receive *all* contributions and write one cheque to each riding, NDP candidates in BC could show as few as 32 contributions! As it is, in 1988, NDP candidates reported 1 224 contributions from individuals versus 2 320 to Liberal party candidates and 4 323 to Conservative party candidates. In 1984, NDP candidates reported 6 933 contributions from individuals versus 2 181 to Liberal and 5 657 to Conservative candidates (Canada, Elections Canada 1985, 251). This raises serious questions about the information reported to the CEO because of the various ways candidates can receive, transfer and hence record revenues.

4. EXPENDITURES BY CANDIDATES

4.1 "Election Expenses" in Perspective

To put the average "election expenses" of candidates in perspective, it is useful to look back to 1974, the last general election *before* the 1974 amendments to the *Canada Elections Act* came into effect. On the basis of the returns filed by 914 of the 1 209 candidates (there were no auditing requirements), average election expenditures in 1974 were $20 416 for Liberals, $19 425 for Conservatives and only $6 010 for New Democratic candidates (table 12.15). However, the CPI increased by 72.8 percent over the period 1974 to 1988. Therefore, in 1988 dollars, the average expenditure per candidate in 1974 was as follows: Liberal, $35 279; Conservative, $33 566; and NDP, $10 385. The average "election expenses" of candidates in 1988, in 1988 dollars, were: Liberal, $32 803; Conservative, $40 218; and NDP, $24 768. In other words, Liberal candidates (on average) spent *less* in real terms in 1988 than those who filed reports in 1974 when there was no limit. On the other hand, Conservative party candidates spent (on average) 20 percent more in real terms in 1988 than they did in 1974. The biggest increase by far was by NDP candidates. In real terms, their average expenditures increased by 138 percent between 1974 and 1988. Care must be used in drawing conclusions here, because there was no detailed definition of "election expenses" in 1974. Some of what was reported may have been what in 1988 was classified as "other expenses" or "personal expenses."

Before analysing the components of candidates' "election expenses," it is useful to recall that in 1988 Conservative party candidates spent an average of $40 217 on "election expenses" (or $11.86 million for the nation), while Liberal party candidates spent an average of $32 803 (a total of $9.68 million) and NDP candidates averaged $24 766 ($7.31 million in total) (tables 12.8, 12.16).

4.2   Components of "Election Expenses"

Taking all candidates together (over 1 400 in each election), it is clear that non-electronic or print advertising has been the largest component of "election expenses" over the past four elections, accounting for between 45 percent and 52 percent of the total (table 12.16). Candidates spent only from 7.1 percent to 13.1 percent on radio or television advertising. Two factors would appear to account for the modest expenditures on electronic media. The first is its high cost, particularly in the case of television advertising. The second is the fact that, in major metropolitan areas, the "footprint" of the electronic media is far larger than that of individual ridings.

The second largest category of candidates' "election expenses" consists of "office expenses." It accounted for 16.5 percent in 1979, 21.1 percent in 1984 and 22.3 percent in 1988. This category apparently includes the rental of space for campaign offices[24] as well as some administrative costs.

Travel expenses have declined in importance for all candidates as a group, from 4.8 percent in 1979 and 1980 to 2.9 percent in 1984 and 2.5 percent in 1988. Note, however, that the candidate's own travel to and from and within the riding may be included in "personal expenses" and hence be subject only to the limitation that they be "reasonable" (see the discussion in chap. 13).

Salaries and wages have been the third or fourth most important category of all candidates' "election expenses," and they declined slightly in importance from 11.7 percent in 1979 and 11.2 percent in 1980 to 9.2 percent in 1984 and 9.5 percent in 1988. However, NDP candidates have consistently spent more on salaries (18.2 percent to 21.7 percent over the past four elections) than their Liberal (7.9 percent to 11.5 percent) and Conservative (4.8 percent to 8.8 percent) party rivals (table 12.16). This occurs because candidates, party headquarters or trade unions pay the wages of party or union officials who volunteer to be campaign organizers for NDP candidates.

Within the largest category of "election expenses," namely print or non-electronic advertising, the variation by party across four elections has been rather modest, but it has been increasing. In 1979, for example, only two percentage points separated any two of the three main parties' share of total expenses devoted to print advertising. In 1980, the difference was 5.7 percentage points, and in 1984 it was 8.2 points, while in 1988 it was 13.6 points. If there is a trend, it appears to be that Conservative candidates have been spending (on average) a slightly higher fraction on print advertising over the past four elections (about 49 percent to 51 percent in 1979, 1980 and 1984 versus 55 percent in 1988), while NDP candidates have spent a somewhat smaller fraction (48 percent to 49 percent in 1979 and 1980, versus about 42 percent in 1984 and 1988). With respect to electronic advertising, NDP candidates have tended to spend slightly less, on average, as a fraction of total election expenses than have Conservative or Liberal party candidates (table 12.16).

Table 12.17 permits an examination of party differences for candidates' average "election expenses" in 1988. On average, Conservative party candidates spent $7 400 more than Liberal party candidates and $15 400 more than NDP candidates. Candidates of other parties spent, on average, from one-seventh to one-ninth as much as candidates for one of the three main parties. Most of the difference in total "election expenses" across the three main parties was accounted for by spending on print advertising. While Conservative candidates spent an average of $22 136, Liberals spent $17 459 and NDP candidates spent $10 264. In other words, of the absolute difference in total spending between Conservative party and NDP candidates ($15 400), some $11 900 was accounted for by the difference in print advertising (more precisely, non-electronic advertising). In the case of Liberal candidates, $4 700 of the $7 400 difference in their total "election expenses" in comparison with Conservative candidates was attributable to lower outlays on print advertising.

"Election Expenses" and "Personal Expenses" by Province
In 1988, there were major differences in candidates' average "election expenses" and "personal expenses" by province (table 12.8). The Conservatives, however, exhibited the least interprovincial variation in candidates' "election expenses." Their range was from $33 516 in the Yukon/NWT to $44 356 in Saskatchewan. In contrast, the range for NDP candidates was $5 003 in PEI to $42 626 in Saskatchewan; the range for

Liberal candidates was $17 466 in Alberta to $37 486 in Quebec. Such results are what one would expect from the party in power and a "regionalized" opposition.

For Progressive Conservative party candidates, the provinces in which their "election expenses" were above the national average for all parties were Saskatchewan, Quebec and Newfoundland, in descending order. NDP candidates concentrated their outlays in Saskatchewan, BC, Ontario and the Yukon/NWT (table 12.8). Despite their effort to run a full campaign in Quebec at the national (party) level, NDP candidates in Quebec were only able to spend an average of $17 053 on "election expenses," far behind their Conservative ($42 474) and Liberal ($37 486) party rivals.

For the Liberals, the provinces in which the average "election expenses" of candidates exceeded the national average for all parties were Quebec, Ontario and all four Atlantic provinces (table 12.8).

Components of "Election Expenses" in Relation to the Limit
In order to get a better sense of the spending priorities of candidates of different parties, it is useful to compare candidates who spent about the same percentage of the statutory limit on "election expenses." This is done in table 12.18. Consider first the outlays by the 74 Liberal, 56 NDP and 148 Conservative candidates in 1988 who spent at least 90 percent of the statutory limit on "election expenses." There are two major differences among the candidates in this cohort. First, while the Liberal and Conservative candidates spent 54 percent of their "election expenses" on "other advertising (print advertising)," NDP candidates spent 38 percent. In absolute terms, the difference was about $6 700. Second, while the Liberals and PCs spent 8 percent and 5 percent of their "election expenses" on "salaries," NDP candidates spent 26 percent. The absolute difference was $8 100 less than Liberal candidates and $9 400 less than Tory candidates. In summary, it appears that, unlike their rivals, when they were close to the constraint on "election expenses" NDP candidates substituted paid campaign organizers for print advertising. This is not a proper understanding of what is occurring, however. The problem for NDP candidates is that trade unions and party headquarters offer contributions in kind rather than in cash. The "salaries" component for NDP candidates in table 12.18 is the payment of the salary of "volunteers," who hold key positions in NDP campaigns. These people cannot afford to go on leave from their jobs without pay in order to engage in their avocation of being campaign organizers. Therefore, either the local candidate pays these organizers for the loss of salary while they are on leave for all or part of the campaign, or a union or party

headquarters pays them. In either case, the payment is both a contribution and an "election expense." The problem for the NDP candidate who needs to "spend the limit" in a marginal riding or in one where he/she must fight hard to retain the seat is to find the best trade-off between having skilled organizers running the campaign and having more money available for advertising. The more volunteers whose salary must be paid, the less money there will be for advertising, travel, office expenses and so on.

The need to pay organizers also shows up on the revenues side in the case of NDP candidates. Table 12.18 indicates that, among the candidates spending 90 percent or more of the limit on "election expenses," NDP candidates received an average of $6 133 (or 15 percent of total revenue) from trade unions, while PC and Liberal candidates averaged only $26 and $14. Notice also that NDP candidates received 29 percent of their revenue ($11 580) from "political organizations," that is, from local riding associations and provincial sections, as compared to only 14 percent for Liberal party candidates ($6 385) and 11 percent for Conservative party candidates ($5 244). Thus, the rules governing the use of volunteers who are continuing to receive an income have an asymmetric effect on the parties. In particular, the NDP is at a disadvantage because its volunteers cannot afford to forego income while working as organizers. This issue is addressed in chapter 13.

An examination of the data for candidates spending 80 percent to 90 percent of the limit on "election expenses" in 1988 reveals a pattern very similar to that of candidates spending over 90 percent of the limit. On average, NDP candidates spent about $8 000 less on print advertising and $7 000 more on salaries than did their rivals in the other two main parties. In the case of candidates spending less than 70 percent of the limit on "election expenses," comparisons are made very difficult because of the big differences in average total "election expenses." In any event, in percentage terms, the differential pattern of spending identified above can still be seen (table 12.18).

4.3 "Election Expenses" Relative to the Limit

One of the most important elements of the federal regulatory regime governing party/candidate financing since 1 August 1974 is the limit placed on "election expenses." The effect of the limit can be examined in several ways. The first is to look at the total "election expenses" of each party's candidates relative to their combined limit. The second is to examine the distribution of candidates by party in terms of their "closeness" to the limit.

The "election expenses" of Progressive Conservative candidates as a whole increased relative to the limit between the 1979 and 1980 elections (77.6 percent and 72.4 percent respectively) and the 1984 (89.0 percent) and 1988 (85.8 percent) elections (table 12.19). Recall from table 12.18 that 148 of 295 PC candidates in 1988 spent more than 90 percent of the limit versus 74 Liberals, 56 NDP candidates and none of the 693 candidates of other parties.

The pattern for the Liberal party was quite different: its candidates spent 78 percent to 80 percent of the limit in the general elections of 1979, 1980 and 1984, but only 70 percent of the limit in 1988. This was also far below the percentage for all Conservative candidates (85.8 percent). Between the 1979 and 1984 elections, NDP candidates' "election expenses" increased slightly (from 34.4 percent in 1979 to 38 percent in the next two elections); then they jumped to 52.8 percent in 1988. This was far below the comparable figure for Liberal or Conservative candidates (table 12.19). Of particular importance is the interprovincial variation for the NDP. In 1988, NDP candidates in PEI spent only 13 percent of their collective limit on "election expenses." In New Brunswick, the comparable figure was 24 percent, while in Quebec it was 36 percent (but this was a big increase from 5 percent in 1984). In contrast, in BC, NDP candidates spent 80 percent of the limit, in Saskatchewan they spent 90 percent, and in the Yukon/NWT, they spent 73 percent (table 12.19).

There is very little information about whether the legal limit on "election expenses" has been "binding," in the sense that, if it had been higher, candidates would have spent more on their campaigns.[25]

Spending on "election expenses" relative to the limit is likely a reflection of one of two variables, or both: (i) the strength of a party in a particular province; (ii) the number of federal seats that are thought to be marginal, that is, that the party could win with extra effort or that it could lose if it fails to make a stronger effort than its rivals. By *province*, the biggest changes in terms of percentage of the limit spent between the 1979 and 1988 elections were as follows. For the NDP, the biggest increases were in Quebec, New Brunswick, Alberta and the Yukon/NWT. By 1988, NDP candidates in BC and Saskatchewan were spending 80 percent and 90 percent of the limit on "election expenses." These are provinces in which the NDP has its greatest strength.

For the Liberal party, the major areas of decline were BC, Saskatchewan and Alberta – although there was a decline in Quebec, long a Liberal stronghold – from 87 percent in 1979 to 79 percent in 1988. For the Conservative party, the opposite case prevailed in Quebec – an increase from 65 percent in 1979 to 92 percent in 1984 and 90 percent in 1988. Major increases were also recorded in Newfoundland, the Yukon/NWT and New Brunswick (table 12.19). In 1988, PC candidates in

Quebec, New Brunswick, PEI and Saskatchewan spent above the national average on "election expenses," reflecting the intensity of competition in those provinces (table 12.8).

Table 12.20 indicates that, between the 1979 and 1988 elections, a growing fraction of candidates of the three major parties spent more than 90 percent of the limit on "election expenses." It rose from 20.7 percent in 1979 to 25.2 percent in 1980 to 31.5 percent in 1988. The biggest change was for the NDP, from 3.2 percent in 1979 to 19.1 percent in 1988, and for the Conservative party, from 30.5 percent in 1979 to 50.2 percent in 1988. Liberal candidates moved in the opposite direction: while 28.4 percent spent more than 90 percent of the limit in 1979 and 34.0 percent in 1980, the fraction fell to 25.1 percent in 1988. At the other end of the spectrum, 35.8 percent of candidates of all three major parties spent less than 70 percent of the limit on "election expenses." The financial strength of Conservative party candidates can be seen in the fact that only 11.2 percent of them spent less than 70 percent of the limit as compared to 37.6 percent of Liberal party and 58.7 percent of NDP candidates.

It is possible that the growing percentage of NDP and Conservative candidates spending over 90 percent of the limit on "election expenses" reflects shifts in the ability of these parties' candidates to raise money. But this, in turn, is likely to be a reflection of their increased political strength measured in terms of a higher probability of winning more seats. However, the rising number of Tory and NDP candidates with "election expenses" equal to at least 90 percent of the limit may be attributable to the failure of the CPI-indexed limit to properly reflect the full increase in the costs of election campaigns. But if this was the case – as the NDP brief to the Royal Commission on Electoral Reform and Party Financing suggested – the same thing should have occurred for Liberal party candidates. Yet the percentage spending 90 percent or more of the limit declined between 1980 and 1988 – despite the fact that even in 1980, a slightly higher percentage of Tory candidates were spending at least 90 percent of the limit (37 percent versus 34 percent).

4.4 "Personal Expenses" in 1988

In 1988, the average level of "personal expenses" for all candidates was $1 098. Progressive Conservative party candidates had the highest average, $2 403, followed by the Liberals, $1 677, and the NDP, $1 249. The almost 700 candidates of other parties averaged only $232 (table 12.17).

The average figures conceal substantial variations in personal expenses across candidates in each party. Table 12.21 indicates that 26.1 percent of PC candidates spent more than $3 000 on personal expenses compared to 16.3 percent of Liberal candidates, 10.1 percent of NDP candidates and 1.0 percent of candidates of other parties. Five Conservative and three Liberal candidates spent over $10 000 on personal expenses. On the other hand, 19.7 percent of Conservative candidates spent less than $500; the comparable figure for the Liberals was 27.9 percent, while for the NDP it was 37.3 percent. As for candidates of other parties, 86.7 percent spent less than $500 on personal expenses. By province, the candidates spending more than $3 000 on personal expenses were most heavily concentrated in Quebec and the three Prairie provinces.

5. CANDIDATES' "OTHER EXPENSES" IN 1988

In the 1988 general election, all candidates spent $31.34 million on "election expenses" and $1.73 million on "personal expenses" according to the Chief Electoral Officer (Canada, Elections Canada 1988c). These figures, however, do *not* include all of the campaign-related expenditures of candidates that the author has called "other expenses." While the Chief Electoral Officer does not include "other expenses" in his post-election *Report of the Chief Electoral Officer Respecting Election Expenses*, he has used the term "campaign expenses" to describe "a default concept which refers to anything not an election expense [or a personal expense]. Such expenses are not covered by the spending limits, but must be reported by parties and candidates" (ibid., 1, 2). This omission is significant, because the author estimates that all candidates' "other expenses" totalled $4.7 million in 1988, an amount equal to 15 percent of the "election expenses" of all candidates. More importantly, the "other expenses" were most unevenly distributed among candidates, even among Progressive Conservative, Liberal and New Democratic candidates. Further, the large amounts of "other expenses" incurred by some candidates (e.g., at least 74 candidates of the three major parties spent more than $15 000 on "other expenses") raise serious questions both about the definition of "election expenses" in the *Canada Elections Act* and about its interpretation by the CEO in his *Guidelines*. With this "big picture" in mind, it is now necessary to explain in detail the quite complex process by which the author's estimate of candidates' "other expenses" was obtained.

5.1 Objectives and Limitations

The primary objectives of the analysis of candidates' "other expenses" in 1988 were to determine: (i) the amount of each candidate's "other expenses"; and (ii) the composition (types of outlays) of each candidate's "other expenses." The following categories of "other expenses" were specified:

1. Pre-writ expenses
2. Campaign-period expenses:
   - Unused materials
   - Fund-raising costs
   - Expenses of volunteers
   - Election-day expenses
   - Polling/research expenses
   - Poll agents' wages/expenses
   - Candidates' wages
   - Other campaign-period expenses
3. Post–election day expenses:
   - Office expenses
   - Bank charges (including interest on loans)
   - Victory party (including thank-you cards, ads, etc.)
   - Contracts
   - Other post-election day expenses.

Figure 12.2 illustrates the relationship among the three categories of expenditures by candidates associated with their election campaigns. All of these categories of "other expenses" are *invisible* to the public because the Chief Electoral Officer does not publish any information on them. In fact, the CEO does not publish even the total "other expenses" for each candidate.

There were two central problems in achieving these two objectives. First, while the CEO does not publish information on each candidate's "other expenses," his staff does compute each candidate's "other expenses" in the course of determining whether each candidate had a surplus or deficit after the campaign. However, the amount of "other expenses" is correctly computed only for those candidates who *also* had a surplus. As will be explained in more detail in section 5.2, the CEO's staff truncates the analysis of each candidate's forms that report "election expenses," "personal expenses" and the default concept of "campaign expenses" (which we have described as "other expenses") once it becomes clear that the candidate will *not* have a surplus. Thus, the CEO could provide the amount of "other expenses" only for those 721 candidates who also had a surplus. However, the CEO's staff does not prepare any analysis of the *types* of expenditures included in the "other expenses" category.

The second problem in trying to determine the amount of "other expenses" arose because of the time and cost of analysing each candidate's file in order to determine, first, the true amount of "other expenses" in the case of candidates with a *deficit*, and, second, to then

Figure 12.2
Relationship between candidate "election expenses" and "other expenses"

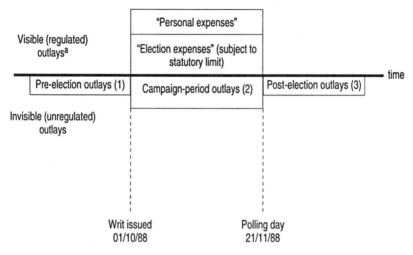

Notes: "Other expenses" = 1 + 2 + 3 (excluding capital items and transfers).
[a]As reported by CEO (1989b).

categorize the *types* of "other expenses." While the candidates with a deficit could be identified easily, there were 853 to be reviewed. Yet, about 600 were unlikely to have spent over $1 000 on "other expenses" because of the modest level of their revenues and their "election expenses." Because sampling was necessary, it was logical and efficient to correctly compute and analyse the types of "other expenses" of the "biggest spenders," defined in terms of their total "other expenses." However, another problem arose, namely, how to identify *all* of the "big spenders," i.e., including those who had a *deficit*. How this was done is explained in section 5.3 below.

5.2 "Other Expenses" of Candidates Who Also Had a Surplus
A limited picture of candidates' "other expenses" can be gained by examining the "other expenses" of the 721 candidates in 1988 who also had a surplus. Unfortunately, this data file contained only the total amount of "other expenses" as computed by the CEO's staff. The data were obtained from an electronic file on the revenues and expenditures of all candidates prepared by the CEO (referred to as file 1). File 1 incorporates more data and more recent data than was used to compile the *Report of the Chief Electoral Officer Respecting Election Expenses, 1988*. Officials responsible for election finances in the CEO's office stated that the final data for some candidates were not received until early 1991!

The CEO's purpose in preparing file 1 was to determine whether each candidate had a surplus or a deficit, so that the CEO could be sure that, where a candidate had a surplus, the surplus had been disposed of in a manner provided for by the *Canada Elections Act* (i.e., that the surplus funds had been transferred to a local association or to the candidate's party). A candidate's surplus (S) or deficit (D) is defined as follows:

$$S \text{ or } D = TR - EE - PE - OE + R$$

where

TR	=	the candidate's total revenues from contributions and transfers from party sources (riding, PTA/PTS and/or headquarters)
EE	=	"election expenses"
PE	=	"personal expenses"
OE	=	"other expenses" = campaign-related expenditures that are not EE or PE
R	=	reimbursement of half the candidate's "election expenses" (if he/she obtained 15 percent of the votes).

A surplus (S) exists if $TR + R > EE + PE + OE$. A deficit (D) exists if $TR + R < EE + PE + OE$.

To determine the correct amount of each candidate's "other expenses," the CEO's staff had to distinguish capital items (e.g., a loan or advance) and transfers (e.g., from or to party headquarters, the riding or provincial association) from campaign-related expenditures that were not defined as "election expenses" or "personal expenses."[26] This time-consuming process was completed *only* if it was clear that the candidate was going to have a surplus, as defined above. Where it was clear that the candidate was going to have a *deficit*, the process of computing "other expenses" was truncated by the CEO's staff. Thus, in file 1, the value of OE is correct only for those candidates who *also* had a surplus, but *not* for those who had a deficit.[27] For those candidates with a deficit, the CEO's staff set $S = 0$ and then derived from the formula above an estimate of "other expenses," which they called "estimated other expenses" (EOE). For candidates with a deficit, this figure is wrong because of the truncation of the process of disentangling capital transactions and transfers from the true "other expense" items recorded in part 7 of the F206A form filed by each candidate.

Tables 12.22 and 12.23 were prepared from the data in file 1 on the "other expenses" of the 721 candidates who *also* had a surplus according to the CEO's calculations. Note that the total "other expenses" of the candidates with a surplus amounted to $3.19 million, while the author's estimate of the total "other expenses" of *all* candidates was $4.7 million. (See section 5.4 below.) Table 12.22 indicates that 26.6 percent of Progressive Conservative candidates, 12.1 percent of Liberal candidates and 2.4 percent of NDP candidates who had a surplus in 1988 each spent more than $10 000 on "other expenses." Thirteen Conservative party and five Liberal party candidates each spent more than $25 000 on "other expenses," the highest being $78 000 by an unsuccessful Conservative party candidate. On the other hand, table 12.22 reveals that 20.6 percent of PC, 29.7 percent of Liberal, 41.8 percent of New Democratic and 80.2 percent of other candidates spent less than $1 000 on "other expenses."

The average level of "other expenses" for candidates who also had a surplus was $7 496 for Conservative party candidates, $4 486 for Liberal party candidates and $1 946 for NDP candidates. The average for all 721 candidates was $4 430. This amount understates the total for *all* candidates, because it excludes those candidates who ended their campaign in 1988 with a deficit. Some of these candidates ($N = 73$) were included in file 2, discussed below.

Table 12.23 indicates that "other expenses" were equal to a substantial fraction of "election expenses" for Conservative party candidates in several provinces. In Quebec, for example, 42 of 75 Conservative party candidates spent an average of $15 666 on "other expenses," while all Conservative candidates averaged $42 474 in "election expenses." In Newfoundland, "other expenses" for six of the seven Conservative candidates averaged $15 617, as compared to "election expenses" of $42 016. In BC, 31 of 32 Conservative candidates added an average of 25 percent ($9 527) to their "election expenses" by means of "other expenses." The figures for "other expenses" for candidates of the Liberal party were typically well below those of their Tory rivals, but above those of New Democratic candidates. In Ontario, 85 of 99 Liberal candidates spent an average of $6 484 on "other expenses," as well as an average $37 415 on "election expenses." Their "other expenses" were slightly above those of rival Conservative candidates in this case. The Liberals' figures for Nova Scotia were similar to those for Ontario, and again they slightly outspent the Tories in respect to "other expenses." For the NDP, average "other expenses" were of some consequence only in BC. There, 30 of 32 candidates spent $3 766 in addition to "election expenses" of $38 156.

5.3 "Other Expenses" of Candidates Who Were "Big Spenders" in Terms of "Other Expenses" (File 2)

The analysis of the data on "other expenses" in file 1 (candidates who also had a surplus) is unsatisfactory for several reasons. First, it omits candidates who had a deficit, and they may have incurred substantial "other expenses." Second, it was not possible to disaggregate "other expenses" into the categories identified in section 5.1 above.

The author sought to overcome these limitations by selecting a sample of candidates who were "big spenders" in terms of their total "other expenses" and then examining each of their files in detail. Unfortunately, it was not possible to identify all the "big spenders" (those above some arbitrary level) *without* also examining in detail the files of hundreds of candidates – in principle, all of those who had a deficit. We knew only the correct "other expenses" for those candidates with a surplus, and we knew that 95 of those 721 candidates had spent over $10 000 on "other expenses" (table 12.22). For the candidates with a deficit, we knew only their "estimated other expenses" (*EOE*) computed from the formula cited in section 5.2 above. But this calculation incorrectly estimates their "other expenses."

There being no practicable alternative, the "big spenders" (in terms of "other expenses") were arbitrarily defined as those candidates whose "estimated other expenses" (*EOE*) were greater than $10 000.[28] Note that this list of 277 candidates (called file 2) included the 204 candidates in file 1 (those with a surplus).

Until *each* candidate's file was reviewed by the author, it was not possible to determine the *correct* amount of his/her "other expenses," i.e., outlays from tax-receipted contributions that were not "election expenses" *or* "personal expenses" for those candidates who had a *deficit*. Therefore, the tabulations of "other expenses" for the 277 candidates in file 2 (the "big spenders") include candidates whose actual "other expenses" were *under* $10 000 because it was *not possible* to know the correct amount of "other expenses" for those candidates who had a deficit, as defined above. For each of the 277 candidates in file 2 (the "big spenders"), the correct amount of their "other expenses" was determined by a careful examination of the various forms in his/her file.[29] Then these "other expenses" were grouped into the categories listed in section 5.1.

While file 2 is a sample selected on the basis that the candidates were "big spenders" in terms of "other expenses," it provides some very useful insights into the amount and composition of "other expenses." Overall, these 277 candidates spent $3.16 million on "other expenses" out of a total of $4.7 million for *all* candidates in 1988 (see section 5.4 below). We turn now to the analysis of the 277 candidates who were "big spenders" on "other expenses" in 1988.

Total "Other Expenses"
As table 12.24 indicates, *after eliminating capital items and transfers* from "estimated other expenses" as calculated by the CEO, only 48 percent

of the 277 candidates in file 2 actually spent over $10 000 on "other expenses." On average, the 277 "big spenders" spent $11 394 on "other expenses" (table 12.24). Candidates who had a deficit ($N = 73$) spent an average of $13 348 on "other expenses," while those who had a surplus ($N = 203$) spent an average of $10 694 on "other expenses." Table 12.24 indicates that 10 Conservative party candidates and 4 Liberal party candidates spent more than $30 000 on "other expenses" in 1988. At the other end of the distribution, 26.7 percent of the 277 candidates spent less than $4 000 on "other expenses," and there was little variation in this percentage among the three main parties.

For two reasons, the remainder of the analysis of candidates' "other expenses" is based on all 277 candidates in file 2 (the "big spenders") even though a substantial number in fact spent less than $10 000 on "other expenses." First, the file does capture the "big spenders" because the average ($11 394) is far more than the average ($4 430) of the 721 candidates who also had a surplus (file 1). Second, the entire sample provides insights into what items were included in candidates' "other expenses."

Of the 277 "big spenders" in file 2, 155 were Progressive Conservatives, 69 were Liberals, 39 were New Democrats and 14 were Christian Heritage party candidates. Average outlays on "other expenses" by party were $14 200 for Tories, $11 400 for Liberals, $3 700 for NDP candidates and $1 500 for Christian Heritage candidates.

Types of "Other Expenses"
The amounts in the 14 detailed categories of "other expenses" defined by the author in section 5.1 are reported in table 12.25 for the 277 candidates in file 2 ("big spenders"). Four categories accounted for 67.7 percent of total "other expenses": poll agents,[30] 27.6 percent; pre-writ expenses, 18.3 percent; victory parties, 13.7 percent; and fundraising costs, 8.1 percent. Payments to poll agents were concentrated in Quebec: 82.9 percent of the total, although only the Liberal and Conservative candidates reported making such payments. In addition, the Conservative and Liberal candidates made sizable outlays for poll agents in Nova Scotia and Newfoundland. One candidate in Nova Scotia spent $21 100 on poll agents. Seven candidates spent over $15 000 on poll agents.

Victory parties (and thank-you cards/ads) cost the 277 candidates an average of almost $2 700. However, six candidates (five Conservatives) spent over $10 000. Given the fact that their official "election expenses" were about $50 000, it behooves us to ask if Canadian taxpayers should subsidize victory parties that cost one-fifth of the amount spent on statutorily limited election expenses. Recall from chapter 8 that the value of tax credits in 1988 was equal to 47 percent of the value of contributions by individuals to parties and candidates.

Fund-raising costs amounted to 8.1 percent of total "other expenses" reported by the 277 candidates in file 2 (the "big spenders"). Only 74 of 277 candidates reported *any* amount in this category and, of these, 15 reported $1 001 to $2 000, 17 reported spending $2 001 to $5 000, while 16 reported spending over $5 000. Five candidates spent more than $10 000 on fund-raising, the highest being $21 600. The expenses for the highest-spending candidate amounted to 42.5 percent of total revenues raised. Another candidate who generated over $92 000 in revenues spent $19 600 on a dinner featuring the leader. In the same riding, another candidate spent $10 400 to raise just over $58 000.

The 277 candidates in file 2 spent an average of $726 (or 6.4 percent) of total "other expenses" on polling and research (table 12.25). However, this average conceals a bipolar distribution: 195 candidates spent nothing on this category, while 21 spent over $3 000 and 10 spent over $5 000. The highest expenditure, $9 500, was incurred by a Conservative candidate who was in a very close race in Western Canada. Indeed, the five highest spenders on polling and research were Conservative party candidates.

Two other categories – although modest in average amount – merit comment. First, there is the payment of wages/salary to candidates. Only 19 of 277 candidates were reimbursed for lost wages/salary: 13 New Democrats, 3 Liberals and 3 Tories. The highest amount was $11 400, but 7 candidates received $2 000 or less and 18 received $6 000 or less. While this category of "other expenses" was not included in the CEO's 1988 *Guidelines,* he later issued a letter to all parties in July 1988 (at the request of the NDP) defining the payment of wages/salary to candidates as "other expenses" rather than "election expenses." If a candidate's agent (or party) reimburses volunteers for lost wages/salary when they are working on an election campaign, such outlays are classified as "election expenses" and are therefore subject to the statutory limit.

The second modest category raises more serious questions. In 1988, 7 of the 277 candidates spent a total of $19 800 on contracts issued after voting day. One candidate spent $14 000 on such contracts.[31] A party official stated that the contracts were, in fact, rewards for work by volunteers *during* the campaign and not for being poll agents. If these individuals had been paid during the campaign, the candidate would have exceeded the limit by about $8 000. The central issue is this: should candidates be permitted to issue contracts after election day to individuals who were highly active "volunteers" during the campaign? Unless it is clear that the work performed *after* election day is commensurate with the payment, it is hard to avoid the inference that such contracts are a means to circumvent the limit on "election expenses."

Temporal Distribution of "Other Expenses"
The distribution of "other expenses" prior to the issue of the writs, during the campaign period and after election day is described in table 12.26. It indicates that Conservative candidates spent 18 percent of "other expenses" prior to the calling of the election, while the Liberals spent 20 percent and the NDP candidates spent 14 percent in this period. Candidates of all three parties spent virtually the same percentage of their "other expenses" during the campaign period: 58 percent for the PCs and New Democrats and 59 percent for the Liberals. There was somewhat more variation in the percentage spent *after* election day: Conservative candidates, 24 percent; Liberals, 21 percent; New Democrats, 29 percent. In absolute terms, however, the differences in pre-writ spending were much greater: an average of $2 554 for Conservative candidates versus $2 276 for Liberal candidates and $504 for the New Democratic candidates. As table 12.26 indicates, pre-writ spending was concentrated in Manitoba, Ontario, BC and Alberta for the Tories, in BC and Ontario for the Liberals and in BC for the NDP.

Table 12.27 indicates that 48 percent of the 277 candidates spent nothing on "other expenses" during the pre-writ period. This fact is consistent with the finding by Carty and Erickson (1991), who indicate that one-third of the winners of nomination contests spent nothing on their campaign, while 70 percent spent $500 or less, and 20 percent were believed to have spent more than $1 000.[32] While the average was $1 200, the median expenditure was only $100.

Of the 277 candidates in file 2 (the "big spenders"), 13.7 percent spent more than $4 000 in the pre-writ period (table 12.27). However, the figures from Carty and Erickson (1991)[33] and those in table 12.27 are not closely comparable because theirs refer to the costs of obtaining the *nomination*, while those in table 12.27 refer to outlays by candidates *prior* to the date the writ was issued.[34] Our analysis indicates that three Conservative and two Liberal candidates spent over $20 000 on pre-writ expenses. Most of the money went into printing brochures, polling and the rental of office space. However, one candidate who spent $34 200 on pre-writ expenses provided no explanation for $23 800 of this amount, and the CEO did not require any details based on the information in the file.

With respect to "other expenses" incurred *during* the campaign period, the differences in absolute terms were much greater: in terms of *average* outlays, the Progressive Conservative party candidates spent $8 205, versus $6 772 for Liberals and $2 117 for New Democrats. By province, the Conservative candidates' "other expenses" were concentrated in Quebec, Nova Scotia and Newfoundland – largely due to the payment of poll agents. Liberal candidates' outlays on "other expenses" during the campaign period were concentrated in Quebec and Nova Scotia, for the same reason. For the NDP, expenditures were concentrated in Ontario and BC. During the campaign period, 32 percent of the 277 candidates spent less than $2 000 on "other expenses," while 27 percent spent more than $10 000 (table 12.28).

The average outlay on "other expenses" *after* voting day was $3 449 for Conservative candidates, $2 400 for Liberal candidates and $1 057 for New Democratic candidates. Table 12.29 indicates that 59.2 percent of all the 277 candidates in file 2 (the "big spenders") spent $2 000 or less on "other expenses" after election day. On the other hand, 7.6 percent spent more than $7 000.

5.4   The Bottom Line: Estimating Total "Other Expenses" for All Candidates

The author's estimate of total "other expenses" for *all* candidates was derived in the following way. For the 721 candidates in file 1 (i.e., those that *also* had a surplus), "other expenses" amounted to $3.194 million, or an average of $4 430 per candidate (table 12.22). The correct amount of "other expenses" of the 277 candidates in file 2 amounted to $3.156 million, or an average of $11 394 per candidate (table 12.25). However, files 1 and 2 overlapped, because file 2 (the "big spenders") contains 204 candidates who also had a surplus and who were therefore included in file 1 (CEO file) as well. The analysis of file 2 revealed that the 73 candidates who also had a deficit averaged $13 348 on "other expenses" for a total of $974 406. Therefore, this figure should be added to the total for file 1 ($3.194 million) to obtain a total of $4.168 million. This figure represents the outlays on "other expenses" by 278 PC candidates, 248 Liberal and 173 New Democratic candidates, as well as 95 candidates from other parties. To estimate the "other expenses" of the *remaining* candidates, the averages reported in table 12.22 were scaled down[35] to reflect the fact that the "big spenders" had already been captured in file 1 or file 2. At the *outside*, it was estimated that these remaining candidates spent $530 000 on "other expenses." When the various estimates were combined, total "other expenses" of candidates in 1988 amounted to $4.7 million.

The purpose of section 5 has been to provide the best possible estimate of the amount of money federal candidates spent on their 1988 campaigns *outside* the legally limited and officially defined categories of "election expenses" and "personal expenses." There are several reasons why the amount of total "other expenses" is important. First, the Chief

Electoral Officer does not publish information on "other expenses" – even though such outlays are financed by contributions for which receipts for the tax credit are issued. Second, the CEO's estimate of "other expenses" made available to the Royal Commission on Electoral Reform and Party Financing is wrong, because the CEO's staff used the truncation rule. Third, if candidates' "other expenses" are large, there is a policy issue relating to the definition of "election expenses" in the *Canada Elections Act* and its interpretation by the CEO in his *Guidelines,* if it is also true that "other expenses" are a reasonably close substitute for "election expenses" in terms of helping a candidate get elected.

Total "other expenses" of all candidates in the 1988 federal election amounted to $4.7 million, the equivalent of 15 percent of all candidates' official "election expenses." Obviously there can be debate about the significance of this figure. If almost every candidate spent 15 percent of the "election expenses" on "other expenses," the electoral consequences are likely to be roughly neutral, although an extra 15 percent on the "election expenses" for a candidate who is at the limit is likely to be more important than it would be for a candidate who is well below the limit. However, on the basis of file 2 (the "big spenders"), it is clear that the "other expenses" were highly concentrated in 1988, i.e., a small percentage of candidates had "other expenses" that were large relative to their "election expenses" (e.g., 74 spent more than $15 000 on "other expenses," of which 55 were PC candidates). In close races, a higher level of "other expenses" may alter the electoral outcome. More research is needed to link the level of "other expenses" to the closeness (ex ante) of electoral races. A priori, one would expect that the largest outlays on "other expenses" would be found in two situations that may overlap: where a challenger tries to overcome an incumbent's advantage by spending more outside the legal definition of "election expenses," and where the candidates believe early on, perhaps before the writ is issued, that the race will be a close one. Then they will try to use "other expenses" to help their campaign, knowing that they (and their rivals) will be going to the limit on "election expenses."[36]

6. FREQUENCY OF REIMBURSEMENT

A candidate must receive at least 15 percent of the popular vote to be eligible for reimbursement of one-half of his/her "election expenses." Over the past three general elections, there has been a slight increase in the percentage of *all* candidates who qualified for reimbursement, from 43 percent in 1980 to 46 percent in 1984 and to 47 percent in 1988 (table 12.30). However, the average conceals more than it reveals. Over three-quarters of the candidates of the three largest parties received reimbursement, but only 1 percent to 2 percent of candidates of other parties or independents received reimbursement. The reimbursement rate for candidates of the three largest parties rose from 76.1 percent in 1980 to 78.0 percent in 1984 and to 82.9 percent in 1988. The comparable percentages for all other candidates were 1.2 percent, 0.7 percent and 1.7 percent respectively.

In 1988, 293 of 295 Conservative candidates received reimbursement. In 1984, all Tory candidates received reimbursement, but only 215 of 282 were reimbursed in 1980. While a higher fraction of New Democratic candidates was eligible for reimbursement in 1988 than in 1980, only 57.6 percent received reimbursement in 1988.[37] A smaller fraction of Liberal party candidates received reimbursement in 1984 (84.4 percent) than in 1988 (89.8 percent) (table 12.30).

Recall from table 12.1 that Progressive Conservative party candidates received $6.06 million in reimbursement from the federal government, and that none of this was "taxed" away by party headquarters. Liberal candidates received $4.66 million in reimbursement, but party headquarters "taxed" away $2.27 million of this amount. NDP candidates received $2.84 million, but party headquarters required the candidates in BC to hand over part to the provincial section to finance their share of the cost of the national campaign.

Table 12.31 shows that, if the threshold for reimbursement had been 10 percent in 1988 instead of 15 percent, the number of candidates eligible for reimbursement would have increased from 739 to 856. However, 100 of the additional 117 candidates who would have been reimbursed with the lower threshold would have come from the three main parties. If the threshold had been reduced to 5 percent of the *popular vote* (instead of 15 percent of the vote on a riding-by-riding basis), an additional 203 candidates would have been eligible for reimbursement in 1988. Virtually all candidates of the three main parties would have been reimbursed, but the biggest beneficiaries would have been candidates of the Reform and Christian Heritage parties (table 12.31).

7. SURPLUS/DEFICIT OF CANDIDATES

7.1 Measures of Surplus/Deficit

It is useful to define three different measures of a candidate's surplus or deficit:

- Campaign Surplus (or Deficit) = $TR - EE - PE$
- Post Reimbursement Campaign Surplus (or Deficit) = $TR - EE - PE + R$
- Surplus (or Deficit) = $TR - EE - PE - OE + R$ where the variables are as defined in section 5.1.

As noted in table 12.1, all candidates combined had a "post-reimbursement campaign surplus" of $6.8 million in 1979, $7.2 million in 1980, $9.9 million in 1984 and $13.2 million in 1988.[38] However, when "other expenses" are taken into account, the CEO states that all candidates had a combined surplus of over $8 million in 1984 (Canada, Elections Canada 1989a, 47) and $9.6 million in 1988 (Canada, Elections Canada 1991, 10). This measure is really the *sum* of all candidates' surplus (after deducting "other expenses"), rather than the algebraic sum of all candidates' surplus or deficit.[39]

Table 12.32 recasts the data in table 12.1 for the three main parties to examine their candidates' surplus as defined by the CEO *after* "other expenses" have been taken into account. "Other expenses" totalled $3.6 million for the three main parties in 1988, but this figure omits the "other expenses" of candidates who did *not* have a surplus (a total of 252 of the 885). Another estimate of candidates' surplus using the estimate of "other expenses" of $4.7 million derived in the previous section is provided below. In any event, on the basis of the data reported in table 12.32, as a group the candidates of each of the three main parties ran a "campaign deficit," i.e., *before* receiving the reimbursement of half their "election expenses." The total "campaign deficit" of $4.2 million was far smaller than the sum of reimbursements, $13.55 million. The result is that, collectively, the candidates of the three main parties ended up with a surplus of $9.4 million when "other expenses" were taken into account. This figure is quite consistent with that of the CEO (Canada, Elections Canada 1991, 10).

For the 1988 general election, over three-quarters of Progressive Conservative and Liberal candidates reported a surplus after their "other expenses" were taken into account (table 12.33).[40] Only 57 percent of NDP candidates reported a surplus. While all but one Conservative candidate reporting a surplus *also* received reimbursement, there were 14 Liberal and 24 NDP candidates who had a surplus, even though they did not receive reimbursement for half of their "election expenses" (table 12.33). Ninety-one (or 13 percent) candidates of parties *other* than the Liberal, PC or NDP reported a surplus – even though only 11 were reimbursed for half of their "election expenses."

The average size of surplus (for those candidates reporting a surplus) was just over $20 000 for Conservative candidates, almost $13 000 for Liberals and $10 000 for NDP candidates in 1988. Twenty-one of 72 Reform Party candidates had a surplus, the average of which was $6 650. One-half of the 63 Christian Heritage party candidates had a surplus, the average was $3 368 (table 12.33; figure 12.3).

Table 12.34[41] provides data on the average surplus of candidates by party and by province. The provinces in which the highest percentage of candidates of the three main parties reported a surplus were BC (90 percent), Saskatchewan (88 percent), Nova Scotia (79 percent) and Ontario (77 percent). A candidate's surplus is dependent primarily on the relationship between (i) total revenues and "election expenses" and (ii) the amount of "other expenses." The relationship between total revenues and "election expenses" can be seen by looking at the candidates' "campaign surplus" by party and province in table 12.8. To put the provincial *averages* in perspective, note that, for Canada as a whole, the average campaign surplus for Conservative party candidates in 1988 was $2 777. The other two main parties had *deficits*: Liberal party ($1 834); NDP ($2 938).

The main reason why so many BC candidates had a surplus is that Conservative ($11 215) and NDP ($5 322) candidates had, on average, a large "campaign surplus" while Liberal candidates had only a slight "campaign *deficit*" ($1 471). Tory candidates had an average campaign surplus of $4 395, while their rivals had deficits. However, in most cases, their reimbursement minus their "other expenses" more than offset their campaign deficit. In Nova Scotia, Tory and Liberal candidates had on average a "campaign surplus," while New Democratic candidates, had on average a deficit. In Ontario, Conservative candidates had on average a "campaign surplus," while Liberals "broke even" and New Democratic candidates had a "campaign deficit" (table 12.8).

At the other end of the spectrum were Quebec (56 percent of candidates reporting a surplus – largely due to the NDP), Newfoundland (62 percent) and Manitoba (62 percent). In Quebec and Manitoba, the candidates of all three parties had, on average, a "campaign deficit," which was larger in Manitoba than in Quebec. In Quebec, the level of "other expenses" was high for the Tories and Liberals; hence, fewer candidates ended up with a surplus (tables 12.23, 12.26). The low percentage with a surplus in Manitoba was largely due to the low level of revenues relative to "election expenses" (table 12.8).

While all Conservative party candidates reporting a surplus in 1988 had an average surplus of $20 080 (table 12.33), the highest surpluses were reported in New Brunswick ($25 556), Saskatchewan ($25 061) and BC ($22 578). Moreover, all but one Conservative candidate in these three provinces reported a surplus. Table 12.8 indicates that the average *campaign* surplus was $11 989 in New Brunswick, $4 395 in Saskatchewan and $11 215 in BC – the highest of all provinces except Newfoundland ($7 577). The provinces in which Conservative candidates had the smallest surpluses were Manitoba ($9 558) and PEI, Newfoundland and

Figure 12.3
Candidate "election expenses," reimbursement and surplus, 1988 general election

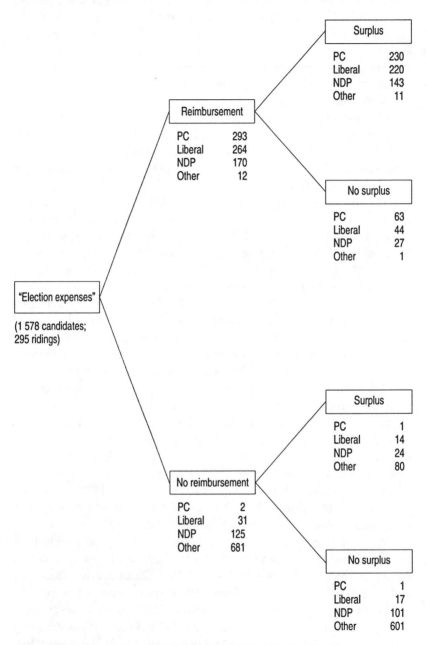

Source: Tabulated from data provided by Frederick B. Slattery, Elections Canada.

the Yukon/NWT – each about $14 000. Moreover, fewer candidates in these provinces reported a surplus. In Manitoba, Conservative candidates had an average campaign *deficit* of $7 886, the second largest in Canada (table 12.8).

The biggest interprovincial variation in both the fraction of candidates reporting a surplus in 1988 and the average size of those doing so occurred among NDP candidates. For example, none of the NDP candidates in New Brunswick reported a surplus, while 30 of 32 candidates in BC reported an average surplus of $19 340, which was almost twice the national average for NDP candidates ($10 421) (table 12.33). Interestingly, 27 of 75 NDP candidates in Quebec reported a surplus that averaged $5 329. Recall, however, that the average "election expenses" of the NDP candidates in Quebec was $17 053, only half that of the other parties (table 12.18). In contrast, 57 Liberal candidates in Quebec reported a surplus; the average was $14 557. Yet table 12.8 indicates that, on average, Liberal candidates had a *campaign deficit* of $3 737. Thus, their reimbursement more than offset "other expenses." Note from table 12.34 that there was far less interprovincial variation in both the percentage of Liberal candidates reporting a surplus and its average size. The highest average surplus was in PEI ($17 171), followed by Newfoundland ($16 388). The lowest were in the Yukon/NWT ($3 989) and Alberta ($5 851).

Table 12.35 provides some descriptive data on the 27 candidates in 1988 who ended up with a surplus of over $40 000 after "other expenses" were deducted.[42] The objective was to determine the relative importance of revenues raised and of various expenditures in determining the existence of the largest surpluses. The highest surplus reported was $96 283, and this was despite the fact that the candidate spent over $7 000 on "other expenses." In general, a large surplus is the result of large revenues rather than of modest expenditures. Seventeen[43] of the 27 candidates with a surplus over $40 000 raised more than $80 000 (excluding reimbursement). Fourteen of the 27 had been cabinet ministers during the previous Mulroney administration and 17 had been a government MP or minister. Overall, 20 of the 27 individuals with a surplus over $40 000 were incumbents, and 15 won re-election. Six of the seven challengers with a large surplus were elected.

Using additional information from the CEO, other measures of candidates' surplus in the 1988 federal election were derived. *Before* "other expenses" were taken into account, 565 of 1 574 candidates had a "post-reimbursement campaign deficit" or broke even (table 12.36). By party, 6.7 percent of Conservative party candidates, 10.9 percent of Liberal party candidates and 29.8 percent of NDP candidates had a "post-reimbursement campaign deficit" or broke even. Recall from table 12.30 that 293 of 295 PC candidates, 264 of 294 Liberal candidates and 170 of 295 NDP candidates received reimbursement. The average "post-reimbursement campaign deficit" (i.e., before "other expenses") was $4 941 for Conservative candidates, $5 828 for Liberals and $3 243 for NDP candidates. The distribution of the size of "post-reimbursement campaign deficits" *before* "other expenses" is given in table 12.37. It indicates that 7 Conservative, 13 Liberal and 19 New Democratic candidates had deficits, before "other expenses" but after reimbursements, of over $5 000. Only a handful of candidates of all parties had a "post-reimbursement deficit" of over $15 000.

7.2 The "Bottom Line"

The figures for total and average surplus by party in table 12.38 are very close to those reported in table 12.33, based on less complete (earlier) data compiled by the CEO. The most important point to note is that, after the dust had settled, 233 Conservative party candidates ended up with an average surplus of $20 000. A similar number of Liberal candidates ended the 1988 election with an average surplus of $12 800. Some 166 New Democratic candidates finished with an average surplus of $10 500, while 92 candidates of other parties ended with an average surplus of $2 700.

The total *net* surplus of all candidates in 1988 was less than $8.26 million,[44] if *both* surpluses and deficits are taken into account rather than the figure of $9.6 million that is used by the CEO (Canada, Elections Canada 1991, 10). Recall, however, that the total amount of reimbursement of candidates' "election expenses" by the federal government was $13.7 million (table 12.1). In other words, even *after* the reimbursement, federal candidates as a group ended up with a net surplus of about $8 million. However, note that this amount is *before* amounts transferred to the party in the case of the Liberals and the NDP. (For example, the Liberal party recovered $2.27 million from its candidates in 1988.) This raises the question of why much of the federal direct subsidy of candidates' "election expenses" should end up going to local associations or to parties, since in most cases the candidates of the Conservative, Liberal and New Democratic parties have been able to raise enough money to cover their election-related outlays (including "other expenses") *before* any reimbursement.

8. CONCLUSIONS

It is clear that, over the past four general elections, candidates of federal parties, as a whole, have been able to become "self-financing." That is, even before reimbursement of half their "election expenses," candidates have been able to raise enough money to cover their "election expenses" and "personal expenses." Perhaps because "election expenses" are limited to fairly modest amounts (the average limit in 1988 was $46 900), the 50 percent reimbursement rate for candidates who get 15 percent of the vote (293 Conservatives, 264 Liberals, 170 New Democrats and 12 other candidates in 1988) far more than covers the tiny shortfall between revenue and total election-related outlays.[45]

A critical point for policy makers is this: about two-thirds of the total reimbursement to federal candidates ($13.2 million in 1988) is surplus to the *total* costs of their election campaigns. This is even *after* taking into account estimated total "other expenses" (*not* reported by the CEO) of $4.7 million in 1988. To summarize, the 1 578 candidates to become MPs in 1988 generated total revenues of $32.5 million. They spent $31.34 million on official "election expenses," $1.73 million on "personal expenses," and $4.7 million on "other expenses." As a group, candidates received $13.42 million in reimbursement. Thus, the "bottom line" is that candidates ended up with a surplus of $8.05 million in 1988 (not the $9.6 million reported by the CEO in his 1991 Statutory Report). While the Liberal and New Democratic parties sought to "capture" part of this amount by requiring some or all of their candidates to transfer to party headquarters part of their reimbursement (the Liberal party collected $2.27 million), it appears that several million dollars of the surplus ended up in the accounts of riding associations.[46] It should be noted, however, that candidates reported to the CEO that local associations had provided them with $4.32 million and that parties had provided $4.48 million (table 12.3) to help them finance their campaigns. (These figures, however, do not agree with those reported by the parties; see table 12.4a.)

The financial strength of the Conservative party candidates in 1988 can be seen in a few key figures. On average, Conservative candidates raised $45 400 or $12 800 *more* than the average for Liberal candidates and $22 300 *more* than that for NDP candidates. The gap was not quite so large in terms of average "election expenses." The Tory candidates spent an average of $40 200, which was on average $7 400 *more* than was spent by their Liberal rivals and $15 400 *more* than was spent by their NDP rivals. While the Conservative candidates' average revenues *exceeded* their average "election expenses" and "personal expenses" by $2 800, the other two parties' candidates had a "campaign deficit": an average of $1 800 for Liberal candidates and of $2 900 for NDP candidates.

The *number* of contributions from individuals to individual candidates rose steadily over the past four general elections, from 67 300 in 1979 to 104 800 in 1988. Over the same period, contributions from individuals formed an increasing fraction of the total number of contributions (i.e., including those from corporations and unions) – from 75.1 percent in 1979 to 89.3 percent in 1984, with a slight drop to 86.9 percent in 1988. (By comparison, the number of contributions from individuals giving to a party in election years increased from 119 300 in 1979 (116 800 in 1980) to 211 000 in 1984, but then fell slightly to 208 300 in 1988 (table 8.1).)

Contributions from individuals accounted for 46 percent of Progressive Conservative party candidates' revenues in 1988, as compared with 39 percent for Liberal party candidates and 34 percent for NDP candidates. However, the most important differences in the sources of candidates' revenues by party lay in two other areas. First, while Tory candidates, as a group, raised 35 percent of their revenues from corporations and Liberal candidates raised 27 percent from corporations, NDP candidates raised only 2.7 percent from this source. On the other hand, trade unions accounted for 16 percent of NDP candidates' revenues, while other parties' candidates received almost no money from unions. Second, Conservative party candidates were less dependent on intraparty sources (ridings, party headquarters) than were their rivals: 18.1 percent of total revenues, versus 32.5 percent for Liberal candidates and 44.1 percent for NDP candidates. However, these figures do *not* take into account transfers from candidates to party headquarters (in the form of part of the reimbursement in the case of Liberals and New Democrats) and transfers of candidates' surplus to their riding association. Unfortunately, the data filed with the CEO or available from the parties do not permit us to determine accurately either the gross or net flows within each party.

The analysis of candidates' campaign-related expenditures indicated that "other expenses" *besides* those reported by the CEO ("election expenses" and "personal expenses") amounted to about $4.7 million in 1988, or some 15 percent of official "election expenses." These "other expenses" were paid for by tax-receipted contributions, and thus should be made public for each candidate. They arise because a number of potentially important campaign-related outlays are not defined as "election expenses" (and hence subject to the limit) or as "personal expenses" in the *Canada Elections Act*, as interpreted by the CEO in his *Guidelines*. If every candidate incurred about the same absolute amount or percentage of "other expenses," and such outlays were not reasonably close substitutes for "election expenses," then these "other expenses" would be of little policy significance. The analysis in this chapter indicates that "other expenses" were highly asymmetrically distributed in 1988. For many candidates, they were modest: for example, for the 630 candidates of the three main parties who *also* reported a surplus, 54 percent had "other expenses" of less than $3 000. However, some 155 Conservative candidates spent an average of $14 208 on "other expenses," while 69 Liberal candidates spent an average of $11 449 on "other expenses," and 39 New Democratic candidates averaged $3 678. Almost 60 percent of these outlays occurred *during* the campaign period, the largest single expense being for "poll agents." In a very few cases, the candidates' "other expenses" *exceeded* their "election expenses." The failure of the CEO to report candidates' "other expenses" is a major gap in the present regulatory regime.

The data for the four general elections reveal that an increasing fraction of candidates of all of the major parties is able to raise more revenue than is necessary to cover their total campaign-related expenditures. In 1988, for example, candidates eligible for the 50 percent reimbursement needed to raise (on average) only about $32 600[47] to cover their campaign-related expenditures, *less* the reimbursement, even if they spent to the limit on "election expenses." Yet in 1988, 82 percent of Tory candidates, 57 percent of Liberal candidates and 34 percent of New Democratic candidates raised *over* $30 000 from various sources. Thus, after all campaign-related outlays and the reimbursement were taken into account, 279 Conservative, 262 Liberal and 207 New Democratic candidates ended up with a surplus. The average surplus of Conservative party candidates was $19 957, while that for the Liberal party candidates was $12 809 and that for NDP candidates was $10 529. The frequency and size of the candidates' surpluses stand in contrast to the ability of parties to finance their campaign-related expenditures in election years and the reimbursement of only 22.5 percent of their "election expenses."

PART V

REFORMING THE REGULATORY REGIME

13

PROBLEMS WITH THE REGULATORY REGIME

1. INTRODUCTION

Most royal commissions are created to address a problem or set of problems either in an existing public policy or in an area that might be addressed by government action. The Royal Commission on Electoral Reform and Party Financing was clearly designed to address a host of concerns and problems related to the financing of federal parties and candidates since the *Election Expenses Act* was adopted in 1974. The purpose of this chapter is to identify and describe the most important problems associated with those aspects of the *Canada Elections Act* that deal with the financing of parties and candidates. Some of these problems were first identified, briefly, in chapter 2. Others became apparent in the detailed analysis of the revenues and expenditures of parties (chaps. 4 to 11) and of candidates (chap. 12). Some problems, however, emerged from the analysis of the literature and public debate on the raising and spending of money in politics. This chapter provides a comprehensive review of the problems, in preparation for the proposals for reform contained in the next chapter.

The problems and potential policy issues are grouped into five categories. Section 2 examines political activities whose financing is not presently regulated, such as campaigns for the leadership of parties and trust funds. Section 3 examines asymmetries in the use of the tax credit and its extension to the financing of leadership campaigns and party conventions. Section 4 analyses the definition of "election expenses" and how the timing of campaign-related expenditures by parties can affect their "election expenses." Section 5 is devoted to an extensive discussion of the definition of "election expenses" of candidates, including the ways in which the Chief Electoral Officer has interpreted the definition in the *Canada Elections Act*. Section 6 touches briefly on two advantages enjoyed by incumbents: the franking privilege and advertising by government departments and Crown corporations. Finally, the conclusions are set out in section 7. The proposals for reform come in the next chapter.

2. ACTIVITIES NOT PRESENTLY REGULATED

Although the regulatory regime governing the financing of federal parties and candidates in Canada is extensive, there are some important political activities whose financing is not regulated. These include leadership campaigns, nomination campaigns, the post-nomination but pre-writ activities of candidates, most of the activities of riding associations, trust funds and the expenditures of advocacy (or "third-party") groups during election campaigns. In this section each is examined with the objective of determining whether regulation is called for. Where regulation seems appropriate, an outline of its nature is provided in chapter 14.

2.1   Leadership Campaigns

Even though they can involve raising and spending millions of dollars and are often financed in part by contributions for which a tax receipt is issued, campaigns for the leadership of federal parties are not regulated under the *Canada Elections Act*.

Expenditures on leadership campaigns have grown rapidly. In 1967, Robert Stanfield spent $150 000 on his campaign to become leader of the Progressive Conservative party.[1] In 1976, Joe Clark won the leadership race and spent little more ($168 353) than did Stanfield nine years earlier, although four other candidates each spent considerably more ($267 000 to $343 000). In 1983, the three leading candidates each spent more than $1 million. This amounted to a six-fold increase in 16 years in terms of nominal dollars. In real terms, the increase was 2.1 times the 1967 level of spending by the winner.

While Pierre Trudeau spent about $300 000 to win the leadership of the Liberal party in 1968, in 1984 John Turner and Jean Chrétien each spent almost $1.6 million, the amount set by the party as the limit on campaign expenditures. For the Liberal party's 1990 leadership race, the two top contenders each spent about $2.4 million, and all candidates together spent about $6 million[2] (table 13.1). Thus, in *real* terms, the winner of the leadership race in 1990 spent 1.9 times the amount the winner did in 1968 – even with a limit set by the party. To put the amounts spent in 1990 into perspective, one should recall that the statutory limit on a *party* running a candidate in every riding in the 1988 federal election was $8 million. The average limit for a candidate was $46 900.[3] In contrast to the Liberal party, the NDP set a limit of $150 000 on the expenditures of candidates for the party leadership to replace Ed Broadbent in 1989. The winner, Audrey McLaughlin, spent $128 576 (table 13.1). One of the reasons why the limit could be set so low was that the party sponsored a series of all-candidates meetings in order to reduce the total costs of contacting delegates or potential delegates to the leadership convention[4] (appendix 13.1).

While the federal government did not regulate the financing of leadership races, the parties made some effort to do so. Apparently the Conservatives' 1976 leadership race was the first in which either of the two older parties required disclosure by the candidates of their total revenues and expenditures and of donations of more than $1 000 (Ontario, Commission 1986, 83). In 1983, however, the Progressive Conservative party did not impose any regulations on the leadership race won by Brian Mulroney. While John Crosbie's expenses in that race were originally estimated to be "about $1 million," his campaign manager later said they were "around $1.5 million" (ibid., 84).[5] Joe Clark spent $800 000 to $850 000, including $200 000 in Quebec, according to his campaign manager (ibid.). Estimates of Mr. Mulroney's spending, which he declined to divulge, ranged from $750 000 to $2 million (ibid.).

The Liberals' rules for leadership candidates in 1984 included an expenditures limit of $1.65 million, but the candidates did not have to publicly disclose their revenues or expenditures and none did. Moreover, the rules to enforce the limit were "weak at best" (quoted in Ontario, Commission 1986, 86). The party published a list of all (1 108) donors of more than $500, but did not indicate which candidate(s) received the contribution(s). Nine months after the convention, the party published a statement that aggregated all the candidates' expenditures. In other words, the Liberals in 1984 disclosed less than the Tories did in 1976 (ibid.).

The most elaborate sets of regulations for a leadership race were those established for the NDP's leadership race in 1989 and for the Liberals' race in 1990 (appendix 13.1). Neither set of rules was entirely satisfactory, however. In the case of the Liberal party,[6] candidates were not required to disclose the name of the person/corporation/union and the amount for all contributions over $100,[7] as are parties or candidates for the House of Commons. The cochairs of the Liberal Party of Canada Leadership Expenses Committee, in their report in November 1990, recommended that party "regulations should provide for full disclosure of contributions," that sanctions for violation of the rules should be more strict and have application after the convention and that the use of the tax credit for contributions made after the vote should be studied.

Of particular concern in the matter of disclosure of expenditures by leadership candidates are those outlays that create *individuated* benefits for delegates to the convention. It is less important to know the expenditures on travel, advertising, posters and computer networks than it is to know how much a candidate spent on buying party memberships for "instant" members in order to "pack" delegate selection meetings, the convention expenses of delegates (fees, travel, accommodation, food) and the contributions made to ethno-cultural or other organizations to gain the support of their members at delegate selection meetings in the ridings.

The failure to regulate the financing of leadership campaigns while closely regulating the financing of campaigns for individual ridings is an anomaly. Wearing (1988a, 72) suggests that "the potential impact of high expenditure and secretive money-gathering on what is supposed to be an open and democratic process raises serious questions about leadership selection in Canada's major political parties." He asks, "Could unregulated, undisclosed campaign fund-raising ultimately undermine the democratic nature and integrity of the leadership selection process?"[8]

Races for the leadership of the three main parties would appear to be at least as important as campaigns in individual ridings during a general election, which are quite strictly regulated. The leader sets the tone for the entire party.[9] The leader has a great deal of influence over the party's internal rewards. Becoming leader is a necessary but not sufficient condition for attaining the apex of power, namely, becoming Prime Minister (or Premier). Arguably, the selection of a party leader is more important today than it was in earlier eras. This is the era of "leadership" politics, in which much more stress is being placed on the characteristics and skills (e.g., the media and linguistic skills) of the leader. In a dynamic world, the leader's ability to handle as-yet-unforeseen problems is of greater importance. The party leader is *the* visible (and vocal) symbol of the party in the media, and often in the minds of the voters.

Is the selection of a party leader "a matter in the public domain" (Ontario, Commission 1986, 78), and hence should it be subject to public regulation, or is it a purely private matter, subject only to whatever rules the party may decide to impose? At present, leadership races make extensive use of public funds, because some contributions to candidates are routed through the party's official agent ($1.95 million in 1990 for the Liberal race; table 5.8) and the donors receive receipts for the tax credit.[10] Further, the registration fee for delegates to the leadership convention ($875 in the case of the Liberals in 1990) can be paid in the form of a tax-receipted contribution. In other words, taxpayers are now subsidizing leadership races for federal parties to a considerable degree, although it is not possible to provide a reliable estimate of the tax expenditures for contributions to the Liberal leadership race in 1990. Wearing (1988a, 82) argues both for the formal extension of tax credits for contributions to leadership campaigns and for more and better disclosure. To ensure full disclosure of revenues and expenditures, he suggests that candidates not be allowed to mail out tax receipts until disclosure has been made. "What candidate could resist the pressure coming from contributors who wanted their tax credits?" he asks.

The Ontario Commission (1986, 92) study argued that the dangers of nonregulation of leadership campaigns are undue influence and excessive spending, so that success has less to do with talent and more to do with campaign efforts.[11] What forms might the regulation of the financing of leadership campaigns take? The Ontario Commission (ibid., 96–109) reviewed the following: disclosure of contributions; contribution limits; blind trusts for contributions; spending limits (but campaign expenses would have to be clearly defined); and subsidies, that is, tax credits for contributions versus direct subsidies. Note that the Camp Commission (whose third report of September 1974 dealt with the regulation of electoral finance) considered the possibility of regulating leadership campaigns, but made no recommendations in this regard (ibid., 90). (A decade later, Camp said the Commission decided it would be an impossible task to regulate the financing of leadership campaigns.) To minimize the chance of undue influence, the Ontario Commission argued that all candidates should have their contributions run through a blind trust so the candidates would not know who had contributed to their campaign (ibid., 91). On the other hand, former MP Douglas Fisher has argued that, even if no public funds are involved, "the choice of leaders is so vital that the process needs to be part of the public domain of politics. It simply is not just the business of a private party" (ibid., 92). The Ontario Commission (ibid., 110) concluded that public regulation should not be undertaken until the practical problems of enforceability are resolved.[12] Moreover, such regulations could be challenged under the *Canadian Charter of Rights and Freedoms*. For example, spending limits might well be held to infringe a candidate's freedom of expression.

In July 1986, Ontario became the first jurisdiction in Canada to regulate the financing of leadership campaigns. Candidates must register with the Commission on Election Finances, file an audited statement of their revenues and expenses and disclose the names of the donors and amounts of all contributions over $100 (Ontario, *Election Finances Act,* 1986, ss. 15, 43(4)). Further, constituency associations (ridings) are prohibited from contributing or transferring funds to a leadership contestant (ibid., s. 30(2)). However, there are no limits on either contributions or expenditures (as there are on total contributions to parties and/or candidates and on expenditures by candidates). It should be noted that contributions to a leadership contestant are *not* eligible for Ontario's individual or corporate tax credits.

2.2 Nomination Campaigns

While the *Canada Elections Act* does not regulate the spending of persons seeking a party's nomination in a particular riding, it appears that only in a handful of cases involving the Progressive Conservative and Liberal parties have large sums been spent on nomination races (chap. 1). Indeed, Carty and Erickson (1991) estimate that, in two-thirds of the ridings in 1988, the candidate won by acclamation. Further, when there was a contest, only a few contestants spent more than $3 000 on their campaigns. The issue for public policy, therefore, is whether it is necessary to regulate the financing of nomination races at all, given the modest amounts of money involved in all but a handful of races. The Reform Commission of the Liberal party has suggested that the party might be willing to issue tax receipts for contributions to be routed to persons seeking the nomination "in return for a commitment to full disclosure of all contributions, and the respecting of spending limits based on a dollar amount for every eligible voting Liberal member in the riding" (1991, 9).

2.3 Post-Nomination, but Pre-Writ Campaigns

One-third of candidates in 1988 were nominated after the writs of election were issued, according to Carty and Erickson (1991). Thus they had an opportunity to campaign before the date on which the limit on "election expenses" came into effect, namely, the day when a candidate filed his/her nomination papers. The issue for public policy is whether candidates should be permitted to use tax-receipted funds (from intraparty transfers) to begin their electioneering prior to the time that such outlays would be classified as "election expenses" subject to the statutory limit. This issue was highlighted in a newspaper article, which revealed that the Liberal party's Trinity–Spadina association had told candidate Antonio Ianno that he could spend up to $2 000 to promote himself after he was nominated on 1 May 1988 (*Vancouver Sun,* 16 August 1990, B6). The writ was not issued until 1 October. Recall from chapter 12 that the

277 candidates with the largest amount of "other expenses" in 1988 spent an average of $2 065 (table 12.26) on *pre-writ* expenses, although 26 spent more than $7 000 (table 12.27). Again, the question is whether the amounts involved are sufficiently large to justify regulation. Note also that candidates can use the pre-writ period to raise funds for the coming campaign. They can accept "blank-dated" cheques on which the date will be filled in after the writ is issued; hence the candidate's agent can issue a receipt for the tax credit. Alternatively, the cheques can be made out to the riding association, which then routes them through the *party*'s agent (e.g., PC Canada Fund, Federal Liberal Agency). However, the party's agent may "tax" part of the contribution, thus reducing the amount flowing through to the candidate. There is a third alternative: the donor can contribute to the riding association (in the name of the candidate) and not request a receipt for the income-tax credit for political contributions. Therefore, the money is not routed through the party's agent. Nor is the identity of the donor subsequently made public, because riding associations do not have to file statements with the Chief Electoral Officer as do parties and candidates.

2.4   Riding Associations

The registration of parties and the requirement that each candidate have an official agent who is responsible for collecting, receipting, disbursing and disclosing the funds associated with an election campaign is at the core of the system of federal regulation of the financial activities of parties and candidates (recall chap. 2). However, riding associations are not registered entities under the *Canada Elections Act* and this fact has a number of important implications for the regulatory system.[13] To begin, very little information about the financial activities of riding associations is required to be made public. The exceptions are those occasions when a riding association transfers money to a candidate (more precisely to his/her agent); then the sources of those funds must be made public. Further, when the riding association routes contributions to it through party headquarters in order to provide the donors with receipts so that they can claim the tax credit, the names of the donors (if their total contributions are over $100) must be reported by the party's agent (e.g., the PC Canada Fund in the case of the Progressive Conservative party).

Riding associations are free to fund pre-nomination activities of would-be candidates and pre-writ activities of their candidate without limit or public disclosure. They can also financially assist an incumbent MP between elections without limit or public disclosure. Riding associations – unlike parties or agents for candidates – need not disclose the identity of donors (see below). It is the party (or candidate) that is responsible for informing the CEO of the sources and amounts of contributions. Riding associations are the major recipient of candidates' surpluses (which the CEO said amounted to $8 million in 1984 and $9.6 million in 1988) (Canada, Elections Canada 1984d, 60; 1991, 10).[14] Once this money is put into the riding association's bank account, all public accountability ends, unless part of the money is "recycled" back to the candidate's agent at the next election.

The absence of registration and public disclosure has meant that the national offices of all parties know very little about the financial operations of their ridings.[15] While riding associations[16] cannot issue receipts for the federal tax credit between elections, they can get the national party agent to issue such receipts. Two of the three main parties levy a "tax" or fee for this service to help finance the national office (NDP, 15 percent; Conservative party, 25 percent).[17] While parties must report transfers to PTAs or riding associations, the amount of money flowing through the national office but raised at the riding association or PTA level need not be identified to the CEO.

Section 232 of the *Canada Elections Act* permits a candidate to transfer surplus funds to a local association or to the registered party. However, the Act does not define a local association.[18] Presently, anyone can organize a local association in a district and transfer the campaign surplus to the association.

An obvious "loophole" in the disclosure provisions occurs in the case of contributions to a local association between elections for which no tax receipt is issued (for the political contribution tax credit).[19] As one party official noted, not all donors want or need the "benefit" of a tax receipt, for with it comes disclosure of their name and amount (if over $100).[20] Further, the riding association, unlike the party and candidates during the campaign period, cannot issue tax receipts. In any event, the executive of the riding may find it convenient to accept money from individuals or corporations that do not want to be identified publicly. Transfers of funds from a local association to the official agent of a candidate during the campaign period must be reported by the agent and the association's sources for that money must be identified. It may not be possible, however, for an association to identify the sources of the particular dollars it transfers to the candidate's agent.

Party officials interviewed for this study indicated that some ridings have set up charitable foundations with money raised by a popular MP who has been able to raise a great deal of money for the local association.[21] The foundation then distributes funds in a way that is likely to be politically beneficial to the MP.

Some MPs raise funds by holding events such as dinners or golf tournaments from which the net proceeds can be considerable, according to party officials. Often, the tickets are not tax-receipted and the proceeds may or may not go to a local riding association. Further, the contributions and subsequent expenditures are not reported to the CEO. Other forms of non-tax-receipted fund-raising include the supply of goods or services by a trade union, for which a tax receipt is irrelevant.

Local associations can solicit cash contributions or those in the form of goods or services sold to the party/candidate at *below* the going market price in an arm's length transaction. Not only is the benefit greater than the amount of the reported contribution in the case of in-kind gifts, but also between election campaigns neither have to be reported to the CEO. Since the maximum tax credit of $500 is reached on a contribution of $1 150, most corporate donors do not need a receipt for tax purposes for either type of contribution. The result is that the local association can build up a "war chest" that is beyond public scrutiny, and donors' names will not be revealed (as they would be if they gave $100 or more to the national party).

Because there is so little regulation of riding associations, it is entirely possible for a small group with control over the executive to use the association's funds for purposes far removed from the operation of the association and to finance election campaigns. Frequently, party officials interviewed for this study alluded to rumours of the possible misuse of funds. No one, however, could or would provide specific details.

The central issue for public policy is the asymmetric treatment of riding associations (relative to candidates and parties) in terms of disclosure of contributions and of expenditures. Yet federal riding associations benefit from federal subsidies and tax credits through the transfer of any surplus from their candidate after elections. They also benefit from funds receipted at the national level and returned to the riding (less any "tax" imposed by the party). For all of the reasons described above, riding associations are the "black holes" of party and candidate financing in Canada.

2.5 Trust Funds

The practice of setting up trust funds to augment the official income of party leaders is an old one. Laurier's biographer states that, in 1896, just before he formed his first government, Laurier received a letter from William Mulock, who was to be appointed Postmaster General, stating: "What the country requires is clean government ... I think steps should be taken *now* to raise a fund that would protect you from want the rest of your days" (Schull 1965, 325). Laurier had no objections to

Mulock raising from $50 000 to $100 000, since "there were no strings. It was an open and honourable arrangement and the same thing had been done for Macdonald by his friends ... [The] wealthy contributors would ask for nothing specific. At worst it was partial assurance that the head of the government would not be easily bribable" (ibid.).

Mackenzie King, Louis St. Laurent and Lester B. Pearson all benefited from trust funds created by anonymous donors (Whitaker 1977, 197). Moreover, the public was not aware of the existence of such funds (at least, until long after they had left office). Pierre Trudeau and subsequent Prime Ministers have benefited from a private fund of $275 000 collected to provide a swimming pool for the Prime Minister's official residence.

The practice of providing a trust fund for party leaders, or even potential leaders, has not gone out of fashion. In 1976, there was some publicity concerning a fund of $300 000 created for Claude Wagner in 1972, designed to induce him to resign his judicial appointment to run as a Progressive Conservative candidate in Quebec. He was runner-up to Joe Clark in the 1976 Tory leadership convention (*Maclean's*, 23 February 1976, 14–15).

In general, the purpose of trust funds for party leaders has been to ensure that the leader's family is able to enjoy the same degree of financial security as it would have had if the leader had not pursued a career in politics. When John Turner left his law practice in 1984 to run for leader of the Liberal party, "a number of his wealthy friends ... formed a secret committee to ease his financial transition into public life ... his friends were willing to pay for the education of his children as the least controversial or detectable way of slipping him support" (Graham 1986, 240). During the leadership race, the existence of this trust fund came to light (Weston 1988, 39–40). The fund was cancelled within 24 hours and the money returned to donors.[22] Mr. Turner was apparently the beneficiary of another trust fund set up shortly after he won the leadership race in 1984 out of the surplus from his leadership campaign.[23] While the surplus from Turner's campaign was about $600 000, the funds made available for Turner's personal use were said to amount to $300 000 (Wallace and Laver 1988, 12).

Trust funds can be created and used for purposes other than to supplement the leader's income. In order to ensure that John Turner's job was not put on the line at a leadership review convention, a group of supporters calling themselves "The Friends of John Turner" raised money to assist Mr. Turner prior to and at the November 1986 Liberal party convention. The money was used to pay for the expenses of some delegates, including their registration fees, travel expenses, accommodation and food. It was also used to equip Turner supporters with "computers, walkie-talkies and convention paraphernalia ... [and it] paid for private polls, hospitality suites and travel by Turner loyalists to win over undecided delegates" (Wallace and Laver 1988, 12). "The Friends" ' efforts were financed by the money they raised and by money from the "Addison Fund," the existence of which was not known to the party's chief fund-raiser, Senator Leo Kolber. "The Friends" were anxious to avoid adverse publicity if money from the Leader's Office budget[24] was used for their efforts to help Turner. Although Turner organizers admit that between $75 000 and $100 000 was spent to support the leader at the national convention, other sources have stated that fund-raiser David Addison, and his team, raised three times that amount.

From time to time, there have been reports that national political parties have provided funds to the leader to supplement his/her official salary and to cover the high costs associated with the position. Between 1984 and 1986, Prime Minister Mulroney received $313 000 from the PC Canada Fund to redecorate 24 Sussex Drive. Some $158 000 was a loan to the Prime Minister, while the rest was used to purchase furnishings now owned by the party (*Maclean's*, 27 April 1987, 13). The Minister of National Revenue said that the *Income Tax Act* did not put restrictions on the disbursement of funds donated to political parties. That is within the jurisdiction of the Chief Electoral Officer (*Globe and Mail*, 1 March 1988, A3). In mid-1985, some $50 000 of the $185 000 in the "Ottawa Fund"[25] was transferred to the federal Liberal party to pay for furniture for Stornoway, the official residence of the Leader of the Opposition. This amount supplemented the more than $500 000 paid by the government to totally remodel and refurnish Stornoway for the Turners.

Trust funds have proven a source of embarrassment to parties and their beneficiaries.[26] They are inconsistent with the general approach to the disclosure of the sources of party revenues and the activities on which party money is spent. Proposals for their regulation are given in chapter 14.

2.6   Expenditures by Advocacy Groups

Since the Alberta court decision in the *National Citizens' Coalition* case in 1984 (described in chapter 2), there have been few legal constraints on advocacy groups participating in federal election campaigns. While such groups cannot *directly* support or oppose the election of a specific candidate or party, they are free to advocate causes, issues or specific public policies. This fact raises very difficult policy problems, because the regulation of advocacy groups' activities during election campaigns in order to preserve the integrity of the controls on "election expenses" by parties and candidates is likely to conflict with the protection of freedom of expression in the *Canadian Charter of Rights and Freedoms* entrenched in the Constitution in 1982.

In 1988, the proposed Free Trade Agreement (FTA) with the United States stimulated the creation of groups for and against the FTA, and it also saw such groups spend large sums advertising their views. During the 1988 general election, advocacy groups spent about $4.73 million on advertising in 14 newspapers (Hiebert 1991).[27] This figure amounted to 8 percent of the total "election expenses" of parties and candidates, but 40 percent of the three major parties' outlays on advertising (ibid.). Most of the groups' advertising dealt with the free trade issue: four times as much was spent in support of the FTA as was spent in opposing it. Pro–free trade advertising amounted to 30 percent of the Progressive Conservative party's advertising expenditures, while anti–free trade advertising amounted to 5 percent of the advertising expenditures of the Liberal and New Democratic parties (which opposed the FTA) (ibid.). The focus of the debate over free trade was at the level of the national party, rather than the candidate. Hiebert found that the pro–free trade groups spent 77 cents for every $1.00 of the Conservative party's advertising budget, while the anti–free trade forces spent only 13 cents for the total advertising budgets of the two parties opposing free trade. Moreover, about 65 percent of the advocacy groups' advertising space was purchased in the last week of the campaign,[28] with 25 percent in the newspapers' final full-circulation day (ibid.). Econometric research suggests that the major effect of the advertisements was to mobilize those Free Trade Agreement supporters intending to vote for the Liberal party to support the Progressive Conservative party (ibid.).

3. USE OF THE TAX CREDIT FOR POLITICAL CONTRIBUTIONS

The federal government – or, more precisely, taxpayers – contributes a great deal to political parties and candidates in the form of tax credits for contributions. Over the four-year electoral cycle ending in 1988, the value of the credits amounted to 29 percent of the income of federal parties (chap. 1). There are, however, several policy issues concerning the use of the tax credit that merit discussion.

3.1 Asymmetry in the Treatment of Contributions with Respect to the Income-Tax Credit

One hundred percent of political contributions made in cash or by cheque (up to $1 150 per year) are eligible for the federal income-tax credit.

However, only the "net revenue" raised at a fund-raising event such as a dinner or social event is eligible for the tax credit because of the Department of National Revenue's rules regarding political tax credits issued for such activities.[29] The rules are set out in DNR's Interpretation Bulletin 110RZ. They specify that, about three months in advance of the event, the party must apply for a ruling, provide all receipts for the event in advance of its occurrence and carefully account for the gross revenues and expenses. Further, only the net revenue is listed in reports to the CEO as a contribution. What this means is that some forms of fund-raising are discriminated against when receipts are issued for the political tax credit, because it costs money to raise "political" money in all forms. Even the personal solicitation of corporations by a party fund-raiser requires some outlays (e.g., telephone calls, letters, secretarial time, stationery), even if the imputed value of the fund-raiser's time is ignored. Yet these costs are not deducted before the value of the contribution for income-tax purposes is reported. More importantly, there is also the case of direct mail. Even when using its house list, a party's cost of raising $1.00 by means of direct mail may well be $0.25 to $0.35 per piece (chap. 9). This is comparable to the costs (food, wine, invitations, telephone calls) of a $500-per-plate dinner featuring the party leader.[30] As noted above, such costs must be deducted in determining what portion of the $500 ticket price constitutes the contribution. As the Reform Party noted in its brief to the Royal Commission on Electoral Reform and Party Financing, "The system favours large, expensive functions put on by experienced fundraisers where the costs and donations are substantial." However, the entire gross value of contributions raised through direct-mail campaigns is eligible for a receipt for the tax credit.

Between election periods, a party cannot provide receipts for the income-tax credit for donations of goods and services. A party official explained how this constraint can be circumvented. The individual/firm "gives" the goods/services to the party, but bills them for, say $500. The party pays the bill of $500. Then the individual gives the party a cheque (donation) for $500 and gets a receipt for an income-tax credit. It is not clear why contributions in the form of goods or services to parties between official campaign periods are not eligible for the tax credit – provided they are valued at their fair market value.

3.2 Extension of the Tax-Receipting Power

The federal income-tax credit for political contributions was designed to provide an incentive for individuals and smaller businesses to make contributions to registered political parties and candidates. The degree to which this has been achieved is still a matter of conjecture, given the small number of Canadians who make political contributions and the data on the percentage of individuals making a contribution who also claim the tax credit (chap. 8). One critically important consequence of the rise of the individual donor (also stimulated by the use of direct-mail appeals) is that the Liberal and Progressive Conservative parties are no longer dependent on a few hundred corporations for the lion's share of their revenues, as they were before 1974.

Because the parties believe the tax credit to be such a powerful incentive (even though the nominal amounts in the tax credit formula have remained unchanged since 1974), it is not surprising that they have extended the issuance of receipts for the tax credit to contributions to be used for the following purposes:

- contributions routed through the national party agency to be passed along in whole or in part to a candidate for the party's leadership;
- the payment by individuals of the registration fee for a party convention; and
- contributions to a party that will be used subsequently to finance activities designed to elect members to a *provincial* legislature or even to a municipal council.

Whether or not these uses of the federal tax credit were contemplated by parliamentarians in 1974 when the *Election Expenses Act* was passed is irrelevant. All parties engage in almost all of these types of "tax receipting."[31] Presumably they do so because they believe it is legally permissible, although the matter has not been subject to a judicial decision. However, Liberal party officials did obtain a legal opinion before they allowed leadership candidates in 1990 to route contributions through the Federal Liberal Agency and thereby make the contributions eligible for a receipt for the tax credit.

Leadership Races

The use of the federal tax credit for political contributions in leadership races is illustrated by the 1990 campaign for the leadership of the Liberal party. Almost one-third of the total amount (about $6 million) raised by the six candidates ($1.95 million) was routed through the Federal Liberal Agency, and therefore the donor received a receipt for the tax credit. It is impossible to determine the amount of tax expenditure involved, because it would also be necessary to know the value of other amounts given to the party by each individual or corporation during the year. For example, if a corporation or individual had already given the Liberal party more than $1 150 in 1990 and also gave a candidate a donation, it would *not* be eligible for additional tax credits. Therefore, the incremental cost to taxpayers would be zero.

Interviews with party officials indicated that they believe the central policy issue is the failure to link full disclosure to the use of the tax receipts for leadership campaigns. For example, in 1990 the Liberal party made public the names of persons who donated a total of over $100 to one or more candidates (see appendix 13.1). Thus no one could identify how much each donor gave to each candidate[32] – except where the contributions were routed through the Federal Liberal Agency, because the party published a list of such contributions on 8 November 1990, five months after the date of the convention.

Registration Fees

As noted in chapter 1, it is the practice of all the major parties to treat the payment of delegate fees for party policy or leadership conventions as contributions for which they issue a tax receipt. Such fees are designed at least to cover the costs of the convention, and have become substantial. For example, each delegate paid a fee of $875 for the 1990 Liberal leadership convention (a total of $4.4 million). With the receipt for the political tax credit, the *net* cost to each delegate was $467. The difference of $408 in effect represents a subsidy to the delegates and party from other taxpayers. Party officials argue that policy and leadership conventions are central activities of the parties and it is entirely appropriate to issue tax receipts for delegate fees. However, in Ontario in 1985, the deputy registrar of the provincial Commission on Election Contributions and Expenses stated that no riding association may issue tax receipts for donations that are clearly intended for convention purposes (*Globe and Mail*, 12 January 1985, 12). This statement was in response to the fact that delegates were making a donation of $335 to their riding association, a sum equal to the registration fee for the forthcoming Progressive Conservative party provincial leadership convention, and were receiving a tax receipt. The riding was then paying the delegate's registration fee to the provincial party. Further, delegates planned to submit their claims for out-of-pocket expenses for the convention to their riding association in order to receive a tax receipt for their outlays. The treasurer of one riding association said that the Ontario Commission told him this was permitted (ibid.). This particular circumvention has not been raised by any of the officials of federal parties.

Federally Receipted Money Used in Provincial Politics

The ways in which parties are organized and the flows of funds within them can result in the use of federally receipted money for provincial politics, i.e., for efforts to elect provincial MLAs, MPPs or MNAs. While Ontario law contains a "double bar" against federal-provincial flows in both directions within a party, most other provinces are not so restrictive.[33] More importantly, the federal government has made no effort to restrict the use of federally receipted contributions to finance provincial political activity. All parties have had to deal with the problems created by legislation in some provinces requiring "hermetical divisions between federal and provincial organizations," to use NDP official Robin Sears' phrase. Sears objected to this approach:

> I really resent what I regard as an intrusion by provincial governments into this field. They're saying that we should set up competitive relationships within our own organizations within a province. From time to time I know more about the PC Ontario Fund and their revenues and operations than the PC Canada Fund does – and that's a bizarre situation created in part by the divisions enforced by Ontario law...
>
> I want to be able to send money to New Brunswick – I want to be able to say, here's some money for your provincial campaign. I can't do it, I'm prohibited by law... in New Brunswick, Ontario and Alberta, with the exception of $100. ("Round Table" 1981, 11)

The organizational structure of the Progressive Conservative party, with its complete separation of federal and provincial parties, is such that no federally receipted funds are used for provincial purposes. The Liberal Party of Canada, however, is a federation of 12 provincial or territorial associations (PTAs) and eight of them are "dual-purpose" in that they work for the election of provincial members and also federal MPs. It is very difficult to determine if federally receipted contributions end up being used for provincial purposes. Senator John Godfrey stated in 1978 that for some years it had been the policy of the Liberal party not to funnel contributions intended to finance provincial elections through the federal party so as to give donors the benefit of the tax credit on contributions.[34]

On the other hand, from 1974 to 1987, most of the Liberal party's revenues were collected by the PTAs, which then transferred most of the money to party headquarters. However, each PTA – which had been delegated authority to issue tax receipts from the Federal Liberal Agency – maintained its own bank accounts. There were frequent battles between headquarters and the PTAs over how much the latter should retain to finance their efforts. In 1987, the PTAs' tax-receipting authority was rescinded so that all revenues for which a tax receipt is issued now pass through the Federal Liberal Agency in Ottawa (recall chap. 5).

The analysis in chapter 6 of federally receipted revenues and the expenditures on federal politics by the NDP revealed that, since 1974, several millions of dollars each year raised by the NDP using the federal income-tax credit for political contributions are spent on *provincial* political activities. In nominal terms, the amounts ranged from $1.4 million to $2.9 million annually between 1974/75 and 1980; $2.6 million to $4.8 million annually between 1981 and 1984; and $2.3 million to $6.5 million annually between 1985 and 1990 (chap. 6).

The basic question for policy makers is the following: Is it appropriate to spend money for which federal income-tax credits are issued on political activities *other* than those directly or indirectly associated with electing members of Parliament?[35] In particular, should a party be able to use such money to elect provincial MLAs? While the matter was not directly addressed by the Barbeau Commission in 1966 or the Chappell Committee in 1971, or even in the debates on the *Election Expenses Act* in 1974, it seems very unlikely that the framers of the present law intended that federal tax money would be used to finance provincial political activity. This issue is addressed again in chapter 14.

4. ACCOUNTING FOR PARTY "ELECTION EXPENSES"

Depending on their circumstances, political parties have an incentive to rearrange their outlays related to general election campaigns in different ways. The core of the problem lies in the intertemporal allocation of party expenditures, the timing of when certain campaign-related expenditures are incurred, the legal definition of "election expenses" and the interpretation of that definition by the Chief Electoral Officer. This section begins by discussing the definition of "election expenses" as applied to federal parties. Then a party's incentive to "pad" its "election expenses" is analysed. Finally, the more common issue of accounting for election-related outlays to ensure that the limit on "election expenses" is not exceeded is discussed.

4.1   Defining the "Election Expenses" of Political Parties

The CEO's 1988 *Guidelines Respecting Election Expenses of Registered Political Parties* are effectively part of the law according to the CEO:

> Adherence to the guidelines will be considered by the Chief Electoral Officer as meeting the statutory requirements for issuing certificates for reimbursement purposes ... Compliance with these guidelines will ensure no prosecution will be initiated by the Commissioner on matters related to the guidelines. (Canada, Elections Canada 1988a, 1)

The definition of "election expenses" is interpreted by the Office of the Chief Electoral Officer as follows: "Election expenses in respect of registered parties include the cost of all those activities and endeavours which directly promote the primary or quantitative advancement or growth of the party as an entity" (Canada, Elections Canada 1988a, 2). The definition of "election expenses" in the *Canada Elections Act* requires that an expense be "for the purpose of promoting or opposing, directly and during an election, a particular registered party." The CEO states that "if an election expense is incurred prior to or during an election and the product of the expense is used during the election, an election expense will have been incurred" (ibid., 6).

Specific Inclusions
The *Guidelines* specify that "election expenses" under the Act include "all those costs incurred in furtherance of the primary objectives of the party for the purpose of: (a) soliciting votes for candidates of the party during an election; (b) adding members or adherents to the party or its policies or programs during an election; or (c) otherwise improving the public image or acceptance of the party, its leader, candidates, members, ideas, programs, principles, or policies during an election" (Canada, Elections Canada 1988a, 3–4). The *Guidelines* go on to state:

> The cost of acquiring broadcasting time or space in a periodical publication is specifically referred to in ... the statutory definition of "election expenses" ...
>
> The net costs to the party of the leader's tour are clearly election expenses within the meaning of that expression in the Act, as they are incurred for the purpose of improving the public image or acceptance of the party[36] ...
>
> If the [travel or transportation] expense is incurred in relation to an activity, the purpose of which is to improve the public image or acceptance of the party, its leader, members, policies or programs, then it is an election expense ...
>
> The party must value the use of a capital asset purchased for the election at the current commercial value. The commercial value to be used is the cost of rental of a similar asset for the period of the election which cost must be recorded as an election expense. (Ibid., 10–12)

Specific Exclusions
The 1988 *Guidelines* for parties state that the "election expenses" of a party do *not* include all those costs that do not promote the primary objectives of the party but are incurred for the purpose of developing

the party's policies or programs, developing the party's strategies, carrying out research and analyses relating to the activities [listed above], and training the party's candidates and workers. The normal administrative costs of maintaining the party as an ongoing entity, and all other internal costs not incurred as an integral part of endeavours furthering the external exposure of the party are excluded from "election expenses" (Canada, Elections Canada 1988a, 3–4). The *Guidelines* go on to provide more detail on several potentially important expenditures:

> The party must *not* report those specific costs to produce an advertisement [e.g., raw film footage] which was not used during the election ...
>
> The cost of collecting and analyzing survey information is not an election expense as the activity does not result in the *direct* promotion of a party, its leader, candidates, members, programs or policies and therefore does not directly support the primary objectives of the party ...
>
> Notwithstanding the importance of this process, the cost of policy research and formulation is not an election expense as the promotion of the party does not *directly* result from these activities ...
>
> Although [expenditures for party worker self-improvement and education] may put the party in a better position to promote itself, its leader and candidates, the activity does not result in the *direct* promotion of the party and therefore such costs are not election expenses ...
>
> Activities such as social functions generally do not promote or oppose the party and therefore the costs are not considered to be election expenses. (Ibid., 5–9; emphasis added)[37]

The words "direct" and "directly" have been italicized to draw attention to the fact that one of the major reasons for these exclusions is the definition of "election expenses" in the *Canada Elections Act*, which uses the key phrase "for the purpose of promoting or opposing, directly and during an election, a particular registered party." Thus, the *Guidelines* reflect the CEO's interpretation of this ambiguous phrase.

Exemption of Polling Costs from "Election Expenses"
The decision of the CEO, at the behest of the Ad Hoc Committee composed of representatives of the parties, to exclude expenditures on polling from a party's "election expenses" has frequently been criticized. An official deeply involved in recent NDP campaigns stated that it was "stupid" to exclude outlays on polling from a party's "election expenses" when virtually all of the fruits of polling (e.g., advertising,

direct mail,[38] and leader's tour) are included. He contends that the Progressive Conservative party spent over $1 million on polling during the 1988 election and almost as much in 1984, but these amounts may be understated (Hoy 1989). In the official's view, the definition of "election expenses" should be made more comprehensive and the limit should be raised to reflect the broader definition.

The CEO is not alone in excluding polling costs from party (or candidate) election expenses. In 1987, the Ontario Commission on Election Finances decided to exclude expenditures on polling from the definition of party "election expenses," which are limited under Ontario law (*Globe and Mail*, 22 April 1987, A3). The representatives of the Liberal and Conservative parties on the Commission argued that doing public surveys is an ongoing political activity and should not be counted as "election expenses." The NDP representative voted against the change. The NDP's provincial secretary said, "I can't think of any other reasons political parties do polling other than as part of an election campaign." It is interesting to note that the rationale for exclusion in Ontario is quite different from that at the federal level, where it is argued that expenditures on polling are not *directly* related to efforts to promote the election of a party or its candidates.

Narrow Definition of "Election Expenses"
The Chief Electoral Officer has interpreted the definition of "election expenses" in the *Canada Elections Act* in a way that excludes many campaign-related expenditures from official "election expenses." If the central activity of parties during election campaigns is, as the CEO suggests, to "attract voters for [its] candidates," then the exclusion of outlays on such important activities as polling and research, the development of party policies and strategies, the training of campaign workers, the costs of preparing ads not used in the campaign, and part of the costs of raising money to finance the campaign seems surprising. It might be argued that, since there is no limit on contributions, it is entirely appropriate to exclude the costs of fund-raising from "election expenses." However, the case for excluding the other outlays is weak. There can be little doubt that they are necessary costs of running an effective campaign. The fact that they do not result in what the CEO calls "the direct promotion of the party" is sophistry. This issue is addressed again in chapter 14.

4.2 "Padding" "Election Expenses"
When a party expects that its outlays on "election expenses" will be below the maximum permitted, it has an incentive to "pad" them so

as to increase the amount of the 22.5 percent rebate provided by the federal government. Paltiel (1989, 68) noted that, for its calculation of party "election expenses" in 1984, the NDP attributed all of its national office expenditures to "election expenses" in order to increase the total and therefore the amount received from the 22.5 percent government rebate. Because its declared 1984 campaign expenses were $1.6 million *below* the statutory limit, the NDP would receive only the 22.5 percent reimbursement on the smaller amount of actual outlays. According to Gray,

> The New Democrats, indeed, have their own "creative" approach to election financing. As the poorest party, their problem is to reach the legal limit on spending in order to get the maximum reimbursement of 22.5 percent under the [*Canada Elections Act*]. Their suppliers are therefore rumoured to charge top-dollar prices for services, then make generous donations to the party – donations for which the supplier gets an additional tax credit. (1989, 11)

The NDP, up to 1988,[39] padded *party* "election expenses" in order to increase the amount of 22.5 percent reimbursement. In their own accounts, pre-writ outlays related to a coming election were carried forward to be included in the official "election expenses" eligible for reimbursement (chap. 6).

4.3 Timing and Allocation of Campaign-related Expenditures

If a party is able to *shift* campaign-related outlays to the period prior to the official campaign period (from the day the writ is issued until election day), it will have more money available during the campaign and still not exceed the limit on "election expenses." The problem arises because of several factors. First, "election expenses" are defined so as to focus on outlays during the official campaign period. Yet expenditures incurred prior to the start of the period may be a close substitute for those incurred during the campaign period. Second, there is an asymmetry between the position of the party in power and that of the others. The Prime Minister may tell top party officials when he is going to call the next election some months before the announcement is made. Hence, his party can arrange its affairs to benefit from this prior knowledge, while rivals cannot. Third, all parties face the problem of how to allocate "normal" overheads to the campaign period and thereby include them in "election expenses." However, the CEO's *Guidelines* are rather vague and accommodating in terms of the method of allocating the "costs of national offices."

The costs of national offices should be divided in accordance with the basic activities carried on by that office. The purpose of each activity should be considered to determine whether the costs incurred to carry on the activity are election expenses ...

The Office of the Chief Electoral Officer will accept the basis of allocation used by the party for reimbursement purposes only, provided that it is reasonable and provided that the party's external auditor agrees that the allocation is reasonable and in keeping with these guidelines. (Canada, Elections Canada 1988a, 7)

Other, less important, allocations are dealt with in more detail in the CEO's *Guidelines*.[40]

If a party fielded a full slate of candidates in 1988, it was entitled to spend $8 million during the 52-day campaign period. However, by adroit timing of certain expenditures, it was possible to reduce the impact of the constraints on "election expenses." According to Gray,

The Liberal and NDP "soft spending" (election expenses not covered by the Election Expenses Act) is chicken feed compared to what the Tories spent – and spent legally. The PC victory cost the party at least $18 million. But we will never discover the precise bill. As Harry Near, director of operations for the 1988 campaign, says with a triumphant grin, "That's none of your business, sweetheart." (1989, 15)[41]

In calendar year 1988, the federal Progressive Conservative party spent $17.8 million on "operating expenses" plus $7.92 million on "election expenses" (chap. 4). The important point is that in 1987 the Tories' "operating expenses" were $11.5 million and in 1989 they were $10.7 million. In other words, during the election year of 1988, the party's nonelection outlays rose by over 50 percent, only to fall by an even greater amount the year after the election. If "operating expenses" simply represent the normal activities of the party not directly connected with general elections,[42] why did they rise from 1987 to 1988 and fall so sharply in 1989? Party officials emphasize that part of these increased outlays relate to items excluded from "election expenses," for example, training of party workers and candidates, the production costs of print and electronic advertisements not used during the campaign, polling and research activities and fund-raising costs. It seems clear that the Tories' planning for the 1988 election began at about the mid-point of Mr. Mulroney's first term as Prime Minister:

Senator Norman Atkin's strategy group was established in 1986 and from then onwards the campaign buzz words were straight out of a

military strategy handbook. Senior organizational meetings with headquarters staff and volunteers who were to work on the campaign
began in January 1988. All three parties ran training schemes for candidates, riding presidents, and party workers before the election was
called, but the Tory schools were the most elaborate. The bulk of the
PC campaign literature was ready before the election was called, and
much of the work on more than thirty television commercials had
been done. (Each opposition party prepared fewer than half that
number.) The party was in a state of campaign readiness from June 1
onwards. In the late summer, at government expense, the prime
minister did a dry run of his electoral tour through the regions, trying
out speech themes such as "managed change" and fine-tuning his
"statesman" image. (Gray 1989, 16)

Perhaps because they had been suffering financial woes, a similar
pattern did not occur for the Liberal party in 1988. Operating expenses
in 1987 were $7.64 million and $6.95 million in 1988, then they fell to
$5.5 million in 1989 (chap. 5). The Liberal party's "election expenses"
in 1988 were $6.84 million, well below the $8 million limit, because of
problems raising more money and the party's concern about increasing
its already large debt.

The figures for the NDP indicate that *total* expenditures by the
"federal office" were $2.52 million in 1987, $3.72 million in 1988 and
$1.53 million in 1989. These figures, however, include $149 878 in pre-
election activities in 1987 and $916 034 in 1988 (chap. 6). The 1988 figure
includes $570 542 in interest on loans to finance the campaign.

With respect to the 1984 election campaign, when the Conservative
party was in opposition, Paltiel observes:

Expense declarations from the ... federal general election in 1984
revealed a lack of uniformity and a great disparity in the treatment of
ongoing party expenses during the national campaign. Thus, whereas
the New Democratic Party attributed all of its national office spending
during the summer of 1984 to election expenses, the Liberals treated
two thirds as such, while the Progressive Conservatives allocated only
slightly more than one quarter of their national office expenditures
during the campaign as election expenses! Had the Liberals and
Conservatives followed the practice of the NDP, both would have been
in serious violation of the legal limits. (1987, 241)

Gray (1989, 16), using material from an interview with Paltiel,
contends that the Conservative party's campaign began about 13 months

before the 1984 election was called and that Paltiel was told by party officials that at least half of the Conservatives' expenditures for the campaign occurred before the writs were issued in July 1984. The Conservative party's "operating expenses" grew rapidly in the two years prior to the 1984 election and then fell by 50 percent in 1985. They rose from $7.3 million in 1982 to $10.98 million in 1983 to $18.2 million in 1984 (the election was held in September). Then the Conservative party's "operating expenses" fell to $9.9 million in 1985. Note that this drop was *greater* than the party's official 1984 "election expenses" of $6.39 million. The pattern for the Liberals in 1984 was rather similar to that of the Tories. Operating expenses rose from $4.1 million in 1982 to $4.62 million in 1983, then increased to $11.2 million in 1984 (however, this figure included a leadership convention that cost about $2.5 million). Then the Liberal party's "operating expenses" fell to $7.25 million in 1985 (chap. 5).

Chapter 6 indicated that the *total* expenditures by the federal office of the NDP rose steadily from 1982 to 1985, but the absolute amounts were modest: between $1.05 million in 1982 and $1.72 million in 1985. More importantly, the NDP's "election expenses" in 1984 ($4.73 million according to reports filed with the CEO) fell *below* the statutory limit, so the party had no incentive to shift campaign-related expenditures into "operating expenses." Indeed, as noted above, it had the *opposite* incentive – to "pad" their "election expenses" in order to increase the 22.5 percent rebate from the federal government.

In 1984, the Progressive Conservative party allocated $619 000 of the $2 303 000 cost of running its national office during the election period to "election expenses."[43] In 1988, the comparable figures were $385 000 and $1 563 000 respectively. In other words, the percentage of running costs allocated to "election expenses" (which are subject to statutory limit) fell slightly from 26.9 percent to 24.6 percent, but the absolute amount fell by $234 000. Put another way, in 1984 some 9.7 percent of total party "election expenses" consisted of national office expenses. In 1988, the comparable amount was 5.0 percent. In 1984, the Conservative party reported total "operating expenses" of $18.2 million, as compared with $17.8 million in 1988. Both these figures *exclude* "election expenses" ($6.39 million in 1984 and $7.92 million in 1988). Therefore, while the party's total "operating expenses" declined by a little over 2 percent (in nominal dollars) between 1984 and 1988, the amount of these operating costs said to be incurred during the election period fell by 32.1 percent. Much of the $740 000 drop in operating costs between 1984 and 1988 is attributable to the following: $299 000 in fund-raising expenses in 1984 that were totally excluded in 1988, a drop of

$267 000 in printing and stationery expenses between 1984 and 1988, and $70 000 in advertising expenses in 1984 that were totally excluded in 1988. The first and third items reflect changes in the CEO's *Guidelines* for the determination of *party* "election expenses."

Parties are not alone in their ability to benefit from shifting campaign-related expenditures to the period before the writs are issued. Riding associations can also "front-end load" their campaign-related outlays and thereby reduce the pressure on the "election expenses" limit. In the pre-writ period, they can rent offices and furnish them – although the rental during the campaign period is an "election expense" – install telephone lines, print and distribute leaflets (in which they can endorse the party or candidate and talk about issues) and pay the production costs of alternative advertising materials that may or may not be used in the campaign. All of these activities are perfectly legitimate under the present legislation and *Guidelines* issued by the Chief Electoral Officer, as indicated in section 4.1 above.

5. "ELECTION EXPENSES" OF CANDIDATES

One of the central elements of the 1974 *Election Expenses Act* was the imposition of a limit on "election expenses" incurred by candidates and parties. In the 1988 general election, for example, parties that ran candidates in all 295 ridings were limited to $8 million in "election expenses," while the average limit for candidates was $46 900. Canadians might think that the administration of such limits is quite straightforward. In fact, it is not, because, since 1979, changes have been made in the interpretation of "election expenses" as defined in the *Canada Elections Act* so as to exclude important categories of outlays by candidates from what is subject to control. The authoritative interpretations of the definition of "election expenses" are those of the Chief Electoral Officer as published in his periodic *Guidelines*. The following discussion begins with a review of the definition of "election expenses" as it applies to candidates and then considers some of the practical problems with the definition.

5.1 Defining the "Election Expenses" of Candidates

A useful way to understand the significance of the definition of "election expenses" as it applies in practice is to ascertain which expenditures by candidates are included and which are excluded from the category.

Specific Inclusions

The Chief Electoral Officer (1988) in his *Guidelines Respecting Election Expenses of Candidates* (Canada, Elections Canada 1988b) indicates that "election expenses" of candidates *include* the following:[44]

1. All expenses incurred to promote the election of a candidate during the writ period (i.e., the official campaign period), even if they were incurred *prior* to the filing of the nomination paper with the returning officer (ibid., 4).

2. The commercial value[45] of goods or services provided free of charge or at discounts not available to other customers (ibid., 6). If a business sells both retail and wholesale, the wholesale price is applied to free goods. These are *both* contributions and election expenses.

3. The production costs associated with political broadcasts or commercials (as well as the paid media time).[46]

4. The cost of printing and mailing an MP's "householder" item after the writ has been issued where it directly promotes or opposes a registered party or the election of a candidate.

5. Costs of the services of an official agent or registered agents at the poll with certain exceptions (ibid., 11).[47]

6. The difference in the costs of renting a limousine or mini-bus as compared to a regular passenger car by the candidate so as to be able to transport more than three campaign workers with the candidate. (The rental cost of a regular car, which would also carry up to three campaign workers, would be a personal expense and is hence excluded from "election expenses.")

7. The commercial value of services of volunteers who are self-employed where the services provided are those for which the person is normally remunerated, for example, a secretary of an insurance agent who is being paid by her employer who works several days in the campaign (hence the commercial value is at least $100). The commercial value is a contribution by the employer and an election expense (ibid., 20). (This issue is addressed in section 5.5 below.)

8. The commercial value of services of regular party employees paid by the party and loaned to assist a candidate (ibid.). The commercial value is to be recorded as a contribution from the employer and as an election expense.

9. The commercial value of services from exempt staff of ministers and party research staff (paid from party research budgets) when working for any candidate during normal working hours. Their salary is a contribution from the government of Canada and an election expense (ibid.).

10. Incidental expenses of volunteers for meals, lodging and travel paid for by the candidate or paid for by the volunteer but reimbursed by the candidate (ibid., 20, 7).[48]

11. The portion of any material purchased to promote the nomi-
    nation of a candidate that is subsequently used to promote the
    candidate's election is both an election expense and a contri-
    bution by the candidate or local association (ibid., 24).
12. Any material purchased by the official agent before or during
    the election, which is used during the election (ibid., 26).
    Moreover, "purchases made and paid for by the local associa-
    tion for goods and services to be used during the writ
    (campaign) period must be considered contributions to and
    expenses incurred by the candidate at the price paid by the
    local association" (ibid., 35).[49]

Specific Exclusions

The CEO states in his 1988 *Guidelines* (Canada, Elections Canada 1988b)
that the following items are *not* included in a candidate's "election
expenses" that are subject to limit under the *Canada Elections Act*:

1. Auditor's fees (ibid., 3).[50]
2. Expenses of a potential candidate for the purpose of obtaining
   the nomination as a candidate, even if incurred during the writ
   period (ibid., 4, 24).
3. Donations by a commercial organization of goods/services it
   normally uses in its business, but does not normally sell, where
   the value of each donation is less than $100 (ibid., 7).
4. The value of volunteer labour (ibid., 9) (addressed in more
   detail in section 5.5 below).
5. Any material (e.g., brochures, signs, etc.) that is not used and
   remains on hand at the end of a campaign (because it does not
   directly promote the election of a candidate) (ibid., 10).
6. The cost of printed material used to directly promote the election of a candidate *before* the issue of the writ (the brochures,
   etc. must be mailed before the writ is issued) (ibid.).
7. Payment of the expenses of poll agents or their salary where it
   is "materially less than the commercial value of their services"
   (ibid., 11).[51]
8. The candidate's "personal expenses,"[52] provided they are a
   "reasonable" amount incurred in respect of such travel, living
   and other related expenses as the Chief Electoral Officer may
   designate (see section 5.4 below).[53]
9. The candidate's deposit on nomination ($200) (ibid., 32).
10. The cost of victory parties held after the close of polls on polling
    day (ibid.).

11. Costs of legal services, including a recount (ibid.).
12. The proportion of rent and other costs of campaign offices before the writ is issued and after polling day (ibid.).
13. Interest on loans after polling day (ibid.).
14. The costs of polls or other types of surveys, because such expenditures do not *directly* promote the election of the candidate.[54]
15. The costs associated with preparing the various reports required under the *Canada Elections Act* (ibid.).
16. Wages/salary paid to the candidate. This provision was made in a letter to all parties from the CEO in July 1988.

This is obviously an extensive list of exclusions. They explain why "other expenses" in 1988 amounted to 15 percent of candidates' "election expenses," but were far more than this percentage for a substantial number of candidates (chap. 12).

5.2 Problems with the Definition of "Election Expenses"

Concerns about the definition of "election expenses" are not new, but they became more serious after the 1984 election. The Chief Electoral Officer stated in his 1985 *Statutory Report* that "the present definition of election expenses is so vague and imprecise that its application to various sections of the Act has become extremely difficult" (Canada, Elections Canada 1986, 10). The CEO argued that:

> Problems relating to pre-writ expenses, the principle of direct promotion of or opposition to a candidate or a political party (third party advertising), the monies paid to agents and campaign workers, fund raising, opinion surveys and the use of capital assets, to name but a few, must be looked at and clarified before the next election. (Canada, Elections Canada 1986, 10)

The CEO indicated that he had discussed his concerns with candidates and agents after the 1984 election and had placed his concerns before the Ad Hoc Committee of representatives of the parties.[55] No doubt his concerns were increased by what came to be called the "Masse affair."

Marcel Masse resigned his Cabinet post when it was announced that he was under investigation with respect to his "election expenses" following the 1984 election. The controversy showed that, under the *Canada Elections Act*, the payment of the expenses of a poll agent need not be included in a candidate's official "election expenses," which are limited by the Act. They must, however, be channelled through the official agent and be labelled "campaign expenses" (or "other expenses") rather than "election expenses." Moreover, it also revealed that there is no provision in the Act with respect to a candidate *asking* a third party such as a business to pay the expenses of a volunteer, even though such payments by a third party are prohibited (*Globe and Mail*, 15 February 1988, A2). After being cleared by the Federal Elections Commissioner,[56] Masse was reappointed to the Cabinet as Minister of Communications.

Columnist Hugh Winsor argued that, with respect to the Masse affair, "the real villain in the piece is the ambiguous legislation." In his view, "the bottom line is that Mr. Masse and his election manager (and other candidates in the last election) discovered a major loophole in the definition of election expenses." That loophole consists of "campaign expenses" that are paid by the official agent out of contributions, but that are not subject to limitation as are "election expenses" (*Globe and Mail*, 15 February 1988, A2). The payment of a volunteer's expenses by the agent is not included in "election expenses," according to Winsor:

> As NDP MP Rod Murphy pointed out, he could pay all costs to fly volunteers around his vast Churchill riding, put them up in motels and feed them steaks every night, and as long as the payments were channeled through the official agent and labelled campaign expenses, they would not count against his election expenses total. (Ibid.)

Masse incurred $19 000 on "campaign expenses," of which $16 876 "was channelled properly and reported." The problem lay with the fact that Masse had asked his former employer Lavalin Inc. to pay about $2 000 worth of travelling expenses of a volunteer who had worked on his campaign.[57] The payment was made directly to the volunteer, not to Masse's agent as a contribution after which the agent could properly pay the volunteer's expenses.

The definition of "election expenses" was not addressed in Bill C-79, which was introduced in June 1987.[58] Why? According to Winsor,

> That is because by tradition, the Government legislates in these areas only by agreement between the parties, and there wasn't agreement. The main reason there wasn't agreement, was that the representatives of the Conservative Party (which has been able to raise more political contributions than the other two parties combined) would not agree to further limitations. (*Globe and Mail*, 15 February 1988, A2)

The Eighth Report of the Standing Committee on Elections, Privileges and Procedure (3 March 1988), however, dealt with the "Masse affair." The Committee concluded that, if the payment by Lavalin Inc. of expenses to some campaign volunteers were "election expenses," an offence had occurred. If they were classified as "campaign expenses," there was no offence – although all expenses are supposed to be paid by the candidate's official agent. Masse said the reimbursement was to be treated as a contribution to his campaign (see now Canada, *Canada Elections Act*, ss. 2(1), 217(1)(*a*)). The Committee recommended that the definition of "election expenses" be amended as quickly as possible to make it clear what outlays are subject to legal constraint. This was not done, however.

The CEO acted to clarify the definition of candidates' "election expenses" in light of the "Masse affair." In a press conference on 5 October 1988, the CEO stated that volunteers' expenses were now to be considered part of a candidate's "election expenses" (*Globe and Mail*, 6 October 1988, A5). He noted, however, that "if it were to come to court, I don't know what a judge would do."

5.3 Importance of "Other Expenses"

Because of the ambiguities associated with the term "campaign expenses," the author uses the term "other expenses" to refer to campaign-related outlays by candidates that are not "election expenses" or "personal expenses." As explained in chapter 12, "other expenses" can be grouped into expenditures incurred prior to the day the election was called, expenditures during the official campaign period that the CEO's *Guidelines* exclude from "election expenses" (or "personal expenses") and expenditures incurred after voting day, such as the cost of victory parties. The author's estimate of "other expenditures" by candidates of all parties in 1988 is $4.7 million or 15 percent of official "election expenses." However, a few candidates spent almost as much on "other expenses" as they did on "election expenses."

It must be emphasized that at least part of these "other expenses" are financed through campaign contributions received by the candidate's agent and for which receipts for the federal tax credit have been issued. However, the *Report of the Chief Electoral Officer Respecting Election Expenses* for each of the general elections in 1979, 1980, 1984 and 1988 did *not* provide any information on these "other expenses." The *Report* did not even note that the outlays reported, namely those on "election" and "personal" expenses did not represent all of the outlays by candidates. In light of the analysis in chapter 12, the failure to report candidates' "other expenses" is a major omission.

5.4 Candidates' "Personal Expenses"

The 1974 *Election Expenses Act* provided for "election expenses" and also provided for another category of campaign-related expenditures, namely, "personal expenses." The candidate must have vouchers for all personal expenditures of $25 or more. In the 1988 *Guidelines,* the CEO stated that "the candidate's personal expenses are election expenses, but are not subject to any limit, i.e., they can be incurred over and above the election expenses limit" (see now Canada, *Canada Elections Act,* s. 209). A candidate's "personal expenses" include "any reasonable amount incurred by the candidate in respect of such travel, living and other related expenses as the Chief Electoral Officer may designate." The CEO has designated the following as categories of "personal expenses" when incurred for the candidate's personal benefit:

- travelling costs to the electoral district;
- cost of rental of a temporary residence necessary for the election;
- transportation costs within the electoral district;
- costs of lodging, meals and incidentals while travelling to and within the electoral district; and
- other expenses related to the above, including the cost of child care (Canada, Elections Canada 1988b).

In 1988, 39 Conservative, 16 Liberal and 8 New Democratic candidates spent more than $5 000 on "personal expenses" in the federal election (chap. 12). The average limit on "election expenses" was $46 900. Therefore, the ability to spend a few thousand dollars more on "personal expenses" might be the difference between winning and losing. In 1988, "personal expenses" for candidates who were winners averaged $2 165, for those who were second, $1 895 and for those who were third, $1 325 (Canada, Government Consulting Group 1990).

A former NDP candidate stated that, in the NDP, candidates tend to be discouraged from submitting vouchers for personal expenses to be reimbursed out of the contributions received by their official agent. There is said to be a pervasive belief that candidates should be prepared to pay their own personal expenses as part of their contribution to the campaign.[59] Presently, if a candidate's "election expenses" are below the statutory limit, their personal expenses *could* be reported as "election expenses." Then they would be eligible for the 50 percent reimbursement (assuming that they obtain 15 percent of the vote). Thus the former NDP candidate suggested that there should be a separate provision reimbursing candidates for part of their "personal expenses."

It seems odd to exclude from the limit on "election expenses" the travel and accommodation expenses of candidates while they are electioneering. In the interests of simplicity, it would seem desirable to include what are now "personal expenses" in a broadened definition of "election expenses" and to increase the limit to reflect this change. This point was discussed in chapter 4.

5.5 Problem of Volunteer Labour

The *Election Expenses Act* of 1974 did not provide a definition of "volunteer labour," although the term was used in the definition of "election expenses." Carter describes how the matter was handled by the Ad Hoc Committee in 1974:

> The guideline distinguishes between employed and self-employed individuals. An employed individual can volunteer his services as long as he is not being paid by his employer for performing services for the candidate. In this way an office or factory worker can work after hours and a salesman or professor can work for a party or candidate during the normal working day if his responsibilities to his employer are fulfilled in his own time. To qualify as volunteer labour, a self-employed person cannot work in excess of sixty hours per week on behalf of the party or candidate. The sixty hours provision was calculated on a basis of an assessment of the time an employed person could reasonably work on a campaign (5 weeknights @ 6 hours each and Saturday and Sunday @ 14 hours/day = 58). If a self-employed person works *more* than sixty hours per week on behalf of the party or candidate, his *total* services shall be regarded as an election expense. Any election worker on vacation can work as many hours as he wishes. (1979, 99)

The CEO's 1988 *Guidelines* specify that volunteer labour means "any service provided free of charge by a person outside that person's working hours, but does *not* include service provided by a person who is self-employed if the service is one that is normally sold or otherwise charged for by that person" (Canada, Elections Canada 1988b, 19). Volunteer labour includes unemployed or retired persons working any time, employees on unpaid leaves of absence and self-employed persons working any time if the service they are providing is one for which they do not normally charge.

Senator Norman Atkins (1990b) has argued that campaign labour donated by the self-employed of the type for which they are normally paid should be exempt from the limits on "election expenses." Palda (1991, 38) contends that Bill C-79 to reform the *Canada Elections Act* failed to pass because the Conservative party insisted that so-called paid volunteer labour – of which it was the greatest user – remains exempt from the limits on "election expenses." Recall that expenditures on labour provided at less than its commercial value are exempt from the definition of "election expenses."

The NDP has a particular problem with "volunteer labour" in those cases where union officials and other persons remain on salary (paid by their union) while working as full-time volunteers (organizers) on federal election campaigns. The party or candidate must then record the amount of their wages as a contribution of goods or services and also as an "election expense." The candidate or party must record as an "election expense" all money paid to or in behalf of these volunteers for their out-of-pocket expenses, such as travel, accommodation and food. On the other hand, the work of self-employed persons (e.g., lawyers, accountants) who work for a campaign doing things *other* than they would do in their normal occupational roles is not counted on either the revenue (contribution) or expenditure side. Yet the salaried union official and the self-employed person may perform services whose value to the campaign ranges from modest to very high. Indeed, some of their campaign-related skills may be nearly indispensable and not available for hire in the labour market, since campaign skills can only be learned "on the job." Such learning may be costly to the candidate or party as well as to the volunteer. In 1988, the NDP's federal office reported that it had received $595 406 in "goods and services" (primarily from trade unions) and a cash contribution of $1 007 897 from the CLC. The goods and services worth $595 406 were recorded as "election expenses" by the party (chap. 6).

The significance of the present treatment of volunteer labour for the NDP at the candidate's level can be seen by looking at the structure of the "election expenses" of candidates who spent at least 90 percent of the limit in 1988. The "salaries" component for the candidates of the three main parties was as follows: NDP, $11 656; Liberals, $3 548; and Conservatives, $2 277. For *all* candidates (i.e., regardless of their level of "election expenses"), the differences were not so dramatic, but they are important nevertheless: NDP, $5 367; Liberals, $2 590; and Conservatives, $1 914 (see chap. 12).

In some ridings, campaign workers were not paid during the official writ period. However, in a very few cases, some were paid a substantial honorarium to perform work *after* voting day, such as cleaning up the candidate's headquarters, handling all the accounting work, preparing a report on the campaign, etc. These outlays are classified as "other expenses" rather than as "election expenses."

6. INCUMBENTS' ADVANTAGES

Incumbent members of Parliament, particularly government members, enjoy a number of advantages over challengers.[60] However, only three relate to the rules governing the financing of parties and candidates.

6.1 Franking Privileges

Because the leader of the party in power determines the date of the general election,[61] the MPs of that party may be able to use the franking privilege to send out a mailing to every constituent in their riding just before the election is called. In 1984, however, it was the opposition Conservative party MPs who were able to do this. A week before John Turner called the election, the Conservatives sent out several hundred copies of campaign-oriented booklets through the House of Commons post office. The booklets carried attacks on the Liberals, as well as campaign instructions for Conservative candidates. Each envelope bore the parliamentary stamp of Mr. Mulroney, as well as a House of Commons postmark (which meant that the mailing was sent at no cost to Mr. Mulroney or his party). A spokesman for Mr. Mulroney initially stated that the materials "easily [fell] within the guidelines for distribution of public policy material" and later added that, as they contained excerpts from Mr. Mulroney's speeches, they were, therefore, public policy material.[62] As noted in chapter 2, Bill C-79 contained an amendment that would have required MPs to count as an "election expense" the costs of mailing out "householders" after the writ was issued. It was not enacted, however.

6.2 Government Advertising

The party in power can induce government departments and Crown corporations to undertake advertising campaigns prior to and during the election period that suggest that the government has been doing a great job and that echo or mimic party advertising themes/colours/slogans.[63] Paltiel (1988a, 158) notes that, in the 1984 campaign, the federal government placed $21 million in advertisements – about three times its normal summer advertising – mainly with agencies that were active in supporting the Liberal party's campaign. In an earlier study the author also made the following observations:

> In the months preceding an election campaign, it is common to observe an increase in government advertising designed to connect the party in power to the beneficial actions of the government. For example, the Conservative MP for Western Arctic wrote to the chief federal officer after the last general election with the following complaint: "The attached brochure entitled 'We're in it Together,' published by the Government of Canada, was circulated throughout the Northwest Territories during the election campaign. It was an insert in the 20th July, 1984 edition of *News/North* and was also an insert in other local papers at or about the same time. The brochure is in Liberal party colours and was evidently designed to complement and be part of the Liberal party campaign." (Stanbury 1986a, 460, 462)

The MP condemned this practice for three reasons: "First, it is a charge against all taxpayers including many of whom may not wish to help finance a party campaign. Secondly, it appears to be a mechanism for circumventing the rules governing the election expenses, and thirdly, it gives an unfair advantage to members of the incumbent party. The practice ought to be prohibited by law." Further, as the author argued previously:

> It may be very helpful for electoral purposes to raise the visibility of MPs and cabinet ministers of the party in power by more travel, more speeches, more policy announcements – all of which are backed up by large-scale communications efforts of government departments. This involves a larger number of publicly-funded official functions that act as an excellent substitute for electioneering. Indeed, in some instances "just doing the public's business" is the best method of campaigning. Ministers can be seen to be "above the rough and tumble" of partisan competition: they can aspire to the title of "statesman" rather than "grasping politician." (Stanbury 1986a, 464)

6.3 Allocation of Time for Paid Broadcast Advertising

As noted in chapter 7, the Reform Party brought a legal action in August 1991 challenging the constitutionality of the formula used to allocate the 6.5 hours of paid broadcast advertising time during the next federal election. The formula, which is administered by the Broadcasting Arbitrator, is entirely retrospective. That is, a party's allocation in the *next* election is based on how well it did in the *previous* one in terms of the number of seats obtained, its percentage of the popular vote and the number of candidates the party ran. Thus, even with the Arbitrator's exercise of discretion, the Reform Party was allocated only 10 minutes (as compared with 193 minutes for the Progressive Conservative party, 110 minutes for the Liberal party and 71 minutes for the NDP). Recall that, in the 1988 general election, the Reform Party ran 72 candidates in the West. It did not win a seat, although it won a by-election in Beaver River, Alberta on 13 March 1989. However, since the general election and by the end of 1991, the Reform Party could point to the following indices of its strength as a party: (i) it was able to raise $6.6 million in 1991, and is in the process of raising much more; (ii) party membership hit 100 000 in January 1992, including 30 000 in Ontario (even though the party only voted in May 1991 to become a national party (outside Quebec)); and (iii) in public opinion polls, support for the party has at times rivalled or exceeded that of the governing Progressive Conservative party. While the political environment in Canada at the end of 1991 was highly dynamic, and the next federal election is not likely to occur until 1993, it is entirely possible that a party that would otherwise be a serious contender for a substantial number of seats will be prevented from purchasing more than 10 minutes of broadcast advertising – even though it has plenty of money and has "room" to spend it in terms of the limit on "election expenses." If competition is to be effective and fair, the rules should be changed (see chap. 14).

7. CONCLUSIONS

After more than a decade and a half of experience with the *Election Expenses Act*, it is evident that the regime for regulating party and candidate financing is in need of a major overhaul. The most significant "problem areas" include important political activities that are not regulated, notably leadership campaigns, trust funds and most of the activities of riding associations. As long as tax credits are issued to finance leadership campaigns, it seems reasonable to insist that such campaigns be regulated to at least provide for disclosure. Riding associations are the "black hole" in the present regulatory regime and provide at least a limited means of avoiding the disclosure of tax-receipted revenues and expenditures.

The federal income-tax credit is the largest federal subsidy to parties and candidates. It is presently being used in ways not contemplated by Parliament when the legislation was enacted in 1974. These include treating fees for party conventions as contributions, routing contributions to leadership candidates through the party official agent and using the federal tax credit receipting power to raise money that is used to attempt to elect *provincial* governments. Policy makers need to address these matters and to confirm or reject present interpretations.

Perhaps the most important issue – one that goes to the heart of the integrity of efforts to control campaign spending – concerns the ambiguous definition of "election expenses" and its interpretation by the Chief Electoral Officer. In 1988, candidates spent about $4.7 million on "other expenses" that were not subject to limit, yet such outlays either helped them get the nomination or helped in their election campaign. Sadly, such expenditures are not publicly reported by the CEO. Moreover, much of the growth in such expenditures appears to be directly attributable to changes in the CEO's interpretation of the definition of "election expenses" in his *Guidelines.*

Further, it appears that the Liberal and Progressive Conservative parties in 1984 and the Conservative party in 1988 greatly increased their "operating expenses" so as to provide a substitute for the controlled "election expenses." The increase in "operating expenses" in all three cases exceeded what the party spent on official "election expenses," although the parties maintain that the increase is attributable to the exclusions specified in the CEO's *Guidelines*. The intricacies of the definition and its important exclusions place a premium on exploitation of the rules, rather than on efficient and effective use of resources to inform and persuade voters.

There are two problems: the ambiguous definition of "election expenses" in the *Canada Elections Act*, and the changes in the interpretation of the definition contained in the CEO's *Guidelines*. The ambiguities in the former have been resolved by interpretation in such a way as to permit candidates, and particularly parties, to spend more on election campaigns than the legal limit on "election expenses" would seem to imply. When the law becomes more form than substance, it is not surprising that the public becomes cynical and disaffected. Moreover, one is left with the distinct impression that the definition of "election expenses" was crafted to serve the *appearance* politicians wish to convey to voters. They want to give voters the impression that party campaign outlays are modest, particularly relative to those in the United States. The result is yet another form of institutional hypocrisy.

APPENDIX 13.1
RECENT EFFORTS BY TWO PARTIES TO REGULATE
LEADERSHIP CAMPAIGNS

The Liberal and New Democratic parties have made considerable effort to regulate the financial aspects of leadership campaigns. In 1989, the federal NDP established a fairly detailed set of rules for the candidates seeking to replace Ed Broadbent at the leadership convention in December (New Democratic Party 1989). The rules included the following provisions with respect to financial matters:

- A limit of $150 000 was placed on each candidate's expenditures but the exemptions included

  - the registration fee of $2 500;

  - expenses incurred in holding a fund-raising function that makes a profit;

  - sums paid as replacement salary for the candidate or for his/her child-care expenses;

  - costs of meeting halls and facilities and travel by candidates for the party-sponsored Cross-Canada tour which consisted of 15 all-candidates meetings.

- Contributions from individuals or organizations, whether in cash or goods/services were limited to $1 000.

- Contributions of staff (i.e., donated labour) could exceed more than $1 000 in value but the full amount had to be included in the list of expenditures.

- No anonymous contributions of $25 or more could be accepted.

- The candidate's official agent had to submit a final statement of contributions and expenses, identifying all contributors of $25 or more, within 75 days after the convention.

- Candidates were permitted to raise money for 60 days after the convention to cover any deficit. Any surplus had to be given to the federal party.

- Donated goods and services (other than donated labour) were to be reported at their "commercial value."

- The party reimbursed each candidate's travel costs for the Cross-Canada tour up to $5 000 provided he/she filed interim statements of contributions and expenditures and received at least 75 votes on the first ballot.

- Candidates had to file an interim statement showing the total amount spent on their campaign and the source of such money or goods and services, including the names of all contributors of $25 or more, at the convention. The statement was made available to all delegates (New Democratic Party 1989).

The Liberal party's rules for the leadership race decided in June 1990 included the following provisions (Liberal Party of Canada 1989a):

- Total "leadership expenses" for each candidate were limited to $1.7 million.

- "Leadership expenses" included expenses incurred or the commercial value of goods and services (over $100) donated prior to, during or after the campaign.

- Certain expenditures were *prohibited*, namely

  - the purchase of a membership in a federal constituency,[64] student club, women's association or provincial/territorial association;

  - outlays for the purpose of facilitating any person's attendance at a delegate selection meeting; or

  - outlays for the purposes of facilitating the attendance of any delegate at the leadership convention.

- A considerable number of expenses were *excluded* from the official "leadership expenses," including

  - the candidate's deposit ($25 000);

  - auditing and legal expenses;

  - interest on loans;

- the "reasonable expenses" in holding fund-raising functions that make a profit;[65]

- the candidate's child-care expenses;

- salary of the candidate or payments in lieu of salary;

- the travel and accommodation costs of the candidate, spouse, children and one aide when travelling together, based on commercial airline rates and hotels at up to $400/day in total;

- any goods produced for a candidate by voluntary labour less the cost of materials;

- services provided by an individual voluntarily, provided the individual provides the labour outside his/her working hours or on unpaid leave, *or*, if the labour is supplied during working hours, the volunteer must not receive compensation from his/her employer or third party in excess of what he/she would normally receive, *and* such individual is not employed for the purposes of supporting or working for a candidate.

- The party imposed a "tax" of 20 percent of all of a candidate's expenditures above $250 000 but below the limit of $1.7 million.

- Each candidate was required to give the party a $25 000 non-refundable deposit (to deter frivolous candidates).

- Each candidate had to file a *quarterly* expenditure report (on 15 December 1989; 15 March 1990; 15 June 1990) and a *final* report within four months of the end of the convention on 23 June 1990.

- Donors could obtain a receipt for their contributions to a candidate by making their cheque payable to the Liberal Party of Canada. The party, in turn, made a cheque payable to the candidate's campaign and issued a tax receipt to the donor.[66]

- Donated goods or services whose "commercial value" was less than $100 did not have to be reported as a contribution or as a "leadership expense."

- Each candidate had to report to the party *all* contributions in cash or the commercial value of goods and services received between 17 June 1989 and the date of his/her report (no later than 23 October 1990). The party, in turn, made *public* the "names of the contributors who donated in aggregate [i.e., to all candidates] more than $100, in the form of a consolidated document," i.e., *not* linking the names of the donor and recipient candidate. It did, however, provide a list of all contributions of $100 or more by candidate, for which tax receipts were requested, in November 1990.

- If a candidate had a surplus of contributions over expenditures, he/she had to give it to the party, any federal constituency association, or to the Receiver General of Canada.

14

CONCLUSIONS AND PROPOSALS FOR REFORM

1. INTRODUCTION

THIS STUDY of the regulation and financing of federal parties and candidates in Canada since the enactment of the *Election Expenses Act* of 1974 is a long one. It is studded with more numbers about party and candidate financing than have ever been assembled before. For most readers there are probably too many numbers – except, of course, in those areas where they would like to know more!

The purpose of this final chapter is twofold. The first is to try to stand back and restate briefly the major themes identified in the myriad details discussed above, in the form of an assessment of the strengths and weaknesses of the present method of financing political parties and candidates in Canada. The key empirical findings have been summarized in chapter 3 and at the end of chapters 4 to 11. The second purpose is to offer some proposals for reforming the present federal regulatory regime that governs party and candidate financing. Rather than the proposals for reform being set out in a single list, they have been integrated into each of the topics or issues where they are relevant.

In thinking about possible changes to the existing regulatory regime, it is useful to keep several points in mind. First, while the regime has flaws – which are being addressed by the Royal Commission on Electoral Reform and Party Financing – its key provisions are remarkably consistent with public opinion. A large-scale public-opinion survey conducted in the fall of 1990 indicated that a majority of Canadians believe that corporations, unions and other interest groups have a right to give money to political parties (Blais and Gidengil 1991).[1] Some 87 percent of those interviewed favour spending limits, and three-quarters believe that parties should be required to disclose who contributes money to them.

constrained the growth in "election expenses" because the limits on such outlays have declined or been constant. Palda (1991, 8) notes that, in real terms, the average limit on candidates' "election expenses" has declined slightly over the past four general elections: $51 402 in 1979; $47 227 in 1980; $48 774 in 1984; and $49 237 in 1988 (all in 1989 dollars using the CPI as the deflator). The spending limit in 1989 dollars for a party that ran a full slate of candidates was less in 1980 ($7 729 000) and 1984 ($7 862 000) than it was in 1979 ($8 339 000) or in 1988 ($8 406 000) (ibid.). Canadian election spending (parties and candidates) remains quite modest by the standards of the United States or Japan. In 1988, all parties spent $22.4 million on official "election expenses," while all candidates spent $31.3 million on "election expenses," $1.73 million on "personal expenses" and $4.7 million on "other expenses." The total amounted to less than $2.30 per capita. Yet none of the 60 current or former party officials interviewed for this study indicated that this level of spending was insufficient to properly inform the electorate. However, Pammett (1990) states that in the 1988 general election, 70 percent of voters surveyed stated that they wanted more information on the proposed Canada–U.S. Free Trade Agreement. This issue was said to be the most important in the campaign. Data on party campaign expenditures in the 1960s and early 1970s indicate that, in real terms, the "election expenses" of parties have *declined* since the 1974 legislation came into effect.[8] For example, in the 1965 election, the Liberal party spent at least $15.8 million in 1989 dollars (chap. 5). In 1979, the first election under the 1974 rules, the party spent $7.3 million in 1989 dollars. Liberal candidates spent virtually the same amount in 1965 and 1979 in real terms (chap. 5). In the 1972 election, the Liberal party spent $22.2 million in 1989 dollars. This was three times what the party spent in each of the four general elections under the 1974 regulations (in 1989 dollars) (chap. 5). As noted in chapter 13, the definition of "election expenses" is rather narrow, and in 1984 and 1988 the Progressive Conservative party, and in 1984 the Liberal party, greatly increased their "operating expenses." These higher outlays seem largely to have been spent on campaign-related activities but were excluded from their "election expenses" as interpreted by the CEO. Thus, it is possible that, while official "election expenses" by parties have been constrained, total campaign-related expenditures in 1984 and 1988 for some parties were greater in real terms than they were in the elections prior to 1974.

All the major parties have made innovations in fund-raising, principally in the use of direct mail. In addition, the Liberal and Progressive Conservative parties have established special "clubs" designed to raise contributions of over $1 000 annually from individuals. These two parties have further developed the traditional fund-raising dinners so that they generate more revenue. However, they are hampered by the Department of National Revenue's rule that only the costs of the dinner must be deducted from the ticket price to determine the amount eligible for the federal income-tax credit. Since 1987, the Reform Party has shown that, with a central membership list, it is possible to raise substantial sums ($5.6 million in 1991) from a party's *members* (as well as from its supporters) using direct mail.

Both the Liberal and Conservative parties have reduced their dependency on contributions from large corporations.[9] Between 1974 and 1990, corporations of all sizes provided, on average, slightly less than one-half of each party's total revenues. They also greatly increased the number of both corporate and individual contributors, although the average annual number of contributors to either party in the period 1985–90 was slightly below that in the period 1980–84.

The NDP has reduced its dependency on contributions from labour organizations (notably trade unions) to finance federal elections. It has also broadened the base of its financial support from individuals. In interelection years, individuals typically account for three-quarters of the NDP's total revenues at the federal level (chap. 6).

The candidates of the Progressive Conservative and Liberal parties have become less dependent on transfers from party headquarters or riding associations to finance their election campaigns.[10] Further, the Liberal and New Democratic parties now make a major effort to "capture" a substantial part of the federal government's reimbursement paid to candidates. For example, the Liberal party collected $2.27 million in this fashion in 1988. The Progressive Conservative party made no effort to obtain part of its candidates' reimbursement in any of the last four general elections.

The rapid growth of the revenues of the Reform Party (the party was founded in May 1987, and in 1991 it generated a total of $6.6 million in revenues) suggests that the admitted barriers to entry *can* be overcome when the party is seen as a serious contender in some regions at least (Manning 1992). However, if the Reform Party is not permitted to purchase an amount of broadcast time for its commercials roughly comparable to that of the Liberal, Progressive Conservative and New Democratic parties, it may be seriously handicapped in the next federal election (see section 3.10 below).

2.2 Problems/Deficiencies

It is apparent that the system of party and campaign financing now in place has certain problems or deficiencies. These include the following.

Over time, the effects of the Chief Electoral Officer's interpretations of the definition of "election expenses" have been to expand the set of campaign-related outlays *outside* the official "election expenses." The result is that these "other expenses" threaten the heart of the regulatory regime, namely, the strict control of election-related outlays. In the case of candidates, "other expenses" in 1988 amounted to 15 percent of "election expenses." However, for a substantial fraction of Liberal and Progressive Conservative party candidates, "other expenses" amounted to one-third of their "election expenses." In the case of parties, exemptions from "election expenses" such as polling and research costs, policy formulation and development, training of campaign workers and the production costs of commercials not used in the campaign may have added as much as 50 percent to the official "election expenses" of the three major parties.[11]

The indexing of expenditure limits using the Consumer Price Index has been inadequate because it seems clear that the prices of campaign "inputs" have risen faster than the CPI.[12] Therefore, in real terms, the limits on candidate and party "election expenses" have fallen since 1980.

There are conspicuous omissions in the purview of the present federal regulatory regime: leadership campaigns, nomination campaigns, the pre-writ activities by candidates, political trust funds and most of the activities of riding associations. Given the amounts of money involved in several of these activities or entities, there is a good case to be made for regulation.

Despite the fairly generous tax credit (unchanged since 1974) and the growing use of direct mail, less than 2 percent of electors (even in the peak years of 1984 and 1988) made a contribution to a party and/or a candidate in any year between 1974 and 1990. Public opinion data suggest that many more people *say* they make political contributions than in fact do so.

It costs money to raise money. A substantial fraction (perhaps one-third) of each party's gross revenue from contributions is absorbed by the cost of generating the revenue. However, the costs of fund-raising have not previously been publicly disclosed in any fashion.[13]

The volume and type of information published by the Chief Electoral Officer are inadequate in a number of respects. For example, each candidate's "other expenses" – which in 1988 amounted to 15 percent of official "election expenses" – are not published in the CEO's report following each general election, nor is each candidate's surplus or deficit, nor the amount that each candidate transferred to the party and/or riding association.[14] Yet the amount of each candidate's "personal expenses" *is* published after each election – although it is likely to be far less than the candidate's "other expenses." (In 1988, the average "personal expenses" of candidates was $1 098.)

There is an unjustified asymmetry in the treatment of party revenues for the issuing of tax credits: while the *gross* amount of all other contributions is eligible for a tax credit, only the *net* revenues of a fund-raising dinner are so eligible. Yet the costs of both, as a percentage of gross revenues, may be the same. Similarly, it seems illogical to prevent parties from issuing a receipt for the tax credit for contributions of goods and services outside the official campaign period, when they can do so during the campaign period.

Parties have extended the use of the federal tax credit to (i) fees paid by delegates to attend party conventions; (ii) contributions to candidates for party leader; and (iii) contributions that are in fact used for *provincial* politics (in the case of the NDP). There is ambiguity concerning the appropriateness of such uses of the tax credit, although none of these uses is prohibited in the *Canada Elections Act*. Regardless, it seems surprising that federal tax expenditures should be used to raise funds to finance the election of provincial members. In any event, it is unlikely that most taxpayers are aware of these uses of the tax credit to subsidize political activity.

Section 232 of the *Canada Elections Act* requires a candidate to transfer the surplus remaining after an election campaign to a local association or to the registered party.[15] However, the Act does not define a local association,[16] and associations do not report on their activities, although a substantial percentage of the money expended by a local association has been provided by taxpayers. Presently, anyone can organize a local association in a district and then receive a candidate's surplus to fund its activities.

The activities of advocacy groups during campaigns – notably during the 1988 general election – appear to threaten the integrity of the regulatory regime's constraints on expenditures and on the timing of advertising messages during the campaign period. At the same time, stringent regulation of the activities of advocacy groups inevitably conflicts with the protection of the right of freedom of expression under the *Canadian Charter of Rights and Freedoms*.

There is some evidence to suggest that there is a "fiscal imbalance" within the Progressive Conservative, Liberal and New Democratic parties. The imbalance exists with respect to the roles/responsibilities and fund-raising capacity of the national party as compared to that of provincial/territorial associations and riding associations. It appears to be attributable to differences in the reimbursement rate of party

(22.5 percent) and candidate (50 percent) "election expenses" and the revenue sharing or division of sources of revenues among units within each party. Further, parties have to finance a substantial set of activities in the interelection years, which candidates do not. As a result, parties have to "go back to the well" every year, while candidates need to do so only every four years or so.[17] The nature of Canada's political system means that the national campaign effort (including the leader's tour) is generally more important than the efforts of individual candidates, although the complementarities are obvious within individual ridings (see Heintzman 1991). In order to help pay for the cost of increasingly expensive national campaigns, the Liberal and New Democratic parties have "taxed" part of their candidates' reimbursement from the federal government. In principle at least, it should be possible for parties to reduce any fiscal imbalance by intraparty transfers. In practice, efforts to redistribute funds within a party tend to be fraught with conflict.

3. MAJOR THEMES AND PROPOSALS FOR REFORM

3.1 Total Party Spending

There has been a vast growth of party spending between elections. In the 1960s, for example, the Progressive Conservative and Liberal parties' annual spending between elections was about 10 percent to 20 percent of campaign expenditures. In 1989 dollars, Conservative party expenditures increased from $6.4 million in 1974/75 to about $11.5 million in 1978, 1981 and 1982. It then increased to $17 million in 1983 and $16.1 million in 1986. In 1989, the Conservative party spent $12.8 million and in 1990 it spent $10.15 million in 1989 dollars. The Liberal party's expenditures increased from $5.1 million in 1974/75 to $10.8 million in 1978, but fell to $7.7 million in 1981. Then expenditures rose to $12.7 million in 1986 but fell to $7.1 million in 1989. The increase to $12.7 million in 1990 was largely attributable to the revenues of the convention and the contributions to candidates routed through the Federal Liberal Agency (over $6 million). The expenditures of the NDP's federal office were much smaller and they grew more slowly in real terms – from $1.5 million in 1977 and 1978 to $2.25 million in 1987 – but they dropped to just under $2 million in 1990 (in 1989 dollars).

Over the course of the four elections between 1979 and 1988, the NDP was able to "close the gap" with Conservatives and Liberals in respect to *party* "election expenses." In 1979, the NDP spent 49.1 percent of the party's limit on "election expenses," while the Liberals spent 86.2 percent and the Conservatives spent 87.7 percent. In 1988, the comparable figures were 88.2 percent, 85.7 percent and 98.9 percent respectively.

In fact, in 1988, the NDP ($7.06 million) slightly outspent the Liberal party ($6.84 million). The Tories ($7.92 million), however, outspent the New Democrats by 12.2 percent.

Despite the substantial (but uneven) increase in party revenues in real terms between 1974 and 1990 and the cap on "election expenses," the Liberals ran a substantial cumulative deficit ($2.57 million) during the last period they were in power (1980-84), and in the period 1985–90 ($2.66 million) – both in 1989 dollars. In 1989 dollars, the Conservative party had a cumulative surplus of $2 million over the years prior to 1980, but then it had a cumulative deficit of $4.8 million in the period 1980–84. This was offset by a cumulative *surplus* of $5.5 million in the first five years of the Mulroney government, 1985–90.

3.2 Broadening of the Parties' Revenue Base

There has been a broadening of the major parties' revenue sources, notably in contributions from individuals and federal subsidies (direct and indirect), in the period since 1974. At the same time, the level of public participation in financing parties/candidates is low. First, less than 2 percent of electors made a contribution to a party or candidate in any year between 1984 and 1990. Yet 18 percent of the adult population said they had made a contribution to a party or candidate according to a survey of 2 947 people conducted in the fall of 1990 (Blais and Gidengil 1991). Second, only 2 percent to 9 percent of corporations made a contribution to a party in any year between 1983 and 1990,[18] but 40 percent of the 500 largest nonfinancial enterprises (FP 500) and 35 percent of the 155 largest financial enterprises (F 155) did so between 1983 and 1990. Third, less than one-half of trade unions are affiliated with the NDP, although they accounted for from 10 percent to 20 percent of the NDP's federal revenue in interelection years – and more in election years.

The dependency of the Liberal and Conservative parties on a few hundred corporations for the bulk of their funds ended with the 1974 legislation. Corporate contributions between 1974 and 1990 averaged just under one-half of total revenues for both parties. The Conservatives increased the number of contributions from corporations from about 2 000 in 1974/75 to over 21 000 in 1984, but in 1987 and 1989 the number was only slightly more than 9 000. In 1990, the number was down to 7 183. The Liberal party increased the number of contributions from corporations from 2 430 in 1974/75 to over 5 000 annually in the late 1970s, but the peak of 7 536 was reached in 1983. While almost the same number of corporations were "tapped" in 1988 (7 238), the number fell sharply to 3 857 in 1989. (The increase to 5 598 in 1990 was in large part due to the leadership race.)

There has been a diversification in the sources and techniques of funding of the Liberal and Progressive Conservative parties since 1974. On average, individuals now provide slightly more than 50 percent of their total revenue – stimulated by growing direct-mail efforts and perhaps by the tax credit. Both parties have been able to obtain funds from small and medium-sized corporations (i.e., *other* than the FP 500 or F 155). The number of contributions by individuals to all federal parties rose from 84 600 in 1975 to 211 000 in 1984 and 208 000 in 1988, the last two years being election years. The peak was 218 000 in 1990, including 38 000 contributions from individuals to *other* than Conservative, Liberal or New Democratic parties. The number of individuals contributing to *candidates* of all parties rose from 67 300 in the 1979 election to 104 800 in the 1988 election.

While contributions from corporations accounted for slightly less than one-half of the revenues of the Liberal and Conservative parties in the period 1974–90, the amount received from the largest 500 nonfinancial and the largest 155 financial enterprises as a fraction of party revenues was far less than their share of economic output. While the FP 500 accounted for 68.2 percent of all corporate assets in 1983, they typically accounted for about one-fifth of the value of contributions to the Liberal and Conservative parties between 1983 and 1990 (table 11.12).

The dependency of the NDP on contributions and other forms of assistance from labour organizations and trade unions has declined since 1974, particularly for national elections. In 1979 and 1980, labour provided 32.5 percent and 30.4 percent of the NDP's federally receipted revenues (including reimbursement). In the next two election years, this fell to 25.6 percent (1984) and 19.8 percent (1988). Labour's contributions to the NDP's federal office *between* elections have varied, from about 14 percent in the period 1975–77 to about 10 percent in 1982–83, to 19.7 percent in 1987 to about 13 percent in 1989 and 1990 (table 6.8).

3.3 The Extent of Public Funding

Public funding of parties and candidates is a central tenet of the present regulatory regime, which was established in 1974. The federal government provides financial assistance in three ways: reimbursement of 22.5 percent of parties' "election expenses," reimbursement of 50 percent of each candidate's "election expenses" (provided he/she gets 15 percent of the votes) and the income-tax credit on contributions by individuals and corporations to parties and candidates.

Michaud and Laferrière (1991) indicate that, over the 1981–84 electoral cycle, the value of federal tax credits amounted to 30.7 percent of total party revenues ($118.9 million).[19] For the last electoral cycle

(1985–88), tax credits amounted to 29.0 percent of total party revenues ($165.3 million).[20] Michaud and Laferrière (ibid.) state that, for the 1984 and 1988 general elections, tax credits (annualized) plus reimbursements to candidates and parties amounted to 43.3 percent of total party and candidate election-related expenditures. For the last electoral cycle (1985–88), total government funding (tax credits plus reimbursements) amounted to 31.4 percent of party and candidate *expenditures* ($212.4 million). In addition, the estimated market value of advertising time on the electronic media provided free to the parties in the 1988 election was $169 500 for radio and $6.145 million for television (ibid.).

The work of the Royal Commission on Electoral Reform and Party Financing has raised the question of the appropriate balance between private and public funding of parties and candidates. Given the fiscal constraints faced by the federal government, there is unlikely to be widespread support for much more public money, whether in the form of direct cash transfers or indirectly through income tax credits. Further, the data in chapter 3 make it clear that the Progressive Conservative, Liberal and New Democratic parties have been able to generate substantial increases in total revenues (and expenditures) in real terms over the period 1974–90. They appear to have been aided by the tax credit, but this has not been changed since 1974, and a substantial fraction of individuals who make contributions do not claim the tax credit. Even if the tax credit is not made more generous, the senior officials of all three major parties have indicated that there is an imbalance in the fiscal capacity of headquarters and the riding association/candidate. They point to the reimbursement of 50 percent of candidates' "election expenses" versus 22.5 percent for parties. Officials also note that, even after "other expenses," many candidates are able to transfer substantial surpluses to their riding association. The implication is that the reimbursement rate should be reduced for candidates and increased for parties (even if the total subsidy is unchanged). In 1988, 293 Progressive Conservative, 264 Liberal and 170 New Democratic candidates (out of 295 in each case) received reimbursement for half their "election expenses." However, only 12 of the 689 candidates of other parties were eligible for reimbursement (table 12.30).

There are several arguments for increasing the federal tax credit for political contributions. First, while all the major parties have increased their expenditures *between* general elections in real terms (and they also almost spend the limit on "election expenses"), it is evident that they are experiencing "fiscal stress" in varying degrees for several reasons:

1. It is clear that the limit on "election expenses," although it has been indexed to the CPI, has not kept up with increases in the prices of campaign-related activities and, to a lesser degree, this appears to be the case for party activities between elections as well; in other words, party revenues have to rise *faster* than the rate of inflation as measured by the CPI if they are not to fall in real terms.

2. It may be that the total number of contributions from individuals to federal parties peaked in the period 1983–85, when the average was 206 200. In contrast, for the last three years (1987–90), which also include a general election, the average was 188 066, although in 1990 the number rose to 218 423 (table 8.1). On the other hand, the number of contributions from individuals to *candidates* has increased in each of the last three elections (from 67 300 in 1979 to 70 600 in 1980, and to 87 500 in 1984 and to 104 800 in 1988).

3. In real terms, average contributions in the late 1980s for all three main parties were less than they were in the mid-1970s.[21]

4. While the Liberal and Conservative parties have increased the number of contributions from corporations (particularly the Tories), the average contribution in the late 1980s was slightly less than it was in the mid-1970s (table 11.2). Moreover, the variation over the period was very noticeable: in the case of the Tories, the average went from $1 293 in 1974/75 to $663 in 1979, then rose to $1 483 in 1980, but fell to $299 in 1983. It then rose to $1 075 in 1988, and fell again to $736 in 1989.[22]

5. There is plenty of evidence in the form of public opinion polls to indicate that the public's level of cynicism about politicians and government (or even alienation) has increased during the 1980s and into the 1990s (see Blais and Gidengil 1991; Gregg and Posner 1990).

The second reason for increasing the income-tax credit for contributions from individuals is that the tax credit is more heavily used by individuals who make contributions than by corporations, perhaps because it is relatively more important as a percentage of the taxes payable. Third, the income-tax credit gives *individuals* an opportunity to direct a government subsidy to the "target" of their choice, rather than having it done by Parliament.[23] Moreover, the tax credit rewards the energy and initiative of party officials (largely volunteers) who have to solicit contributions from individuals or corporations. Larger reimbursement for expenses or pure cash subsidies do not have this effect.[24]

Proposals for Reform

- The federal income-tax credit should be increased to reflect part of the inflation since 1974, for example, 70 percent on the first $300, plus 50 percent on contributions between $301 and $600, plus 30 percent on contributions between $601 and $2 000.[25] The maximum credit would be $780 on contributions totalling $2 000 in any year.
- The reimbursement by the federal government of candidates' "election expenses" should be reduced to 33.3 percent (from 50 percent). However, the 33.3 percent rate would be applied to a new, broader definition of "election expenses"(see section 3.5 below).
- The federal government's reimbursement on the broader definition of party "election expenses" should be increased from 22.5 percent to 33.3 percent.
- In general, total cash subsidies to parties and candidates should not be increased. The object of the proposals is to shift the value of such subsidies from candidates to parties.

3.4 Local or Riding Associations

The importance of riding associations in all parties has increased. Yet the financing of their activities is largely unregulated. Their resources have increased because they are the main recipients of candidate surpluses, which grew from $8 million in 1984 to $9.6 million in 1988 according to the Chief Electoral Officer.[26] They also benefit from the tax credit if contributions are routed through the party's official agent, although both the Liberal party and the NDP "tax" such revenues.

As the only unregistered and virtually unregulated entity in the federal system regulating political finance, riding associations are, in effect, the "black hole" of party and candidate financing in Canada. Riding associations enter into the financing picture in at least the following ways: they finance the pre-writ activities of the candidate in some cases; they raise money between elections from nonreceipted sources; and they are the primary recipients of their candidate's surplus. Yet party officials at the national and provincial/territorial association level are ignorant of riding associations' revenues and expenditures, balance sheet and trust funds. In contrast to the federal position, Ontario, Quebec, Alberta and New Brunswick require that local or riding associations register and publicly report their revenues, expenditures and transfers to the party or to candidates. They must also make public their balance sheets.

One of the problems with electoral finance in Canada is the pressures created by the ability of most riding associations to raise far more money than they need to cover their candidate's "election expenses," "personal expenses" and "other expenses" when the reimbursement by the federal government is taken into account. For example, in 1988, 231 of 295 Conservative party candidates had a surplus (average of $20 080), while 234 Liberals had a surplus (average of $12 727) and 167 NDP candidates had a surplus (average of $10 421) (table 12.33). Twenty-seven candidates, all Liberals or Conservatives, had a surplus of at least $40 000 in 1988 (table 12.35).

Officials in the Progressive Conservative and Liberal parties stated that *some* ridings have bank balances, trust funds or charitable trusts in the six-figure range. Cabinet ministers are more likely to have a surplus after the campaign. Their riding associations are likely to be financially stronger. Similarly, the riding associations of incumbents with a "safe seat" are more likely to benefit from a larger surplus and to have more money in the bank. On the other hand, some candidates/riding associations are poor because they "sit on their hands." Yet, if the seat is winnable, the party will transfer money to the candidate for "election expenses." In general, it should be appreciated that, for about one-third of the 295 federal constituencies, the riding association is a rather modest organization with few members and very little money (Carty and Erickson 1991).

There has been a large reduction in the dependency of candidates on party headquarters, particularly in the case of the Conservative party. However, in 1988 Conservative and Liberal candidates in Quebec were more dependent upon transfers from within the party than were candidates in other provinces.[27] As a whole, candidates have become a *net* contributor to parties and riding associations through the transfer of surpluses to both. In 1979, 1980 and 1988, the Liberal party "taxed" part of many candidates' reimbursement of their "election expenses." In some cases (e.g., the NDP in BC in 1988), parties require that contributions to candidates be passed through the provincial/territorial section, which then retains part of the revenue.

Proposals for Reform

- Each riding association should be required to become a registered entity, as are parties and candidates. Hence they would be required to publicly disclose their revenues and expenditures and provide each year to the Chief Electoral Officer a list of the names of donors contributing more than $100.

- No candidate's surplus should be permitted to be transferred to other than a properly constituted riding association (or to his/her party). Each party's rules for this purpose should have to be approved by the Chief Electoral Officer.
- The total amount of a candidate's surplus paid to the party and/or riding association following an election campaign should be limited to $10 000[28] (indexed). The excess should be remitted to the government of Canada.

3.5 "Election Expenses"

Campaign-related spending *other* than official "election expenses" by parties and candidates has become substantial. For example, in 1988, candidates' "other expenses" amounted to $4.7 million, or 15 percent of "election expenses." These outlays were highly concentrated: of the 277 candidates with the largest "other expenses," the average for 155 Conservative party candidates was $14 200; for 69 Liberals the average was $11 400; and for 39 NDP candidates the average was $3 700 (table 12.25). Eighteen percent of these "other expenses" were incurred prior to the issue of the writ, 59 percent during the campaign and 23 percent after voting day. For a very few candidates, their "other expenses" exceeded their official "election expenses." The growth in candidates' "other expenses" is largely due to the definition of "election expenses" in the *Canada Elections Act*, and the CEO's interpretation of it in his *Guidelines*. As has been noted in chapter 13, a rather long list of items is not included in official "election expenses" that are subject to limit under the *Canada Elections Act*. Some of the most important of these are: expenses of a potential candidate for the purpose of obtaining the nomination as a candidate, even if incurred during the writ period; any material (e.g., brochures, signs, etc.) that is not used and remains on hand at the end of a campaign; payment of the expenses of poll agents or their salary where it is "materially less than the commercial value of their services"; the cost of victory parties; and the costs of campaign offices before the writ is issued and after voting day.

A common reaction of MPs and other observers to the revelation that a number of important campaign-related expenditures are *not* defined as "election expenses" and are therefore not controlled is to propose that *all* direct and indirect expenditures on behalf of a candidate or party be included and controlled (albeit perhaps at a higher level). It has been suggested that even a comprehensive definition of "election expenses" for candidates would "catch" only two or three potentially important outlays, for example, payments to poll agents (largely in Quebec and Atlantic Canada) and the costs of polling and other forms of research. There are two issues here, however. One has to do with controlling total election-related spending. The other is the failure to publish the details on the use of tax-receipted moneys used for campaign-related activities but outside the official campaign period.[29]

With respect to *parties*, the "election expenses" problem takes at least two forms. First, there is the possibility that a party is able to shift what would otherwise be "election expenses" to outside the official campaign period, during which they are limited. It is impossible to determine for sure if this has been done. But the data indicate that, in calendar year 1988, the federal Progressive Conservative party spent $17.8 million on "operating expenses" plus $7.92 million on "election expenses." The important point is that, in 1987, the Conservatives' "operating expenses" were $11.5 million and, in 1989, they were $10.7 million. A similar pattern occurred for the 1984 election for both the Conservative and Liberal parties. If "operating expenses" simply represent the normal activities of the party not directly connected with the general election, why did they rise from 1987 to 1988 and fall so sharply in 1989?

The second form – and the heart of the problem – is the fact that a number of potentially important election-related outlays have been *excluded* from a party's "election expenses" by the CEO in his *Guidelines*. As noted in more detail in chapter 13, these include: polling and research expenses (which could amount to $400 000 to $800 000 during the campaign);[30] fund-raising costs; costs of developing party policies or election strategy; costs of training candidates or election organizers; and all the party's internal costs "not incurred as an integral part of endeavours furthering the external exposure of the party" (Canada, Elections Canada 1988a, 4). These exclusions might easily have totalled $4 million in the case of the Conservative party in 1988 and somewhat smaller amounts for the Liberal party and the NDP. Surely most of these expenditures are closely related to fighting an election campaign and should be included in the definition of "election expenses."

Proposals for Reform

- Parliament should establish a clear and more comprehensive definition of "election expenses" for both parties and candidates. Any exemptions should be specified, and the amount spent on each should be publicly reported after the election. The analysis of the campaign-related expenditures by parties suggests that the limit for a better, broader definition of "election expenses" in 1988 should have been about $12 million instead of $8 million. Thus, all parties' "election expenses" would have amounted to less than $1.50 per capita. This is hardly an exorbitant amount for a national election campaign. The broader definition should include the following types of expenditures: polling and research; training of party officials and volunteers for the campaign; costs of developing party policy and election strategy; and costs of production of campaign commercials/ads, even if they are not used. Some of these activities naturally occur *before* the election is called. However, election dates are at the discretion of the leader of the governing party. Even though it is arbitrary, expenditures incurred for any of the categories listed above should be included in a party's "election expenses" if they are incurred in the 12 months preceding the day on which the election is called.

A broader definition, it should be noted, would *not* eliminate the problem of how to allocate the ongoing overhead and operating expenses to the campaign period. Any solution would be somewhat arbitrary, but Parliament should request the Chief Electoral Officer to establish a formula based on a standardized set of accounts subject to independent audit. If the integrity of the regulatory regime designed in 1974 is to be restored, it is essential that the legislation be changed.

• Both parties and candidates should be required to distinguish (and report) the following categories of campaign-related outlays: all pre-writ expenditures (in the 12 months prior to the date the election is called); all outlays *during* the campaign period, whether official "election expenses" or not; *post*–election day outlays; and *exempt* expenditures by category.

• The statutory limits on party and candidates' "election expenses" should be increased to reflect the failure to keep up with inflation over and above the increase in the limit due to the broader definition of "election expenses" proposed above. The increase should be about 25 percent to reflect increases in the prices of election activities over and above those captured by the Consumer Price Index.

• The inflation-adjustment mechanism for the limits on party and candidate "election expenses" should be modified to better reflect the true rate of inflation in outlays on election campaigns. This could be done by having Statistics Canada prepare a special index to reflect the major types of expenditures that parties/candidates make.

• A precise definition of candidates' "personal expenses" should be established by Parliament. It should not be left to the Chief Electoral Officer's discretion as published in his *Guidelines*, as at present.[31]

3.6 Volunteer Labour

This study has focused on the revenues and expenditures of federal parties and candidates. It has not been possible to add to the money amounts of both the value of volunteer labour supplied to parties and candidates.[32] Nor has it been possible to determine the number of hours of volunteer labour provided. Yet, as noted in chapter 1, the work of volunteers – and not just during election campaigns – is central to political activity in Canada.

Public policy concerning the use of volunteer labour by parties and candidates ought to recognize three things. First, the quality of democracy is almost certainly improved by encouraging individuals to participate in political parties by doing volunteer work for them. Second, it should recognize that any regulations concerning volunteer labour should be "user friendly," that is, easy for the individuals and for the party or candidate to administer. Third, public policy should recognize that, where skilled individuals apply their skills in working for a party or candidate and where considerable time is devoted to such volunteer work, the party or candidate is receiving a substantial donation (in kind) and that therefore it is able to substitute voluntary for paid labour. The issue on the "contributions" side is to achieve parity in the *disclosure* of cash contributions and those in kind. While cash contributions of more than $100 to a party or riding must be publicly disclosed, the value (or even the amount) of volunteer labour is not disclosed – unless the free service is provided by a person who is self-employed, if the service is one that is normally sold or otherwise charged for by that person (Canada, Elections Canada 1988a, 19).

On the expenditure side, a problem arises because the "election expenses" of parties and candidates are limited by law. If an unpaid volunteer can do work that would normally be done by an employee (or fee-for-service consultant), then the value of his/her services is not included in official "election expenses." Thus there is more money left to spend on other activities. However, under the CEO's 1988 *Guidelines*, volunteer labour is *not* an "election expense," provided that it is performed by otherwise unemployed or retired persons, or by employees on an unpaid leave of absence or, in the case of self-employed persons, that the volunteer labour is work for which they do not normally charge. Therefore, as Senator Norman Atkins notes, communications consultants "can't do anything remotely related to communications for fear that their voluntary activity will have adverse effects on the campaign budget and that their time will be assessed against [official 'election expenses'] at a 'fair market value' " (1990a, 11). Thus the services of a union official on a paid leave of absence working for a candidate or of a self-employed communications consultant handling a candidate's publicity (if that is part of what he/she does professionally) would have to be included in the candidate's "election expenses." Not surprisingly, all these subtle distinctions escape almost everyone.

A newspaper report during the 1988 election stated that partners in many of the government relations consulting firms in Ottawa "abandon their desks to help their friends retain or get into power" (*Financial Post*, 11 October 1988, 11). Bill Lee, who managed John Turner's campaign in 1984 and who was chairman of Executive Consultants Ltd., noted that "it's certainly helpful to know the political people of both major parties. When you are talking to a client about behind-the-scenes policy development, they feel better if you have been in the game and know the big players at both the political and bureaucratic level" (ibid.). The chairman of Public Affairs International (a major government-relations consulting firm) noted that up to a half a dozen of his senior staff will be involved in political campaigns on a full- or nearly full-time basis.

Elaborate regulatory requirements regarding volunteer labour could easily create a compliance nightmare that would make campaigns more expensive. At the same time, it is clear that failure to require disclosure of the amount or value of donated labour can and has led to practices that are inconsistent with the spirit and intent of the 1974 legislation. These include the following: (i) situations whereby corporations, law firms, trade unions, lobbying firms and other organizations provide a leave of absence with or without pay to employees (partners) to work full time on political campaigns for extended periods of time;[33] or (ii) situations like those described in (i), but where the problem is exacerbated by having the employer organization (or other third party) pay the out-of-pocket expenses of the person whose labour is being donated; such expenses can be considerable where the individual is working away from the city in which he/she resides; or (iii) situations where a candidate's official agent pays the living and other expenses of volunteers. These are difficult situations to identify and regulate, although the CEO on 25 October 1988 stated that volunteers' expenses are to be included in a candidate's "election expenses" (*Globe and Mail*, 6 October 1988, A5).

In the case of lobbyists, lawyers, advertising executives and other skilled professionals, the market value of their "free labour" is high – at least $1 000 per day and probably closer to $2 000 a day. The point is that a campaign that attracts three or four very skilled individuals each working for 30 days on it receives contributions totalling about $150 000. This is clearly an amount to be reckoned with. It is too important not to include within the amount of any required disclosure of contributions.

How might the matter of volunteer or donated labour be handled? One possibility would be to require each candidate or party to declare the estimated fair market value of *all* volunteer labour of more than, say, 20 hours per individual, or $500 in value. Obviously, the height of the threshold is arbitrary. The objective is not to impose an excessive burden on those subject to the regulation. A second regulatory approach would be to require all candidates or parties to disclose the fair market value of volunteer labour where it exceeds 20 percent (or some other percentage) of other contributions in total, or where an individual volunteers more than, say, five days of his/her time, regardless of its fair market value. A third relatively simple and nonburdensome approach to the disclosure of volunteer labour to parties and candidates would be to require each candidate or party to report the following information for all individuals who provide more than, say, 20 hours of volunteer labour: name, address of employer, total number of hours of volunteer labour donated, whether or not the individual had to forgo employment income (or vacation pay) during the period in which his/her labour was donated to the campaign and the total value of the volunteer's expenses paid by the volunteer, advocacy groups or by the candidate's official agent. This information would be publicly disclosed. This would avoid the problem of having to determine the fair market value of donated labour, but it would identify those persons who gave a great deal of their time to assist a candidate or party and whether they were at the same time forgoing salary or vacation time to do so. If an individual works full time for several weeks on a campaign, but is being paid his/her regular salary by the employer, then it is the latter who is, in effect, making the donation, because the individual is sacrificing no pecuniary advantage in order to help the candidate.

3.7 Asymmetric Treatment of Revenue Sources

The Department of National Revenue's rules concerning the issuing of receipts for the income-tax credit for political contributions provide that the total or gross amount of contributions raised from direct mail or personal solicitation is eligible for the tax credit. However, only the net revenue from fund-raising dinners is eligible, despite the fact that the cost of raising money via direct mail may exceed the costs of putting on a dinner as a percentage of the gross revenue (see chaps. 9 and 10).

Proposals for Reform

- The Department of National Revenue should permit parties, ridings or the candidate's agent to issue a receipt for the gross amount of the ticket price for any fund-raising dinner.

• Parties should be permitted to issue a receipt for the tax credit for contributions of goods or services, at their fair market value, contributed at *any* time (not just during campaign periods, as at present).

3.8 Costs of Raising Funds

While parties (and candidates) have been able to raise considerable sums over the period 1974–90 (rising in real terms), they have learned that it costs money to raise money, even with the help of the income-tax credit. The data in chapter 9 indicate that, for the Conservative party, the costs of direct-mail fund-raising amounted to from 18 percent to 28 percent of annual gross revenue between 1983 and 1990. They were from 40 percent to 65 percent in the case of the federal office of the NDP between 1987 and 1990, and from 34 percent to 78 percent in the case of the Liberal party between 1985 and 1990. For the Conservative party, the costs of national fund-raising dinners featuring the leader amounted to from 26 percent to 40 percent of gross revenue between 1985 and 1990. For the Liberal party, the comparable figures were 32 percent to 38 percent (chap. 10). No party publicly discloses its costs of fund-raising. When these figures are published, there may be pressure for them to do so, including disclosing the costs in their direct-mail appeals and other forms of solicitation.

Proposal for Reform

• Parties, candidates and ridings should be required to publicly report the *costs* of fund-raising for each major source of revenue (e.g., individuals, corporations, trade unions, etc.) and for each major fund-raising technique (e.g., direct mail, leader's dinners, major-donor programs, etc.).

3.9 *Financement Populaire*/Limits on Contributions

In the late 1980s, some Progressive Conservative party MPs from Quebec called on the federal government to adopt the *financement populaire* system that has prevailed in the province of Quebec since 1977. The chairman of Canada's largest bank has recommended that this option be carefully considered (Stanbury 1991). *Financement populaire* has two main elements: only *electors* may make political contributions (not corporations, trade unions or other interest groups); and each person is limited to contributing $3 000 annually to each party, including its candidates. Given the fact that over the past decade both the Liberal and Conservative parties relied on corporations for almost one-half of their total revenues, and that trade unions and other labour organizations provided up to one-fifth of the NDP's federally receipted revenues in interelection years and more in election years, the adoption of *finance-ment populaire* would require major changes in the way federal parties and candidates raise money (chap. 8).

Consideration of the *financement populaire* approach raises the question of whether limits should be placed on the total amount of contributions from any or all sources (individuals, corporations, trade unions, etc.). Under the present regulatory regime, "election expenses" are capped, but contributions are not. In general, under U.S. federal regulations, there are no limits on expenditures,[34] but there are a series of limits on contributions (see Alexander 1991). Palda (1991, 105) argues that "a contribution [to a party or candidate] is the best weapon the individual has against special interests" because the latter are better able to lobby government between elections. A low limit on contributions may reduce the "contributing public's hold on the candidate for two reasons. The ceiling may stop any one person from making a very intense show of preference [e.g., Mrs. Irene Dyck] ... The more important reason is that people often give to public interest groups who use their accumulated money to sway politicians" (ibid.). However, this does not happen in Canada, unlike the United States with its political action committees. Aside from corporations, the only organizations that make substantial contributions to parties are trade unions. The sum of all interest-group contributions – excluding unions and corporations – in any year in the period 1983–90 was less than the average contribution of the five largest banks in Canada, that is, under $50 000.

There is considerable public support (57 percent) for a limit on contributions to parties, based on a major opinion poll in the fall of 1990. Further, 35 percent of those polled think the limit should be $1 000 or less. Moreover, the vast majority (84 percent) of people think such controls are *not* "a waste of time and energy" (Blais and Gidengil 1991).[35] In modern times, however, Canadians have no direct experience with limits on political contributions at the federal level. However, several provinces have legislated limits on contributions: Ontario, 1976; Quebec, 1977; Alberta, 1977; and New Brunswick, 1978. More importantly, the experience of the United States should make Canadians very sceptical about the *practicality* of being able to limit contributions from any source.

In the United States, the term "soft money" refers to contributions that are essentially exempt from federal statutory limits on contributions, reporting requirements and restrictions on the sources of contributions.[36] Goldstein (1991, 1) found that the Republican National Committee (RNC) received $18.5 million in soft money in 1989–90, while the Democratic National Committee (DNC) received $6.5 million. Reported contributions to the RNC totalled $68.7 million, while those to the DNC totalled $14.5 million (*New York Times*, 18 May 1991, 10). Goldstein (1991, 4) found that 56 percent of the soft money going to the RNC came from business (largest donation, $291 360), while 42 percent came from individuals (largest contribution $130 000). The sources of the DNC's soft money were business, 42 percent (largest contribution $75 325), unions, 28 percent (largest contribution $222 550), and individuals, 25 percent (largest contribution $280 000). Goldstein concludes that

> the soft money loophole has been stretched so wide that it threatens to explode the entire structure of our campaign finance system – a system designed to limit who can contribute, how much they can contribute and to put it all on the public record. The raising of soft money by the political parties undercuts every one of these basic tenets of our campaign finance laws. (Ibid., 17)

Limits on contributions and on the *sources* of contributions would be very difficult to enforce. In the case of corporations, the existence of subsidiaries and affiliated companies would make it easy to avoid any limit placed on a single legal entity. Limits on unions that did not also include all their locals would suffer from the same problem. Party officials interviewed for this study suggested that efforts to limit contributions to individuals (electors) in Quebec have not been entirely successful in preventing organizations from making contributions through individuals. Laws that are not properly enforced tend to increase cynicism and to bring into disrepute laws that can be properly enforced.

In general, disclosure – particularly where legally (and hence economically) related entities such as corporations and trade unions are required to disclose the *combined* amount of their contributions[37] – is the best practicable protection the public has against the efforts of those individuals or organizations that would use large donations to influence the political process.[38]

Proposals for Reform

- The federal government should *not* adopt the *financement populaire* proposal, even if the limit on the amounts of each elector's contributions is raised well above that which currently prevails in Quebec.
- All business enterprises with sales exceeding $100 million (or assets exceeding $100 million) should be required to report to

the Chief Electoral Officer (who would make public) the political contributions of each of its affiliates or subsidiaries (where the parent company or an affiliate owns at least 50 percent of the voting shares).[39]

- All trade unions with more than 5 000 members should be required to report to the Chief Electoral Officer (who would make public) the political contributions by each of its locals (or other organizational entity associated with the union).[40]

3.10 Allocation of Time for Paid Broadcast Advertising

As noted in chapter 13, the formula for allocating the total permitted amount of paid broadcast advertising during election campaigns (6.5 hours) is retrospective; it depends largely on a party's allocation, on the number of seats it won and on its popular vote in the previous general election. The result is that a new party (one that has become registered since the previous election) or one whose support and activities have grown rapidly since the previous election, is at a serious disadvantage in communicating with the electorate because it cannot purchase much broadcast advertising. In 1988, the three main parties spent an average of 46 percent of their "election expenses" on radio or television advertising (table 3.5). In the case of the Liberal party at least, the lack of funds limited its television advertising, rather than the limit on the amount of time it was permitted to purchase. In the next election, however, the Reform Party may have the money, but not be able to purchase broadcasting time if the present allocation formula is upheld by the courts. It would be entitled to purchase 10 minutes, versus 173 minutes for the Conservative party. (The Reform Party won its constitutional challenge to the formula at the trial level in late 1992.)

In the course of interviews with senior officials of the Conservative, Liberal and New Democratic parties, questions concerning the formula for broadcast advertising often elicited interesting responses. Several officials argued that "once the writs are issued, all parties should have the same opportunity to advertise." Thus the only limit on broadcast or other forms of advertising would be the limit on total "election expenses." In the view of these officials, the relatively tight limit on "election expenses" and the high cost of television commercials[41] would force all parties to think carefully about where to spend their money for best effect. In their view, it is unnecessary – and unfair – to control one particular campaign technique.[42] Other officials, particularly those in parties with a large allocation, thought that the current allocation formula is "just fine." They recognized the value to their party of what they acknowledge is a barrier to entry to new or rapidly growing parties.

One official, a lawyer, suggested that the formula is "constitutionally questionable," but he liked having it in place as long as possible to benefit his party.

Proposals for Reform

- There should be *no limit* on the amount of broadcast time a party is able to purchase for advertising, except that determined by the legal limit on its "election expenses."
- Parties should be permitted to purchase broadcast advertising at any time after the writs are issued, except in the 48 hours prior to the opening of the polls on voting day.[43]
- The present rules regarding the pricing of broadcast ads purchased by parties or candidates should be retained.
- The role of the Broadcasting Arbitrator should be confined to mediating conflicts between parties and broadcasters, for example, conflicts over the allocation of the limited number of advertising minutes when there is excess demand for those minutes (and the total number of minutes cannot be increased due to CRTC regulations). (Care must be exercised here to ensure that the Arbitrator does not have too much discretion, however.)

3.11 Activities of Advocacy Groups

In 1988, the proposed Free Trade Agreement with the United States stimulated the creation of advocacy groups both for and against the FTA, but it also saw such groups spend large sums advertising their views. Hiebert (1991) found that the pro–free trade groups spent 77 cents for every $1.00 of the Conservative party advertising budget, while the anti–free trade forces spent only 13 cents for every $1.00 of the total advertising budgets of the two parties opposing free trade. Moreover, about two-thirds of the advocacy groups' advertising space was purchased in the last week of the campaign, with one-quarter of the space appearing on the last full-circulation day. Econometric research indicates that the most important effect of the advertisements was apparently to convince those Free Trade Agreement supporters intending to vote for the Liberal party to support the Conservative party.

Palda (1991) argues that advocacy groups make political parties and candidates more responsive to the interests of voters by highlighting issues about which they feel strongly. Such groups, if they were allowed to directly endorse candidates and parties, would help overcome the barriers to entry faced by new/small parties.

The issue of advocacy-group activities during election campaigns is one of the most difficult to address. A balance must be struck between the regulation of these activities in order to preserve the integrity of the controls on "election expenses" by parties and candidates and the constitutional protection of freedom of expression in the *Canadian Charter of Rights and Freedoms.*

Four policy options are outlined in figure 14.1, together with some comments on the implications of adopting each one.

3.12 Unregulated Activities

The importance of expenditures on political activities that are not presently regulated has grown substantially. Such activities include leadership campaigns, nomination campaigns and pre-election writ activities. For example, in the 1983 Conservative party leadership race, the five leading candidates spent about $4.3 million. In 1990, the six candidates for leader of the Liberal party spent about $6 million. In the latter race, some $1.95 million in contributions were routed through the Federal Liberal Agency; hence they were eligible for the tax credit on political contributions, and were subject to more detailed disclosure than was made of other contributions to candidates under the rules established by the party.

Wearing (1988a, 72) suggests that unregulated, undisclosed campaign fund-raising could ultimately undermine the democratic nature and integrity of the leadership selection process. The Reform Commission of the Liberal party (1991, 19) has sought comment in respect to the following possible reforms in the party's regulation of the financing of leadership races:

- full public disclosure of all amounts spent by leadership candidates;
- spending limits established based on a dollar amount per every paid up member of the Liberal Party of Canada;
- spending limits established in specific areas of leadership activity such as advertising;
- specific activities prohibited (based on guidelines drawn up by a Leadership Election Expenses Committee);
- sanctions applied for violations of regulations, including the withdrawal of a candidate;
- certain services such as mailings and joint meetings provided from a common pool of funds;
- all funding for candidates channelled through the national party; and

Figure 14.1
Options for regulating activities of advocacy groups in federal election campaigns

Option	Comments/likely effects
1. Status quo: advocacy groups are permitted to spend money without limit to advance their views on policy issues, but not to directly endorse or oppose a party or candidate during election campaigns.	• There could be a repeat of the 1988 election with big expenditures by advocacy groups on specific *issues*, on which parties may have taken positions. • It is not clear if expenditures by advocacy groups in 1988 affected electoral outcome. • This form of limitation may be constitutional.
2. Prevent all advocacy groups from spending money to advance their views on policy issues during campaign periods.	• Such a restiction would very likely be held to violate the protection of freedom of expression in the 1982 *Charter of Rights and Freedoms.*

3. Place a limit on expenditures by advocacy groups during election campaigns
  a. to push policy issues, but not directly endorse or oppose a party or candidate(s);
  b. to push policy issues *or* to endorse or oppose a party or candidate.
	• Any limit for either a. or b., other than amount for a political party running a full slate of candidates ($8 million in 1988), would be arbitrary.
	• Parties could get around the limit on their "election expenses" by "inspiring" advocacy groups to support their issues a. or their candidates b.

4. Eliminate legal limit on party and candidate "election expenses" and place no limit on expenditures by advocacy groups during campaigns. (However, parties, candidates and advocacy groups could be required to publicly disclose the names of donors (over $100) and account for their expenditures.)	• This would eliminate what is believed to be the single most important element of the 1974 legislation on financing of federal parties/candidates in Canada. • Disclosure might constrain efforts by donors of large amounts of money to influence elections. • Single interest groups would likely become more important in election campaigns at national and local levels. • Parties would likely have to become more responsive to various interest groups able to attract money to advance their views.

• full disclosure of financial contributions to be made periodically during the leadership campaign as a way to control overspending.

While the amount of "election expenses" that a candidate (or party) may incur during an election campaign is limited under a formula in the *Canada Elections Act*, expenditures to obtain a party's nomination as its candidate are not regulated. In a few cases, such expenditures can be substantial. For example, Gray (1989, 18) notes that in Metro Toronto some of the winners of Liberal party nominations in 1988 spent from $50 000 to $100 000. However, research by Carty and Erickson (1991) suggests that, even in contested nomination races (only one-third of the total), very few individuals incur substantial expenditures. It seems unnecessary to regulate such activity, *provided* candidates are not able to use the tax credit in soliciting contributions.

In Canada, the practice of setting up secret trust funds to augment the official income of federal party leaders (in part to ensure that their family is not called upon to sacrifice an appropriate standard of living) has existed since the time of Sir John A. Macdonald (Schull 1965, 325). (Such trust funds also exist at the provincial level; see chapter 13.) The existence of such funds is totally inconsistent with the spirit of the government regulation of party and candidate finances. The money going to party leaders is not (apparently) used for electoral purposes. However, it does confer a benefit on its recipient. As long as such money comes from secret sources (even if the source is not known to the beneficiaries), there will be the suspicion that donors to the trust fund may be able to exercise improper political influence. No wonder that some party officials would like to abolish trust funds, or see them regulated in much the same way that parties and candidates are regulated!

Proposals for Reform

• Legitimate uses of the federal income-tax credit for political contributions should be clearly specified in legislation. These should include contributions to leadership campaigns (which would also be subject to disclosure) and delegate fees for party conventions. However, the use of the tax credit to finance transfers to other party organizations to be used to elect provincial members should be prohibited.
• Political trust funds operated by any organization or person should be prohibited. However, existing trust funds should be "grandmothered," that is, existing funds should not be permitted to increase in size through new contributions.

- All transfers of interest or capital from existing trust funds to a party, riding association, a candidate or to a public office holder must be publicly disclosed by the recipient.
- Parties should be permitted to supplement the income of their leader out of tax-receipted revenues, but the amount should be publicly disclosed annually.
- Legislation should specify that any surplus from a leadership campaign must be transferred to the candidate's party and the amount should be disclosed publicly.

3.13 Disclosure

Both the observers of and participants in the financing of parties and candidates agree that one of the cornerstones of the regulation of such financing is public disclosure. Disclosure involves not only what is disclosed, but also when it is made public and in what form it is made public. For example, the annual list of donors of over $100 to each party that is filed with the CEO is filed only in the form of a printed list in alphabetical order. In 1990, these lists contained the names of 218 400 individuals and 13 000 corporations. Any useful analysis of these donors (e.g., the number who gave more than $X, etc.) had to be done by hand because the information was not available in a machine-readable form (e.g., computer tape or diskette).

The Chief Electoral Officer does not publish any information on each candidate's surplus (or to whom it was transferred, i.e., party and/or local association), or on each candidate's "other expenses," that is, outlays for which tax credits were issued over and above official "election expenses" and "personal expenses" (some $4.7 million in 1988). The forms on revenues and expenditures that parties must fill out and file annually have not been changed since 1974. Further, the forms are not very detailed and they are filed six months after the end of the relevant calendar year. Moreover, there is no indication *when* a donation was made during a year; for example, a corporation may wait until after the election results are in before making a large contribution in the hope that it will improve its relations with the party in power.

Proposals for Reform

- Parties that use the tax credit for contributions to leadership campaigns should be required to identify the amount (over $100) given by each contributor to each candidate, and the candidate's expenses, shortly after the end of the campaign.[44]

- Parties and riding associations should be required to identify pre-writ and post-election day spending by or on behalf of candidates.
- Parties, riding associations and candidates should be required to identify and publicly disclose the gross amount of transfers to or from any other registered entity during each year.
- Parties should be required to separate federal and provincial/local revenues and expenditures in the data reported to and by the Chief Electoral Officer.
- All reports to the Chief Electoral Officer should be available in the same *electronic* format (e.g., computer diskettes or tapes), as well as in traditional paper form.
- The Chief Electoral Officer should publish all campaign-related expenditures for each party and candidate in reasonable detail, regardless of whether any category of expenditures is subject to limit (e.g., "election expenses").
- The Chief Electoral Officer should be required to publish amounts and disposition of each candidate's *surplus* or the amount of his/her deficit.
- The Chief Electoral Officer should be required to publish the amount of any *assignment* of each candidate's reimbursement and the identity of the recipient.
- Each candidate's agent should be required to specifically identify contributions (over $100) postmarked (or delivered) *after* voting day.

3.14 Administration of the Regulatory Regime

The focus of this study has been on the revenues and expenditures of federal parties and candidates in Canada since the *Election Expenses Act* was passed in 1974. However, in the course of the study, the author has become aware of certain problems with the administration of the regulatory regime other than the ones identified above. These include the threats to the independence of the Chief Electoral Officer, the secrecy associated with the Ad Hoc Committee that advises the CEO and the fact that it was 15 years before a systematic public review of the 1974 legislation was undertaken.

The Chief Electoral Officer has an important, wide-ranging and difficult job, only part of which involves administering the regulations governing the financing of parties and candidates. In theory, because he/she reports directly to Parliament, the CEO has a high degree of independence in carrying out his/her responsibilities. In practice, however, the CEO has chosen to rely heavily on the informal Ad Hoc

Committee of party representatives. The nature and role of the Committee raise several serious questions about matters of institutional design. First, the Committee has no formal recognition: it was not set up pursuant to any statutory provision. It was created for the entirely practical reason of assisting the CEO in implementing the 1974 legislation, but it has continued to function since then. Second, the Committee consists only of representatives of federal parties, primarily of the Conservative, Liberal and New Democratic parties. Surely there are other interests – most importantly the public interest – that should be represented.[45] The obvious danger is that the CEO will find it easier to "go along" with the wishes of the parties on many of the detailed matters that are entailed in any system of regulation. The potential problem is exacerbated when one realizes that the CEO is very unlikely to be criticized in Parliament for decisions/actions that have been approved by the Ad Hoc Committee. The public, however, is unlikely to be well served by a regulatory regime under which the regulatees have unusual opportunities to shape the actions of the regulator (Paltiel 1987).

Third, the minutes of the meetings of the Ad Hoc Committee are secret,[46] unlike, for example, those of parliamentary committees. While the membership of a parliamentary committee would necessarily be limited to MPs, it could call witnesses and thus gain advice from whatever source it saw fit. Secret committees smack of the Star Chamber. Surely the CEO would be better able to assert his/her independence if the means by which advice was obtained were more broadly based and conducted in a fashion that was accessible to the public.[47]

The CEO presently has the power to, in effect, make "regulations" concerning the financing provisions of the *Canada Elections Act*. These regulations are set out in the *Guidelines* for parties and candidates. They specify the way in which the CEO will interpret the statute in the course of carrying out electoral responsibilities. The potential problem, however, is that, unlike subordinate legislation, the *Guidelines* have not been submitted to Cabinet and approved by the committee of Cabinet that makes new regulations and other forms of subordinate legislation (Special Committee of Council). In the case of an appointed official responsible to Parliament, the idea of requiring his/her proposed regulations to be approved by the Cabinet may seem anomalous. But surely no official should, in effect, be able to "make law" without the authority of either the Cabinet (government of the day) or Parliament. Perhaps the problem could be resolved by having the CEO submit proposed regulations (now called *Guidelines*) to an all-party committee, with the clear understanding that cabinet approval will be automatic once the committee approves the regulations. This process would have several advantages. First, the status of the *Guidelines* would be clear – they would be enforceable regulations. Second, the independence of the CEO would be reinforced, as would the role of the CEO as a servant of Parliament. Third, the process of making new laws (in the form of regulations) would be clear and open. The general objective is to open up the process and to try to overcome the institutional bias in favour of accommodating the interest of the major parties due to the large amount of contact the representatives of the parties have with the CEO.

Proposals for Reform

- The *Canada Elections Act* (and related provisions) should be subject to decennial review like the *Bank Act*. In this way it can be modified periodically to ensure that it meets current needs.
- Canada should establish a new regulatory body, the Election Finances Commission, responsible for the administration and enforcement of all the laws and regulations dealing with the financing of *federal* parties and candidates in Canada. Without attempting to specify the legal mechanics,[48] the central functions and characteristics of the Commission should be as follows:

  - The Commission would replace the Chief Electoral Officer as the sole regulatory authority, although the CEO might be appointed as chairman of the Commission. The members of the Commission would be appointed by the Governor in Council.
  - Members would include representatives of parties and public members. Public members should make up a majority of members of the Commission and they should be chosen for their independence from any party to represent the broader public interest in the regulation of party/candidate financing.
  - Any guidelines for the interpretation of the legislation issued by the Commission should have the force of law; for example, they could be tabled in Parliament and would automatically have the force of statutory regulations subject only to amendment after debate in Parliament.
  - The meetings of the Commission should be conducted in public to the greatest possible extent and the minutes of its meetings would also be public as far as is possible.[49]
  - The Commission should report annually to Parliament and also promptly after every general election (such reports to be made public as soon as they are transmitted).

- The *Canada Elections Act* should be changed to include both civil remedies and criminal penalties for violations of its provisions. In general, violations that are not as serious or deserving of criminal sanction would be treated as civil matters where both the stigma and standard of proof would be lower. Prosecution under criminal law would be reserved for violations that have the requisite mental element (*mens rea*), as required under the *Canadian Charter of Rights and Freedoms*, and for which fines and/or imprisonment are suitable penalties. Further, where a civil-law approach is used, the Commission itself might well be the appropriate adjudicatory body. The staff-proposed Commission should have the power to conduct investigations of violations of the civil-law provisions in its legislation. Criminal-law provisions would continue to be investigated as they are at present.

TABLES

Table 1.1
Canadians' participation in politics, 1988

1. Which of the following best describes your participation in organized political party politics?	60%	Have not been and are not involved at all.
	21%	Have been involved but are not any more.
	12%	Have been involved and continue to be involved.
	7%	Have become involved fairly recently.
2. In the years ahead do you expect to become more or less active in politics, or will your involvement not change?	70%	Involvement will not change.
	23%	More active.
	7%	Less active.
3. What is the most important reason why you are not now more actively involved in politics?	47%	You are preoccupied with other things (family, job, etc.).
	31%	You are simply not the type of person who would become involved in politics.
	18%	You don't have much respect for the political party system in Canada.
	3%	You are as involved as you possibly could be.
4. Have you worked for a political party on a federal election campaign in the past, or are you planning to do so in the next campaign?	7%	Yes, in the past.
	4%	Yes, in the next election.
	4%	Yes, both in the past and in the next campaign.
	80%	No.
5. If you plan to work in the next campaign, to which party will you volunteer your services?	28%	Progressive Conservatives.
	28%	Liberals.
	22%	New Democrats.
	11%	Other.
	12%	No opinion/Refused to answer.
6. If you aren't planning to work in the next campaign, what's your main reason for not doing so?	26%	Not interested.
	24%	No time. Too busy.
	7%	Too old.
	6%	Haven't been asked.
	5%	No party affiliation.
	4%	Dislike politicians.
	4%	Lack of knowledge.
	24%	Other.

Sources: Financial Times, 21 March 1988, 3; 3 October 1988, 3.

Notes: Questions 1–3 were from a Decima Research poll of 1 200 randomly selected Canadians age 18+ conducted in mid-February 1988. Questions 4–6 came from a Decima poll of 1 100 Canadians age 18+, for which no date was given but it appears to have been in 1988, prior to election.

Percentages may not add to 100 because of rounding.

Table 1.2
Major sources of federal government funding of political activity in Canada
(thousands of dollars)

	General election			
	1979	1980	1984	1988
Reimbursement of parties				
PC	794	978	1 437	1 782
Liberal	718	910	1 416	1 539
NDP	496	678	1 064	1 589
Others	8	2	0	49
Total	2 016	2 568	3 917	4 959
Reimbursement of candidates				
PC	2 868	2 871	5 117	6 056
Liberal	3 594	3 656	4 081	4 656
NDP	1 671	1 885	1 917	2 839
Others	385	112	55	184
Total	8 518	8 524	11 170	13 735
	1974–79	1980	1981–84	1985–88
Tax credits paid to				
Individuals	19 593	6 379	33 003	43 733
Corporations	2 835[a]	1 247	3 454	4 231
Total	22 428	7 626	36 457	47 964
Total government funding per electoral cycle	32 959[c]	18 717[d]	51 545[c]	66 658[c]
Government funding in 1989 dollars[b]	61 606[c]	31 832[d]	63 636[c]	70 019[c]

Sources: Canada, Elections Canada (1980b, 1981, 1984c, 1988c); and Department of National Revenue data supplied to Royal Commission on Electoral Reform and Party Financing.

[a]Data available only for 1976–79; previous election was in 1974.

[b]Deflated using year of election, i.e., tax credits in years after previous election were accumulated to election year in nominal terms and then adjusted for changes in CPI from election year. This procedure slightly understates cost in 1989 dollars.

[c]Includes year of election and years preceding it. For example, cost of electoral cycle ending in 1988 includes reimbursements for 1988 election plus tax credits for 1985 through 1988.

[d]1980 only.

Table 3.1
Major parties' revenues and expenditures, 1974–90
(thousands of dollars)

Period	Liberal		PC		NDP		
	Revenue	Expend-itures	Revenue	Expend-itures	Total revenue[a]	Provincially receipted revenue[g]	Expend-itures[h]
1974	2 217[b]	1 936[b]	1 721[b]	1 597[b]	1 437[c]	n.a.	1 270[c]
1975	[included in 1976]		1 203[e]	889[e]	2 580	n.a.	2 570
1976	5 823[d]	4 707[d]	4 084	3 497	2 925	644	2 381
1977	4 587	4 187	3 774	4 233	3 525	519	3 105
1978	5 018	5 283	5 465	5 470	4 184	784	3 514
1979E	6 302	2 771	8 376	5 184	6 020	1 279	4 678
EE		3 913		3 845			2 190
R	718		794		496		
1980E	7 457	3 702	7 564	4 923	6 101	1 180	5 992
EE		3 846		4 407			3 086
R	910		978		677		
1981	5 592	5 116	6 950	7 542	6 003	2 147	6 491
1982	6 746	6 781	8 521	8 521	7 108	2 342	4 871
1983	7 736	6 277	14 767	13 199	8 669	2 697	8 009
1984E	11 598	11 999	21 979	20 777	10 513	3 156	7 407
EE		6 293		6 389			4 731
R	1 416		1 438		1 064		
1985	6 163[f]	8 149	15 073	11 654	10 152	3 688	11 071
1986	10 719[f]	11 166	15 639	14 141	14 639[f]	7 655	15 188
1987	8 882	9 274	13 058	13 490	12 608[f]	5 775	14 012

Table 3.1 (cont'd)
Major parties' revenues and expenditures, 1974–90
(thousands of dollars)

	Liberal		PC		NDP		
Period	Revenue	Expend-itures	Revenue	Expend-itures	Total revenue[a]	Provincially receipted revenue[g]	Expend-itures[h]
1988E	16 358	10 176	25 231	21 124	18 754[f]	6 592	14 933
EE		6 840		7 922			7 061
R	1 539		1 782		1 589		
1989	6 397	7 115	14 521	12 824	13 865[f]	6 119	12 507
1990	13 778[i]	13 327[i]	11 298	10 635	15 439	6 396	14 262

Sources: Calculated from Canada, Elections Canada (1980b, 1981, 1984c, 1988c); and annual returns filed by parties with CEO, 1979–90.

[a]Prior to 1980, CEO did *not* include provincially receipted revenue in NDP revenue figure. This revenue has been included here. All CEO revenue figures after 1980 did include provincially receipted revenue and also include provincial rebates and subsidiaries.

[b]1 Aug. 1974 to 31 July 1975 (12 months).

[c]1 Aug. 1974 to 31 Dec. 1974 (5 months).

[d]1 Aug. 1975 to 31 Dec. 1976 (17 months).

[e]1 Aug. 1975 to 31 Dec. 1975 (5 months).

[f]Includes 1985 item "(1984 general election expense)" = $111 444 *and* portion of reimbursement for 1986, $8 452, labelled "reimbursement." These figures do *not* appear in CEO source.

[g]Includes provincial rebates and subsidies; largest amount was $811 in 1986.

[h]Total expenditure for party including most of its provincial sections (does not include Ontario).

[i]Reflects almost $7 million in revenues and expenditures associated with 1990 leadership race and convention.

E = Election year revenue or expenditures excluding "election expenses" or reimbursement.
EE = "Election expenses" for party.
n.a. = Data not available.
R = Reimbursement of election expenses by federal government, that is, one-half allowed outlays on electronic media for advertising in 1979 and 1980, and 22.5 percent of total allowable expenditures in 1984 and 1988.
Revenue = Contributions plus other income, for example, interest and reimbursement of "election expenses" in election years.

Table 3.1a
Sources of party revenues, number of contributors and total expenditures, 1991
(thousands of dollars)

	PC	Liberal	NDP	Reform
Source of revenue				
Individuals	5 367	3 353	7 318	4 737
Business organizations	6 660	3 412	759[a]	491
Governments	0	2	0	0
Trade unions	0	4	1 083[b]	0
Provincial sections	N/A	N/A	9 301	N/A
Other organizations	9	6	131	0
Interest	104	0	422	63
Other	130	428	919[c]	1 297[d]
Total revenue	12 261	7 205	19 933	6 588
Total expenditures	11 768	7 197	18 771	6 289
Number of contributors				
Individuals	27 391	26 396	94 080	43 176
Business organizations	7 401	3 799	715	2 286
Governments	0	12	0	0
Trade unions	0	10	987	0
Other organizations	7	39	58	0
Total contributors (N)	34 799	30 256	95 840	45 462

Source: Annual returns filed by parties with CEO.

[a]Includes $467 000 from sale of Woodsworth House (Ottawa) Corp.

[b]Includes $671 052 in affiliation dues and $411 908 in contributions.

[c]Includes $264 352 in subsidies from provinces; $645 742 in miscellaneous fund-raising for which no receipts were issued.

[d]Includes sale of memberships ($721 679), merchandise sales ($275 108) and assembly fees ($300 000).

N/A = Not applicable.

Table 3.2

New Democratic Party federal office estimates of revenues and expenditures, 1974–90
(thousands of dollars)

Year	Federal revenue[a]	Federal office revenue[b]	Federal office expenses[c]
1974–75[d]	4 017	1 175[e]	1 100
1976	2 282	547	476
1977	3 006	656	688
1978	3 400	641	714
1979E	5 237	3 315	3 343
1980E	5 595	3 780	4 224
1981	3 856	1 185	984
1982	4 766	1 058	1 055
1983	5 972	1 716	1 130
1984E	9 021	6 880	6 663
1985	6 284	1 922	1 720
1986	6 985	2 114	1 973
1987	6 833	1 803	2 522
1988E	13 752	8 962	11 459
1989	7 746	2 565	1 530
1990	9 043	2 685	2 082

Sources: Table 3.1 and tables relating to chapter 6.

[a]Federally receipted contributions plus other income plus reimbursement of party "election expenses."

[b]Includes revenue for general elections including federal rebate.

[c]Includes "election expenses" as measured by party — see chapter 6. Party's figure is slightly above figure reported by CEO.

[d]1 Aug. 1974 to 31 Dec. 1975.

[e]Includes 1974 election revenue of $372.

E = Election year.

Table 3.3
Political parties' nominal and real revenues and expenditures, 1974–90
(thousands of 1989 dollars)

	1974–75	1976	1977	1978	1979E	1980E	1981	1982	1983	1984E	1985	1986	1987	1988E	1989	1990
PC																
Revenue[a]																
Nominal	2 924[c]	4 084	3 774	5 465	9 170	8 542	6 950	8 521	14 767	23 417	15 073	15 639	13 058	27 013	14 521	11 298
Real	7 556	9 817	8 405	11 153	17 140	14 527	10 499	11 625	19 030	28 909	17 901	17 832	14 271	28 375	14 521	10 781
Expenses																
Nominal	2 486[c]	3 497	4 233	5 470	8 929	9 330	7 542	8 521	13 199	27 165	11 654	14 141	13 490	29 046	12 824	10 635
Real	6 424	8 406	9 428	11 163	16 690	15 867	11 393	11 625	17 009	33 537	13 841	16 124	14 743	30 511	12 824	10 148
Excess of R over E																
Nominal	438[c]	587	(459)	(5)	241	(788)	(592)	0	1 568	(3 748)	3 419	1 498	(432)	(2 033)	1 696	663
Real	1 132	1 411	(1 023)	(10)	450	(1 340)	(894)	0	2 021	(4 628)	4 060	1 708	(472)	(2 136)	1 696	633
Liberal																
Revenue[a]																
Nominal	2 217[d]	5 823[e]	4 587	5 018	7 020	8 367	5 592	6 747	7 736	13 014	6 163	10 719	8 882	17 897	6 397	13 778
Real	5 729	13 998	10 216	10 241	13 122	14 230	8 447	9 205	9 969	16 067	7 320	12 222	9 707	18 799	6 397	13 147
Expenses[b]																
Nominal	1 963[d]	4 707[e]	4 187	5 283	6 684	7 548	5 116	6 781	6 277	18 292	8 149	11 166	9 274	17 016	7 115	13 327
Real	5 072	11 315	9 325	10 782	12 494	12 837	7 728	9 251	8 089	22 583	9 678	12 732	10 136	17 874	7 115	12 717
Excess of R over E																
Nominal	254[d]	1 116[e]	400	(265)	336	819	476	(34)	1 459	(5 278)	(1 986)	(447)	(392)	881	(718)	451
Real	657	2 683	891	(541)	628	1 393	719	(46)	1 880	(6 516)	(2 358)	(510)	(429)	925	(718)	430

Table 3.3 (cont'd)
Political parties' nominal and real revenues and expenditures, 1974–90
(thousands of 1989 dollars)

	1974–75	1976	1977	1978	1979E	1980E	1981	1982	1983	1984E	1985	1986	1987	1988E	1989	1990
NDP |g																
Revenue[h]																
Nominal	4 017[f]	2 925	3 525	4 184	6 517	6 778	6 003	7 108	8 669	11 577	10 152	14 639	12 608	20 343	13 865	15 439
Real	10 380	7 031	7 851	8 539	12 181	11 527	9 068	9 697	11 171	14 293	12 057	16 692	13 779	21 369	13 865	14 732
Expenses[b]																
Nominal	3 840[f]	2 381	3 105	3 514	6 867	9 078	6 491	4 872	8 009	12 138	11 071	15 188	14 012	21 994	12 507	14 262
Real	9 922	5 724	6 915	7 171	12 836	15 438	9 805	6 647	10 321	14 985	13 149	17 318	15 314	23 103	12 507	13 609
Excess of R over E																
Nominal	177[f]	544	420	670	(350)	(2 300)	(488)	2 236	660	(561)	(919)	(549)	(1 404)	(1 651)	1 358	1 177
Real	458	1 307	936	1 368	(655)	(3 911)	(737)	3 050	851	(692)	(1 092)	(626)	(1 535)	(1 734)	1 358	1 123
CPI Index (1989 = 100)	34.9 (1974) 38.7 (1975)	41.6	44.9	49.0	53.5	58.8	66.2	73.3	77.6	81.0	84.2	87.7	91.5	95.2	100.0	104.8

NDP II[i]

Revenue[a]																
Nominal	1 175[f]	547	656	642	3 315	3 780	1 185	1 058	1 716	6 880	1 922	2 114	1 803	8 962	2 565	2 685
Real	3 117	1 315	1 461	1 310	6 196	6 429	1 790	1 443	2 211	8 494	2 283	2 411	1 971	9 414	2 565	2 562
Expenses[b]																
Nominal	1 100[f]	476	688	714	3 343	4 224	984	1 055	1 130	6 663	1 720	1 973	2 522	11 459	1 530	2 082
Real	2 918	1 144	1 532	1 457	6 249	7 184	1 486	1 439	1 456	8 226	2 043	2 250	2 789	12 037	1 530	1 987
Excess of R over E																
Nominal	75[f]	71	(32)	(72)	(28)	(444)	201	3	586	217	202	141	(719)	(2 497)	1 035	603
Real	199	171	(71)	(147)	(53)	(755)	304	4	755	268	240	161	(818)	(2 623)	1 035	575

Sources: Canada, Elections Canada (1980b, 1981, 1984c, 1988c); Registered parties fiscal period returns (1974–90); NDP financial statements as provided to author.

[a]Includes election reimbursement.
[b]Includes election expenses.
[c]1 Aug. 1974 to 31 Dec. 1975 (17 months).
[d]1 Aug. 1974 to 31 July 1975 (12 months).
[e]1 Aug. 1975 to 31 Dec. 1976 (17 months).
[f] 1 Aug. 1974 to 31 Dec. 1975 (17 months).
[g]NDP I = NDP figures as reported to CEO plus certain adjustments.
[h]Includes provincially receipted revenue and provincial government subsidies and reimbursement.
[i]NDP II = Federal office revenue and expenditures plus election revenue and expenditures.

E = Election year.

Table 3.4
Election expenses by parties, 1979, 1980, 1984 and 1988 general election campaigns
(thousands of dollars)

	1979	1980	1984	1988
Election expenses				
PC	3 845	4 407	6 389	7 922
Liberal	3 913	3 846	6 293	6 840
NDP	2 190	3 086	4 731	7 061
Total	9 948	11 339	17 413	21 823
Other parties	166	202	205	604
All parties	10 114	11 541	17 618	22 427
Total election expenses in 1989 dollars	18 907	19 628	21 751	23 557
Party election expenses as percentage of statutory limit				
PC	87.7	96.9	99.96	98.95
Liberal	86.2	84.6	98.5	85.7
NDP	49.1	68.1	74.0	88.2
Reimbursement from federal government to parties[a]				
PC	794	977	1 438	1 782
Liberal	718	910	1 416	1 539
NDP	496	677	1 064	1 589
Other	8	2	0	49
All parties	2 016	2 567	3 918	4 959
Reimbursement as % of total party election expenses	19.9	22.2	22.2	22.1

Source: Canada, Elections Canada (1980b, 1981, 1984c, 1988c).

[a]These figures do not include reimbursement of candidates. See table 1.1.

Table 3.5
Analysis of party election expenses, 1979, 1980, 1984 and 1988
(thousands of dollars)

Expenditure category	1979 $	1979 %	1980 $	1980 %	1984 $	1984 %	1988 $	1988 %
Print advertising								
PC	267	7.0	578	13.1	207	3.2	722	10.2
Liberal	576	14.7	403	10.4	763	12.1	812	11.9
NDP	315	14.4	426	13.8	154	3.3	156	2.2
Radio advertising								
PC	939	24.4	652	14.8	1 236	19.3	1 555	19.6
Liberal	563	14.4	579	15.1	1 069	17.0	1 024	15.0
NDP	248	11.3	233	7.6	495	10.4	477	6.8
Television advertising								
PC	1 539	40.0	1 876	42.6	1 758	27.5	2 441	30.8
Liberal	1 295	33.1	1 613	41.9	1 695	26.9	2 025	29.6
NDP	771	35.2	1 167	37.8	1 158	24.5	2 495	35.3
Total advertising								
PC	2 745	71.4	3 106	70.5	3 201	50.1	4 718	59.5
Liberal	2 434	62.2	2 595	67.5	3 527	56.0	3 861	56.4
NDP	1 334	60.9	1 826	59.2	1 807	38.2	3 128	44.3
Travelling								
PC	632	16.4	639	14.5	1 130	17.7	1 552	19.6
Liberal	691	17.7	421	10.9	881	14.0	1 219	17.8
NDP	233	10.6	378	12.2	146	3.1	1 037	14.7
Other expenses								
PC	468	12.2	662	15.0	2058	32.2	1 652	20.9
Liberal	788	20.1	830	21.6	1 885	30.0	1 761	25.8
NDP	623	28.4	882	28.6	2 779	58.7	2 895	41.0
Total expenses								
PC	3 845	100.0	4 407	100.0	6 389	100.0	7 922	100.0
Liberal	3 913	100.0	3 846	100.0	6 293	100.0	6 840	100.0
NDP	2 190	100.0	3 086	100.0	4 731	100.0	7 061	100.0

Source: Tabulations from Canada, Elections Canada (1980b, 1981, 1984c, 1988c).

Table 3.6
Party expenditures on radio and television advertising, 1965–88 general elections
(thousands of dollars)

Election year	Expenditures on radio and TV advertising		Total party expenses (nominal $)	Broadcast advertising as % of total election expenses
	Nominal dollars	1989 dollars		
1965	1 212[a]	5 385	5 934[c]	20.4
1968	1 426[a]	5 657	6 569[c]	21.7
1972	2 681[a]	9 151	9 671[d]	27.7
1974	2 714[a]	7 776	10 310[e]	26.3
1979	5 355[b]	10 009	9 948	53.8
1980	6 120[b]	10 408	11 339	54.0
1984	7 411[b]	9 149	17 413	42.6
1988	10 017[b]	10 522	21 823	45.9

Source: See table 3.5 and Paltiel (1970b, 1974, 1975).
[a]All parties, from Paltiel (1974, 352; 1975, 199).
[b]PC, NDP and Liberal parties only (expenditure by other parties was too small to measure.
[c]From Paltiel (1970b).
[d]From Paltiel (1974).
[e]From Paltiel (1975).

Table 3.7
Accumulated surplus (deficit) of federal parties by period
(thousands of dollars)

Party	1989 dollars				Nominal dollars			
	1974–78 Liberal (Trudeau)	1979 PC (Clark)	1980–84 Liberal (Trudeau)	1985–90 PC (Mulroney)	1974–78 Liberal (Trudeau)	1979 PC (Clark)	1980–84 Liberal (Trudeau)	1985–90 PC (Mulroney)
PC	1 510	450	(4 841)	5 490	561	241	(3 560)	4 811
Liberal	3 690	628	(2 570)	(2 660)	1 505	336	(2 558)	(2 211)
NDP I[a]	4 069	(655)	(1 439)	(2 506)	1 811	(350)	(453)	(1 988)
NDP II[b]	152	(53)	576	(1 430)	42	(28)	563	(1 235)

Source: Table 3.2.

[a] NDP as a whole as reported to CEO after a few minor adjustments.

[b] NDP federal office including election revenue and "election expenses."

Table 3.8
Federal party revenues and expenditures by period
(thousands of 1989 dollars)

Period: Party in power (prime minister)	PC	Liberal	NDP
Revenue			
1974–78: Liberal (Trudeau)	36 931	40 184	29 947[a]
1979[c]: PC (Clark)	17 140	13 122	9 789[a]
1980–84[d]: Liberal (Trudeau)	84 590	57 918	40 762[a]
1985–90[e]: PC (Mulroney)	103 681	67 592	45 970[a]
Expenditures			
1974–78: Liberal (Trudeau)	35 421	36 494	7 051[b]
1979[c]: PC (Clark)	16 690	12 494	6 249[b]
1980–84[d]: Liberal (Trudeau)	89 431	60 488	19 791[b]
1985–90[e]: PC (Mulroney)	98 191	70 252	22 636[b]
Surplus (deficit)			
1974–78: Liberal (Trudeau)	1 510	3 690	22 896[f]
1979: PC (Clark)	450	628	3 540[f]
1980–84: Liberal (Trudeau)	(4 841)	(2 570)	20 971[f]
1985–90: PC (Mulroney)	5 490	(2 660)	23 334[f]

Source: Tabulated from tables 3.2 and 3.3 (converted to 1989 dollars).

[a]Federally receipted revenue plus other non-receipted federal revenue plus reimbursement of election expenses.

[b]Federal office only plus "election expenses."

[c]Includes general election in 1979.

[d]Includes general elections in 1980 and 1984.

[e]Includes general election in 1988.

[f]"Surplus" is transferred to NDP's provincial sections where almost all of it is used in provincial politics.

Table 4.1
Progressive Conservative party revenues and expenditures, 1974–82

	1974–75[a]	1976	1977	1978	1979E	1980E	1981	1982
Contributions	2 793 605	3 906 908	3 545 446	5 363 536	8 375 716	7 564 120	6 949 797	8 193 660
Individuals	1 280 659	1 909 951	1 742 964	2 661 175	3 182 897	3 043 829	4 319 604	5 181 016
Corporations	1 447 968	1 926 732	1 723 939	2 625 341	5 020 285	4 367 936	2 573 208	2 922 661
Trade unions	0	0	432	0	1 190	0	0	0
Other organizations	.64 978	70 225	78 111	77 020	171 344	152 355	56 985	89 983
Other income	130 643	177 250[b]	229 002	100 974	0	0	0	327 276
Reimbursement[c]	0	0	0	0	793 967	977 835	0	0
Total revenue[d]	2 924 248	4 084 158	3 774 448	5 464 510	9 169 683	8 541 955	6 949 797	8 520 936
Operating expenses	1 233 095	2 455 313	2 921 103	3 617 030	3 664 661	3 759 282	6 800 348	7 307 662
By-election expenses	0	18 293	55 645	129 479	23 578	14 312	81 865	31 746
General election expenses[c]	0	0	0	0	3 845 217	4 407 207	0	0

Table 4.1 (cont'd)
Progressive Conservative party revenues and expenditures, 1974–82

	1974–75a	1976	1977	1978	1979E	1980E	1981	1982
Transfers to party associationsᵉ	730 485	856 143	1 256 624	1 723 321	1 395 111	1 148 998	659 334	1 181 686
Other expenditures	522 538	167 282	0	0	0	0	0	0
Total expenditures	2 486 118	3 497 031	4 233 372	5 469 830	8 928 567	9 329 799	7 541 547	8 521 094
Excess of revenue over expenditures (158)	438 130	587 127	(458 924)	(5 320)	241 116	(787 844)	(591 750)	

Sources: Canada, Elections Canada (1980b, 1981, 1984c, 1988c); and Registered Parties Fiscal Period Returns (1974–90).

a1974–75 figures combine (1 Aug. 74–31 July 75) and (1 Aug. 75–31 Dec. 75).

bOther income not listed on party's fiscal period return.

cReimbursement and election expenses not included in CEO's tables.

dTotal is higher than "total revenue" as reported by CEO as it includes "other income" and "reimbursement" of part of party's "election expenses."

eTransfers to riding associations and provincial associations; consists largely of riding's share of revenue raised at riding level – see table 4.6.

E = Election year.

Table 4.1a
Progressive Conservative party revenues and expenditures, 1983–90

	1983	1984E	1985	1986	1987	1988E	1989[a]	1990
Contributions	14 108 012	21 145 920	14 565 652	15 177 750	12 761 155	24 542 036	13 801 368	11 046 654
Individuals	9 105 732	10 142 398	7 872 289	7 874 533	6 065 219	10 181 404	6 850 205	4 686 453
Corporations	4 819 737	11 003 522	6 693 363	7 301 230	6 695 571	14 358 842	6 942 728	6 349 996
Trade unions	0	0	0	1 987	365	1 790	790	0
Other organizations	182 543	0	0	0	0	0	7 645	10 205
Other income	659 155	833 420	507 294	461 562	297 067	688 271	719 257	251 289
Reimbursement[b]	0	1 437 512	0	0	0	1 782 391	0	0
Total revenue[c]	14 767 167	23 416 852	15 072 946	15 639 312	13 058 222	27 012 698	14 520 625	11 297 943
Operating expenses	10 977 197	18 155 542	9 913 209	11 507 465	11 488 370	17 768 512	10 676 787	8 798 016
By-election expenses	44 712	0	0	42 274	50 990	20 849	14 188	44 200
General election expenses"[b]	0	6 388 941	0	0	0	7 921 738	0	0

Table 4.1a (cont'd)
Progressive Conservative party revenues and expenditures, 1983–90

	1983	1984E	1985	1986	1987	1988E	1989[a]	1990
Transfers to party associations[d]	2 177 281	2 620 938	1 740 815	2 591 254	1 950 916	3 335 311	2 133 300	1 792 750
Other expenditures	0	0	0	0	0	0	0	0
Total expenditures	13 199 190	27 165 421	11 654 024	14 141 173	13 490 276	29 046 410	12 824 275	10 634 966
Excess of revenue over expenditures	1 567 977	(3 748 569)	3 418 922	1 498 139	(432 054)	(2 033 712)	1 696 350	662 977

Sources: Canada, Elections Canada (1980b, 1981, 1984c, 1988c); and Registered Parties Fiscal Period Returns (1974–90).

[a]1989 data taken from fiscal period returns (Source 2).

[b]Reimbursement and election expenses not included in CEO's tables.

[c]Total is higher than "total revenue" as reported by CEO as it includes "other income" and "reimbursement" of part of party's "election expenses."

[d]Transfers to riding associations and provincial associations; consists largely of riding's share of revenue raised at riding level – see table 4.6.

E = Election year.

Table 4.2
Analysis of operating expenses, Progressive Conservative party, 1974–90
(percentages)

Category	1974–75[a]	1975–76[b]	1977	1978	1979E	1980E	1981	1982	1983	1984E	1985	1986	1987	1988E	1989	1990
Salaries, wages and employee benefits	39.8	23.9	31.9	29.4	30.8	30.9	26.8	33.2	27.4	28.8	34.0	34.8	37.4	27.9	35.9	37.8
Travelling expenses	15.0	11.8	13.0	15.1	15.1	14.6	14.2	18.5	11.9	20.6	14.4	11.5	15.7	15.3	12.5	14.4
Party conventions/ meetings	5.3	33.8	14.7	1.4	4.8	3.8	11.3	6.3	23.9	0.0	1.6	8.3	0.0	0.0	8.7	0.6
Rent, heat, light and power	8.3	4.2	3.4	4.2	8.6	4.9	4.0	5.6	3.6	3.5	4.3	4.3	5.0	4.7	6.0	6.7
Advertising and broadcasting	0.2	0.0	0.0	14.8	2.9	2.9	1.9	1.0	0.6	6.3	0.3	0.5	0.4	1.2	0.2	0.1
Printing and stationery[c]	6.9	6.5	13.8	18.3	23.8	30.6	25.8	24.5	23.4	28.9	31.4	27.0	27.0	36.9	24.6	26.7

Table 4.2 (cont'd)

Analysis of operating expenses, Progressive Conservative party, 1974–90

(percentages)

Category	1974–75[a]	1975–76[b]	1977	1978	1979E	1980E	1981	1982	1983	1984E	1985	1986	1987	1988E	1989	1990
Telephone and telegraph	11.0	3.7	3.7	5.1	5.5	6.4	5.4	5.6	4.3	6.2	5.2	4.8	4.5	5.5	4.4	4.9
Legal and audit fees	1.3	0.5	1.3	1.1	1.6	1.3	0.9	1.1	0.7	0.4	1.1	0.8	0.3	0.4	0.4	0.3
Other expenses	12.2	15.6	18.3	10.7	7.0	4.7	9.6	4.3	4.2	5.4	7.7	8.0	9.6	8.0	7.2	8.5
Total	100.0	100.0	100.0	100.0	100.0	100.0	100.0	100.0	100.0	100.0	100.0	100.0	100.0	100.0	100.0	100.0
Total in $000	749	2 455	2 921	3 617	3 665	3 759	6 800	7 308	10 977	18 156	9,913	11 508	11 488	17 759	10 677	8 798

Source: Annual returns filed by party with CEO, 1974–90.

Notes: Analysis excludes "election expenses" and transfers to candidates and riding associations.

[a]1 Aug. 1974 – 31 July 1975 (12 months).

[b]1 Aug. 1975 – 31 Dec. 1976 (17 months).

[c]See table 4.3 for more details on 1987, 1988 and 1989.

Percentages may not total 100.0 because of rounding.

Table 4.3
Details of expenditures on printing and stationery by Progressive Conservative party, 1987–90
(thousands of dollars)

Category	1987	1988	1989	1990
Direct mail (printing/mailing)	818	1 537	802	737
Internal printing (net)	139	155	11	21
Postage	230	285	139	122
Courier	85	223	50	39
Office supplies	100	241	74	61
Photographic supplies	21	30	16	15
Publications	36	46	35	27
Other office and supply costs	24	42	24	16
Professional, polling and other outside services	1 080	3 045	1 142	962
Computer services	112	168	25	20
Newswire services	8	52	1	2
Outside printing	288	307	150	122
Outside photocopying	6	18	3	2
Outside translation	94	132	37	28
Outside photography	61	265	122	174
Total	3 102	6 546	2 631	2 348

Source: Data supplied to author by Progressive Conservative party, Ottawa.

Table 4.4
Analysis of Progressive Conservative party revenues, 1983–90
(thousands of dollars)

Source of gross revenue	1983	1984E	1985	1986	1987	1988E	1989	1990
Direct mail	5 729	7 571	5 611	4 307	3 763	6 517	3 529	2 434
Corporate[a]	1 982	9 120	4 119	4 101	4 299	10 834	4 099	3 491
Major donor ("FP500")	319	1 688	1 936	1 513	1 222	2 477	1 353	1 224
National fund-raising events[b]	1 551	996	1 009	1 152	996	927	1 615	1 703
Constituencies (gross)[c]	2 674	2 122	1 947	3 349	2 344	3 686	2 168	2 148
Other income	2 511	481	450	1 217	434	789	1 756	298
	14 766	21 978	15 072	15 639	13 058	25 230	14 520	11 298
Reimbursement of election expenses		1 438				1 782		
Total party revenue	14 767	23 417	15 072	15 639	13 058	27 013	14 521	11 298
Total contributions from individuals	9 106	10 142	7 872	7 875	6 065	10 181	6 850	4 686
Contributions from individuals as % of total revenue	61.7	43.3	52.2	50.4	46.4	37.7	47.2	41.5
Direct-mail revenue as % of contributions from individuals	63.0	75.0	71.0	55.0	62.0	64.0	52.0	52.0

Source: Data supplied to author by Progressive Conservative party, Ottawa, and table 4.1.

[a]Defined by party as contributions in form of cheques from corporations.

[b]Events featuring party leader; amounts are after expenses deducted.

[c]This is before PC Canada Fund's share, but after expenses of fund-raising events.

E = Election year.

Table 4.5
Details of corporate contributions to Progressive Conservative party, 1983–90
(thousands of dollars)

Category	1983	1984E	1985	1986	1987	1988E	1989	1990
Total contributions from business organizations[a]	4 820	11 004	6 693	7 304	6 696	14 359	6 943	6 350
"Corporate" contributions[b]	1 982	9 120	4 119	4 101	4 299	10 834	4 099	3 491
FP500 (non-financial corporations)[c]	820	1 925	890	991	1 139	2 043	1 309	1 408
FP155 (financial corporations)[d]	300	698	401	528	665	1 143	620	397
Corporate contributions ≥ $10 000	781	4 362	1 983	2 294	2 612	6 871	2 671	2 462
Average ($000)	18.2	22.0	20.9	22.1	21.9	23.0	22.6	23.0
Number	43	198	95	104	119	299	118	107
Total party revenue	14 767	23 417	15 073	15 639	13 058	27 013	14 521	11 298
Total FP500 + FP155 as % of total party revenue	7.6	11.2	8.6	9.7	13.8	11.8	13.3	16.0
Total contributions from corporations as % of total party revenue	32.6	47.0	44.4	46.7	51.3	53.2	47.8	56.2
Corporate contributions ≥ $10 000 as % of party revenue	5.3	18.6	13.2	14.7	20.0	25.4	18.4	21.8
"Corporate" revenue as % of total contributions from corporations	41.0	83.0	62.0	56.0	64.0	75.0	59.0	55.0

Source: Data supplied to author by Progressive Conservative party, Ottawa, and tables 11.12 and 11.17.

[a]Data provided by CEO.

[b]Data provided by party. Defined as contributions in form of cheques from corporations.

[c]500 largest non-financial enterprises in Canada as compiled by *Financial Post.*

[d]Group of 100 largest financial institutions, 25 largest life insurers, 15 largest property and casualty insurers, and 15 largest investment dealers as compiled by *Financial Post.*

E = Election year.

Table 4.6
Revenues of federal riding associations processed through PC Canada Fund, 1985–90
(thousands of dollars)

Description	1985	1986	1987	1988E	1989	1990
Fund-raising events[a]						
Gross revenue	1 029	1 841	1 198	2 143	1 404	1 740
Expenses	357	627	393	651	467	546
Net revenue (profit)	672	1 214	805	1 492	937	1 194
Returned to ridings						
$	496	877	609	1 131	702	900
%	73.8	72.2	75.7	75.8	74.9	75.4
Net revenue to PC Canada Fund	176	337	196	361	235	294
Contributions						
Gross revenue	1 275	2 135	1 539	2 194	1 231	953
Returned to ridings						
$	1 005	1 610	1 161	1 864	953	728
%	78.8	75.4	75.4	85.0	77.4	76.4
Total net revenue to PC Canada Fund	270	525	378	330	278	225
Total net revenue to PC Canada Fund	446	862	574	691	513	519
Total net revenues to ridings	1 501	2 487	1 770	2 995	1 655	1 628

Source: Data supplied to author by Progressive Conservative party, Ottawa.

Notes: Except during election periods (and then it's through candidate's agent), ridings cannot issue tax receipts except through PC Canada Fund, the party's official agent.

[a]Local dinners, golf outings, etc.

E = Election year.

Table 4.7

Analysis of transfers to constituencies and other party organizations, Progressive Conservative party, 1985–90

(thousands of dollars)

	1985	1986	1987	1988E	1989	1990
Fund-raising						
Straight donations[a]	1 005	1 610	1 161	1 864	952	728
Net revenue from events[b]	496	877	609	1 131	702	900
Total	1 501	2 487	1 770	2 995	1 654	1 628
Riding/candidate support	152	25	0	232	384	58
Cost-sharing agreements with provincial parties[c]	87	79	124	107	95	106
Share of national events[d]	0	0	56	0	0	0
Total transfers to constituencies and other party organizations	1 740	2 591	1 950	3 334	2 133	1 792
% of total transfers to constituencies attributable to PC Canada Fund's receipted revenues	86.3	96.0	90.8	89.8	77.5	90.8

Source: Data supplied to author by Progressive Conservative party, Ottawa.

[a]Amount returned to constituencies after deduction of about 25% for PC Canada Fund.

[b]Amount returned to constituencies after deduction of about 25% for PC Canada Fund from *net* revenue from local fund-raising events.

[c]Shared cost of provincial offices, field organizers and the like in P.E.I. and Nova Scotia.

[d]Fund-raising dinners staged by PC Canada Fund. See chapter 10.

E = Election year.

Table 4.8
Analysis of Progressive Conservative party revenues available to party headquarters, 1983–90
(thousands of dollars)

	1983	1984E	1985	1986	1987	1988E	1989	1990
Total party revenue[a]	14 767	23 417	15 072	15 639	13 058	27 013	14 521	11 298
Deductions								
Direct costs of fund-raising								
Direct mail	1 160	1 337	1 342	1 211	839	1 600	777	641
Major donor	n.a.	n.a.	265	191	12	41	48	96
Other sources	n.a.	n.a.	n.a.	n.a.	n.a.	n.a.	n.a.	n.a.
Total	1 160	1 337	1 607	1 402	851	1 641	825	737
Amount returned to ridings[b]	2 006[c]	1 592[c]	1 501	2 487	1 770	2 995	1 654	1 628
Net revenue available to head-quarters	11 601	20 488	11 964	11 740	10 437	22 377	12 042	8 933

Source: Data supplied to author by Progressive Conservative party, Ottawa.

[a]See table 4.1.

[b]Constituencies' 75% share of contributions to local associations and 75% share of net revenue from fund-raising events.

[c]Estimated by author based on 75% of constituency revenue based on experience of 1985–89.

E = Election year.
n.a. = Data not available.

Table 5.1
Liberal party revenues and expenditures, 1974–82

	1974–75[a]	1975–76[b]	1977	1978	1979E	1980E	1981	1982
Contributions	2 148 659	5 599 496	4 423 566	4 779 694	5 220 520	6 217 795	5 095 158	6 104 367
Individuals	1 104 462	2 955 700	1 983 687	2 101 716	1 184 755	2 277 650	2 101 350	3 195 283
Corporations	993 177	2 574 536	2 291 555	2 488 014	3 875 567	3 730 983	2 705 385	2 521 810
Trade unions	555	740	1 154	400	1 663	1 697	1 627	2 745
Other organizations[c]	50 465	68 520	147 170	189 564	158 535	207 465	286 796	384 529
Other income	68 041	223 411	163 040	237 817	1 081 513	1 239 360	496 951	642 227
Reimbursement[d]	0	0	0	0	718 020	909 923	0	0
Total revenue[e]	2 216 700	5 822 908	4 586 606	5 017 511	7 020 054	8 367 078	5 592 109	6 746 594
Operating expenses	1 016 778	2 411 345	2 363 712	3 391 406	2 758 789	3 306 955	3 428 162	4 107 781
By-election expenses	0	0	83 063	29 016	4 700	6 278	62 195	39 537
General election expenses[d]	0	0	0	0	3 912 826	3 846 223	0	0

Table 5.1 (cont'd)
Liberal party revenues and expenditures, 1974–82

	1974–75[a]	1975–76[b]	1977	1978	1979E	1980E	1981	1982
Transfers to party associations	941 290	2 295 200	1 739 933	1 862 604	7 134	388 572	1 625 925	2 663 578
Other expenditures	4 738	0	0	0	0	0	0	0
Total expenditures	1 962 807	4 706 545	4 186 708	5 283 026	6 683 449	7 548 028	5 116 282	6 780 896
Excess of revenue over expenditures	253 893	1 116 362	399 898	(265 515)	336 605	819 050	475 827	(34 302)

Sources: Canada, Elections Canada (1980b, 1981, 1984c, 1988c); and "Registered Parties Fiscal Period Returns, 1974–90."

[a] 1 Aug. 1974–31 July 1975 (12 months).
[b] 1 Aug. 1975–31 Dec. 1976 (17 months).
[c] Includes "government" contributions.
[d] "Reimbursement" and "election expenses" not included in original tables (see Sources).
[e] This total is higher than "total contributions" as reported by CEO as it includes "other income" and "reimbursement" of part of party's "election expenses."
E = Election year.

Table 5.1a
Liberal party revenues and expenditures, 1983–90

	1983	1984E	1985	1986	1987	1988E	1989	1990
Contributions	7 285 115	10 553 316	5 570 822	10 619 007	8 832 377	13 211 364	6 324 012	12 038 486
Individuals	3 261 950	5 181 097	3 129 232	5 752 902	3 471 932	4 748 305	2 385 223	7 441 191
Corporations	3 542 895	5 339 729	2 432 398	4 845 901	5 343 968	8 449 440	3 931 263	4 567 820
Trade unions	3 223	2 499	1 055	5 203	8 898	5 264	2 883	3 443
Other organizations[d]	477 047[f]	29 991	8 137	15 001	7 579	8 355	4 642	26 032
Other income	451 246	1 044 974	398 281	91 279	49 327	3 146 688[c]	54 039	1 729 776
Reimbursement[e]	0	1 415 921	193 908[a]	8 452[a]	0	1 538 972	19 229[a]	9 714
Total revenue[g]	7 736 361	13 014 211	6 163 001	10 718 738	8 881 704	17 897 024	6 397 280	13 777 976
Operating expenses	4 616 117	11 205 819	7 253 851	9 608 242	7 639 926	6 949 519	5 496 344	9 892 905
By-election expenses	27 679	0	0	36 814	57 040	0	68 639	117 395
General election expenses[e]	0	6 292 983	0	0	0	6 839 875	0	0
Transfers to party associations	1 633 213	793 487	894 741[b]	1 521 209	1 508 120	2 572 393	1 550 168	3 316 348[h]

Table 5.1a (cont'd)
Liberal party revenues and expenditures, 1983–90

	1983	1984E	1985	1986	1987	1988E	1989	1990
Other expenditures	0	0	0	0	69 227	653 700	0	0
Total expenditures	6 277 009	18 292 289	8 148 592	11 166 265	9 274 313	17 015 487	7 115 151	13 326 648
Excess of revenue over expenditures	1 459 352	(5 278 078)	(1 985 591)	(447 527)	(392 609)	881 537	(717 871)	451 328

Sources: Canada, Elections Canada (1980b, 1981, 1984c, 1988c); and "Registered Parties Fiscal Period Returns, 1974–90."

aReimbursement appears in 1985 and 1986 for 1984 general election. 1985 also includes revenue item labelled "'1984 general election expense" of $111 414.

bNumber differs from "Registered Political Parties Fiscal Return" Report. CEO *Election Expenses* figure used here (see Source 1).

cIncludes approximately 50% of federal government reimbursement of candidates' election expenses ($2 273 684) assigned to party by candidates.

dIncludes "government" contributions.

e"Reimbursement" and "election expenses" not included in original tables (see Sources).

fIncludes $457 822 from "unincorporated organizations (excluding unions)." This category was not used after 1983. Amount from unincorporated organizations ranged from $47 828 in 1974–75 to $371 240 in 1982.

gThis total is higher that "total contributions" as reported by the CEO as it includes "other income" and "reimbursement" of part of the party's "election expenses."

hIncludes $578 086 transferred to riding associations, $788 000 transferred to provincial associations and $1.95 million transferred to leadership candidates.

E = Election year.

Table 5.2

Comparison of contributions from individuals, Liberal Party of Canada and Quebec Liberal Party, 1983–89

Year	Liberal Party of Canada				Quebec Liberal Party		
	Contributors (*N*)	Amount ($000)	Average contribution ($)	Receipts (*N*)	Contributors (est. *N*)	Amount[a] ($000)	Average contribution[b] ($)
1983	33 649	3 262	97	50 009	49 941	1 807	36
1984	29 056	5 181	178	54 120	54 088	3 459	64
1985	28 545	3 129	110	61 791	56 814	6 407	104
1986	35 369	5 753	163	45 286	40 938	6 550	145
1987	28 972	3 472	120	66 524	60 373	6 544	98
1988	30 642	4 748	155	53 349	48 145	7 243	136
1989	19 970	2 385	119	11 824	n.a.	2 997	253

Sources: Tables 8.2 and A8.1, and Massicotte (1991), table 1.A6.

[a]Contributions from individuals.

[b]Based on number of receipts issued, which is larger than number of individuals making a contribution to party.

n.a. = Not available.

Table 5.2a
Sources of Liberal party revenues, 1989 and 1990

Sources	1989 ($)		1990 ($)	
Corporate donations	2 344 635		1 821 595	
Popular fund-raising	1 252 471		1 001 443	
Direct mail	1 041 636		1 731 667	
Laurier Club	184 775		94 500	
Leader's dinners	1 038 268		776 394	
Special events	462 227		265 986	
Sub-total A[a]		6 324 012		5 691 585
Candidate levies[b]	0		608 151	
Sub-total B[c]		6 324 012		6 299 736
Leadership candidates[d]	0		1 954 958	
Convention fees[d]	0		4 391 943	
Total revenue		6 324 012[f]		12 646 637[g]

	$	%	$	%
Sources[e]				
Individuals	2 385 224	37.6	7 441 191	61.8
Corporations	3 931 264	62.1	4 567 820	37.9
Governments	1 715	0.1	4 351	0.1
Unions	2 883	0.1	3 443	0.1
Other	2 926	0.1	21 681	0.1
Total	6 324 012	100.0	12 038 486[e]	100.0

	Number	Average ($)	Number	Average ($)
Individuals	19 970	119	36 361	205
Corporations	3 857	1 019	5 598	816
Governments	13	132	15	290
Unions	4	721	6	574
Other	15	195	55	394
Total	23 859		42 035	

Source: Liberal Party of Canada, Reform Commission (1991,16); return filed by party with CEO.

[a]Sub-total A represents all non-convention related income.

[b]Non-receipted revenue.

[c]Sub-total B represents all monies available to party.

[d]Receipted, but no net revenue to party. Figure is $4 402 392 in table 5.8.

[e]Excludes $608 151 in non-receipted revenue.

[f]Figure in table 5.1 (as reported to CEO) is $3 397 280.

[g]Figure in table 5.1 (as reported to CEO) is $13 777 796.

Table 5.2b

Transfer of funds within Liberal party, 1979, 1980, 1984 and 1988 general elections
(dollars)

Election year	Transfers[a] to candidates from		Transfers[b] from party headquarters to		
	Party headquarters	PTA/riding associations	Candidates	Ridings	PTAs (& other party organizations)
	(1)	(2)	(3)	(4)	(5)
1979	2 700 669	465 841	(810 386)[c]	732 123	85 397
1980	1 545 858	667 142	(1 098 249)[c]	874 996	611 825
1984	2 765 899	719 598	474 212	194 887	124 388
1988	1 681 488	1 445 030	485 146[d]	1 155 796	931 451

Sources: Annual returns filed by party with CEO; and Canada, Elections Canada (1980b, 1981, 1984c, 1988c).

[a]As reported by CEO in his data on each general election.

[b]As reported by party to CEO.

[c]Figures in brackets indicate negative amounts, meaning candidates transferred more money to headquarters than headquarters transferred to candidates.

[d]*Excludes* amounts candidates transferred to party headquarters ($2 273 684) after 1988 election.

PTA = Provincial/territorial association.

Table 5.3
Analysis of Liberal party operating expenses, 1974–90
(percentages)

Category	1974–75[a]	1975–76[b]	1977	1978	1979E	1980E	1981	1982	1983	1984E	1985	1986	1987	1988E	1989	1990
Salaries, wages and employee benefits	42.6	38.6	38.4	33.9	36.3	25.4	29.2	31.9	28.6	11.3	28.2	31.9	39.4	40.9	38.5	19.1
Travelling expenses	9.9	8.7	7.9	11.7	4.7	3.6	6.2	6.3	5.3	3.0	6.7	7.5	9.6	7.9	6.6	4.6
Party conventions/ meetings	2.5	15.6	10.2	11.4	7.7	25.0	13.8	13.9	9.9	38.9	14.0	18.4	2.6	2.7	2.0	46.4
Rent, heat, light and power	5.5	4.3	4.0	3.0	4.4	3.1	3.5	5.7	4.3	2.3	4.1	4.5	6.3	5.1	5.9	3.4
Advertising/broadcasting	2.9	4.6	6.8	6.3	7.9	3.0	3.8	.5	.2	1.4	12.3	12.0	11.6	11.1	11.8	7.5

Printing, stationery and postage	10.0	10.3	9.6	8.1	7.9	6.6	6.9	8.0	6.5	3.3	5.1	2.8	4.5	3.1	1.4	1.0
Telephone and telegraph	5.4	4.8	5.3	4.2	4.8	3.8	4.4	4.4	3.5	3.0	3.8	1.9	3.3	3.3	3.4	2.2
Legal and audit fees	2.8	3.3	1.8	1.6	4.0	2.6	1.9	2.8	2.1	1.0	2.6	.7	.7	1.2	1.2	0.6
Other office expenses	6.2	2.1	0	0	12.1	0	0	0	0	0	0	4.6	7.6	1.0	12.1	5.8
Consulting fees	9.4	0	10.5	13.7	0	.3	1.0	2.5	3.6	12.8	2.8	0	0	0	0	0
Bank charges and interest	0	0	0	0	0	3.9	3.0	5.1	3.5	2.3	6.6	5.2	5.3	7.7	11.8	6.1
Miscellaneous	2.8	7.6	5.5	6.2	10.3	22.6	26.6	19.1	32.6	20.8	13.8	10.4	9.1	7.1	5.3	3.3
Total operating expenses	100.0	100.0	100.0	100.0	100.0	100.0	100.0	100.0	100.0	100.0	100.0	100.0	100.0	100.0	100.0	100.0
Total in $000	1 017	2 411	2 370	3 391	2 759	3 307	3 428	4 108	4 616	11 206	7 260	9 608	7 640	6 950	5 496	9 893

Source: Annual returns filed by party with CEO.

Notes: Excludes "election expenses" and transfers to PTAs and candidates. Percentages may not add up to 100.0 because of rounding.

[a] 1 Aug. 1974 to 31 July 1975 (12 months).
[b] 1 Aug. 1975 to 31 Dec. 1976 (17 months).

Table 5.4
Liberal party revenues and expenditures, 1983–90
(dollars)

	1983	1984E	1985	1986	1987	1988E	1989	1990
Revenue								
Contributions receipted 086h	7 825 115	10 553 316	5 570 822	10 815 424	8 832 377	13 211 364	6 323 558	12 037
Interest	343 102	329 581	174 169	127 999	41 381	36 784	63 186	85 499
Election rebates	0	1 415 921	115 878	8 452	0	3 813 144[d]	108 078	13 680
Unreceipted contributions	0	0	151 763	56 668	766 415	938 952	683 329	2 240 336
Event costs	0	0	0	(226 033)	(1 062 729)	(1 364 485)	(851 204)	(558 455)
Other revenue	105 859	715 394	71 839	(63 773)	144 606	1 261 653[e]	123 918	0
Total revenue	7 734 076	13 014 212	6 084 981	10 718 737	8 722 050	17 897 512	6 450 865	13 818 146
Expenses								
Party administration	3 095 927[a]	5 193 313[b]	2 949 716	3 870 409	3 879 881	3 169 892	2 694 777	2 887 616
Agency administration	459 741	2 279 227	556 881	691 644	495 301	350 774	346 635	393 716
Liberal party of Canada Fund/ provincial fund-raisers	0	0	0	802 469	844 926	622 122	453 484	278 060
Office of leader	78 199	138 174	1 137 879	1 121 846	954 994	994 273	478 617	512 733
Caucus expense	0	0	64 242	59 554	67 966	63 521	30 815	47 427
Direct-mail campaign	1 009 929	747 878	1 041 586	1 367 547	925 217	744 690	663 520	766 039
Interest	0	.	439 375	464 049	400 825	516 149	637 145	571 995
Legal and settlements and professional fees	0	0	0	0	0	44 748	28 349	12 037
Conventions/conferences	0	2 847 228	671 004[c]	1 152 637	23 345	29 817	0	4 402 392
Pre-election: election readiness	0	0	0	0	72 767	425 582	0	0
Elections: Victory campaign	0	0	0	0	0	29 822	0	0

Election expenses								
Rebatable	0	6 292 983	0	0	0	6 839 875	0	0
Non-rebatable	0	0	0	0	0	611 830	0	0
Closing	0	0	(78 025)	0	0	0		
By-election expenses	0	0	0	0	0	0	68 639	87 270
Post-election expenses	0	0	0	0	0	0	163 002	18 490
Revenue committee	0	0	457 392	0	0	0	0	0
Transfers to other party organizations	649 840	124 388	543 509	894 441	1 181 621	931 451	882 339	2 738 262[i]
Transfers to constituencies	983 373	194 887	286 990	618 627	314 578	1 155 796[f]	667 829	578 086
Transfers to candidates	0	474 212	(111 414)	8 141	0	485 146	0	30 125
Miscellaneous				114 901	52 292	0	0	3 966
Total expenses	6 277 009	18 292 290	7 959 153	11 166 265	9 213 313	17 015 488	7 169 190	13 328 214
Surplus (deficit)	1 457 067	(5 278 078)	(1 874 172)	(447 528)	(491 263)	881 536	(718 325)[g]	489 932

Source: Derived from Federal Liberal Agency of Canada, Statement of Revenue and Expense (1983–90).

a Comprised $1 154 083 (national party office) and $1 941 844 (administrative expenses).

b Comprised $1 119 143 (national party office) and $4 074 170 (administrative expenses).

c Includes $646 927 for 1985 Reform Conference.

d Figure includes 22.5% rebate from Government ($1 538 972) plus party's share of government reimbursement of candidates' "election expenses" ($2 273 684).

e Includes $935 783 in election revenue and the rest from Ontario, Quebec and Alberta provincial associations.

f *Net* of transfers of $626 740 and $357 689 from constituencies to Ontario and Quebec provincial associations.

g $453 difference is interest on loan of $20 000 made to Quebec association; had to accrue $453 interest as if an interest-bearing loan.

h Includes $1.95 million in contributions transferred to leadership candidates and $4.4 million in fees for 1990 leadership convention.

i Includes $1.95 million transferred to leadership candidates.

E = Election year.

Table 5.5

Estimates of Liberal party net revenue available to party headquarters, 1983–90
(thousands of dollars)

Category	1983	1984E	1985	1986	1987	1988E	1989	1990
Total revenue[a]	7 736	13 014	6 163	10 727	5 881	17 897[b]	6 397	13 778
Less								
Direct-mail costs	1 010	748	1 042	1 368	925	745	664	776
Agency administration[c]	460	2 279	557	692	495	351	347	394
PTA fund-raising costs				802	845	622	454	278
Revenue committee	0	0	457	0	0	0	0	0
Conventions and conferences	0	2 847	671	1 153	23	29	0	4 402
Transfers to PTAs	650	125	544	894	1 182	931	882	2 738[e]
Transfers to constituencies	983	195	287	619	315	1 156	668	578
Transfers to candidates	0	474	(111)	8	0	485	0	30
Total	3 103	6 668	3 447	5 536	3 785	4 319	3 015	9 196
Net revenue available to party headquarters[d]	4 633	6 346	2 716	5 191	2 096	13 578	3 382	4 582
Party election expenses		6 293				6 738		
Net revenue available after election expenses		53				6 767		

Source: Derived from tables 5.1, 5.4 and tables relating to chapter 9.

[a]Excludes costs of staging an event or dinner because party may issue a tax receipt only for net revenue from events such as a dinner, but includes delegate fees for conventions.

[b]Includes $2 274 transferred *from* candidates, half of federal government's reimbursement of their "election expenses."

[c]Costs of Liberal Agency of Canada – party's official agent.

[d]Before "election expenses" in 1984 and 1988.

[e]Includes $1.95 million transferred to leadership candidates and routed through Federal Liberal Agency so tax receipts could be issued.

E = Election year.
PTA = Provincial/territorial association.

Table 5.6
Liberal party revenues by method raised, 1988 and 1989
(dollars)

	1988E	1989
Revenue per Chief Electoral Officer		
Contributions	13 211 364	6 324 012
Other income	873 004	19 229
Total	14 084 368[a]	6 343 241
Revenue by level at which it was raised		
National		
Raised in PTA — donations	7 812 469	2 787 389
Raised in PTA — events	1 313 835	1 038 267
Direct mail (gross revenue)	2 174 638	1 041 636
Miscellaneous	140 139	57 880
Popular campaign	116 843	0
Victory campaign	28 900	0
Convention	0	146 369
Other (unreceipted) revenue	873 004	19 229
Total	12 459 828	5 090 770
Provincial/territorial associations	0	0
Riding		
Donations	825 709	512 444
Events	798 831	740 027
Total	1 624 540	1 252 471
Total revenue	14 084 368[a]	6 343 241

Source: Liberal party internal statements, Federal Liberal Agency of Canada office.

[a]Excludes reimbursement of party "election expenses" ($1 538 972) and approximately half of federal government's reimbursement of candidates' "election expenses" transferred to party head-quarters ($2 273 694) by candidates.

E = Election year.
PTA = Provincial/territorial association.

Table 5.7
Liberal party balance sheet at year end, 1983–90
(dollars)

	1983	1984E	1985ᵃ	1986	1987	1988E	1989	1990
Assets								
Current	9 104 884	5 272 804	3 484 295	2 970 387	1 590 018	8 349 982ᶜ	1 511 363	1 359 119
Fixedᵇ	0	0	0	0	825 000	825 000	825 000	825 000
Total	9 104 884	5 272 804	3 484 295	2 970 387	2 415 018	9 174 982ᵉ	2 336 363	2 184 119
Liabilities								
Current	5 721 137	7 191 780	7 356 296	7 289 916	6 400 810	12 279 237	6 158 943	5 516 767
Long termᵇ	0	0	0	0	825 000	825 000	825 000	825 000
Total	5 721 137	7 191 780	7 356 296	7 289 916	7 225 810	13 104 237	6 983 943	6 341 767
Unallocated funds (members' equity)	3 383 747	(1 918 971)	(3 872 001)	(4 319 529)	(4 810 792)	(3 929 255)ᶠ	(4 648 580)	(4 157 648)
Total liabilities and unallocated funds	9 104 884	5 272 809	3 484 295	2 970 387	2 415 018	9 174 982	2 336 363	2 184 119

Source: Liberal Party of Canada, financial statements, 1984–90.

ᵃIn 1986, accounting policies changed and 1985 statements were re-cast to reflect this; re-cast figure is presented here.

ᵇIn 1988, accounting policy vis-à-vis fixed assets changed. Office premises were capitalized and related mortgage payments recorded as a liability. The 1987 statements were re-cast to reflect this change and are presented here. Statements to 1987 show no similar fixed asset treatment.

ᶜIncludes $6 086 339 in "rebates receivable." Note amount recovered was $1 538 972 from 22.5% rebate on party election expenses plus $2 274 684 from candidates required to transfer half their "election expenses" reimbursement to party.

ᵈIncludes $5 341 845 in "marketable investments and accrued interest".

ᵉOverstated by $2.273 million, see note c.

ᶠ Understated by $2.273 million, see note c.

E = Election year.

Table 5.8

Revenues and expenditures for Liberal party's leadership convention and leadership candidates, 1990

(dollars)

Revenue	
Delegates/alternates	2 871 177
Youth delegates/alternates	1 095 595
Observers' fees	268 502
Leadership forums	136 450
Leader's night	12 950
Miscellaneous	17 720
Total	4 402 394[a]
Expenses	
Travel assistance	2 202 817
Finance and administration	561 115
Leadership forums	203 203
Opening/leader's night	147 936
Delegate services	326 235
Constitution and legal	202 324
Technical services	374 361
Communications	204 460
Special committees	119 717
Honorary delegates	14 242
1989 convention costs	45 982
Total	4 402 392[b]

Candidate	Leadership expenses subject to $1.7 million limit	Levy to Liberal party	Excluded and pre-call expenses	Total expenses	Amount of contributions routed through Federal Liberal Agency
Jean Chrétien	1 671 768	284 354	489 914	2 446 036	940 000
Paul Martin	1 637 147	277 429	457 114	2 371 690	400 000
Sheila Copps	481 838	46 368[c]	277 858	806 064	550 000
John Nunziata	166 076	0	0	166 076	160 000
Tom Wappell	143 186	0	0	143 186	
Clifford Lincoln	not filed	—	—	—	—
Total	4 100 015	608 151	1 224 886	5 933 052	1 950 000

Sources: Liberal Party of Canada, Ottawa; *Globe and Mail*, 8 November 1990, A1, A4.

[a]Reported as $4 391 943 in convention fees in table 5.6.

[b]Total reported to CEO was $4 585 660.

[c]Includes amounts owing and in dispute.

Table 6.1
Use of federal and provincial income-tax credits by B.C. section of New Democratic Party, 1988–90

Category	1988[a] $	%	1989 $	%	1990 $	%
Federally receipted	1 744 654	43.7	846 977	27.1	1 164 298	29.6
Provincially receipted	2 218 354	55.5	2 253 723	72.2	2 764 264	70.2
Non-receipted[b]	30 597	0.8	21 265	0.7	8 257	0.2
Total	3 993 605	100.0	3 121 965	100.0	3 936 819	100.0

Source: Dr. Roger Howard, treasurer of B.C. section of NDP.

[a]Federal election on 21 November 1988.

[b]Small contributions for which a receipt was not requested and name of donor was not required to be reported.

Table 6.2
New Democratic Party revenues and expenditures, 1974–82

	1974–75[a]	1976	1977	1978	1979E	1980E	1981	1982
Contributions								
Federally receipted	4 017 239	2 206 446	2 860 838	3 259 347	4 597 112	4 646 090	3 534 958	4 537 112
Provincially receipted		643 737	519 238	783 152	1 278 885	1 180 210	2 146 770	2 341 715
Other income[b]	0	75 031	145 295	141 223	144 169	274 357	320 854	229 370
Reimbursement[c]	0	0	0	0	496 350	677 481	0	0
Provincial rebates/ subsidies	0	0	0	0	0	0	0	0
Total revenue	4 017 239	2 925 214	3 525 371	4 183 722	6 516 516	6 778 138	6 002 582	7 108 197
Operating expenses	2 603 643	2 035 120	2 848 181	3 008 952	3 365 009	3 139 014	4 455 900	4 850 076
By-election expenses	2 000	4 610	8 926	19 105	14 100	11 505	17 648	21 458
General election expenses[c]	0	0	0	0	2 190 093	3 086 176	0	0
Transfers to party associations[d]	1 234 135	340 955	247 773	486 077	1 298 727	2 841 104	2 017 891	1 075 483

Table 6.2 (cont'd)
New Democratic Party revenues and expenditures, 1974–82

	1974–75[a]	1976	1977	1978	1979E	1980E	1981	1982
Total expenditures	3 839 778	2 380 685	3 104 880	3 514 134	6 867 929	9 077 799	6 491 439	4 871 534
Surplus (deficit)	177 461	544 529	420 491	669 588	(351 413)	(2 299 661)	(488 857)	2 236 663

Sources: Canada, Elections Canada (1980b, 1981, 1984c, 1988c); registered parties' fiscal period returns (1974–89).

[a]Includes (1 Aug. 1984 to 31 Dec. 1974) plus (1 Jan. 1975 to 31 Dec. 1975).

[b]Includes miscellaneous federal fund-raising for which no tax credit receipts were issued.

[c]Reimbursement and election expenses not included in CEO report.

[d]Transfers to provincial sections plus transfers to provincial ridings.

E = Election year.

Table 6.2a
New Democratic Party revenues and expenditures, 1983-90

	1983	1984E	1985	1986	1987	1988E	1989[c]	1990
Contributions								
Federally receipted	5 746 066	7 149 680	5 644 056	6 466 102	6 206 685	10 978 300	7 196 713	8 569 177[e]
Provincial receipted	2 697 121	3 155 793	3 687 695	6 843 667	5 447 255	6 144 875	6 026 988	6 396 172
Other income[a]	225 645	807 223	640 260	518 561	625 619	1 184 696	548 811	0
Reimbursement[b]	0	1 064 413	0	0	0	1 588 627	0	0
Provincial rebates/ subsidies	0	0	0	810 995	327 917	446 899	92 182	473 559
Total revenue	8 668 652	11 577 109	10 152 011	14 639 325	12 607 476	20 343 397	13 864 694	15 438 908
Operating expenses	5 638 742	6 498 935	10 125 277	12 483 048	12 720 080	12 092 132	8 873 830	10 910 966
By-election expenses	25 214	0	0	26 071	58 570	21 533	19 573	97 804
General election expenses[c]	0	4 730 723	0	0	0	7 060 563	0	0
Transfers to party associations[d]	2 344 807	908 425	945 232	2 678 476	1 233 011	2 819 537	3 613 347	3 253 053

Table 6.2a (cont'd)
New Democratic Party revenues and expenditures, 1983–90

	1983	1984E	1985	1986	1987	1988E	1989c	1990
Total expenditures	8 008 763	12 138 083	11 070 509	15 187 595	14 011 661	21 993 765	12 506 750	14 261 823
Surplus (deficit)	659 889	(560 974)	(918 498)	(548 270)	(1 404 185)	(1 650 368)	1 357 944	1 177 095

Sources: Canada, Elections Canada (1980b, 1981, 1984c, 1988c); Registered parties fiscal period returns (1974–89).

aIncludes miscellaneous federal fund-raising for which no tax credit receipts were issued.

bReimbursement and election expenses not included in CEO report.

c1989 data from source b.

dTransfers to provincial sections plus transfers to provincial ridings.

eIncludes $934 013 in non-receipted contributions from fund-raising events.

E = Election year.

Table 6.3
Analysis of New Democratic Party revenues, 1974–82

	1974	1975[a]	1976	1977	1978	1979E[c]	1980E	1981	1982
Federally receipted contributions									
Individuals	1 285 505	2 067 848	1 772 534	2 209 500	2 552 866	2 448 397	2 817 387	2 868 724	3 774 971
Corporations	14 204	143 590	92 113	189 910	206 646	170 398	96 501	109 062	144 324
Trade unions	133 664	366 537	338 329	436 214	490 359	1 701 616	1 702 828	515 186	473 139
Other organizations[d]	3 486	2 405	3 470	25 214	9 476	102 353	29 374	41 986	144 678
Other income	58 749[b]	164 530[b]	75 031	145 295	141 223	182 556	274 357	320 854	229 370
Reimbursement	0	0	0	0	0	496 350	677 481	0	0
Provincially receipted revenues	0	0	643 737	519 238	783 512	1 278 885	1 180 210	2 146 770	2 341 715

Table 6.3 (cont'd)
Analysis of New Democratic Party revenues, 1974–82

	1974	1975[a]	1976	1977	1978	1979E	1980E	1981	1982
Provincial rebates and subsidies	0	0	0	0	0	0	0	0	0
Total	1 495 608	2 744 910	2 925 214	3 525 371	4 183 722	6 516 516	6 778 138	6 002 582	7 108 197

Sources: Canada, Elections Canada (1980b, 1981, 1984c, 1988c); annual returns filed by party with CEO (1974–89).

Notes: See special notes on CEO *Report* below.

[a]1 Aug. 1974–31 Dec. 1974 (5 months).

[b]Not included in CEO figures.

[c]See special notes on CEO *Report.*

[d]Includes "government" contributions.

Notes to NDP figures as given in CEO *Report.*
CEO does not include provincially receipted revenue in revenue figure prior to 1980. For consistency they have been added, where necessary, to revenues 1974–79.
CEO does not include provincial rebates/subsidies in revenue figures. They have been included here.
Treatment of "other income" as published by CEO has varied as follows:
  1976–78: Miscellaneous fund-raising (no receipt); interest income; rental income.
  1979: Government; interest and rental income; N.B. Miscellaneous fund-raising (no receipt) included individual contributions (although *not* a receipted item).
  1980–84: Miscellaneous fund-raising (no receipt); provincially receipted revenue; interest and other income.
  1985–88: Other organizations; provincially receipted revenue; miscellaneous fund-raising (no receipts).

E = Election year.

Table 6.3a
Analysis of New Democratic Party revenues, 1983–90

	1983	1984E	1985	1986	1987	1988E	1989[c]	1990
Federally receipted contributions								
Individuals	4 998 350	4 156 000	4 611 704	5 036 131	4 782 200	7 844 753	5 981 989	6 034 726
Business/commercial organizations	41 432	51 665	58 417	177 960	47 476	262 524	54 323	141 509
Trade unions	636 539	2 159 055	869 401	1 172 784	1 345 227	2 718 009	1 006 689	1 170 766
Other organizations[d]	69 745	182 960	104 534	79 227	31 782	153 114	153 712	20 676
Other income	225 645	807 223[a]	640 260	518 561	625 619	1 184 696[b]	548 811	1 201 500[c]
Reimbursement	0	1 064 413	0	0	0	1 588 627	0	0
Provincially receipted revenues	2 697 121	3 155 793	3 687 695	6 843 667	5 447 255	6 144 875	6 026 988	6 396 172

Table 6.3a (cont'd)
Analysis of New Democratic Party revenues, 1983–90

	1983	1984E	1985	1986	1987	1988E	1989c	1990
Provincial rebates and subsidies	0	0	0	810 995	327 917	446 899	92 182	473 559
Total	8 668 652	11 577 109	10 152 011	14 639 325	12 607 476	20 343 497	13 864 694	15 438 908

Sources: Canada, Elections Canada (1980b, 1981, 1984c, 1988c); annual returns filed by party with CEO (1974–89).

Notes: See special notes on CEO *Report* below.

aIncludes "government" contributions.

bIncludes $740 652 in non-receipted revenues.

cIncludes $655 545 in non-receipted revenues.

Notes to NDP figures as given in CEO *Report.*
CEO does not include provincially receipted revenue in revenue figure prior to 1980. For consistency they have been added, where necessary, to revenues 1974–79.
CEO does not include provincial rebates/subsidies in revenue figures. They have been included here.
Treatment of "other income" as published by CEO has varied as follows:
    1976–78: Miscellaneous fund-raising (no receipt); interest income; rental income.
    1979: Government; interest and rental income; N.B. Miscellaneous fund-raising (no receipt) included individual contributions (although *not* a receipted item).
    1980–84: Miscellaneous fund-raising (no receipt); provincially receipted revenue; interest and other income.
    1985–88: Other organizations: provincially receipted revenue; miscellaneous fund-raising (no receipts).

E = Election year.

Table 6.4
New Democratic Party federally receipted revenues and federal office expenditures, 1974–90
(thousands of dollars)

	1974–75[a]	1976	1977	1978	1979E	1980E	1981	1982	1983	1984E	1985	1986	1987	1988E	1989	1990
Federally receipted contributions	4 017	2 207	2 861	3 259	4 597	4 646	3 535	4 537	5 746	7 150	5 644	6 466	6 207	10 978	7 197	7 367
Other income	0	75	145	141	144	274	321	229	226	807	640	519	626	1 185	549	1 202
Reimbursement of election expenses	N/A	0	0	0	496	675	0	0	0	1 064	0	0	0	1 589	0	0
Total federal revenue	4 017	2 282	3 006	3 400	5 237	5 595	3 856	4 766	5 972	9 021	6 284	6 985	6 833	13 752	7 746	8 569
Federal office expenses	720	476	688	714	788	1 070	984	1 055	1 130	1 413	1 720	1 973	2 522	3 717	1 530	2 082
General election expenses[b]	380	0	0	0	2 555	3 154	0	0	0	5 250	0	0	0	7 742	0	0
Total federal expenses	1 100	476	688	714	3 343	4 224	984	1 055	1 130	6 663	1 720	1 973	2 522	11 459	1 530	2 082
Difference[c]	2 917	1 806	2 318	2 686	1 894	1 371	2 872	3 771	4 842	2 358	4 564	5 012	4 311	2 293	6 216	6 487

Table 6.4 (cont'd)
New Democratic Party federally receipted revenues and federal office expenditures, 1974–90
(thousands of dollars)

	1974–75[a]	1976	1977	1978	1979E	1980E	1981	1982	1983	1984E	1985	1986	1987	1988E	1989	1990
Transfers to provincial sections[d]	68	105	225	266	664	276	1 419	701	1 090	141	32	138	236	12	163	355
Transfers to provincial ridings[d]	587	237	491	669	635	789	599	1 265	1 254	768	913	2 541	997	2 808	3 451	2 898
PTS quotas in election years[e]	115	0	0	0	459	364	0	0	0	1 582	0	0	0	2 200	0	0
Provincially receipted revenues[d]	N/A	644	519	783	1 279	1 180	2 147	2 342	2 697	3 156	3 688	6 844	5 447	6 145	6 027	6 396

Sources: Annual returns filed by NDP with CEO, 1974–90; Financial statements for NDP federal office, 1974–90.

[a] 1 Aug. 1974 to 31 Dec. 1975 (17 months).

[b] Figures as provided by NDP. They are greater than "election expenses," per CEO: 1979 = 2 190; 1980 = 3 086; 1984 = 4 371; 1988 = 7 061. For more detail on NDP election expenses, see chapter 4.

[c] Apparent amount of federally receipted revenues used by provincial level of NDP, i.e., to elect provincial members rather than federal MPs.

[d] As reported to CEO.

[e] See table 6.7. These amounts are transferred to federal office to pay for party "election expenses."

N/A = Not applicable.
PTS = Provincial/territorial section.

Table 6.5
New Democratic Party federal office statement of revenues and expenditures, 1974–82

	1974	1975[a]	1976	1977	1978	1979E	1980E	1981	1982
Revenue									
Individual memberships	138 003	272 990	0	0	0	0	0	0	0
Revenue sharing	0	0	315 021	377 451	379 938	423 176	495 385	871 812	788 764
Affiliated members' dues[a]	157 366	183 252	182 990	190 602	191 369	191 455	202 961	211 980	189 664
Other contributions	23 653	16 479	34 269	63 892	53 034	44 997	100 155	89 878	56 097
Interest and sundry income	5 848	5 194	15 015	24 408	17 111	13 290	4 121	3 132	22 264
Literature sales	0	0	0	0	0	0	6 232	8 338	1 605
Transfer federal finance drive	0	0	0	0	0	0	0	0	0
Forum 2000 (policy development)	0	0	0	0	0	0	0	0	0
Goods and services	0	0	0	0	0	0	0	0	0
Contributions to rent	0	0	0	0	0	0	0	0	0
Special fund-raising	0	0	0	0	0	0	0	0	0
Convention	0	0	0	0	0	0	0	0	0
Total revenue	324 870	477 915	547 295	656 353	641 452	683 918	808 854	1 185 140	1 058 394
Expenses									
Administration	142 020	201 894	244 530	312 547	315 476	385 592	425 706	452 920	458 809
Leader/caucus	17 031	38 882	82 668	101 143	109 756	126 709	67 328	75 325	80 262
Executive/council/ committees	27 994	0	0	20 118	15 199	16 899	102 359	102 699	128 849

Table 6.5 (cont'd)
New Democratic Party federal office statement of revenues and expenditures, 1974–82

	1974	1975[a]	1976	1977	1978	1979E	1980E	1981	1982
Expenses (cont'd)									
Organization	72 247	122 779	111 730	168 965	217 874	264 102	168 158	208 737	249 032
Publications and research	4 500	9 943	21 065	25 380	21 457	12 078	15 859	33 564	47 870
Policy development	0	0	0	0	0	0	22 725	0	0
Communications	0	0	0	0	0	0	0	0	0
Conventions	0	53 394	0	48 384	0	33 451	0	27 493	0
Election activities (federal)	8 494	0	0	0	0	(76 801)	183 360	0	0
Provincial activities (between elections)	0	0	0	0	0	0	0	0	0
International activities	4 684	6 306	5 198	6 463	30 883	24 317	21 860	48 069	24 232
Miscellaneous	5 001	4 647	10 771	5 288	3 560	1 791	62 428	34 746	65 917
Total expenses	281 971	437 845	475 962	688 288	714 205	787 868	1 069 783	983 553	1 054 971
Surplus (deficit)	42 899	40 070	71 333	(31 935)	(72 753)	(103 950)	(260 929)	201 587	3 423

Source: NDP financial statements as provided to author.

Notes: Excludes election year revenues and election expenses.

[a]From affiliated trade unions.

E = Election year.

Table 6.5a
New Democratic Party federal office statement of revenues and expenditures, 1983–90

	1983	1984E	1985	1986	1987	1988E	1989	1990
Revenue								
Individual memberships	0	0	0	0	0	0	0	0
Revenue sharing	1 143 535	985 888	1 495 278	1 580 267	1 285 323	1 276 444	1 407 269	1 485 080
Affiliated members' dues[a]	179 813	256 931	340 089	380 543	354 989	379 940	403 920	364 540
Other contributions	386 557	301 835	80 042	95 686	119 895	126 127	133 240	229 925
Interest and sundry income	4 091	2 340	3 907	4 222	3 505	7 018	11 991	0
Literature sales	2 280	2 817	2 315	827	1 014	0	2 989	0
Transfer federal finance drive	0	130 000	0	0	0	0	0	0
Forum 2000 (policy development)	0	0	0	0	0	0	0	0
Goods and services	0	0	0	3 446	9 142	0	0	0
Contributions to rent	0	0	0	27 813	10 859	0	0	0
Special fund-raising	0	0	0	21 120	18 705	0	583 974	605 159
Convention	0	0	0	0	0	0	21 663	0
Total revenue	1 716 166	1 679 811	1 921 631	2 113 924	1 803 432	1 789 529	2 565 046	2 684 704

Table 6.5a (cont'd)
New Democratic Party federal office statement of revenues and expenditures, 1983–90

	1983	1984E	1985	1986	1987	1988E	1989	1990
Expenses								
Administration	508 211	630 167	646 876	745 572	919 328	1 780 391	998 623	879 785
Leader/caucus	77 195	84 227	107 162	116 977	132 800	115 607	63 734	86 307
Executive/council/committees	118 256	121 550	162 337	196 709	184 813	139 587	181 292	218 711
Organization	209 764	283 199	201 891	191 750	299 374	246 157	0	460 717
Publications and research	44 313	63 414	0	0	0	0	8 847	0
Policy development	35 835	0	69 061	262 265	53 980	48 922	0	123 753
Communications	0	0	0	88 674	106 251	154 779	0	103 492
Conventions	(9 857)	0	24 715	0	123 531	0	0	0
Election activities (federal)	0	49 687	13 725	0	149 878	916 004	0	129 578
Provincial activities (between elections)	0	29 758	446 747	283 762	504 195	267 416	228 223	0
International activities	32 569	34 743	47 386	50 022	48 194	47 812	49 073	47 787
Miscellaneous	113 331	115 919	0	36 875	0	0	0	31 977
Total expenses	1 129 617	1 412 664	1 719 900	1 972 546	2 252 344	3 716 675	1 529 802	2 082 147
Surplus (deficit)	586 549	267 147	201 731	141 378	(718 912)	(1 927 146)	1 035 244	602 557

Source: NDP financial statements as provided to author.

Notes: Excludes election year revenues and election expenses.

aFrom affiliated trade unions.

E = Election year.

Table 6.6
New Democratic Party federal office balance sheet, 1974–82

	1974	1975[a]	1976	1977	1978	1979E	1980E	1981	1982
Current assets									
Cash and deposits	54 084	103 283	164 850	185 571	118 991	280 505	29 068	53 214	110 844
Accounts receivable	26 815	11 515	18 225	25 012	35 342	56 605	52 953	30 412	18 733
Due from PTS	0	0	0	0	0	0	266 808	536 203	610 048
Inventory, at cost	4 042	6 165	12 387	12 728	34 964	10 890	19 849	16 979	12 933
Prepaid expenses	11 279	1 061	13 976	56 950	87 909	22 791	425	2 395	27 151
Special funds	54 826	83 102	93 720	0	0	0	0	0	0
Total current assets	151 046	205 126	303 158	280 261	277 206	370 791	369 103	639 203	779 709
Fixed assets (at cost)									
Furniture and equipment	14 453	18 195	25 281	35 001	42 742	49 400	50 659	51 659	64 896
Depreciation	10 049	10 830	12 106	14 386	17 865	22 010	26 281	30 652	33 200
Total fixed assets	4 404	7 365	13 175	20 615	24 877	27 390	24 378	21 007	31 696
Total assets	155 450	212 491	316 333	300 876	302 083	398 181	393 481	660 210	811 405

Table 6.6 (cont'd)
New Democratic Party federal office balance sheet, 1974–82

	1974	1975[a]	1976	1977	1978	1979E	1980E	1981	1982
Current liabilities									
Bank loans	0	0	0	0	20 000	0	124 000	89 000	235 000
Accounts payable	12 196	20 891	46 317	108 370	156 859	238 165	154 694	163 081	183 540
Loans payable	7 000	7 000	7 000	7 000	8 825	5 325	5 320	3 500	3 500
Revenue received in advance	5 000	5 000	1 465	0	0	0	0	0	0
Fund contributions	0	0	0	0	0	0	0	10 974	0
Election/pre-election	0	0	0	0	0	144 067	0	0	0
Funds relating to federal financial drive	0	0	0	0	0	0	0	0	67 313
Total current liabilities	24 196	32 891	54 782	115 370	185 684	387 557	284 014	266 555	489 353

Long-term assets									
Lien payable, net of current portion	0	0	0	0	3 646	1 821	0	0	0
Total liabilities	24 196	32 891	54 782	115 370	189 330	389 378	284 014	266 555	489 353
Members' equity									
Members' equity	76 428	91 498	160 331	125 506	62 753	(41 197)	59 467	343 655	322 052
Restricted equity	54 826	88 102	101 220	60 000	50 000	50 000	50 000	50 000	0
Total members' equity	131 254	179 600	261 551	185 506	112 753	8 803	109 467	393 655	322 052
Total liabilities and members' equity	155 450	212 491	316 333	300 876	302 083	398 181	393 481	660 210	811 405

Source: New Democratic Party financial statements, as provided to author.

E = Election year.

Table 6.6a
New Democratic Party federal office balance sheet, 1983–90

	1983	1984E	1985	1986	1987	1988E	1989	1990
Current assets								
Cash and deposits	510 511	0	313 048	588 749	677 402	153 902	1 245 969	602 465
Accounts receivable	22 162	1 383 937	41 094	75 415	20 852	1 553 068	40 283	12 237
Due from PTS	1 014 190	1 062 177	1 455 602	1 753 654	1 628 368	1 353 993	1 093 281	1 115 649
Inventory, at cost	9 092	0	0	0	0	0	0	0
Prepaid expenses	5 425	2 421	0	38 686	166 868	6 320	63 414	16 468
Special funds	0	0	0	0	0	0	0	0
Total current assets	1 561 380	2 448 535	1 809 744	2 456 504	2 493 490	3 067 283	2 442 947	1 746 819
Fixed assets (at cost)								
Furniture and equipment	88 651	91 755	93 652	126 788	253 267	426 412	427 331	506 109
Depreciation	41 270	49 651	58 221	68 966	93 498	135 344	177 282	227 098
Total fixed assets	47 381	42 104	35 431	57 822	159 769	291 068	250 049	279 011
Total assets	1 608 761	2 490 639	1 845 175	2 514 326	2 653 259	3 358 351	2 692 996	2 025 830

Current liabilities							
Bank loans	0	0	180 000	500 000	2 330 944	1 475 000	660 000
Accounts payable	95 238	183 032	367 601	572 624	1 836 411	876 674	363 994
Loans payable	0	0	0	0	0	0	0
Revenue received in advance	0	0	0	0	0	0	0
Fund contributions	0	0	0	199 317	140 883	255 965	13 922
Election/pre-election	0	284 664	447 868	312 243	0	0	0
Funds relating to federal financial drive	604 922	0	0	0	0	0	0
Total current liabilities	700 160	467 696	995 469	1 584 184	4 308 238	2 607 639	1 337 916
Long-term assets							
Lien payable, net of current portion	0	0	0	0	0	0	0
Total liabilities	700 160	467 696	995 469	1 584 184	4 308 238	2 607 639	1 337 916
Members' equity							
Members' equity	908 601	1 377 479	1 518 851	1 069 075	(949 887)	85 357	687 914
Restricted equity	0	0	0	0	0	0	0
Total members' equity	908 601	1 377 479	1 518 851	1 069 075	(949 887)	85 357	687 914
Total liabilities and members' equity	1 608 761	1 845 175	2 514 326	2 563 259	3 358 351	2 692 996	2 025 830

Source: New Democratic Party financial statements, as provided to author.

E = Election year.

Table 6.7
Provincial elections, 1974–91
(thousands of dollars)

		NDP	
Year	Provincial general election	Provincially receipted revenues	Transfers from federal to PTS or provincial ridings
1974	New Brunswick, Nova Scotia, Prince Edward Island	n.a.	1 234[a]
1975	Alberta, *British Columbia*, Newfoundland, Ontario, *Saskatchewan*		
1976	Quebec	644	341
1977	*Manitoba, Ontario*	519	248
1978	New Brunswick, Nova Scotia, Prince Edward Island, *Saskatchewan*, Yukon	784	486
1979	Alberta, *British Columbia*, Newfoundland, Prince Edward Island	1 279	1 299
1980	None	1 180	2 841
1981	*Manitoba*, Nova Scotia, *Ontario*, Quebec	2 147	2 018
1982	Alberta, New Brunswick, Newfoundland, Prince Edward Island, *Saskatchewan*, Yukon	2 342	1 075
1983	*British Columbia*	2 697	2 345
1984	Nova Scotia	3 156	908
1985	Newfoundland, *Ontario*, Quebec, Yukon	3 687	945
1986	Alberta, *British Columbia*, *Manitoba*, Prince Edward Island, Saskatchewan	6 844	2 678
1987	New Brunswick, *Ontario*	5 447	1 233
1988	*Manitoba*, Nova Scotia	6 145	2 820
1989	Newfoundland, Prince Edward Island, Yukon	6 027	3 613
1990	*Manitoba, Ontario*	6 396	3 608
1991	*British Columbia, Saskatchewan*, New Brunswick	n.a.	n.a.

Notes: Italicized provinces are more important to NDP. Most extensive efforts have usually been made in British Columbia, Saskatchewan, Manitoba and Ontario.

[a] 1 Aug. 1974–31 Dec. 1975.

n.a. = Data not available.
PTS = Provincial/territorial section.

Table 6.8

Labour contributions relative to total New Democratic Party federal revenues, 1974–90
(thousands of dollars)

Year	Union			Total federal revenue[a]	Labour contributions as % of total federal revenue
	Affiliation dues	Union contributions	Total		
1974[b]	114	20	134	1 496	9.0
1975	305	61	367	2 745	13.4
1976	305	33	338	2 281	14.8
1977	318	119	436	3 006	14.5
1978	319	171	490	3 400	14.4
1979E	319	1 382	1 702	5 238	32.5
1980E	338	1 365	1 703	5 598	30.4
1981	353	162	515	3 856	13.4
1982	316	157	473	4 767	9.9
1983	300	337	637	5 972	10.7
1984E	417	1 742	2 159	8 421	25.6
1985	567	303	869	6 464	13.4
1986	634	539	1 173	6 985	16.8
1987	625	720	1 345	6 832	19.7
1988E	633	2 085	2 718	13 752	19.8
1989	673	334	1 007	7 746	13.0
1990	608	563	1 171	8 569	13.7

Sources: Tables 6.2 and 6.3; annual returns filed by party with CEO.

[a]Includes reimbursement of party "election expenses." Main source is federally receipted contributions.

[b]1 Aug. 1974 to 31 Dec. 1974 (5 months).

E = Election year.

Table 6.9
Contributions of $1 000 or more from labour organizations to New Democratic Party, 1988

Federations of labour		
Alberta	4 000	
British Columbia	9 875	
Ontario	25 661	
Saskatchewan	10 200	
		49 736
District Labour Councils		
Brampton/Mississauga	2 000	
Medicine Hat	1 500	
North Okanagan	1 000	
Peace River	3 000	
Port Alberni	1 100	
Prince George	2 338	
South Cariboo	1 100	
		12 038
Canadian Labour Congress		1 014 192
Other		
B.C. Building Trades		3 100
Unions		
Amalgamated Transit (incl. 1 local)		6 270
AUPE	2 500	
AUPE locals (2)	2 200	
		4 700
B.C. Council of Carpenters		17 500
B.C. Staff Union		5 000
Bricklayers, L2		1 000
CMPL		1 250
Canadian Machinists		16 000
CAW	5 384	
CAW locals (13)	11 579	
		16 933
CBRT	12 500	
CBRT locals (2)	1 300	
		13 800
CPU	4 250	
CPU locals (4)	2 900	
		7 150
CUPE	5 767	
CUPE locals (12)	6 692	
		12 459

Table 6.9 (cont'd)
Contributions of $1 000 or more from labour organizations to New Democratic Party, 1988

ECWU	13 961	
ECWU locals (8)	6 000	
		19 961
Hospital Employees L180		8 850
IWA	11 000	
IWA locals (7)	7 750	
		18 750
IAM & AW locals (8)		6 182
Int. L & W Union		3 850
Labourers' Adv. Fund		1 500
LCUC locals (3)		1 170
LIU, L832		1 000
OPEIU, L491		1 000
P & PUA, L488		3 000
Pipe Trades		4 500
Plumbers L170		1 300
RWDSU	8 550	
RWDSU locals (5)	12 440	
		20 990
SEIU	30 660	
SEIU locals (4)	4 550	
		35 210
TWA, L1-423		1 000
TWU		22 000
UFCW	58 383	
UFCW locals (12)	22 994	
		81 377
USWA	63 136	
USWA locals	9 599	
		72 735
URW (incl. 1 local)		3 125
Total contributions over $1 000		1 491 628

Source: Tabulation from 1988 annual return filed by NDP with CEO.

Table 6.10

Contributions of $1 000 or more from labour organizations to New Democratic Party, 1989

Federations of Labour		
Ontario	40 924	
Saskatchewan	20 000	
		60 924
District Labour Councils		
Brampton/Mississauga		1 300
Canadian Labour Congress		18 471
Unions		
ACTU		3 100
CAW	11 707	
CAW Family Ed. Cnt.	3 750	
CAW Locals (58)	36 781	
		52 238
CBRT & GW	9 200	
CBRT locals (4)	1 200	
		10 400
Canadian Machinists		1 140
CPU	6 884	
CPU local (1)	600	
		7 484
CUPE	18 074	
CUPE locals (11)	4 191	
		22 265
ECWU (3 regional councils)	7 045	
ECWU locals (6)	7 100	
		14 145
IWA regional council	2 200	
IWA locals (12)	6 470	
		8 670
IAM & AW	950	
IAM & AW local (1)	500	
		1 450
MFL	3 548	
MFL local (1)	675	
		4 223
OPEIU (and 1 local)		1 200
RWDSU	5 050	
RWDSU locals (6)	2 510	
		7 560

Table 6.10 (cont'd)
Contributions of $1 000 or more from labour organizations to New Democratic Party, 1989

SEIU locals (4)		2 351
UFCW	22 671	
UFCW locals (15)	13 160	
		35 831
USWA	20 250	
USWA districts (3)	3 180	
USWA locals (73)	30 269	
USWA area councils (4)	5 099	
		58 798
Total contributions over $1 000		308 450
Total union contributions of all sizes		334 112

Source: Tabulation from 1989 annual return filed by NDP with CEO.

Table 6.10a
Contributions of $1 000 or more from labour organizations to New Democratic Party, 1990

Federation of Labour		
Ontario		162 343
Canadian Labour Congress	40 000	
CLC COPE	8 100	
		48 100
Unions		
Canadian Machinists Pol. League		1 400
CMPL local 764		2 526
CAW National Headquarters	68 780	
CAW Com. Nat. Auto Aero Agr. Impl.	300	
CAW locals (10)	2 782	
		71 862
CBRT & GW National Headquarters	8 000	
CBRT & GW local 226	200	
		8 200
CPU	4 450	
CPU local 1178	300	
		4 750
CUPE National Headquarters	15 820	
CUPE Manitoba Division	3 068	
CUPE locals (3)	820	
		19 708
CWC National Rep.	500	
CWC Ontario Regional Office	1 000	
CWC locals (2)	6 650	
		8 150
STCC		2 000
ECWU Ontario Regional Office	3 250	
ECWU Ontario Area Council	570	
ECWU 0001	330	
		4 150
HEU – local 180		34 850
LIUNA locals (3)		15 720
RWDSU National Headquarters	2 760	
RWDSU locals (5)	4 090	
		6 850
SEIU National Headquarters	26 000	
SEIU locals (2)	11 000	
		37 000

Table 6.10a (cont'd)
Contributions of $1 000 or more from labour organizations to New Democratic Party, 1990

UFCW National Headquarters	3 000	
UFCW locals (3)	15 932	
		18 932
USWA National Office	155	
USWA Political Action Fund	2 940	
USWA TA PAC	500	
USWA districts (3)	83 470	
USWA locals (10)	2 159	
		89 224
Total contributions over $1 000		535 765
Total union contribution of all sizes		563 127

Source: Tabulation from 1990 annual return filed by NDP with CEO.

Table 6.11
Contributions of $2 000 or more from business organizations to New Democratic Party, 1988

John Labatt Limited	25 000
Nova Corp. of Alta.	17 500
McDonalds Restaurants of Canada	10 000
91619 Canada Inc.	10 000
Associated Printers Ltd.	8 778
Government Consultants International (lobbying firm)	5 000
Westcoast Energy	5 000
Molson Companies Ltd.	5 000
NIM Management	5 000
Novalta Resources	5 000
Olympia & York Developments	5 000
Power Corp. of Canada	5 000
Doane Raymond (accountants)	5 000
G. Brent Gawne Prof. Corp.	5 000
Carling O'Keefe Breweries Ltd.	4 500
Gowling & Henderson (law firm)	4 500
Philippon Forage AD	4 500
Union Communications	3 000
Agra Industries Ltd.	2 500
Osler, Hoskin & Harcourt (law firm)	2 490
Coopers & Lybrand National Ltd. (accountants)	2 150
Balfour Moss (law firm)	2 000
Peat Marwick (accountants)	2 000
Tricil Ltd.	2 000
H.A. Simons Ltd. (engineers)	2 000
Total	147 918

Source: Tabulated by author from annual return filed by NDP with CEO.

Note: Includes law, accounting and engineering firms.

Table 6.12
New Democratic Party federal office election expenses, 1974–88 general elections

	1974[a]	1979	1980	1984	1988
Revenue					
Contributions	22 197	0	0	25 512	137 070
Provincial quotas	115 000	459 069	363 500	1 581 703	2 200 000
Contributions from labour	234 745	449 803	357 971	602 056	1 192 423
Leader's tour[b]	0	171 767	170 742	265 726	540 717
Direct mail	0	0	75 489	409 800	742 236
Goods and services[c]	0	697 919	930 385	1 121 071	595 406
Sales	0	31 810	12 735	57 790	82 386
Miscellaneous	0	324 804[d]	382 672[e]	72 270	98 801
Rebate from federal government	0	496 307	677 481	1 064 413	1 588 627
Total revenue	371 942	2 631 479	2 970 975	5 200 341	7 171 666
Expenses					
Pre-election	0	0	0	718 831	520 991
Administration	23 279	92 094	83 937	142 074	363 590
Leader's tour	42 849	249 464	342 816	531 094	1 258 490
Media	126 426	1 274 767	1 533 994	1 919 447	3 174 637
Organization	150 200	192 048	133 455	273 051	420 801
Direct mail	0	0	0	166 070	382 685
Goods and services	0	697 919	930 385	1 118 231	595 406
Riding materials	0	0	0	0	340 428
Surveys	0	0	0	0	250 718
Miscellaneous	37 682	48 386	129 748	380 230[f]	434 462[g]
Total expenses	380 436	2 554 678	3 154 335	5 250 028	7 742 208
Surplus (deficit)	(8 494)	76 801	(183 360)	(48 687)	(570 542)
Election expenses per CEO	N/A	2 190 093	3 086 176	4 730 723	7 060 563
1989 dollars	1 090 000	4 093 000	5 248 000	5 841 000	7 417 000

Sources: NDP financial statements as provided to author; Canada, Elections Canada (1980b, 1981, 1984c, 1988c).

[a]Last federal election before *Election Expenses Act* of 1974 came into effect.

[b]Revenue from media personnel on tour.

[c]Largely donations of services of campaign organizers by trade unions.

[d]Includes "media co-op," $299 866.

[e]Includes "media co-op," $369 947.

[f] Includes "federal finance drive and debt reduction," $224 104.

[g]Includes "bad debts," $354 348.

N/A = Not applicable.

Table 7.1

Reform Fund Canada statement of revenues and expenditures, 1988 and 1989

(dollars)

	1988	1989
Revenue		
Donations and memberships	688 419	1 055 365
Merchandise sales	108 402	37 257
Assembly	0	16 415
Other	2 313	7 608
Total	799 134	1 116 645
Expenses[a]		
Accommodation and meetings	8 516	2 306
Advertising and promotional materials	153 790	44 132
Amortization of organization and development costs	29 536	29 537
Bank charges	439	2 282
Beaver River by-election	0	13 520
Clerical	39 155	0
Computer costs	10 255	25 848
Deliveries	9 978	4 648
Equipment purchases	0	23 906
Equipment rental	10 596	8 320
Fees and dues	1 400	564
Fund-raising expense	0	169 982
Insurance	1 125	21
Media relations	0	5 539
Office equipment	2 388	0
Photocopying	19 118	6 487
Postage	30 521	35 867
Professional fees	22 670	21 887
Rent	23 998	29 009
Special projects	0	7 470
Supplies	14 493	37 696
Tabloid	81 237	47 110
Team of eight	7 405	0
Travel	56 015	63 847
Telephone and utilities	46 005	46 129
Wages and benefits	143 952	271 412
Total	712 592	897 339
Net operating surplus for the year	86 542	219 306

Source: Attachment to annual returns filed by Reform Party with CEO.

Note: Fund is business agent for Reform Party of Canada and is incorporated under Part II of Canada Corporations Act, R.S.C. 1970, c. C-32.

[a]Excludes transfers to constituencies.

Table 7.1a
Reform Party expenditures, 1989–91
(dollars)

Expenditure category	1989	1990	1991
Operating expenses			
Salaries, wages, benefits	318 964	400 724	804 146
Travelling expenses	59 393	128 570	219 964
Party conventions and meetings	2 775	0	296 880
Rent, heat, light, power	32 595	42 852	131 925
Advertising	104 029	115 786	13 163
Broadcasting	0	0	0
Printing and stationery	277 572	194 248	221 472
Telephone and telegraph	51 375	57 525	131 995
Legal and audit fees	21 887	35 678	81 062
Miscellaneous	48 290	153 185	0
Equipment purchases	35 389	100 499	0
Postage and mailhouse	0	220 042	0
Commission	0	60 000	0
Special project	0	155 113	28 020
Tabloid	0	57 246	0
Fund-raising costs not included above	0	0	836 361
Cost of merchandise sales	0	0	220 086
Policy, strategy and communication not included above	0	0	197 680
Finance, administration and member services not included above	0	0	483 342
Pre-writ election outlays not included above	0	0	267 001
Depreciation	0	0	56 061
Total operating expenses	952 268	1 721 468	4 170 461
Other expenditures			
Transfers to constituency associations	n.a.	653 145[a]	2 118 130
Total expenditures	952 268+	2 374 613	6 288 591

Source: Annual returns and amended 1990 return filed by Reform Party with CEO.

[a]Consists of $486 970 in the form of constituencies' 95% share of donations routed through Reform Fund Canada and $166 175 for constituencies' 50% share of $10 annual membership dues. Comparable figures for 1989 were not available from party.

n.a. = Not available.

Table 7.2
Analysis of Reform Party revenues, 1988–91
(dollars)

Category[a]	1989[b]	1990	1991
Contributions by individuals			
Amount	1 205 734	2 075 723[c]	4 737 307
Number of contributions	7 360	23 462	43 176
Average contribution	154	88	110
Contributions by business organizations			
Amount	141 184	138 039	490 743
Number of contributions	245	274	2 286
Average contribution	533	504	215
Contributions by other organizations			
Amount	4 000	0	0
Number of contributions	1	0	0
Average contribution	4 000	0	0
Total amount of contributions	1 350 918	2 213 762	5 228 050
Other revenue			
Sale of memberships	n.a.[d]	479 860	721 679
Merchandise sales	37 257	26 821	275 108
Assembly fees	16 415	0	300 000
Interest and other	7 608	24 705	63 398
Total revenues	1 412 198	2 745 148	6 588 235

Sources: Table 7.1, annual returns and amended 1990 return filed by Reform Party with CEO.

[a]Party did not receive any contributions from governments or trade unions.

[b]Includes contributions under $100.

[c]Party states its constituencies raised $512 600 in 1990, for which tax receipts were issued (letter to author, 26 March 1992). Party headquarters retained only 5% of this amount.

[d]Included in contributions from individuals.

n.a. = Not available.

Table 7.3
Comparison of Reform Party candidates' revenues and expenditures, 1988 general election
(dollars)

	Reform	PC	Liberal	NDP
Alberta				
Number of candidates	26	26	26	26
Average revenue	19 922	44 949	16 273	20 421
Average number of contributors	129	207	90	14[a]
Average "election expenses"	19 375	35 603	17 466	21 162
Average personal expenses	1 027	2 383	959	1 232
Average reimbursement	6 235	17 798	4 335	9 201
British Columbia				
Number of candidates	30	32	32	32
Average revenue	12 349	53 152	24 600	44 782
Average number of contributors	80	204	92	56[a]
Average "election expenses"	12 169	39 331	24 846	38 156
Average personal expenses	506	2 606	1 225	1 304
Average reimbursement	0[b]	20 107	10 808	17 441
Manitoba				
Number of candidates	12	14	14	14
Average revenue	7 794	31 973	26 396	17 215
Average number of contributors	49	204	162	5[a]
Average "election expenses"	8 765	38 131	28 842	24 381
Average personal expenses	735	1 728	1 585	1 175
Average reimbursement	0[b]	19 545	14 759	9 989
Saskatchewan				
Number of candidates	4	14	14	14
Average revenue	4 911	51 285	19 412	40 495
Average number of contributors	38	235	133	36[a]
Average "election expenses"	5 422	44 356	19 960	42 626
Average personal expenses	1 749	2 534	1 416	1 895
Average reimbursement	0[b]	22 590	9 162	21 225

Source: Calculated from Canada, Elections Canada (1988c, 3–315, 3–223, 3–259, 3–285).

[a]Figure is not comparable to other parties as most contributions from individuals or others were routed through provincial/territorial sections; sections then sent cheques to candidate's agent.
[b]No candidates were eligible for reimbursement.

Table 7.4
Order of finish of Reform Party candidates, 1988 general election

		Order of finish				
Province	N	1	2	3	4	5
Alberta	26	0	9	6	11	0
British Columbia	30	0	0	1	24	5
Manitoba	12	0	0	1	10	1
Saskatchewan	4	0	0	0	4	0
Total	72	0	9	8	49	6

Source: Calculated from Canada, Elections Canada (1988c).

Table 7.5
Ten Reform Party candidates who raised the most revenue, 1988 general election

Candidate	Riding	Revenue
Ken Copithorne	Macleod (Alta)	53 443
Preston Manning	Yellowhead (Alta)	49 992
Val Meredith	Surrey–White Rock–South Langley (BC)	38 586
Dan Fletcher	Peace River (Alta)	32 789
Dal Brown	Wild Rose (Alta)	32 708
Bob Slavik	Saanich–Gulf Islands (BC)	32 638
John Hamilton	Calgary Centre (Alta)	32 600
Terry Volb	Victoria (BC)	32 431
Jay Hill	Prince George–Peace River (BC)	29 906
Werner Schmidt	Okanagan Centre (BC)	28 892

Sources: Canada, Elections Canada (1988c); and Elections Canada data as supplied to author.

Note: Reform Party became a federally registered party on 21 October 1988, a month before election day. It was only during that period that candidate agents could issue receipts for political tax credit.

Table 8.1
Number of contributions from individuals to parties and candidates, 1974–91

Year	PC, Liberal and NDP	Other parties	All parties	All candidates	Total
1974 (5 months)	34 703	7 796[a]	42 499		42 499
1975	82 603	2 007[b]	84 610		84 610
1976	97 812	11 432	109 244		109 244
1977	101 571	2 754	104 325		104 325
1978	125 098	5 040	130 138		130 138
1979E	111 632	7 701	119 333	67 323	186 656
1980E	112 908	3 865	116 773	70 528	187 301
1981	129 405	1 600	131 005		131 005
1982	147 327	1 538	148 865		148 865
1983	198 537	6 556	205 093		205 093
1984E	202 282	8 700	210 982	87 456	298 438
1985	201 026	1 622	202 648		202 648
1986	178 642	2 442	181 084		181 084
1987	156 219	2 603	158 822		158 822
1988E	202 925	5 410	208 335	104 807	313 142
1989	149 451	17 232[c]	166 683		166 683
1990	180 511	37 837[d]	218 348		218 348
1991	147 867	46 926[e]	194 793		194 793

Sources: Canada, Elections Canada (1980b, 1981, 1984c, 1988c); and annual returns filed by parties with CEO.

[a]1 Aug. 1974 to 31 July 1975.

[b]1 Aug. 1975 to 31 Dec. 1975.

[c]Includes 7 541 for Christian Heritage party (22 Oct. 88 to 31 Dec. 89) and 7 360 for Reform Party. Total number of individual contributors to Confederation of Regions Western Party was not disclosed. Number included here, 265, is based on those contributing $100 or more and so is understated.

[d]Includes Reform Party, 23 462; Christian Heritage party, 9 226; and Confederation of Regions party, 2 956.

[e]Includes Reform Party, 43 176, and seven other parties, 3 750.

E = Election year.

Table 8.1a

Number of contributions from individuals to parties and candidates in election years

Election year	PC	Liberal	NDP	All other parties	Total
1979					
Party	34 952	13 025	63 655	7 701	119 333
Candidates	27 597	18 525	13 765	7 436	67 323
Total	62 569	31 550	77 420	15 137	186 656
1980					
Party	32 720	17 670	62 428	3 865	116 773
Candidates	23 489	25 823	16 778	4 438	70 528
Total	56 209	43 493	79 206	8 303	187 301
1984					
Party	93 199	29 056	80 027	8 700	210 982
Candidates	42 247	21 185	18 690	5 334	87 456
Total	135 441	50 241	98 717	14 034	298 438
1988					
Party	53 893	30 642	118 390	5 410	208 335
Candidates	40 329	27 106	22 497	14 875	104 807
Total	94 222	57 748	140 887	20 285	313 142

Sources: Canada, Elections Canada (1980b, 1981, 1984c, 1988c).

Table 8.2
Number and average size of contributions from individuals to federal parties, 1974–91

Year	PC[a] N	PC[a] Average ($)	Liberal[b] N	Liberal[b] Average ($)	NDP N	NDP Average ($)
1974 (5 months)	6 423[c]	99[c]	4 117	112	27 910	46
1975	10 341	98	13 373	113	58 889	35
1976	23 409	82	18 261	114	56 142	32
1977	20 339	86	21 063	94	60 169	37
1978	35 615	75	22 350	94	67 133	38
1979E	34 952	91	13 025	91	63 655	43
1980E	32 720	98	17 670	141	62 428	52
1981	48 125	90	24 735	85	56 545	51
1982	52 694	98	27 968	114	66 665	57
1983	99 264	92	33 649	97	65 624	76[c]
1984E	93 199	109	29 056	178	80 027	52[d]
1985	75 117	105	28 545	110	97 364	47
1986	52 786	149	35 369	163	90 487	56
1987	39 320	154	28 972	120	87 927	54
1988E	53 893	189	30 642	155	118 390	66
1989[e]	40 191	170	19 970	119	89 290	67
1990	27 702	169	36 361[f]	205	116 448	52
1991	27 391	196	26 396	127	94 080	78

Sources: Canada, Elections Canada (1980b, 1981, 1984c, 1988c); and annual returns filed by parties with CEO.

Notes: Figures are in nominal dollars. Number does not include individuals contributing to candidates in election years.

[a]Original figures for Progressive Conservative party were for 1 Aug. 1974 to 31 July 1975 and 1 Aug. 1975 to 31 Dec. 1975. They were recomputed on a pro rata basis to fit calendar year.

[b]Original figures for Liberal party were for 1 Aug. 1974 to 1 July 1975 and 1 Aug. 1975 to 31 Dec. 1976. They were recomputed on a pro rata basis to fit calendar year.

[c]If $453 365 donation from Irene Dyck is eliminated, average is $69.

[d]If $215 767 donation from Irene Dyck is eliminated, average is $49.

[e]Average for nine other parties was $154, including average of $333 for Communist party.

[f]Increased due to leadership convention and fact that $1.95 million in contributions to leadership candidates were routed through Federal Liberal Agency.

E = Election year.

Table 8.3
Average size of contributions from individuals to federal parties, 1974–91
(constant 1989 dollars)

Year	PC	Liberal	NDP	CPI deflator
1974	284	321	132	34.9
1975	253	292	90	38.7
1976	197	274	77	41.6
1977	192	209	82	44.9
1978	153	192	78	49.0
1979E	170	170	80	53.5
1980E	167	240	88	58.8
1981	136	128	77	66.2
1982	134	156	58	73.3
1983	119	125	98	77.6
1984E	135	220	64	81.0
1985	125	131	56	84.2
1986	170	186	64	87.7
1987	168	131	59	91.5
1988E	199	163	69	95.2
1989	170	119	67	100.0
1990	161	196	50	104.8
1991	180	117	72	109.0

Source: Derived from table 8.2. Nominal dollar amounts were rounded to nearest dollar before being converted to 1989 dollars.

E = Election year.

Table 8.4

Number of individuals making political contributions and number claiming federal political tax credit, 1974–88

Year	Number of individuals claiming tax credits	Tax expenditure[a] ($000)	Average individual credit[b] ($)	Total number of contributions by individuals to parties and candidates	Number claiming tax credit as % of total number of contributions by individuals
1974	19 584	1 273	65	42 499	46.1
1975	36 227	2 394	66	84 610	42.8
1976	48 313	2 800	58	109 244	44.2
1977	48 027	3 114	65	104 325	46.0
1978	64 547	3 901	60	130 138	49.6
1979E	92 353	6 111	66	186 656	49.6
1980E	95 547	6 379	67	187 301	51.0
1981	77 114	4 910	64	131 005	58.9
1982	85 941	6 268	73	148 865	57.7
1983	104 599	8 237	79	205 093	51.0
1984E	151 308	13 588	90	298 438	50.7
1985	109 310	8 624	79	202 648	53.9
1986	117 566	9 934	85	181 084	64.9
1987	102 824	7 660	75	158 822	64.7
1988E	184 410	17 515	95	313 142	58.9

Sources: Revenue Canada Taxation, Statistical Services Division, as provided to Royal Commission on Electoral Reform and Party Financing. Earlier versions of some of the data can be found in Seidle and Paltiel (1981, 276) and Seidle (1985, 122); annual returns filed by parties with CEO; table 8.1.

[a]Value of tax credits to individuals.
[b]Nominal dollars.

E = Election year.

Table 8.5
Political contributions from individuals, by party, 1974–91
(thousands of dollars)

Year	Contributions by individuals to parties			Total contributions	
	PC	Liberal	NDP[a]	N	1989 dollars
1974 (5 months)	264[b]	460[c]	1 286	2 010	5 759
1975	1 016[b]	1 514[c]	2 068	4 598	11 881
1976	1 910	2 086[b]	1 773	5 769	13 868
1977	1 743	1 984	2 210	5 937	13 223
1978	2 661	2 102	2 553	7 316	14 931
1979E	3 183	1 185	2 448	6 816	12 740
1980E	3 044	2 278	2 817	8 139	13 842
1981	4 320	2 101	2 869	9 290	14 033
1982	5 181	3 195	3 775	12 151	16 577
1983	9 105	3 262	4 998	17 366	22 379
1984E	10 142	5 181	4 156	19 479	24 048
1985	7 872	3 129	4 612	15 613	18 543
1986	7 875	5 753	5 036	18 664	21 282
1987	6 065	3 472	4 782	14 319	15 649
1988E	10 181	4 748	7 845	22 774	23 922
1989	6 850	2 385	5 982	15 217	15 217
1990	4 686	7 441	6 035	18 162	17 330
1991	5 367	3 353	7 318	16 038[d]	14 714

Sources: Tables 8.2 and 3.1.

[a]Federally receipted revenues from individuals only (excludes provincially receipted contributions from individuals). See chapter 6.

[b]Pro-rated, see note 3, table 8.2.

[c]Pro-rated, see note 2, table 8.2.

[d]Excludes 4.738 million received by Reform party.

E = Election year.

Table 8.6

Value of political contributions from individuals and value of income-tax credit, 1974–90

(thousands of dollars)

Year	Contributions by individuals to parties			Contributions to all candidates	Total contributions by individuals	Total value of tax credits	Tax credit as % of total contributions	Total value of tax credits 1989 dollars
	PC, Liberal NDP	Other parties	All parties					
1974ª	2 010	1 988	3 998			1 273	31.8	3 648
1975	4 598	244	4 842			2 394	49.4	6 186
1976	5 769	442	6 211			2 800	45.1	6 731
1977	5 937	287	6 244			3 114	50.0	6 935
1978	7 316	353	7 669			3 901	50.9	7 961
1979E	6 816	325	7 141	5 639	12 780	6 111	47.8	11 422
1980E	8 139	316	8 455	5 736	14 191	6 379	45.0	10 849
1981	9 290	296	9 586			4 910	51.2	7 417
1982	12 151	301	12 452			6 268	50.3	8 551
1983	17 366	1 146	18 512			8 327	45.0	10 731
1984E	19 479	645	20 124	9 215	29 339	13 588	46.3	16 775
1985	15 613	329	15 942			8 264	51.8	9 815
1986	18 664	416	19 080			9 934	52.1	11 327
1987	14 319	435	14 754			7 660	51.9	8 372
1988E	22 774	625	23 399	14 033	37 432	17 515	46.8	18 398
1989	15 217	2 659	17 876			n.a.	n.a.	n.a.
1990	18 612	3 213	21 825			n.a.	n.a.	n.a.

Sources: Tables 8.1, 8.4; Canada, Elections Canada (1980b, 1981, 1984c, 1988c); and annual returns filed by parties with CEO.

ª1 Aug. to 31 Dec. 74. (5 months)

E = Election year.

n.a. = Not available.

Table 8.7
Number of filers receiving federal political tax credit, by sex, 1980–88

Taxation year	Female			Male			Total		
	N	$000	% of tax filers[a]	N	$000	% of tax filers[a]	N	$000	% of tax filers[a]
1980E	18 020	1 192	0.5	72 540	5 187	1.2	90 560	6 380	0.9
1981	14 690	876	0.4	62 430	4 034	1.0	77 110	4 909	0.8
1982	17 910	1 186	0.4	68 030	5 083	1.1	85 940	6 269	0.8
1983	21 560	1 611	0.5	83 040	6 627	1.3	104 600	8 237	1.0
1984E	34 530	2 702	0.8	116 780	10 886	1.8	151 310	13 588	1.4
1985	25 410	1 687	0.6	83 900	6 937	1.3	109 310	8 624	1.0
1986	29 340	2 301	0.6	88 230	7 633	1.2	117 570	9 934	0.9
1987	29 950	1 820	0.5	72 870	5 840	1.0	102 820	7 661	0.8
1988E	50 310	3 970	n.a.	134 100	13 545	n.a.	184 410	17 515	n.a.

Sources: Department of National Revenue data as supplied to Royal Commission on Electoral Reform and Party Financing; and Canada, Revenue Canada, Taxation 1989 (table 5 and historical tables 2, 3 and 4).

[a]Based on number of taxable returns. In 1987, 67% of female and 85% of male tax filers had a taxable return.

E = Election year.
n.a. = Not available.

Table 8.8
Federal political tax credits received by individuals, by income class, 1980–88

Taxation year	Up to $15 000	$15 000– 30 000	$30 000– 50 000	$50 000– 100 000	$100 000– 250 000	Over $250 000	Total[a]
1980E							
$	783	2 014	1 493	1 267	637	186	
380[b]							
N[c]	15 650	33 980	21 740	13 560	4 730	890	90 560
Average $[d]	50	59	69	93	135	209	70
1981							
$	534	1 266	1 382	1 097	507	124	4 909
N	10 910	25 060	22 170	13 510	4 650	800	77 110
Average $	49	51	62	81	109	155	64
1982							
$	490	1 714	1 791	1 480	594	199	6 269
N	8 920	27 340	26 680	16 290	5 520	1 200	85 940
Average $	55	63	67	91	108	166	73
1983							
$	565	2 064	2 316	1 859	1 086	348	8 237
N	10 030	31 950	31 930	20 340	8 500	1 850	104 600
Average $	56	65	773	91	128	188	79
1984E							
$	847	3 130	3 617	3 418	1 958	618	13 588
N	13 720	44 590	44 890	32 570	12 980	2 560	151 310
Average $	62	70	81	105	151	241	90
1985							
$	500	1 897	2 263	2 218	1 320	427	8 624
N	10 510	30 300	34 570	22 920	9 070	1 940	109 310
Average $	48	63	66	97	146	220	79
1986							
$	874	2 267	2 810	2 176	1 425	383	9 934
N	14 890	33 250	34 500	23 740	9 310	1 880	117 570
Average $	59	68	82	92	153	204	85
1987							
$	590	1 832	1 951	1 869	1 061	358	7 661
N	13 730	29 720	30 340	19 850	7 460	1 720	102 820
Average $	43	62	64	94	142	208	75
1988E							
$	1 079	3 749	4 393	4 656	2 574	1 064	17 515
N	16 740	52 180	54 320	41 720	14 890	4 560	184 410
Average $	65	72	81	112	173	233	95

Source: Department of National Revenue data as supplied to Royal Commission on Electoral Reform and Party Financing.

[a]Due to confidentiality procedures, Revenue Canada totals may be different from actual row totals. Revenue Canada totals have been used.

[b]Total amount of tax credit in $000.

[c]Number of individual tax filers.

[d]Average size of individual tax credit received.

E = Election year.

Table 8.9
Federal political tax credit by total income class: percentage number of contributors and total tax credit received, 1980–88

Taxation year	Up to $15 000	$15 000–30 000	$30 000–50 000	$50 000–100 000	$100 000–250 000	Over $250 000	Total[a]
1980E							
N	17.3	37.5	24.0	15.0	5.2	1.0	100
$	12.3	31.6	23.4	19.9	10.0	2.9	100
1981							
N	14.1	32.5	28.8	17.5	6.0	1.0	100
$	10.9	25.8	28.2	22.3	10.3	2.5	100
1982							
N	10.4	31.8	31.0	19.0	6.4	1.4	100
$	7.8	27.3	28.6	23.6	9.5	3.2	100
1983							
N	9.6	30.5	30.5	19.5	8.1	1.8	100
$	6.9	25.1	28.1	22.6	13.2	4.2	100
1984E							
N	9.1	29.5	29.7	21.5	8.6	1.7	100
$	6.2	23.0	26.6	25.2	14.4	4.6	100
1985							
N	9.6	27.7	31.6	21.0	8.3	1.8	100
$	5.8	22.0	26.2	25.7	15.3	5.0	100
1986							
N	12.7	28.3	29.3	20.2	7.9	1.6	100
$	8.8	22.8	28.3	21.9	14.3	3.9	100
1987							
N	13.4	28.9	29.5	19.3	7.3	1.7	100
$	7.7	23.9	25.5	24.4	13.8	4.7	100
1988E							
N	9.1	28.3	29.5	22.6	8.1	2.5	100
$	6.2	21.4	25.1	26.6	14.7	6.1	100

Sources: Department of National Revenue data as supplied to Royal Commission on Electoral Reform and Party Financing and table 8.8.

[a]Due to confidentiality procedures, Revenue Canada totals may be different from actual row totals. Revenue Canada totals have been used.

E = Election year.

N = Distribution of number of individual tax filers.

$ = Distribution of amount of political tax credit received by individuals.

Table 8.10
Percentage distribution of political tax credits, all returns by income group, 1980, 1985, 1987

Taxation year	Up to $15 000	$15 000– 30 000	$30 000– 50 000	$50 000– 100 000	$100 000– 250 000	Over $250 000	Loss and nil	Total[a]
1980E								
Tax credits[c]	12.3	31.6	23.4	19.9	10.0	2.9	n.a.	100
Taxable returns[d]	46.4	42.2	9.0	2.0	0.4[b]	n.a.	n.a.	100
All returns[e]	57.1	28.6	6.1	1.4	0.2	0.05	6.5	100
1985								
Tax credits	5.8	22.0	26.2	25.7	15.3	5.0	n.a.	100
Taxable returns	30.0	41.9	22.1	5.2	0.8	0.1	n.a.	100
All returns	45.1	30.1	15.8	3.7	0.6	0.1	4.7	100
1987								
Tax credits	7.7	23.9	25.5	24.4	13.8	4.7	n.a.	100
Taxable returns	32.2	37.8	22.7	6.3	0.9	0.1	n.a.	100
All returns	43.2	29.2	17.5	4.8	0.7	0.1	4.5	100

Source: Canada, Revenue Canada, Taxation (1983–1989, table 2 and historical table 2).

[a] Total may be affected by rounding.
[b] 1980 breakdown to "$250 000" not available.
[c] Percentage of tax credits for political contributions in terms of dollars.
[d] Percentage of taxable returns.
[e] Percentage of all income tax returns.

E = Election year.
n.a. = Not available.

Table 8.11
Federal political tax credits received by individuals, by region, 1980–88

Taxation year	Atlantic[a]	Quebec	Ontario	Manitoba/Saskatchewan	Alberta	British Columbia	Other[b]	Total
1980E								
$	391	717	2 456	1 311	454	1 027	24	6 380c
N[d]	4 060	6 950	33 960	20 800	5 210	19 270	310	90 560
Average $[e]	96	103	72	63	87	53	77	70
1981								
$	261	479	1 438	1 074	530	1 103	24	4 909
N	3 630	6 190	22 330	16 020	7 690	20 960	290	77 110
Average $	72	77	64	67	70	53	83	64
1982								
$	373	569	1 832	1 535	525	1 405	30	6 269
N	3 620	8 450	26 220	19 460	7 200	20 650	340	85 940
Average $	103	67	70	79	73	68	88	73
1983								
$	506	915	2 930	1 427	760	1 649	50	8 237
N	5 440	11 730	35 570	18 060	8 200	25 070	530	104 600
Average $	93	78	82	79	93	66	94	79
1984E								
$	1 076	1 665	5 320	2 019	1 294	2 136	78	13 588
N	9 100	16 050	58 080	27 260	12 820	27 270	730	151 310
Average $	118	104	92	74	101	78	107	90

1985								
$	560	946	2 968	1 666	895	1 546	43	8 624
N	5 870	11 310	35 090	22 440	8 980	25 070	550	109 310
Average $	95	84	85	74	100	62	78	79
1986								
$	671	1 246	3 281	2 357	866	1 460	53	9 934
N	5 820	13 100	36 460	29 970	8 590	23 210	420	117 570
Average $	115	95	90	79	101	63	126	84
1987								
$	474	1 054	2 477	1 676	681	1 267	32	7 661
N	4 950	11 500	29 380	26 890	6 580	23 120	400	102 820
Average $	96	92	84	62	104	55	80	75
1988E								
$	947	2 997	6 692	2 502	1 641	2 666	70	17 515
N	9 530	25 280	66 650	32 900	14 780	34 530	740	184 410
Average $	99	116	100	76	111	77	95	95

Source: Department of National Revenue data as supplied to Royal Commission on Electoral Reform and Party Financing.

[a] Atlantic includes Newfoundland, Prince Edward Island, Nova Scotia and New Brunswick.

[b] Includes Yukon, Northwest Territories and taxpayers outside Canada jurisdiction.

[c] Total amount of tax credit in $000.

[d] Number of individual tax filers.

[e] Average size of individual tax credit received.

E = Election year.

Table 8.12
Percentage distribution of federal political tax credits received by individuals and number of individual filers, by region, 1980, 1985, 1987

Taxation year	Atlantic[a]	Quebec	Ontario	Manitoba/Saskatchewan	Alberta	British Columbia	Other[b]	Total[c]
1980E								
$[d]	6.1	11.2	38.5	20.5	7.1	16.1	0.4	100
N[e]	4.5	7.7	37.5	23.0	5.8	21.3	0.3	100
Taxable returns[f]	8.4	25.1	37.0	8.3	9.2	11.6	0.5	100
1985								
$	6.5	11.0	34.4	19.3	10.4	17.9	0.5	100
N	5.4	10.3	32.1	20.5	8.2	22.9	0.5	100
Taxable returns	8.3	25.0	37.5	8.3	9.4	11.1	0.5	100
1987								
$	6.2	13.8	32.3	21.9	8.9	16.5	0.4	100
N	4.8	11.2	28.6	26.2	6.4	22.5	0.4	100
Taxable returns	8.5	25.3	37.5	8.0	8.9	11.3	0.5	100

Sources: Department of National Revenue data as supplied to Royal Commission on Electoral Reform and Party Financing; Canadian Economic Observer, *Historical Statistical Supplement, 1989/90* (Ottawa: Supply & Services Canada), 96–97.

[a] Newfoundland, Prince Edward Island, Nova Scotia and New Brunswick.
[b] Yukon, Northwest Territories and taxpayers outside Canada.
[c] Total may be affected by rounding.
[d] Percentage of total amount of tax credit received.
[e] Percentage of individual tax filers.
[f] Percentage of taxable returns.

E = Election year.

Table 8.12a
Tax filers claiming federal political tax credit,
as percentage of electors, 1984 and 1988

Area	1984	1988
Atlantic	0.59	0.59
Quebec	0.35	0.53
Ontario	0.99	1.06
Manitoba and Saskatchewan	1.98	2.34
Alberta	0.87	0.95
British Columbia	1.48	1.77
Canada	0.91	1.05

Source: Calculated using data in table 8.11 and number of electors reported by CEO.

Table 8.13
Contributions of $2 000 or more from individuals to federal parties, 1983–90

Amount	1983			1984E			1985			1986			1987			1988E			1989				1990			
	PC	Lib.	NDP	PC	Lib.	NDP	PC	Lib.	NDP	PC	Lib.	NDP	PC	Lib.	NDP	PC	Lib.	NDP	PC	Lib.	NDP	Reform	PC	Lib.	NDP	Reform
$2 000–4 000	39	26	17	231	23	9	44	15	9	35	49	8	56	30	8	211	78	37	55	14	22	8	69	85	16	7
$4 001–6 000	3	8	0	20	3	1	3	0	0	5	6	0	6	3	0	53	12	0	18	2	1	2	14	14	1	2
$6 001–8 000	1	0	1	6	0	0	4	0	0	2	1	1	3	0	0	13	2	0	5	0	0	0	0	0	1	0
$8 001–10 000	1	3	1	4	2	0	5	0	0	0	0	0	4	0	0	9	1	1	2	1	1	0	0	2	0	0
$10 001–15 000	1	0	0	8	0	0	3	0	0	1	2	0	2	2	0	3	0	0	0	0	0	1	1	0	0	0
$15 001–20 000	0	0	0	0	0	0	0	0	0	1	0	0	0	1	0	3	0	0	0	0	0	0	0	0	0	0
$20 001–25 000	0	0	1	7	0	0	1	0	0	1	1	0	0	0	1	1	2	0	1	0	0	0	0	0	0	0
Over $25 000	0	1	1	2	0	1	1	0	1	1	5	1	0	1	1	2	1	1	0	0	2	0	0	0	1	0
Total	45	38	21	278	28	11	62	15	10	46	64	10	71	37	10	295	96	39	82	17	26[a]	11	84	101[c]	19	9
Highest ($000)	15	10	453[b]	50	10	216[b]	26	3	23[b]	25	27	94[b]	15	26	107[b]	40	40	103[b]	55	12	148[b]	16	10	10	84[b]	5.7
Average ($000)	3.0	3.8	25.4	3.9	3.2	21.9	4.8	2.3	4.5	4.4	5.2	12.2	3.5	4.1	15.2	3.8	3.9	5.3	4.3	3.4	12.3	4.2	3.1	2.9	15.0	3.1

Source: Tabulation by author from annual returns filed by parties with CEO.

Notes: Between 1983 and 1989, CPI rose by 29%.

[a] Includes 4 estates: $100 000, $15 000, $2 000, $2 000.

[b] In each case, highest individual contributor was Irene Dyck.

[c] Includes 33 contributions of $2 000 or more to leadership candidates routed through Federal Liberal Agency.

E = Election year.

Table 8.14
Importance of contributions of $2 000 or more from individuals to Liberal and Progressive Conservative parties, 1983–90

	1983		1984E		1985		1986		1987		1988E		1989		1990	
	PC	Lib.	PC	Lib.	PC	Lib.	PC	Lib.	PC	Lib.	PC	Lib.	PC	Lib.	PC	Lib.
Number of individual contributors ≥ $2 000	45	38	278	28	62	15	46	64	71	37	295	96	82	17	84	101
Total large contributions by individuals ($000s)	134	143	1 086	88	298	35	200	335	249	153	1 153	375	349	56	259	290[a]
Average large contribution ($)	2 978	3 758	3 906	3 150	4 800	2 323	4 356	5 233	3 507	4 131	3 908	3 906	4 267	3 293	3 083	2 801
Total contributions by individuals ($000)	9 106	3 262	10 142	5 181	7 872	3 129	7 875	5 753	6 065	3 472	10 181	4 748	6 850	2 385	4 686	7 441
Large contributions as % of all contributions from individuals	1.5	4.4	10.7	1.7	3.8	1.1	2.5	5.8	4.1	4.4	11.3	7.9	5.1	2.3	5.5	3.9

Source: Tabulation from annual returns filed by parties with CEO.

[a] Includes $103 050 in contributions of $2 000 or more to leadership candidates routed through Federal Liberal Agency.

E = Election year.

Table 8.A1
Analysis of Quebec Liberal party and Parti québécois revenues, 1978–89

Year P.Q.	No. of receipts		Average contribution ($)		Contributions of $100 or less as % of total contributions		Quebec Liberal party		Total revenues ($000)		Contributions as % of total revenues	
	Liberal[c]	P.Q.	Liberal	P.Q.	Liberal	P.Q.	No. of social events	% of total contributions	Liberal	P.Q.	Liberal	P.Q.
1978[b]	64 535	93 941	27	20	82	75	n.a.	n.a.	2 195	2 266	80	84
1979	124 439	107 569	21	22	78	73	n.a.	n.a.	3 151	2 918	82	82
1980	103 337	154 170	23	23	74	73	n.a.	n.a.	3 106	4 296	77	84
1981	11 049	168 910	65	20	69	75	n.a.	n.a.	1 077	4 928	67	69
1982	29 815	77 748	33	25	73	72	n.a.	n.a.	2 632	3 537	38	56
1983	50 009	49 143	36	33	69	60	112	n.a.	3 747	2 910	48	56

1984	44 963	54 120	64	38	45	55	79	n.a.	5 864	2 902	59	59
1985	61 895	61 791	104	64	23	40	139	30,4	10 130	6 906	63	57
1986	23 620	45 286	145	35	19	58	211	66,7	8 802	2 010	74	42
1987	22 118	66 524	98	38	17	60	221	73,5	8 364	1 805	78	
1988	34 355	53 349	136	36	15	66	264	82,6	9 774	2 241	74	55
1989[d]	66 582	11 821	254	49	8	55	32	6,0	6 717	5 803	45[e]	56[e]

Source: Massicotte (1991, tables 1.6 to 1.13); Directeur général des élections du Québec, *Rapports financiers* pour l'exercice terminé le 31 décembre 1989 (Quebec City, 1990).

[a] Contributions at social events as percentage of total contributions to party.

[b] April to December.

[c] Massicotte (1991, tables 1.A1 and 1.A2) estimates that beginning in 1985, number of contributions to Liberal party is only about 70% of number of receipts. Difference for P.Q., however, was only 0.6 to 3.4% during this period.

[d] Data from Directeur général des élections, *Rapports financiers* pour l'exercice terminé le 31 décembre 1989.

[e] Excludes Transferts des instances aux agents officiels: $50 380 for Liberal party and 3 044 145 for P.Q.

Table 8.A2
Revenues of political parties in Quebec, 1978–88
(percentages)

Source of revenues	Liberal party	Parti québécois	All parties
Contributions	66.3	62.8	64.9
Membership fees	10.3	15.8	12.4
Admission/registration fees	5.2	2.4	4.2
Anonymous donors	0.3	0.3	0.4
Reimbursement of "election expenses"*	4.8	6.9	5.6
Other	13.1	11.9	12.5
Total	100.0	100.0	100.0
Amount ($000)	65 538	42 523	110 962

Source: Massicotte (1991, tables 1.5, 1.6 and 1.7)

Note: Percentages do not add to 100.0 due to rounding.

*Includes annual subsidy of $0.25 per elector.

Table 9.1
Significance of direct-mail revenue, Progressive Conservative, Liberal and New Democratic parties, 1983–90
(thousands of dollars)

Year	PC					Liberal				
	Total contributions from individuals	Direct mail (gross revenue)	Direct mail as % of individual contributions	Total party revenue	Direct mail as % of party revenue	Total contributions from individuals	Direct mail (gross revenue)	Direct mail as % of individual contributions	Total party revenue	Direct mail as % of party revenue
1983	9 106	5 729	62.9	14 767	38.8	3 262	n.a.	n.a.	7 736	n.a.
1984E	10 142	7 571	74.6	23 417	32.3	5 181	n.a.	n.a.	13 014	n.a.
1985	7 872	5 611	71.2	15 073	37.2	3 129	1 445	46.1	6 163	9.6
1986	7 875	4 307	54.6	15 639	27.5	5 753	1 742	30.3	10 719	16.3
1987	6 065	3 763	62.0	13 058	28.8	3 472	1 664	47.9	8 882	18.7
1988E	10 181	6 517	64.0	27 013	24.1	4 748	2 178	45.9	17 897	12.2
1989	6 850	3 529	51.5	14 521	24.3	2 385	1 042	43.7	6 397	16.3
1990	4 686	2 434	51.9	11 298	21.5	7 441	1 743	23.4	13 778	12.7

Table 9.1 (cont'd)
Significance of direct-mail revenue, Progressive Conservative, Liberal and New Democratic parties, 1983–90
(thousands of dollars)

Year	Total contributions from individuals[a]	NDP			
		Direct mail (gross revenue)	Direct mail as % of individual contributions	Total party revenue[b]	Direct mail as % of party revenue
1983	4 998	n.a.	n.a.	5 972	n.a.
1984E	4 156	n.a.	n.a.	9 021	n.a.
1985	4 612	n.a.	n.a.	6 284	n.a.
1986	5 036	n.a.	n.a.	6 985	n.a.
1987	4 782	1 495	31.3	6 833	21.9
1988E	7 845	2 113	26.9	13 752	15.4
1989	5 982	1 460	24.4	7 746	18.8
1990	6 035	1 596	26.4	8 569	18.6

Sources: Data provided by parties and tables 3.7, 3.13, 3.15.

[a]Federally receipted contributions.
[b]Total revenue at federal level.

E = Election year.
n.a. = Not available.

Table 9.2
Net revenue from direct mail, by party, 1985–90
(thousands of dollars)

Year	PC	Liberal	NDP[a]	Difference PC–Lib	Difference PC–NDP
1985	4 269	404	n.a.	3 865	n.a.
1986	3 096	378	n.a.	2 718	n.a.
1987	2 924	666	524	2 258	2 400
1988	4 917	1 433	910	3 484	4 007
1989	2 752	378	877	2 374	1 875
1990	1 793	766	784	1 027	1 009

Sources: Tables 9.1 and 9.6.

[a]NDP federal office.

n.a. = Not available.

Table 9.3

Direct-mail revenues and expenses, Progressive Conservative, Liberal and New Democratic parties, 1983-90

(thousands of dollars)

Description	1983	1984E	1985	1986	1987	1988E	1989	1990
Progressive Conservative Party								
Gross revenue								
In house	n.a.	n.a.	4 940	3 918	3 638	5 631	3 314	2 243
Promotional	n.a.	n.a.	671	390	125	886	215	191
Total	5 729	7 571	5 611	4 307	3 763	6 517	3 529	2 434
Expenses								
In house	n.a.	n.a.	730	728	764	860	489	443
Promotional	n.a.	n.a.	612	483	75	740	288	198
Total	1 160	1 337	1 342	1 211	839	1 600	777	641
% gross revenue	20.2	17.7	23.9	28.1	22.3	24.6	22.0	26.3
Net revenue	4 569	6 234	4 269	3 096	2 924	4 917	2 752	1 793
Liberal Party								
Gross revenue	n.a.	n.a.	1 445	1 742	1 664	2 178	1 042	1 743
Expenses[a]	1 010	748	1 041	1 364	998	745	664	766
% gross revenue	n.a.	n.a.	72.0	78.3	60.0	34.2	63.7	43.9
Net revenue	n.a.	n.a.	404	378	666	1 433	378	976
New Democratic Party								
Gross revenue	n.a.	n.a.	n.a.	n.a.	1 495	2 113	1 460	1 596
Expenses	n.a.	n.a.	n.a.	n.a.	971	1 203	583	812
% gross revenue	n.a.	n.a.	n.a.	n.a.	64.9	56.9	39.9	50.9
Net revenue	n.a.	n.a.	n.a.	n.a.	524	910	877	784

Sources: Data supplied by three parties.

[a]Includes direct and indirect expenses.

E = Election year.

Table 9.4
Direct-mail revenues and expenses, Liberal party, 1986–90
(thousands of dollars)

Type	1986	1987	1988E	1989	1990 (to 31 Aug.)	Total 1986–90
Regular	173/44[a]	—	—	—	—	
	82/13					
	157/27					
	224/18					
	78/21					
	184/38					
	195/10					
Total R/E	1 093/171					1 093/171
Prospect	100/136	240/196	171/238	44/231	220/36	
	193/255	52/25	241/93	44/100	45/49	
	67/89	146/231				
	108/176	65/220				
	176/148					
Total R/E	644/804	503/672	412/331	88/331	265/85	1 912/2 223
Special	—	216/23	255/42	119/74	71/37	
		177/28	157/46	71/37	31/50	
		183/39	296/73	135/38	168/62	
		200/41	97/65	122/26	132/24	
				161/22	249/131	
				183/29		
				136/34		
Total R/E	—	776/131	805/226	927/260	651/304	3 159/921
Renewal	—	236/27	234/41	—	—	
		63/23	381/43			
		74/13	257/64			
Total R/E		373/63	872/148			1 245/211
Direct mail Visa	—	—	—	—	6/3	6/3
Previous year	6/4	14/8	91/9	26/1	47/1	184/23
Grand total R/E	1 743/979	1 666/874	2 180/714	1 041/592[b]	969/393[c]	7 599/3 552

Source: Data provided to author by Liberal party, Ottawa.

[a]Read as 173 000 in revenues and 44 000 in direct expenses. Indirect expenses are given in table 9.5.
[b]An additional $54 000 expense incurred on a campaign not run. With expense included, total equals $1 041/646.
[c]An additional $11 000 expense incurred on campaigns not run. With expense included, total equals $959/404.

E = Election year.
R/E = Revenues and expenses.

Table 9.5
Direct-mail activity, Liberal party, 1985–90

	1985	1986	1987	1988E	1989	1990
Direct-mail revenue (gross)	1 445 392	1 742 231	1 663 902	2 178 313	1 041 535	1 742 532
Direct expenses	797 971	978 125	873 679	714 154	647 219	766 039
Indirect expenses	243 618[a]	386 137[a]	124 397	31 438	16 302	n.a.
Direct-mail net revenue	403 803	377 969[b]	665 826	1 432 721	378 014	976 493
Type of mailing (*N*)						
Regular	n.a.	7	0	0	0	0
Prospect	n.a.	5	4	2[d]	2	2
Telemarketing	n.a.	0	1	0	0	0
Special	n.a.	0	4	4	7	5[e]
Renewal	n.a.	0	3	3	0	0
Direct mail Visa	n.a.	0	0	0	0	1
Total number	n.a.	12	12[c]	9	9	8

Source: Federal Liberal Agency of Canada, financial statements, 1986–90, and combined condensed financial statements, 1986–90; Liberal Party of Canada, fiscal period returns, 1986–90.

[a]Includes consultant fees, salaries, travel, office expenses, computer expenses, costs of acquiring lists.

[b]Before revenue sharing of $7 541.

[c]In 1987, 6 specials were scheduled: only 4 were run; 7 renewals were listed: only 3 were run.

[d]1988 Prospect labelled Prospect 1, 3 and 4 with no Prospect 2 listed. Prospect 4 was not run.

[e]1990 had scheduled: 8 specials; 2 prospects; 1 Visa; 1 year-end, but as of 31 Aug. 1990 only 5 mailings had been sent out, and specials 6 and 7 were still being prepared (small amount expensed with no revenue recorded).

E = Election year.

n.a. = Not available.

Table 9.6
Direct-mail revenues and expenses, New Democratic Party federal office, 1987–90

	1987	1988	1989	1990
Revenues				
House list mailings	404 884	1 278 603	1 061 227	1 050 207
Prospect mailings	663 461	505 999	163 909	377 106
Leader's circle	22 640	0	0	0
Agnes MacPhail appeal	237 526	134 213	121 214	168 566
Tommy Douglas appeal	166 618	26 300	25	0
Ed Broadbent appeal	0	0	113 183	0
Sweepstakes	0	168 195	0	0
Total revenues	1 495 129	2 113 310	1 459 558	1 595 879
Expenses				
House list mailings	0	252 666	185 602	263 797
Prospect mailings	0	503 519	146 376	329 307
Professional fees	42 178	33 739	40 364	44 682
Purchase lists of names	45 155	0	0	0
Processing	52 218	49 894	45 928	65 859
Printing and postage	626 697	133 979	44 908	24 860
Agnes MacPhail appeal	145 681	95 943	59 880	83 133
Tommy Douglas appeal	59 146	0	0	0
Ed Broadbent appeal	0	0	59 460	0
Sweepstakes	0	133 287	0	0
Total expenses	971 075	1 203 027	582 518	811 638
Net revenue	524 054	910 283	877 040	784 241
Expenses as % of gross revenue	64.9	56.9	39.9	50.9

Source: Data provided by Audrey Kari, NDP federal office, Ottawa, February 1992.

E = Election year.

Table 10.1

Revenues and expenses of national fund-raising events featuring party leader, Progressive Conservative party, 1983–90

(thousands of dollars)

Description	1983	1984E	1985	1986	1987	1988E	1989	1990
Gross revenue	n.a.	n.a.	1 461	1 918	1 703	1 244	2 240	2 313
Expenses	n.a.	n.a.	452	766	707	317	625	610
Net revenue[a]	1 551	996	1 009	1 152	996	927	1 615	1 703
Expenses as % of gross revenue	n.a.	n.a.	30.9	39.9	41.5	25.5	27.9	26.4
Total party revenue	14 767	23 417	15 073	15 639	13 058	27 013	14 521	11 298
Net revenue as % of total party revenue	10.5	4.3	6.7	7.4	7.6	3.4	11.1	15.1

Source: Data supplied to author by Progressive Conservative party, Ottawa, and tables relating to chapters 3 and 4.

Notes: Events include brunches and dinners.

[a]Only this amount, contribution component as specified by Department of National Revenue, is included in "receipts" on party's statement of receipts and expenditures.

E = Election year.

n.a. = Not available.

Table 10.2

Revenues and expenses of dinners featuring party leader, Liberal party, 1987-90
(thousands of dollars)

Description	1987	1988E	1989	1990
All dinners				
Gross revenue	2 631	3 350	2 024	974
Expenses	834	1 150	734	310
Net revenue	1 797	2 200	1 290	664
Expenses as % of gross revenue	31.7	34.3	36.3	31.9
Total party revenue	8 882	17 897	6 397	13 778
Net revenue as a % of total party revenue	20.2	12.3	20.2	4.8[a]
Confederation dinner[b]				
Gross revenue	881	1 232	627	455
Expenses	401	620	243	135
Net revenue	479	612	384	320
Expenses as a % of gross revenue	45.5	50.3	38.8	29.6
Net revenues as % of total net revenue from leader's dinners	26.7	27.8	29.8	48.2

Source: Data provided by Liberal Party of Canada, Ottawa.

[a]Drop is largely due to increase in total party revenues attributable to leadership convention (about $6.4 million). If these are removed, figure is 9.0%.

[b]Included in total figures given above.

E = Election year.

Table 10.3

"The 500" revenues, Progressive Conservative party, 1983–90

(thousands of dollars)

Year	Major-donor program			Total party revenue	Gross revenue as % of total party revenue
	Gross revenue	Reported expenses	Net revenue		
1983	319	n.a.	< 319	14 767	2.2
1984E	1 688	n.a.	< 1 688	23 417	7.2
1985	1 936	265	1 661	15 073	12.8
1986	1 513	191	1 322	15 639	9.7
1987	1 222	12	1 210	13 058	9.4
1988E	2 477	41	2 436	27 013	9.2
1989	1 353	48	1 305	14 521	9.3
1990	1 224	96	1 128	11 298	10.8

Sources: Data supplied to author by Progressive Conservative party, Ottawa, and tables relating to chapters 3 and 4.

E = Election year.

n.a. = Not available.

Table 10.4
Laurier Club revenues and expenses, Liberal party, 1985–90

Year	Gross revenue	Reported expenses	Net revenue	Gross revenue as % of total party revenue
1985	n.a.[a]	n.a.	n.a.	n.a.
1986	458 939	148 297	310 642	4.3
1987	421 150	119 228	301 922	4.7
1988E	442 596	26 284	416 312	2.5
1989	184 775	30 690	154 085	2.9
1990	94 000	n.a.	n.a.	0.7

Source: Liberal Party of Canada financial statements as supplied to author.

[a]Club was announced in May 1985 (see *Vancouver Sun*, 3 May 1985, A12), but financial statements for 1985 do not provide details of Laurier Club.

E = Election year.

n.a. = Not available.

Table 10.5

Number of larger contributions from individuals to New Democratic, Progressive Conservative and Liberal parties, 1987–90

Party	1987	1988E	1989	1990
NDP				
$1 000–1 999	199	380	311	269
$2 000 +	10	39[a]	26[c]	19
Average $2 000 +	4 100	5 277[b]	12 348[d]	7 119[e]
PC				
$2 000 +	71	295	82	84
Average $2 000 +	3 507	3 906	4 267	3 083
Liberal				
$2 000 +	37	96	17	101[f]
Average $2 000 +	4 131	3 908	3 293	2 801

Sources: Tabulated by author from annual returns filed by parties with CEO and table 8.14.

[a]Only two donors exceeded $3 700: $12 500 and $103 480. Leader gave $2 000 (versus $1 700 in 1988).

[b]Average without Irene Dyck's contribution of $103 480 = $2 692.

[c]Includes four estates over $2 000, one of which was $100 000 (total value $119 000).

[d]Average without Irene Dyck's contribution of $147 669 and $100 000 estate = $3 058.

[e]Average without Irene Dyck's contribution of $84 086 = $2 843.

[f]Includes 33 contributions to leadership candidates routed through Federal Liberal Agency.

E = Election year.

Table 11.1
Contributions by business and commercial organizations to federal parties, 1974–91
(thousands of dollars)

Year	Progressive Conservative			Liberal Party				NDP			1989 dollars[d]	
	Business organization	Total	%	Business organization	Total	%	Corporate contributions PC–Liberal	Business organization	Total[c]	%	PC	Liberal
1974								14	1 496	0.9		
1974–75[a]	975	1 721	56.6	939	2 217	42.4	36	144	2 745	5.2	2 642	2 545
1975–76[b]	2 403	5 287	45.5	2 595[d]	5 823[d]	44.6	(192)	92	2 281	4.0	5 904	6 376
1977	1 724	3 774	45.7	2 292	4 587	50.0	(568)	190	3 006	6.3	3 840	5 105
1978	2 625	5 465	48.0	2 488	5 018	49.6	137	207	3 400	6.1	5 357	5 078
1979E	5 020	9 170	54.7	3 876	7 020	55.2	1 144	170	5 238	3.2	9 383	7 245
1980E	4 368	8 542	51.1	3 731	8 367	44.6	637	97	5 598	1.7	7 429	6 345
1981	2 573	6 950	37.0	2 705	5 592	48.4	(132)	109	3 856	2.8	3 887	4 086
1982	2 923	8 521	34.3	2 522	6 747	37.4	401	144	4 766	0.9	3 988	3 441
1983	4 820	14 767	32.6	3 543	7 736	45.8	1 277	41	5 972	0.7	6 211	4 566
1984E	11 004	23 417	47.0	5 340	13 014	41.0	5 644	52	8 421	0.6	13 585	6 593
1985	6 693	15 073	44.4	2 432	6 163	39.5	4 261	58	6 464	0.9	7 949	2 888
1986	7 301	15 639	46.7	4 846	10 719	45.2	2 455	178	6 984	2.5	8 325	5 526

Table 11.1 (cont'd)

Contributions by business and commercial organizations to federal parties, 1974–91

(thousands of dollars)

Year	Progressive Conservative			Liberal Party				NDP			1989 dollars[d]	
	Business organization	Total	%	Business organization	Total	%	Corporate contributions PC–Liberal	Business organization	Total[c]	%	PC	Liberal
1987	6 696	13 058	51.3	5 344	8 882	60.2	1 352	47	6 832	0.7	7 318	5 840
1988E	14 359	27 013	53.2	8 449	17 897	47.2	5 910	263	13 751	1.9	15 083	8 875
1989	6 943	14 521	47.8	3 931	6 397	61.5	3 012	54	7 746	0.7	6 943	3 931
1990	6 350	12 298	51.6	4 560[e]	13 778[f]	33.2	1 782	141	8 569	0.2	6 059	4 359
1991	6 660	12 271	54.3	3 412	7 204	47.4	3 248	759[g]	10 368	0.7	6 110	3 130

Source: Derived from annual returns filed by parties with CEO.

a 1 Aug. 1974–31 Jul. 1974 (12 months); 1975 only for NDP.

b 1 Aug. 1975–31 Dec. 1976 (17 months); 1976 only for NDP.

c Excludes provincially receipted revenues and provincial rebates and subsidies. See chapter 6.

d Using Consumer Price Index as deflator.

e Includes substantial amounts contributed to leadership candidates routed through Federal Liberal Agency.

f Includes $1.95 million in individual and corporate contributions routed through Federal Liberal Agency, plus $4.4 million in fees paid by delegates for June 1990 leadership convention.

g Includes $467 000 from sale of Woodsworth House (Ottawa) Corp.

E = Election year.

Table 11.2

Contributions by corporations to federal Liberal and Progressive Conservative parties, 1974–91

	PC			Liberal		
		Average			Average	
Year	N^a	Nominal dollars	1989 dollars^d	N^a	Nominal dollars	1989 dollars^d
1974–75^b	2 046	477	1 293	2 430	410	1 111
1975–76^c	7 045	341	838	5 173	510	1 253
1977	4 501	386	860	5 685	404	900
1978	8 105	325	663	5 026	495	1 010
1979E	7 752	651	1 218	3 737	1 037	1 938
1980E	5 011	872	1 483	4 420	844	1 435
1981	7 312	352	532	6 039	448	677
1982	9 432	310	423	5 652	446	608
1983	18 067	232	299	7 536	352	454
1984E	21 286	517	638	6 494	822	1 015
1985	15 789	424	504	3 775	644	765
1986	12 680	576	657	6 221	779	888
1987	9 198	729	797	6 073	880	962
1988E	14 032	1 023	1 075	7 238	1 167	1 226
1989	9 435	736	736	3 857	1 019	1 019
1990	7 183	884	845	5 598	816	779
1991	7 401	900	826	3 799	898	824

Source: Tabulation by author from Canada, Elections Canada (1980b, 1981, 1984c, 1988c); and annual returns filed by parties with CEO.

[a]From 1974 to 1979, the number is the sum of "private corporations" plus "public corporations," and "corporations without share capital." It excludes "unincorporated organizations." From 1980, the category is "business and commercial organizations."

[b]1 Aug. 1974 to 31 Jul. 1975 (12 months).

[c]1 Aug. 1975 to 31 Dec. 1976 (17 months).

[d]Using Consumer Price Index as deflator.

E = Election year.

Table 11.2a

Contributions by corporations to Liberal and Progressive Conservative parties, by period of party in power, 1974–91

Period	PC	Liberal
1974–78		
Liberal/Trudeau		
Total number of contributors	21 697	18 314
Average number of contributions	4 909	4 143
Total contributions ($000)[a]	17 743	19 104
Average[b]	818	1043
1979		
PC/Clark		
Total number of contributors	7 752	3 737
Average number of contributions	7 752	3 737
Total contributions ($000)[a]	9 383	7 245
Average[b]	1 210	1 939
1980–84		
Liberal/Trudeau[c]		
Total number of contributors	61 108	30 141
Average number of contributions	12 222	6 028
Total contributions ($000)[a]	35 100	25 031
Average[b]	574	830
1985–91		
PC/Mulroney		
Total number of contributors	75 718	36 561
Average number of contributions	10 817	5 223
Total contributions ($000)[a]	57 787	34 549
Average[b]	763	945

Sources: Tables 11.1; 11.2.

[a]In 1989 dollars.

[b]Average contribution during the period in 1989 dollars.

[c]John Turner became Leader and Prime Minister in June 1984.

Table 11.3
Number and size of contributions by corporations to candidates, 1979, 1980, 1984 and 1988 general elections

Election year	PC	Liberal	NDP	Others	Total
1979					
N^a	9 515	7 028	296	709	17 548
Total ($000)	2 075	1 457	36	119	3 687
Average	218	207	12	17	210
Average (1989 $)	407	387	22	32	393
1980					
N^a	8 137	8 867	416	520	17 940
Total ($000)	1 838	1 779	51	90	3 758
Average	226	201	12	17	209
Average (1989 $)	384	342	20	29	355
1984					
N^b	17 639	8 052	286	401	26 378
Total ($000)	4 488	2 317	69	130	6 995
Average	254	288	21	32	265
Average (1989 $)	314	356	26	40	327
1988					
N^b	13 849	8 209	774	1 801	24 633
Total ($000)	4 652	2 629	182	492	7 956
Average	336	320	24	27	323
Average (1989 $)	353	336	25	28	339

Sources: Canada, Elections Canada (1980b, 1981, 1984c, 1988c).

[a]Includes "public corporations," "private corporations" and "corporations without share capital."
[b]"Businesses and commercial organizations."

Table 11.3a
Comparison of corporate contributions to parties and candidates, 1979, 1980, 1984 and 1988 general elections

Election year	PC	Liberal
1979		
Number to party	7 752	3 737
Number to candidates	9 515	7 028
Average/party (1989 $)	1 218	1 938
Average/candidates (1989 $)	407	387
1980		
Number to party	5 011	4 420
Number to candidates	8 137	8 867
Average/party (1989 $)	1 483	1 435
Average/candidates (1989 $)	384	342
1984		
Number to party	21 286	6 494
Number to candidates	17 639	8 052
Average/party (1989 $)	638	1 015
Average/candidates (1989 $)	314	356
1988		
Number to party	14 032	7 238
Number to candidates	13 849	8 209
Average/party (1989 $)	1 075	1 226
Average/candidates (1989 $)	353	336

Sources: Tables 11.3, 12.2, 12.3.

Table 11.4

Largest contribution to federal parties by a corporation, 1983–91

Year	PC		Liberal	
1983	50 000	(Canadian Pacific Ltd.)	51 958	(Canadian Pacific Ltd.)
1984E	150 000	(Candor Investments Ltd.)	78 822	(Power Corp.)
1985	75 000	(Candor Investments Ltd.)	56 500	(Canadian Pacific Ltd.)
1986	62 145	(Deloitte, Haskins & Sells)	62 125	(Power Corp.)
1987	77 149	(Candor Investments Ltd.)	75 951	(Clarkson Gordon)
1988E	136 500[b]	(Agra Industries Ltd.)	80 501[a]	(Canadian Imperial Bank of Commerce)
1989	61 890[d]	(Coopers & Lybrand)	65 200[c]	(Canadian Pacific Ltd.)
1990	75 000	(Imperial Oil Ltd.)	75 000	(Imperial Oil Ltd.)
1991	65 000	(Canadian Pacific Ltd.)	64 639	(Bombardier)

Source: Tabulation by author from annual returns filed by parties with CEO.

[a]Fifteen contributions of $50 000 or more.

[b]Six contributions of $100 000 or more and 29 of $50 000 or more.

[c]Two contributions of $50 000 or more.

[d]Five contributions of $50 000 or more.

E = Election year.

Table 11.5

**Large contributions to Liberal party by firms
with headquarters in Ontario, 1968 and 1972**

Corporation	1968	1972
Non-financial		
Gulf Oil Canada	22 500	50 000[a]
Hiram Walker	50 000	60 000
Noranda Mines	10 000	15 000
Southam Press	—	10 000
Fodor & Associates	2 000	10 000
IBM	5 000	12 500
George Weston	—	20 000
Interprovincial Pipe Line	5 000	10 000
Comstock International	10 000	15 000
Canadian General Electric	5 000	15 000
Bramalea Corp.	10 000	15 000
Shell Canada	10 000	25 000
Steel Co. of Canada	45 000	75 000
Brascan Ltd.	10 000	20 000
John Labatt Ltd.	10 000	45 000
General Motors	50 000	60 000
Canadian Breweries	10 000	35 000
Imperial Oil Ltd.	90 000	85 000
Dofasco	50 000	50 000
International Nickel	75 000	75 000
Hawker Siddeley	7 000	25 000
Massey Ferguson	10 000	10 000
Ontario Jockey Club	—	15 000
Ford Motor Co.	25 000	40 000
Rio Algom	12 000	15 000
Simpsons-Sears	17 500	17 500
Falconbridge Nickel	15 000	13 000
Olympia & York Develop.	2 000	15 000
Chrysler Canada	7 500	12 500
Consumers Gas Co.	15 000	15 000
Northern & Central Gas	3 500	10 000
Coca-Cola	—	15 000
Sun Oil	—	25 000
Abitibi Paper Co.	10 000	10 000
Texas Gulf Sulphur	5 000	15 000
Canada Packers	15 000	20 000
Union Gas	10 000	18 000
Newconex Holdings	—	13 000
Douglas Aircraft	—	12 000
T. Eaton Co.	25 000	20 000
Boise Cascade	—	10 000
John C. Parkin (architects)	5 000	10 800
Banister Pipelines	—	10 000

Table 11.5 (cont'd)
Large contributions to Liberal party by firms with headquarters in Ontario, 1968 and 1972

Corporation	1968	1972
Financial		
Canadian Imperial Bank of Commerce	80 000	125 000
Household Finance	10 000	15 000
Bank of Nova Scotia	40 000	75 000
Toronto Dominion Bank	40 000	75 000
National Trust	2 500	10 000
General Insurance Assn.	—	10 000
Number ≥ 10 000	29	50

Source: Files of Senator John Godfrey who was Liberal party's chief fund-raiser in Ontario for 1968, 1972 and 1974 general elections.

Notes: Large was defined as $10 000 or more in one or both years.

[a]Nominal dollars.

Table 11.6
Large contributions to Progressive Conservative and Liberal parties by corporations, 1983–90

| Year | Large corporate contributions[a] | | | | | | Total corporate contributions ($000) | | Amount of large contributions PC–Liberal ($000) | Large contribution as % of corporate contributions | | Large corporate contributions as % of party revenue[b] | |
| | N | | Amount ($000) | | Average ($000) | | | | | | | | |
	PC	Liberal	PC	Liberal	PC	Liberal	PC	Liberal		PC	Liberal	PC	Liberal
1983	43	45	781	899	18.2	20.0	4 820	3 543	(118)	16.2	25.4	5.3	11.6
1984E	198	113	4 362	2 370	22.0	21.0	11 004	5 340	1 992	39.6	44.4	18.6	18.2
1985	95	54	1 983	1 101	20.9	20.3	6 693	2 432	882	29.6	45.3	13.2	17.9
1986	104	102	2 294	2 283	22.1	22.4	7 301	4 846	11	31.4	47.1	14.7	21.3
1987	119	104	2 612	2 216	21.9	21.3	6 696	5 344	396	39.0	41.5	20.0	24.9
1988E	302	174	6 941	3 951	23.0	22.7	14 359	8 449	2 990	48.3	46.8	25.7	22.1
1989	118	83	2 671	1 782	22.6	21.5	6 943	3 931	889	38.5	45.3	18.4	27.9
1990	107	86[c]	2 462	1 848[d]	23.0	21.5	6 350	4 568	614[e]	38.8	40.5[f]	20.0	13.4[g]

Sources: Tabulation by author from annual returns filed by parties with CEO.

Notes: Large is defined as $10 000 or more in nominal dollars.

[a]Large is defined as $10 000 or more in a year (in nominal dollars).

[b]See chapter 3.

[c]Includes 17 contributions to leadership candidates routed through the Federal Liberal Agency.

[d]Includes $198 250 in contributions to leadership candidates.

[e]$812 excluding contributions $10 000 or more to leadership candidates.

[f] 37.8% excluding contributions of $10 000 or more to leadership candidates.

[g]12.2% excluding contributions of $10 000 or more to leadership candidates.

E = Election year.

Table 11.6a
Distribution of corporate contributions of $10 000 or more in 1988

Range	PC	Liberal	NDP
10 000–11 999	83	46	2
12 000–14 999	32	23	0
15 000–19 999	54	32	1
20 000–24 999	29	22	0
25 000–29 999	45	23	1
30 000–39 999	21	5	0
40 000–49 999	11	8	0
50 000–69 999	14	7	0
70 000 and over	13	8	0
Total	302	174	4
Average contribution ($)	22 984	22 707	15 625
Total amount ($000)	6 941	3 951	625

Source: Electronic data file provided to author by D.K. Heintzman, Royal Commission on Electoral Reform and Party Financing, August 1991.

Table 11.7

Number of corporations making political contributions and number claiming tax credit, 1977–88

Year	Corporate contributions to Parties[a] (1)	Corporate contributions to Candidates[b] (2)	Number of corporate contributions per DNR[c] (3)	Number of corporations claiming tax credit[d] (4)	% claiming tax credit[e] (5)	Value of tax credits[f] ($000) (6)	Average value of credit[g] (7)	Total number of corporations (8)	% of corporations making a contribution[h] (9)
1977	10 186		n.a.	n.a.	n.a.	504	n.a.	n.a.	n.a.
1978	13 131		n.a.	n.a.	n.a.	653	n.a.	n.a.	n.a.
1979E	11 489	17 548	n.a.	n.a.	n.a.	1 213	n.a.	n.a.	n.a.
1980E	9 431	17 940	6 803	n.a.	n.a.	1 247	n.a.	479 109	5.7
1981	13 351		3 576	n.a.	n.a.	530	n.a.	511 315	2.6
1982	15 084		3 439	3 507	23.2	567	162	557 507	2.7
1983	25 603		4 224	4 178	16.3	762	182	579 925	4.4
1984E	27 780	26 378	7 414	7 561	14.0	1 595	211	597 893	9.1
1985	19 564		5 716	5 995	30.5	1 254	209	599 613	3.3
1986	18 901		3 938	3 979	21.1	836	210	618 222	3.1
1987	15 271		4 232	3 647	23.9	808	222	641 470	2.4
1988E	21 270	24 633	4 820	5 471	11.9	1 333	244	688 507	6.7

Sources: Tables 11.2 and 11.3a, and data provided by Department of National Revenue to Royal Commission on Electoral Reform and Party Financing.

[a]Total number of business organizations making a contribution to the Liberal or Progressive Conservative parties. The number giving to other parties is very small, e.g., *N* = 54 in 1988.

[b]All parties. See table 11.3a.

[c]Number of corporations making a political contribution according to DNR. Data provided by DNR to Royal Commission on Electoral Reform and Party Financing, tabulations dated 14 and 17 September 1990.

[d]Data provided by DNR the Royal Commission, 24 July 1990 and 1 October 1990.

[e]Column 4 divided by the sum of columns 1 and 2.

[f] Data supplied to Royal Commission by DNR.

[g]Column 6 divided by column 4.

[h]Column 1 plus column 2 divided by column 8.

DNR = Department of National Revenue.

E = Election year.

n.a. = Not available.

Table 11.8
Federal political contributions by size of corporations, 1980–88

Taxation year	"Small" corporations[a]			"Other" corporations[c]			Total all corporations		Corporate contributions to 3 main parties ($000)	Corporate contributions to candidates ($000)	Number of corporations (DNR)		% of corporations making a contribution (DNR)	
	N	Amount[b] ($000)	Average ($)	N	Amount[b] ($000)	Average ($)	N	Amount[b] ($000)			Small	Other	Small	Other
1980E	4 747	1 677	353	2 056	4 661	2 267	6 803	6 338	8 196	3 759	180 868	298 241	2.6	0.7
1981	2 411	520	216	1 164	1 547	1 329	3 576	2 067	5 387		169 777	341 538	1.4	0.3
1982	1 957	549	281	1 482	1 824	1 231	3 439	2 374	5 589		169 962	387 545	1.2	0.4
1983	2 791	500	179	1 433	2 103	1 468	4 224	2 603	8 404		184 408	395 516	1.5	0.4
1984E	4 514	1 703	377	2 900	6 339	2 186	7 414	8 042	16 396	6 995	192 821	405 072	1.5	0.4
1985	4 704	3 399	723	1 012	2 460	2 431	5 716	5 859	9 183		209 034	390 579	2.3	0.3
1986	3 034	1 988	655	894	2 365	2 645	3 938	4 353	12 325		229 977	388 245	1.3	0.2
1987	3 410	1 936	568	822	2 878	3 501	4 232	4 813	12 087		265 734	375 736	1.3	0.2
1988E	3 488	2 144	615	1 332	4 974	3 734	4 820	7 119	23 071	7 956	279 112	409 395	1.2	0.3

Sources: Department of National Revenue data as supplied to Royal Commission on Electoral Reform and Party Financing; table 11.1; Canada, Elections Canada (1980b, 1981, 1984c, 1988).

Notes: Table is based on corporations that claimed the tax credit for political contributions. See columns (3) and (4) of table 11.7.

[a]Corporations claiming the Small Business Deduction (SBD). For 1980–84 this was $200 000 annual income and $1 million lifetime income. For 1985–88, all corporations could claim SBD on the first $200 000 of active business income.

[b]Amount of political contribution (not tax credit).

[c]All other corporations.

E = Election year.

Table 11.9

Political contributions by corporations, by size of corporation and size of contribution, 1980–88

Taxation year	0.01–$100	$100–499	$500–1 999	$2 000–9 999	over $10 000	Total
1980						
Small (N)[a]	203	3 404	1 093	47	n.a.	4 747
Small ($000)[b]	11.8	571.7	957.0	136.2	n.a.	1 676.8
Other (N)[c]	82	747	842	282	102	2 056
Other ($000)[d]	3.1	148.8	756.5	1 084.1	2 668.4	4 660.9
1981[e]						
Small (N)	378	1 792	241		n.a.	2 411
Small ($000)	19.7	311.9	188.2		n.a.	519.8
Other (N)	202	537	394		31	1 164
Other ($000)	9.9	108.3	758.4		670.6	1 547.1
1982						
Small (N)	410	1 211	336	n.a.	n.a.	1 957
Small ($000)	20.3	224.4	304.5	n.a.	n.a.	549.2
Other (N)	410	557	353	133	29	1 482
Other ($000)	29.5	97.5	323.1	541.7	832.6	1 824.4
1983[e]						
Small (N)	650	1 997	144		n.a.	2 791
Small ($000)	38.7	330.3	131.3		n.a.	500.3
Other (N)	100	524	768		41	1 433
Other ($000)	8.4	116.7	1 091		886.4	2 102.5
1984						
Small (N)	548	3 117	708	132	9	4 514
Small ($000)	27.1	577.5	595.3	352.5	150.4	1 702.9
Other (N)	196	1 099	1 122	347	136	2 900
Other ($000)	14.6	247.2	1 322.3	1 239.9	3 515.1	6 339.1
1985						
Small (N)	432	2 807	1 115	314	37	4 704
Small ($000)	21.5	652	918.4	1 307	499.8	3 398.6
Other (N)	66	453	271	173	49	1 012
Other ($000)	3.3	98.1	253.9	782.7	1 322.3	2 460.3
1986						
Small (N)	339	1 912	633	135	25	3 044
Small ($000)	17.0	407.5	550.8	519.9	492.7	1 988
Other (N)	73	239	390	138	54	894
Other ($000)	5.0	43.1	254.7	533.6	1 528.8	2 365
1987						
Small (N)	470	2 143	694	81	22	3 410
Small ($000)	27.9	441.4	762.2	290.4	413.9	1 935.9
Other (N)	5	110	451	195	60	822
Other ($000)	0.2	21.9	482.5	676.6	1 696.3	2 877.5

Table 11.9 (cont'd)

Political contributions by corporations, by size of corporation and size of contribution, 1980–88

Taxation year	0.01– $100	$100– 499	$500– 1 999	$2 000– 9 999	over $10 000	Total
1988E						
Small (N)	1 365[f]	1 035[g]	911	163	15	3 488
Small ($000)	152.9[f]	315.0[g]	756.6	586.1	333.8	2 144.4
Other (N)	592[f]	128[g]	328	169	114	1 332
Other ($000)	99.7[f]	45.2[g]	280.4	757.0	3 791.9	4 974.3

Source: Department of National Revenue data supplied to Royal Commission on Electoral Reform and Party Financing.

Notes: Omits the over 95% of corporations that made no political contribution.

[a]Number of "small" corporations, i.e., those receiving the Small Business Deduction (SBD) for their political contribution.

[b]Total amount of political contributions.

[c]Number of other corporations, i.e., those not receiving SBD for their political contribution.

[d]Total amount of political contributions by "large" corporations.

[e]For 1981 and 1983 tax years, "500–1 999" and "2 000–9 999" categories were combined by Department of National Revenue for confidentiality purposes.

[f]0.01–$199.

[g]$200–499.

E = Election year.
n.a. = Not available.

Table 11.10

Average sales revenues of firms in *Financial Post 500*, 1983–90
(thousands of dollars)

Rank by revenues	1983	1984	1985	1986	1987	1988	1989	1990
1–50	3 979 744	4 450 187	4 704 796	4 622 241	4 860 426	5 382 999	5 411 683	5 462 400
51–100	1 144 580	1 264 498	1 284 875	1 207 442	1 397 534	1 579 938	1 603 290	1 659 560
101–150	603 716	692 480	725 022	775 885	865 212	886 466	886 204	905 420
151–200	394 215	446 494	475 583	498 406	545 131	565 328	574 113	566 900
201–250	290 545	323 844	342 284	367 708	394 231	406 575	404 910	424 760
251–300	230 109	251 280	273 773	281 324	309 079	321 744	325 789	329 300
301–350	181 548	195 683	214 146	210 187	242 695	251 812	251 820	258 880
351–400	148 670	151 884	163 711	170 222	194 216	200 700	196 275	201 900
401–450	120 841	120 930	128 155	136 384	157 190	160 682	154 377	167 000
451–500	90 404	95 013	101 937	113 877	127 495	128 827	127 349	136 698

Sources: Tabulated by author from *Financial Post 500* (various years; data for 1983 were published in mid-1984, and so on.)

Note: Financial Post 500 are 500 largest nonfinancial corporations in Canada.

Table 11.11
Number of firms in *Financial Post 500* contributing to federal parties, 1983–90

Rank by revenues	1983			1984E			1985			1986			1987			1988E			1989			1990		
	Both	PC only	Lib. only	Both	PC only	Lib. only	Both	PC only	Lib. only	Both	PC only	Lib. only	Both	PC only	Lib. only	Both	PC only	Lib. only	Both	PC only	Lib. only	Both	PC only	Lib. only
1–50	23	3	2	23	3	2	17	6	4	19	2	3	24	2	2	25	2	3	20	6	1	19	3	3
51–100	25	6	2	29	3	0	20	9	2	22	5	4	18	4	4	17	6	1	15	5	3	22	4	3
101–150	15	4	5	23	4	1	18	4	4	13	8	4	17	2	3	17	4	2	12	6	6	18	13	3
151–200	20	7	3	20	7	1	12	3	6	15	2	3	12	4	2	12	3	0	8	6	4	8	5	4
201–250	10	9	6	13	8	5	5	9	2	14	10	3	13	3	2	8	8	2	9	8	4	11	10	5
251–300	8	8	5	6	10	1	5	8	1	9	4	2	8	7	1	7	7	2	8	6	2	10	6	3
301–350	7	10	2	16	10	3	8	6	1	6	6	1	12	3	2	12	2	2	6	9	0	9	7	4
351–400	4	7	4	5	12	4	2	10	2	8	6	2	4	5	0	5	6	2	5	3	3	4	9	4
401–450	9	8	3	7	12	2	5	6	3	4	9	4	7	5	1	3	4	0	2	5	4	5	4	0
451–500	9	9	2	8	9	5	4	10	2	4	4	3	2	1	2	4	4	1	3	5	4	3	9	2
Total	130	71	34	150	78	24	96	71	27	114	56	29	117	36	19	110	46	15	88	59	31	109	70	31

Sources: Tabulated by author from *Financial Post 500* (various years) and annual returns filed by parties with CEO.

E = Election year.

Table 11.11a

Frequency of contributions by firms in *Financial Post 500*, by party, 1983–90

	Both		PC		Liberal		Total		Part rate (%)
	N	%	N	%	N	%	N	%	
1983	130	55.3	71	30.2	34	14.5	235	100	47.0
1984E	150	59.5	78	31.0	24	9.5	252	100	50.4
1985	96	49.5	71	36.7	27	13.9	194	100	38.8
1986	114	57.3	56	28.1	29	14.6	199	100	39.8
1987	117	68.0	36	20.9	19	11.0	172	100	34.4
1988E	110	64.3	46	26.9	15	8.8	171	100	34.2
1989	88	49.4	59	33.1	31	17.4	178	100	35.6
1990	109	51.9	70	33.3	31	14.8	210	100	42.0
Total	914	58.3	487	30.2	219	13.0	1 611	100	40.3

Source: Tabulated from table 11.11.

E = Election year.

Table 11.11b

Average participation rate of firms in *Financial Post 500*, 1983–85 and 1986–90

Rank by revenues	1983–85				1986–90			
	Both	PC only	Liberal only	Total	Both	PC only	Liberal only	Total
1–100	45.7[a]	10.0	4.0	59.6	40.2	7.8	5.4	53.4
101–200	36.0	9.7	6.7	52.3	26.4	10.2	6.2	42.8
201–300	15.7	17.3	6.7	39.7	19.0	13.6	5.2	37.8
301-400	14.0	18.3	5.3	37.7	14.2	11.2	4.0	29.4
401–500	14.0	18.0	5.7	37.7	7.4	10.0	4.2	21.6
1–500	25.1	14.7	5.7	45.4	21.4	10.6	5.0	37.0

Source: Tabulated from table 11.11.

[a]Read as follows: Of firms ranked in top 100 nonfinancial firms in Canada, 45.7% made a contribution to both Liberal and Progressive Conservative parties during period 1983–85.

Table 11.11c

Number and average contributions by firms in *Financial Post 500* and 140 largest financial enterprises, 1990

| | FP500 | | | | 140 largest financial enterprises[a] | | | |
| | PC | | Liberal | | PC | | Liberal | |
	N	Average ($)	*N*	Average ($)	*N*	Average ($)	*N*	Average ($)
No contribution	320	0	361	0	99	0	112	0
Contribution to PC only	71	3 256	N/A	N/A	15	2 547	N/A	
Contribution to Liberal only	N/A	N/A	30	2 380	N/A		2	1 500
Contribution to both parties								
Identical	17 (		17 (		2 (		2 (	
		(13 471		(13 564		(17 442		(17 960
Within 10%[b]	(		(		15 (		15 (	
PC > Liberal[c]	57	11 615	57	5 204	5	6 055	5	3 549
Liberal > PC[d]	35	5 256	35	11 695	4	10 955	4	20 383
	180	7 866	139	7 935	41	9 693	28	14 042

Source: Tabulated by author from *Financial Post 500* (summer 1991) and annual returns filed by parties with CEO.

[a]Data available for only 140 firms in 1990.

[b]Contribution to one party within 10% of contribution to other party.

[c]Contribution to Progressive Conservative party at least 10% greater than contribution to Liberal party (excluding zero contributions).

[d]Contribution to Liberal party at least 10% greater than contribution to Progressive Conservative party (excluding zero contributions).

N/A = Not applicable.

Table 11.12

Importance of contributions by firms in *Financial Post 500* to federal Progressive Conservative and Liberal parties, 1983–90

Contributions	1983		1984E		1985		1986		1987		1988E		1989		1990	
	PC	Lib.	PC	Lib.	PC	Lib.	PC	Lib.	PC	Lib.	PC	Lib.	PC	Lib.	PC	Lib.
FP 500 firms ($000)	820	726	1 925	1 387	890	738	991	1 139	1 139	1 012	2 043	1 598	1 309	907	1 408	1 088
All businesses ($000)	4 820	3 543	11 004	5 340	6 695	2 432	7 301	4 846	6 696	5 344	14 359	8 449	6 943	3 931	6 350	4 568
All sources[a] ($000)	14 767	7 736	23 417	13 014	15 073	6 163	15 639	10 718	13 058	8 882	27 013	17 897	14 521	6 397	12 298	13 778[b]
Contributions by FP 500 firms as % of																
All business contributions	17.0	20.5	17.5	26.0	13.3	30.3	13.6	23.5	17.0	18.9	14.2	18.9	18.9	23.1	22.2	23.8
Party revenue from all sources	5.6	9.4	8.2	10.7	5.9	12.0	6.3	10.6	8.7	11.4	7.6	8.9	9.0	14.2	11.4	7.9
FP 500 firms in 1989 dollars (000)	1 057	936	2 377	1 712	1 057	876	1 130	1 299	1 245	1 106	2 524	1 678	1 309	907	1 344	1 038

Source: Tabulated by author from *Financial Post 500* (various years) and annual returns filed by parties with CEO, 1983–90.

[a] Total party revenue from all sources including reimbursement from federal government of part of party's "election expenses."

[b] Includes $4.4 million in delegates fees for June 1990 leadership convention and $1.95 million in contributions to leadership candidates routed through Federal Liberal Agency.

Table 11.12a

Total and average contributions by firms in *Financial Post 500*, by party, 1983–90
(in 1989 dollars)

Year	Total contributions (000)			Number of firms contributing to		Average contribution[a] per firm	
	PC	Liberal	PC–Liberal	PC	Liberal	PC	Liberal
1983	1 057	936	121	201	164	5 259	5 707
1984E	2 377	1 712	665	228	174	10 425	9 839
1985	1 057	876	181	167	123	6 329	7 122
1986	1 130	1 299	(169)	170	143	6 647	9 084
1987	1 245	1 106	139	153	136	8 137	8 132
1988E	2 524	1 678	846	156	125	16 169	13 424
1989	1 309	907	402	147	119	8 905	7 622
1990	1 344	1 038	306	179	140	7 507	7 414

Sources: Tables 11.11 and 11.12.

[a]Average of firms making any contribution to either or both parties.

E = Election year.

Table 11.13
Average size of contributions to federal parties by firms in *Financial Post 500*, 1983–90

Rank by revenues	1983		1984E		1985		1986		1987		1988E		1989		1990	
	PC	Lib.	PC	Lib.	PC	Lib.	PC	Lib.	PC	Lib.	PC	Lib.	PC	Lib.	PC	Lib.
1–50																
All firms[a]	5 325	5 587	11 349	10 150	7 014	6 878	7 377	8 294	8 343	7 895	13 341	11 897	10 625	8 804	9 752	9 028
Actual contributors[b]	10 241	11 175	21 824	20 299	15 248	16 376	17 565	18 851	16 044	15 183	24 706	21 245	20 433	20 962	22 163	20 519
N[c]	26	25	26	25	23	21	21	22	26	26	27	28	26	21	22	22
51–100																
All firms[a]	4 669	3 597	7 549	6 324	3 507	2 542	2 287	3 756	3 583	3 406	7 658	4 186	4 778	2 288	6 034	4 423
Actual contributors[b]	7 531	6 661	11 795	10 903	6 047	5 777	4 235	7 222	8 142	7 742	16 648	11 629	11 945	6 355	11 604	8 845
N[c]	31	27	32	29	29	22	27	26	22	22	23	18	20	18	26	25
101–150																
All firms[a]	948	1 474	6 330	3 461	2 011	1 845	2 914	1 692	3 013	2 942	4 743	5 520	2 761	2 500	4 032	2 466
Actual contributors[b]	2 496	3 685	11 722	7 210	4 570	4 193	6 937	4 976	7 930	7 356	11 292	14 525	7 670	6 944	6 502	5 871
N[c]	19	20	27	24	22	22	21	17	19	20	21	19	18	18	31	21
151–200																
All firms[a]	1 180	1 021	2 720	2 055	929	1 246	1 808	4 009	1 923	1 518	3 871	2 399	1 967	696	614	443
Actual contributors[b]	2 186	2 219	5 038	4 892	3 096	3 461	5 316	11 137	6 010	5 423	12 902	9 997	7 026	2 901	2 362	1 847
N[c]	27	23	27	21	15	18	17	18	16	14	15	12	14	12	13	12
201–250																
All firms[a]	1 181	755	3 551	1 870	425	201	1 133	1 117	1 572	1 531	2 636	1 004	1 280	781	1 346	1 244
Actual contributors[b]	3 107	2 359	8 454	5 195	1 517	1 437	2 361	3 287	4 913	5 104	8 237	5 018	3 764	3 004	3 204	3 888
N[c]	19	16	21	18	14	7	24	17	16	15	16	10	17	13	21	16

Category	Measure	1	2	3	4	5	6	7	8	9	10	11	12	13	14	15	16
251–300	All firms[a]	1 100	1 242	769	395	856	144	843	893	1 089	612	2 495	2 618	906	805	1 731	1 526
	Actual contributors[b]	3 436	4 776	2 402	2 825	3 292	1 203	3 242	4 058	3 631	3 401	8 912	14 546	3 235	4 025	5 409	5 870
	N[c]	16	13	16	7	13	6	13	11	15	9	14	9	14	10	16	13
301–350	All firms[a]	697	271	3 054	2 296	1 248	1 356	1 013	1 052	1 204	1 483	4 315	3 188	2 681	1 262	2 110	1 495
	Actual contributors[b]	2 049	1 503	5 873	6 043	4 459	7 533	4 219	7 518	4 012	5 296	15 411	11 386	8 938	10 517	6 595	5 748
	N[c]	17	9	26	19	14	9	12	7	15	14	14	14	15	6	16	13
351–400	All firms[a]	496	283	1 402	416	463	35	1 250	1 473	1 079	132	813	800	585	637	756	570
	Actual contributors[b]	2 254	1 770	4 124	2 310	1 930	432	4 464	7 365	5 997	1 648	3 695	5 715	3 658	3 981	2 907	3 565
	N[c]	11	8	17	9	12	4	14	10	9	4	11	7	8	8	13	8
401–450	All firms[a]	519	143	1 003	195	695	147	399	147	854	572	377	100	232	152	839	284
	Actual contributors[b]	1 525	595	2 639	1 084	3 161	917	1 534	920	3 556	3 576	2 690	1 675	1 654	1 271	4 658	2 838
	N[c]	17	12	19	9	11	8	13	8	12	8	7	3	7	6	9	5
451–500	All firms[a]	276	150	776	580	647	365	796	343	114	154	613	240	373	213	950	286
	Actual contributors[b]	766	682	2 282	2 231	2 310	3 046	4 977	2 450	1 895	1 926	3 832	2 400	2 329	1 519	3 960	2 863
	N[c]	18	11	17	13	14	6	8	7	3	4	8	5	8	7	12	5

Sources: Tabulated by author from *Financial Post 500* (various years) and annual returns filed by parties with CEO, 1983–1990.

[a]Average contribution for all firms in category.

[b]Average contribution for all firms making any contribution.

[c]Number of firms making a contribution to one or both parties.

E = Election year.

Table 11.14
Political contributions relative to total revenues for firms in *Financial Post 500*, 1983–90
(contributions per million dollars of revenues)

FP rank by revenues	1983	1984E	1985	1986	1987	1988E	1989	1990
1–50								
All[a]	2.74	4.83	2.95	3.39	3.34	4.69	3.07[d]	3.43
PC[b]	2.98	5.91	3.88	4.05	3.54	5.15	3.51[d]	3.82
Liberal[c]	3.16	5.28	3.66	4.11	3.20	4.05	3.67[d]	3.45
51–100								
All	7.22	10.97	4.71	4.76	5.00	7.50	4.41	6.30
PC	6.55	9.52	4.90	3.35	5.77	10.67	7.43	7.01
Liberal	5.69	8.79	4.68	5.67	5.41	7.61	4.07	5.11
100–150								
All	4.01	14.14	5.32	5.94	6.88	11.58	5.94	7.18
PC	4.26	16.81	6.42	8.95	8.90	12.95	8.89	7.19
Liberal	6.26	10.40	5.86	6.41	8.32	16.55	7.90	6.25
151–200								
All	5.58	10.69	4.57	11.67	6.31	11.09	4.64	1.87
PC	5.60	11.26	6.43	10.21	10.71	21.29	11.84	4.15
Liberal	5.52	10.92	7.19	21.43	9.44	16.78	4.79	3.37
201–250								
All	6.66	16.74	1.83	6.12	7.87	8.95	5.09	6.10
PC	10.49	26.53	4.49	6.46	12.46	20.75	9.30	7.45
Liberal	7.97	16.01	4.19	9.03	12.70	12.58	7.24	9.13
251–300								
All	10.17	4.63	3.65	6.17	5.51	15.89	5.25	9.89
PC	14.93	9.64	12.13	11.53	11.71	27.13	9.86	16.03
Liberal	20.68	11.26	4.52	14.21	11.28	44.34	12.55	17.32
301–350								
All	5.16	27.34	12.16	9.83	11.07	29.80	15.66	13.92
PC	11.24	30.05	20.76	20.18	16.79	62.71	35.48	25.30
Liberal	8.33	30.98	35.76	35.69	22.87	46.27	41.09	24.79
351–400								
All	5.24	11.97	3.04	16.00	6.24	8.04	6.23	6.57
PC	15.26	27.90	12.05	26.47	31.46	18.05	18.42	14.33
Liberal	12.12	15.21	2.77	43.25	8.91	29.57	20.24	18.03
401–450								
All	5.47	9.90	6.57	4.00	9.07	2.97	2.49	6.74
PC	12.84	21.58	24.61	11.21	22.43	16.58	10.55	28.64
Liberal	5.00	8.74	7.00	6.70	22.60	10.33	8.17	17.63

Table 11.14 (cont'd)
Political contributions relative to total revenues for firms in *Financial Post 500*,
1983–90
(contributions per million dollars of revenues)

FP rank by revenues	1983	1984E	1985	1986	1987	1988E	1989	1990
451–500								
All	4.71	14.27	9.93	10.00	2.10	6.62	4.60	9.03
PC	8.67	24.29	22.30	42.63	15.82	30.81	18.59	28.66
Liberal	7.55	23.79	29.58	20.94	15.50	18.66	11.96	21.89

Sources: Compiled by author from *Financial Post 500* (various years) and annual returns filed by parties with CEO, 1983–1990.

[a]Contributions by all firms (i.e., *N* = 50) to *either* party or both divided by total sales of all firms in category.

[b]Only firms contributing to Conservative party divided by total sales of all firms giving to Progressive Conservative party.

[c]Only firms contributing to Liberal party divided by total sales of all firms giving to Liberal party.

[d]These figures are slightly understated and will be corrected.

Table 11.15
**Political contributions and foreign ownership among largest 250 firms
in *Financial Post 500*, 1984–86**

	1984		1985		1986	
	0–49%[a]	50–100%[a]	0–49%	50–100%	0–49%	50–100%
Size of contribution						
$0–99	37	57	28	48	34	55
$100–9 999	28	28	17	18	27	26
$10 000 +	35	14	56	33	39	20
Total	100	100	100	100	100	100
N	120	104	131	98	134	96
Pearson correlation coefficients						
Propensity to donate and % Canadian ownership	.170		.208		.201	
% foreign ownership and whether corporation makes a contribution	–.223		–.235		–.259	
Percentage of firms making contribution						
British	86		50		77	
Canadian	71		65		68	
American	56		49		48	
Japanese	0		9		11	

Source: Wearing and Wearing (1990, tables 1 and 3, p. 119).

[a]Percentage foreign ownership.

Table 11.16
Average assets of financial enterprises in *Financial Post* annual ranking, 1983–90
(millions of dollars)

Category	Rank by assets	1983	1984	1985	1986	1987	1988	1989	1990
Financial institutions	1–25	18 186	20 259	22 081	23 542	25 670	27 446	32 759	32 219
	26–50	1 408	1 439	1 448	1 437	1 756	1 869	3 031	2 047
	51–75	596	632	619	691	787	877	1 232	948
	76–100	344	359	372	429	471	503	692	541
Life insurance companies	1–25	3 066	3 521	4 240	5 028	5 696	6 424	7 335	8 362
Property and casualty insurance companies[a]	1–15	429	460	559	645	762	850	1 117	678
Investment dealers[b]	1–15	32	34	49	89	123	132	2 139[c]	n.a.

Source: Tabulated by author from *Financial Post 500* (various years).

[a]Ranked by revenue.

[b]Investment dealers ranked by capital from 1983 to 1988.

[c]In 1989, ranking was by assets and only ten dealers appeared in *Financial Post* list.

n.a. = Not available.

Table 11.17

Importance of contributions to federal parties by 155 financial enterprises in *Financial Post* annual ranking, 1983–90

Rank by revenues	1983 PC	1983 Lib.	1984E PC	1984E Lib.	1985 PC	1985 Lib.	1986 PC	1986 Lib.	1987 PC	1987 Lib.	1988E PC	1988E Lib.	1989 PC	1989 Lib.	1990 PC	1990 Lib.
FP financial enterprises ($000s)	300	235	698	621	401	322	528	531	665	566	1 143	919	620	550	397[b]	393[d]
All businesses ($000s)	4 192	3 543	11 004	5 340	6 693	2 432	7 301	4 846	6 696	5 344	14 359	8 449	6 943	3 931	6 350	4 568
All sources[a] ($000s)	14 767	7 736	23 417	13 014	15 073	6 163	15 639	10 719	13 058	8 882	27 013	17 897	14 521	6 397	12 298	13 778[c]
Contributions by FP financial enterprises as % of																
All business contributions	7.2	6.6	6.3	11.6	6.0	13.2	7.2	11.0	9.9	10.6	8.0	10.9	8.9	14.0	6.3	8.6
Party revenue from all sources	2.0	3.0	3.0	4.8	2.7	5.2	3.4	5.0	5.1	6.4	4.2	5.1	4.3	8.6	3.2	2.9
FP financial enterprises in 1989 dollars (000)	387	303	862	767	476	382	602	605	727	619	1201	965	620	550	379	375

Sources: Tabulated by author from *Financial Post 500* (various years) and annual returns filed by parties with CEO (1983–1990).

[a] Total party revenue from all sources including reimbursement from federal government of part of party's "election expenses."

[b] Excludes top 10 investment dealers.

[c] Includes $1.95 million in individual and corporate contributions routed through Federal Liberal Agency, plus $4.4 million in delegate fees for June 1990 leadership convention.

E = Election year.

Table 11.17a
Total and average contributions by 155 financial enterprises in *Financial Post* annual ranking, 1983–90

Year	Total contributions (000)			Number of firms contributing to		Average[a] contribution per firm	
	PC	Liberal	PC–Liberal	PC	Liberal	PC	Liberal
1983	387	303	84	52	41	4 607	5 827
1984E	862	767	95	58	48	14 862	15 979
1985	476	382	94	51	37	9 333	10 324
1986	602	605	(3)	50	44	12 040	13 750
1987	727	619	108	49	41	14 837	15 098
1988E	1 201	965	236	51	42	23 549	22 976
1989[b]	620	550	70	45	42	13 778	13 095
1990[c]	379	375	4	41	28	9 244	13 393

Sources: Tables 11.17 and 11.18a.

[a]Average of firms making a contribution to one or both parties.

[b]Only 150 firms.

[c]Only 140 firms; 15 missing firms are all investment dealers that normally make above average contributions.

E = Election year.

Table 11.18
Number of financial enterprises in *Financial Post* annual ranking contributing to federal parties, 1983–90

Category	Rank by assets	1983 Both	PC only	Lib. only	1984E Both	PC only	Lib. only	1985 Both	PC only	Lib. only	1986 Both	PC only	Lib. only	1987 Both	PC only	Lib. only	1988E Both	PC only	Lib. only	1989 Both	PC only	Lib. only	1990 Both	PC only	Lib. only
Financial institutions	1–25	7	3	2	11	2	0	11	3	0	12	3	0	12	1	0	12	1	0	12	1	0	9	3	0
	26–50	4	2	1	3	2	1	3	3	0	4	2	1	2	4	4	2	3	1	3	0	0	3	2	0
	51–75	5	2	3	0	5	3	0	4	1	1	1	2	1	2	0	0	1	0	1	2	1	1	2	1
	76–100	0	3	0	0	3	2	0	1	0	1	2	0	1	4	0	1	1	2	0	0	1	1	2	0
	Total	16	10	6	14	12	6	14	11	1	18	8	3	16	11	4	15	6	3	16	3	2	14	9	1
Life insurance companies	1–25	9	1	1	12	0	0	9	3	2	10	1	0	7	2	2	9	4	0	11	1	0	8	3	1
Property and casualty insurance companies[a]	1–15	1	2	0	4	2	0	2	1	0	1	1	0	1	0	1	4	1	0	3	1	0	4	3	0
Investment dealers	1–15[b]	8	5	0	12	2	0	9	2	0	11	0	1	9	3	1	10	2	1	10	0	0	n.a.		

Sources: Tabulated by author from *Financial Post 500* (various years) and annual returns filed by parties with CEO, 1983–1990.

[a] Ranked by revenues.

[b] Only 10 in 1989.

E = Election year.

Table 11.18a
Frequency of contributions by 155 largest financial institutions, by party, 1983–90

	Both		PC		Liberal		Total		Partici-pation rate (%)
	N	%	N	%	N	%	N	%	
1983	34	18	7	59	57.6	30.5	11.9	100	38.1
1984E	42	16	6	64	65.6	25.0	9.4	100	41.3
1985	34	17	3	54	63.0	31.5	5.6	100	34.8
1986	40	10	4	54	74.1	18.5	7.4	100	34.8
1987	33	16	8	57	57.9	28.1	14.0	100	36.8
1988E	38	13	4	55	69.1	23.6	7.3	100	35.5
1989[a]	40	5	2	47	85.1	10.6	4.3	100	31.3
1990[a]	26	15	2	43	60.5	34.9	4.7	100	30.7
Total	287	110	36	433	66.3	25.4	8.3	100	35.5

Source: Table 11.18.
[a]150 firms total.
[b]140 firms total.
E = Election year

Table 11.19
Average size of contributions to federal parties by financial enterprises in *Financial Post* annual ranking, 1983–90

Rank by assets	1983		1984E		1985		1986		1987		1988E		1989		1990	
	PC	Lib.	PC	Lib.	PC	Lib.	PC	Lib.	PC	Lib.	PC	Lib.	PC	Lib.	PC	Lib.
Financial institutions																
1–25																
All firms	7 008[a]	5 290	18 767	18 063	9 493	8 680	10 717	10 522	12 410	11 595	23 234	22 219	11 998	11 899	11 523	11 816
Actual contributors	17 521[b]	14 695	36 090	41 053	16 952	19 727	17 862	21 922	23 865	24 155	44 681	46 290	23 054	24 791	24 006	32 821
N	10[c]	9	13	11	14	11	15	12	13	12	13	12	13	12	12	9
26–50																
All firms	715	973	1 506	407	1 816	562	129	1 195	1 560	1 140	1 587	716	1 565	323	345	280
Actual contributors	2 979	4 865	7 529	2 544	7 569	4 687	538	5 975	9 750	5 701	7 936	5 970	13 042	2 694	1 726	2 336
N	6	5	5	4	6	3	6	5	4	5	5	3	3	3	5	3
51–75																
All firms	659	489	920	148	653	20	36	444	168	198	170	0	291	90	349	168
Actual contributors	2 353	1 527	4 602	1 233	4 084	500	445	3 700	1 053	2 478	4 240	0	2 428	1 119	2 907	2 100
N	7	8	5	4	4	1	2	3	4	2	1	0	3	2	3	2
76–100																
All firms	60	0	367	85	9	0	1 307	89	1 515	60	60	105	0	20	239	60
Actual contributors	501	0	3 057	1 060	213	0	10 889	2 218	6 314	1 500	1 500	875	0	500	1 992	1 500
N	3	0	3	2	1	0	3	1	6	1	1	3	0	1	3	2

Life insurance companies																
1-25																
All firms	1 465	1 708	3 322	3 482	2 310	2 461	2 894	3 466	2 489	3 035	5 338	3 449	2 897	2 841	2 820	2 862
Actual contributors	3 663	4 269	6 921	7 255	4 814	5 594	6 577	8 665	6 914	8 431	10 266	9 582	6 036	6 456	6 409	7 950
N	10	10	12	12	12	11	11	10	9	9	13	9	12	11	11	9
Property and casualty insurance companies[d]																
1-15																
All firms	354	167	632	400	296	167	200	167	89	256	782	834	869	815	1 035	907
Actual contributors	1 772	2 500	1 581	1 500	1 479	1 253	1 500	2 500	1 333	1 917	2 347	3 128	3 260	4 075	2 218	3 385
N	3	0	6	4	3	2	2	1	1	2	5	4	4	3	7	4
Investment dealers																
1-15																
All firms	3 127	1 403	4 456	4 030	2 667	1 739	9 864	9 033	14 017	10 781	24 759	16 301	18 791[e]	15 869[e]	n.a.	n.a.
Actual contributors	3 608	2 630	4 774	5 037	3 637	2 898	13 451	11 291	17 521	16 172	30 949	22 228	18 791	15 869		
N	13	8	14	12	11	9	11	12	12	10	12	11	10	10		

Sources: Tabulated by author from *Financial Post 500* (various years) and annual returns filed by parties with CEO, 1983–1990.

[a] Average contribution for all firms in category.

[b] Average contribution for all firms making *any* contribution.

[c] Number of firms making contribution to one or both parties.

[d] Ranked by revenues.

[e] Only 10 investment dealers listed in 1989.

E = Election year.

n.a. : Not available.

Table 11.20
Political contributions relative to total assets for financial enterprises in *Financial Post* annual ranking, 1983–90
(contributions per million dollars of assets)

Rank by assets	1983	1984E	1985	1986	1987	1988E	1989	1990
Financial institutions 1–25								
All	0.68[a]	1.82	0.82	0.90	0.94	1.66	0.72	0.72
PC	0.49[b]	1.15	0.52	0.54	0.59	1.04	0.46	0.58
Liberal	0.56[c]	1.15	0.52	0.71	0.57	1.06	0.50	0.53
26–50								
All	1.20	1.33	1.64	0.92	1.54	1.23	0.76	0.31
PC	1.85	4.30	4.42	0.36	6.64	4.72	3.22	0.90
Liberal	2.68	1.30	2.81	4.46	3.79	3.47	0.74	1.07
51–75								
All	1.93	1.69	1.09	0.69	0.47	0.19	0.25	0.55
PC	3.79	6.96	6.63	0.60	1.17	4.43	1.80	2.92
Liberal	2.58	1.99	0.99	5.12	2.55	0.00	0.23	2.12
76–100								
All	0.17	1.26	0.02	3.25	3.34	0.33	0.03	0.55
PC	1.42	8.54	0.58	25.68	13.07	3.05	0.00	3.66
Liberal	0.00	3.22	0.00	4.93	3.46	1.65	0.59	2.40
Life insurance companies 1–25								
All	1.03	1.93	1.13	1.26	0.97	1.37	0.78	0.68
PC	0.71	1.25	.93	0.75	0.65	1.05	0.54	0.46
Liberal	0.97	1.31	.81	0.99	0.78	0.80	0.63	0.49
Property and casualty insurance companies[d] 1-15								
All	1.21	2.24	0.83	0.57	0.45	1.90	1.51	2.86
PC	3.40	3.15	2.00	1.75	2.78	2.34	2.93	3.68
Liberal	3.06	2.85	1.66	2.20	2.09	2.94	3.42	5.02

Table 11.20 (cont'd)
Political contributions relative to total assets for financial enterprises in *Financial Post* annual ranking, 1983–90
(contributions per million dollars of assets)

Rank by assets	1983	1984E	1985	1986	1987	1988E	1989	1990
Investment dealers[e] 1–15								
All	141.56	249.59	89.92	212.33	201.61	311.06	16.20[f]	n.a.
PC	103.09	136.40	59.62	141.59	124.26	202.28	8.78[f]	
Liberal	62.62	125.92	42.62	122.73	114.70	139.80	7.42[f]	

Sources: Tabulated by author from *Financial Post 500* (various years) and annual returns filed by parties with CEO, 1983–1990.

[a]Contributions by *all* firms in category to one or both parties.

[b]Any firm contributing to Progressive Conservative party.

[c]Any firm contributing to Liberal party.

[d]Ranked by revenues.

[e]Investment dealers ranked by capital from 1983 to 1988 and assets in 1989.

[f]Only 10 firms listed in 1989.

n.a. = Not available.

Table 12.1
Revenues, expenses and reimbursement of candidates, 1979, 1980, 1984, and 1988 general elections
(thousands of dollars)

	Candidates N	Total revenue (TR)	Election expenses (EE)	Personal expenses (PE)	Campaign surplus (S) TR-EE-PE[a]	Reimburse- ment (R)	Post reim- bursement campaign surplus/deficit TR-EE-PE+R
1988							
PC	295	13 392	11 864	709	819	6 056	6 875
Liberal	295	9 631	9 677	495	(541)	4 656	4 115
NDP	295	6 807	7 306	368	(867)	2 839	1 972
3 main parties	885	29 830	28 847	1 572	(589)	13 551	12 962
Others	693[b]	2 702	2 494	161	47	184	231
Total	1 578	32 532	31 341	1 733	(542)	13 735	13 193
1984							
PC	282	11 345	9 951	775	619	5 117	5 736
Liberal	282	8 391	8 836	611	(1 056)	4 081	3 025
NDP	282	3 724	4 227	252	(755)	1 917	1 162
3 main parties	846	23 460	23 014	1 638	(1 192)	11 115	9 923
Others	603[c]	867	860	123	(116)	56	(60)[a]
Total	1 449	24 327	23 874	1 761	(1 308)	11 171	9 863
1980							
PC	282	5 888	5 680	542	(334)	2 871	2 537
Liberal	282	6 293	6 074	494	(275)	3 656	3 381
NDP	280	2 674	2 987	180	(493)	1 885	1 392
3 main parties	844	14 855	14 741	1 216	(1 100)	8 412	7 312
Others	653[d]	541	628	123	(210)	112	(98)[a]
Total	1 497	15 396	15 369	1 339	(1 310)	8 524	7 214
1979							
PC	282	6 087	6 016	488	(417)	2 868	2 451
Liberal	282	6 558	6 186	527	(155)	3 594	3 439
NDP	282	2 307	2 665	186	(544)	1 671	1 127
3 main parties	846	14 952	14 867	1 201	(1 116)	8 133	7 017
Others	581[e]	671	1 055	185	(569)	385	(184)[a]
Total	1 427	15 623	15 922	1 386	(1 684)	8 518	6 834

Source: Canada, Elections Canada (1980b, 1981, 1984c, 1988c).

Notes: Bracketed numbers indicate negative sums, i.e., deficit.

[a]Calculation omits "other expenses," but figure is not published by CEO.

[b]Nine parties with 539 candidates plus 154 other candidates.

[c]Eight parties with 519 candidates plus 84 other candidates.

[d]Six parties with 543 candidates plus 110 other candidates.

[e]Six parties with 511 candidates plus 70 independent candidates.

Table 12.2
Analysis of candidate revenues, 1979 and 1980 general elections
(thousands of dollars)

Source of revenue	1979[a]					1980[a]				
	PC	Lib.	NDP	Other parties	Total	PC	Lib.	NDP	Other parties	Total
Individuals										
$	2 643	1 758	813	425	5 639	2 220	2 180	1 021	315	5 736
%	43.4	26.8	35.2	63.2		37.7	34.6	38.2	58.2	
Corporations										
$	2 075	1 457	36	119	3 687	1 838	1 779	51	90	3 758
%	34.1	22.2	1.6	17.7		31.2	28.3	1.9	16.6	
Governments										
$	16	2	—	4	22	11	—	—	1	12
%	0.3	—	—	0.6		0.2	—	—	—	
Trade unions										
$	—	—	420	2	422	1	1	469	—	471
%	—	—	18.2	0.3		—	—	17.5	—	
Political organizations[b]										
$	470	466	421	5	1362	756	667	404	11	1 838
%	7.7	7.1	18.2	0.7		12.8	10.6	15.1	2.0	
Registered parties										
$	776	2 701	553	74	4 104	970	1 546	655	100	3 271
%	12.8	41.2	24.0	11.0		16.5	24.6	24.5	18.5	
Fund-raising functions										
$	52	88	35	10	185	35	38	55	20	148
%	0.9	1.3	1.5	1.5		0.6	0.6	2.0	3.7	
Other[c]										
$	54	86	28	34	202	59	81	20	3	163
%	0.9	1.3	1.2	5.1		1.0	1.3	0.7	0.6	
Total	6 086	6 558	2 307	672	15 623	5 888	6 293	2 674	541	15 396

Sources: Canada, Elections Canada (1980b, 1981).

[a]Totals in each category rounded to nearest $1 000 and hence may not add.
[b]Local riding associations and provincial/territorial associations (sections).
[c]Unincorporated organizations.

Table 12.3
Analysis of candidate revenues, 1984 and 1988 general elections
(thousands of dollars)

Source of revenue	1984[a]					1988[a]				
	PC	Lib.	NDP	Other parties	Total	PC	Lib.	NDP	Other parties	Total
Individuals										
$	4 714	2 384	1 607	510	9 215	6 124	3 716	2 316	1 877	14 033
%	41.6	28.4	43.2	58.8	37.9	45.7	38.6	34.0	69.4	43.1
Corporations										
$	4 488	2 317	60	130	6 995	4 652	2 629	182	492	7 956
%	39.6	27.6	1.6	15.0	28.8	34.7	27.3	2.7	18.2	24.5
Governments										
$	11	29	1	0	40	9	17	10	6	42
%	—	0.3	—	—	0.2	—	0.2	0.1	0.2	0.1
Trade unions										
$	7	3	499	0	509	3	10	1 113	0	1 125
%	—	—	13.4	—	2.1	—	0.1	16.4	—	3.5
Political organizations[b]										
$	702	720	527	16	1 965	1 383	1 445	1 425	69	4 322
%	6.2	8.6	14.2	1.8	8.1	10.3	15.0	20.9	2.6	13.3
Registered parties										
$	1 234	2 766	915	179	5 093	1 040	1 681	1 576	181	4 477
%	10.9	33.0	24.6	20.6	20.9	7.8	17.5	23.2	6.7	13.8
Fund-raising functions										
$	142	104	62	31	338	90	93	156	66	405
%	1.3	1.2	1.7	3.6	1.4	0.7	1.0	2.3	2.4	1.2
Other[c]										
$	47	69	52	3	171	92	39	31	11	172
%	0.4	0.8	1.4	0.3	0.7	0.7	0.4	0.5	0.4	0.5
Total	11 345	8 391	3 724	867	24 327	13 392	9631	6 807	2 703	32 532

Source: Canada, Elections Canada (1984c, 1988c).

[a]Totals in each category rounded to nearest $1 000 and hence may not add.
[b]Local riding associations and provincial/territorial associations (sections).
[c]Unincorporated organizations.

Table 12.3a
Average revenues of candidates by source, 1984 and 1988 general elections

Source of revenue	1984				1988			
	PC	Lib.	NDP	Other parties	PC	Lib.	NDP	Other parties
Individuals								
$	16 690	8 408	5 719	846	20 758	12 597	7 850	2 709
%	42	29	44	59	45	39	34	69
Corporations								
$	15 880	8 110	215	215	15 771	8 913	616	710
%	40	28	2	15	35	27	3	18
Governments								
$	39	101	3	—	29	57	34	9
%	0	0	0	—	0	0	0	0
Trade unions								
$	26	10	1 776	—	9	33	3 772	1
%	0	0	14	—	0	0	16	0
Political organizations[a]								
$	2 470	2 552	1 871	26	4 689	4 898	4 830	100
%	6	9	14	2	10	15	21	3
Registered parties								
$	4 367	9 661	3 243	296	3 524	5 700	5 341	261
%	11	33	25	21	8	18	23	7
Fund-raising functions								
$	502	422	221	51	305	316	528	95
%	1	1	2	4	1	1	2	2
Other								
$	n.a.	n.a.	n.a.	4	310	133	104	—
%	—	—	—	—	1	—	1	—
Total	39 975	29 263	13 047	1 437	45 395	32 647	23 074	3 900

Sources: Canada, Bureau of Management Consulting (1985); Canada, Government Consulting Group (1990); Canada, Election Expenses (1988c).

[a]Includes local associations or riding associations and provincial/territorial associations (sections).

Table 12.4

Importance of transfers from parties and riding associations to candidate revenues, 1979, 1980, 1984 and 1988 general elections

(thousands of dollars)

Contributions to candidates	1979	1980	1984	1988
PC				
Total revenue	6 086	5 888	11 345	13 392
From party	776[b]	970	1 234	1 040
From riding associations[a]	470	756	702	1 383
Liberal				
Total revenue	6 558	6 293	8 391	9 631
From party	2 701[c]	1 546	2 766[e]	1 681
From riding associations[a]	466	667	720	1 445
NDP				
Total revenue	2 307	2 674	3 724	6 807
From party	553[d]	655	915	1 576
From riding associations[a]	421	404	527	1 425
Other parties				
Total revenue	670	541	867	2 703
From party	74	100	178	181
From riding associations[a]	5	11	16	69

Sources: Tabulated from Canada, Elections Canada (1980b, 1981, 1984c, 1988c).

[a]Includes provincial/territorial associations (sections).

[b]Ontario 161; Quebec 318; Manitoba 79; Alberta 74.

[c]Ontario 759; Quebec 898; Nova Scotia 134; New Brunswick 92; British Columbia 282; Alberta 185; Newfoundland 97.

[d]Ontario 324; British Columbia 61; Alberta 36; Manitoba 50.

[e]Ontario 735; Quebec 1148; Manitoba 195; British Columbia 155.

Table 12.4a

Transfer of funds within federal parties, 1979, 1980, 1984 and 1988 general elections
(thousands of dollars)

Election year	Transfers[a] to candidates from		Transfers[b] from party headquarters to		
	Party headquarters (1)	PTA/riding association (2)	Candidates (3)	Ridings (4)	PTAs (and other party organizations) (5)
Liberal					
1979	2 701	466	(810)[c]	732	85
1980	1 546	667	(1 098)[c]	875	612
1984	2 766	720	474	195	124
1988	1 681	1 445	485[d]	1 156	931
PC					
1979	776	470	0	1 395	N/A
1980	970	756	(see col. 4)	1 149[e]	N/A
1984	1 234	702	912	1 709	N/A
1988	1 040	1 383	3 335	0	N/A
NDP					
1979	553	421	0	635	6646
1980	655	404	0	789	2766
1984	915	527	0	768	140
1988	1 576	1 425	0	2 809	12

Sources: Annual returns filed by parties with CEO; and Canada, Elections Canada (1980b, 1981, 1984c, 1988c).

[a]As reported by candidates to CEO and published in his volume after each general election.

[b]As reported by party to CEO in parties' annual returns.

[c]Figures in brackets indicate negative amounts, meaning candidates transferred more money to headquarters than headquarters transferred to candidates.

[d]*Excludes* amounts candidates transferred to party headquarters ($2 273 684).

[e]Includes transfers to candidates.

[f]For "extraordinary organizing expenses."

N/A = Not applicable.

Table 12.5
**Number of contributions to candidates by party, 1979, 1980, 1984 and 1988
general elections**

Party and category	1979	1980	1984	1988
PC				
Individuals[a]	27 597	23 489	42 247	40 329
Total[b]	37 979	32 501	60 660	55 025
Percentage[c]	72.7	72.3	69.6	73.3
Liberal				
Individuals	18 525	25 823	21 185	27 106
Total	26 531	35 730	29 915	36 009
Percentage	69.8	72.3	70.8	75.3
NDP				
Individuals	13 765	16 778	18 690	22 497
Total	15 420	18 505	20 106	25 073
Percentage	89.3	90.7	93.0	89.7
Other parties				
Individuals	7 436	4 438	5 334	14 875
Total	9 895	5 276	5 972	17 121
Percentage	75.1	84.1	89.3	86.9
Total individuals	67 323	70 528	87 456	104 807
Total contributions	88 431	92 012	116 653	133 328

Sources: Canada, Elections Canada (1980b, 1981, 1984c, 1988c).

[a]Number of contributions from individuals. An individual may make more than one contribution.

[b]Total number of contributions, i.e., from individuals, business organizations, trade unions, local riding associations and political parties.

[c]Contributions from individuals as percentage of total number of contributions.

Table 12.6
Size distribution of candidates' total revenue, 1988 general election

Category	PC N	PC %	Liberal N	Liberal %	NDP N	NDP %	Other parties N	Other parties %	Total N	Total %
Under $10 000	3	1.0	15	5.1	72	24.7	384	80.3	474	34.9
$10 001–20 000	19	6.4	54	18.4	67	22.9	45	9.4	185	13.6
$20 001–30 000	32	10.8	58	19.8	54	18.5	32	6.7	176	13.0
$30 001–40 000	74	25.1	95	32.4	50	17.1	10	2.1	229	16.9
$40 001–50 000	69	23.4	35	11.9	37	12.7	2	0.4	143	10.5
$50 001–60 000	44	14.9	18	6.1	8	2.7	5	1.0	75	5.5
$60 001–70 000	23	7.8	9	3.1	3	1.0	0	0	35	2.6
$70 001–80 000	12	4.1	3	1.0	1	0.3	0	0	16	1.2
$80 001–100 000	10	3.4	4	1.4	0	0	0	0	14	1.0
Over 100 000	9	3.1	2	0.7	0	0	0	0	11	0.8
Total	295	100	293[c]	100	292[b]	100	478	100	1 358[c]	100

Source: Tabulated from electronic data file provided by CEO.

Notes: Total revenue includes cash contributions plus donations of goods and services, but excludes reimbursement of "election expenses" by federal government.

[a]Data missing for one candidate.

[b]Data missing for three candidates.

[c]Data file provided by CEO had 216 missing cases, 211 of which were candidates of "other" parties.

Table 12.7
Analysis of candidate revenues by party and amount of revenue, 1988 general election

Category	PC	Liberal	NDP	Other parties
Under $10 000				
Total revenue ($)	18 113	96 688	389 098	626 207
Candidates (*N*)	3	15	72	384
Contributions of $100 or less (%)	43.8	26.8	23.2	28.1
Contributions of over $100 (%)	51.4	64.4	61.9	51.5
Goods and services (%)	3.8	8.8	12.0	17.5
Fund-raising functions (%)	0	0	2.9	2.9
$10 001–20 000				
Total revenue ($)	291 246	839 429	981 836	592 062
Candidates (*N*)	19	54	67	45
Contributions of $100 or less (%)	17.3	27.6	22.7	32.5
Contributions of over $100 (%)	63.9	65.8	65.0	58.5
Goods and services (%)	17.1	6.1	10.5	7.1
Fund-raising functions (%)	1.7	0.5	1.8	1.8
$20 001–30 000				
Total revenue ($)	792 993	1 484 426	1 338 303	781 131
Candidates (*N*)	32	58	54	32
Contributions of $100 or less (%)	22.1	22.2	19.9	33.0
Contributions of over $100 (%)	69.3	69.8	65.7	55.8
Goods and services (%)	8.2	7.2	11.8	7.7
Fund-raising functions (%)	0.5	0.9	2.6	3.4
$30 001–40 000				
Total revenue ($)	2 601 079	3 331 316	1 755 156	335 929
Candidates (*N*)	74	95	50	10
Contributions of $100 or less (%)	21.2	18.6	15.9	33.6
Contributions of over $100 (%)	73.1	73.1	62.0	57.4
Goods and services (%)	5.1	7.8	20.4	7.2
Fund-raising functions (%)	0.6	0.4	1.7	1.7
$40 001–50 000				
Total revenue ($)	3 035 298	1 541 198	1 654 716	95 354
Candidates (*N*)	69	35	37	2
Contributions of $100 or less (%)	19.9	13.6	8.9	27.8
Contributions of over $100 (%)	75.3	78.5	75.6	70.5
Goods and services (%)	4.3	7.8	13.1	0.5
Fund-raising functions (%)	0.4	0.1	2.4	1.2
$50 001–60 000				
Total revenue ($)	2 373 760	978 490	427 338	273 384
Candidates (*N*)	44	18	8	5
Contributions of $100 or less (%)	20.1	15.8	7.6	23.0
Contributions of over $100 (%)	73.5	78.7	71.3	73.3
Goods and services (%)	5.7	3.7	18.1	2.5
Fund-raising functions (%)	0.7	1.8	3.0	1.3

Table 12.7 (cont'd)
Analysis of candidate revenues by party and amount of revenue, 1988 general election

Category	PC	Liberal	NDP	Other parties
$60 001–70 000				
Total revenue ($)	1 478 345	570 206	193 192	0
Candidates (N)	23	9	3	0
Contributions of $100 or less (%)	19.7	14.8	0.9	
Contributions of over $100 (%)	73.2	79.1	82.5	
Goods and services (%)	6.3	5.0	14.2	
Fund-raising functions (%)	0.8	1.1	2.4	
$70 001–80 000				
Total revenue ($)	884 354	219 879	70 332	0
Candidates (N)	12	3	1	0
Contributions of $100 or less (%)	14.2	6.9	0.4	
Contributions of over $100 (%)	80.7	89.9	91.4	
Goods and services (%)	4.4	3.0	3.2	
Fund-raising functions (%)	0.7	0.2	5.1	
$80 001–100 000				
Total revenue ($)	889 565	342 152	0	0
Candidates (N)	10	4	0	0
Contributions of $100 or less (%)	13.7	6.9		
Contributions of over $100 (%)	83.3	77.4		
Goods and services (%)	1.7	3.3		
Fund-raising functions (%)	1.3	12.3		
Over $100 000				
Total revenue ($)	1 027 088	226 259	0	0
Candidates (N)	9	2	0	0
Contributions of $100 or less (%)	14.3	7.7		
Contributions of over $100 (%)	82.9	90.8		
Goods and services (%)	2.2	1.6		
Fund-raising functions (%)	0.7	0		

Source: Tabulated from electronic data file provided by CEO that had 216 missing cases, 211 of which were candidates of "other" parties.

Table 12.8
Average level of total revenue, "election expenses" and personal expenses for candidates, by province, 1988 general election

Province and category	PC	Liberal	NDP
B.C. (*N* = 32)			
Total revenue	53 152	24 600	44 782
Election expenses	39 331	24 846	38 156
Personal expenses	2 606	1 225	1 304
Campaign surplus	11 215	(1 471)	5 322
Alberta (*N* = 26)			
Total revenue	44 949	16 273	20 421
Election expenses	35 603	17 466	21 162
Personal expenses	2 383	959	1 232
Campaign surplus	6 963	(2 178)	(1 973)
Saskatchewan (*N* = 14)			
Total revenue	51 285	19 412	40 495
Election expenses	44 356	19 960	42 626
Personal expenses	2 534	1 416	1 895
Campaign surplus	4 395	(1 964)	(4 026)
Manitoba (*N* = 14)			
Total revenue	31 973	26 396	17 215
Election expenses	38 131	28 842	24 381
Personal expenses	1 728	1 585	1 175
Campaign surplus	(7 886)	(4 031)	(8 341)
Ontario (*N* = 99)			
Total revenue	44 251	38 482	25 382
Election expenses	40 098	37 415	28 067
Personal expenses	1 672	1 362	1 097
Campaign surplus	2 481	(295)	(3 782)
Quebec (*N* = 75)			
Total revenue	43 820	35 735	14 071
Election expenses	42 474	37 486	17 053
Personal expenses	2 827	1 986	1 367
Campaign surplus	(1 481)	(3 737)	(4 349)
New Brunswick (*N* = 10)			
Total revenue	55 255	35 193	10 154
Election expenses	40 657	36 074	10 896
Personal expenses	2 609	1 153	1 129
Campaign surplus	11 989	(2 034)	(1 871)
P.E.I. (*N* = 4)			
Total revenue	35 809	35 802	6 426
Election expenses	36 121	33 461	5 003
Personal expenses	1 234	1 556	447
Campaign surplus	(1 546)	785	976

Table 12.8 (cont'd)

Average level of total revenue, "election expenses" and personal expenses for candidates, by province, 1988 general election

Province and category	PC	Liberal	NDP
Nova Scotia (*N* = 11)			
Total revenue	45 245	40 428	13 210
Election expenses	38 564	36 631	17 106
Personal expenses	1 772	1 047	343
Campaign surplus	1 979	2 750	(4 239)
Newfoundland (*N* = 7)			
Total revenue	55 647	35 622	15 846
Election expenses	42 016	35 178	17 901
Personal expenses	6 054	5 742	1 265
Campaign surplus	7 577	(5 298)	(3 320)
Yukon/N.W.T. (*N* = 3)			
Total revenue	35 391	33 412	27 773
Election expenses	33 516	28 413	32 340
Personal expenses	11 081	10 906	4 946
Campaign surplus	(9 206)	(5 907)	(9 513)
Canada (*N* = 295)			
Total revenue	45 397	32 647	23 075
Election expenses	40 217	32 803	24 766
Personal expenses	2 403	1 678	1 247
Campaign surplus	2 777	(1 834)	(2 938)

Source: Tabulated from Canada, Elections Canada (1988c).

Notes: Total revenue excludes reimbursement of part of candidates' "election expenses."
Campaign surplus = total revenue – election expenses – personal expenses.

Table 12.9
Total revenue raised by candidates ranked by total contributions, 1988 general election

Rank among all candidates based on total revenue generated	Total contributions received
1	130 626
50	66 615
100	55 648
150	50 035
200	45 361
250	42 261
300	39 899
350	37 393
400	35 314
450	33 153
500	31 272

Source: Tabulated from Canada, Elections Canada (1988c).

Table 12.10
Candidates by party ranked by amount of revenue raised, 1988 general election

Ranking	PC	Liberal	NDP	Other parties	Total
1–100	68	24	6	2[a]	100
101–200	50	23	22	5[b]	100
201–300	51	26	23	0	100
Total N	169	73	51	7	300
%	56.3	24.3	17.0	2.3	100

Source: Tabulated from Canada, Elections Canada (1988c).

[a]Two Christian Heritage party candidates.
[b]Three Christian Heritage party candidates and two Reform party candidates.

Table 12.11
Distribution of 100 candidates raising largest amount of revenue, 1988 general election

			Electoral result	
			Won	
Status	N	Lost	N	%
--------	---	------	---	---
Incumbent, cabinet minister[a]	28	3	25	89
Incumbent, government party MP	24	10	14	58
Incumbent, opposition party MP	15	1	14	93
Challenger	33	15	18	55
Total	100	29	71	71

Source: Tabulated from Canada, Elections Canada (1988c); and *Canadian Parliamentary Guide, 1988, 1990.*

[a]Held cabinet post or equivalent (e.g., Speaker) sometime during period 1984–88.

Table 12.12
Top 200 candidates by amount of revenue raised, by province and party, 1988 general election

Province	PC 1–100	PC 101–200	Liberal 1–100	Liberal 101–200	NDP 1–100	NDP 101–200	Other parties 1–100	Other parties 101–200	Total 1–100	Total 101–200	Total candidates
B.C. (N = 32)[a]	13	4	1	12	4	1	0	0	18	18	266
Alta. (N = 26)	8	0	0	0	0	1	0	3[b]	8	4	168
Sask. (N = 14)	3	4	1	0	1	4	0	0	5	8	57
Man. (N = 14)	1	2	1	0	0	0	0	0	2	2	86
Ont. (N = 99)	22	18	12	9	1	4	2[c]	2[c]	37	33	515
Que. (N = 75)	13	13	8	7	0	1	0	0	21	21	386
N.B. (N = 10)	4	2	0	1	0	0	0	0	4	3	43
P.E.I. (N = 4)	0	0	0	0	0	0	0	0	0	0	14
N.S. (N = 11)	2	3	0	4	0	0	0	0	2	7	47
Nfld. (N = 7)	2	4	1	0	0	0	0	0	3	4	23
Yukon/ N.W.T. (N = 3)	0	0	0	0	0	0	0	0	0	0	13
Total	68	50	24	23	6	22	2	5	100	100	1 578

Source: Tabulated from Canada, Elections Canada (1988c).

[a]Number of ridings in province.

[b]Two Reform Party and one Christian Heritage party.

[c]Both Christian Heritage party.

Table 12.13
Analysis of candidate revenues by place of finish, 1984 and 1988 general elections

	Winning candidates				Second place				Third place			
	Ridings[a] (N)		% of total		Ridings (N)		% of total		Ridings (N)		% of total	
	1988	1984	1988	1984	1988	1984	1988	1984	1988	1984	1988	1984
Most revenue	182	185	61.7	65.6	87	84	29.5	29.8	20	10	6.8	3.5
Second highest revenue	94	85	31.9	30.1	154	148	52.2	52.5	39	44	13.2	15.6
Third highest revenue	18	11	6.1	3.9	46	44	15.6	15.6	193	178	65.4	63.1

Sources: Canada, Bureau of Management Consulting (1985); and Canada, Government Consulting Group (1990).

Notes: The odds against winning were 16 to 1 in 1988 and 25 to 1 in 1984 if you obtained the third highest revenue in a riding.

[a]282 in 1984; 295 in 1988.

Table 12.14

Analysis of candidate revenues in Ontario, Quebec and British Columbia, 1988 general election
(thousands of dollars)

Sources of revenue	Ontario[a]				Quebec[b]				British Columbia[c]			
	PC	Liberal	NDP	Other parties	PC	Liberal	NDP	Other parties	PC	Liberal	NDP	Other parties
Individuals												
$	2 045	1 694	1 332	700	1 999	780	634	59	647	350	53	415
%	46.7	44.5	53.0	73.3	60.8	29.1	60.1	68.6	38.0	44.4	3.7	70.1
Corporations												
$	1 592	1 039	50	155	197	724	81	10	898	231	19	98
%	36.3	27.3	2.0	16.2	6.0	27.0	7.6	11.6	52.8	29.4	1.3	16.6
Governments												
$	1	4	1	—	2	5	—	6	—	—	5	—
%	—	0.1	—	—	0.1	0.2	—	7.0	—	—	0.3	—
Trade unions												
$	1	6	583	—	—	2	121	—	—	—	260	—
%	—	0.2	23.2	—	—	0.1	11.5	—	—	—	18.1	—

Political organizations											
$	72	619	340	28	414	322	53	4	70	41	272	14
%	1.6	16.2	13.5	2.9	12.6	12.0	5.0	4.7	4.1	5.2	19.0	2.4
Registered parties											
$	128	363	154	47	604	839	137	6	68	144	775	51
%	2.9	9.5	6.1	4.9	18.4	31.3	13.0	7.0	4.0	18.3	54.1	8.6
Other organizations											
$	7	13	6	8	54	5	5	—	3	14	10	—
%	0.2	0.3	0.2	0.8	1.6	0.2	0.5	—	0.2	1.8	0.7	—
Fund-raising functions											
$	34	71	48	18	16	3	25	2	14	7	37	74
%	0.8	1.9	1.9	1.9	0.5	0.1	2.4	2.3	0.8	0.9	2.6	12.5
Total											
$	4 381[d]	3 810	2 513	944	3 286	2 680	1 055	86	1 701	787	1 433	592
%	100[d]	100	100	100	100	100	100	100	100	100	100	100

Source: Tabulated from Canada, Elections Canada (1988c).

[a]Ninety-nine federal ridings.

[b]Seventy-five federal ridings.

[c]Thirty-two federal ridings.

[d]Totals in each category rounded to nearest $1000 and hence may not add.

Table 12.15

Expenditures reported by candidates, 1974 general election

	Total expenditures ($)	Average per candidate ($)	Number of candidates	
			Filing a return	Not filing a return
Party				
PC	4 215 180	19 425	217	47
Liberal	4 961 127	20 416	243	21
NDP	1 262 018	6 010	210	52
Social Credit	138 497	1 610	86	66

Source: Seidle (1980, 263).

Table 12.16

Analysis of candidates' "election expenses" by party, 1979, 1980, 1984 and 1988 general elections
(thousands of dollars)

Category	1979 PC	Lib.	NDP	Other parties	Total	1980 PC	Lib.	NDP	Other parties	Total	1984 PC	Lib.	NDP	Other parties	Total	1988 PC	Lib.	NDP	Other parties	Total
Advertising Print (non-electronic)																				
$	2 980	2 934	1 314	502	7 730	2 768	2 612	1 305	304	6 988	5 046	4 194	1 795	534	11 570	6 530	5 151	3 028	1 584	16 292
%	49.5	47.4	49.3	47.6	48.5	48.7	43.0	43.7	48.4	45.5	50.7	47.5	42.5	62.1	48.5	55.0	53.2	41.4	63.5	52.0
Radio and TV																				
$	639	579	165	136	1 519	755	794	373	90	2 013	867	945	357	98	2 266	933	707	385	192	2 216
%	10.6	9.4	6.2	12.9	9.5	13.3	13.1	12.5	14.3	13.1	8.7	10.7	8.4	11.4	9.5	7.9	7.3	5.3	7.7	7.1
Salaries and wages																				
$	531	711	498	118	1 858	395	696	544	82	1 718	555	773	850	17	2 195	565	764	1 583	74	2 986
%	8.8	11.5	18.7	11.2	11.7	7.0	11.5	18.2	13.1	11.2	5.6	8.7	20.1	2.0	9.2	4.8	7.9	21.7	3.0	9.5
Office expenses																				
$	993	1 031	474	137	2 635	1 036	1 069	540	70	2 715	2 249	1 743	916	129	5 037	2 826	2 082	1 643	425	6 976
%	16.5	16.7	17.8	13.0	16.5	18.2	17.6	18.1	11.1	17.7	22.6	19.7	21.7	15.0	21.1	23.8	21.5	22.5	17.0	22.3
Travel expenses																				
$	286	329	82	89	772	261	346	98	30	734	262	267	148	27	704	235	190	305	45	775
%	4.8	5.2	3.1	8.4	4.8	4.6	5.7	3.2	4.8	4.8	2.6	3.0	3.5	3.1	2.9	2.0	2.0	4.2	1.8	2.5

Table 12.16 (cont'd)

Analysis of candidates' "election expenses" by party, 1979, 1980, 1984 and 1988 general elections

(thousands of dollars)

Category	1979					1980					1984					1988				
	PC	Lib.	NDP	Other parties	Total	PC	Lib.	NDP	Other parties	Total	PC	Lib.	NDP	Other parties	Total	PC	Lib.	NDP	Other parties	Total
Other expenses																				
$	586	600	133	90	1 409	465	557	127	52	1 201	973	913	162	55	2 102	775	784	362	175	2 096
%	9.7	9.7	5.0	8.5	8.8	8.2	9.2	4.3	8.3	7.8	9.8	10.3	3.8	6.4	8.8	6.5	8.1	5.0	7.0	6.7
Total	6 016	6 186	2 665	1 055	15 922	5 680	6 074	2 987	628	15 369	9 952	8 835	4 227	860	23 874	11 864	9 677	7 306	2 494	31 341

Source: Tabulated from Canada, Elections Canada (1980b, 1981, 1984c, 1988c).

Note: Totals in each category rounded to nearest $1 000 and hence may not add.

Table 12.17
Analysis of candidates' average "election expenses," 1988 general election

Category	PC (N = 295)	Liberal (N = 295)	NDP (N = 295)	Other parties (N = 693)	All (N = 1 578)
Advertising					
Print (non-electronic)	22 136	17 459	10 264	2 286	10 324
Radio and TV	3 162	2 395	1 306	277	1 405
Salaries and wages	1 914	2 590	5 367	107	1 892
Office expenses	9 581	7 056	5 569	613	4 421
Travel expenses	797	644	1 034	64	491
Other expenses	2 628	2 658	1 228	252	1 328
Total "election expenses"	40 218	32 803	24 768	3 599	19 862
Average personal expenses	2 403	1 677	1 249	232	1 098

Source: Tabulated from Canada, Elections Canada (1988c).

Table 12.18

Average revenues and expenses by candidates in relation to percentage of statutory limit, 1988 general election

	PC		Liberal		NDP[b]	
	Average ($)	% total[a]	Average ($)	% total[a]	Average ($)	% total[a]
Candidates spending more than 90% of limit						
Revenues						
Individuals	23 526	48	14 823	34	11 131	27
Corporations	15 765	32	13 108	30	933	2
Governments	16	—	52	—	99	—
Trade unions	14	—	26	—	6 133	15
Political organizations	5 244	11	6 385	14	11 580	29
Registered parties	4 319	9	9 329	21	9 912	24
Other organizations	112	—	179	0.4	88	—
Fund-raising	397	1	201	0.5	738	2
Total	49 393	100	44 103	100	40 614	100
Expenses						
Radio and TV advertising	3 794	9	2 741	6	2 336	5
Other advertising	23 720	54	23 293	54	16 790	38
Salaries and wages	2 277	5	3 548	8	11 656	26
Office expenses	10 520	24	9 205	21	9 732	22
Travel expenses	850	2	711	2	1 868	4
Other expenses	3 074	7	3 914	9	1 954	4
Total	44 235	100	43 412	100	44 336	100
Candidates (N)	148		74		56	
Candidates spending 80–90% of limit						
Revenues						
Individuals	22 107	47	15 530	39	8 570	24
Corporations	17 501	37	11 631	29	770	2
Government	49	—	10	—	80	—
Trade unions	6	—	50	—	6 987	20
Political organizations	3 828	8	5 996	15	7 833	22
Registered parties	3 168	7	5 803	15	10 640	30
Other organizations	63	—	171	—	299	1
Fund-raising	261	1	254	1	587	2
Total	46 983	100	39 539	100	35 766	100

Table 12.18 (cont'd)
Average revenues and expenses by candidates in relation to percentage of statutory limit, 1988 general election

	PC		Liberal		NDP[b]	
	Average ($)	% total[a]	Average ($)	% total[a]	Average ($)	% total[a]
Expenses						
Radio and TV advertising	3 079	8	3 143	8	3 069	8
Other advertising	22 773	57	22 126	55	14 268	37
Salaries and wages	1 853	5	2 515	6	9 224	24
Office expenses	8 952	22	8 261	21	7 931	20
Travel expenses	972	2	666	2	1 927	5
Other expenses	2 422	6	3 344	8	2 414	6
Total	40 051	100	40 055	100	38 833	100
Candidates (*N*)	79		72		41	
Candidates spending 70–80% of limit						
Revenues						
Individual	16 586	40	13 525	49	9 625	29
Corporations	16 376	40	7 387	22	668	2
Government	5	—	0	—	0	—
Trade unions	0	—	47	—	6 300	19
Political organizations	5 443	13	6 794	20	6 928	21
Registered parties	765	2	6 257	18	8 835	27
Other organizations	1 885	5	42	—	125	—
Fund-raising	128	—	149	—	632	2
Total	41 188	100	34 201	100	33 113	100
Expenses						
Radio and TV advertising	2 510	7	1 963	6	1 293	4
Other advertising	19 769	55	18 360	52	14 904	42
Salaries and wages	1 210	3	4 057	12	7 482	21
Office expenses	9 316	26	7 302	21	8 615	24
Travel expenses	542	2	672	2	1 206	3
Other expenses	2 422	7	2 671	8	1 962	6
Total	35 769	100	35 025	100	35 462	100
Candidates (*N*)	35		38		24	

Table 12.18 (cont'd)
Average revenues and expenses by candidates in relation to percentage of statutory limit, 1988 general election

	PC		Liberal		NDP[b]	
	Average ($)	% total[a]	Average ($)	% total[a]	Average ($)	% total[a]
Candidates spending less than 70%						
Revenues						
Individuals	9 538	34	8 893	45	6 453	49
Corporations	11 017	39	4 875	25	476	4
Government	65	—	111	1	7	—
Trade unions	0	—	23	—	1 928	15
Political organizations	3 462	12	2 546	13	1 680	13
Registered parties	3 740	13	3 024	15	2 165	16
Other organizations	123	—	108	1	61	1
Fund-raising	189	1	129	1	378	3
Total	28 134	100	19 709	100	13 148	100
Expenses						
Radio and TV advertising	1 221	5	1 827	9	568	4
Other advertising	16 017	59	10 236	51	6 656	48
Salaries and wages	1 179	4	1 499	7	2 167	16
Office expenses	7 163	26	4 758	24	3 291	24
Travel expenses	411	2	577	3	538	4
Other expenses	1 339	5	1 371	7	620	4
Total	27 330	100	20 268	100	13 840	100
Candidates (N)	33		111		172	

Source: Tabulated from Canada, Elections Canada (1988c).

[a]Totals may be affected by rounding.

[b]Two NDP candidates did not file return before volume was published.

Table 12.19
Candidates' "election expenses" on aggregate basis as percentage of statutory limit, 1979, 1980, 1984 and 1988 general elections

Party	1979	1980	1984	1988
PC	77.6	72.4	89.0	85.8
Liberal	79.8	77.5	79.0	70.0
NDP	34.4	38.4	37.8	52.8
Other parties[a]	6.5	3.4	3.6	7.7

Source: Canada, Elections Canada (1980b, 1981, 1984c, 1988c).

[a]Five hundred and eighty-one candidates in 1979, 653 in 1980, 603 in 1984 and 693 in 1988.

Table 12.19a
Candidates' "election expenses" as percentage of statutory limit, by province, 1979, 1980, 1984 and 1988 general elections

Party and year	B.C.	Alta.	Sask.	Man.	Ont.	Que.	N.B.	P.E.I.	N.S.	Nfld.	Yukon/ N.W.T.	Canada
PC												
1988	82	74	94	83	86	90	91	97	85	86	75	86
1984	89	70	89	87	90	92	93	94	92	94	67	89
1980	84	70	87	83	86	42	89	91	90	82	60	72
1979	83	79	88	79	84	65	84	94	86	58	66	78
Liberal												
1988	52	36	42	63	80	79	81	90	81	72	64	70
1984	55	56	71	70	87	83	89	94	90	89	80	79
1980	69	59	67	66	86	75	94	88	84	89	63	78
1979	74	65	75	66	80	87	90	86	85	79	74	80
NDP												
1988	80	44	90	53	60	36	24	13	38	37	73	53
1984	79	17	82	65	50	05	34	05	38	03	53	38
1980	73	16	83	63	51	05	31	10	44	40	51	38
1979	67	09	81	58	48	04	09	10	36	53	45	35

Source: Canada, Bureau of Management Consulting (1985); and Canada, Government Consulting Group (1990); Seidle and Paltiel (1981).

Table 12.20

"Election expenses" as percentage of statutory limit, by party, 1979, 1980 and 1988 general elections

% of statutory limit	1979 PC	1979 Liberal	1979 NDP	1980 PC	1980 Liberal	1980 NDP	1988 PC	1988 Liberal	1988 NDP
90–100									
N	86	80	9	104	96	13	148	74	56
%	30.5	28.4	3.2	36.9	34.0	4.6	50.2	25.1	19.1
80–90									
N	80	75	33	64	69	33	79	72	41
%	28.4	26.6	11.7	22.7	24.5	11.8	26.8	24.4	14.0
79–80									
N	50	50	15	31	36	21	35	38	24
%	17.7	17.7	5.3	11.0	12.8	7.5	11.9	12.9	8.2
< 70									
N	65	67	225	83	81	213	33	111	172
%	23.0	23.8	79.8	29.4	28.7	76.1	11.2	37.6	58.7
Total	282	282	282	282	282	2801	295	295	2932

Sources: Table 12.15 and Canada, Elections Canada (1983, 6).

[a]NDP did not run full slate in 1980.

[b]Electronic version of CEO (1989b) reports only 293 candidates, but NDP ran 295.

Table 12.21
Distribution of candidates' personal expenses, by party and by province, 1988 general election

Amount	PC N	PC %	Liberal N	Liberal %	NDP N	NDP %	Other parties N	Other parties %	Total N	Total %
Under $500	58	19.7	82	27.9	110	37.3	598	86.7	848	53.9
$501–1 000	28	9.5	47	16.0	55	18.6	42	6.1	172	10.9
$1 001–1 500	45	15.3	46	15.7	34	11.5	25	3.6	150	9.5
$1 501–2 000	40	13.5	34	11.6	37	12.5	14	2.0	125	7.9
$2 001–3 000	47	15.9	37	12.6	29	9.8	4	0.6	117	7.4
$3 001–5 000	38	12.9	32	10.9	22	7.5	6	0.9	98	6.2
$5 001–10 000	34	11.5	13	4.4	8	2.7	1	0.1	56	3.6
Over $10 000	5	1.7	3	1.0	0	0	0	0	8	0.5
Total	295	100.0	294	100.0	295	100.0	690	100.0	1574	100.0

Province of those with personal expenses over $3 000	PC	Liberal	NDP	Other parties	Total
B.C. (*N* = 32)	10	3	2	0	15
Alberta (*N* = 26)	6	5	1	0	12
Saskatchewan (*N* = 14)	6	1	4	4	15
Manitoba (*N* = 14)	2	3	2	0	7
Ontario (*N* = 99)	12	11	8	1	32
Quebec (*N* = 75)	28	19	9	1	57
New Brunswick (*N* = 10)	4	1	0	0	5
P.E.I. (*N* = 4)	4	2	2	1	9
Nova Scotia (*N* = 11)	2	1	0	0	3
Newfoundland (*N* = 7)	2	2	2	0	6
Yukon/N.W.T. (*N* = 3)	0	0	0	0	0
Total	76	48	30	7	161

Source: Tabulated from electronic data file no. 1 provided by CEO.

Table 12.22
Distribution of "other expenses" of 721 candidates who also had a surplus, 1988 general election

Amount	PC	Liberal	NDP	Other parties	Total
Under $1 000	48	69	69	73	259
1 001–3 000	38	61	53	13	165
3 001–5 000	36	35	25	2	98
5 001–7 000	21	25	10	1	57
7 001–10 000	28	14	4	1	47
10 001–15 000	30	12	3	0	45
15 001–20 000	11	8	0	1	20
20 001–25 000	8	3	1	0	12
25 001–40 000	11	3	0	0	14
Over $40 000	2	2	0	0	4
Total	233	232	165	91	721
Average "other expenses"[a] ($)	7 496	4 486	1 946	939	4 430
Total "other expenses"[a] ($)	1 746 479	1 040 712	321 118	85 433	3 193 742
Candidates for whom no estimate is available	62	62	130	599[b]	853
Total candidates	295	294[c]	295	690	1 574

Source: Tabulated from electronic data file no. 1 provided by CEO.

Notes: CEO truncates calculation of "other expenses" at point where it is clear candidate has a deficit.

[a]Only for candidates who *also* had a surplus.

[b]For most of these, "other expenses" would be zero or under $1 000.

[c]One candidate withdrew shortly before election day but remained on ballot.

Table 12.23
Average level of "other expenses" of 721 candidates who also had a surplus, by province, 1988 general election

Province	PC $	PC N	Liberal $	Liberal N	NDP $	NDP N	Other parties $	Other parties N
B.C. (N = 32)[a]	9 527	31	1 612	25	3 766	30	445	8
Alberta (N = 26)	4 026	25	902	13	2 015	16	985	25
Saskatchewan (N = 14)	1 814	14	1 494	10	1 973	13	200	1
Manitoba (N = 14)	8 456	8	1 916	12	1 037	6	109	4
Ontario (N = 99)	4 352	81	6 484	85	1 725	62	1 529	31
Quebec (N = 75)	15 666	41	4 866	57	1 049	27	253	2
New Brunswick (N = 10)	7 277	10	4 166	9	0	0	—	—
P.E.I. (N = 4)	2 663	4	1 027	4	400	1	—	—
Nova Scotia (N = 11)	6 022	10	6 109	11	640	5	390	3
Newfoundland (N = 7)	15 617	6	3 110	4	1 132	3	—	—
Yukon/N.W.T. (N = 3)	9 655	2	497	2	884	2	—	—

Source: Tabulated from electronic data file no. 1 provided by CEO.

Notes: Level calculated excluding cases where surplus was equal to zero and "other expenses" was zero or negative.

[a]Total number of federal ridings in province.

[b]Number of candidates for whom "other expenses" were computed. Note "other expenses" could be derived only for those candidates who also had a surplus.

Table 12.24
Distribution of total "other expenses" of 277 candidates ("big spenders"), by party, 1988 general election

Amount	PC	Liberal	NDP	CHP	Total
Under $2000	12	8	16	10	46
$2 001–4 000	10	5	10	3	28
$4 001–7 000	20	10	9	1	40
$7 001–10 000	14	14	1	0	29
$10 001–15 000	44	14	2	0	60
$15 001–20 000	25	9	1	0	35
$20 001–30 000	20	5	0	0	25
$30 001–50 000	7	4	0	0	11
Over $50 000	3	0	0	0	3
Total	155	69	39	14	277
Average	14 208	11 449	3 678	1 470	11 394

Source: Tabulated from electronic data file no. 2 ("big spenders" in terms of "other expenses"). See discussion in text.

Notes: Candidates are those whose "estimated other expenses" exceeded $10 000 before capital items and transfers were excluded.

CHP = Christian Heritage party.

Table 12.25

Details of "other expenses" of 277 candidates ("big spenders"), 1988 general election
(dollars)

Category	PC	Liberal	NDP	CHP	Total
Pre-writ expenses	2 554	2 276	504	445	2 090
Campaign period expenses (total)	8 205	6 772	2 117	602	6 607
Unused materials	573	387	81	169	437
Fund-raising costs	841	1 403	681	39	918
Election-day expenses	427	378	84	0	345
Polling/research	866	948	35	0	726
Poll agents	4 461	2 594	0	0	3 143
Volunteers' expenses	131	9	9	0	77
Candidates' wages	66	113	1 136	0	225
Other	840	940	91	395	737
Post-election day expenses (total)	3 449	2 400	1 057	422	2 698
Office expenses	551	249	153	158	400
Bank charges	124	56	195	3	111
Victory party	1 918	1 434	638	192	1 564
Contracts	106	32	16	51	72
Other post-election day expenses	690	629	55	19	551
Total other expenses	14 208	11 449	3 678	1 470	11 394
Candidates (N)	155	69	39	14	277

Source: Tabulated from electronic data file no. 2 ("big spenders" in terms of "other expenses"). See discussion in text.

Notes: Average expenditure in each category. Candidates are those whose "estimated other expenses" exceeded $10 000 before capital items and transfers were excluded.

CHP = Christian Heritage party.

Table 12.26
"Other expenses" of 277 candidates ("big spenders"), by party and by province, 1988 general election

Party and province	Candidates (*N*)	Pre-writ ($)	During campaign period ($)	Post-election day ($)	Total ($)
PC					
British Columbia	17	4 299	5 051	4 728	14 077
Alberta	7	3 576	1 832	2 702	6 461
Saskatchewan	5	96	2 142	1 890	4 128
Manitoba	7	6 497	5 973	3 011	15 482
Ontario	36	4 961	4 057	4 152	13 164
Quebec	65	1 025	12 821	3 201	17 047
New Brunswick	6	0	5 113	1 555	6 668
Nova Scotia	5	118	11 602	1 772	13 491
Newfoundland	6	698	10 322	4 710	15 730
Yukon/N.W.T.	1	1 808	2 237	837	4 882
Total	155	2 554	8 205	3 449	14 208
Liberal					
British Columbia	2	5 123	232	2 594	7 949
Manitoba	3	1 461	1 350	874	3 685
Ontario	34	4 030	5 756	2 877	12 664
Quebec	20	160	10 738	2 293	13 191
New Brunswick	3	0	3 338	391	3 729
Nova Scotia	4	62	8 870	1 382	10 313
Newfoundland	2	723	1 446	2 846	5 015
Yukon/N.W.T.	1	520	3 916	1 721	6 157
Total	69	2 276	6 772	2 400	11 449
NDP					
British Columbia	7	192	2 656	2 176	5 025
Alberta	2	4 727	1 609	1 170	7 505
Saskatchewan	2	219	952	520	1 690
Manitoba	6	258	281	1 094	1 633
Ontario	19	351	3 002	675	4 028
Quebec	1	0	0	885	885
Nova Scotia	1	203	0	1 074	1 277
Newfoundland	1	0	129	1 264	1 393
Total	39	504	2 117	1 057	3 678

Table 12.26 (cont'd)
"Other expenses" of 277 candidates ("big spenders"), by party and by province, 1988 general election

Party and province	Candidates (N)	Pre-writ ($)	During campaign period ($)	Post-election day ($)	Total ($)
CHP					
British Columbia	3	0	12	488	500
Alberta	3	745	1 985	184	2 914
Ontario	8	500	305	487	1 292
Total	14	445	602	422	1 470
Average all parties	277	2 065	6 697	2 631	11 393
Total "other expenses"		578 816	1 830 029	747 385	3 156 230

Source: Tabulated from electronic data file no. 2 ("big spenders" in terms of "other expenses"). See discussion in text.

Notes: Average expenditure in each category. Candidates are those whose "estimated other expenses" exceeded $10 000 before capital items and transfers were excluded.

CHP = Christian Heritage party.

Table 12.27
Distribution of pre-writ expenses of 277 candidates ("big spenders"), by party, 1988 general election

Amount	PC	Liberal	NDP	Other parties	Total
$0	65	34	23	11	133
$1–2 000	53	18	14	1	86
$2 001–4 000	10	5	1	2	18
$4 001–7 000	8	6	0	0	14
$7 001–10 000	7	3	1	0	11
$10 001–15 000	7	0	0	0	7
$15 001–20 000	2	1	0	0	3
Over $20 000	3	2	0	0	5
Total	155	69	39	14	277

Source: Tabulated from electronic data file no. 2 ("big spenders" in terms of "other expenses"). See discussion in text.

Notes: Included in "other expenses" are pre-writ expenses made prior to day writs of election were issued (1 October 1988) and paid out of contributions eligible for income-tax credit. Candidates are those whose "estimated other expenses" exceeded $10 000 before capital items and transfers were excluded.

Table 12.28
Distribution of "other expenses" of 277 candidates ("big spenders")
during campaign period,1988 general election

Amount	PC	Liberal	NDP	Other parties	Total
Under $2000	36	15	25	13	89
$2 001–4 000	14	16	9	0	39
$4 001–7 000	24	7	3	1	35
$7 001–10 000	25	13	1	0	39
$10 000–15 000	34	12	0	0	46
$15 001–20 000	12	3	1	0	16
$20 001–30 000	9	3	0	0	12
Over $30 000	1	0	0	0	1
Total	155	69	39	14	277

Source: Tabulated from electronic data file no. 2 ("big spenders" in terms of "other expenses"). See discussion in text.

Notes: "Other expenses" include outlays made between day writs were issued (1 October 1988) and voting day (21 November 1988) and paid out of contributions eligible for income-tax credit. Candidates are those whose "estimated other expenses" exceeded $10 000 before capital items and transfers were excluded.

Table 12.29
Distribution of post-voting day expenses of 277 candidates ("big spenders"), by party, 1988 general election

Amount	PC	Liberal	NDP	Other parties	Total
$0	5	9	3	2	19
$1–2 000	70	33	30	12	145
$2 001–4 000	41	14	5	0	60
$4 001–7 000	22	9	1	0	32
$7 001–10 000	7	2	0	0	9
$10 001–15 000	6	1	0	0	7
$15 001–20 000	3	1	0	0	4
Over $20 000	1	0	0	0	1
Total	155	69	39	14	277

Source: Tabulated from electronic data file no. 2 ("big spenders" in terms of "other expenses"). See discussion in text.

Notes: "Other expenses" include post-voting day expenses made after voting day (21 November 1988) and paid out of contributions eligible for income-tax credit. Candidates are those whose "estimated other expenses" exceeded $10 000 before capital items and transfers were excluded.

Table 12.30
Number of candidates eligible for reimbursement of "election expenses" by federal government, 1980, 1984 and 1988 general elections

Party	1980 N	1980 %	1984 N	1984 %	1988 N	1988 %
PC	215/282	76.2	282/282	100	293/295	99.3
Liberal	275/282	97.5	238/282	84.4	264/294	89.8
NDP	152/280	54.3	140/282	49.6	170/295	57.6
Social Credit	8/81	9.9	0/51	0	——	—
Confederation of Regions Western	——	—	3/55	5.5	0/51	0
Reform Party	——	—	——	—	11/72	15.3
Independent/no affiliation	0/111	0	1/84	1.2	1/154	0.6
Other parties	0/461	0	0/413	0	0/413	0
Total	650/1 497	43.4	664/1 449	45.8	739/1 574	46.95

Source: Canada, Elections Canada (1984d, 71; 1989a, 60)

Table 12.31

Number of candidates for each party receiving various minimum percentages of vote, 1988 general election

| | Percentage | | | | Candidates |
Party	15	12.5	10	5	(N)
PC	293	295	295	295	295
Liberal	264	275	287	294	295
NDP	170	209	245	292	295
Christian Heritage	0	0	0	11	63
Confederation of Regions Western	0	0	3	7	52
Libertarian	0	0	0	1	88
Reform	11	18	25	39	72
Rhino	0	0	0	1	74
Independent	1	1	1	1	154
No affiliation	0	0	0	1	186
Total	739	798	856	942	1 574

Source: Frederick B. Slattery, Elections Canada, presentation to Royal Commission on Electoral Reform and Party Financing, 1990.

Table 12.32

Surplus (deficit) of candidates before and after reimbursement, 1988 general election
(thousands of dollars)

Party	Total revenue (TR)	Election expenses (EE)	Personal expenses (PE)	Other expenses (OE)[a]	Campaign surplus (deficit)[b] (CS)	Reimburse- ment (R)	Surplus (S)[c]
PC	13 392	11 864	709	2 236	(1 417)	6 056	4 639
Liberal	9 631	9 677	495	1 137	(1 678)	4 656	2 978
NDP	6 807	7 306	368	232	(1 099)	2 839	1 740
Total	29 830	28 847	1 572	3 605	(4 194)	13 551	9 357[d]

Sources: Canada, Elections Canada (1988c); and data provided by Frederick B. Slattery, Elections Canada.

[a]"Other expenses" are not publicly reported by CEO. Figures here were derived from those candidates with a surplus, using formula OE = TR – EE – PE + R – S.

[b]CS = TR – EE – PE – OE

[c]S = CS + R

[d]CEO stated total surplus of *all* candidates was $9.61 million.

Table 12.33
Analysis of candidates' surplus, by party, 1988 general election

Party	Candidates (N)	Number reporting a surplus	Number receiving reimbursement[a]	Percentage reporting a surplus	Total surplus[b] reported ($000)	Average amount of surplus reported[c]
PC	295	231	230	78	4 639	20 080
Liberal	295[c]	234	220	79	2 978	12 727
NDP	295	167	143	57	1 740	10 421
Reform	72	21	11	29	140	6 650
Christian Heritage	63	31	0	49	104	3 368
Confederation of Regions Western	52	9	0	17	2.4	262
Communist	52	8	0	15	1.8	223
Green	68	9	0	13	1.3	143
Libertarian	88	8	0	9	1.9	242
Social Credit	9	1	0	11	—	81
Rhino	74	0	0	0	—	—
Party for the Commonwealth	61	0	0	0	—	—
Independent	154	4	0	3	—	63

Source: Data provided by Frederick B. Slattery, Elections Canada.

[a]Number of candidates reporting surplus who *also* received reimbursement.

[b]Surplus = Total revenue – election expenses – personal expenses – other expenses + reimbursement from federal government.

[c]Only for those candidates reporting surplus. Amounts may vary slightly due to rounding.

[d]Two hundred and ninety-five names appeared on ballot but one candidate withdrew from election.

Table 12.34

Average size of surplus after "other expenses" for candidates, by party and by province, 1988 general election

Province	PC		Liberal		NDP		Other parties	
	$	N	$	N	$	N	$	N
B.C. (N = 32)[a]	22 578	31[b]	10 583	25[b]	19 340	30[b]	763	25
Alberta (N = 26)	21 634	25	5 851	13	8 862	16	5 666	25
Saskatchewan (N = 14)	25 061	14	8 565	10	16 705	13	92	1
Manitoba (N = 14)	9 558	8	11 123	12	7 767	6	286	4
Ontario (N = 99)	22 029	81	13 558	85	9 271	62	2 696	31
Quebec (N = 75)	13 726	42	14 557	57	5 329	27	190	1
New Brunswick (N = 10)	25 556	10	13 748	9	0	0	—	—
P.E.I. (N = 4)	13 841	4	17 171	4	1 050	1	—	—
Nova Scotia (N = 11)	19 418	10	14 899	11	1 754	5	1 273	3
Newfoundland (N = 7)	14 656	6	16 388	4	2 568	3	—	—
Yukon/N.W.T. (N = 3)	14 084	2	3 989	2	7 641	2	—	—

Source: Tabulated from electronic data file provided by Frederick B. Slattery, Elections Canada.

Notes: Surplus = Total revenue – election expenses – personal expenses – other expenses + reimbursement. Table includes only candidates with surplus.

[a]Total number of ridings in province. All three parties ran candidates in all ridings in all provinces.
[b]Only for those candidates reporting surplus.

Table 12.35
Candidates reporting surplus greater than $40 000 after "other expenses," 1988 general election

Name	Party	Riding	Status[a]	% of limit spent	Total revenue (TR)	Election expenses (EE)	Personal expenses (PE)	Other expenses (OE)[i]	Reimbursement (R)	Total surplus (TR-EE-PE-OE+R)	PE/EE (%)	OE/EE (%)
Larry Schneider	PC	Regina–Wascana (Sask.)[b]	C-W[g]	93.1	124 788	40 098	2 415	7 250	21 258	96 283	6.0	18.1
Barbara McDougall	PC	St. Paul's (Ont.)	INC-CM-W	98.8	130 626	45 346	2 020	14 874	22 959	91 345	4.5	32.8
Jim Peterson	Lib.	Willowdale (Ont.)	C-W	87.1	112 188	39 861	2 596	2 696	20 661	87 696	6.5	6.8
Paul Dick	PC	Lanark–Carleton (Ont.)	INC-CM-W	88.9	105 989	44 086	4 288	(762)[j]	24 188	82 565	9.7	1.7
Jim Kelleher	PC	Sault Ste. Marie (Ont.)	INC-CM-L	94.4	110 409	40 538	0	10 096	20 134	79 909	0	24.9
Gerry St. Germain	PC	Mission–Coquitlam (B.C.)[b]	INC-CM-L	86.6	123 427	38 691	5 362	22 911	21 385	77 848	13.9	59.2
Gerry G.S. Merrithew	PC	Saint John (N.B.)	INC-CM-W	91.8	108 015	39 738	3 280	9 660	21 510	76 847	8.3	24.3
Michael Wilson	PC	Etobicoke–Centre (Ont.)	INC-CM-W	89.9	105 568	40 501	1 264	7 216	19 434	76 021	3.1	17.8
Paul Martin	Lib.	Lasalle–Émard (Que.)[b]	C-W[e]	83.8	114 070	39 415	1 039	17 956	19 853	75 513	2.6	45.6
David MacDonald	PC	Rosedale (Ont.)	C-W[f]	87.4	89 275	41 945	6 984	(84)[j]	21 601	62 031	16.7	0.2
Stewart MacInnes	PC	Halifax (N.S.)	INC-CM-L	92.4	87 093	44 228	1 992	9 192	22 475	54 156	4.5	20.8
John A. Fraser	PC	Vancouver South (B.C.)	INC-CM-W[g]	81.5	101 770	37 768	5 111	22 368	17 633	54 156	13.5	59.2
Perrin Beatty	PC	Wellington–Grey–Dufferin–Simcoe (Ont.)[b]	INC-CM-W	89.7	83 617	42 919	1 820	10 887	22 371	50 362	4.2	25.4
Lucien Bouchard	PC	Lac-Saint-Jean (Que.)	INC-CM-W	73.0	82 558	37 722	7 172	12 367	22 448	47 745	19.0	32.8
Terry Clifford	PC	London–Middlesex (Ont.)	INC-GMP-W	96.3	76 050	44 845	2 223	4 447	22 535	47 070	5.0	9.9
Dennis H. Cochrane	PC	Moncton (N.B.)	INC-GMP-L	86.2	73 334	39 796	3 338	4 988	20 530	45 742	8.4	12.5
Raymond Garneau	Lib.	Ahuntsic (Que.)[c]	INC-OPP-L	97.7	82 997	45 688	1 200	15 206	23 380	44 283	2.6	33.3
Ralph Goodale	Lib.	Regina–Wascana (Sask.)[b]	C-L[h]	91.9	64 290	39 553	608	1	19 960	44 088	1.5	0
Joe Clark	PC	Yellowhead (Alta.)	INC-CM-W	87.7	69 797	47 001	7 306	(1 348)[j]	26 792	43 630	15.5	2.9
Sergio Marchi	Lib.	York West (Ont.)	INC-OPP-W	86.5	81 244	36 188	1 005	18 701	17 635	42 985	2.8	51.7

Table 12.35 (cont'd)
Candidates reporting surplus greater than $40 000 after "other expenses," 1988 general election

Name	Party	Riding	Status[a]	% of limit spent	Total revenue (TR)	Election expenses (EE)	Personal expenses (PE)	Other expenses (OE)[i]	Reimbursement (R)	Total surplus (TR-EE-PE-OE+R)	PE/EE (%)	OE/EE (%)
Jim Edwards	PC	Edmonton Southwest (Alta.)[b]	INC-GMP-W	83.1	67 456	40 146	558	3 932	19 911	42 731	1.4	10.0
Lee Richardson	PC	Calgary Southeast (Alta.)[b]	C-W	68.4	72 820	33 064	3 576	8 108	14 272	42 344	10.8	24.5
John Turner	Lib.	Vancouver Quadra (B.C.)	INC-OPP-W	86.8	66 777	40 529	0	4 637	20 202	41 813	0	11.4
Don Mazankowski	PC	Vegreville (Alta.)	INC-CM-W	74.9	60 872	36 407	2 538	(34)[j]	19 473	41 434	7.0	0.09
Jean Corbeil	PC	Anjou–Rivière-des-Prairies (Que.)	C-W	89.4	99 289	43 927	2 699	34 025	23 314	41 952	6.1	77.5
Harvie Andre	PC	Calgary Centre (Alta.)	INC-CM-W	58.0	66 313	28 614	3 824	6 578	14 064	41 361	13.4	23.0
Frank Oberle	PC	Prince George–Peace River (B.C.)	INC-CM-W	91.2	74 480	47 758	10 159	1 807	26 180	40 936	21.3	3.8

Source: Tabulated from data provided by Frederick B. Slattery, Elections Canada; and *Canadian Parliamentary Guide, 1988, 1990.*

[a]Key for status:
GMP = MP in governing party between 1984 and 1988.
INC = Incumbent in 1988 election.
CM = Held cabinet position, or equivalent, between 1984 and 1988.
C = Challenger.

OPP = Opposition.
W = Won seat.
L = Lost seat.

[b]Boundary change resulted in new riding or new riding name.

[c]Garneau was sitting member for Laval-des-Rapides but lost seat in new riding Ahuntsic (Île-de-Montréal–Île-Jésus). Also elected to Quebec Legislature 1970, 1973, 1976.

[d]Merrithew was member of provincial legislature 1972, 1978 and 1982. First elected to House of Commons in 1984.

[e]Martin is son of late prominent Liberal Paul Martin, Sr., and ran for Liberal leadership in 1990.

[f]MacDonald was elected to House in 1965, 1968, 1972, 1974 and 1979 and defeated in 1980. He did not run in 1984 and was made ambassador to Ethiopia in 1986. Re-elected in 1988.

[g]Fraser resigned from Privy Council in 1985 and was elected Speaker of the House in 1986.

[h]New riding, no sitting member.

[i]Campaign expense tabulated from CEO formula: Surplus = Contributions – election expenses – personal expenses – "other" expenses + reimbursement. All information provided by CEO except campaign expense, which was tabulated from other data.

[j]Anomalies being checked by CEO.

Table 12.36
Distribution of "post-reimbursement campaign surplus" (deficit) (before "other expenses") for candidates, 1988 general election

Amount of surplus (deficit)[a]	PC	Liberal	NDP	Other parties	Total
Deficit	20	32	88	425[b]	565
$1–3 000	14	23	59	228	106
$3 001–7 000	17	35	33	21	78
$7 001–10 000	17	30	27	4	78
$10 001–15 000	36	63	27	6	132
$15 001–20 000	43	51	20	3	117
$20 001–30 000	75	32	37	2	146
$30 001–40 000	30	15	3	1	49
$40 001–60 000	26	9	1	0	36
Over $60 000	17	4	0	0	21
Total candidates	295	294	295	690	1 574
Sum of Post-reimbursement campaign deficits ($)	98 819	186 494	285 419	238 522	809 254
Post-reimbursement campaign surpluses ($)	6 922 757	4 227 751	2 192 975	426 657	13 770 140
Average Post-reimbursement campaign deficit ($)	4 941	5 828	3 243	561	1 432
Post-reimbursement campaign surplus ($)	25 174	16 136	10 594	1 610	13 647

Source: Tabulated from electronic data file no. 1 provided by CEO.

[a]Campaign post-reimbursement surplus or deficit = Total revenue + reimbursement – election expenses – personal expenses; therefore omits "other expenses."
[b]Includes 245 candidates who broke even, i.e., surplus or deficit = 0.

Table 12.37
**Size of "post-reimbursement campaign deficit" (before "other expenses")
for candidates, 1988 general election**

Amount of deficit	PC	Liberal	NDP	Other parties	Total
Under $500	0	6	20	367[a]	393
$501–1 000	1	4	11	14	30
$1 001–2 000	5	3	11	13	32
$2 001–5 000	7	6	27	18	58
$5 001–7 000	3	6	7	4	20
$7 001–10 000	1	2	6	6	15
$10 001–15 000	1	1	4	2	8
Over $15 000	2	4	2	1	9
Total	20	32	88	425	565
Candidates with surplus (*N*)	275	262	207	265	1 009
Total candidates	295	294	295	690	1 574

Source: Tabulated from electronic data file no. 1 provided by CEO.

[a]Includes 244 candidates who broke even, i.e., surplus or deficit = 0.

Table 12.38
Distribution of surplus (deficit) (after "other expenses") for candidates, 1988 general election

Amount of surplus (deficit)[a]	PC	Liberal	NDP	Other parties	Total
Deficit[b]	62	60	129	598	849
$1–3 000	17	28	38	69	152
$3 001–7 000	30	43	29	14	116
$7 001–10 000	22	33	21	0	76
$10 001–15 000	37	65	30	5	137
$15 001–20 000	41	30	26	2	99
$20 001–30 000	41	24	18	2	85
$30 001–40 000	24	5	4	0	33
$40 001–60 000	13	4	0	0	17
$over $60 000	8	2	0	0	10
Total candidates	295	294	295	690	1574
Amount of surplus	4 650 071	2 971 769	1 737 242	249 727	9 608 809
Average surplus (excluding deficits)	19 957	12 809	10 529	2 744	13 327

Source: Tabulated from electronic data file no. 1 provided by CEO.

[a]Surplus (deficit) = Total revenue + reimbursement – election expenses – personal expenses – other expenses.

[b]Size of deficit cannot be computed because CEO truncates calculation of "other expenses" when it is clear candidate will have a deficit.

Table 13.1
Expenditures on selected federal leadership campaigns, 1967 to 1990

1967: Robert Stanfield, Progressive Conservative party, $150 000[a]

1968: Pierre Trudeau, Liberal party, about $300 000[b]

1976: Progressive Conservative party[c]
      Joe Clark (winner), $168 353
      Claude Wagner (runner-up) $266 538
      Brian Mulroney, $343 000 est.
      Sinclair Stevens, $294 106
      Paul Hellyer, $287 788
      Flora MacDonald, $152 704
      John Fraser, $116 107

1983: Progressive Conservative party[d]
      Brian Mulroney (winner), $1 million ($750 000–$2 million)[e]
      Joe Clark (runner-up), $1 million ($850 000)[f]
      John Crosbie, $1 million ($1.5 million)[f]
      David Crombie, $325 000
      Peter Pocklington, $730 000 (plus $235 000 on a precampaign speaking tour)

1984: Liberal party[g]
      John Turner (winner), $1.6 million
      Jean Chrétien (runner-up), $1.5 million
      Donald Johnston, between $900 000 and $1 million
      John Roberts, $550 000
      Mark MacGuigan, $475 000
      John Munro, $625 000
      Eugene Whelan, $160 000

1989: New Democratic Party[h]
      Audrey McLaughlin (winner), $128 576
      David Barrett, $113 987
      Howard McCurdy, $78 312
      Steven Langdon, $52 462
      Simon de Jong, $42 517
      Ian Waddell, $39 256
      Roger Lagasse, $11 892

1990: Liberal party[f]
      Jean Chrétien (winner), $2 446 000
      Paul Martin (runner-up), $2 372 000
      Sheila Copps, $806 000
      Thomas Wappel, $143 000
      John Nunziata, $166 000
      Clifford Lincoln, under $100 000

Sources:

[a]*Maclean's* (28 June 1976, 17).
[b]Ibid.
[c]Ibid.
[d]*Maclean's* (3 October 1983, 16).
[e]Ontario, Commission (1986, 84).
[f]*Globe and Mail* (8 November 1990, A1, A4).
[g]*Globe and Mail* (31 August 1984, 5); and *Globe and Mail* (18 December 1984, 5).
[h]New Democratic Party, letter to chairman, Royal Commission on Electoral Reform and Party Financing, 30 November 1990.

NOTES

This study was completed in April 1992.

CHAPTER 1 INTRODUCTION

1. Very little party money is spent on research, other than that spent on public-opinion polling. Obviously, the latter focuses on the perception of problems and the acceptability of various "solutions." Because of its high and rising cost, the three main parties were able to convince the CEO that polling was not an "election expense" (hence not subject to the statutory limit). Rather, expenditures on polling were excluded from "election expenses" because they were a form of "research" and hence deemed not to be *directly* promoting the party or a candidate (see chap. 13).

2. For example, for the 1990 race for the leadership of the Liberal party, the candidates spent $6 million, including $608 151 paid to the party itself (table 5.8). The delegates' fees for the leadership convention in Calgary in June 1990 totalled $4.4 million. To put these figures into perspective, note that the Liberal party raised $6.3 million in 1990 outside the convention fees and $1.95 million in contributions to leadership candidates routed through the national agency in order to give donors receipts for the income-tax credit (see chap. 5).

3. It might be argued that the Chief Electoral Officer's changes in interpretation of such key terms as "election expenses" in the *Guidelines* he issues periodically for candidates and parties have been more important than the formal amendments (see chap. 13).

4. The registration of political parties was introduced in 1970. Note that the doctrine of agency (all of a candidate's revenues and expenditures must be made to and by his/her official agent) and the requirement that candidates disclose their revenues and expenditures in summary form predated the 1974 reforms (Seidle 1980).

5. This stands in sharp contrast to the federal level in the United States where *direct* contributions from corporations and unions are banned and contributions from individuals are constrained, but outlays on election campaigns are not, except in presidential campaigns, and only if the candidate accepts public funding (Alexander 1991).

6. It has been argued that, even with limits on election expenses, challengers may be at a disadvantage, since they need to spend more to overcome the advantages of incumbency (Palda 1991, chap. 3; more generally, see Heintzman 1991).

7. A related objective is to encourage parties and candidates to develop multiple sources of campaign funds so as to diversify sources and lessen dependence on a relatively few large contributors.

8. A somewhat different perspective can be found in the Chief Electoral Officer's 1989 statutory report (Canada, Elections Canada 1989a).

9. Note that some volunteers, particularly at the riding level during a campaign, may not even be party members. Many members never participate in the party as volunteers.

10. For example, in 1988 all federal candidates in Canada ($N = 1\ 574$) spent some $31.3 million on "election expenses" (see chap. 12). In 1990, the two candidates for a U.S. Senate seat in North Carolina together are reported to have spent about $30 million (U.S.). In several previous Senate races, the candidates spent over $25 million.

11. To reduce complexity, campaigns for the leadership of the party and the financing of nomination races are analysed separately; see figures 1.2 and 1.4.

12. Matters are complicated when the PC Canada Fund receives contributions earmarked for a candidate. Part or all of such contributions is transferred to the candidate (see chap. 4).

13. The limit for a party running candidates in all 295 ridings was $8 million in 1988. Therefore the threshold was $800 000.

14. The tax credit is equal to 75 percent of the first $100 of contributions to a party and/or candidate, plus 50 percent of donations between $100 and $500, plus 33.3 percent of amounts above $500 with a maximum tax credit of $500 for a contribution or contributions totalling $1 150 in the year (see chap. 8).

15. Thus, it is *other* taxpayers who are effectively subsidizing part of the contribution made by an individual or corporation.

16. Although Ontario bans the transfer of provincial party funds to the federal level, the Ontario PTS did meet its quota of $585 000 in 1988.

17. This was done by the Liberal party for a substantial number of candidates in 1979 and 1980, and for all candidates in 1988. It was done for Quebec candidates only in 1984. The Tories have not imposed this requirement.

18. The amounts are given in chapter 4. If no tax receipt is requested, the riding not only can receive "100-cent dollars," but the donor's name will not be publicly reported, even if the amount is over $100. All donations over $100 passing through the federal agents such as the PC Canada Fund must be reported to the CEO, who makes the list public about seven months after the end of the calendar year.

19. A decade ago, Seidle and Paltiel (1981, 255) observed that "Many local associations have grown rich through dedicated fund raising and the surplus that can accumulate from campaigns assisted by public funds. The national party organizations have access to some of the public funding provisions, but, as shown above, they have varied in the way they approached the advantages of the tax credit. Party officials have commented

over and over again that the parties are rich at the local level and starved at the center. The Liberals succeeded in 1979 and 1980 in recapturing some of the surplus funds from candidates' campaigns."

20. Apparently, this was done for the first time in the 1983 Conservative party leadership race (Ontario, Commission 1986, 80–81).

21. Note that the total value of tax-receipted donations by each donor is reported to and by the CEO annually. Therefore, one cannot identify who gave how much to each leadership candidate from this source. However, for the 1990 leadership race, the Liberal party made public the names of the donors and the amounts of their contribution to leadership candidates where the donation was routed through the Federal Liberal Agency.

22. However, in 1985, the deputy registrar of the Ontario Commission on Election Contributions and Expenses stated that no riding association may issue tax receipts for donations that are clearly intended for convention purposes (*Globe and Mail*, 12 January 1985, 12). Delegates were making a donation of $335 to their riding association, a sum equal to the registration fee for the forthcoming Conservative party provincial leadership convention, and receiving a tax receipt. Then the riding was paying the delegates' registration fee to the provincial party. Further, delegates planned to submit their expense claims for the convention to their riding association in order to receive a tax receipt for their outlay. The treasurer of one riding association said that the Ontario Commission told him this was permitted (ibid.). It appears that this technique has not been used by a federal party.

23. The sum of $4.4 million divided by $875 equals 5 017 delegates. (Some 4 658 delegates voted on the first and only ballot.) The tax credit per delegate, as noted in the text, was $408 – assuming they had made no other contributions during 1990.

24. The CEO's report on the 1988 election was on computer disk, but only in a word-processing format. It had to be converted to permit analysis. In addition, the CEO supplied an electronic file on the revenues, expenditures and surplus/deficit of each candidate in the 1988 election (referred to as file 1 in chap. 12). Beginning with the data for 1990, which are filed with the CEO in June 1991, the parties will provide data in a machine-readable form, and copies in this format (as well as "hard copies") will be available to the public.

25. Moreover, the parties' methods of recording contributions make this task rather difficult. A company may be reported in up to three different ways in any year depending upon the number of cheques it sent and the way the information was reported. For example, contributions from the Royal Bank of Canada to the Liberal party in 1989 were found in three places in the listing: under "R" for Royal Bank of Canada; under "B" for Banque royale du Canada; and under "T" for The Royal Bank of Canada.

26. Most of these could *not* be resolved by reference to additional data provided by the parties.

27. As chapter 12 makes clear, most of these outlays were made by about 200 candidates and the largest amounts of "other expenses" were incurred by Progressive Conservative candidates.

28. For example, the Liberal party, the Reform Party and the NDP provided balance sheets; the Progressive Conservative party declined to do so.

29. See chapter 5 and the Reform Commission of the Liberal Party of Canada (Liberal Party, Reform Commission 1991).

CHAPTER 2   EVOLUTION OF THE REGULATORY REGIME

1. Any regulatory regime has a number of elements. The core is the enabling legislation – in this case the *Election Expenses Act* of 1974, which contained a number of amendments to the *Canada Elections Act* and other statutes, such as the *Income Tax Act*. However, the regime is shaped by any regulations or other forms of subordinate legislation enacted by the Cabinet pursuant to the enabling legislation. Other elements include formal and informal interpretations of the statutes or regulations by the Chief Electoral Officer (see his *Guidelines* for candidates and political parties) and decisions of the courts that interpret the statutes or regulations.

2. More comprehensive discussions of the history of election finance regulation can be found in Seidle (1980), and Canada, Committee (1966).

3. However, in virtually every election from 1874 to 1900, some MPs were unseated for corrupt practices.

4. In 1907, the U.S. Congress prohibited corporations from making political contributions or expenditures in an election, convention or caucus (Atkey 1985, 133).

5. Registration was first provided for in 1970.

6. One might begin by referring to the fact that in 1964 NDP MP Andrew Brewin offered a private member's bill calling for strict limits on campaign expenditures by candidates and parties. It was reintroduced in 1966, but not enacted (Canada, Committee 1966, 24).

7. Barbeau had chaired the Quebec Liberal Party Commission, which recommended the reforms enacted in Quebec in 1963.

8. The pioneering Quebec *Election Act* was enacted in Quebec effective 1 January 1964. It imposed ceilings on expenditures by parties and candidates; provided for reimbursement of a substantial fraction of permitted candidate expenditures where they received at least 20 percent of the popular vote; applied the doctrine of agency to all candidates and parties; required all parties to apply for recognition and to be so recognized as official parties they had to field at least 10 candidates; and required reporting and disclosure of all campaign income and expenditures.

9. Sears was a member of the Ad Hoc Committee that dealt with the implementation of the *Election Expenses Act* of 1974.

10. In Bill C-203, introduced in June 1973, "election expenses were defined to include virtually all possible expenditures" (Seidle 1980, 193).

11. Frank Howard (NDP, Skeena) conducted a filibuster against the bill (Acker 1979, 80).

12. Sears describes some of the factors that shaped the 1974 reforms as follows: "It came out of the Barbeau Commission in the mid-60s which produced some very thoughtful research on how expenditures affect decisions, how public financing in other jurisdictions affects electoral outcome, and so on. Then there were three closely related phenomena in the early 70s; the Quebec election in 1970, the Ontario election in 1971 and the American presidential election in 1972, in which election expenditures mushroomed beyond anything anyone had conceived of previously. Then there were all the ramifications of Watergate following the 1972 election. These built up a head of steam about the impact of those expenditure levels on democracy. In 1972 it's estimated that the Nixon campaign spent over $70 million; today presidential campaigns are limited to less than half that – $29.3 million" ("Round Table" 1981, 7).

13. The threshold for reimbursement of candidates' election expenses was 20 percent in Bill C-203 in 1973. It was reduced to 15 percent after much discussion in the Committee reviewing the bill and in the House. The NDP had sought 10 percent (Seidle 1980, 200–201).

14. This provision was modified in October 1983 by "indexing" the maximum allowable expenditure by the increase in the Consumer Price Index. Each year, effective 1 April, the Chief Electoral Officer must publish a fraction (F) based on the following formula: $F =$ (average CPI during the previous January to December)$/88.9$, where the CPI is based on 1981 = 100, and 88.9 was the average CPI in 1980. Note that the 1983 amendment had the effect of indexing the spending limit from 1980, the year of the previous federal election.

15. This ceiling was also indexed in October 1983 in the same way as the limit on party expenditures; see note 14.

16. This was changed by Bill C-169 in October 1983 to reimburse candidates for one-half of their actual expenses (not to exceed 50 percent of the maximum allowable expenses), provided that the candidate obtained 15 percent of the votes cast and had filed the appropriate forms with the Chief Electoral Officer.

17. Candidates were to be reimbursed for 50 percent of the sum of their "election expenses" and "personal expenses" up to 50 percent of the spending limit. Therefore travel expenses were to be reimbursed in any riding, because they were classified as "personal expenses."

18. In the 1979 general election the allocation to parties of 6.5 hours of prime time for paid political advertising was as follows: Liberal party, 155 minutes; Conservative party, 134 minutes; NDP, 63 minutes; Social Credit party, 22 minutes; Communist party, 8 minutes and Marxist-Leninist party, 8 minutes. Note that no party could buy *more* than the amount allotted under the legislation (Boyer 1983, 465).

19. In the 1979 election, the total time for each network was distributed as follows: (i) Television, CBC English, 3.5 hours; CBC French, 3.5; CTV, 3.5; and TVA, 1 hour; (ii) Radio, CBC-AM English, 2 hours; CBC-AM French, 2; Radiomutuel, 1; and Telemedia, 1 (Boyer 1983, 469–70).

20. While these lengthy lists were available for public inspection at the office of the Chief Electoral Officer and could be obtained on request, only summary data were published in the CEO's report on each general election.

21. The party's return detailed "election expenses" only on a form provided by the CEO. Candidates were to provide details of revenue and spending.

22. The national party often took a fraction of the contribution, e.g., for the Progressive Conservative party, the amount was 25 percent. It appears that a local association could raise funds between elections for which no receipts were issued and then make a large donation to the national party and not have to reveal the names of donors (see Murray 1975, 43).

23. Seidle and Paltiel note that "the parties were able to agree on an elaborate set of guidelines for candidates and their agents. These guidelines were later published by the Chief Electoral Officer, with a note in the introduction that they had been specifically approved by the party representatives on the ad hoc committee" (1981, 263); see also Canada, Elections Canada (1980a).

24. Seidle and Paltiel state that "in an electoral district where the number of names on the preliminary list of electors is less than the average number of names on the preliminary lists for all electoral districts, the number of names for that electoral district is deemed to be increased by one-half of the difference between that number of names and the average number of names on the list for all electoral districts ... In electoral districts where the number of names on the list is less than the average of all electoral districts, the amount of the reimbursement is adjusted upward in a way similar to the provisions for the candidates' spending limit" (1981, 234).

25. Amendments to the *Canada Elections Act* in 1982 reduced the minimum length of federal elections from 60 to 50 days (Canada, *An Act to Amend the Canada Elections Act,* 1982, s. 2(1)).

26. The 1974 legislation prohibited individuals or groups other than candidates and registered parties from incurring "election expenses." However, section 70.1(4) of the *Canada Elections Act* stated that if the spending was

for the purpose of gaining support on an issue of public policy and was done in "good faith," the accused would not be convicted. According to Seidle (1985b, 125), this defence "had received a broader application than may have been intended and prosecutions were not assured." On the matter of the activities of advocacy groups during election campaigns, Sears, a member of the Ad Hoc Committee for several years, noted that "We attempted to tackle that in Section 70.1 and then tried to revise it in the fall of 1977 to make it a little more precise but we failed. Increasingly we're seeing the development of organizations and individuals whose function is to take shots at political parties and candidates through the expenditure of money in the media during a campaign period. If this continues, we have inadvertently created a loophole you can drive a truck through; if I'm constrained in my expenditures as a candidate at the local level, I'll form the 'Citizens for Social Democracy' and we'll go out and raise some money and I'll defy any legislation to deal with that after the fact in the way that Section 70.1 tries to" ("Round Table" 1981, 8).

27. Charles Dalfen, a former vice-chairman of the Canadian Radio-television and Telecommunications Commission (CRTC), was appointed as the first Broadcasting Arbitrator (Canada, Broadcasting Arbitrator 1984, 1989).

28. "While an additional potential total of 39 minutes of broadcast time was made available for allocation among "new" parties, the allocation system distinctly favoured the three parliamentary parties. Thus, in 1984, the Liberals, Progressive Conservatives, and New Democrats were allocated 173, 129 and 69 minutes respectively, whereas apart from the Rhinoceros Party, which was granted eight minutes, no other party was accorded more than five and a half minutes" (Paltiel 1987, 239).

29. Note that in a case in Quebec, Mr. Justice Bernier of the Cour des Sessions de la paix made the following ruling in regard to section 101 of *An Act to Govern the Financing of Political Parties:* "les dispositions de l'article 101 ne restreignent pas le droit de s'exprimer mais bien le droit de *dépenser pour s'exprimer*" (*Boucher* 1982, 1005).

30. A useful summary of the recommendations is contained in "Changes Proposed to Canada Elections Act" (Canada, Elections Canada 1987, 2–3, 5).

31. Both opposition parties objected to the fact that annual reporting of revenues and expenditures by riding associations was to be *voluntary.* Given the fact that such associations benefit from the income-tax credit, this distinction from the national party and candidates seemed illogical to them.

32. The central issue was whether payment of the expenses of poll agents was an "election expense" (see chap. 13).

33. According to the Chief Electoral Officer, Bill C-79 died on the Order Paper "because the members of the House of Commons could not reach a consensus on *one issue,* namely that related to election expenses" (Canada, Elections Canada 1989a, 44) [emphasis in the original].

CHAPTER 3   PARTY REVENUES AND EXPENDITURES, 1974–90:
AN OVERVIEW

1. One of the best discussions is contained in the NDP's submission to the Royal Commission on Electoral Reform and Party Financing (New Democratic Party 1990).

2. The Reform Party did not become a registered federal party until October 1988, so it is excluded from the analysis in this chapter. Its finances are the subject of chapter 7.

3. As noted in table 3.1, this period is 1 August 1974 to 31 July 1975 because, until 1977, the Liberal and Conservative parties reported to the Chief Electoral Officer on a fiscal- rather than a calendar-year basis.

4. See note 3, chapter 1.

5. The Ontario provincial section of the NDP is excluded because Ontario law prohibits money raised in Ontario by provincial parties to be transferred to federal parties (or to the federal wing of the party). It also prohibits money raised outside Ontario from being used in provincial politics. In the case of the Progressive Conservative party, there is a clear separation of the federal party from the various provincial PC parties. The Liberal party is a federation of 12 provincial or territorial associations, only four of which (Ontario, Quebec, Alberta and BC) focus exclusively on electing MPs, while the others are "dual purpose," that is, they attempt to elect provincial members as well as federal members (see chap. 5). However, the revenues of the Liberal party reported to the CEO and described in this study do not include those relating solely to electing provincial members. The NDP, however, is an integrated party in all provinces except Quebec. Historically, the federal wing grew out of the provincial sections. As a result, there is little effort to separate revenues or expenditures that relate exclusively to electing federal MPs (see chap. 6).

6. The information filed with the Chief Electoral Officer for 1974 and 1975 did not indicate the amount of provincially receipted revenues.

7. Note, however, that the Liberal party's revenues in 1988 included almost $2.3 million obtained from candidates in the form of half their "election expenses" reimbursement.

8. Using a four-year moving average, Michaud and Laferrière (1991) estimated the increase in all three major parties' "non-electoral expenses" to be $13.9 million in 1984 and $7.96 million in 1988. The purpose of the calculation was to try to determine if, in election years, parties systematically increase their nonelection spending. This appears to be the case, suggesting that considerable election-related spending occurs outside the "election expenses" in an election year.

9. It is assumed here that one of the objectives of the reporting requirements is to provide information on the *federal* activities of the parties.

10. See the notes to table 6.2.

11. For example, one of the referees who reviewed this study stated that "while *some* of that money undoubtedly does get used for provincial and even municipal purposes, the charge [that the NDP diverts federally receipted funds into provincial activities] is not entirely fair, because *some* of the money going back to the provincial sections *does* get used to elect federal members. Where the NDP can be faulted is that the public has no way of knowing what the proportions are." Not only does the public not know, but it is evident that many NDP officials were not aware of the size of these intraparty transfers before parts of an earlier draft of this study were given to them for review and comment. NDP officials stated that virtually all of the difference between federally receipted revenues and the federal office's expenditures was used by the provincial sections for provincial political activities outside of federal election campaigns.

12. The year 1989 was chosen because, when the study began in the spring of 1990, 1989 was the last year for which party finance data were available. In July 1991, however, the 1990 data were released by the Chief Electoral Officer.

13. In its brief to the Royal Commission on Electoral Reform and Party Financing, the NDP noted that while the CPI increased by 17.5 percent between election years 1984 and 1988, its costs increased by 38 percent for commercial travel, 42 percent for charter aircraft travel, between 20 percent and 54 percent for accommodation (depending on location), upwards of 20 percent increase in advertising costs, and 20 percent for salaries and benefits (NDP 1990, 6).

14. It is generally agreed that some of these outlays, e.g., on polling and other forms of research, are election-related, but are not included in official "election expenses" (see the discussion in chap. 13).

15. The reasons for this are discussed in chapter 6.

16. Michaud and Laferrière (1991) estimate the market value of free media time in the 1988 election to be $169 500 for radio (excluding the CBC-AM English and CBC-AM French networks) and $4.1 million for television (excluding the CBC English network).

17. For the latest internal assessment of the party, see Liberal Party of Canada, Reform Commission (1991).

18. For example, in 1989 and 1990 the Liberal Party of Canada (LPC) reduced its bank debt by about $2 million, but the members' equity is still negative. As important, beginning in 1989 various sources of funds were divided between LPC headquarters and the PTAs and ridings. Headquarters now has exclusive use of the Revenue Committee's list of large firms, the Laurier Club (individuals who contribute over $1 000), nationwide direct mail and the leader's dinners. The PTAs and the riding associations retain all the

revenues from door-to-door canvassing, solicitation of individuals and small to medium-sized businesses, membership dues, local dinners, social events and direct mail within their own area (chap. 5).

19. In 1990, the NDP came to power in Ontario, and in the fall of 1991, it came to power in BC and Saskatchewan.

20. In 1984, 730 of 8 744 union locals affiliated with the Canadian Labour Congress were affiliated with the NDP. However, only 56.1 percent of all union members are in unions affiliated with the CLC (Archer 1990, 51, 53). Overall, 7.3 percent of union members in 1984 were in locals affiliated with the NDP.

21. The NDP's federal office's expenditures in 1977 were less than one-sixth of the Liberal and Conservative parties. In 1989 they had fallen to 12 percent of the Conservatives' expenditures, and amounted to 21.5 percent of the Liberals' expenditures.

CHAPTER 4   PROGRESSIVE CONSERVATIVE PARTY

1. The Reform Party has experienced extraordinary growth in revenues – from $799 500 in 1988 to $6.6 million in 1991 (see chap. 7).

2. During campaign periods, each candidate's agent can issue tax receipts directly to donors; hence the candidate keeps the entire amount of the contribution.

3. For example, in April 1991 the Alberta Conservatives under Premier Don Getty voted 178 to 144 in favour of deleting a number of references to their federal counterpart from the party constitution. The provincial party is no longer compelled to support Tory candidates in federal elections, and members of the federal party will no longer automatically be members of the Alberta party (*Globe and Mail*, 8 April 1991, A5).

4. Transfers from PC party headquarters to candidates amounted to 12.8 percent of candidates' total revenues in 1979, 16.5 percent in 1980, 10.9 percent in 1984 and 7.8 percent in 1988 (see tables 12.2 and 12.3). However, these figures, at least in 1988, overstate the dependence of candidates on funds provided by party headquarters.

5. Progressive Conservative party officials stated that they do not alternate dinners in Ontario. Rather, the federal party holds at least one annual event in the province. There is no evidence from the financial statements filed with the CEO or supplied by the party to the author that the federal PC party transfers money to provincial Conservative parties.

6. The Priorities Committee (composed of extraparliamentary notables and a few MPs) was established in early February 1981 and it had its first meeting in March. The Committee was initially chaired by Terry Yates, who was formerly chairman of the PC Canada Fund, and later by Lowell Murray, the 1979 and 1980 campaign chairman. It established five subcommittees

dealing respectively with policy (Arthur Tremblay), administration (Don McDougall), finance (Finlay MacDonald), organization (Don Mazankowski) and communications (Don Hamilton). The Committee chairman together with the chairmen of the five subcommittees became the chief extra-parliamentary force in the party. Their work began the transformation of the Conservative party into a more sophisticated and professional organization, although they had to contend with a series of leadership-related events that redirected much attention of the caucus, extraparliamentary notables, national headquarters staff and local association members away from the less glamorous work of the committee.

7. To put these figures in perspective, note that Dalton Camp is quoted as saying that he ran the national Conservative office for $30 000 a month – under $400 000 annually – in the mid-1960s (Hoy 1989, 25).

8. The importance of corporate contributions to the Conservative and Liberal parties is discussed in more detail in chapter 11.

9. Prior to amendments in 1983, parties were reimbursed for 50 percent of their expenditures on electronic media (recall chapter 2).

10. This figure was obtained in confidence from a knowledgeable source. Party officials stated that such outlays also tend to fluctuate depending upon a number of factors, including who is acting as liaison between the pollster and party. In general, after Norman Atkins was appointed as campaign chairman in 1983, polling activity increased greatly.

11. Party officials indicated that Tory riding associations want headquarters to spend more money in the field on hiring party organizers, despite the increase in the number of organizers from 4 to 5 in the late 1970s, to 19 in 1990.

12. In 1989 dollars, the Conservative party's conventions in 1983 cost $3.38 million, as compared with $4.2 million (in 1989 dollars) for the Liberals' leadership convention in 1990.

13. In contrast, the Liberal party's leadership convention in 1990 cost $4.4 million, excluding what the candidates spent on the race ($6 million) (see table 5.8). Both parties try to ensure that the delegates' fees cover the cost of their conventions.

14. The size of the debt cannot be ascertained because, unlike the Liberal party and NDP, the Progressive Conservative party declined to provide balance sheets to the author.

15. "The 500" is a vehicle for raising contributions of at least $1 000 annually from individuals (see chap. 10).

16. The cost centres are the following: leader's office, PC caucus services, organization (the largest cost centre), PC Canada Fund (substantial sums are required in order to raise money for the party), women's bureau, national

executive, multicultural programs, youth, finance and administration and regional operations.

17. Most dinners feature a speech by the leader of the party. Both individuals and corporations purchase tickets. They receive a tax receipt based on the price of the ticket (from $150 to $500 over the last few years) *less* the costs of the event (see chap. 10).

18. What the party describes as "corporate" revenues (donations on what appear to be corporate cheques) amounted to from 41 percent to 75 percent of total contributions from business and commercial organizations between 1983 and 1990.

19. PMAC's annual contributions have typically been in the range of $2 000 to $4 000.

20. Revenue Canada permits political activity that is incidental to a charity's main activities, but there is ambiguity concerning how much political activity is permitted before the organization loses its tax-deductible status.

21. This figure is in nominal dollars and is the *net* amount the riding associations received *after* deducting the PC Canada Fund's 25 percent (see table 4.6).

22. In the case of fund-raising events, only the revenue after expenses is included in party revenue, because that is the amount for which tax receipts must be issued according to the *Income Tax Act*.

23. Except for rounding errors, it is not clear why the percentage returned to ridings is not 75 percent. In 1988, for example, it was 85.0 percent of contributions (table 4.6).

24. Thus the data in table 4.6 are *not* comparable to those in table 5.5 for the Liberal party because a much more complete picture has been obtained for the latter.

25. Several books have been written on the campaigns of 1984 and 1988. See Lee (1989), Fraser (1989), Frizzell et al. (1989), and Caplan et al. (1989) regarding the 1988 campaign. See Penniman (1988) on the 1984 election.

26. A Progressive Conservative party official stated that during the last two general elections, the party billed representatives of the media a flat fee if they wished to take advantage of transportation provided by the party as part of the leader's tour. This charge covered transportation, both by air and by bus, as well as some food and media facilities. The party recovered $594 038 from these billings during and after the 1988 general elections.

27. Targeted voter mail (other than fund-raising) was first used by the Tories in 1984 and was used again in 1988. Mailings are combined with telephone calls (see chap. 9).

28. Campaign staff work 12 to 16 hours per day to get the "right" 45 seconds on the evening news, particularly on the national news programs at 10 PM (CBC) or at 11 PM (CTV).

29. A senior Progressive Conservative party campaign official noted that, in most campaigns, the party runs three "flights" of ads: soft/low key, tough and upbeat. In 1988 the party ran nine *sets* of commercials reflecting better polling information and shifts in preferences during the campaign. The "comic insert" sponsored by the anti–Free Trade Agreement (FTA) coalition had "ten times" the impact of the material put out by the coalition of business firms supporting the FTA. This came through in the Tories' focus groups. The Tories' advertising response to John Turner's effectiveness in the leadership debates is described in Lee (1989).

30. For example, one west coast riding association had only 163 members in early 1987, even though its candidate had held the riding since 1972. A new executive was able to increase the membership to 1 500 (large even by national standards) by September 1988 with the help of four well-qualified individuals who ran for the nomination. However, the Conservative party candidate did not win the 1988 election. The riding membership had atrophied from a peak just prior to the 1984 election to the point where only 65 members attended the annual meeting in February 1987 – and they constituted one-third (average turnout) of the membership. To put this example in a broader context, see Carty and Erickson (1991).

31. If a campaign is to make the best use of volunteers, they must be recruited and screened to ensure they are not opposition "plants." Their campaign-related skills and interests must be ascertained, and they must be put to work. The failure of a campaign to accept the volunteers' offer and put them to work has negative consequences: motivation drops and volunteers get "turned off." They may even offer their services to an opponent.

32. For example, in Vancouver Centre in 1988, riding volunteers did phone canvassing in three waves: 90 percent to 95 percent of electors received a single call that sought to elicit voter preferences; 30 percent to 40 percent received a second call close to voting day – those identified as "undecided" in the first canvass – and all electors identified as Tory supporters received a call on election day.

33. Headquarters officials stated that candidates' agents are not prevented from soliciting funds from these sources.

34. The president of the Vancouver Centre riding association emphasized that it is not wise for a local association to "look flush." It may discourage contributors who like to feel their money will be put to good use and that most of those working for the party are volunteers. Worse, a big bank balance (or large term deposits) could create an incentive for a small group to try to dislodge the current executive and use the funds on causes or activities of their own choosing. For example, this president stated that he regularly scans the lists of new members to see if known anti-abortion activists are joining the association. If they were to "pack" the annual meeting, they might elect an executive willing to put the association's funds into right-to-life campaigns or to back a candidate with similar views.

35. The major figures include the campaign manager, election-day coordinator, chief fund-raiser, candidate's coordinator, head of communications, coordinator of the phone bank, coordinator of door-to-door distribution/canvassing, sign coordinator, recruiter/coordinator of volunteers and youth coordinator.

36. According to a former PC official, "PC Metro" has a written constitution that entitles it to send delegates to general meetings and conventions.

37. The author is indebted to David Marley for most of the information on which this account is based.

38. The facts were as follows: in 1980 the five PC candidates spent 97.3 percent, 91.6 percent, 87.2 percent, 81.9 percent and 76.3 percent of the statutory limit on "election expenses" (about $30 000). In that year the five candidates raised an average of $24 861 per riding (versus $26 986 for NDP candidates). The PC candidates spent an average of $26 083 on "election expenses." This was only very slightly more than NDP candidates ($25 937). These data indicate that Tory candidates in 1980 spent, on average, only $1 222 more on "election expenses" than they raised in contributions. In 1979, the PC candidates on Vancouver Island spent 78.0 percent, 94.4 percent, 77.3 percent, 86.6 percent and 83.9 percent of the limit on "election expenses."

39. This figure was provided by a party official. The CEO indicates that the five PC candidates raised $341 970, which is greater than 75 percent of $428 000 ($321 000). In chapter 8, the data indicate that, even in election years, no more than 3 percent of the voting-age population makes a contribution to a federal party and/or candidate.

40. While a very senior party official disagreed with this interpretation, he declined to offer an alternative one, despite repeated requests by the author.

41. The average revenue of the six NDP candidates in 1988 was $47 776 (Canada, Elections Canada 1989a).

42. In 1990, the Liberal party reported contributions from 36 361 individuals, versus 27 702 for the Conservatives, 116 448 for the NDP and 23 462 for the Reform Party. However, the Liberal party figure is inflated by the 1990 leadership convention and the fact that $1.95 million in contributions to leadership candidates was routed through the Federal Liberal Agency and was thus counted in the data reported by the party to the Chief Electoral Officer.

43. The Liberal party did the same thing in 1984, but failed to have the resources to do it in 1988.

CHAPTER 5   THE LIBERAL PARTY OF CANADA

1. Between 1958 and 1962, when the Liberal party was out of office, it was nearly bankrupt and was faced with the threat of closing some of its offices (Paltiel 1970b, 37). In 1969, the Liberal party national headquarters had a

budget of $363 000, including $100 000 for a national meeting and special projects (ibid., 39). Wearing (1981, 148) put the party's cost of operations in 1969 at $377 000. In 1973, the net disbursements of the Liberal Party of Canada were $407 130 (or about $1.2 million in 1989 dollars). For the 11 months ending 31 July 1974, the outlays were $392 409. The expenditures for the year ending 31 July 1975 were $517 399 (Paltiel 1975, 193). In contrast, the Progressive Conservative party spent $900 195 in 1973 (about $2.7 million in 1989 dollars). The NDP's regular (nonelection, federal office) budget in 1973 was $223 350 and it was $279 700 in 1974 (ibid., 197).

2. This was still the case at the end of 1991, although the latest Reform Commission (1991) recommended that a national list be compiled.

3. This point was made by senior officials of both the Liberal and Progressive Conservative parties interviewed by the author and by Wearing (1981).

4. In the words of two party officials, "The Liberal Party as we know it today originated in the 1960s. Prior to the 1950s, the party was a loose coalition of provincial organizations held together by an alliance between parliamentary leaders, regional barons and a non-parliamentary elite – politically successful, but not the mass party that we have today" (Banister and Gibson 1984, 8).

5. In 1964, the name National Liberal Federation was changed to Liberal Federation of Canada.

6. For example, in 1933 only half the $50 000 sought from wealthy Liberals to create a capital fund to sustain the national office could be raised (Canada, Committee 1966). In 1960, the operating costs of the national office of the LPC had risen to $150 000. In 1989 dollars this would amount to about $750 000 – only one-ninth the LPC's expenditures in 1989.

7. In 1957, Gordon Dryden, later treasurer of the LPC, wrote that "while the federal field holds the glamour of the big league, it is in the Provinces that one finds the basis of political power in Canada." He favoured a single party, federally and provincially (Wearing 1981, 13).

8. An extreme case occurred early in 1974. Ian Sinclair, chairman of the CPR, told both the Liberal and Tory fund-raisers that the CPR and all of its subsidiaries would no longer contribute to any political party. Apparently Sinclair was unhappy with the Liberal government's policies (see letter from Senator John Godfrey to Mr. Sinclair, dated 22 February 1974). He had threatened in 1972 to cut off the Liberal party for the 1972 election unless CP Air was given the Milan route. Later Sinclair "backed down completely and said he never had any intention to blackmail the Liberal Party or the government" (letter from Senator Godfrey to Hon. G.C. van Roggen, dated 31 August 1972). Senator Godfrey then told Robert Andras, the Minister of Consumer and Corporate Affairs, that the government was free to deal with the route decision entirely on its merits. In Godfrey's view, Sinclair's talk of making his company's contribution conditional on

.

the government's decision "would not just hurt his cause but make it practically impossible for the government to decide in favour of CP [Air]" (ibid.).

9. Paltiel (1974, 344) states that, in the 1965 election, the expenditures of Liberal party headquarters (excluding Quebec and other provincial committees) were $525 000; this figure rose to $657 000 in 1968 and to $1 322 000 in the 1972 election.

10. Note that there were 295 ridings in 1988, but only 265 in 1965.

11. This amount includes funds that were raised for national and provincial campaign committees; $600 000 went to cover overdrafts, $1 322 000 was used by the national office and $3 978 000 was disbursed to provincial campaign committees (Paltiel 1974, 343). Note that Senator John Godfrey (1974) put the Liberals' net outlays in 1972 at $5.3 million. In the same year, the Conservative party spent $3.93 million, while the NDP spent only $371 000 (Paltiel 1974).

12. "The Federal Liberal Agency technically receives and receipts all contributions to the party. Most of the actual cash flows are held in accounts managed by the official agent in each province/territory. All are appointed by, and report, through the chairman, to the leader. Each agent upon appointment must provide the leader with a signed, but undated, letter of resignation, which is then available for enactment at the leader's discretion. The Agency, on the basis of a series of individual negotiations, directs the disposition of most party funds" (Banister and Gibson 1984, 15). Beginning in 1987, when the Federal Liberal Agency retracted the official agent status delegated to an individual in each province/territory, the cash flows were deposited in accounts in each province/territory but managed by the Federal Liberal Agency.

13. Wearing (1981, 232) states that, in the four and one-half years after the 1974 legislation came into effect, the Liberals collected almost $17 million from all sources, of which it transferred $4.3 million to ridings under the formula whereby 75 percent of money raised at the riding level was returned to them. He therefore infers from the formula that $6.7 million was raised at the PTA and riding levels and $11.3 million was raised by the national office.

14. Seidle and Paltiel continue: "The subject was raised during the Liberal party's national convention in July 1980 and, according to one press report, MPs and party workers claimed that the scheme had been 'imposed from on high.' They complained that candidates who opposed the plan to transfer part of their reimbursement to the national organization were told they might lose their endorsement as official Liberal candidates. In interviews, leading Liberals involved in the 1979 and 1980 campaigns did not deny that pressure was applied to candidates who appeared unwilling to agree to this plan" (1981, 255).

15. In the Progressive Conservative party, membership lists are maintained at the riding level.

16. See Banister and Gibson (1984, 12). The Reform Commission of the LPC (1991, 20) recommended that a national membership list be created and maintained because "the national Party cannot identify individual members and therefore does not have the ability to communicate with all its members on a regular basis" (ibid., 5). This is a huge disadvantage in raising money by means of direct mail. The official membership list would be maintained by the national party in Ottawa and would be shared through the use of a computerized network (ibid., 24).

17. Since March 1991 when the BC Liberal party established a separate provincial Liberal party, the four separate provincial Liberal parties are in BC, Quebec, Alberta and Ontario.

18. Former party president Michel Robert, in an interview with the author, suggested that the LPC central office has increasingly become a service agency for the PTAs and riding associations in the conduct of elections. It provides campaign manuals, trains official agents and campaign managers, recruits candidates, sometimes runs/oversees nomination meetings and provides funds for some ridings.

19. Section 3(1)(h) of the LPC Constitution as amended in November 1986 requires PTAs to provide for full and fair financial disclosure and requires all constituency associations to provide the provincial or territorial associations with financial statements within three months of the end of each calendar year. Party officials indicated that few local associations have complied with this provision. PTAs were reminded of this requirement each year between 1987 and 1990.

20. In 1979 and 1980, many Liberal candidates were required to assign half of the federal reimbursement of their "election expenses" to party headquarters to help finance the national campaign. In 1984, only candidates from BC, Alberta, Ontario and Quebec were requested to make the assignment. Why? Because, as Michel Robert, party president from 1987 to 1989, said, "We thought we were rich." Only modest amounts of money were turned over to headquarters. In 1988, all candidates were *required* to transfer half their reimbursement to the party (a total of about $2.27 million). The assignment was made a condition of obtaining the leader's signature on the candidate's nomination papers, a stipulation required by the *Canada Elections Act*.

21. The complexity can be seen by comparing figure 5.1 to figure 4.1 (chap. 4) for the Progressive Conservative party.

22. The Quebec tax credit was (and is) 50 percent of contributions up to $280. The federal tax credit is 75 percent of the first $100 and reaches a maximum of $500 on a contribution of $1 150.

23. Party officials stated that the Ontario Liberal party holds its Heritage Dinner in the spring, while the federal Liberal party holds its leader's dinner in the fall each year.

24. The Laurier Club seeks donations of at least $1 000 annually from individuals (see chap. 10).

25. There are also *regional* Liberal associations, which are units within the PTAs (for example, the Ottawa and District Liberal Association covers some 15 ridings).

26. Headquarters puts the name of any person who becomes a donor on its "house list," and the name is removed from the list from which donations are shared 50/50.

27. These changes in the party's financial arrangements were made in several stages between early 1987 and 1 January 1989. The key change (effective 1 January 1989) was that the PTAs and constituency associations were given the right to use all "popular fund-raising sources," such as direct mail, personal solicitation from individuals and from small and medium-sized enterprises, dinners and social events. They were allowed to keep *all* of the revenues from these sources.

28. In general, Liberal party membership dues are higher than those for the Conservative party.

29. The Quebec association's membership list has about 350 000 names, versus only 23 000 in Alberta's list. Note that ridings or PTAs can run their own direct-mail campaigns provided that the "targets" live in the riding or the PTA respectively.

30. Party officials indicated that there are several types of trust funds associated with the LPC: those in existence before the 1974 legislation, such as the big one in Nova Scotia, and those created by candidates from campaign surpluses routed through riding associations.

31. While data provided by the party in table 5.4 indicate that $2.85 million was spent on "conventions and conferences" in 1984, as compared to zero in 1983, on the other hand, the comparable figure for 1984 (derived from table 5.3) is $4.36 million. The latter is the figure that the party filed with the CEO. The difference could not be reconciled with party officials.

32. This category includes several types of transfers: those to candidates, those to riding associations, those to PTAs and (in 1990) those to leadership candidates, i.e., money routed through the Federal Liberal Agency in order to be eligible for a receipt for the income-tax credit for political contributions. Moreover, the amount reported in table 5.1 is a *net* amount, reflecting transfers from PTAs and candidates to headquarters (except in 1988) (see table 5.2b).

33. While table 5.1 reports that $3.32 million was transferred to party organizations in 1990, $1.95 million of this amount consisted of funds transferred to leadership candidates for contributions routed through the Federal Liberal Agency (table 5.8).

34. Party officials were not able to explain why the Agency administration costs rose so much in 1984 when there was both a leadership convention and a general election.

35. This would also apply to the four PTAs (Quebec, Ontario, Alberta, BC) that are *not* dual-purpose. They focus only on federal politics.

36. This figure, according to party records, is net of transfers of $626 740 and $347 685 from constituencies to the Ontario and Quebec PTAs.

37. In 1982, Banister and Gibson pointed out, the Treasury Committee generated $1.0 million, "sectoral" contributions and revenue raised by ridings totalled $3.6 million, leader's dinners generated $600 000 and registration fees for the national convention (required to break even) amounted to $1.0 million. They also said that "the 'sectoral' fundraising referred to is undertaken by provincial/territorial finance committees and is raised from mid-sized corporate and professional donors. Provincial offices receive much of their funding from this source. Of the riding total, over two-thirds was raised in the province of Quebec" (1984, 18). They noted that the party's debt was close to being paid off.

38. According to Weston, "the common belief that Pierre Trudeau had walked away from a party with no red ink on its books was a myth. In February 1984, a warchest of close to $900 000, salted away for an election, was completely emptied to reduce the party's debts. Based on projected fundraising figures at the time, Liberal president Iona Campagnolo assured Trudeau that he would be leaving behind an organization in the black" (1988, 114). Liberal party balance sheets indicate that at the end of 1983 the members' equity was $3.4 million (table 5.7).

39. In 1984, when Senator Keith Davey replaced Bill Lee as head of the Liberal party's national campaign, Davey was "astounded to discover that most members of the Ontario campaign committee were being paid for their services. This was a regrettable first" (1986, 344).

40. To put these figures in context, note that between 1985 and 1988 the federal office of the NDP spent a total of $473 000 to supplement the funds provided by Parliament for Ed Broadbent's office and for the caucus (see chap. 6).

41. Table 5.7 indicates that, at the end of 1984, the Liberal party's members' equity was *minus* $1.92 million, while its total liabilities were $7.2 million. These figures suggest that the debt was much larger than the reported $3.5 million.

42. At that time, senior officials considered having the Liberal party declare bankruptcy, leaving the bank to swallow the $6 million debt (based on interviews by the author conducted in 1990).

43. Senator Kolber indicates that some 40 to 45 names were on the Quebec list, and that in 1984 he raised $1 million in Quebec.

44. Senator Kolber said he consulted lawyers to see if it would be possible to dissolve the Nova Scotia trust fund (under the direction of Senator Henry Hicks, the former premier of Nova Scotia) and obtain part of its assets for the national party. The fund's objective is to "advance the cause of

Liberalism." Kolber had asked Hicks for $250 000. Hicks refused to help. Former party president Michel Robert confirmed that trustees of the Nova Scotia trust fund, which was said to have assets of about $5 million, refused to help. He noted that, at election time, the trust fund gave only $40 000 to the Nova Scotia Liberal party.

45. Senator Kolber stated that he paid most of the costs of his fund-raising drive himself (except for Metcalfe's salary).

46. In fact, Senator Kolber gave the LPC a total of $27 337 in 1986. In that year, five individuals gave $25 000 or more to the party, while 12 gave $5 000 or more.

47. Note also that in 1986 the number of contributions of $2 000 or more to the Liberal party by individuals increased to 64 from 15 in 1985. However, the number fell to 37 in 1987. See table 8.14.

48. There is no doubt that Senator Kolber was greatly frustrated by Turner's failure to "back him up" in his efforts to take over and change both fund-raising and spending activities. It points out the fundamental contradiction with which political parties must contend: they must be open, democratic and encourage popular participation in their operation, *and* they must be well-managed organizations that are able to raise money efficiently and spend it for best political effect. The latter usually requires clear mandates, hierarchical relationships, a limited number of participants in decision making and continuity.

49. The President's Committee on Reform was struck in January 1983 under Iona Campagnolo. Its co-chairmen, Armand Banister and Gordon Gibson, produced a discussion paper in January 1984. The planned 1984 convention became a leadership convention after Pierre Trudeau resigned. The President's Committee produced its final report in August 1985 (Banister and Gibson 1985). At the national convention in November 1986, the report resulted in some amendments to the LPC constitution. For an assessment, see Wearing (1989).

50. LPC headquarters did not get the Quebec list as promised.

51. The 1988 federal election resulted in Liberal candidates receiving a total of $4 655 526 in reimbursements (Canada, Elections Canada 1988c, 3–339). Some $2 273 694 was transferred to LPC headquarters.

52. The Senator was thought to be part of the "dump Turner" movement at the 1986 convention. Senator Kolber was reported to have been unhappy with Turner's lack of support for changes necessary "to overhaul the party's financial operations" (*Vancouver Sun*, 5 February 1987, B8).

53. The decisions of the Financial Management Committee came after serious clashes between veteran party insiders and fund-raisers and those newer to the party and fund-raising activities (*Globe and Mail*, 9 March 1988). According to Liberal sources, one "cautious group," fearing that banks

would not extend further credit for the upcoming election, looked to drastic cost-cutting measures to enable money to be banked immediately. The other "traditional group" argued that, once the writ was dropped, it was up to the leading fund-raisers to get the money rolling in and, therefore, there was no need to worry at that time. "Do you cut zero and assume that you'll raise everything in the campaign or do you cut 50 percent on the assumption that you've got to have everything ready before the campaign begins?" one source was quoted as asking (ibid.). In the end the party compromised.

54. Such a large cut was deemed by Turner's principal secretary to be far too severe, as it would have "political ramifications" (Weston 1988, 270). It was not until after the Conservative party's victory in the November 1988 election that the cuts could be made. Expenditures on the Leader's Office in 1989 ($479 000) were half those in 1988 and 1987 (table 5.4).

55. In early May, while appearing on an open-line radio program in Vancouver, John Turner moved to distance himself from the financial problems of the party. He told listeners that, although he had not threatened to fire Michel Robert, the ultimate responsibility for the party's money woes rested with Robert as the party's chief financial officer (*Financial Post*, 6 May 1988, 5). He also was upset at the blame placed on his office for overspending and stated that his office and his personal budgets were not exceeding their yearly targets.

56. *Globe and Mail*, 20 June 1988, A3. At the meeting of the executive committee in June, no decision was reached as to who should replace Michel Robert as chief financial officer (he had been removed from this position after the failed caucus revolt in April).

57. According to a *Maclean's* story, "by August 1989, six months before he officially entered the race [on 23 January 1990], Chrétien's campaign was in high gear. Two paid organizers quietly opened a Toronto office and within three months there was a full time staff of seven." Chrétien paid the expenses of 75 "influential party members" to come to Ottawa for a two-day campaign strategy meeting before he formally announced his decision to run (*Maclean's*, 2 July 1990, 20).

58. The party official who prepares the party's financial statements told the author that the debt was $3.8 million at the end of 1990. Note, however, that the Liberal party's total liabilities exceeded its total assets by $4.16 million at the end of 1990 (table 5.7).

59. 1990 is omitted because the 1990 Liberal leadership race and convention roughly doubled the Liberal party's revenues and expenditures in 1990.

60. Computed from table 3.1 and converted into 1989 dollars.

61. Others argue that the problem does not lie in the fact the LPC is a federation, but in the failure of the PTAs and local associations to do the neces-

sary organizational work at their level. This work cannot be done effectively out of the Ottawa office.

62. For example, at the 1990 Convention the LPC established an Aboriginal Peoples' Commission within the party to promote the interests of Aboriginals.

CHAPTER 6 NEW DEMOCRATIC PARTY

1. The weakness and dependency of the "federal wing" of the CCF (i.e., the federal office) on money provided by the provincial/territorial sections can be seen in the federal office's tiny budgets. Sixteen years after the party was established (1948/49), its budget was only $53 005 (Paltiel 1970b). Only $21 000 and $22 000 was received for the 1957 and 1958 federal elections (Seidle 1980, 166). Even today, the finances of the federal office of the NDP are largely controlled by the party's provincial/territorial sections (PTSs).

2. Paltiel (1975, 196) notes that because of the decentralized structure of the NDP, the figures for 1972 ($371 000) and 1974 understate markedly the party's total outlays on the last two general elections before the reforms of 1974.

3. In 1989, the NDP's constitution was altered to indicate that the leader and two of the president, secretary and treasurer are to sit on the federal council.

4. However, one writer has argued that individuals in the NDP owe their "direct allegiance to provincial riding associations and to the provincial sections of the national party ... Members are only incidentally members of the national party" (Surich 1975, 136).

5. For example, a donation of $100 to the Vancouver Centre federal riding in 1990 was distributed as follows: $70 to the BC PTS, $15 to the federal office and $15 to the federal riding.

6. The data reported by the CEO include *all* provincial activity (ongoing and elections), except that of Ontario, but distinguish between provincially and federally receipted revenues (omitting Ontario provincial revenues). However, senior party officials stated that in some years considerable amounts of money raised in Ontario are reported as federal revenue.

7. Party officials pointed out that the provinces and territories do not send union affiliation fees to the federal office. The federal office receives 100 percent of the affiliation fees from a local union and remits to the province or territory where that local is located 40 percent of the affiliation fee. With that explanation, Dyck's sentence concerning the Ontario party is inaccurate.

8. The NDP's official agent under the *Canada Elections Act* is in the federal office. However, authority to issue receipts for the income-tax credit is delegated to officials within each PTS.

9. In Saskatchewan, for example, money raised at the provincial level is allocated as follows: 15 percent to the federal office, 5 percent to federal ridings in the province and 80 percent to the Saskatchewan office. This is split equally among provincial ridings, but the latter benefits *both* provincial and federal candidates/members. Saskatchewan PTS officials are free to mingle money and to apply it to the election of provincial MLAs or federal MPs. Morley (1991, table 3.2) states that, in 1989, the major recipients of the BC section's net income of $2.76 million were as follows: federal office, $413 000; constituency quotas, $1 566 000; BC section, $160 400; provincial ridings, $473 200; federal ridings, $28 600; central by-election, $111 100; and other, $3 700.

10. The 15 percent federal, 85 percent provincial/local split of federally receipted revenues raised at the local level was established in 1975. One party official stated that 30 percent of tax-receiptable contributions made to local associations between elections is kept by the local association, while the balance goes to the PTS, which remits part to the central office. However, during the 1984 and 1988 federal elections, 85 percent was kept by the candidate's agent and 15 percent went to the central office in Ottawa. Provincial sections object to the fact that 15 percent of moneys raised to fight provincial elections – including provincially receipted funds – must be paid to the federal office. In Ontario, however, during provincial elections, all contributions are receipted by the ridings rather than by the PTS. Further, legislation in Ontario, Alberta and New Brunswick makes it illegal to make payments to a federal party from provincially received money. Note that under changes approved by the party's Federal Finance Committee in 1989, the federal party may not collect its normal 15 percent revenue-sharing from the time a provincial/territorial election writ is dropped until 30 days after that election campaign has finished. In exchange, the federal party is entitled to do three direct-mail appeals to that provincial/territorial membership list over the next four years above the normal number, in consultation with the PTS as to the timing.

11. In the NDP, it is policy to require incumbent MPs to be financially self-sufficient, as they have considerable advantages as an incumbent – including raising funds. They are not to receive money, people or materials from party headquarters.

12. For example, in 1988 the PTSs were given quotas so as to provide $2.2 million to the national campaign committee: BC and Ontario were each responsible for 26.5 percent ($585 000), while Saskatchewan, Manitoba and Alberta provided 22.7 percent, 14.7 percent and 4 percent respectively. The other provinces were supposed to collectively pay 5 percent, but made only token payments (Morley 1991, 111). The party's "election expenses" in 1988 were just over $7 million.

13. The complexity of financial flows within the NDP is illustrated by the case of federal organizers who are sent to assist in a provincial campaign. The

provincial or territorial section pays their salary, while the ridings in which they work pay their expenses.

14. In its annual financial statements to the Chief Electoral Officer, it has regularly included this note: "Since 1974, the New Democratic Party has reported all the revenue raised by it as a Party across Canada. Despite the passage of provincial/territorial legislation which requires separate reporting in different jurisdictions, we continue to do so. We believe it is important for the voters of Canada to see the actual revenues of national political parties at every level of their operation. Those separately reported sums are noted on our return."

15. This is the case because, in the Conservative party, there is a complete split between the federal and provincial wings and the federal wing does not have any provincial entities. Of the 12 PTAs of the Liberal party, four are devoted exclusively to federal politics. Of the eight "dual" PTAs, party officials stated that very little federally receipted money is used for provincial politics.

16. In its letter to the CEO accompanying the filing of its financial statements for 1989 (dated 27 June 1990) the NDP's federal secretary noted that "most of our revenue [is] raised in the provinces and territories with a percentage of those funds being forwarded to finance the Federal Party's operations; ... since the Party was founded in 1961, the NDP has accepted the principle that, if you are a member in good standing in a province or territory, you are automatically a member of the Federal Party; ... and the amounts reported to the CEO include the revenues and expenses of all provinces including those that require separate reporting of revenues received."

17. The phrase "activity at the provincial level" is used to refer to efforts that are directly and indirectly designed to elect members (e.g., MLAs), and to form a government in a province. "Activity at the federal level" refers to efforts designed to elect federal MPs, regardless of at which level it occurs.

18. The party need not report the names of contributors of less than $100. Some fund-raising events involve "passing the hat" or selling tickets of less than $100 for which no receipts are issued.

19. Because of the high degree of integration between federal and provincial activities, there is never a four-year gap between elections. The leadership cadre tries to coordinate and focus its limited financial and human resources for the party as a whole, i.e., both at the federal level and within most provinces. Therefore, somewhere in the country, the NDP is almost always in a pre-election period (see table 6.7).

20. The Federal Finance Committee agreed in November 1990 that there should be sharing of federal "house list" direct-mail revenues in terms of the net revenues. Prospect mail and special programs such as the Agnes MacPhail appeal were excluded from this agreement.

21. Note that the phrase "federally receipted contributions" in table 6.3 should more properly be "contributions that may be eligible for the federal tax credit." Some types of contributions, notably those from trade unions, are not eligible for the tax credit, because they have no taxes payable from which to deduct the credit.

22. The cost of such organizers is a modest fraction of the transfer to PTSs reported in table 6.4.

23. There is no question that, during federal elections, the provincial sections play a major role. Dyck (1989, 209) states that "when it comes to federal elections, the national party relies very heavily on the provincial party's campaign team, usually headed by the provincial secretary, and the whole staff is normally turned over to the federal election effort."

24. In BC, for example, a contribution of $200 to the NDP is eligible for a federal tax credit of $75 and a provincial tax credit of $75, since individuals belong to a PTS that gives them membership at both the provincial and federal levels. It is possible, therefore, that money intended by the donor to be used for the purpose of electing provincial MLAs ends up being used for a campaign in a federal riding, or vice versa. This activity is prohibited in Ontario, New Brunswick and Alberta, but not in BC.

25. The fact that the CEO lumps together federally and provincially receipted revenues is his choice. The party provides separate figures for each.

26. Telephone interview by the author in October 1990.

27. A poll by Decima Research in the late spring of 1990 found that 72 percent of Canadians are opposed to union affiliation with political parties. At the same time, a majority have favourable views of trade unions. The research was conducted for the 220 000-member Canadian Federation of Labour which is non-partisan. The 2.3 million-member Canadian Labour Congress officially supports the NDP (*Vancouver Sun*, 15 June 1990, E8).

28. Archer (1990, 37) notes that only 29.8 percent of nonagricultural paid workers were unionized in 1963.

29. Some 39.2 percent of paid agricultural workers were unionized in 1984. Therefore, only 2.8 percent of the labour force belonged to NDP-affiliated union locals (Archer 1990, 41).

30. Of the 730 union locals affiliated with the NDP, 702 are locals of national and international unions. Their 267 348 members comprise 20.8 percent of the non-public sector CLC locals affiliated with the NDP (Archer 1990, 53). In 1990, the NDP received $607 639 in affiliation dues from 684 contributors according to the party's return filed with the CEO.

31. While the National Union of Provincial Government Employees (NUPGE) and Public Service Alliance of Canada (PSAC) are usually prohibited by legislation, the Canadian Union of Public Employees (CUPE) locals are generally not prohibited from affiliating with the NDP. In 1990, for example,

the largest local in CUPE representing the Ontario Hydro Workers Union affiliated a portion of its membership to the party.

32. The three largest unions in 1984 were public sector unions, jointly accounting for 19.6 percent of all union members in Canada (Archer 1990, 43).

33. Archer (1990, 28) points out that at the 1987 federal convention, 17.3 percent of the delegates were from affiliated unions and 5.2 percent were from central labour bodies. The party convention (held every two years) is the supreme governing body of the NDP and has final authority on "all matters of federal policy, programme and constitution." Between conventions, the party is governed by the Federal Council ($N = 116$–21), which meets at least twice annually at the call of the executive ($N = 34$). Twelve members represent affiliated organizations (ibid., 29).

34. According to one senior NDP official, the unions are more integrated into the party on paper than they are in practice. When CLC representatives sit on party organizations they tend to wear their "NDP hat" rather than the hat of "pure delegates of the CLC," their employer.

35. In 1961, BC enacted legislation that prohibited the use for political purposes of any money deducted from an employee's wages or paid as a condition of membership of a union. While this legislation did not prohibit political donations, it did discourage unions from collecting the money for political donations. The legislation was upheld in *O.C.A.W. v. Imperial Oil Ltd.* (1963). However, the restriction was removed in 1973 by the NDP government of David Barrett. In *Lavigne v. Ontario Public Service Employees Union*, the Supreme Court of Canada in June 1991 upheld the use of union dues for political purposes, even when membership is compulsory or when the individuals pay dues according to the Rand formula (i.e., they do not have to belong to the union, but must pay the same dues as do members).

36. In 1982–83, unions made special contributions to a fund to eliminate the party's debt.

37. In addition, labour organizations contributed $1.113 million to NDP candidates out of their total revenues of $6.8 million (Canada, Elections Canada 1988c, 3–339).

38. In 1984, also an election year, there were only eight contributions from labour organizations exceeding $20 000. The largest amount was $122 500 from the Canadian Steelworkers' Union.

39. Note, however, that in 1968 the NDP spent $569 000 or $2.26 million in 1989 dollars, versus $380 436 in 1974 or $1.09 million in 1989 dollars. (Deflation by the author using the Consumer Price Index.)

40. The figure was $7.47 million in 1989 dollars less $2 million, versus $5.84 million in 1984 in 1989 dollars. The reason for making this comparison is that the NDP spent only $50 000 in Quebec during the 1984 election.

41. However, the NDP won its first seat in Quebec in the by-election in Chambly only a few months after the general election.

42. Note that in 1974, before the current legislation came into effect, the PTSs provided 31 percent of the funds for the federal election.

43. The quota set for each PTS is typically paid in three instalments: a fraction before the writ is issued, another fraction when the writ is issued and the balance about halfway through the campaign. Sometimes there is a fourth round when more funds are needed. It is common for the PTS, in turn, to put a quota on the riding associations to help them meet the quota for the national campaign.

44. The BC and Ontario quotas were the same in 1988, namely $585 000.

45. In 1988, the federal office of the NDP obtained an assignment of all of each candidate's reimbursement in BC ridings. This was done to retire the BC section's debt to the federal office. Despite the assignment, almost all candidates ended up breaking even on the general election campaign. Morley (1991) states that at the end of 1987, the BC section owed $700 000 to the federal office and could not borrow more. BC had borrowed $300 000 to pay off its $600 000 debt in the federal office in the form of arrears in revenue-sharing. It was this situation that moved the BC section to require all candidates in the 1988 federal election to pay all of their reimbursement to the BC section. The complexity of the intraparty flows at election time is extraordinary. For example, for the 1988 federal election, the BC section generated $260 000 in quota payments from federal ridings, and $558 000 from the 100 percent "tax" on candidate reimbursements. Morley (1991, table 3.4) indicates that the BC section spent $794 300 on the election, of which its election quota of $585 000 was the largest outlay. In addition, $45 300 was spent on a fund-raising coordinator, $46 900 was spent on literature and signs, $28 400 on data processing and $16 300 on clerical staff.

46. In 1984, 56.1 percent of union members in Canada were in unions affiliated with the CLC (Archer 1990, 51).

47. For the 1990 Ontario election, the services of over 100 people were provided to the NDP through the Ontario Federation of Labour.

48. A senior CLC official argued that the limits on a candidate's "election expenses" need to be doubled. He said that about $100 000 is needed to "run a decent campaign" in a major urban riding with 80 000 people. He pointed out that it costs $1 000 per week to cover the wages and benefits of a skilled organizer on leave from his/her position to act as a campaign organizer. Moreover, the CLC brief to the Royal Commission on Electoral Reform and Party Financing advocated an increase of 50 percent in *party* "election expenses." (This would have put the limit at $12 million in 1988, if a party ran a candidate in all 295 ridings.)

49. In 1990, the CLC's fund for political contributions was financed by a levy of $.02 per union member per month. The $.02 is part of the CLC's "nickel fund." The other $.03 is used by the CLC to lobby for or against legislative or other government actions.

50. The party expected to win three to five seats in Quebec and increase its popular vote – perhaps as much as 25 percent.

51. These figures ignore both "other expenses" (campaign-related outlays that need not be included in "election expenses" – see chap. 13), and increases in operating expenditures during the election year which are helpful in the campaign.

52. The contrast between the NDP's efforts in Quebec in 1984 and 1988 could hardly be greater. In 1984, the NDP had only 4 000 paid members in Quebec, and only one dedicated campaign worker. In that year, the federal office spent only $50 000 in Quebec and the leader made only one or two appearances in the province. In 1988, Mr. Broadbent made three "passes" in Quebec, visiting at least six cities, some more than once, and focusing on some key ridings, such as Chambly. Each "pass" got national media attention for the party's efforts in Quebec and it served to throw the local media spotlight on some candidates.

53. In 1988, NDP candidates in Quebec received $393 873 in reimbursement from the CEO for their "election expenses" (Canada, Elections Canada 1988c, 3–178). In contrast, Liberal candidates received $1.42 million and PC candidates received $1.64 million.

54. The party developed a new model in its training for 1988 which gave the stamp of approval to the new technologies: phone banks, direct mail, new techniques to make the candidates visible (e.g., shopping mall walks versus all-candidates meetings). There was also more emphasis on the use of electronic media *outside* major urban areas.

CHAPTER 7   THE REFORM PARTY OF CANADA

1. For a party created since the previous general election to become registered, the *Canada Elections Act* specifies that it must nominate at least 50 candidates. Although parties may name candidates prior to the day the writs are issued, they can only be officially nominated after that date.

2. In addition, there were 54 independent candidates and 100 candidates with no affiliation for a total of 1 578 candidates.

3. Preston Manning has been called the product of "a political tradition made up of equal parts of evangelical Christianity and fervent conservatism." His father, Ernest Manning, leader of the Social Credit Party of Alberta, was the premier of Alberta from 1943 to 1968. Preston Manning graduated in 1964 from the University of Alberta with a B.A. (Economics). He worked for a conservative Albertan think-tank and an American aerospace consult-

ing firm before founding M&M Consultants (later Manning Consultants Ltd.) with his father in 1968. The firm specialized in producing "long-range planning reports for a blue-chip list of clients with major interests in Alberta." Manning is committed to his Christianity, and until recently spoke regularly on the "Back to the Bible Hour." He remains in close contact with his father, to whom he admits he owes a "huge political debt" (*Maclean's*, 29 October 1990, 30–32). For more detail on Manning and the origins of the Reform Party, see Dobbin (1991), Manning (1992) and Sharpe and Braid (1992).

4. Manning (1992, 134) states that the Reform Association of Canada was created to sponsor the assembly in Vancouver in May 1987 and to collect funds to defray expenses. Two other persons had an important role in establishing the Association: Ted Byfield, editor of *Alberta Report*, and Francis Winspear, a prominent Edmonton accountant. Among those prominent in their early support for the Reform Association and its ideas were Jack Gallagher, chairman of Dome Petroleum, Dr. Clay Gilson (agricultural economist at the University of Manitoba) and Dr. David Elton (political scientist and president of the Canada West Foundation). The assembly also attracted political observers such as MPs Alex Kindy (PC – Calgary Northeast) and Nelson Riis (NDP – Kamloops), as well as Mel Smith, Premier Vander Zalm's chief advisor, Peter White, a senior official in the Prime Minister's Office, and Charles Crichton, an employee of the Federal-Provincial Relations Office in Ottawa dealing with Liaison (*Financial Post* 1987, 1–2). The development of Preston Manning's ideas, which now shape Reform Party policy, is traced in Sharpe and Braid (1992, 64–75; see also Manning 1992).

5. The author of a Ph.D. dissertation on the Reform Party states that:

> It is not clear to me that the RAC was formed in 1986. Nor did the RAC "establish" core groups in Edmonton, Calgary, and Vancouver. Rather, the roots of the RAC (and later the party) are to be found in somewhat spontaneously-formed and separate groups that arose in each of these areas (and the southern ranchlands of Alberta) in the Fall of 1986–early 1987. When these groups became aware of each other (primarily through Roberts, Manning, and Winspear), a series of meetings were held in Edmonton and Calgary in the Spring of 1987. It was at this time, I believe, that the RAC was formed for the purposes of organizing the Vancouver Assembly." (Letter from Trevor Harrison, Department of Sociology, University of Alberta, 6 April 1992, 1)

6. In 1984, the Progressive Conservatives elected 58 MPs from the West and the same number in Quebec. However, in the view of many westerners, the influence of the latter was much greater than the former. The reason is that the Tories' support in the West was seen as inframarginal (i.e., unlikely to shift even if little rewarded) while the party's support in Quebec was seen as marginal (easily shifted back to the Liberal party or

to separatism/sovereignty association). However, the rise of the Reform Party can be seen as evidence that the Conservative party's support in the West could be lost, that is, its voters could move from the inframarginal to marginal column.

7. According to Manning (1992, 130–34), Winspear provided $50 000 to help finance the assembly. According to the *Globe and Mail* (1 December 1987, A10), Mr. Winspear donated $100 000 to the Reform Party late in 1987. It is not clear if he made one or two such contributions. Because the party did not become registered until October 1988, the list of its donors prior to that time is not in the public domain.

8. Manning (1992, v) put the number at less than 3 000. Sharpe and Braid (1992, 7) state that the party had "fewer than 1 000 members" in November 1987.

9. Roberts was then running his own economics consulting firm. He had been president of the Canadian Chamber of Commerce, the first president of the Canada West Foundation, had been a Liberal MLA in Manitoba and had been president of Simon Fraser University.

10. Roberts' friends and other observers described his behaviour as uncharacteristic and possibly due to illness (Sharpe and Braid, 1992, 26–28).

11. Manning left his consulting firm effective 1 January 1988 to work full-time as leader of the party. According to Sharpe and Braid (1992, 2), Manning's "meek demeanour masks a political will cast in iron, skills as polished as a tap dancer's shoes, and beliefs so radical they would entirely change the nature of Canada."

12. Winspear is described as a lifelong supporter of the Liberal party, who had left it "over the central-Canadian bias and fiscally irresponsible behaviour of the Trudeau administration." He financially backed the Conservatives in 1984 but had become disillusioned by 1986. He had been a "long-time supporter of the Canada West Foundation and a member of its governing council." It was there that he met Stan Roberts (Manning 1992, 129–30).

13. Letter from Grace Dimion, Reform Party, to the author, 26 March 1992.

14. Preston Manning refused to allow Doug Collins, a controversial newspaper columnist, to run in the 1988 federal election, even though Collins was nominated for the riding of Capilano–Howe Sound at a meeting of 165 party members and another 600 of Collins' supporters. Collins refused to sign a pledge committing him to follow the party's opposition to racism. Manning refused to endorse his nomination as a Reform Party candidate as required under the *Canada Elections Act* (Manning 1992, 167–68).

15. However, Clark's vote fell from 37 500 in 1984 to 17 800 in 1988, but note that the total number of votes fell by 10 000 between 1984 and 1988.

16. Manning (1992, 183) states that Reform Party ridings collected $848 000, spent $923 000 on the 1988 campaign and received $173 000 in reimbursements.

17. The information on each candidate's surpluses was supplied to the author by the CEO (see chap. 12).

18. In the 1988 general election, Ms. Grey had finished fourth in the Beaver River riding.

19. Waters received 74 percent of the votes at the party's nominating meeting attended by 210 voting delegates from Reform Party constituency associations and over 600 delegates at large. Waters had been a fund-raiser for the Progressive Conservative party in 1984 (Manning 1992, 203).

20. The evolution of the idea of electing senators is traced in Manning (1992, chap. 11).

21. Manning (1992, 212) states that Waters received 257 523 votes or about 42 percent of the total, 120 000 ahead of Liberal Bill Code.

22. Sharpe and Braid (1992, 152) state that 94 percent of Reform Party members wanted to scrap the Accord even if the result was that Quebec separated.

23. There appears to be an error in the data filed by the Reform Party with the CEO. If the number of individuals said to be contributing less than $100 (7 360 − 3 806 = 3 554) is divided into the amount they contribute ($1 205 733 − $767 856 = 437 877), the average is $123. Party officials could not provide an explanation for this inconsistency.

24. The Fund's statement includes $28 537 for the amortization of costs incurred up to and including the founding convention. The statement required to be filed with the CEO includes $104 029 for "Advertising," while the Fund's statement indicates $44 132 for "Advertising and promotional materials." "Wages and benefits" were $318 964, as reported to the CEO, but only $271 412 as indicated by the Fund. Party officials could not provide an explanation of this inconsistency. Note also that, in 1989, the party did not indicate to the CEO the amount it transferred to riding associations reflecting their 95 percent share of donations they received but which were routed through the Reform Canada Fund so that donors could receive receipts.

25. Sharpe and Braid (1992, 31) state that a poll leaked to the Edmonton *Journal* early in 1990 indicated that 72 percent of Reform Party members were men; 48 percent were over age 60; and 38 percent were retired.

26. *Maclean's,* 29 October 1990. No date was given for Gallup Canada's poll.

27. *Maclean's,* 29 October 1990. On the conflicts over the early efforts to organize for the Reform Party in Ontario, see Dobbin (1991, 128–29; 148–53).

28. Sharpe and Braid (1992, 106) state that as a result of the meeting, Sterling Newspapers, owned by Conrad Black, made a donation of $5 000.

29. Based on the party's amended annual return for 1990 filed with the CEO.

30. A "mailhouse" is a firm that handles mass mailings for political parties, charities or businesses.

31. It is possible that the amount of revenue in the form of contributions from individuals reported in table 7.2 substantially *understates* the total amount of Reform Party revenues provided by individuals because membership dues ($10 per year) appear to have been *excluded*, as well as the net revenue on the sales of merchandise to individuals. In 1990, memberships brought in $479 860 and the sale of merchandise and interest revenues totalled $51 526.

32. Amended party return for 1990 filed with the CEO.

33. This figure includes membership dues (which probably amounted to over $900 000) (*Vancouver Sun*, 3 April 1992, A5).

34. This raises a question about the quality of the auditing by the CEO of the statements filed by the Reform Party (and perhaps others). Part of the problem is probably attributable to the incomplete and antiquated forms (unchanged since 1974) supplied by the CEO to the parties for their annual returns. In particular, in the space below "total operating expenses," only two categories are specified: "transfers to party candidates for general election purposes" and "by-election expenses reported by polling day." It is left up to party officials to know that in the blank spaces they are to record transfers to riding associations (or to other units within the party).

35. Interview with Grace Dimion, 3 April 1992.

36. In some cases, the fee was $5 (Sharpe and Braid 1992, 40).

37. In this case, the rally was co-sponsored by headquarters and some local riding associations, so the net revenue was split equally.

38. When Quebec is dropped from the national results, Reform's share rises to 22 percent or seven points above the Tories (*Vancouver Sun*, 10 May 1991, A12).

39. *Globe and Mail*, 2 April 1991, A8. There were also 128 media people and observers (*Vancouver Sun*, 6 April 1991, A11).

40. These are party members who were not elected as voting delegates, but if they pay the registration fee, they can participate in all aspects of the assembly, except voting.

41. He developed this theme in his "The Road to New Canada" speech to the Assembly (Manning 1992, 282–84).

42. The drive to organize Ontario began in mid-1990 before the members in western Canada approved the change in the party's constitution (May 1991). Manning supported the unofficial efforts but made it clear that the effort had to be "self-financing," i.e., not require money or people from party headquarters (Sharpe and Braid 1992, 28–29).

43. In his book, Manning (1992, 327) indicates that the Reform Party expects to have 200 000 members and $15 million in the bank before the next federal election.

44. This figure, which appears to include revenues from the "Save Canada Campaign," which was suspended at the end of 1991, was given by Preston Manning (*Vancouver Sun*, 4 February 1992, A5). Cliff Fryers told the author in December 1991 that *regular* revenues in 1991 were expected to be $4.1 million.

45. Fryers was also described as chairman of the party and its chief operating officer (*Vancouver Sun*, 30 October 1991, A5).

46. Cliff Fryers was quoted in the *Vancouver Sun* as saying,

> If we don't make use of the political tax credit like other people are doing, we will find ourselves at an incredible disadvantage ... In order to maintain a level playing field for the next election we are going to take advantage of that mechanism. We will take away the political tax credit if we ever have the opportunity to do so. The Reform Party is opposed to allowing income tax deductions for money donated to political parties. (30 October 1991, A5)

47. The "Save Canada Campaign," as of December 1991, did not contain any plan for a direct-mail solicitation, either of party members or of other persons. However, party officials do not rule out the possibility of using direct mail in the near future, depending upon the success of the campaign.

48. The strategy was developed for the party by the Australia-based fund-raising consulting firm Compton's International.

49. See "Pickering rally draws 4000 as party seeks to expand base," *Globe and Mail*, 23 January 1992, A6; "Manning show SRO in Ontario," *Globe and Mail*, 25 January 1992, A1, A4.

50. According to Sharpe and Braid,

> The Reform Party is not simply a home for disillusioned Conservatives. To a startling extent it is a party of newcomers and outsiders, of Canadians who have never been involved in politics before ... for years they have watched governments do things they do not like, growing more frustrated until they could keep silent no longer. Over and over one hears the same refrain: I've never been active in a party before, but something has to be done. (1992, 34)

51. The original constitution (created in November 1987) of the Reform Party "contained a unique sunset clause declaring that the party constitution would be dead in the year 2000 unless two-thirds of the delegates at an assembly voted to re-enact it. This ... clause was included because so many of the delegates had belonged to political parties that had outlived their usefulness" (Manning 1992, 148).

52. Dobbin (1991) contends that the Reform Party is not a populist party, but a consistent right wing, conservative party. Manning, it is argued, "has tapped into and nurtured powerful forces of western discontent in order to build his conservative project. His way has been made easier by a prime minister reviled in much of the country" (ibid., 119). A former Calgary alderman is quoted as saying "if we look backwards and look at the Reform Party, it wasn't a group picking a leader; it was a leader picking a group" (quoted in ibid., 120). Sharpe and Braid comment on the party's ability to be well organized: "The party shows remarkable competence for its stage of development, and what it lacks it makes up for in pure enthusiasm. Meetings are invariably well organized and smoothly run ... The tables selling membership and buttons are staffed by hordes of eager volunteers" (1992, 39–40).

53. Note that the Social Credit party, which ran only nine candidates in 1988, *continued* to be a registered party, reflecting the exercise of discretion by the Chief Electoral Officer.

CHAPTER 8   CONTRIBUTIONS FROM INDIVIDUALS
           AND THE IMPORTANCE OF THE TAX CREDIT

1. To the extent that a party (or candidate) aggregates all contributions from an individual during the year (campaign) before reporting the information to the CEO, then the number of contributions from individuals is the same as the number of individuals (as opposed to corporations) making a contribution.

2. The number of electors was 16 700 565 for the 1984 election and 17 635 201 in 1988.

3. Of course, non-voters may make political contributions, but it is reasonable to believe they are far less likely to do so than voters.

4. The calculation for 1988 used the number of contributions in 1988 divided by the number of votes in the 1989 election.

5. It is possible that contributions to the party fell off because they went to the early efforts of leadership candidates.

6. Annual average is based on 3.42 years because the legislation did not come into effect until 1 August 1974.

7. In the case of the NDP, federally receipted contributions by individuals were divided by total federally receipted contributions from all sources, plus other income (non-receipted), plus the federal "election expenses" rebate.

8. A slight amount is due to reimbursement, but it is a smaller fraction of Conservative party revenues than it is of Liberal party or NDP revenues. Recall chapter 4.

9. Data are taken from tables 5.1 through 5.9.

10. Seidle and Paltiel (1981, 253–54) put the amount at about $830 000 in 1979, and about $1 million in 1980. More generally, see chapter 5.

11. The same threshold was used in 1983 as in 1989. During this period, the CPI increased by 29 percent – hence $2 000 in 1989 is the equivalent of $1 552 in 1983.

12. The data in table 8.13 on the largest single contribution have been rounded to the nearest thousand dollars.

13. Note that in 1930 Tory leader R.B. Bennett contributed $750 000 to the Conservative party's election campaign (Paltiel 1970b, 29). That is the equivalent of roughly $4.2 million in terms of 1989 prices.

14. The sequence of the tables follows that of an earlier version of this volume, which formed part of the research used in the Final Report of the Royal Commission, released in February 1992.

15. Derived by the author from data made public by the Liberal party on 7 November 1990.

16. Corporate donations in 1990 totalled $406 million, down 4.3 percent from 1989, but pre-tax corporate profits were down 24.7 percent. Corporate contributions to charity in Canada amounted to 0.9 percent of pre-tax profits in 1990 (0.71 percent in 1989). Americans were much more generous than Canadians in terms of contributions to charity. In 1990, individuals gave 2.2 percent of their pre-tax income (U.S. $101.8 billion) or almost three times the Canadian level. U.S. corporations donated 1.67 percent of their pre-tax income, or almost twice the Canadian level (*Financial Post*, 16 December 1991, 17).

17. The Quebec tax credit is equal to 50 percent of contributions up to $280.

18. The province of Ontario recognized the potential effects of inflation on political contributions in 1986 when it changed its tax credit provisions from those that were the same as the federal government to the following: 75 percent of contributions up to $200; $150 plus 50 percent of contributions between $200 and $800; and $450 plus 33.3 percent of contributions between $800 and $1 700, with a maximum tax credit of $750.

19. The median could not be computed from the data from the original sources. Some care must be exercised in interpreting this number, since it is simply the total value of tax credits for political contributions divided by the number of individuals claiming the credit on their income tax return.

20. Note that a tax credit is of no value to someone who does not have any taxable income, because it is a deduction from the amount of tax payable.

21. The peak years were 1984 (1.78 percent) and 1988 (1.77 percent).

22. See chapter 9. Note also that a fund-raiser in a cabinet minister's riding sent a letter to the members of the riding association soliciting contributions of $100 in December 1991. The letter emphasized that donors could receive

a tax credit of $75, thereby reducing their net cost to $25. Further, the fund-raiser proposed to have the riding association give each donor a cheque for $25 to reduce the net cost of the $100 contribution to zero. However, the riding would net $50, the PC Canada Fund would get $25 for issuing the receipt for the tax credit, while other taxpayers would cover the cost of the $75 tax credit (*Globe and Mail*, 3 February 1992, A4).

23. While BC and Manitoba have their own provincial tax credit for political contributions, Saskatchewan does not. In Saskatchewan, the NDP issues federal tax receipts for contributions to provincial sections or candidates. In the other provinces, it divides contributions and issues tax receipts for both levels so as to maximize the credit to the donor, according to party officials.

24. Michaud and Laferrière (1991) estimated that 2.4 percent of persons voting in the 1989 Quebec provincial election made a contribution to a party and/or candidate. Further, Massicotte (1991, table 1.16) estimated that 47 percent of Quebeckers making a contribution to a provincial party claimed the provincial tax credit in 1988. Therefore, these data suggest that residents of Quebec are more likely to make contributions to a provincial party than to a federal party.

25. Derived from the federal tax credits by province given in table 8.11.

26. They are not alone in advocating such a position. For example, in mid-1987, NDP leader Ed Broadbent called upon the Conservatives to change the *Canada Elections Act* to permit only electors to make political contributions (*Globe and Mail*, 22 August 1987). In 1981, a Liberal MPP introduced Bill 206 in the Ontario legislature, which would have, among other things, allowed only electors to make political contributions. In the United States, there is a limit of $1 000 on contributions by individuals to each candidate per election and a $25 000 limit on an individual's donations to all candidates in a calendar year. These limits have not been increased since they were set in 1974. (Note that the limit on contributions to *party* committees is $20 000 annually for an individual and $15 000 for a multicandidate political action committee) (Alexander 1991).

27. Between 1978 and 1983, the Quebec Liberal party raised an average of $2.65 million annually in Quebec. Between 1984 and 1989, it raised an average of $8.0 million annually. The Parti québécois was initially more successful in using *financement populaire* than was the Liberal party: it raised an average of $3.5 million annually between 1978 and 1983. However, the average fell to $3.3 million annually between 1984 and 1989 (all figures in nominal dollars) (Massicotte 1991).

28. Note that, to give individuals a receipt for the tax credit, their contributions would have to be routed through the PC Canada Fund, which would have retained 25 percent.

29. Commenting on Mr. Gérin's efforts, W. David Angus, president of the PC Canada Fund, said that, while he did not dispute the need to broaden the

base of support for the party, he drew the line "at fellow Tories under-cutting his efforts to raise money from corporations" (*Globe and Mail*, 13 November 1987, A1). He called Gérin and his supporters "short-sighted and negative" and questioned whether they were really "team players." In the same article, Gérin was quoted as saying that he was not swayed by Mr. Angus's comments and that, by Christmas, there would be at least 20 Quebec ridings where corporate donations would not be accepted – which would give him a lot of personal satisfaction.

30. These arguments have force, but it is essential to distinguish between allowing only electors to make contributions to parties, candidates or lead-ership campaigns, and limiting the size of contributions from any source. It seems logical that the expectation of reciprocity for political contribu-tions is much greater for *large* contributions, regardless of their source. Further, if contributions can come only from individuals, corporations, unions or other organizations could "get around" the law by requesting their executives to make donations for which they would be reimbursed. While this would increase the effective after-tax cost of their political contribu-tions, organizations intent upon making them would still be able to do so. Moreover, public disclosure of all contributions from individuals over, say, $100 would still obscure direct linkages between corporations or unions and political parties. It would be necessary for people to be able to iden-tify donors in terms of their employer and then be able to determine that the individuals were, in fact, reimbursed for their donation.

31. In August 1988, the Quebec Conservative caucus had adopted a resolu-tion specifying that the next general election should be financed solely through *financement populaire*.

32. "Election expenses" averaged $42 474 and "personal expenses" averaged $2 827 – see chapter 12.

33. In 1988 the Quebec Liberal party held 264 social activities ("access oppor-tunities") for which they charged admission. The number of such social events had risen from 79 in 1984 to 139 in 1985 (an election year) to 221 in 1987. These activities, which included suppers, brunches, "Bavarian nights," trips, cocktail parties, lunches, golf days, fashion shows, corn roasts, sugaring-off parties, dances and a bowl-a-thon, raised a total of $5.9 million. This amounted to 82 percent of the total of $7.2 million the QLP raised in contri-butions in 1988. Note that 87 percent of the amount raised through social activities came from contributions over $100. The highest price of any event was $2 500 for a dinner (Angell 1990a, 20). The impact of the Liberals' social activities fund-raising strategy can be seen in the fraction of the contribu-tions under $100. In the period 1978–83, about three-quarters of the total value of contributions to the QLP came in amounts less than $100. However, in the period 1986–88, such small contributions accounted for about one-sixth of total contributions. In contrast, over three-fifths of the PQ's contributions came from donations under $100. In general, see Massicotte (1991).

34. This amounts to only $33 300 per riding, but the CEO (Canada, Elections Canada 1988c, 3–178) indicates that Quebec PC candidates raised an average of $43 820 in contributions from all sources.

35. See Toronto *Star*, 27 February 1991, and *Financial Post* (editorial), 11 March 1991, 7. An analysis of Taylor's arguments can be found in Stanbury (1991).

36. As noted in chapter 7, between 1988 and 1991 contributions from individuals accounted for over 90 percent of the total revenue of the Reform Party.

37. It cannot be computed from the data available from the Department of National Revenue.

38. Massicotte (1990, 5) notes that, while 35 parties have been authorized since the legislation reforming party financing came into effect in 1978, two parties (Liberal party and Parti québécois) have collected 97.5 percent of revenues and contributions and accounted for 96.3 percent of party expenditures. In 1989, 17 parties were authorized. Only the QLP and PQ had authorized associations in all ridings.

39. Note that an increase from $20 in 1978 to $38 in 1987 (90 percent) was only very slightly above the rate of inflation (86.7 percent).

40. In 1985, the Liberal party had some 190 100 members; in 1987, it had 105 800 according to Massicotte (1990). The PQ had 102 200 members in May 1988.

41. In absolute terms, the amounts were $4.3 million in 1987 and $4.8 million in 1988.

42. See the discussion in chapter 10 with respect to "The 500" fund-raising program of the federal Conservative party.

43. In September 1989, the Liberal party was returned to power in Quebec, but lost seven seats to hold 92. It obtained 54 percent of the popular vote (Angell 1990a, 14).

CHAPTER 9 DIRECT-MAIL FUND-RAISING AND ELECTIONEERING

1. Direct marketing sales in Canada totalled $7.8 billion and the industry grew by 10 percent each year between 1982 and 1990, according to John Gustavson, president and chief executive officer of the Canadian Direct Marketing Association. The biggest direct mailers in Canada are the banks, insurance companies, publishers, catalogue sales companies, airlines and charities. Direct-response television commercials (e.g., Canadian Home Shopping Club) and telephone marketing are other branches of this form of marketing (*Vancouver Sun*, 8 December 1991).

2. In the parlance of marketing, this is known as "market demassification." For example, Compusearch Market and Social Research Ltd. of Toronto has combined Statistics Canada census data with postal codes (there are 700 000 in total) to produce a detailed database grouped into 70 kinds of

neighbourhoods. Marketers or political parties can target their direct mail by grouping postal codes with similar characteristics (income, family size, education, expenditure patterns) (Mitchell 1990, 67).

3. In 1989, 63.7 billion pieces of third-class or "bulk business" mail were sent in the United States. This type of mail accounted for 39 percent of total postal volume. An estimated 92 million Americans responded to a direct-mail "pitch," a 60 percent increase in six years. They spent or donated some $183 billion. "Today, more money is invested in direct-mail pitches, promotions and appeals than is spent on advertising in magazines or on radio or network television" (Smolowe 1990). It is estimated that "over the course of a lifetime, the average American professional will devote eight months to sifting through mail solicitations" (ibid.). Despite all the effort devoted to making the envelopes appealing, it is hard to get people to open direct mail. It is estimated that 44 percent of such mail ends up unopened. The electronic version of direct mail is growing in the United States. Some 180 000 businesses use automatic dialing telephones to reach as many as 7 million people daily (ibid.).

4. In 1916, the Democratic Party, with Woodrow Wilson in the White House, sponsored a mail solicitation drive that is believed to have resulted in donations from 300 000 persons (Canada, Committee 1966, 199). Note that the large-scale use of direct-mail political fund-raising had its origins in the frustration and alienation in the United States during the late 1960s.

5. Paltiel states that the Liberal party used direct mail in the 1972 election, but "abandoned the use of the expensive computerized direct mail technique [in the 1974 election] because of the adverse publicity it had brought in 1972" (1975, 193). Note that, in 1961–62, the Liberal party in Ontario sent letters seeking funds to 75 000 Liberal sympathizers at a cost of $4 000. Net receipts were about $6 600. A second mailing in 1965 cost $4 500 but there was a net loss of $800 on this appeal. The mailing list was the Ontario section of the national party (Canada, Committee 1966, 200, n. 156).

6. One study found that 87 percent of direct-mail appeals by nonprofit organizations are thrown away unopened. Hence the envelope must be designed to get the recipient to open it and read the appeal (Berry 1989, 57–58).

7. The premium is a gift of modest value that is designed to draw upon the deeply embedded cultural value of reciprocity, i.e., to increase the odds that the recipient will send a contribution. On reciprocity, see Gouldner (1961) and Noonan (1984).

8. Information provided by Stephen Thomas, consultant to the NDP. Thomas operates a direct-mail firm in Toronto.

9. Recall that the Reform Party has focused almost exclusively on party members under its "sustainer program" (chap. 7).

10. In the United States, the renting of lists for both political and commercial direct mail is a $3 billion business. The *Direct Mail List Rates and Data*

volume contains descriptions of 10 258 mailing lists available for rent at a cost of $50 to $150 per 1 000 names (Smolowe 1990, 46).

11. Berry notes that a "good" return on a prospecting list can be 2 percent of the recipients making a contribution: "A 'house list' generally gets a response from 8 to 15 percent of those solicited" (1989, 61).

12. Warwick (1990, 114) states that in U.S. direct-mail fund-raising for charitable and interest groups, the average "life" of donors is 2.6 years (31 months). The typical donor will make two or three renewal gifts that average about 20 percent to 25 percent above the initial donation.

13. Recall from chapter 6 that (except for election years) the revenues of the NDP's *federal office* are a modest fraction of the total revenues raised by the federal wing, i.e., using the federal tax credit.

14. Another perspective on the Conservatives' success with direct mail is to note that its net revenues from this source alone greatly exceeded the *total* revenues of the NDP's federal office in the years between elections in the 1980s.

15. The parties' expense ratio can be compared to the experience of charitable organizations. A review of the fund-raising costs of 46 charities in the United States in 1987 found that they absorbed an average of 7.8 percent of total revenue (Plawin 1988). The range was from 1.5 percent (National Kidney Foundation; income of $3.3 million) to 33 percent (Epilepsy Foundation; income of $8.8 million). About 60 percent of these charities could be described as "cause" groups (e.g., Greenpeace USA, Environmental Defense Fund, Mothers Against Drunk Driving), while the rest fall into the category of medical-related charities (e.g., American Cancer Society, American Lung Association, March of Dimes Birth Defects Foundation). The distribution of costs of fund-raising for the two groups of charities as given by Plawin (ibid.) was as follows:

	Medical-related	"Cause" groups
≤ 3%	2	2
4–6%	2	6
7–10%	5	5
11–15%	4	4
16–20%	2	6
21–25%	1	3
26%+	2	1
Total	18	27

These figures may not be comparable to political parties' costs of raising money by direct mail for several reasons: the charities may also raise money by other means (e.g., foundation grants) whose costs are much lower; many of the charities' direct-mail appeals have been operating for a much longer period than have those of the political parties and have found the most efficient techniques; in the case of the Liberal party, large changes in the level of direct-mail activity have undoubtedly increased costs (see below).

16. Terry O'Grady, the Communications Director of the NDP's federal office, states that the "ratio of expenses to gross revenues for the federal party's direct mail is approximately 20 percent for the House list and upwards of 35–40 percent overall, depending on the amount of prospecting done. To my knowledge, the party has always broken even or made modest profits on direct mail" (letter to the author, 9 May 1991). However, the figures provided by the federal office (table 9.6) indicate that the costs were usually much higher than "upwards of 35–40 percent overall."

17. Letter from Rosemary Dahlman to the author, October 1990.

18. One-half of what was raised was placed in the riding's election "trust fund," 25 percent went to the riding's ongoing expenses and 25 percent went to the PTA (Seidle and Paltiel 1981, 237).

19. While the Treasury Committee is said to have 150–325 companies on its various provincial lists, party officials believe that solicitation of those on the list was not done systematically (at least annually). As important, little or no effort was made to expand the number of firms to be solicited. In any event, the Progressive Conservative party outdistanced the Liberal party in terms of large donations ($10 000+) from corporations of all sizes, as the data in chapter 11 make clear.

20. PTAs do, however, use them for other kinds of fund-raising: annual dues, dinners, special events and personal solicitation. That is why they guard them so zealously. They feel that the "well only has so much water." If the far-off "feds" get more, the PTA won't be able to raise as much money. Previously, the PTAs would raise money and *then* tell the centre how much they were willing to give it. However, in 1987, headquarters took away the PTAs' tax receipting authority, which had been delegated to them by the Federal Liberal Agency (chap. 5).

21. Three PTAs that *do* use their membership lists for direct-mail solicitations, according to former party president Michel Robert, are New Brunswick, Manitoba and Quebec.

22. Note that, even where a PTS uses the federal tax credit (delegated to it by the federal office) to provide receipts for contributions, the federal office receives only 15 percent of the revenues raised (recall chap. 6).

23. Presumably there is an exception for Ontario where provincial law prohibits transfers from the provincial party to the federal level.

24. Even the more generous donors seem to prefer to send smaller amounts several times a year. "Most direct mail donors write checks to charity when they're paying their bills on a weekly or monthly basis" (Warwick 1990, 17). Parties, therefore, try to send out regular "bills" in the hope of receiving almost monthly donations from individuals.

25. Thomas was first hired by the federal office in 1985.

26. The NDP's financial statements for the 1988 election (chap. 6) indicate that direct-mail revenue was $742 200, while associated expenses totalled $382 700. However, table 9.6 indicates that the federal wing generated $2.1 million in 1988 from direct mail (expenses were $1.2 million).

27. When the party is down in the polls, the NDP's direct-mail effort stresses "movement" themes (including mention of such revered leaders as Woodsworth, Douglas and Lewis) rather than themes that focus on the party.

28. Considerable effort goes into two to four "special appeals" each year. The logic is based on the idea that people want to see their money used to achieve a particular purpose. The NDP has a separate program aimed at women that seeks money for the Agnes MacPhail Fund earmarked for women candidates (table 9.6). Prospect, specials and house-list mailings have been used for this fund.

29. A senior official stated that this list contained 30 000 names in 1990.

30. In the fall of 1990, the Quebec wing took one riding and applied a targeted, individualized direct-mail appeal to raise money. As a Quebec official emphasized, the Tories are far ahead of all other parties on segmenting voters by social, economic and demographic characteristics and then on tailoring the message to reflect the individual's characteristics, thereby increasing the probability of receiving a donation and increasing the average size of donations.

31. In the United States, these calls can be made by a computer-driven machine using a recorded message which is capable of recording the voter's responses to the recording!

32. "Those who've contributed most generously, most frequently and most recently are your best prospects for additional gifts" (Warwick 1990, 128). Direct-mail fund-raising is subject to a version of "Pareto's Law": 20 percent of donors are likely to account for 80 percent of the total value of contributions (ibid., 131).

33. For example, the Ontario NDP sent out four direct-mail appeals during the 1990 provincial election: The first emphasized the need for funds to finance the election campaign. The second provided "inside information" on the leader's tour and asked for money to pay for the tour; the third was sent out two weeks before voting day and focused on the possibility of winning more seats; the fourth went out a few days before voting day, thanked people for supporting the party and asked them to get out and vote NDP.

34. The federal office's communications director stated that it refrains from mailing during provincial elections and for 30 days thereafter.

35. Of the 23 mailings examined, nine were signed by the leader, eight by the federal secretary, three by the campaign director and three by others, such as MPs.

36. A BC section direct-mail piece in May 1990 emphasized that "if you pay income tax, you can get back 75 percent of the first $200 you donate each year." This is because the federal and provincial tax credits are the same and the party divides the contributions and issues two receipts.

37. The NDP has occasionally used a regular stamp with good effect.

38. Stephen Thomas & Associates won a prize given by the Canadian Direct Marketing Association for a federal NDP direct-mail piece using a "sweepstakes" theme. Recipients who returned a card were eligible for a draw for two tickets for a holiday in Australia.

39. The NDP has thought of asking for smaller donations, e.g., $10, but it received an average of $31 from donors responding to a prospect mailing to BC residents featuring a "sweepstakes" prize of a trip to Australia. Noted artist Robert Bateman gave prints to Amnesty International to be offered as a draw prize in a direct-mail campaign for the organization. The mailing raised about $250 000. According to Stephen Thomas, Amnesty International is able to net $45 per year per donor from six or seven mailings annually.

40. However, the figures in table 9.6 indicate sweepstakes revenues of $168 195 in 1988 and costs of $133 287.

41. In November 1990 the *Deceptive Mailings Prevention Act of 1990* was enacted in the United States. It "bans solicitations that masquerade as government notices and prey particularly upon the fears of the elderly" (Smolowe 1990, 46).

42. The mailings were provided to the author by Stephen Thomas & Associates in October 1990.

43. Officials at Conservative party headquarters stated that this is one of the least important characteristics of direct mail, and one that many of their campaign people find *least* attractive. They emphasized that Conservative party direct-mail copy is written to elicit a financial commitment. Direct-mail content for voter solicitation is substantially different from that used for fund-raising purposes. They said that the Conservative party's message is not communicated using fund-raising direct mail.

44. The theoretical and empirical basis in applied psychology of this approach is discussed in Pratkanis and Aronson (1991, chap. 7).

45. Generally, see Lee (1989) and Fraser (1989). Target '88 used a "demassification" technique. Close targeting based on numerous standard responses can get over the differing shifts in support. More generally, see Axworthy (1991).

46. The techniques of Target '88, which is now called the "Incumbency Protection Program," were adapted for the 1990 Manitoba election.

47. See the discussion in chapter 13.

48. Data provided by the CEO. More generally, see chapter 12.

CHAPTER 10   TWO FUND-RAISING TECHNIQUES: DINNERS
                         AND MAJOR-DONOR PROGRAMS

1. The NDP makes very little use of fund-raising dinners and it does not have a major-donor program.

2. A senior official in the Conservative party argues that, while certain events may not be accessible to those who make smaller contributions, other social events are open to them, such as barbecues or golf tournaments organized by a riding or a group of ridings.

3. This figure seems high. It implies that some 4 000 people attended dinners at an average ticket price of $500.

4. Based on an Angus Reid-Southam news poll of 1 505 Canadians conducted on 19–27 November 1991 (*Vancouver Sun*, 7 December 1991, A3).

5. Such paid staff might well help with the mailing lists, design the invitations, handle negotiations with the hotel and so forth.

6. Mrs. Dyck, it should be noted, has been a party supporter for many years and does not represent any interest group. She gave almost $127 000 to the NDP in 1991.

7. Gallery is president and owner of Gallery Publications, which publishes "Seaports and Shipping World" and "Canadian Sailings." He is the former mayor of Westmount (1983–87). He was also the former chairman and director of CN Hotels (1987–88), CN Tower (1988–89), CN (France) (1986–90), and vice-chairman and a director of Canadian National (1987–89). He is a director of the PC Canada Fund.

8. In 1983, "The 500" raised $319 000 (table 10.3).

9. Note that the Department of National Revenue indicates that in 1987 only 3 410 of 265 734 businesses claiming the small business deduction (SBD) and 4 232 of the 641 470 other (larger) corporations made *any* contribution to a political party. Moreover, for 76.6 percent of the SBD corporations and 64.5 percent of the larger corporations making a donation, the amount was *under* $500. (see chap. 11).

10. Wearing (1981, 62, 185–86) notes that the Ontario Liberal party set up a "Liberal Union" in 1959 to get 1 000 donations of $100 each. In terms of 1989 dollars, the target contribution was over $500. In the early 1970s, the federal Liberal party set up the Red Carnation Fund to obtain larger donations from individuals.

11. Individuated or exclusive benefits (in contrast to collective benefits) are obtained only by those persons who pay to belong to the organization. They help to overcome the "free rider" problem faced by groups that produce collective benefits that are available even to those who have not contributed to the group. Individuals can gain the benefits of the policies of the party in power (or the positions of an opposition party) without making a donation. However, where a party is able to provide individuated benefits, only those who contribute the required amount can gain access to these benefits. Thus the provision of such benefits is likely to encourage larger contributions. Generally, see Olson (1965) and Dunleavy (1990).

12. An individual who contributes $3 000 or more (either on a personal basis or through a personal corporation) beyond the $1 000 membership fee is placed on the Honour Roll, as is one who recruits three new members.

13. Gallery's willingness to volunteer considerable time to the Conservative party to run "The 500" is based on the idea that those who do well in society should "give something back." He identifies himself as a small businessman who is a strong believer in a competitive market economy. Describing himself as "right-of-centre," he says it is logical for him to identify with the Progressive Conservative party.

14. Gallery believes that a more generous income-tax credit would increase membership in "The 500."

15. Note that such letters from MPs whose assistance has been sought by a constituent – individual or corporate – are a routine fact of political life.

16. The Quebec Liberal party's use of "access opportunities" to raise money is described in Angell (1990a, 1990b).

17. The reason that gross rather than net revenues are used is that the proportion of gross revenues absorbed by the costs of raising that revenue vary greatly by fund-raising technique *and* because such costs are available only for "The 500" and for direct mail. Therefore, we cannot compare the net revenue from "The 500" to the net revenue from *all* sources for the Conservative party.

18. The size distribution of contributions by individuals of $2 000 or more to the NDP can be found in table 8.13.

19. Three of the 39 contributions of $2 000 or more to the NDP in 1988 came from NDP MPs.

20. During an interview with the author, Conservative Senator Norman Atkins said that "The 500" is unobjectionable as a fund-raising technique because all contributions are disclosed, and there is "no undue influence." However, he suggested that "The 500" may create too high a profile, hence attract unfavourable media attention. In his view, the success of "The 500" shows "there is a market for ego and artificial status."

21. A senior Conservative party official points out that most ministers, including the Prime Minister, attend far more meetings with groups of individuals in their official role than they do fund-raising meetings.

CHAPTER 11   CONTRIBUTIONS FROM BUSINESS AND COMMERCIAL ORGANIZATIONS

1. In the period 1974–80 the Chief Electoral Officer provided several categories: public corporations, private corporations, corporations without share capital and unincorporated organizations that might include corporations. Later, the CEO used the category "businesses, commercial organizations," which appears to include the first three of the four categories listed above. For convenience, the term "corporations" has been used to refer to all business and commercial organizations.

2. Senator Godfrey stated that, in raising money for the Liberal party during election years prior to 1974, he tried hard to hold back enough money to finance the national office over the next four years until the next election. Prior to 1974, very little effort was made to collect funds from corporations to finance interelection activities (interview with the author in September 1990).

3. The average of the annual percentages (i.e., not weighted by size) was 46.4 percent for the Conservative party and 46.6 percent for the Liberal party.

4. Convention revenues (delegates' fees) totalled $4.4 million (30.5 percent of the party's total revenues), very largely in the form of contributions for which tax receipts were issued to individuals. In addition, $1.95 million in contributions by individuals and corporations to leadership candidates were routed through the Federal Liberal Agency and these were included in total party revenues.

5. The NDP does, however, receive substantial sums from trade unions, unlike its two main rivals (chap. 6).

6. To put the $4.1 per annum *difference* into perspective, note that the NDP's federal office *total* revenues amounted to $2.6 million in 1989 (chap. 6).

7. After the *Election Expenses Act* came into effect, Prime Minister Trudeau imposed an annual limit of $25 000 on contributions to the Liberal party from any corporation and twice that in an election year. Party fund-raisers were not pleased (chap. 6).

8. For the 1968 election, the Liberal party raised $4.5 million, of which $1.3 million was raised from about 350 corporations whose head office was in Ontario (letter from Senator John Godfrey to the *Financial Times of Canada* dated 22 December 1972). More was raised from corporations whose head office was in Quebec than from those based in Ontario. In 1972, Senator Godfrey raised over $2.25 million from corporations whose headquarters were in Ontario. In 1974 he raised $2.26 million from this source (Senator John Godfrey, "Memorandum to File," 2 December 1974, 4).

9. Corporate contributions to the three main parties in 1988 totalled $23.07 million, while corporate contributions to all candidates totalled $7.96 million (Canada, Elections Canada 1988c).

10. Corporate contributions to the three main parties in 1984 totalled $16.4 million, while corporate contributions to all candidates amounted to $7.0 million. Note that the total amount of tax credits claimed by corporations peaked in 1984 at $1.6 million (table 11.7).

11. The average rank of those giving to both parties but at least 10 percent more to the Conservative party than to the Liberal party is 205. The average rank for those giving more than 10 percent more to the Liberals than to the Tories in 1990 was 178. Overall, the average rank of firms giving to the Liberal party (188) was lower than that of firms giving to the Conservative party (210). This suggests that Liberals focus more of their efforts on larger firms or, in any event, it is larger firms that give to them rather than to the Tories.

12. In Ontario, however, corporate political contributions up to $7 000 are tax-deductible in computing the province's corporate income tax payable.

13. Some 14 corporations made contributions of $5 000 or more to the NDP in 1988 (table 6.6).

14. The F 155 was created from the following lists compiled by the *Financial Post*: 100 largest financial institutions in Canada (ranked by assets); 25 largest life insurers (ranked by assets); 15 largest property and casualty insurers (ranked by revenue); and the 15 largest investment dealers (ranked by total capital). In 1990, the *Financial Post* changed its listings somewhat (for 1989 results), but it was possible to compile a list comparable to that of previous years (1983–88), except that data for only 10 investment dealers could be obtained and they had to be ranked by assets instead of by total capital. In 1990, the *Financial Post* did not provide information on investment dealers, so only 140 firms are on the list.

15. The data in table 11.18a suggest that it is not necessary to separate election from nonelection years, because the participation rate (as opposed to the average size of contributions) did not increase in election years, or it increased only slightly (1984).

16. The Bank of Nova Scotia gave $55 875 to the Liberal party and $40 000 to the Conservative party.

17. This figure is based on all 25 firms in the cohort. Hence it includes the firms making no contribution to *either* party.

18. Stevenson (1981, 31–32) reports that, when Senator John Godfrey was a major fund-raiser for the Liberal party in the late 1960s and early 1970s, he requested that firms contribute 0.2 percent of their profits in election years.

19. A telephone survey of 2 947 Canadians conducted between 13 September and 5 November 1990 by the Institute for Social Research indicates that a

majority (or plurality) of citizens believe that corporations, unions and interest groups have a right to give money to political parties (Blais and Gidengil, 1991). Forty-three percent believe there should *not* be a limit on the amount of contributions a person can make, while 35 percent favour a limit of $1 000 or less. At the same time, 55 percent believe that unions/corporations should get the approval of members/shareholders before making political donations. Three-quarters of those interviewed believe that parties should be required to disclose who contributes money to them. At the same time, 55 percent "basically agree" with the statement "It is impossible to control what political parties receive and spend in an election."

CHAPTER 12   CANDIDATE REVENUES AND
              EXPENDITURES, 1979–88

1. In 1988, one Liberal candidate withdrew before election day, but his name remained on the ballot; he filed his post-election return on revenues and expenditures.

2. The Chief Electoral Officer uses the term "contributions" to refer to *all* forms of revenues received by candidates. Candidates often receive *transfers* from their riding association and provincial and territorial associations as well as from party headquarters in Ottawa. The term "total revenues" is used to refer to all sources of revenues other than the reimbursement of part of a candidate's "election expenses."

3. Between 1979 and 1988, the CPI increased by 78 percent.

4. In 1983, the requirement that the candidate's "personal expenses" exceeding $2 000 be included in "election expenses" for the purpose of calculating the limit was eliminated (recall chap. 2).

5. The term "campaign surplus" is the author's. It is not the same as "surplus" as defined by the CEO, which is computed by taking into account "other expenses." Note again that all campaign-related outlays are not captured here, because we have no data on "other expenses" except for 1988. See section 5 below.

6. Note that both figures are the sum of all candidates who had a surplus. The deficits of those candidates who had a deficit were not deducted, so the *net* surplus is overstated – see section 7 below.

7. However, for the reasons discussed in section 5, the CEO understated the candidates' "other expenses" in 1988 and therefore overstated the total surplus of candidates.

8. In 1984, the Liberal party did *not* seek to obtain part of its candidates' reimbursement, except in Quebec, according to party officials.

9. Table 12.2 is based on total revenues for all of each party's candidates; the three main parties all ran a full slate of 282 candidates, except for the NDP in 1980, which ran 280 candidates. Therefore, the percentages in table 12.2 are directly comparable to those in table 12.3 for the three main parties.

10. Note that it is impossible to properly sort out the flows of funds within the parties. In 1988, Liberal candidates transferred $2.27 million to party head-quarters (table 12.4a) while Liberal candidates reported receiving $1.68 million from party headquarters (table 12.3). However, the transfer to the party from candidates took the form of the assignment of one-half of each candidate's reimbursement of his/her "election expenses" by the federal government. Thus the money apparently went from the CEO to the party.

11. The NDP refers to these as provincial and territorial sections (PTSs).

12. Seidle and Paltiel (1981, 253–55) indicate that, in 1979, the Liberal party obtained $830 000 from candidates in Ontario and Quebec and a total of "about $1 million" from all provinces.

13. In his 1989 Statutory Report, the Chief Electoral Officer (Canada, Elections Canada 1989a, 47) states:

    Subsection 63(5.1) of the [*Canada Elections*] *Act* states that these surplus funds must be transferred either to the registered party or to any local organization or association of members of the party in the elec-toral district where the candidate ran. The expression "any local organization or association of members of the party" is not defined by the *Act* and no controls are placed on the funds once they have been received by these "undefined" organizations. Because a major portion of these surplus funds comes from the public treasury, I consider that the public has a right to know the use that is being made of these funds. A few provinces have resolved this problem by requiring constituency associations to register formally and to account on an annual basis for the funds they have received. Conversely, these funds could be turned over to the registered party who sponsored the candidate involved in each case, or to the Receiver General.

14. An NDP candidate in BC in 1988 stated that the BC section also kept a frac-tion of each candidate's revenues (which had to be routed through the PTS) to help finance national campaign activities in BC.

15. Note that the data in table 12.5 are for the number of contributions by indi-viduals, not for the number of individuals making a contribution (which is the way the parties record and report contributions from individuals).

16. The CEO puts the number of electors at 16 700 565 in 1984 and 17 635 201 in 1988.

17. These figures for the NDP may be misleading. In 1988 in BC all NDP candi-dates had to route all contributions through the provincial section. It then made transfers to the candidates. As a result, Johanna den Hertog, the NDP candidate in Vancouver Centre, reported only 28 contributions, versus 334 for the PC candidate and 145 for the Liberal candidate (Canada, Elections Canada 1988c, 3-254).

18. Raising far more money than the limit on expenditures does not appear to be useful unless it can be spent on campaign-related activities. However,

since any surplus must be given to the candidate's party or a local association, these entities have an interest in any surplus. See section 7 below.

19. This calculation assigns 211 of the 216 missing cases in the file obtained from the CEO to the under $10 000 category. CEO staff indicate that virtually all the missing cases were candidates who raised very little money.

20. Prime Minister Mulroney ranked forty-fifth. He raised $68 551 in 1988 (Canada, Elections Canada 1988c, 3-115).

21. The incumbency rate is calculated excluding deaths, retirements and failures to obtain the nomination, that is, it includes only those MPs who ran again and won. With respect to the incumbency rate, Blake (1991, 256) states that "until 1984, it appeared that Canadian elections [between 1962 and 1979] had become very stable affairs with only minor net shifts between elections." He continues, "it now appears that 1984 may have ushered in a new era of competition." Blake (ibid., 257–58) concludes that "it is clear that electoral volatility in Canada has been higher than that in the United States and is higher, on average, than that in Britain."

22. However, table 12.8 indicates that, in six provinces, PC candidates were able to raise more revenue.

23. Further, the BC section of the NDP required that all candidates sign over to it all of the reimbursement of their "election expenses" by the federal government. This amounted to $558 127 (Canada, Elections Canada 1988c, 3-259). This was used to pay the BC section's "quota" of $585 000 to the federal office to help finance the party's national campaign (chap. 6).

24. In major urban areas, the rent for a campaign office may be quite high. In rural ridings, lower rents may be offset by the need to have two or more campaign offices.

25. Shortly after the 1979 election, the Office of the Chief Electoral Officer surveyed the agents of all candidates (Seidle 1980, 271–72). Based on a 56 percent response rate, the survey indicated that 15 percent of Conservative agents, 10 percent of Liberal agents and 1 percent of NDP agents found the limits "very restrictive," while 39 percent, 38 percent and 13 percent respectively found them to be "somewhat restrictive." Three-quarters thought that the limits should be increased to reflect the increased cost of campaigns. Recall that, overall, Tory and Liberal candidates spent 78 percent and 80 percent of the limit in 1979, while the New Democratic candidates spent only 34 percent. The second bit of evidence, the amount candidates spent on "other expenses," will be discussed in section 5.

26. This was necessary because the relevant parts of the form filed by each candidate require that all financial transactions be recorded. Some of these, such as the receipt and repayment of a loan, are capital items rather than expenditures *other* than "election expenses" or "personal expenses." Of course, the interest on the loan is an "other expense."

27. Because the calculation of *OE* was truncated, the size of the candidate's deficit was also not correctly determined by the CEO's staff.

28. The threshold of $10 000 was, of course, arbitrary. It was chosen based on the need for a substantial sample and in recognition of the time and cost of analysing candidate files.

29. The analysis of the files for candidates in file 1 (candidates who had a surplus) revealed that serious errors had been made by the CEO's staff in computing the true "other expenses" for some candidates. For example, in one case, a loan of $10 000 had been incorrectly recorded as an "other expense." Hence, the candidate's surplus was misstated by the same amount. The errors went in both directions, so that some candidates were ordered to pay over amounts of surplus to their party or to a local association that they did not have. In others, the true surplus was more than the amount the CEO ordered the candidate's agent to dispose of. The problem appears to lie, in large part, in the confusing jumble of different types of entries recorded in part 7 of the F206A form filed by candidates. In 1991, the CEO was designing new forms that are likely to be less confusing and should reduce the likelihood of such errors.

30. In some provinces, notably Quebec and the Maritimes, it is the practice of candidates to pay individuals to act as poll agents. In other provinces, poll agents are not paid.

31. Seven individuals received one or more contracts paying them from $1 000 to $5 000.

32. Only 14.2 percent of constituency associations had guidelines concerning expenditures to obtain the nomination (Carty and Erickson 1991).

33. Note that Carty and Erickson's (1991) figures are based on amounts reported by the candidate's agent or other riding association official. Hence, care must be used in interpreting such data.

34. Carty and Erickson (1991) found that 20.4 percent of riding association nomination meetings took place after the 1988 election was called, while 35.7 percent took place in the three months prior to the day the writs were issued (1 October), and 42.4 percent were held between 1 January and 30 June. The rest took place prior to 1 January 1988.

35. The figure used for the 17 remaining Conservative candidates was $6 000, while that for the 46 Liberals was $4 000 and that for the 122 NDP candidates was $2 000. Candidates of other parties were assigned a value of zero for "other expenses."

36. Large "other expenses" might also be important in nomination contests to drive possible opponents out of the race.

37. There could be an irony here: the greater effort a party makes to run a truly national campaign by having a candidate in all ridings, the more likely it is that a substantial fraction will not be eligible for reimbursement.

38. Note that the "post-reimbursement campaign surplus" measure reported in table 12.1, while it omits "other expenses," is a *net* measure, that is, it incorporates candidates who had a *deficit*.

39. All candidates have to complete a form that calculates their surplus, because any surplus must be transferred to their party or to a local association.

40. Note that these figures were provided by the CEO and were based on an earlier analysis of candidates' returns than was made available to the author in file 1. As we shall see, subsequent filings had the effect of slightly reducing the number of candidates with a surplus.

41. Note that the data in table 12.34 are based on an electronic file that updates the data reported in table 12.33.

42. Derived from the data provided by Frederick B. Slattery, Elections Canada, *prior* to the preparation of file 1 (CEO file).

43. In 1988, 25 candidates each raised more than $80 000 (derived from Canada, Elections Canada 1988c).

44. Calculated by taking the sum of surpluses ($13.770 million), deducting the sum of deficits before *OE* ($809 000) (both in table 12.36), then deducting the author's estimate of total "other expenses" ($4.7 million).

45. That is, the sum of "election expenses," "personal expenses" and "other expenses."

46. The amount "captured" by the NDP from its candidates could not be determined.

47. Total campaign-related expenditures amounted to, on average, $46 900 (the average limit on "election expenses," plus $2 000 in "personal expenses" (average) plus an average of 15 percent in "other expenses" ($7 200)). Then deduct 50 percent of "election expenses" for reimbursement to obtain the net amount a candidate has to raise from individuals, corporations, unions or from the party/riding association.

CHAPTER 13   PROBLEMS WITH THE REGULATORY REGIME

1. In 1989 dollars this amounts to $620 000.

2 The expenses subject to the party's limit totalled $4.1 million for all candidates, but candidates spent a total of about $6 million (table 5.8).

3. Calculated by taking each of the three leading federal parties' limit on candidates' "election expenses" ($13.8 million) and dividing by the total number of candidates (295). Data from Chief Electoral Officer (Canada, Elections Canada 1988c, 3–339). Note that the average outlay for "election expenses" was $40 200 for the Conservatives, $32 800 for the Liberals and $24 800 for NDP candidates.

4. While the NDP leadership convention in 1989 cost $1.46 million, the Liberal party leadership convention in 1990 cost $4.4 million. (Both figures are

based on the cost of the conventions themselves financed by delegates' fees and excluding outlays by candidates.)

5. These figures are different from those in table 13.1, as they come from a different source.

6. Article 17 of the LPC Constitution specifies that the party will establish a spending limit for leadership candidates and establish a set of regulations to govern expenditures by candidates and disclosure of contributions to candidates.

7. Where contributions were routed through the Federal Liberal Agency, such disclosure did occur, although it is impossible to distinguish them on the party's return filed with the CEO. On 7 November 1990, however, the Liberal party did publish a list of contributions to each candidate, indicating the name of the donor and the amount contributed, but this was for contributions routed through the Federal Liberal Agency.

8. A former Conservative party official contends that leadership races and the nomination process are the true fulcrums in the political process. It is here that individuals/groups can obtain the greatest leverage for their efforts (money, organization/campaign work, etc.) on behalf of a candidate. Note that the motives of the backers may be benign (such as helping a friend to gain a position of power, with no desire for reward other than being appreciated), or they may be questionable (such as hoping to gain access or information to be used in one's business or profession).

9. An editorial in the *Globe and Mail* (24 October 1984, 6) argued that "leaders in government must demonstrate, for the benefit and guidance of all who serve under them, the ideal of unassailable integrity to which they might aspire."

10. Public money is used in leadership campaigns in other ways: where publicly paid staff of the candidate work on his/her campaign instead of at their regular jobs; and where a cabinet minister is a candidate and uses part of his/her travel and related expenses (government phone lines, mailing privileges) to benefit his/her campaign for the leadership.

11. The concerns that led the Ontario Commission on Election Contributions and Expenses (now the Commission on Election Finances) to undertake a study of the financing of leadership campaigns were their high cost, the amount of tax-deducted funds finding their way into such races and the question of whether or not government should be involved.

12. The Ontario Conservative party made a token effort to regulate the financing of the January 1985 leadership race, but "the effort failed completely" (Ontario, Commission 1986, 87). For the November 1985 race, the party executive set a limit of $500 000, but provided no penalties for noncompliance.

13. In Ontario, riding associations must be registered and file reports annually on their revenues and expenditures and balance sheet with the Commission on Election Finances.

14. Recall, however, that the amount for 1988 was overstated (chap. 12) and that the Liberal party and the NDP were able to "tax" part of the reimbursement and thus reduce the amount of the surplus available to transfer to riding associations.

15. According to senior party officials, some NDP local associations have real property that is very valuable. They received these originally as donations in kind years ago, sometimes from the estates of supporters. Today, in a few cases, the property is worth millions of dollars. Although the Liberal party constitution requires ridings to give copies of their financial statements to party headquarters, very few actually do so, according to headquarters' officials.

16. The *Canada Elections Act* (s. 2(1)) refers to "electoral district agents," but no party has made use of the relevant section.

17. The Liberal party restructured its intraparty arrangements effective January 1989 so as to give headquarters and the PTAs or riding associations separate sources of revenue. The PTAs and ridings make use of the Federal Liberal Agency's tax-receipting authority, but all of the money they raise is returned to them by the agency (see chap. 5). Note that, in the case of the NDP, the federal office obtains only 15 percent of federally receipted contributions where a PTS or riding uses the federal office's tax-receipting authority to raise funds (see chap. 6).

18. While Bill C-79 in 1987 would have permitted an association to register itself through the party, it did not require a local association to publicly report all funds received and what use was made of those funds, although most of this money was provided out of public funds (recall chap. 2).

19. Under legislation in five provinces (Ontario, Quebec, Alberta, Manitoba and New Brunswick), local party associations register and report annually on contributions and spending. As a result, the public in those provinces can have a more complete picture of political financing than is possible under the federal rules, but only with respect to provincial riding associations in those provinces where federal and provincial riding associations are separate.

20. Recall from chapter 11 that only 12 percent to 31 percent of corporations making a contribution claim the income-tax credit, perhaps because it is worth a maximum of $500. The average tax credit for the corporations that claimed it rose from $162 in 1982 to $244 in 1988 (table 11.7).

21. No officials provided any details.

22. Public accounts of this fund are confusing, to say the least. Although rumours of the fund's existence were strongly denied at the time, Ottawa accountant James Ross, in a 1988 *Maclean's* interview, stated that he was retained to close the fund when all the money had been spent (Wallace and Laver 1988, 10). The purpose of the fund, according to Mr. Ross, was

to provide for "extraneous expenses" when Mr. Turner returned to public, and political, life. However, some of those involved in the raising of money for the fund later confessed that they were not completely sure of its purpose. Said long-time Turner friend William Sommerville, "I know Addison [one of the leading fund-raisers for the fund] came to me and asked me to join his team but I forget what the devil it was all about. Everyone was vague, but I remember a meeting in the back of Addison's car dealership and I remember that I raised a fair amount of money. But I have no idea what the money was for" (ibid., 11). The fund, according to the former chair of Turner's leadership committee, Warren Chippindale, was not in the leader's direct control, but was under the guardianship of five trustees who approved requests for money spent.

23. In the United States, surpluses from *election* campaigns have been used for purely personal purposes, although federal law requires disclosure of how any surplus is spent. The 1979 legislation allows members of Congress to give unused campaign money to a charity, to the member's political party or to return it to contributors. Members elected before 1980, however, can keep surplus campaign funds for personal use upon their retirement (see *Time*, 4 July 1988, 2; *Newsweek*, 6 June 1988, 41).

24. Between 1985 and 1989, the Liberal party made large transfers to the Leader's Office (see chap. 5).

25. Weston (1988, 124) describes the origins of the "Ottawa Fund," which had its beginnings under Mackenzie King and was directed by George McIlraith for many years prior to 1972. The donors to the fund remained secret, as it existed prior to the 1974 election financing reforms. The fund, established in the 1960s as an election war chest, was reported to have helped as many as 13 Ontario ridings during elections. The current administrator, James Ross, has said that some of the money is used for elections, but a certain portion is allotted to the riding associations for use at their own discretion (Wallace and Laver 1988). The influence that the administrators of these secret accounts hold must not be underestimated. Former Liberal treasurer Gordon Dryden, in a 1988 interview, stated, "Those who control the trusts are a law unto themselves and answer only to God. The money gives them enormous political heft and clout" (ibid.).

26. Political trust funds exist also at the provincial level. For example, a Liberal party trust fund in Nova Scotia came to light in the fall of 1990. It was used to supplement the provincial leader's salary by $46 800 annually (*Globe and Mail*, 12 October 1990, A4). This made the leader, Vincent MacLean, the highest paid politician in Nova Scotia at $129 000 per annum, including his salary as Opposition Leader. It was revealed that the fund had received no new donations since it was set up in 1957 as an income supplement for the party. The fund contained $250 000 in 1957. It was one of several trust funds in existence at one time. Mr. MacLean agreed to give up his salary supplement after receiving it for 4.5 years (*Financial Post*, 25 October 1990).

Senator Leo Kolber, then chief Liberal fund-raiser, apparently once tried to get money from the trust to reduce the federal party's debt, but was told that the funds were for the provincial wing only and that none would be forthcoming. Kolber even considered launching a lawsuit to "smash the trusts open," according to a former assistant to the Senator, but did not follow through (Wallace and Laver 1988). In April 1991, press reports revealed that, when John Buchanan was Premier and leader of the Progressive Conservative party in Nova Scotia, he received about $3 300 per month from the party (*Vancouver Sun*, 13 April 1991, A13; 16 April 1991, A14). This money was to supplement his salary as MLA and Premier, which in 1990 was $97 000. While (now) Senator Buchanan emphasized that income taxes were paid on the extra income, columnist Dalton Camp noted that "it is the surmise of some that the secrecy [of the payments] was in violation of Nova Scotia law, which would require disclosure by the premier of any outside income in order to avoid the appearance of conflict of interest" (*Toronto Star*, 21 April 1991, B3). From 1978, when he became Premier, to 1990, Buchanan received a total of about $588 000 from a trust fund controlled by the Conservative party. That amount was $156 000, paid by the party on Mr. Buchanan's behalf after Revenue Canada demanded that income tax be paid on the money he received from the trust fund (*Globe and Mail*, 10 May 1991, A6). Further, in early May 1991, the Halifax *Chronicle-Herald* reported that the party trust fund gave Buchanan about $300 000 in the early 1980s to pay off bank debts.

27. The figure excludes voluntary labour and internal organizational or administrative costs. The largest expenditures were by the Canadian Alliance for Trade and Job Opportunities ($2.31 million), the Pro-Canada Network ($799 321) and the Province of Alberta ($727 000).

28. Note that the Canadian Alliance for Trade and Job Opportunities, funded by large business firms, had no intention of becoming financially involved during the 1988 campaign, but intervened following the leaders debate on 24 and 25 October as an attempt to save the FTA (Hiebert 1991). Note that support for the Liberal party rose very sharply after the debates, and as late as the second to last weekend of the campaign, the numbers were too close to call. Hiebert (ibid.) indicates that, during the final week of the campaign, there was a significant shift in support to the Conservatives.

29. The political tax credit is set out in s. 127(4) of the federal *Income Tax Act*. The credit is based on "amounts contributed."

30. For example, the Liberal party states that its Confederation Dinner in October 1990 generated $455 000 in gross revenues. The cash expenses (ignoring the imputed value of staff and volunteers' time) were $135 000 or 29.6 percent of gross revenue (table 10.2).

31. The Progressive Conservative party does not use federally receipted contributions to finance provincial political activities.

32. Note that the total value of tax-receipted donations by each donor of amounts over $100 must be reported to the CEO annually, and he makes such data public. Therefore, one cannot identify who gave how much to each leadership candidate from this source.

33. Seidle and Paltiel (1981, 247) note, "Although the other parties have used the tax credit scheme to benefit some of their provincial operations, the division of revenues in the NDP is weighted fairly strongly in favor of the provincial organizations. It is widely felt that the NDP's decision to use the federal tax credit for provincial purposes encouraged the passage of the *Election Finances Reform Act* in Ontario in 1975. That act, with its emphasis on controls on contributions, prohibits transfers from a federal party to a provincial party, candidate, or constituency association, except for relatively small amounts during a provincial election. Similar prohibitions have been introduced in Alberta and New Brunswick."

34. Letter to J.W.E. Mingo, dated 31 October 1978.

35. Ken Carty, for example, argues that this is a narrow definition of parties and their activities.

36. The *Guidelines* state that, "In addition to the direct transportation costs of leasing an aircraft, buses, etc., the party must ensure to include all other related costs that it is required to pay for such things as meals, refreshments, salaries of party staff assigned to the tour, communications equipment, if any, rented for the media, and baggage handling charges. A party must offset these charges with all the revenue received from media representatives present on the tour in order to arrive at the net cost to the party which is to be recorded as an election expense" (Canada, Elections Canada 1988a, 10–11).

37. This is qualified as follows: "Provided that there is a fixed fee charged for the event which exceeds the proportionate cost of each participant, the net revenue (i.e. total revenue less total costs) is considered to be a contribution to the party. Very often, however, a fundraising activity, such as a mass mailing will also include an advocacy of the party's views or a solicitation of memberships. In such a case, the substance of the matter must be considered and, where the activity promotes or opposes a party and/or its candidates, the inclusion of a request for funds will be insufficient to exclude the cost of the activity from the definition of election expenses. In those instances, where there are more than one purpose, i.e. promote and/or oppose a party and solicit funds, the party must allocate a portion of the gross costs of the activity as an election expense. In all these cases, the Chief Electoral Officer will accept an allocation of 50% of the cost of this activity as an election expense and as meeting the requirements of the Act" (Canada, Elections Canada 1988a, 9–10).

38. There is only a partial exclusion, as indicated in the previous note.

39. The padding of NDP "election expenses" in 1979 and 1980 was admitted by Robin Sears, then a senior NDP official, in an interview in *Parliamentary Government* ("Round Table" 1981).

40. For example, the 1988 *Guidelines* provide that "if a Minister or other member of Parliament travels on behalf of the party, the cost of travelling and accommodation are election expenses of the party. Also, if the Minister's trip is carried out in conjunction with an official government function using government paid transportation, a proportionate share of the transportation, accommodation and any other expenses must be allocated to the party as an election expense and also recorded as a contribution from the Government of Canada. The allocation must be based on the proportionate time spent by the Minister on each activity" (Canada, Elections Canada 1988a, 11–12). Further, the *Guidelines* state that "if a member of the Minister's exempt staff engages in election campaign work for the party, during normal working hours, a proportionate share of that person's salary together with any direct costs, such as travel and living expenses, must be included as election expenses of the party" (ibid., 12).

41. Officials of the Progressive Conservative party interviewed by the author said that the party "does not use any techniques to 'front-end load' election expenses. It is our policy and indeed our practice to recognize expenses in the period they are consumed, rather than in the period they are incurred. That is, materials which are purchased in the period before a general election is called, but which are used during a general election and qualify as an election expense based on our interpretation of the statute, are recorded as election expenses in the Party's return."

42. Carty argues that this is too simplistic in that a party's activities in an election year are not "normal" in the sense of what they do in interelection years. In his view, the core of the problem lies in the election period of 50-odd days.

43. These figures and those in the rest of the section are taken from or derived from the Progressive Conservative party's annual returns filed with the Chief Electoral Officer.

44. In general, "election expenses" are outlays (or liabilities incurred) during an election, whose objective is to directly promote or oppose the election of the candidate. See s. 2(1), (3) of the *Canada Elections Act*.

45. "Commercial value" is defined as the lowest amount charged by the supplier to another customer for the same type and quantity of goods or services, where the supplier is normally in the business of selling such goods or services. If the supplier sells at both wholesale and retail, the free or specially discounted goods are valued at the wholesale price. If the supplier is not normally in the business of selling such goods or services, and the value of goods or services donated is under $100, the contribution and election expense is recorded as nil.

46. But recall that the *Guidelines* for parties indicate that the production costs of commercials *not* used are not "election expenses."

47. If poll agents are not paid for their services, any expenses they receive are *excluded* from "election expenses." If these agents are paid a salary, then their expenses are also included in "election expenses." During the 1984 election, the CEO had to provide further interpretations "on the run" as problems arose. For example, the payment of a salary and expenses of poll agents (scrutineers) was not clear in the Act. (Note that the definition of "election expenses" refers to the cost of acquiring services "or otherwise.") The CEO's interpretation was issued only three days before voting day by means of a telex or facsimile message to all parties. This interpretation was later incorporated into the 1988 edition of the *Guidelines.*

48. Where the volunteer absorbs such incidental expenses, then the matter of their commercial value comes into question. If the commercial value is under $100, the expense is excluded from "election expenses." If the amount exceeds $100, the incidental expenses paid by the volunteer are recorded as a contribution in kind and as an election expense. The *Guidelines* are not clear on this point. See the discussion in section 5.2 below.

49. Further, "the local association must indicate the source of the funds used to pay for the purchase" (Canada, Elections Canada 1988b, 35).

50. Auditor's fees are subsidized out of public funds as follows: the lower of the amount of the auditor's fees or 3 percent of election expenses with a maximum of $750 and a minimum of $100 (Canada, Elections Canada 1988b, 3).

51. The commercial value is the provincial minimum wage for up to 15 hours on polling day. If the payment is less than two-thirds of this definition of commercial value, it is considered to be "materially less" – hence excluded (Canada, Elections Canada 1988b, 12).

52. The outlays may be made from the candidate's personal resources or out of funds advanced by his/her official agent.

53. However, in the 1988 *Guidelines,* the CEO states that "the candidate's personal expenses are election expenses, but are not subject to any limit, i.e., they can be incurred over and above the election expenses limit" (Canada, Elections Canada 1988b, 26). Section 209 of the *Canada Elections Act* specifically excludes from the "election expenses" *limit* the personal expenses of the candidate.

54. Note that the 1988 *Guidelines* do not state that outlays on polls can be excluded from "election expenses," but this is the practice and it is not challenged by the Chief Electoral Officer. Most outlays for polls are made by the party and they *are* excluded from "election expenses" (see section 4.1 above).

55. Despite this, the Conservatives' White Paper in 1986 did not address the definition of "election expenses" (chap. 2). Hoy (1989, 62) notes that a legal

opinion obtained by the CEO from A.E. Ayers of the Toronto law firm of Borden and Elliott stated that the definition of "election expenses" is "so troublesome, cumbersome and ambiguous" that it is "virtually impossible" to determine what constitutes a proper return. Ayers recommended that the Act be amended if "rigid controls [are to] be maintained on election spending" because the existing definition "is fraught with so many difficulties and is so vague and uncertain in so many respects" (ibid.).

56. The Commissioner's reasoning in this matter is discussed in the *Proceedings* of the House of Commons Committee on Elections, Privileges and Procedure (1988, 20:24–20:34).

57. Lavalin Inc. and two campaign workers pleaded guilty to three charges of making illegal contributions to Mr. Masse's campaign by paying the expenses of some volunteers working on the campaign. Such expenses must be paid by the candidate's official agent. Lavalin was fined $800 plus costs for a total of $2 400 (*Globe and Mail*, 18 February 1986, A3).

58. Speakers for both the Liberal and New Democratic parties indicated their frustration with the fact that Bill C-79 did not address what they saw as the most important problem with campaign-financing regulations, namely, the vague but vital distinction between "election expenses" (subject to constraint) and "campaign expenses" (not limited by the *Canada Elections Act*). In short, one of the major problems identified in the Marcel Masse affair of 1985–86 was not addressed in Bill C-79 (see Canada, House of Commons, *Debates*, 16 March 1988, 13816–25).

59. Therefore, the former candidate proposed that candidates be *directly* reimbursed by the CEO for, say, 75 percent of personal expenses (properly vouchered), that a limit of, say, $2 500 be placed on "personal expenses" subject to partial reimbursement, and that the candidate's official agent certify (subject to the CEO's rules) that the candidate has provided the necessary expense vouchers.

60. Palda (1991, 26) argues that there is plenty of Canadian and U.S. empirical support for two conclusions: incumbents start their election races with a large block of voters already favourably disposed to them; and incumbents gain fewer votes from advertising than do challengers. Thus expenditure limits keep down the challengers' spending on advertising, which is a more effective method of gaining them voters than it is for incumbents. For a very careful analysis, see Heintzman (1991).

61. The 1982 Constitution provides that Parliament cannot continue longer than five years before an election is called. However, an election might not be called for several months.

62. On 9 July 1984, the day that the federal election writs were issued, a spokesman for Brian Mulroney announced that the federal Conservative party would stop using Mulroney's parliamentary privileges to mail campaign material (*Globe and Mail*, 11 July 1984, 3).

63. Perhaps the "best" example is the Ontario government "Preserve it. Conserve it" campaign in 1981. See Paltiel (1987).

64. Carty states that this ban didn't work. Several candidates spent large sums paying the fees for new members pledged to support them.

65. "Provided that there is a fixed fee for the event which exceeds the proportionate cost of each participant, the net revenue is considered to be a contribution to the candidate" (Liberal Party of Canada 1989b, 2).

66. Hence donors were eligible for the federal tax credit ($75 on the first $100 for a maximum of $500 on a contribution of $1 150). During the 1983 federal Tory leadership campaign, contributions earmarked for candidates, but sent to the party in order to obtain the benefit of the tax credit, were "taxed" at a rate of 25 percent by the party. Yet Revenue Canada insisted that only the 25 percent retained by the PC Canada Fund was eligible for the tax credit (*Maclean's*, 3 October 1983, 16). Similarly, there appears to be a loophole in Ontario that allows riding associations to raise tax-receipted contributions for regular election expenses and then donate these funds to leadership campaigns (*Globe and Mail*, 24 June 1986, A9).

CHAPTER 14   CONCLUSIONS AND PROPOSALS FOR REFORM

1. At the same time, 55 percent of those polled believe that unions/corporations should get the approval of members/shareholders before making political donations (Blais and Gidengil 1991). At present, there is no such requirement in the legislation. Moreover, in the *Lavigne* case in 1991, the Supreme Court of Canada ruled that trade unions are free to use the dues collected from members or under the Rand formula for political purposes, even if the individual objects to such use. In July 1986, a Gallup poll of 1 040 adults found that 38 percent believe that both unions and corporations should be able to make donations to the party of their choice, while 37 percent believe that neither of these groups should be allowed to donate to political parties. A higher fraction of union members (44 percent) disapproves of either union or corporate donations than nonmembers (35 percent) (The Gallup Report, Press Release, 11 September 1986).

2. Lee argues that "Canadian election law is a byzantine regulatory tangle that attempts to steer a course between vote-buying and legitimate campaign expense" (1989, 220).

3. This point is illustrated by the creation of the Ad Hoc Committee shortly after the 1974 *Election Expenses Act* was passed to advise the Chief Electoral Officer on matters related to the administration of the new regulatory regime (see Carter 1979; Seidle and Paltiel 1981). The influence of the regulated (parties) on the regulator (CEO) is criticized by Paltiel (1987).

4. Palda defines cost as the "monetary and material expense of achieving a certain result" (1991, 21). In the case of an election, this is "communication with the public" to some standard.

5. Heintzman's (1991) study for the Royal Commission on Electoral Reform and Party Financing indicates that the first argument has not yet been proved and that the turnover rate among federal candidates in Canada has increased since 1974.

6. As noted in chapter 6, the NDP raises far more money using the federal tax credit than it spends on federal politics – except during general elections. However, the outlays of the NDP's federal office are those most closely comparable to the interelection expenditures of the Conservative and Liberal parties.

7. Palda (1991, 18) indicates that the "election expenses" of the three main parties in 1989 dollars amounted to $1.22 per adult in 1979, $1.24 in 1980, $1.26 in 1984 and $1.18 in 1988. The "election expenses" of candidates of these parties amounted to $1.82 per adult in 1979, $1.58 in 1980, $1.70 in 1984 and $1.56 in 1988.

8. Note that, in the precedent-setting case of *Buckley v. Valeo*, the U.S. Supreme Court concluded that a restriction on campaign expenditures "necessarily reduces the quantity of expression by restricting the number of issues discussed, the depth of their exploration, and the size of the audience reached" (1976, 19).

9. Palda (1991, 91) suggests that parties and candidates may be moving away from a reliance on large contributions because it is easier/less costly for opponents to "stir voters' resentment." In particular, television helps interest groups of all types to communicate with people in major cities and to mobilize them on political issues. Parties/candidates have an incentive to "take only honest, moderate contributions" because "the cost of secretive behaviour rises as the cost of publicity falls." It should be noted that Seidle does not find this argument clear or convincing.

10. Recall, however, that the data in table 12.4a show that large inconsistencies exist in such transfers.

11. This problem was most severe in the case of the Progressive Conservative party in 1984 and 1988 (see chaps. 4, 13) and the Liberal party in 1984 (see chaps. 5, 13).

12. This point was documented in the NDP's (1990) brief to the Royal Commission on Electoral Reform and Party Financing. The author's analysis of the prices of electronic and print advertising (magazines and newspapers) in major markets indicates that they generally rose at a faster rate than the Consumer Price Index over the period 1974–89. Further, Atkins stated that "unusual increases in certain campaign costs ... were experienced in advertising and transportation costs prior to the last [1988] election" (1990a, 21).

13. There is one exception: the BC section of the NDP indicates the costs of direct-mail fund-raising.

14. The various reports filed by the candidates with the CEO contain much of this information and they are obtainable from the CEO. However, the "other expenses" figure can only be derived from the reports by removing capital items and transfers (see section 5 of chap. 12).

15. Note that, where a party has required the candidate to assign part of the federal reimbursement of "election expenses" to it, the amount of the surplus available to transfer to a local association is reduced.

16. While Bill C-79 in 1987 would have required an association to register with the CEO, it did not require a local association to publicly report all funds received and what use is made of those funds, although part of this money was provided out of funds raised using the federal tax credit or from the surplus of the candidate, which is often attributable to the reimbursement of one-half of his/her "election expenses."

17. Of course, incumbents find it useful to maintain the "election machinery" in their riding association in a way that will increase their odds of re-election. Most are able to do this out of the surplus transferred to the riding association after the previous election.

18. In election years, the percentage is at the higher end of the range: 5.7 percent in 1980, 9.1 percent in 1984, 6.7 percent in 1988.

19. In nominal dollars, not discounted.

20. In nominal dollars, not discounted.

21. Table 8.3 indicates that, for Conservative party candidates, the average in 1974 and 1975 was $284 and $253 respectively in 1989 dollars. The comparable figures in 1988 and 1989 were $199 and $170 (also in 1989 dollars). The average for the Liberal party in 1974 and 1975 was $321 and $292. In 1988, it was $163 and in 1989 it was $119. For the NDP, the average was $132 in 1974 and $90 in 1975, but only $69 in 1988 and $67 in 1989.

22. The ups and downs are closely associated with the "election-year effect" of much larger average contributions in election years.

23. One of the most astute observers of campaign financing, Alexander notes the likely consequences of too much public funding of parties in the form of direct cash subsidies: "By protecting parties from the failure which results from a lack of public enthusiasm for their platforms, public financing may make it less necessary for parties to respond to the real political issues of the day, thereby interfering with the effectiveness and responsiveness of the political system as a whole" (1989, 16).

24. Other consequences of different ways of providing government subsidies to parties/candidates are discussed in Palda (1991, chap. 8).

25. The new levels are intended to be indicative. Detailed simulations of the effects would have to be done before the final version of the new formula could be established.

26. The author's estimate of the surplus of candidates in 1988 is $8.05 million (chap. 12).

27. Progressive Conservative party candidates in Quebec, as a group, received 31 percent of their total revenues from party headquarters or riding associations, as compared with 18.1 percent for all Conservative candidates in Canada. The comparable figure for Liberal candidates in Quebec was 43.3 percent, versus 32.5 percent for all Liberal candidates. NDP candidates in Quebec received 18.0 percent from within party sources, versus 44.1 percent for all NDP candidates in the 1988 election. Data from chapter 12 and the CEO (Canada, Elections Canada 1988c). Recall, however, the discussion of the problems with the data on intraparty transfers in chapter 12.

28. Obviously, any limit is arbitrary. The objective is to limit the accumulation of substantial reserves financed in large part by taxpayers. By having to raise most of the costs of each election in the year or two prior to that election, candidates will be more responsive to the interests of voters.

29. One wonders how many Canadians support the idea of using money raised using the federal income-tax credit for victory parties. Of the 277 candidates with the largest amount of "other expenses" in 1988, the average expenditure on their victory party was $1 564 (table 12.25). However, a few candidates spent more than $5 000.

30. Figures obtained from interviews with party pollsters.

31. The basis for a separate limit on "personal expenses" is not obvious to the author (recall chap. 12).

32. A study prepared for the federal government estimated that the value of work done by volunteers in Canada in 1990 was $13.2 billion. About 5.3 million people volunteer about 1 billion hours for churches, unions, schools and political parties. The hours were valued at the average wage rate of the service sector of the province in which the work was done. The number of hours of work by volunteers was equivalent to about 6 percent of the labour force (*Vancouver Sun*, 27 November 1990, C8).

33. When a partner is on leave without pay, it is easy for his/her firm to adjust future payments to offset the loss of income during the leave.

34. However, in order to become eligible for federal subsidies, presidential candidates have to agree to spending limits (see Alexander 1991).

35. On the other hand, 55 percent "basically agree" with the proposition that "It is impossible to control what political parties receive and spend in an election" (Blais and Gidengil 1991).

36. The *Federal Election Campaign Act of 1971* limits contributions by individuals to an aggregate of $25 000 a year, of which up to $20 000 may be contributed to a national party, $5 000 to a political action committee, and/or $1 000 per election to a congressional candidate. Since 1907, corporations have

been prohibited from taking directly from their treasuries for use in federal elections. Since 1943, labour unions have been prohibited by federal law from contributing money for use in federal elections directly from their treasuries and pension funds. Corporations, unions and other interest groups, however, operate political action committees to raise funds that are contributed to parties and candidates. Effective 1 January 1991, the Federal Election Commission (FEC) established regulations requiring that soft money contributions to national parties be reported to the FEC and be made available to the public. Generally, see Alexander (1991).

37. In a previous paper I reported that eight firms controlled by Edward and Peter Bronfman in 1987 gave a total of $116 296 to the Conservative party *and* $111 873 to the Liberal party. However, such data are seriously incomplete because the "Bronfman empire" includes hundreds of firms. Thus, a great deal of effort is necessary to determine the combined contributions of various corporate complexes in Canada (Stanbury 1990a, 17–18).

38. Wittman (1989) suggests that campaign contributions are endorsements of the candidate (party) that carry information to voters. They may support a candidate precisely because he/she has received contributions from particular individuals, firms, unions, etc.

39. Obviously, the threshold is arbitrary. The objective, however, is to ensure that the combined contributions of affiliated firms are apparent to the public.

40. To the extent that each local writes a cheque, the total amount can presently be identified in the annual data filed by each party, but it is laborious work, subject to error.

41. Palda (1991) suggests that, on a cost-per-impression basis, television advertising may be the least costly method of communicating with voters.

42. These officials, however, supported regulations designed to prevent "rate gouging" by the radio and television stations, and to ensure that stations make available sufficient time during the campaign if parties wish to purchase it.

43. The case for this proposal is explained in Palda (1991, 36).

44. Parties would be free to impose a limit on expenditures if they wished. See appendix 13.1 at the end of chapter 13.

45. This point was repeatedly emphasized by the late Professor Paltiel in his publications.

46. The author was denied copies of the minutes by the CEO, although they were given to the chairman of the Royal Commission on Electoral Reform and Party Financing.

47. An obvious exception occurs where the CEO (or one of his/her subordinates) is receiving legal advice with respect to possible violations of the law.

48. In terms of the details of the institutional design, Parliament would probably want to examine the Ontario Election Finances Commission and the U.S. Federal Election Commission.

49. Obviously, when the Commission is considering alleged violations of the statute/regulations, it would be necessary to conduct its meetings in camera.

BIBLIOGRAPHY

ABBREVIATIONS

c.	chapter
C.L.L.C.	Canadian Labour Law Cases
C.S.P.	Recueils de jurisprudence, Cour des sessions de la paix (Que.)
D.L.R.	Dominion Law Reports
Pub. L.	Public Law (U.S.)
R.S.C.	Revised Statutes of Canada
S.C.	Statutes of Canada
S.C.C.	Supreme Court of Canada
S.C.R.	Supreme Court Reports
S.O.	Statutes of Ontario
S.Q.	Statutes of Quebec
s(s).	section(s)
U.S.	United States Civil Law

Acker, Eric C. 1979. "The Birth of the Election Expenses Bill." In *The Canadian House of Commons Observed*, ed. J.P. Gaboury and J.R. Hurley. Ottawa: University of Ottawa Press.

Albert, Alain. 1981. "La Participation politique: les contributions monétaires aux partis politiques québécois." *Canadian Journal of Political Science* 14:397–410.

Alexander, Herbert E. 1989. "Money and Politics: A Conceptual Framework." In *Comparative Political Finance in the 1980s*, ed. Herbert E. Alexander and Joel Federman. Cambridge: Cambridge University Press.

———. 1991. "The Regulation of Election Finance in the United States and Proposals for Reform." In Comparative Issues in Party and Election Finance, ed. F. Leslie Seidle. Vol. 4 of the research studies of the Royal Commission on Electoral Reform and Party Financing. Ottawa and Toronto: RCERPF/Dundurn.

Angell, Harold M. 1966. "The Evolution and Application of Quebec Election Expense Legislation 1960–66." In Canada, Committee on Election Expenses. *Report*. Ottawa: Queen's Printer.

———. 1982a. "Political Finance in Quebec." Paper presented to the Political Finance Panel, International Political Science Association, Rio de Janiero, 9–14 August.

———. 1982b. "Le financement des partis politiques provinciaux québécois." In *Personnel et Partis politiques au Québec*, ed. V. Lemieux. Montreal: Boréal Express.

————. 1985. "The Decline of the PQ: A Mass Party, the Polls and Political Financing." Paper presented to the 13th World Congress of the International Political Science Association, Paris, July.

————. 1987. "Duverger, Epstein and the Problem of the Mass Party." *Canadian Journal of Political Science* 20:363–78.

————. 1988. "Financing Quebec's Parties: Further Organizational and Financial Decline of the PQ: Buoyancy of the QLP." Paper presented to the 14th World Congress of the International Political Science Association, Washington, DC, August.

————. 1990a. "The Quebec Liberal Party as a Mass/Cadre Party." Paper presented at a memorial conference in honour of Professor K.Z. Paltiel, Carleton University, Ottawa, 8–10 February.

————. 1990b. "Provincial Party Financing in Quebec, 1963 to Date." Paper submitted to the Royal Commission on Electoral Reform and Party Financing, 6 March.

Archer, Keith. 1985. "The Failure of the New Democratic Party: Unions, Unionists and Politics in Canada." *Canadian Journal of Political Science* 18:353–66.

————. 1987. "Canadian Unions, the New Democratic Party and the Problem of Collective Action." *Labour/Le Travail* 20:173–84.

————. 1990. *Political Choices and Electoral Consequences: A Study of Organized Labour and the New Democratic Party.* Montreal and Kingston: McGill-Queen's University Press.

Atkey, Ronald G. 1985. "Corporate Political Activity." *Western Ontario Law Review* 23:129–43.

Atkins, Norman K. 1990a. "Notes for a Submission to the Royal Commission on Electoral Reform and Party Financing." Ottawa, 13 March.

————. 1990b. "Reforming the Canada Elections Act." *Canadian Parliamentary Review* 13 (Autumn): 2–4.

Atkinson, Michael M., and Maureen Mancuso. 1985. "Do We Need a Code of Conduct for Politicians? The Search for an Elite Political Culture of Corruption in Canada." *Canadian Journal of Political Science* 18:459–80.

Axworthy, Thomas S. 1991. "Capital-Intensive Politics: Money, Media and Mores in the United States and Canada." In *Issues in Party and Election Finance in Canada,* ed. F. Leslie Seidle. Vol. 5 of the research studies of the Royal Commission on Electoral Reform and Party Financing. Ottawa and Toronto: RCERPF/Dundurn.

Banister, Armand, and Gordon Gibson. 1984. "Towards a Better Liberal Party." Discussion paper on reform of the Liberal Party of Canada. Ottawa, Liberal Party of Canada, January.

————. 1985. *Final Report of the President's Committee on Reform of the Liberal Party of Canada*. Ottawa, Liberal Party of Canada, August.

Bedelington, Anne H., and Lynda W. Powell. 1986. "Money and Elections." *Research in Micropolitics* 1:161–87.

Benson, Richard V. 1987. *Secrets of Successful Direct Mail*. Savannah, GA: The Benson Organization.

Bercuson, David. 1986. *Sacred Trust? Brian Mulroney and the Conservative Party in Power*. Toronto: Doubleday Canada.

Berry, Jeffrey. 1989. *The Interest Group Society*. 2d ed. Glenview, IL/Boston: Scott, Foresman/Little Brown.

Berton, Pierre. 1976. "The Pacific Railway Scandal." In *Political Corruption in Canada: Cases, Causes and Cures*, ed. K.M. Gibbons and D.C. Rowat. Toronto: McClelland and Stewart.

Bertram, Eric. 1991. "Independent Candidates in Federal General Elections." In *Issues in Party and Election Finance in Canada*, ed. F. Leslie Seidle. Vol. 5 of the research studies of the Royal Commission on Electoral Reform and Party Financing. Ottawa and Toronto: RCERPF/Dundurn.

Biersack, Robert, and Clyde Wilcox. 1990. "Financing National Campaigns." *American Politics Quarterly* 18:215–41.

Black, Edwin. 1979. "Federal Strains Within a Canadian Party." In *Party Politics in Canada*, 4th ed., ed. H.G. Thorburn. Scarborough, Ont.: Prentice-Hall Canada.

Black, Jerome. 1984. "Revisiting the Effects of Canvassing on Voting Behaviour." *Canadian Journal of Political Science* 17:351–74.

Blais, André, and Elisabeth Gidengil. 1991. *Making Representative Democracy Work: The Views of Canadians*. Vol. 17 of the research studies of the Royal Commission on Electoral Reform and Party Financing. Ottawa and Toronto: RCERPF/Dundurn.

Blake, Donald E. 1991. "Party Competition and Electoral Volatility: Canada in Comparative Perspective." In *Representation, Integration and Political Parties in Canada*, ed. Herman Bakvis. Vol. 14 of the research studies of the Royal Commission on Electoral Reform and Party Financing. Ottawa and Toronto: RCERPF/Dundurn.

Blake, Donald E., R.K. Carty and Lynda Erickson. 1991. *Grassroots Politicians: Party Activists in British Columbia*. Vancouver: University of British Columbia Press.

Bonafede, Dom. 1982. "Part Science, Part Art, Part Hokum: Direct Mail Now a Key Campaign Tool." *National Journal*, 31 July.

Bouchard, Lucien. 1988. *Report to the Prime Minister on Measures to Foster Political Ethics*. Ottawa: Department of the Secretary of State.

Boucher c. Centrale de l'enseignement du Québec, [1982] C.S.P. 1003.

Boyer, J. Patrick. 1978a. "The Legal Status of Corporate Political Contributions in Canada Today." *Business Quarterly* 43 (Spring): 67–76.

———. 1978b. "The Legal Status of Union Political Contributions in Canada Today." *Business Quarterly* 43 (Autumn): 20–35.

———. 1979. "Legal Aspects of the Corporate Political Contribution in Canada." *Canadian Business Law Journal* 3:161–92.

———. 1981. *Political Rights: The Legal Framework of Elections in Canada.* Toronto: Butterworths.

———. 1982. "Political Rights and the Charter." *Canadian Lawyer* 6:4.

———. 1983. *Money and Message: The Law Governing Election Financing, Advertising, Broadcasting and Campaigning in Canada.* Toronto: Butterworths.

British Columbia. Royal Commission on Electoral Reform. 1978. *Report.* Victoria: Queen's Printer.

Bruton, Peter. 1964. "Graft Never Hurt a Politician at the Polls." *Maclean's* 77, 25 January, 18–19, 31–32. Also in *Political Corruption in Canada: Cases, Causes and Cures,* ed. K.M. Gibbons and D.C. Rowat. Toronto: McClelland and Stewart.

Buckley v. Valeo 424 U.S. 1 (1976).

Byfield, Ted. 1991. *Act of Faith.* Edmonton: BC Report Books.

Cairns, Alan C. 1968. "The Electoral System and the Party System in Canada, 1921–1965." *Canadian Journal of Political Science* 1:55–80.

Cairns, Alan C., and Daniel Wong. 1985. "Socialism, Federalism and the B.C. Party System." In *Party Politics in Canada.* 5th ed., ed. Hugh G. Thorburn. Scarborough, Ont.: Prentice-Hall Canada.

Canada. *An Act to amend the Canada Elections Act,* S.C. 1977–78, c. 3.

———. *An Act to amend the Canada Elections Act,* S.C. 1980–81–82–83, c. 96, s. 2(1).

———. *An Act to amend the Canada Elections Act* (No. 3), S.C. 1980–81–82–83, c. 164, s. 6(1).

———. *An Act to amend the Dominion Elections Act,* S.C. 1908, c. 26.

———. Bill C-79, ss. 1(6), 15, 55(2.1)(*d*), 56, 57(2), 98.1. *An Act to Amend the Canada Elections Act,* 2nd Session, 33rd Parliament, 1986–87.

———. *Broadcasting Act,* S.C. 1967–68, c. 25.

———. *Canada Elections Act,* R.S.C. 1970, c. 14 (1st Supp.), ss. 2.1(*f*), 13.7, 23(2)(*h*), 62.1(4), 63(3), 63(5.1), 70.1(1), (4), 72, 99, 99.3(*a*).

———. *Canada Elections Act*, R.S.C. 1985, c. E-2, ss. 2(1), (3), 209, 217(1)(*a*), 232, 307, 309(3), 310(7).

———. *Canada Post Corporation Act*, S.C. 1980–81–82–83, c. 54, s. 34.

———. *Canadian Charter of Rights and Freedoms*, s. 2(*b*), Part I of the *Constitution Act, 1982*, being Schedule B of the *Canada Act 1982* (U.K.), 1982, c. 11.

———. *Dominion Elections Act*, S.C. 1874, c. 9.

———. *Dominion Elections Act*, S.C. 1920, c. 46.

———. *Election Expenses Act*, S.C. 1973–74, c. 51.

———. *Income Tax Act*, R.S.C. 1952, c. 148, s. 127(4).

Canada. Broadcasting Arbitrator. 1984. "Broadcasting Guidelines, Canada Elections Act, Federal General Election, September 4, 1984." In *Statutory Report of the Chief Electoral Officer as per subsection 59(1) of the Canada Elections Act, 1984*. Ottawa: Minister of Supply and Services Canada.

———. 1989. "Broadcasting Guidelines, Canada Elections Act, Federal General Election, November 21, 1988." In *Statutory Report of the Chief Electoral Officer as per subsection 195(1) of the Canada Elections Act, 1989*. Ottawa: Minister of Supply and Services Canada.

Canada. Bureau of Management Consulting. 1985. *Summary of Candidate Election Financing*. Report prepared for the Chief Electoral Officer. Ottawa: Minister of Supply and Services Canada.

Canada. Committee on Election Expenses. 1966a. *Report*. Ottawa: Queen's Printer.

———. 1966b. *Studies in Canadian Party Finance*. Ottawa: Queen's Printer.

Canada. House of Commons. Committee on Election Expenses. 1971a. *Journals*. Vol. 117, no. 146, 4 June, 605-17.

Canada. Department of National Revenue. *Interpretation Bulletin 110RZ*.

Canada. Department of National Revenue. 1978a. "Registered Charities: Political Objects and Activities." Information Circular No. 78-3. 27 February. Ottawa: Department of National Revenue.

———. 1978b. "Contributions to a Candidate at a Federal Election." Information Circular No. 75-2R2. 24 April. Ottawa: Department of National Revenue.

Canada. Elections Canada. 1973. "Declared Election Expenses of Candidates in the General Election of October 30, 1972." Tabled by Chief Electoral Officer in House of Commons 8 March.

———. 1974. "Declared Expenditures of Candidates in the General Election of July 8, 1974. Tabled by the Chief Electoral Officer in the House of Commons 28 November.

———. 1979a. *Guidelines and Procedures Respecting Election Expenses.* Ottawa: Elections Canada.

———. 1979b. *Manual of Information Respecting Candidates, Official Agents, and Auditors.* Ottawa: Elections Canada.

———. 1979c. *Statutory Report of the Chief Electoral Officer of Canada as per subsection 59(1) of the Canada Elections Act.* Ottawa: Minister of Supply and Services Canada.

———. 1980a. *Guidelines and Procedures Respecting Election Expenses.* Ottawa: Elections Canada.

———. 1980b. *Report of the Chief Electoral Officer Respecting Election Expenses, 1979.* Ottawa: Minister of Supply and Services Canada.

———. 1980c. "Special Report to the Speaker of the House of Commons Respecting Election Expenses of Registered Parties and Candidates." Tabled in House of Commons 14 April.

———. 1981. *Report of the Chief Electoral Officer Respecting Election Expenses, 1980.* Ottawa: Minister of Supply and Services Canada.

———. 1983. *Statutory Report of the Chief Electoral Officer of Canada as per subsection 59(1) of the Canada Elections Act.* Ottawa: Minister of Supply and Services Canada.

———. 1984a. *Guidelines and Procedures Respecting Election Expenses.* Ottawa: Elections Canada.

———. 1984b. *Manual of Information: A Digest Intended for Candidates, Official Agents, Auditors.* Ottawa: Elections Canada.

———. 1984c. *Report of the Chief Electoral Officer Respecting Election Expenses.* Ottawa: Minister of Supply and Services Canada.

———. 1984d. *Report of the Chief Electoral Officer as per subsection 59(1) of the Canada Elections Act.* Ottawa: Minister of Supply and Services Canada.

———. 1985. *Report on Proposed Legislative Changes.* Ottawa: Minister of Supply and Services Canada.

———. 1986. *Report of the Chief Electoral Officer as per subsection 59(1) of the Canada Elections Act.* Ottawa: Minister of Supply and Services Canada.

———. 1987. "Changes Proposed to Canada Elections Act." *Contact*, No. 64 (August): 2–3, 5.

———. 1988a. *Guidelines Respecting Election Expenses of Registered Political Parties.* Ottawa: Chief Electoral Officer.

———. 1988b. *Guidelines Respecting Election Expenses of Candidates.* Ottawa: Chief Electoral Officer.

———. 1988c. *Report of the Chief Electoral Officer Respecting Election Expenses, Thirty-Fourth General Election, 1988.* Ottawa: Minister of Supply and Services Canada.

———. 1988d. "The Rules of the Game." Video. Ottawa: Elections Canada.

———. 1989a. *Report of the Chief Electoral Officer of Canada as per subsection 195(1) of the Canada Elections Act.* Ottawa: Minister of Supply and Services Canada.

———. 1989b. *Electoral, Campaign Finance, Lobbying and Ethics/Conflict of Interest Legislation and Litigation in Canadian Federal, Provincial and Territorial Jurisdictions.* Ottawa: Elections Canada.

———. 1991. *Report of the Chief Electoral Officer of Canada as per subsection 195(1) of the Canada Elections Act.* Ottawa: Minister of Supply and Services Canada.

Canada. Government Consulting Group. 1990. "Summary of Candidate Election Financing, 1988." Report prepared for Chief Electoral Officer. Ottawa: Minister of Supply and Services Canada.

Canada. House of Commons. Various years. *Debates.* Ottawa. (Please see text for specific days, pages.)

Canada. House of Commons. Special Committee on the Beauharnois Power Project. 1931. *Report.* In House of Commons, *Journals,* Vol. 69, no. 618-45. Also *Evidence.* In *Journals,* 1931, Appendix, No. 5.

Canada. House of Commons. Special Committee on Election Expenses. 1971a. *Journals.* Vol. 117, no. 146, 4 June, 607–17.

———. 1971b. *Report.* Ottawa: Information Canada.

Canada. House of Commons. Standing Committee on Elections, Privileges and Procedure. 1988. *Eighth Report.* Ottawa: Queen's Printer.

Canada. House of Commons. Standing Committee on Privileges and Elections. 1973. *Report.* In *Minutes of Proceedings and Evidence,* No. 26, 13 December 1973.

Canada. Privy Council Office. 1986. *White Paper on Election Law Reform.* Ottawa: Queen's Printer.

Canada. Revenue Canada, Taxation. Various years. *Taxation Statistics.* Ottawa: Minister of Supply and Services Canada.

Canada. Senate. 1974. *Debates,* 10 January, 1428–34.

Canada. Royal Commission in Reference to Certain Charges against Sir A.P. Caron. 1893. *Report.* Ottawa: Queen's Printer.

Canada. Statistics Canada. 1991. *Canadian Economic Observer: Historical Statistical Supplement, 1989/90.* Ottawa: Minister of Supply and Services Canada.

Canadian Bar Association (Ontario), Continuing Legal Education. 1983. *The Clean Campaign: How to Run an Election Campaign Without Running Afoul of the Law*. Toronto: Canadian Bar Association.

Canadian Broadcasting Corporation. 1965. *CBC White Paper: Political and Controversial Broadcasting*. Program Policy No. 65–1. 19 January.

Canadian Radio-television and Telecommunications Commission. 1985. "Allocation of Federal Election Broadcast Time." 12 December. Ottawa: CRTC.

———. 1986. "Political Programs, Advertisements and Announcements." Public Notice 1986–294. Ottawa: CRTC.

———. 1987a. "Political Broadcasting – Complaints re: free time and editorial time allocations." Circular No. 334. Ottawa: CRTC.

———. 1987b. "Political Programs, Advertisements and Announcements." Public Notice 1987–26. Ottawa: CRTC.

———. 1988. "A Policy With Respect to Election Campaign Broadcasting." Public Notice 1988–142. Ottawa: CRTC.

Canadian Study of Parliament Group. 1990. *Reform of Electoral Campaigns*. Proceedings from the Toronto Conference, 23–24 March.

Caplan, Gerald, Michael Kirby and Hugh Segal. 1989. *Election: The Issues, the Strategies, the Aftermath*. Scarborough, Ont.: Prentice-Hall Canada.

Carter, D. 1979. "Implementation of the Election Expenses Act." In *The Canadian House of Commons Observed*, ed. J.P. Gaboury and J.R. Hurley. Ottawa: University of Ottawa Press.

Carty, R.K. 1988. "Campaigning in the Trenches: The Transformation of Constituency Politics." In *Party Democracy in Canada*, ed. George Perlin. Scarborough, Ont.: Prentice-Hall Canada.

Carty, R.K., and Lynda Erickson. 1991. "Candidate Nomination in Canada's National Political Parties." In *Canadian Political Parties: Leaders, Candidates and Organization*, ed. Herman Bakvis. Vol. 13 of the research studies of the Royal Commission on Electoral Reform and Party Financing. Ottawa and Toronto: RCERPF/Dundurn.

Chapman, R.G., and K.S. Palda. 1984. "Assessing the Influence of Campaign Expenditures on Voting Behaviour with a Comprehensive Electoral Market Model." *Marketing Science* 3, no. 3 (Summer): 207–26.

———. 1986. "An Econometric Analysis of the 1984 Canadian Federal Election in Ontario." Working Paper 86–11, School of Business, Queen's University, Kingston.

———. 1989. "Econometric Models of Voting and Campaigning." In *Manipulating Public Opinion*, ed. M. Margolis and G.A. Mauser. Pacific Grove, CA: Brooks/Cole Publishing Co.

Clarkson, Stephen. 1973. "More Reform for the Candidate, Please!" *Canadian Business* 46 (August): 13–14, 16.

Colwell, Randy, and Paul Thomas. 1987. "Parliament and the Patronage Issue." *Journal of Canadian Studies* 22 (Summer): 163–76.

Constantinou, Peter P. 1991. "Public Funding of Political Parties, Candidates and Elections in Canada." In *Issues in Party and Election Finance in Canada,* ed. F. Leslie Seidle. Vol. 5 of the research studies of the Royal Commission on Electoral Reform and Party Financing. Ottawa and Toronto: RCERPF/Dundurn.

Courtney, John C. 1973. *The Selection of National Party Leaders in Canada.* Toronto: Macmillan.

———. 1978. "Recognition of Canadian Political Parties in Parliament and in Law." *Canadian Journal of Political Science* 11:33–60.

———. 1988. "Reinventing the Brokerage Wheel: The Tory Success in 1984." In *Canada at the Polls, 1984,* ed. H.R. Penniman. Durham, NC: Duke University Press.

Davey, Keith. 1986. *The Rainmaker: A Passion for Politics.* Toronto: Stoddart.

Dion, Gerard, and Louis O'Neill. 1956. *Two Priests Censure Political Immorality in the Province of Quebec.* Montreal: The Public Morality Committee of Montreal.

Dobbin, Murray. 1991. *Preston Manning and the Reform Party.* Toronto: James Lorimer.

Donovan, S.J., and R.B. Winmill. 1976. "The Beauharnois Power Scandal." In *Political Corruption in Canada: Cases, Causes and Cures,* ed. K.M. Gibbons and D.C. Rowat. Toronto: McClelland and Stewart.

Dunleavy, Patrick. 1990. *Democracy, Bureaucracy and Public Choice.* New York: Prentice-Hall.

Dyck, Rand. 1989. "Relations Between Federal and Provincial Parties." In *Canadian Parties in Transition,* ed. A.G. Gagnon and A.B. Tanguay. Toronto: Nelson Canada.

Easterbrook, Gregg. 1988. "Junk-Mail Politics." *New Republic,* 25 April, 17–21.

Epstein, Leon. 1986. *Political Parties in the American Mold.* Madison: University of Wisconsin Press.

Etherington, Brian. 1987. "Freedom of Association and Compulsory Union Dues: Towards a Purposive Conception of a Freedom Not to Associate." *Ottawa Law Review* 19:1–48.

Ewing, K.D. 1982. "Campaign Financing: A Dilemma for Liberal Democracy." Toronto: Osgoode Hall Public Law Workshops.

———. 1987a. "Freedom of Association in Canada." *Alberta Law Review* 25:437–60.

———. 1987b. *The Funding of Political Parties in Britain*. Cambridge: Cambridge University Press.

———. 1988. "The Legal Regulation of Campaign Financing in Canadian Federal Elections." *Public Law* (Winter): 577–608.

Falardeau, Denise. 1990. "Notes pour une intervention" before the Royal Commission on Electoral Reform and Party Financing (Chicoutimi, Que., 1 May).

Feigert, Frank. 1989. *Canada Votes, 1935–1988*. Durham, NC: Duke University Press.

Fotheringham, Allan. 1986. "Calling Cards of Troubled Tories." *Maclean's* 99, 31 March, 64.

Fraser, Blair. 1949. "Election Campaign Backstage Ottawa." *Maclean's* 62, 15 August.

———. 1953. "Our Illegal Federal Elections." *Maclean's* 66, 15 April, 12, 83–86.

Fraser, Graham. 1989. *Playing for Keeps: The Making of the Prime Minister, 1988*. Toronto: McClelland and Stewart.

Frizzell, Alan, Jon H. Pammett and Anthony Westell, eds. 1989. *The Canadian General Election of 1988*. Ottawa: Carleton University Press.

Galbraith, J. Kenneth. 1983. *The Anatomy of Power*. Boston: Houghton Mifflin.

Gérin, François. 1990. "Notes for Remarks before the Royal Commission on Electoral Reform and Party Financing." Ottawa, 12 May.

Gibbons, K.M. 1976. "The Political Culture of Corruption in Canada." In *Political Corruption in Canada: Cases, Causes and Cures*, ed. K.M. Gibbons and D.C. Rowat. Toronto: McClelland and Stewart.

Goldfarb, Martin. 1990. "Polls on Political Events." Paper for the Inauguration of the Goldfarb Lecture, Institute for Social Research, York University, 4 April.

Goldfarb, Martin, and Thomas Axworthy. 1988. *Marching to a Different Drummer*. Toronto: Stoddart.

Goldstein, Joshua. 1991. *The Fat Cats' Laundromat: Soft Money and the National Parties*. Washington, DC: Center for Responsive Politics.

Gouldner, Alvin W. 1960. "The Norm of Reciprocity: A Preliminary Statement." *American Sociological Review* 25:161–78.

Grafftey, H. 1969. "Open End: Politics, Elections and Money." *Canadian Dimension* 5 (December–January): 11–12.

———. 1973. "Who Will Bear the Brunt of Election Expenses?" *Canadian Business*, 46 (September): 80.

Graham, Ron. 1986. *One-Eyed Kings: Promise and Illusion in Canadian Politics.* Toronto: Collins.

Granatstein, Jack L. 1966. "Conservative Party Finances: 1939–1945." In Canada, Committee on Election Expenses, *Studies in Canadian Party Finance.* Ottawa: Queen's Printer.

Gray, Charlotte. 1989. "Purchasing Power." *Saturday Night*, March, 15–18.

Gregg, Allan, and Michael Posner. 1990. *The Big Picture: What Canadians Think About Almost Everything.* Toronto: Macfarlane Walter and Ross.

Harrill, Ernest E. 1958. "The Structure of Organization and Power in Canadian Political Parties: A Study in Party Financing." Ph.D. dissertation, University of North Carolina.

Harrison, Robert. 1988. *And Justice for Some: Power and Patronage in Ottawa.* Montreal: Eden Press.

Heard, Alexander. 1960. *The Costs of Democracy.* Chapel Hill, NC: University of North Carolina Press.

Heintzman, D. Keith. 1991. "Electoral Competition, Campaign Expenditure and Incumbency Advantage." In *Issues in Party and Election Finance in Canada*, ed. F. Leslie Seidle. Vol. 5 of the research studies of the Royal Commission on Electoral Reform and Party Financing. Ottawa and Toronto: RCERPF/Dundurn.

Heintzman, Ralph. 1976. "Politics and Corruption in Quebec." In *Political Corruption in Canada: Cases, Causes and Cures*, ed. K.M. Gibbons and D.C. Rowat. Toronto: McClelland and Stewart.

Hiebert, Janet. 1989–90. "Fair Elections and Freedom of Expression Under the Charter." *Journal of Canadian Studies* 24 (4): 72–86.

———. 1991. "Interest Groups and Canadian Federal Elections." In *Interest Groups and Elections in Canada*, ed. F. Leslie Seidle. Vol. 2 of the research studies of the Royal Commission on Electoral Reform and Party Financing. Ottawa and Toronto: RCERPF/Dundurn.

Howse, John. 1990. "The Man and His Mission." *Maclean's* 103, 29 October, 30–32.

Howse, John, Anthony Wilson-Smith and Brian Bergman. 1990. "On the March." *Maclean's* 103, 29 October, 26–28.

Hoy, Claire. 1987. *Friends in High Places: Politics and Patronage in the Mulroney Government.* Toronto: Key Porter Books.

———. 1989. *Margin of Error: Pollsters and the Manipulation of Canadian Politics.* Toronto: Key Porter Books.

Hutchinson, Maryanne McNellis. 1991. "Reform's Bay Man." *Financial Post Magazine*, September, 18–26.

Institute of Chartered Accountants of Ontario. 1977. *Guidelines to Members Appointed as Auditors Under the Election Finances Reform Act, 1975.* Toronto: ICAO.

Irvine, William. 1982. "Does the Candidate Make a Difference? The Macro-Politics and Micro-Politics of Getting Elected." *Canadian Journal of Political Science* 15 (December): 755–82.

Isenberg, Seymour. 1980. "Can You Spend Your Way into the House of Commons?" *Optimum* 11 (1): 29–39.

———. 1981. "Spend and Win? Another Look at Federal Election Expenses." *Optimum* 12 (4): 5–15.

Johnston, R.J. 1987. *Money and Votes: Constituency Campaign Spending and Election Results.* New York: Methuen.

Johnston, Richard. 1990. "The Volume and Impact of Third Party Advertising in the 1988 Election." Paper prepared for the Royal Commission on Electoral Reform and Party Financing, December.

———. 1991. "Free Trade and the Dynamics of the 1988 Election." In *The Ballot and Its Message: Voting in Canada,* ed. Joseph Wearing. Toronto: Copp Clark Pitman.

Klein, Kim. 1988. *Fundraising for Social Change.* 2d ed. Inverness, CA: Chardon Press.

Krashinsky, Michael, and William J. Milne. 1985. "Increasing Incumbency?" *Canadian Public Policy* 11:107–10.

———. 1986. "The Effects of Incumbency in the 1984 Federal and 1985 Ontario Elections." *Canadian Journal of Political Science* 19:337–43.

———. 1991. "Some Evidence on the Effects of Incumbency in the 1988 Canadian Federal Election." In *Issues in Party and Election Finance in Canada,* ed. F. Leslie Seidle. Vol. 5 of the research studies of the Royal Commission on Electoral Reform and Party Financing. Ottawa and Toronto: RCERPF/Dundurn.

Kuniholm, Roland. 1986. *Maximum Gifts by Return Mail.* Ambler, PA: Fund Raising Institute.

La Calamita, John. 1984. "The Equitable Campaign: Party Political Broadcasting Regulation in Canada." *Osgoode Hall Law Journal* 22:543–79.

Lautman, Kay, and Henry Goldstein. 1990. *Dear Friend: Mastering the Art of Direct Mail Fund Raising.* 2d ed. Washington, DC: The Taft Group.

Lavigne v. O.P.S.E.U. (1991) C.L.L.C. 14,029 (S.C.C.).

Lee, Robert Mason. 1989. *One Hundred Monkeys: The Triumph of Popular Wisdom in Canadian Politics.* Toronto: Macfarlane Walter and Ross.

Levesque, Terence J. 1983. "On the Outcome of the 1983 Conservative Leadership Convention: How They Shot Themselves in the Other Foot." *Canadian Journal of Political Science* 16:779–94.

Lewis, David. 1981. *The Good Fight: Political Memoirs, 1909–1958.* Toronto: Macmillan.

Liberal Party of Canada. 1985a. "1984 Liberal Leadership Expenses Report." 1 March. Ottawa: Liberal Party of Canada.

———. 1985b. "Consolidated Report of Contributors of Individual Donations to Leadership Candidates in Excess of $500." 1 March. Ottawa: Liberal Party of Canada.

———. 1986a. *Questions for Discussion on Reform of the Liberal Party of Canada.* Ottawa: Liberal Party of Canada.

———. 1986b. *Constitution* [as amended at the 1986 National Convention]. Ottawa: Liberal Party of Canada.

———. 1989a. "Regulations to Govern Expenditures By and Disclosure of Contributions to Candidates For the Leadership of the Liberal Party of Canada." 29 September. Ottawa: Liberal Party of Canada.

———. 1989b. "Guidelines for Official Agents of Candidates for the Leadership of the Liberal Party of Canada, August 31, 1989 as amended September 14 and 29, 1989." Ottawa: Liberal Party of Canada.

———. 1990. *The Liberal Party of Canada Constitution Amended at the 1990 National Convention.* Ottawa: Liberal Party of Canada.

———. 1991. *The Liberal Party of Canada: Its Philosophy, History and Structure.* Ottawa: Liberal Party of Canada.

Liberal Party of Canada. Reform Commission. 1991. *Agenda for Reform.* Interim Report. 31 July. Ottawa: Liberal Party of Canada.

Little, Bruce. 1980. "Nova Scotia: The Money and the Mounties." *Maclean's* 93, 31 March, 16–17.

MacDonald, Donald C. 1990. "1988 Election Expenditures: A Canadian–American Comparison." Unpublished paper.

McDonald, Lynn. 1987. *The Party That Changed Canada: The New Democratic Party, Then and Now.* Toronto: Macmillan.

MacKay, R.A. 1931. "After Beauharnois – What?" *Maclean's* 15 October.

MacKenzie, Hilary, Mary Janigan and Lisa Van Dusen. 1988. "Debt and dissension." *Maclean's* 101, 21 March, 14–15.

McPherson, W.D. 1905. *The Law of Elections in Canada.* Toronto: Canada Law Book.

Magleby, David B., and Candice J. Nelson. 1990. *The Money Chase: Congressional Campaign Finance Reform.* Washington, DC: Brookings Institution.

Manitoba. Law Reform Commission. 1977. *Working Paper on Political Financing and Election Expenses.* February. Winnipeg: The Commission.

———. 1979. *Report on Political Financing and Election Expenses.* Winnipeg: The Commission.

Manning, Ernest. 1967. *Political Realignment: A Challenge to Thoughtful Canadians.* Toronto: McClelland and Stewart.

Manning, Preston. 1992. *The New Canada.* Toronto: Macmillan.

Marfels, Christian. 1988. "Aggregate Concentration in International Perspective: Canada, Federal Rebulic of Germany, Japan and the United States." In *Mergers, Corporate Concentration and Power in Canada*, ed. R.S. Khemani, D.M. Shapiro and W.T. Stanbury. Halifax: Institute for Research on Public Policy.

Martin, Patrick, Allan Gregg and George Perlin. 1983. *Contenders: The Tory Quest for Power.* Scarborough, Ont.: Prentice-Hall Canada.

Massicotte, Louis. 1984. "Une réforme inachevée: Les règles du jeu électoral." *Recherches sociographiques* 25 (1): 43–81.

———. 1990. "Financement Populaire in Quebec: An Analysis of the Financial Reports of Parties, 1977–1988." Paper presented at a memorial conference in honour of Professor K.Z. Paltiel, Carleton University, Ottawa, 8–10 February.

———. 1991. "Party Financing in Quebec: An Analysis of the Financial Reports of Political Parties, 1977–89." In *Provincial Party and Election Finance in Canada*, ed. F. Leslie Seidle. Vol. 3 of the research studies of the Royal Commission on Electoral Reform and Party Financing. Ottawa and Toronto: RCERPF/Dundurn.

Matasar, Ann. 1986. *Corporate PACs and Federal Campaign Financing Laws: Use or Abuse of Power?* New York: Quorum Books.

Matthews, Christopher. 1988. *Hardball.* New York: Harper and Row/Perennial Library.

Matsusaka, John G., and Filip Palda. 1990. "Why Do People Vote?" Department of Economics, Working Paper #9004. Ottawa: University of Ottawa.

Meisel, John. 1962. *The Canadian General Election of 1957.* Toronto: University of Toronto Press.

Meisel, John, and Richard Van Loon. 1966. "Canadian Attitudes to Election Expenses 1965–1966." In Canada, Committee on Election Expenses, *Studies in Canadian Party Finance.* Ottawa: Queen's Printer.

Michaud, Pascale, and Pierre Laferrière. 1991. "Economic Analysis of the Funding of Political Parties in Canada." In *Issues in Party and Election Finance in Canada*, ed. F. Leslie Seidle. Vol. 5 of the research studies of the Royal Commission on Electoral Reform and Party Financing. Ottawa and Toronto: RCERPF/Dundurn.

Mitchell, Jared. 1990. "Nowhere to Hide." *Report on Business Magazine*, May, 65–72.

Morley, Terry. 1991. "Paying for the Politics of British Columbia." In *Provincial Party and Election Finance in Canada*, ed. F. Leslie Seidle. Vol. 3 of the research studies of the Royal Commission on Electoral Reform and Party Financing. Ottawa and Toronto: RCERPF/Dundurn.

Morton, Desmond. 1986. *The New Democrats 1961–1986: The Politics of Change.* Toronto: Copp Clark Pitman.

Mulgrew, Ian. 1991. "The Making of a Premier." *Vancouver* [Magazine] December, 37–46, 114.

Murray, Grant G. 1975. "Canada's New Election Laws: Counting the Dollars and Making Them Count." *Canadian Business Review* 2:41–43.

Nassmacher, Karl-Heinz. 1989. "The Cost of Party Democracy in Canada." In *Corruption and Reform.* Dordrecht: Kluwer Academic Publishers.

National Citizens' Coalition Inc. v. Canada (Attorney General) 1985, 11 D.L.R. (4th) 481.

New Brunswick. Select Committee on the Elections Act. 1974. *Report.* Fredericton: Queen's Printer.

New Democratic Party. 1989. "New Democratic Party Leadership Rules, 1989." June. Ottawa: New Democratic Party.

———. 1990. "Submission to the Royal Commission on Electoral Reform and Party Financing." Ottawa.

New Democratic Party of British Columbia. 1989. "Direct Ask Fundraising Manual." Vancouver.

Noel, S.J.R. 1987. "Dividing the Spoils: The Old and New Rules of Patronage in Canadian Politics." *Journal of Canadian Studies* 22 (Summer): 72–95.

Noonan, John T. 1984. *Bribes.* New York: Macmillan.

Nova Scotia. Election Commission. 1981. *Report.* Halifax: Queen's Printer.

Nova Scotia. House of Assembly. Select Committee on Electoral Matters. 1981. *Report.* Halifax: Queen's Printer.

Nova Scotia. Royal Commission on Election Expenses and Associated Matters. 1969. *Report.* Halifax: Queen's Printer.

O.C.A.W. v. Imperial Oil Ltd., [1963] S.C.R. 584.

Olson, Mancur. 1965. *The Logic of Collective Action.* Cambridge, MA: Harvard University Press.

Ontario. *Election Expenses Act, 1986,* S.O. 1986, c. 33, ss. 15, 30(2), 43(4).

Ontario. Commission on Election Contributions and Expenses. 1978. *A Comparative Survey of Election Finance Legislation.* Toronto: The Commission.

———. 1982a. *Canadian Election Reform: Dialogue on Issues and Effects.* December. Toronto: The Commission.

———. 1982b. *Consolidation of Recommended Amendments to the Election Finances Reform Act, 1975.* 15 November. Toronto: The Commission.

———. 1983. *Comparative Survey of Election Finance Legislation.* Toronto: The Commission.

——— 1985. *The Commission: Ten Years Later, 1975–1985; Reflections on Political Financing in Ontario.* January. Toronto: The Commission.

———. 1986. *Political Financing: Studies on Election Spending Limits and Party Leadership Campaigns.* January. Toronto: The Commission.

Ontario. Commission on Election Finances. 1988. *A Comparative Survey of Election Finance Legislation, 1988.* Toronto: The Commission.

Ontario. Commission on the Legislature. 1974. *Third Report.* September. Toronto: Queen's Printer.

Ornstein, Norman J., and Mark Schmitt. 1990. "The Buck Stop: The End of California's Political Gold Rush." *New Republic* 202 (5 February): 14–16.

Osborn, David E. 1975. "Business and Political Donations: A Framework for Decision." *Business Quarterly* 40 (Spring): 86–89.

Palda, Filip. 1989. "Electoral Spending." Ph.D. dissertation, University of Chicago.

———. 1990. "What Advantage do Incumbents Have Over Challengers?" Research paper for the Royal Commission on Electoral Reform and Party Financing.

———. 1991. *Election Finance Regulation in Canada: A Critical Review.* Vancouver: The Fraser Institute.

Palda, Filip, and Kristian S. Palda. 1985. "Ceilings on Campaign Spending: Hypothesis and Partial Test with Canadian Data." *Public Choice* 45:313–31.

———. 1990. "Campaign Spending and Campaign Finance Issues: An Economic View." Issues paper submitted to the Royal Commission on Electoral Reform and Party Financing.

Palda, Kristian S. 1973. "Does Advertising Influence Votes? An Analysis of the 1966 and 1970 Quebec Elections." *Canadian Journal of Political Science* 6:638–55.

————. 1975. "The Effect of Expenditure on Political Success." *Journal of Law and Economics* 18:745–71.

————. 1985. "Does Canada's Election Act Impede Voters' Access to Information?" *Canadian Public Policy* 11:533–42.

Paltiel, Khayyam Z. 1967. "The Proposed Reform of Canadian Election Finance: A Study and Critique." *Jahrbuch des Öffentlichen Rechts der Gegenwart*, Neue Folge/Band 16:379–409.

————. 1970a. "Contrasts Among Several Canadian Political Finance Cultures." In *Comparative Political Finance*, ed. A.J. Heidenheimer. Lexington, MA: D.C. Heath.

————. 1970b. *Political Party Financing in Canada*. Toronto: McGraw-Hill.

————. 1974. "Party and Candidate Expenditures in the Canadian General Election of 1972." *Canadian Journal of Political Science* 7:341–52.

————. 1975. "Campaign Financing in Canada and its Reform." In *Canada and the Polls: The General Election of 1974*, ed. H. Penniman. Washington: American Enterprise Institute.

————. 1976a. "Federalism and Party Finance." In *Political Corruption in Canada: Cases, Causes and Cures*, ed. K.M. Gibbons and D.C. Rowat. Toronto: McClelland and Stewart.

————. 1976b. "Election Expenses." In *The Provincial Political Systems: Comparative Essays*, ed. D.J. Ballamy, J.H. Pammett and D.C. Rowat. Toronto: Methuen.

————. 1976c. "Improving Laws on Financing Elections." In *Political Corruption in Canada: Cases, Causes and Cures*, ed. K.M. Gibbons and D.C. Rowat. Toronto: McClelland and Stewart.

————. 1977. *Party, Candidate and Election Finance*. Study No. 22 for the Royal Commission on Corporate Concentration. Ottawa: Minister of Supply and Services Canada.

————. 1979a. "Canadian Election Expenses Legislation: Recent Developments." In *Party Politics in Canada*. 4th ed., ed. H. Thorburn. Scarborough, Ont.: Prentice-Hall Canada.

————. 1979b. "The Impact of Election Expenses Legislation in Canada, Western Europe and Israel." In *Political Finance*, ed. H.E. Alexander. Beverly Hills: Sage Publications.

————. 1981. "Campaign Finance: Contrasting Practices and Reforms." In *Democracy at the Polls*, ed. David Butler, H.R. Penniman and Austin Ranney. Washington, DC: American Enterprise Institute.

————. 1985. "The Control of Campaign Finance in Canada: A Summary and Overview." In *Party Politics in Canada*. 5th ed., ed. Hugh G. Thorburn. Scarborough, Ont.: Prentice-Hall Canada.

————. 1987. "Canadian Election Expense Legislation, 1963–1985: A Critical Appraisal or Was the Effort Worth It?" In *Contemporary Canadian Politics*, ed. R.J. Jackson et al. Scarborough, Ont.: Prentice-Hall Canada.

————. 1988. "The 1984 Federal General Election and Developments in Canadian Party Finance." In *Canada at the Polls, 1984*, ed. H. Penniman. Chapel Hill, NC: Duke University Press.

————. 1989a. "Political Marketing, Party Finance and the Decline of Canadian Parties." In *Canadian Parties in Transition*, ed. A.G. Gagnon and A.B. Tanguay. Toronto: Nelson Canada.

————. 1989b. "Canadian Election Expense Legislation, 1963–85: A Critical Appraisal, or Was the Effort Worth It?" In *Comparative Political Finance in the 1980s*, ed. Herbert E. Alexander and Joel Federman. Cambridge: Cambridge University Press.

Paltiel, Khayyam Z., and Jean Brown Van Loon. 1966. "Financing the Liberal Party, 1867–1965." In Canada, Committee on Election Expenses, *Studies in Canadian Party Finance*. Ottawa: Queen's Printer.

Paltiel, Khayyam Z., and L.G. Kjosa. 1970. "The Structure and Dimensions of Election Broadcasting in Canada." *Jahrbuch des Öffentlichen Rechts der Gegenwart*, Neue Folge/Band 19:355–380.

————. 1966. "Federalism and Party Finance: A Preliminary Sounding." In Canada, Committee on Election Expenses, *Studies in Canadian Party Finance*. Ottawa: Queen's Printer.

Paltiel, Khayyam Z., Howat P. Noble and Reginald A. Whitaker. 1966. "The Finances of the Cooperative Commonwealth Federation and the New Democratic Party, 1933–1965." In Canada, Committee on Election Expenses, *Studies in Canadian Party Finance*. Ottawa: Queen's Printer.

Paltiel, Khayyam Z., Jill McCalla Vickers and Raoul P. Barbe. 1966. "Candidate Attitudes Toward the Control of Election Expenses." In Canada, Committee on Election Expenses, *Studies in Canadian Party Finance*. Ottawa: Queen's Printer.

Pammett, Jon H. 1990. "Third-Party Advertising." Issue paper prepared for the Royal Commission on Electoral Reform and Party Financing. Ottawa.

Pappin, J. Maureen. 1976. "Tax Relief for Political Contributions." *Canadian Tax Journal* 24:298–305.

Pearson, Ian. 1990. "Thou Shalt Not Ignore the West." *Saturday Night*, December, 34, 43, 74–75.

Penniman, Howard R., ed. 1981. *Canada at the Polls, 1979 and 1980: A Study of the General Elections*. Washington, DC: American Enterprise Institute.

————. 1988. *Canada at the Polls, 1984*. Durham, NC: Duke University Press for the American Enterprise Institute.

Perlin, George C., ed. 1988. *Party Democracy in Canada: The Politics of National Party Conventions*. Scarborough, Ont.: Prentice-Hall Canada.

Plawin, Paul. 1988. "Sweet Charities." *Changing Times*, 42 (May): 95–100.

Power, C.G. 1949. "Wanted a Ceiling on Election Spending." *Maclean's* 62, 1 February, 8.

Pratkanis, Anthony, and Elliot Aronson. 1991. *Age of Propaganda: The Everyday Use and Abuse of Persuasion*. New York: W.H. Freeman.

Pratt, Larry, and Garth Stevenson, eds. 1981. *Western Separatism: The Myths, Realities and Danger*. Edmonton: Hurtig Publishers.

Qualter, T.H. 1970. *The Election Process in Canada*. Toronto: McGraw-Hill.

Quebec. *An Act to Govern the Financing of Political Parties and to Amend the Election Act*, S.Q. 1977, c. 11, s. 101.

———. *Quebec Election Act*, S.Q. 1963, c. 13.

Reform Party of Canada. 1990a. *Principles and Policies*. Calgary: Reform Party of Canada.

———. 1990b. "Strengthening Democracy in Canada: A Submission to the Royal Commission on Electoral Reform and Party Financing." Calgary: Reform Party of Canada.

———. 1991. "Constituency Organization and Procedures Manual." Draft. June. Calgary.

Robb, W. 1968. "Politics Cost Money." *Canadian Business* 41 (June): 11–12.

"Round Table: The Party Perspectives on Election Expenses." 1981. *Parliamentary Government* 2, no. 2 (Winter/Spring): 7–11.

Sabato, Larry. 1987. "Real and Imagined Corruption in Campaign Financing." In *Elections American Style*, ed. A.J. Reichley. Washington, DC: Brookings Institution.

Schull, Joseph. 1965. *Laurier: The First Canadian*. Toronto: Macmillan Canada.

Sclanders, I. 1964. "The Real Cost of Expensive Campaigns." *Maclean's* 77, 8 February, 2–3.

Scott, J.R. 1961. "Political Slush Funds Corrupt All Parties." *Maclean's* 74, 9 September, 67–70.

Sécor Group. 1991a. "Alternative Systems of Political Party Financing in Canada." Paper presented to the Royal Commission on Electoral Reform and Party Financing. January.

———. 1991b. "The Impact of New Technologies on the Electoral Process and Party Management in Canada." Paper presented to the Royal Commission on Electoral Reform and Party Financing. January.

————. 1991c. "Economic Aspects of Political Party Financing in Canada." Study for the Royal Commission on Electoral Reform and Party Financing. May.

Seidle, F. Leslie. 1980. "Electoral Law and Its Effects on Election Expenditure and Party Finance in Great Britain and Canada." D. Phil. dissertation, Oxford University.

————. 1985a. "The Regulation of Political Advertising on Canadian Television." Paper prepared for the Committee for the Study of the American Electorate.

————. 1985b. "The Election Expenses Act: The House of Commons and the Parties." In *The Canadian House of Commons: Essays in Honour of Norman Ward*, ed. J.C. Courtney. Calgary: University of Calgary Press.

————. 1987. "Controlling Federal Election Finances." In *Politics Canada*, ed. Paul W. Fox and Graham White. Toronto: McGraw-Hill Ryerson.

————. 1989. "The Canadian Electoral System and Proposals for Reform." In *Canadian Parties in Transition*, ed. A.G. Gagnon and A.B. Tanguay. Toronto: Nelson Canada.

Seidle, F. Leslie, and Khayyam Z. Paltiel. 1981. "Party Finance, the Election Expenses Act and Campaign Spending in 1979 and 1980." In *Canada at the Polls, 1979 and 1980*, ed. H. Penniman. Washington, DC: American Enterprise Institute.

Sharpe, Sydney, and Don Braid. 1992. *Storming Babylon: Preston Manning and the Rise of the Reform Party*. Toronto: Key Porter Books.

Simpson, Jeffrey. 1980. *Discipline of Power: The Conservative Interlude and the Liberal Restoration*. Toronto: Personal Library.

————. 1984. "The Most Influential Private Citizen in Canada." *Saturday Night*, December, 11–18.

————. 1988. *Spoils of Power: The Politics of Patronage*. Toronto: Collins.

Smolowe, Jill. 1990. "Read This!!!!" *Time*, 26 November, 44–50.

Snider, Norman. 1985. *The Changing of the Guard: How the Liberals Fell From Grace and the Tories Rose to Power*. Toronto: Lester and Orpen Dennys.

Somerville, David. 1989. "The Pros and Cons of Election Finance Administration – Promoting or Impeding the Democratic Process?" Paper presented at the 1989 Conference of Canadian Election Officials, Regina, 19 July.

Sorauf, Frank. 1988. *Money in American Elections*. Glenview, IL: Foresman/Little Brown.

Spafford, Duff. 1981. "Highway Employment and Provincial Elections." *Canadian Journal of Political Science* 14:135–42.

Stanbury, W.T. 1986a. *Business–Government Relations in Canada.* Toronto: Methuen.

———. 1986b. "The Mother's Milk of Politics: Political Contributions to Federal Parties in Canada, 1974–84." *Canadian Journal of Political Science* 19:795–821.

———. 1988a. "Financing Federal Political Parties in Canada, 1974–1986." In *Canadian Parties in Transition,* ed. A.G. Gagnon and A.B. Tanguay. Toronto: Nelson Canada.

———. 1988b. "Privatization and the Mulroney Government, 1984–1988." In *Canada Under Mulroney: An End-of-Term Report,* ed. A.B. Gollner and D. Salee. Montreal: Vehicule Press.

———. 1990a. "Should Government Regulate the Financing of Campaigns for the Leadership of Political Parties?" Paper submitted to the Royal Commission on Electoral Reform and Party Financing. Rev. ed. April.

———. 1990b. "Data on Contributions to Federal Political Parties in Canada, 1974–1989." Vancouver: University of British Columbia, Faculty of Commerce and Business Administration. August.

———. 1991. "Comments on Allan R. Taylor's Proposals for Reforming Political Finance in Canada." Paper prepared for the Royal Commission on Electoral Reform and Party Financing. March.

Surich, J. 1975. "Purists and Pragmatists: Canadian Democratic Socialism at the Crossroads." In *Canada at the Polls: The General Election of 1974,* ed. H. Penniman. Washington, DC: American Enterprise Institute.

Taylor, Allan R. 1991. "Business, Politics and Politicians." Eighth Annual James C. Taylor Distinguished Lecture in Finance, School of Business Administration, University of Western Ontario. 26 February.

Thomas, Paul G. 1985. "The Role of National Party Caucuses." In *Party Government and Regional Representation in Canada,* ed. Peter Aucoin. Vol. 36 of the research studies of the Royal Commission on Economic Union and Development Prospects for Canada. Toronto: University of Toronto Press.

Toner, Glen. 1986. "Stardust: The Tory Energy Program." In *How Ottawa Spends, 1986–87: Tracking the Tories,* ed. M.J. Prince. Toronto: Methuen.

Underhill, Frank. 1935. "The Development of National Political Parties in Canada." *Canadian Historical Review* 16:367–87.

United States. *Deceptive Mailings Prevention Act of 1990,* Pub. L. 101-524, Nov. 24, 1990.

———. *Federal Election Campaign Act of 1971,* Pub. L. 92-225, Feb. 7, 1972.

Urquhart, Ian. 1976. "How Big Oil Provides for Its Friends in High Places." *Maclean's* 89, 9 February, 47–48.

———. 1978. "The Bucks Start Here: Behind Every Great Leader is an Equally Great Bagman." *Maclean's*, 91, 15 May, 44b–44p.

Walker, David C. 1989. "Pollsters, Consultants and Party Politics in Canada." In *Canadian Parties in Transition*, ed. A.G. Gagnon and A.B. Tanguay. Toronto: Nelson Canada.

Wallace, Bruce, and Ross Laver. 1988. "Private Funds and the Parties" and "Turner's Private Trusts." *Maclean's* 101, 12 September, 10–12.

Ward, Norman. 1972. "Money and Politics: The Costs of Democracy in Canada." *Canadian Journal of Political Science* 5 (3): 335–47.

Warwick, Mal. 1990. *Revolution in the Mailbox*. Berkeley, CA: Strathmoor Press.

Wearing, Joseph. 1981. *The L-Shaped Party: The Liberal Party of Canada 1958–1980*. Toronto: McGraw-Hill Ryerson.

———. 1987. "Political Bucks and Government Billings: A Preliminary Enquiry into the Question of Linkage between Party Donations by Business and Government Contracts." *Journal of Canadian Studies* 22 (Summer): 135–49.

———. 1988a. "The High Cost of High Tech: Financing the Modern Leadership Campaign." In *Party Democracy in Canada: The Politics of National Party Conventions*, ed. George Perlin. Scarborough, Ont.: Prentice-Hall Canada.

———. 1988b. *Strained Relations: Canadian Parties and Voters*. Toronto: McClelland and Stewart.

———. 1989. "Can an Old Dog Teach Itself New Tricks? The Liberal Party Attempts Reform." In *Canadian Parties in Transition*, ed. A.G. Gagnon and A.B. Tanguay. Toronto: Nelson Canada.

———, ed. 1991. *The Ballot and Its Message: Voting in Canada*. Toronto: Copp Clark Pitman.

Wearing, Joseph, and Peter Wearing. 1990. "Mother's Milk Revisited: The Effect of Foreign Ownership on Political Contributions." *Canadian Journal of Political Science*, 3:115–23.

Weston, Greg. 1988. *Reign of Error*. Toronto: McGraw-Hill Ryerson.

Whitaker, Reginald. 1977. *The Government Party: Organizing and Financing the Liberal Party of Canada 1930–1958*. Toronto: University of Toronto Press.

Wishart, David H. 1975–76. "The Election Expenses Act: A New Challenge for Auditors." *CA Magazine*, No. 104, March, 32–36.

Wittman, Donald. 1989. "Why Democracies Produce Efficient Results." *Journal of Political Economy* 97:1395–424.

Young, W.D. 1978. *Democracy and Discontent*. 2d ed. Toronto: McGraw-Hill Ryerson.

Young, Walter. 1969. *The Anatomy of a Party: The National CCF, 1932–1961*. Toronto: University of Toronto Press.

Zardkoohi, A. 1985. "On the Political Participation of the Firm in the Electoral Process." *Southern Economic Journal* 51:804–17.

ACKNOWLEDGEMENTS

The Royal Commission on Electoral Reform and Party Financing and the publishers wish to acknowledge with gratitude the permission of the following to reprint and translate material:

American Enterprise Institute for Public Policy Research; Nelson Canada; *Parliamentary Government*; University of Calgary Press.

Care has been taken to trace the ownership of copyright material used in the text, including the tables and figures. The authors and publishers welcome any information enabling them to rectify any reference or credit in subsequent editions.

~

Consistent with the Commission's objective of promoting full participation in the electoral system by all segments of Canadian society, gender neutrality has been used wherever possible in the editing of the research studies.

THE COLLECTED RESEARCH STUDIES

COMMISSION ORGANIZATION

CHAIRMAN
Pierre Lortie

COMMISSIONERS
Pierre Fortier
Robert Gabor
William Knight
Lucie Pépin

SENIOR OFFICERS

Executive Director
Guy Goulard

Director of Research
Peter Aucoin

Special Adviser to the Chairman
Jean-Marc Hamel

Research
F. Leslie Seidle,
  Senior Research Coordinator

Coordinators
Herman Bakvis
Michael Cassidy
Frederick J. Fletcher
Janet Hiebert
Kathy Megyery
Robert A. Milen
David Small

Assistant Coordinators
David Mac Donald
Cheryl D. Mitchell

Legislation
Jules Brière, Senior Adviser
Gérard Bertrand
Patrick Orr

Communications and Publishing
Richard Rochefort, Director
Hélène Papineau, Assistant
  Director
Paul Morisset, Editor
Kathryn Randle, Editor

Finance and Administration
Maurice R. Lacasse, Director

Contracts and Personnel
Thérèse Lacasse, Chief

EDITORIAL, DESIGN AND PRODUCTION SERVICES

ROYAL COMMISSION ON ELECTORAL REFORM AND PARTY FINANCING

Editors   Denis Bastien, Susan Becker Davidson, Ginette Bertrand, Louis Bilodeau, Claude Brabant, Louis Chabot, Danielle Chaput, Norman Dahl, Carlos del Burgo, Julie Desgagners, Chantal Granger, Volker Junginger, Denis Landry, André LaRose, Paul Morisset, Christine O'Meara, Mario Pelletier, Marie-Noël Pichelin, Kathryn Randle, Georges Royer, Eve Valiquette, Dominique Vincent.

LE CENTRE DE DOCUMENTATION JURIDIQUE DU QUÉBEC INC.

Hubert Reid, *President*

Claire Grégoire, *Comptroller*

Lucie Poirier, *Production Manager*
Gisèle Gingras, *Special Project Assistant*

Translators   Pierre-Yves de la Garde, Richard Lapointe, Marie-Josée Turcotte.

Technical Editors   Stéphane Côté Coulombe, *Coordinator*;
Josée Chabot, Danielle Morin.

Copy Editors   Martine Germain, Lise Larochelle, Elisabeth Reid, Carole St-Louis, Isabelle Tousignant, Charles Tremblay, Sébastien Viau.

Word Processing   André Vallée.

Formatting   Typoform, Claude Audet; Linda Goudreau, *Formatting Coordinator*.

WILSON & LAFLEUR LTÉE

Claude Wilson, *President*

DUNDURN PRESS

J. Kirk Howard, *President*
Ian Low, *Comptroller*
Jeanne MacDonald, *Project Coordinator*

Avivah Wargon, *Managing and Production Editor*
Beth Ediger, *Managing Editor*
John St. James, *Managing Editor*
Karen Heese, *Special Project Assistant*

Ruth Chernia, *Tables Editor*
Victoria Grant, *Legal Editor*
Michèle Breton, *Special Editorial Assistant*

Editorial Staff   Elliott Chapin, Peggy Foy, Lily Hobel, Marilyn Hryciuk, Madeline Koch, Elizabeth Mitchell, John Shoesmith, Nadine Stoikoff, Anne Vespry.

Copy Editors   Carol Anderson, Elizabeth d'Anjou, Jane Becker, Diane Brassolotto, Elizabeth Driver, Curtis Fahey, Tony Fairfield, Freya Godard, Frances Hanna, Kathleen Harris, Andria Hourwich, Greg Ioannou, Carlotta Lemieux, Elsha Leventis, David McCorquodale, Virginia Smith, Gail Thorson, Louise Wood.

Formatting   Green Graphics; Joanne Green, *Formatting Coordinator;*
Formatters   Linda Carroll, Mary Ann Cattral, Gail Nina, Eva Payne, Jacqueline Hope Raynor, Shawn Syms, Andy Tong, Carla Vonn Worden, Laura Wilkins.

Printed and bound in Canada by
Best Gagné Book Manufacturers